Advances in Computer Vision and Pattern Recognition

More information about this series at http://www.springer.com/series/4205

Rogerio Schmidt Feris · Christoph Lampert
Devi Parikh
Editors

Visual Attributes

Springer

Editors
Rogerio Schmidt Feris
IBM T.J. Watson Research Center
Yorktown Heights, NY
USA

Devi Parikh
Georgia Tech
Atlanta, GA
USA

Christoph Lampert
Computer Vision and Machine Learning
IST Austria
Klosterneuburg
Austria

ISSN 2191-6586 ISSN 2191-6594 (electronic)
Advances in Computer Vision and Pattern Recognition
ISBN 978-3-319-50075-1 ISBN 978-3-319-50077-5 (eBook)
DOI 10.1007/978-3-319-50077-5

Library of Congress Control Number: 2016958717

Printed on acid-free paper

This Springer imprint is published by Springer Nature
The registered company is Springer International Publishing AG
The registered company address is: Gewerbestrasse 11, 6330 Cham, Switzerland

Preface

Visual attributes are generally defined as mid-level semantic visual concepts or properties that are shared across categories, e.g., furry, striped, metallic, young. They have recently gained significant popularity in computer vision, finding applications in zero-shot classification (where a machine can recognize a concept even without having seen it before), image ranking and retrieval, fine-grained categorization, human–machine interaction, and many others.

This book provides an overview of and summarizes recent advances in machine learning and computer vision related to visual attributes, while exploring the intersection with other disciplines such as computational linguistics and human–machine interaction. It contains a collection of chapters written by world-renowned scientists, covering theoretical aspects of visual attribute learning as well as practical computer vision applications.

We would like to express our sincere gratitude to all chapter contributors for their dedication and high-quality work, as well as to Simon Rees and Wayne Wheeler from Springer for their support and help throughout the book's preparation.

Yorktown Heights, NY, USA — Rogerio Schmidt Feris
Vienna, Austria — Christoph Lampert
Atlanta, GA, USA — Devi Parikh
September 2016

Contents

Chapter 1
Introduction to Visual Attributes

Rogerio Schmidt Feris, Christoph Lampert and Devi Parikh

Visual recognition has significantly advanced in recent years, particularly through the widespread adoption of deep convolutional neural networks [22, 28] as the main tool for solving computer vision problems. The recognition accuracy recently obtained in standard benchmark datasets, such as Imagenet [7], has even surpassed human-level performance [15].

The fuel to power up these neural network models is training data. In fact, current methods often require at least thousands of manually annotated training examples for learning robust classifiers for new categories. While it is easy to obtain a large number of example images for common categories, such as images of vehicles or dogs, it is not straightforward to obtain annotated training sets for other infrequent categories, such as a particular vehicle model or a specific dog breed. There are tens of thousands of basic categories in the world (and significantly more subordinate categories) [3]. For many of them, only a few or *no examples at all* are available.

Zero-data or zero-shot classification refers to the problem of recognizing categories for which no training examples are available [26, 30]. This problem happens in many practical settings. As an example, for the task of predicting concrete nouns from neural imaging data [30], many nouns may not have corresponding neural image examples because of the costly label acquisition process. In the visual surveillance domain, while conducting a criminal investigation, the police may have only

R.S. Feris (✉)
IBM T. J. Watson Research Center, New York, USA
e-mail: rsferis@us.ibm.com

C. Lampert
Institute of Science and Technology Austria, Klosterneuburg, Austria
e-mail: chl@ist.ac.at

D. Parikh
Georgia Tech, Atlanta, GA, USA
e-mail: parikh@gatech.edu

R.S. Feris et al. (eds.), *Visual Attributes*, Advances in Computer Vision and Pattern Recognition, DOI 10.1007/978-3-319-50077-5_1

eyewitness descriptions available for searching a targeted suspect, instead of example images [13, 40]. Many *fine-grained* visual categorization tasks have classes for which only a few or no training images exist. For instance, the ImageNet dataset has 30 mushroom synsets, each with 1000 images, whereas there are more than ten thousand mushroom species found in nature. The zero-shot classification problem is also common in other fields. In large vocabulary speech recognition systems, it is infeasible to acquire training samples for each word. Recommender systems face issues when new apps are released without any user ratings (also known as the cold-start problem [35]).

Visual attributes, which are generally defined as mid-level semantic properties that are shared across categories (e.g., furry, yellow, four-legged), provide an effective way of solving the zero-shot classification problem. As initially demonstrated by Lampert et al. [25, 26], a novel unseen category with an associated description based on semantic attributes (either provided by experts or mined from language sources, such as Wikipedia [33, 34]) can be recognized by leveraging visual attribute classifiers, which can be learned using existing training data from known categories. This process is aligned with human capabilities of identifying objects only based on descriptions. For example, when given a sentence like "large gray animals with long trunks," we can reliably identify elephants [26]. Currently, the highest-performing methods for zero-shot learning rely on visual attributes, often in connection with other forms of semantic embedding such as distributional word vector representations [1, 2, 14, 33].

Visual attributes are both semantic (human-understandable) and visual (machine-detectable). In addition to zero-shot learning, they have proven effective in various other applications. As a communication channel between humans and machines, attributes have been used for interactive recognition of fine-grained categories [4], active learning [21], and image search with humans in the loop [20]. Attributes discretize a high dimensional feature space into a simple and readily interpretable representation that can be used to explain machine decisions to humans [16] and predict user annoyance [5]. Conversely, humans can provide rationales to machines as a stronger form of supervision through visual attributes [10]. Along this direction, attributes can serve as a form of privileged information [36] for improving recognition, especially when only a few training examples are available.

Another area in which attributes have recently played a major role is visual analysis of people. In the visual surveillance domain, state-of-the-art person reidentification systems [27, 37, 39] benefit from human attributes as features for improving matching of people across cameras. The extraction of face and clothing attributes enable search for suspects or missing people based on their physical description [13, 40]. In e-commerce applications, attributes are very effective in improving clothing retrieval [17] and fashion recommendation [29]. It has also been shown that facial attribute prediction is helpful as an auxiliary task for improving face detection [42] and face alignment [43]. Methods for image ranking and retrieval also benefit from attributes as a compact and semantic image representation [11, 23, 38].

Other applications of visual attributes include describing unfamiliar objects [12], scene analysis [32], material classification [6], and image virality prediction [8].

Beyond semantics, attributes have been used for understanding and predicting the memorability and aesthetics of photographs [9, 18, 19]. Finally, attributes have been recently used for image editing (e.g., allowing users to adjust the attributes of a scene to be "snowy" or "sunset") [24] and for conditional image generation in the context of generative adversarial networks [41].

This book's goal is to summarize the main ideas related to visual attributes that were proposed in the past few years, and to cover recent research efforts related to this emerging area in an accessible manner to a wider research community. Next, we provide an overview of the chapters of the book, which comprise both theoretical aspects of attribute learning and practical applications.

1.1 Overview of the Chapters

Part I: Attribute-Based Recognition

The first part of the book covers attribute-based methods for *recognition of unseen classes* for which training examples are unavailable (i.e., zero-shot classification), *recognition of seen classes*, where attributes are used as privileged information during the training stage, and methods for *multitask attribute learning*.

Chapter 2, by Bernardino Romera-Paredes and Philip H.S. Torr, introduces the problem of zero-shot learning and proposes a general framework that models the relationships between features, attributes, and classes, so the knowledge learned at the training stage can be transferred to the inference stage. The method is easily implemented: one line of code for training and another for inference; yet, it achieves impressive results on standard benchmark datasets.

In Chap. 3, Viktoriia Sharmanska and Novi Quadrianto consider the problem of visual recognition of categories when their attributes are used as privileged information during training time. In particular, they address whether attributes are still useful privileged data when modern deep convolutional features are used for visual classification. Their analysis shows that the answer to this question depends on the classification task's complexity.

In Chap. 4, Chao-Yeh Chen, Dinesh Jayaraman, Fei Sha, and Kristen Grauman address the problem of multitask attribute learning, exploring when and to what extent sharing is useful for attribute learning. They introduce the idea of selective sharing during multitask learning of attributes, using semantic knowledge to decide what to share and what not to share during learning.

Part II: Relative Attributes and Their Application to Image Search

The second part of the book introduces the concept of relative attributes [31], which consists of measuring the relative strength of properties (for example, "bears are furrier than giraffes") instead of simply determining whether they are present or not, and demonstrates the effectiveness of modeling relative attributes in image search applications.

In Chap. 5, Adriana Kovashka and Kristen Grauman show how semantic attributes can be effectively used for interactive image search with user feedback based on relative attribute comparisons. They present a system called "WhittleSearch," which can answer queries such as "show me shoes like these, but more formal." This chapter also covers techniques for actively selecting images for feedback and adapting attribute models for personalized user queries.

Chapter 6, by Aron Yu and Kristen Grauman, addresses the problem of fine-grained visual comparisons with attributes, which is valuable for sophisticated image search systems that may need to distinguish subtle properties between highly similar images. They develop computational models based on *local learning* for fine-grained visual comparisons, where a predictive model is trained on the fly using only the data most relevant to a given input. They also address the problem of determining when an image pair is indistinguishable in terms of a given attribute.

In Chap. 7, Fanyi Xiao and Yong Jae Lee introduce a weakly supervised method for automatically discovering the spatial extent of relative attributes in images. This is achieved by mining a set of local, transitive connections ("visual chains") that establish correspondences between the same object parts across images. They show that the proposed localized approach better models relative attributes than baselines that either use global appearance features or stronger supervision.

Part III: Describing People Based on Attributes

Automatically describing people based on their fine-grained semantic attributes is important for many application domains, such as visual surveillance and e-commerce. The third part of the book covers state-of-the-art methods for estimation of human attributes and their use in different applications.

Chapter 8, by Chen Change Loy, Ping Luo, and Chen Huang, presents recent progress and cutting-edge methods based on deep learning for solving problems in estimating facial attributes such as gender, age, presence of facial hair, eyewear, hairstyle, and others. They cover approaches for handling class imbalance in attribute prediction, and demonstrate the use of facial attribute classification as an auxiliary task for improving face detection and face alignment.

In Chap. 9, Si Liu, Lisa Brown, Qiang Chen, Junshi Huang, Luoqi Liu, and Shuicheng Yan introduce methods that leverage facial and clothing attributes as a mid-level representation for applications related to fashion. In particular, they show that modeling attributes is crucial for fashion recommendation systems. In addition, they show that attributes play a major role in a system for clothing retrieval from online shopping catalogs.

Part IV: Defining a Vocabulary of Attributes

After covering multiple uses of visual attributes, as described earlier, we address the problem of discovering them, i.e., how to define a vocabulary of attributes.

In Chap. 10, Subhransu Maji surveys recent methods and defines a taxonomy of techniques for discovering a vocabulary of parts and attributes. The approaches discussed in this survey consider a vocabulary of attributes defined by experts and based on discovery methods, such as non-semantic embeddings, text mining, similarity comparisons, and others.

In Chap. 11, Genevieve Patterson and James Hays use crowdsourcing to generate a vocabulary of discriminative scene attributes related to affordances, materials, and spatial layout. After the attributes are discovered, they annotate more than ten thousand images with individual attribute labels, and show that attribute models derived from this data serve as an effective intermediate representation for zero-shot learning and image retrieval tasks.

Part V: Attributes and Language

We conclude our volume with a forward-looking topic: the connection of visual attributes and natural language.

In Chap. 12, Marcus Rohrbach discusses using visual attributes as semantic units between natural language and visual recognition. In particular, he covers methods for mining attributes from language resources, generating sentences from images and video, grounding natural language in visual content, and visual question answering.

In Chap. 13, Carina Silberer states that distributional models of word meaning have been criticized as "disembodied" in that they are not grounded in perception, and show that visual attributes predicted from images can be used as a way of physically grounding word meaning. Silberer introduces a new large-scale dataset of images annotated with visual attributes and a neural network-based model, which learns higher-level meaning representations by mapping words and images, represented by attributes, into a common embedding space.

References

1. Akata, Z., Malinowski, M., Fritz, M., Schiele, B.: Multi-cue zero-shot learning with strong supervision. In: Conference on Computer Vision and Pattern Recognition (CVPR) (2016)
2. Akata, Z., Perronnin, F., Harchaoui, Z., Schmid, C.: Label embeddings for image classification. IEEE Trans. Pattern Anal. Mach. Intell. (PAMI) **38**(7), 1425–1438 (2016)
3. Biederman, I.: Recognition by components—a theory of human image understanding. Psychol. Rev. **94**(2), 115–147 (1987)
4. Branson, S., Wah, C., Schroff, F., Babenko, B., Welinder, P., Perona, P., Belongie, S.: Visual recognition with humans in the loop. In: European Conference on Computer Vision (ECCV) (2010)
5. Christie, G., Parkash, A., Krothapalli, U., Parikh, D.: Predicting user annoyance using visual attributes. In: Conference on Computer Vision and Pattern Recognition (CVPR) (2014)
6. Cimpoi, M., Maji, S., Kokkinos, I., Mohamed, S., Vedaldi, A.: Describing textures in the wild. In: Conference on Computer Vision and Pattern Recognition (CVPR) (2014)
7. Deng, J., Dong, W., Socher, R., Li, L.J., Li, K., Fei-Fei, L.: Imagenet: A large-scale hierarchical image database. In: Conference on Computer Vision and Pattern Recognition (CVPR) (2009)

8. Deza, A., Parikh, D.: Understanding image virality. In: Conference on Computer Vision and Pattern Recognition (CVPR) (2015)
9. Dhar, S., Ordonez, V., Berg, T.: High level describable attributes for predicting aesthetics and interestingness. In: Conference on Computer Vision and Pattern Recognition (CVPR) (2011)
10. Donahue, J., Grauman, K.: Image recognition with annotator rationales. In: International Conference on Computer Vision (ICCV) (2011)
11. Douze, M., Ramisa, A., Schmid, C.: Combining attributes and fisher vectors for efficient image retrieval. In: Conference on Computer Vision and Pattern Recognition (CVPR) (2011)
12. Farhadi, A., Endres, I., Hoiem, D., Forsyth, D.A.: Describing objects by their attributes. In: Conference on Computer Vision and Pattern Recognition (CVPR) (2009)
13. Feris, R.S., Bobbit, R., Brown, L., Pankanti, S.: Attribute-based people search: lessons learnt from a practical surveillance system. In: International Conference on Multimedia Retrieval (ICMR) (2014)
14. Gan, C., Yang, T., Gong, B.: Learning attributes equals multi-source domain generalization. In: Conference on Computer Vision and Pattern Recognition (CVPR) (2016)
15. He, K., Zhang, X., Ren, S., Sun, J.: Delving deep into rectifiers: Surpassing human-level performance on imagenet classification. In: International Conference on Computer Vision (ICCV) (2015)
16. Hendricks, L., Akata, Z., Rohrbach, M., Donahue, J., Schiele, B., Darrell, T.: Generating visual explanations. In: European Conference on Computer Vision (ECCV) (2016)
17. Huang, J., Feris, R.S., Chen, Q., Yan, S.: Cross-domain image retrieval with a dual attribute-aware ranking network. In: International Conference on Computer Vision (ICCV) (2015)
18. Isola, P., Xiao, J., Parikh, D., Torralba, A., Oliva, A.: What makes a photograph memorable? IEEE Trans. Pattern Anal. Mach. Intell. (PAMI) **36**(7), 1469–1482 (2014)
19. Kong, S., Shen, X., Lin, Z., Mech, R., Fowlkes, C.: Photo aesthetics ranking network with attributes and content adaptation. In: European Conference on Computer Vision (ECCV) (2016)
20. Kovashka, A., Parikh, D., Grauman, K.: Whittlesearch: interactive image search with relative attribute feedback. Int. J. Comput. Vis. (IJCV) **115**, 185–210 (2015)
21. Kovashka, A., Vijayanarasimhan, S., Grauman, K.: Actively selecting annotations among objects and attributes. In: International Conference on Computer Vision (ICCV) (2011)
22. Krizhevsky, A., Sutskever, I., Hinton, G.: Imagenet classification with deep convolutional neural networks. In: Conference on Neural Information Processing Systems (NIPS) (2012)
23. Kumar, N., Belhumeur, P.N., Nayar, S.K.: FaceTracer: A search engine for large collections of images with faces. In: European Conference on Computer Vision (ECCV) (2008)
24. Laffont, P.Y., Ren, Z., Tao, X., Qian, C., Hays, J.: Transient attributes for high-level understanding and editing of outdoor scenes. In: ACM SIGGRAPH (2014)
25. Lampert, C., Nickisch, H., Harmeling, S.: Learning to detect unseen object classes by between-class attribute transfer. In: Conference on Computer Vision and Pattern Recognition (CVPR) (2009)
26. Lampert, C., Nickisch, H., Harmeling, S.: Attribute-based classification for zero-shot learning of object categories. IEEE Trans. Pattern Anal. Mach. Intell. (PAMI) **36**(3), 453–465 (2013)
27. Layne, R., T., H., Gong, S.: Re-id: Hunting attributes in the wild. In: British Machine Vision Conference (BMVC) (2014)
28. LeCun, Y., Bottou, L., Bengio, Y., Haffner, P.: Gradient-based learning applied to document recognition. Proc. IEEE **86**(11), 2278–2324 (1998)
29. Liu, L., Xu, H., Xing, J., Liu, S., Zhou, X., Yan, S.: Wow! you are so beautiful today! In: International Conference on Multimedia (ACM MM) (2013)
30. Palatucci, M., Hinton, G., Pomerleau, D., Mitchell, T.M.: Zero-shot learning with semantic output codes. In: Conference on Neural Information Processing Systems (NIPS) (2009)
31. Parikh, D., Grauman, K.: Relative attributes. In: International Conference on Computer Vision (ICCV) (2011)
32. Patterson, G., Hays, J.: Sun attribute database: discovering, annotating, and recognizing scene attributes. In: Conference on Computer Vision and Pattern Recognition (CVPR) (2012)

33. Qiao, R., Liu, L., Shen, C., van den Hengel, A.: Less is more: zero-shot learning from online textual documents with noise suppression. In: Conference on Computer Vision and Pattern Recognition (CVPR) (2016)
34. Rohrbach, M., Stark, M., Szarvas, G., Gurevych, I., Schiele, B.: What helps where and why? Semantic relatedness for knowledge transfer. In: Conference on Computer Vision and Pattern Recognition (CVPR) (2010)
35. Schein, A., Popescul, A., Ungar, L., Pennock, D.: Methods and metrics for cold-start recommendations. In: International Conference on Research and Development in Information Retrieval (ACM SIGIR) (2002)
36. Sharmanska, V., Quadrianto, N., Lampert, C.: Learning to rank using privileged information. In: International Conference on Computer Vision (ICCV) (2013)
37. Shi, Z., Hospedales, T., Xiang, T.: Transferring a semantic representation for person re-identification and search. In: Conference on Computer Vision and Pattern Recognition (CVPR) (2015)
38. Siddiquie, B., Feris, R.S., Davis, L.: Image ranking and retrieval based on multi-attribute queries. In: Conference on Computer Vision and Pattern Recognition (CVPR) (2011)
39. Su, C., Zhang, S., Xing, J., Gao, W., Tian, Q.: Deep attributes driven multi-camera person re-identification. In: European Conference on Computer Vision (ECCV) (2016)
40. Vaquero, D., Feris, R.S., Brown, L., Hampapur, A.: Attribute-based people search in surveillance environments. In: Winter Conference on Applications of Computer Vision (WACV) (2009)
41. Yan, X., Yang, J., Sohn, K., Le, H.: Attribute2image: Conditional image generation from visual attributes. In: European Conference on Computer Vision (ECCV) (2016)
42. Yang, S., Luo, P., Loy, C., Tang, X.: From facial part responses to face detection: a deep learning approach. In: International Conference on Computer Vision (ICCV) (2015)
43. Zhang, Z., Luo, P., Loy, C., Tang, X.: Learning deep representation for face alignment with auxiliary attributes. IEEE Trans. Pattern Anal. Mach. Intell. (PAMI) **38**(5), 918–930 (2015)

Part I
Attribute-Based Recognition

Chapter 2
An Embarrassingly Simple Approach to Zero-Shot Learning

Bernardino Romera-Paredes and Philip H. S. Torr

Abstract Zero-shot learning concerns learning how to recognise new classes from just a description of them. Many sophisticated approaches have been proposed to address the challenges this problem comprises. Here we describe a zero-shot learning approach that can be implemented in just one line of code, yet it is able to outperform state-of-the-art approaches on standard datasets. The approach is based on a more general framework which models the relationships between features, attributes, and classes as a network with two linear layers, where the weights of the top layer are not learned but are given by the environment. We further provide a learning bound on the generalisation error of this kind of approaches, by casting them as domain adaptation methods. In experiments carried out on three standard real datasets, we found that our approach is able to perform significantly better than the state of the art on all of them.

2.1 Introduction

Zero-shot learning (ZSL) is a relatively recent machine learning paradigm that was introduced in the works [21, 28], and quoting the latter, it aims to tackle the following question:

> Given a semantic encoding of a large set of concept classes, can we build a classifier to recognise classes that were omitted from the training set?

That is, ZSL consists in recognising new categories of instances without training examples, by providing a high-level description of the new categories that relate them to categories previously learned by the machine. This can be done by means of

---

B. Romera-Paredes (✉) · P.H.S. Torr
Department of Engineering Science, University of Oxford, Parks Road, Oxford OX1 3PJ, UK
e-mail: bernard@robots.ox.ac.uk; bernardino.romeraparedes@eng.ox.ac.uk

P.H.S. Torr
e-mail: philip.torr@eng.ox.ac.uk

R.S. Feris et al. (eds.), *Visual Attributes*, Advances in Computer Vision and Pattern Recognition, DOI 10.1007/978-3-319-50077-5_2

learning an intermediate encoding describing each class, referred to as attributes. In words of [1]:

> Attributes correspond to high-level properties of the objects which are shared across multiple classes, which can be detected by machines and which can be understood by humans.

One recurrent example that we mention in this chapter is the use of attributes such as *white*, *strong*, *furry*, and *quadrupedal*, to describe and learn classes of animals.

Zero-shot learning has attracted considerable attention due to both its wide applicability to many real- world situations and the singular challenges it presents. An example of ZSL happens when dealing with an ever growing set of classes, such as detecting new species of living beings, using attributes such as the ones mentioned in the previous example. Another scenario occurs when the granularity of the description of the categories to be distinguished makes it infeasible to obtain training instances for each of them, e.g. when a user wants to recognise a particular type of shoe (we refer to Chap. 9 for more on this topic). The main challenge ZSL poses is to design a model able to exploit the relations between features, attributes, and classes, so that the knowledge learned at the training stage can be transferred to the inference stage, in a similar way as human beings are able to understand a new concept, if it is described as a combination of previously known attributes or concepts [27]. Hereafter, we use the term signature to refer to this attribute description of a class.

Zero-shot learning is inherently a two-stage process: training and inference. In the training stage, knowledge about the attributes is captured, and in the inference stage this knowledge is used to categorise instances among a previously unseen set of classes. Many efforts have been made to improve the training stage [10, 15, 17], whereas the inference stage has received little attention [16]. For example many approaches blindly assume that all attributes convey the same amount of information, and can be predicted with the same accuracy, thus, they are evenly utilised in the inference rule. However these assumptions rarely hold true in real world cases.

We study a framework that is able to integrate both stages, overcoming the need to make strong and unrealistic assumptions, as the ones previously described. This framework, introduced in [1], is based on modelling the relationship between features, attributes, and classes as a (linear) model composed of two layers. The first layer contains the weights that describe the relationship between the features and the attributes, and is learned at the training stage. The second layer models the relationship between the attributes and the classes and is fixed using the prescribed attribute signatures of the classes. Given that the seen classes and the unseen classes are different, this second layer is interchangeable.

The main contributions of this work are:

- Given the framework in [1], we derive a principled choice of the regularizer, which has three nice properties:
  1. It performs comparably or better than the state of the art.
  2. It is efficient both at the training and at the inference stages.
  3. It is extremely easy to implement: one line of code for training and another one for inference (without calling any external functions).

- We provide a bound on the generalisation error of the approaches comprised in this framework. This is done by bridging the gap between zero-shot learning and domain adaptation, and making use of previous results in the latter [4, 5].

The remainder of the chapter is organised as follows. In Sect. 2.2 we briefly review methods proposed to deal with zero-shot learning. In Sect. 2.3 we describe the above ZSL framework, and present our method. In Sect. 2.4 we analyse its learning capabilities. In Sect. 2.5 we report the results of our experiments on one synthetic and three standard real datasets. Finally in Sect. 2.6 we discuss the main contributions of this work and propose several research lines that can be explored.

2.2 Related Work

Zero-shot learning relies on learning how to recognise several properties or attributes from objects, so that these learned attributes can be harnessed when used in the description of new, unseen classes. Indeed, it is attributes learning that drives the possibility of learning unseen classes based only on their description [27]. Within the context of machine learning, an antecedent of the notion of attribute learning can be found in [9] in the form of binary descriptors. The aim was using these binary descriptors as error-correcting codes, although these did not convey any semantic meaning. Recently, there has been an increasing interest in attributes learning, partially due to the availability of data containing tags or meta-information. This has proved to be particularly useful for images [10, 11, 21], as well as videos [13, 24].

Many papers focus on attributes learning, namely the training stage in zero-shot learning methods, putting special emphasis on the need to disentangle the correlations between attributes at the training stage, because these properties may not be present in the target data [17]. For example in [10] the authors focus on the feature extraction process with the aim of avoiding confusion in the learning process of attributes that often appear together in the training set instances.

With regard to the inference stage in which the predicted attributes are combined to infer a class, many approaches are variants of 1-nearest neighbour, or probabilistic frameworks. Approaches that resemble 1-nearest neighbour consist in looking in the attribute space for the closest unseen class signature to the predicted attribute signature of the input instance. It is used in [10], and in [28] the authors study risk bounds of this approach when using the Hamming distances between the predicted signature and the signatures of the unseen classes. Whereas 1-nearest neighbour is an intuitive way for inferring classes from the attributes, it presents several drawbacks. Namely, it treats equally all dimensions of the attribute space, which may be suboptimal, as some attributes are more important than others for discriminating between classes, and metrics such as Hamming distance ignore quantitative information in the prediction of the attributes.

In [21, 22] the authors propose a two-stage probabilistic framework in which the predictions obtained in the first stage can be combined to determine the most likely unseen class. Within this framework two approaches are proposed: directed attribute prediction (DAP), and indirect attribute prediction (IAP). In DAP a probabilistic classifier (e.g. logistic regression model) is learned at the training stage for each attribute. At the inference stage, the previous estimators are used to infer among the unseen classes provided their attributes signatures. In IAP one probabilistic classifier is learned for each seen class, whereas at the inference stage the predictions are combined accounting for the signatures of both seen and unseen classes. The DAP approach has been widely used by many other methods. In [35] the authors extend DAP by weighting the importance of each attribute, based on its frequency of appearance. These probabilistic approaches bring a principled way of combining the attribute predictions of a new instance in order to infer its class. However, in addition to being unable to estimate the reliability of the predicted attributes, they introduce a set of independence assumptions that hardly ever hold in real world, for example, when describing animals the attributes "terrestrial" and "farm" are dependent, but are treated as independent in these approaches.

Very recently, the authors of [16] proposed an approach that acknowledges uncertainty in the prediction of attributes, having mechanisms to deal with it. The approach is based on random forests that classify attribute signatures into the unseen classes, using a validation partition from the training set. The resultant model empirically proves to be superior to previous inference methods, such as DAP, and it obtains state-of-the-art results in the benchmark datasets. One of the limitations of this model is the need to have the attribute signatures of the unseen classes at the training stage. In other words, the model learned at the training stage is tailored to work with a predefined set of unseen classes.

The approach we describe in Sect. 2.3 bypasses the limitations of these methods by expressing a model based on an optimisation problem which relates features, attributes and classes. There are some works which follow a similar strategy. A relevant approach is the one described in [1], where the authors propose a model that implicitly learns the instances and the attributes embeddings onto a common space where the compatibility between any pair of them can be measured. The approach we describe here is based on the same principle, however we use a different loss function and regularizer which not only makes the whole process simpler and efficient, but also leads to much better results. Another related approach is proposed in [14], where the authors use the information regarding the correlations between attributes in both training and test instances. The main differences are that they focus on attribute prediction, and they employ a max-margin formulation that leads to a more complex approach. These approaches [1, 14], as well as the one we propose, can be seen as particular instances of the general framework described in [37], which unifies a wide range of multitask learning and multi-domain learning methods.

Other approaches consider the attributes as latent variables to be learned. For example in [36], an explicit feature map is designed to model the relationships between features, attributes and classes. Other approaches, such as [24, 26], consider different schemes where attributes representations are to be learned.

The approach we describe is grounded on the machine learning areas of transfer learning and domain adaptation. The term transfer learning encompasses several machine learning problems, and has received several names, such as learning to learn [23] or inductive transfer [7, 31, 33]. Here, we refer to transfer learning in the lifelong learning sense, that is, the aim is to extract knowledge from a set of source tasks, so that it can be applied to learn future tasks more efficiently. Zero-shot learning problems share the necessity to extrapolate the knowledge gained previously to tackle a new learning scenario. The main difference is that in transfer learning the information about the new tasks is given as a set of labelled instances, whereas in zero-shot learning this information takes the form of descriptions of the unseen classes. An extensive review of transfer learning methods can be found in [29].

The aim of domain adaptation is to learn a function from data in one domain, so that it can be successfully applied to data from a different domain [4, 8, 19]. It resembles transfer learning but there are important differences to note. In transfer learning the marginal input distribution (domain) in both source and target tasks is supposed to be the same, whereas each task comprises a different objective predictive function. For example, given a set of journal documents sampled from a fixed marginal distribution, a source task may consist in classifying documents between different topics, and the target task could be about classifying each document in terms of its author. Domain adaptation makes the reverse assumption, that is, the objective predictive function is the same but the marginal distributions for source and target tasks are different. Following the previous example, now we have a common function to learn: classifying documents in terms of different topics. However the source and target tasks receive documents from two different journals, that is, from two different marginal distributions. The link between our approach and domain adaptation becomes clear in Sect. 2.4.1.

2.3 Embarrassingly Simple ZSL

In order to explain our approach, we start by describing a standard linear supervised learning method, and then extend that model to tackle the ZSL scenario. In the following, we adopt the convention of using lower-case letters to denote scalars, lower-cases bold letters to denote vectors, and higher-case bold letters to denote matrices.

Supervised linear model

Let us denote by $\mathbf{X} \in \mathbb{R}^{d \times m}$ the instances available at the training stage, where d is the dimensionality of the data, and m is the number of instances. Similarly we use

$\mathbf{Y} \in \{0, 1\}^{m \times z}$ to denote the ground truth labels of each training instance belonging to any of the z classes. In most cases, each row of $\mathbf{Y}$ contains only one positive entry indicating the class it belongs to. Nevertheless, the present framework allows an instance to belong to several classes simultaneously.

If we were interested in learning a linear predictor for z classes, we would optimise the following problem:

$$\underset{W \in \mathbb{R}^{d \times z}}{\text{minimise}} \; L\left(\mathbf{X}^\top \mathbf{W}, \mathbf{Y}\right) + \Omega\left(\mathbf{W}\right), \tag{2.1}$$

where $\mathbf{W}$ contains the parameters to be learned, L is a convex loss function, and Ω a convex regularizer. Problem (2.1) encompasses several approaches, depending on the choice of L and Ω. For example if L is the sum of hinge losses, and Ω is the Frobenius norm, this would lead to a standard support vector machine (SVM), but one can consider other loss functions such as logistic loss, and other regularizers, such as the trace norm, leading to multitask learning methods [2, 32].

ZSL model

Quoting [21], the formal definition of the ZSL problem can be described as follows:

> Let $(\mathbf{x}_1, y_1), \ldots, (\mathbf{x}_m, y_m) \subset \mathcal{X} \times \mathcal{Y}$ be training samples where $\mathcal{X}$ is an arbitrary feature space and $\mathcal{Y}$ consists of z discrete classes. The task is to learn a classifier $f : \mathcal{X} \longrightarrow \mathcal{Y}'$ for a label set $\mathcal{Y}'$ of z' classes, that is disjoint from $\mathcal{Y}$.

In order to accomplish that, we are given the attributes of all classes as additional information. We assume that each class is described by a known signature composed of a attributes. We can represent the training signatures in a matrix $\mathbf{S} \in [0, 1]^{a \times z}$. This matrix may contain boolean entries, when the description of classes is defined as a list of attributes, or more generally, it may contain for each attribute any value in $[0, 1]$ providing a soft link between attributes and classes. Together matrices $\mathbf{Y}$ and $\mathbf{S}$ provide enough information so that one can obtain the ground truth attributes for each instance.

In problem (2.1) the attributes are not used, and therefore, there is no way to perform knowledge transfer from this set of classes to new classes. One can introduce the given information about the attributes, $\mathbf{S}$, by introducing a mapping from the attributes to the feature space, $\mathbf{V}$, such that $\mathbf{W} = \mathbf{VS}$, where $\mathbf{V} \in \mathbb{R}^{d \times a}$. That leads to the following problem, similar to the one proposed in [1]:

$$\underset{\mathbf{V} \in \mathbb{R}^{d \times a}}{\text{minimise}} \; L\left(\mathbf{X}^\top \mathbf{VS}, \mathbf{Y}\right) + \Omega\left(\mathbf{VS}\right). \tag{2.2}$$

At the inference stage, given the features of an instance, $\mathbf{x} \in \mathbb{R}^d$, we wish to determine to which class it belongs to, among a new set of z' unseen classes, $\mathcal{Y}'$, disjoint from the set of seen classes, $\mathcal{Y}$. To do so, we are provided with their attributes signatures, $\mathbf{S}' \in [0, 1]^{a \times z'}$. The prediction is then given by

$$\underset{i \in [1,\ldots,z']}{\operatorname{argmax}} \ \mathbf{x}^\top \mathbf{V} \mathbf{s}'_i, \tag{2.3}$$

where $\mathbf{s}'_i \in [0, 1]^a$ denotes the i-th column of matrix $\mathbf{S}'$.

One interpretation of this model is provided in [1]. There, each class is represented in the attribute space by means of its signature. Thus, the learning weights, $\mathbf{V}$, map any input instance, $\mathbf{x}$, into this attribute space. Given that both classes and instances are mapped into a common space, one can estimate the *compatibility* between them. Thus, at the inference stage, the model predicts the class in $\mathcal{Y}'$ that is most compatible with the input instance, by making use of (2.3). Note that if all given signatures are normalised, $\|\mathbf{s}'_1\|_2 = \|\mathbf{s}'_2\|_2 = \ldots \|\mathbf{s}'_{z'}\|_2$, then the notion of maximum compatibility among the signatures corresponds to finding the minimal Euclidean distance with respect to $\mathbf{V}^\top \mathbf{x}$ in the attribute space.

It is important to note the advantage of this model with respect to typical ZSL approaches reviewed in Sect. 2.2. Recall that these approaches were based on first estimating the attributes of a given instance, and then finding the class that best matches the predicted attributes, using some probabilistic or distance measure. In this way, all attributes are assumed to convey the same amount of information, an assumption that is likely detrimental, as often some attributes have more discriminative power than others. On the other hand, the approach in (2.2) is able to learn and exploit the relative importance of each of the attributes for discriminating between classes. For example, if the i-th attribute has less discriminative powers than the others, then the i-th column of the learned weights $\mathbf{V}$ should have a smaller norm than the others, so that it has a smaller contribution in the classification decision.

The method above makes the implicit assumption that for each attribute, its reliability to discriminate between seen classes is similar to its reliability to distinguish between unseen classes. In order to explain why this assumption is reasonable, let us recall the example of animals classification, and let us assume that we are given the attributes *it has teeth*, and *is white*. The former attribute may be more difficult to recognise than the latter, given that some instances of animals may not show the mouth, whereas the colour of an animal is easy to infer. Hence the importance of the attribute *it has teeth* for the final classification decision should be low, independently of the classes at hand, given that it is more difficult to learn a reliable predictor for that attribute. This assumption is relevant whenever the reliability on estimating the attributes remain constant, regardless of the classes considered. The key point of this framework is that it does not try to minimise explicitly the classification error of the attributes, which are an intermediate layer that we are not directly interested in. Instead, it minimises the multiclass error of the final classes, by both learning implicitly how to recognise attributes, and also pondering the importance of each of them in the decision of the class.

There are several points to note from problem (2.2). First, if the regularizer Ω is of the form $\Omega(\mathbf{B}) = \Psi\left(\mathbf{B}^\top \mathbf{B}\right)$ for an appropriate choice of the function Ψ, then by using the representer theorem [3], this leads to a kernel version of the problem, where only inner products between instances are used:

$$\underset{\mathbf{A}\in\mathbb{R}^{m\times a}}{\text{minimise}}\; L\left(\mathbf{KAS}, \mathbf{Y}\right) + \Psi\left(\mathbf{S}^\top \mathbf{A}^\top \mathbf{KAS}\right), \tag{2.4}$$

where $\mathbf{K} \in \mathbb{R}^{m\times m}$ is the Gram matrix, $k_{i,j} = \langle \phi(\mathbf{x}_i), \phi(\mathbf{x}_j)\rangle$, being $\phi(\mathbf{x})$ the representation of $\mathbf{x}$ in a given feature space. Secondly, problem (2.2) and its equivalent problem (2.4) are convex, thus its globally optimal solution can be found.

A scheme of this framework is shown in Fig. 2.1. This framework is utilised in its linear form (Eq. 2.2) in [1], for a particular choice of the loss function (based on the hinge loss function), and the regularizer (based on the Frobenius norm of the learning weights). In the following, we describe and justify a different choice for those elements, which leads to a more efficient and effective training model.

2.3.1 Regularisation and Loss Function Choices

We now come to the first contribution of this chapter. The framework described above comprises several approaches, which vary depending on their regularizers and loss functions. Here we design a regularizer which accomplishes the following desiderata:

- Given any (training) attribute signature, $\mathbf{s}_i \in [0, 1]^a$ for some $i \in [1, \ldots, z]$, its mapping to the d-dimensional feature space is given by $\mathbf{V}\mathbf{s}_i \in \mathbb{R}^d$. This representation must be controlled so that ideally the mapping of all signatures on the feature space have a similar Euclidean norm. This allows fair comparisons between signatures, and prevents problems that stem from highly unbalanced training sets.
- Conversely, the mapping of each training instance $\mathbf{x}_i$, for $i \in [1, \ldots, m]$, into the a-dimensional attribute space is given by $\mathbf{V}^\top \mathbf{x}_i \in \mathbb{R}^a$. Similarly to the previous point, it would be interesting to bound the Euclidean norm of that term. The aim here is to map all instances to a common region in the attribute space. In this way, we can encourage the generalisation of the model to test instances, if their representation into the attribute space fall into the same region where the training instances lie.

A regularizer that accomplishes the previous points can be written as follows:

$$\Omega\left(\mathbf{V}; \mathbf{S}, \mathbf{X}\right) = \gamma \left\|\mathbf{VS}\right\|_{\text{Fro}}^2 + \lambda \left\|\mathbf{X}^\top \mathbf{V}\right\|_{\text{Fro}}^2 + \beta \left\|\mathbf{V}\right\|_{\text{Fro}}^2, \tag{2.5}$$

where the scalars γ, λ, β are the hyper-parameters of this regularizer, and $\|\cdot\|_{\text{Fro}}$ denotes the Frobenius norm. The first two terms account for the above points, and we have added one further term consisting in a standard weight decay penalising the Frobenius norm of the matrix to be learned.

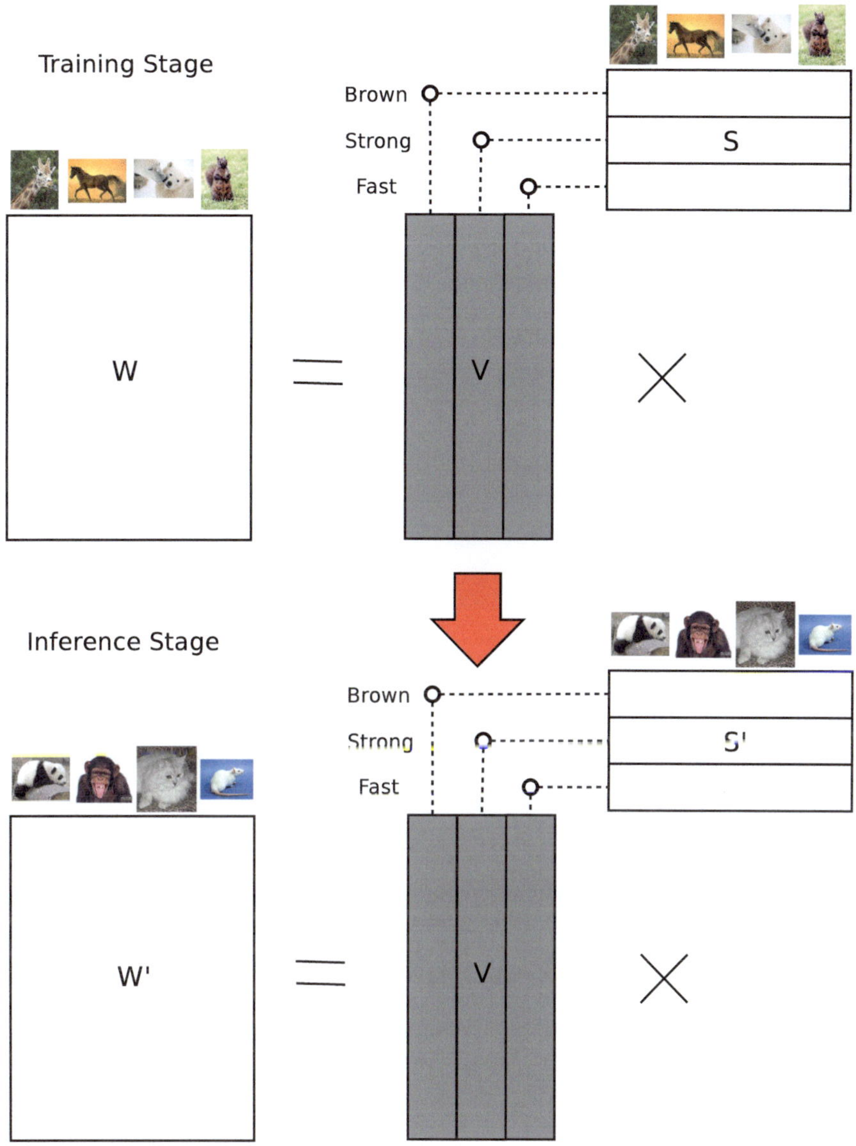

Fig. 2.1 Summary of the framework described in Sect. 2.3. At the training stage, we use the matrix of signatures **S** together with the training instances to learn the matrix **V** (in *grey*) which maps from the feature space to the attribute space. At the inference stage, we use that matrix **V**, together with the signatures of the unseen classes, **S**$'$, to obtain the final linear model **W**$'$

Having made these choices, we note that if:

- $L(\mathbf{P}, \mathbf{Y}) = \|\mathbf{P} - \mathbf{Y}\|_{\text{Fro}}^2$.
- $\beta = \gamma\lambda$

then the solution to problem (2.2) can be expressed in closed form:

$$\mathbf{V} = \left(\mathbf{X}\mathbf{X}^\top + \gamma\mathbf{I}\right)^{-1} \mathbf{X}\mathbf{Y}\mathbf{S}^\top \left(\mathbf{S}\mathbf{S}^\top + \lambda\mathbf{I}\right)^{-1}. \tag{2.6}$$

This, and the corresponding kernel version that can be derived from (2.4), are the one-line-of-code solutions we mentioned in the introduction.

2.4 Risk Bounds

In this section we provide some theoretical guarantees about our approach, bounding the expected error on the inference stage with respect to the training error. In order to do so, we first transform our problem into a domain adaptation one.

2.4.1 *Simple ZSL as a Domain Adaptation Problem*

Let us assume that problem (2.2) can be expressed in the following way:

$$\underset{\mathbf{V}\in\mathbb{R}^{d\times a}}{\text{minimise}} \sum_{i=1}^{m}\sum_{t=1}^{z} \ell\left(\mathbf{x}_i^\top \mathbf{V}\mathbf{s}_t^\top, y_{t,i}\right) + \Omega(\mathbf{V}), \tag{2.7}$$

where $\ell(\cdot,\cdot) : \mathbb{R} \times \{-1, 1\} \longrightarrow [0, 1]$. That implies that one instance may be classified to belong to zero, one, or more than one classes. Such an assumption may be realistic in some cases, for example when there are some instances in the training set that do not belong to any seen class. Then, problem (2.7) can be expressed in a more conventional form:

$$\underset{\mathbf{v}\in\mathbb{R}^{da}}{\text{minimise}} \sum_{i=1}^{m}\sum_{t=1}^{T} \ell\left(\widetilde{\mathbf{x}}_{t,i}^\top \mathbf{v}, y_{t,i}\right) + \Omega(\mathbf{v}), \tag{2.8}$$

where

$$\widetilde{\mathbf{x}}_{t,i} = \text{vec}\left(\mathbf{x}_i \mathbf{s}_t^\top\right) \in \mathbb{R}^{da}. \tag{2.9}$$

Note that at the inference time, given a new instance, $\mathbf{x}$, the predicted confidence of it belonging to an unseen class t with attribute signature $\mathbf{s}_t$, is given by $\widetilde{\mathbf{x}}_t^\top \mathbf{v} = \mathbf{v}^\top \text{vec}\left(\mathbf{x}\mathbf{s}_t^\top\right)$. Therefore, even if the original test instances $\mathbf{x}$ were sampled from the same distribution as the training instances, the transformation of them using attributes signatures makes the training and test instances come from different distributions. Note also that in the current settings, we are learning a unique common function across domains. As a consequence, we are facing a domain adaptation problem.

2.4.2 *Risk Bounds for Domain Adaptation*

Domain adaptation has been analysed from a theoretical viewpoint in several works [4, 5]. Here we apply these developments to our problem.

In a domain adaptation problem we assume that the training instances are sampled from a source distribution $\mathcal{D}$, and the test instances are sampled from a target distribution $\mathcal{D}'$. Following the definition of [4], a function h is said to be a predictor if it maps from the feature space to $\{0, 1\}$, and f is the ground truth labelling function for both domains, mapping from the feature space to $[0, 1]$. Then the expected error of h with respect to the source distribution is defined as:

$$\varepsilon(h) = \mathbb{E}_{\mathbf{x}\sim\mathcal{D}}\left[|f(\mathbf{x}) - h(\mathbf{x})|\right],$$

and the expected error of h with respect to the target distribution, $\varepsilon'(h)$, is defined accordingly.

Theorem 2 in [4] states that given a hypothesis space $\mathcal{H}$ of VC-dimension $\bar{d}$, and sets $\mathcal{U}, \mathcal{U}'$ of $\bar{m}$ instances sampled i.i.d. from $\mathcal{D}$ and $\mathcal{D}'$, respectively, then with probability at least $1 - \delta$, for every $h \in \mathcal{H}$:

$$\varepsilon'(h) \le \varepsilon(h) + 4\sqrt{\frac{2\bar{d}}{\bar{m}}\left(\log\frac{2\bar{m}}{\bar{d}} + \log\frac{4}{\delta}\right)} + \alpha + \frac{1}{2}\hat{d}_{\mathcal{H}\Delta\mathcal{H}}\left(\mathcal{U}, \mathcal{U}'\right), \qquad (2.10)$$

where

- α is an upper-bound of $\inf\limits_{h\in\mathcal{H}}\left[\varepsilon(h) + \varepsilon'(h)\right]$. In particular if the ground truth function f is contained in $\mathcal{H}$, then $\alpha = 0$.
- $d_{\mathcal{H}}\left(\mathcal{D}, \mathcal{D}'\right)$ is known as the $\mathcal{A}$-distance between distributions $\mathcal{D}$ and $\mathcal{D}'$ over the subsets defined in $\mathcal{H}$ [20]:

$$d_{\mathcal{H}}\left(\mathcal{D}, \mathcal{D}'\right) = 2\sup_{h\in\mathcal{H}}\left|P_{\mathcal{D}}(h) - P_{\mathcal{D}'}(h)\right|,$$

  where $P_{\mathcal{D}}(h)$ denotes the probability of any event in h, under the distribution $\mathcal{D}$. This is equivalent to the expected maximal accuracy achieved by a hypothesis in $\mathcal{H}$ separating the instances generated by the two different distributions $\mathcal{D}$ and $\mathcal{D}'$. In a similar vein, $\hat{d}_{\mathcal{H}}\left(\mathcal{U}_S, \mathcal{U}_T\right)$ is defined as the empirical distance between the samples $\mathcal{U}$ and $\mathcal{U}'$.

- $\mathcal{H}\Delta\mathcal{H}$ is the symmetric difference hypothesis space of $\mathcal{H}$ and it is defined as: $\mathcal{H}\Delta\mathcal{H} = \{h(x) \oplus h'(x) : h, h' \in \mathcal{H}\}$, $\oplus$ being the XOR operator. That is, a hypothesis g is in $\mathcal{H}\Delta\mathcal{H}$, if for a couple of hypothesis h,h' in $\mathcal{H}$, $g(x)$ is positive if and only if $h(x) \neq h'(x)$ for all x.

In our case $\mathcal{H}$ is the hypothesis space composed of all linear classifiers, $\bar{m} = mz$, and $\bar{d} = da + 1$. Let us assume that both train and test instances are sampled from the same distribution, $\mathcal{C}$. When we do the transformation specified in Eq. (2.9) using $\mathbf{S}$ and $\mathbf{S}'$ for the training and test instances, we end up having two different distributions, $\mathcal{D}$, and $\mathcal{D}'$ and we are interested in quantifying the $\mathcal{A}$-distance between them over our symmetric difference hypothesis space, $d_{\mathcal{H}\Delta\mathcal{H}}\left(\mathcal{D}, \mathcal{D}'\right)$. The assumption about both train and test instances are sampled from the same distribution (before the transformation) may not hold true in many cases, however it can be a fair approximation in the standard case where the contribution of the differences of training and test distributions of the feature spaces is negligible in comparison to the differences between $\mathbf{S}$ and $\mathbf{S}'$ when quantifying the distance between distributions $\mathcal{D}$ and $\mathcal{D}'$.

We observe two extreme cases. The first one contemplates the trivial scenario where $\mathbf{S} = \mathbf{S}'$, so that both distributions are similar and thus the distance is 0. In that case, if $\alpha = 0$, the bound given in Eq. (2.10) becomes equivalent to the Vapnik–Chervonenkis bound on a standard classifier. The second case arises when each attribute signature of the seen classes is orthogonal to each attribute signature of the unseen classes, that is, for each $i \in \{1 \ldots z\}$, $j \in \{1 \ldots z'\}$, $\langle \mathbf{s}_i, \mathbf{s}'_j \rangle = 0$.

To make the explanation of the latter case clearer let us denote by $\mathbf{x} \in \mathbb{R}^d$ any training instance in the original feature space, and similarly let $\mathbf{x}' \in \mathbb{R}^d$ be any test instance. Then, by applying equation (2.9) using the training signature $\mathbf{s}_i$, and test signature $\mathbf{s}'_j$ we have

$\widetilde{\mathbf{x}}_i = \mathrm{vec}\left(\mathbf{x}\mathbf{s}_i^\top\right) \in \mathbb{R}^{da}$

$\widetilde{\mathbf{x}}'_j = \mathrm{vec}\left(\mathbf{x}'\mathbf{s}'^\top_j\right) \in \mathbb{R}^{da}$

Note that because of the orthogonality assumption between training and test signatures the following holds true:

$$\langle \widetilde{\mathbf{x}}_i, \widetilde{\mathbf{x}}'_j \rangle = \mathrm{trace}\left(\mathbf{x}\mathbf{s}_i^\top \mathbf{s}'_j \mathbf{x}'^\top\right) = 0. \quad (2.11)$$

Equation (2.11) implies that in the new feature space any training instance is orthogonal to any test instance. Because of that, the following lemma becomes useful.

Lemma 1 *Let us consider $\mathcal{H}$ be the hypothesis space composed of all linear classifiers. Then given two orthogonal sets $\mathcal{P}$, $\mathcal{Q}$, in which the element* 0 *is not in either of them, there exists a hypothesis $g \in \mathcal{H}\Delta\mathcal{H}$ which separates them.*

Proof Let us consider any couple of points $\mathbf{p} \in \mathcal{P}$, $\mathbf{q} \in \mathcal{Q}$ with the only condition that they are not zero. We define

$h(\mathbf{x}) = \mathrm{sign}\left((\mathbf{p} + \mathbf{q})^\top \mathbf{x}\right)$, and

$h'(\mathbf{x}) = \mathrm{sign}\left((\mathbf{p} - \mathbf{q})^\top \mathbf{x}\right)$.

For any point $\mathbf{p}' \in \mathcal{P}$, $h(\mathbf{p}') = h'(\mathbf{p}')$, given that by definition $\mathbf{p}'$ and $\mathbf{q}$ are orthogonal. Similarly, for any point $\mathbf{q}' \in \mathcal{Q}$, $h(\mathbf{q}') = -h'(\mathbf{q}')$.

Therefore, for any point in $\mathcal{Q}$, $g \in \mathcal{H}\Delta\mathcal{H}$ associated to functions $h, h' \in \mathcal{H}$ will be positive, and for any point in $\mathcal{P}$, the same function g will be negative. □

As a consequence of Lemma 1, when the orthogonality assumption holds, the right-hand side term in Eq. (2.10) becomes bigger than 1, so that the bound is vacuous. One illustrative instance of this case happens when $\mathbf{S} = [\mathbf{B}, \mathbf{0^{a,c}},]$, and $\mathbf{S}' = \left[\mathbf{0^{a,b}}, \mathbf{C}\right]$ for some non-zero matrices $\mathbf{B} \in \mathbb{R}^{a \times b}$, $\mathbf{C} \in \mathbb{R}^{a \times c}$. In that case, the set of attributes that describe the seen classes are completely different from the ones describing the unseen classes, thus no transfer can be done.

All real scenarios lay between the previous cases. One interesting question is to characterise the value $d_{\mathcal{H}\Delta\mathcal{H}}\left(\mathcal{D}, \mathcal{D}'\right)$ as a function of solely $\mathbf{S}$ and $\mathbf{S}'$. We leave this question open.

2.5 Experiments

In order to assess our approach and the validity of the statements we made, we conducted a set of experiments on one synthetic and three real datasets, which comprise a standard benchmark of evaluation of zero-shot learning methods.[1]

2.5.1 *Synthetic Experiments*

First we used synthetically generated data with the aim of both checking the correctness of the described method, which we refer to as ESZSL (embarrassingly simple zero-shot learning), and comparing it with the baseline algorithm DAP on a controlled set-up. All hyper-parameters required by these methods were tuned by a validation process. This process is based on leaving out one subset of validation classes, so that the performance of the model is validated against them. In all cases the range of values tried for the hyper-parameters was 10^b, for $b = -6, -5, \ldots, 5, 6$. This set of values was chosen after performing preliminary experiments which empirically showed that the optimal performance for both approaches is found within this interval.

The data were generated as follows. Initially, we created the signatures for the classes by sampling each element of $\mathbf{S}$ from a Bernoulli distribution with 0.5 mean. We created the ground truth mapping from the attributes to the features, $\mathbf{V}^{+} \in \mathbb{R}^{a \times d}$, where we have fixed $a = 100$ and $d = 10$, by sampling every element of it from a Gaussian distribution $\mathcal{G}(0, 1)$. The value of d is intentionally low so that there appear correlations between the attributes, as is usually the case in real data. For each class t,

[1] The code can be found at http://romera-paredes.com/zsl.

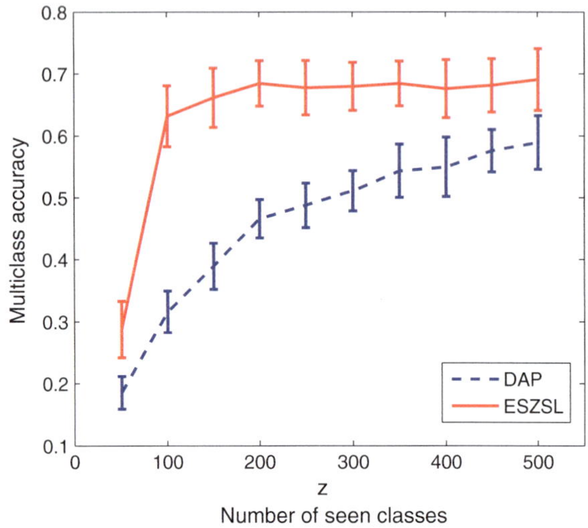

Fig. 2.2 Multiclass accuracy obtained by DAP [21], and ESZSL (Sect. 2.3.1), when varying the number of seen classes, z. *Vertical bars* indicate ± 1 standard deviation

we created 50 instances by first generating their representation in the attribute space by adding Gaussian noise, $\mathcal{G}(0, 0.1)$ to the attribute signature $\mathbf{S}_t$, then we brought them back onto the original feature space by using $\mathbf{V}^+$. Following this process, we generated a training set composed of z seen classes, and a test and validation set composed of 100 unseen classes each.

In the first experiment, we evaluated how the number of seen classes affected the performance of the methods on unseen classes. To do so, we varied the number of seen classes from 50 to 500 in intervals of 50. According to the results shown in Fig. 2.2, we can see that ESZSL significantly outperforms DAP in all cases. It is remarkable that the performance of ESZSL with 100 seen classes is superior to the performance of DAP with 500 seen classes. We also observe that the performance of ESZSL plateaus when the number of seen classes is above 200, possibly because there is no further margin of improvement.

In Sect. 2.3 we argue that the described approach should be robust to attributes having different discriminative capabilities for characterising the classes. In the second experiment, we assess how the approaches perform in the extreme case where some attributes provide no information at all about the classes at hand. The way we have implemented this is by first, synthesising a dataset just as described above, and second, by randomly selecting a set of attributes (without replacement) so that their information in all signatures is corrupted. In particular let us define by $\mathcal{A}$ the set of all attributes, with cardinality $|\mathcal{A}| = a$. From this set $\mathcal{A}$ we randomly sample ψ misleading attributes, creating the set $\Psi \subseteq \mathcal{A}$, $|\Psi| = \psi$. The way each of the inputs of the attributes in Ψ is corrupted is again by sampling from a Bernoulli distribution with 0.5 mean. In this experiment we have tried different values of ψ in the range of 5–45 attributes (out of 100), in intervals of 5. The results, reported in Fig. 2.3, show that our method significantly outperforms the baseline. For example we observe that when

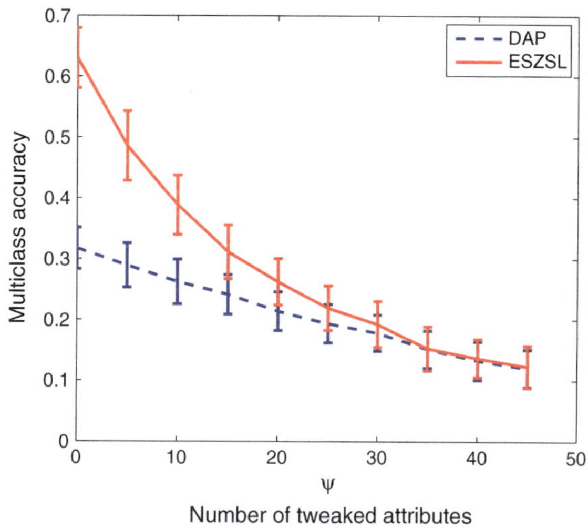

Fig. 2.3 Multiclass accuracy obtained by DAP [21], and ESZSL (Sect. 2.3.1), when varying the number of corrupted attributes, ψ. *Vertical bars* indicate ± 1 standard deviation

having 15 misleading attributes, our method achieves a comparable performance as the baseline with none misleading attributes.

2.5.2 *Real Data Experiments*

We have tried the same real datasets as the ones reported in [16] which are the Animals with Attributes dataset (AwA) [21], the SUN scene attributes database (SUN) [30] described in Chap. 11, and the aPascal/aYahoo objects dataset (aPY) [10]. These consist of collections of images comprising a varied set of categories in different scopes: animals, scenes, and objects, respectively. The AwA dataset contains attribute-labelled classes, which we will use as **S** in the model. The datasets aPY and SUN are attribute-labelled instances datasets, so the attribute signature of each class is calculated as the average attribute signature of the instances belonging to that class. The characteristics of each of these datasets are summarised in Table 2.1.

Table 2.1 Summary of the real datasets employed in the experimental section

	AwA	aPY	SUN
Attributes	85	65	102
Seen classes	40	20	707
Unseen classes	10	12	10
Instances	30, 475	15, 339	14, 340

In the following we perform three sets of experiments. In the first one, we compare our approach with alike methods that also belong to the framework described in Fig. 2.1. In the second set of experiments, we compare our approach against the current state of the art. Finally in the last experiment, we compare our approach and a standard classification method, for attributes prediction. The aim here is to assess whether the good results in zero-shot learning come at the expense of attribute prediction performance. In all cases, in order to tune the hyper-parameters of the methods, we use the following validation procedure. We create the validation set by grouping all instances belonging to 20 % of the classes in the training partition, chosen at random (without replacement). Once the hyper-parameters are tuned, we pool the validation set instances together with the training set instances in order to train the final model. We use the range of values, 10^b for $b = -3, -2, \dots, 2, 3$ to tune all hyper-parameters.

2.5.2.1 Preliminary Experiments

Here we present an experiment comparing our approach to [1]. We used the recently provided VGG network features [34], of the AwA dataset. This dataset also provides both binary and continuous versions of the attributes signatures. Here, we compare these two scenarios. We utilised the best configuration reported on [1], using different training set sizes of 500, 1000, and 2000 instances. The results are shown in Table 2.2. As expected, both approaches perform better when the attributes signatures are continuous. In any case, our approach clearly outperforms [1] in all cases. It is also worth mentioning that the approach in [1] took more than 11 hours to run the scenario with 2000 training instances, whereas ours only took 4.12 s.

2.5.2.2 Comparison with the State of the Art

In order to make our approach easily comparable with the state of the art, we used the set of standard features provided by the authors of the data [16, 21, 30], including SIFT [25], and PHOG [6]. We used combined χ^2-kernels, one for each feature

Table 2.2 Comparison between the approach in [1] and ESZSL, using VGG features extracted from the AwA dataset, utilising binary attributes signatures (Left), and continuous attributes signatures (Right)

Training instances	Binary attributes		Continuous attributes	
	[1]	ESZSL	[1]	ESZSL
500	33.30 %	**33.85** %	47.31 %	**51.63** %
1000	39.02 %	**43.16** %	49.40 %	**53.87** %
2000	41.02 %	**46.89** %	54.09 %	**56.99** %

Table 2.3 Multiclass accuracy obtained by DAP [21], ZSRwUA [16], the method described in Sect. 2.3.1 ESZSL, and its modification ESZSL-AS, on the three real datasets described in Table 2.1

Method/Dataset	AwA	aPY	SUN
DAP	40.50	18.12	52.50
ZSRwUA	43.01 ± 0.07	26.02 ± 0.05	56.18 ± 0.27
ESZSL	**49.30 ± 0.21**	15.11 ± 2.24	**65.75 ± 0.51**
ESZSL-AS	–	**27.27 ± 1.62**	61.53 ± 1.03

channel,[2] following the procedure explained in [16, 21]. In all cases, we used the same attributes signatures, and the same standard partitions between seen and unseen classes, as the ones employed in [16].

In these experiments we compare 4 methods: DAP [21], ZSRwUA [16], ESZSL (Sect. 2.3.1), and a small modification of the latter that we call ESZSL All Signatures (ESZSL-AS).

ESZSL-AS can be applied in attribute-labelled instances datasets (aPY and SUN), and consists in treating each training attribute signature as a class in its own right. That is effectively done by removing Y in Eq. (2.6), where now $S \in \mathbb{R}^{a \times m}$ contains as many signatures as the number of training instances. The inference process remains the same, and the unseen class signatures are used to predict the category.

For each dataset we ran 20 trials, and we report the mean and the standard deviation of the multiclass accuracy in Table 2.3. Overall we notice that the approaches described in Sect. 2.3 significantly outperform the state of the art.

In the AwA dataset, ESZSL achieves an absolute improvement over 6 % over the state of the art. Even more surprising, this performance is better than state-of-the-art approaches applied to discovered (non-semantic) attributes, which according to [16] is 48.7. Let us recall that this dataset contains attribute-labelled classes, and so, ESZSL-AS cannot be applied here.

Regarding the aPY dataset, the standard ESZSL approach has struggled and it is not able to outperform the DAP baseline. One hypothesis is that the small number of classes in comparison to the number of attributes has probably affected negatively the performance. In contrast we see that ESZSL-AS obtains state-of-the-art results, achieving a 1.25 % of improvement over the previous best approach. Its success can be explained by reversing the previous reasoning about why standard ESZSL failed. Indeed, ESZSL-AS effectively considers as many seen classes as the number of training instances.

Finally, in the SUN dataset both ESZSL approaches obtain extremely good results, significantly outperforming the current state of the art. ESZSL leads the table, achieving an improvement of 9.6 %. We note that here the number of seen classes is much bigger than the number of attributes, therefore the advantages obtained by ESZSL-AS in the previous experiment vanish.

[2] Available at www.ist.ac.at/chl/ABC.

Table 2.4 Comparison between SVM (Learning attributes directly), and ESZSL, for attributes prediction, using mean average precision as a measure

Mean Average Precision	AwA	aPY	SUN
Learning attributes directly	**56.95** %	**30.78** %	**79.36** %
Using $\mathbf{X}^\top\mathbf{V}$ from ESZSL	50.73 %	29.51 %	68.53 %

2.5.2.3 Attributes Prediction

The focus of our model is on maximising the multiclass accuracy among the classes at hand. However, as a byproduct of the learning process, we can also use V as a way to predict attributes. In this experiment we check whether these attribute predictors are effective, or on the contrary, the gain in zero-shot performance comes at the expense of attribute prediction. In order to do so, we compare the described option with a simple approach that learns an SVM for each attribute directly. The results are reported in Table 2.4.

The gain in ZSL performance comes at the expense of attribute prediction. This may be because our approach tends to neglect the attributes that are unreliable or useless for class prediction, whereas in attribute prediction all are considered equally important. These results are in the same vein as the ones reported in [1].

2.6 Discussion

In this work, we have described an extremely simple approach for ZSL that is able to outperform by a significant margin the current state of the art approaches on a standard collection of ZSL datasets. It combines a linear model together with a principled choice of regularizers that allow for a simple and efficient implementation.

We have also made explicit a connection between ZSL and domain adaptation. In particular, we have expressed the framework described in Sect. 2.3 as a domain adaptation problem. As a consequence, we are able to translate theoretical developments from domain adaptation to ZSL.

Given the simplicity of the approach, there are many different research lines that can be pursued. In this work we focus on semantically meaningful attributes, but the development of similar ideas applied to word embeddings as in [12], is both promising and straightforward within this framework. Another interesting research line is to study the addition of nonlinearities and more layers into the model, leading to a deep neural network where the top layer is fixed and interchangeable, and all the remaining layers are learned. Recent works exploring this direction are [18, 37].

As a concluding comment, we acknowledge that many problems require complex solutions, but that does not mean that simple baselines should be ignored. On the contrary, simple but strong baselines both bring light about which paths to follow in order to build more sophisticated solutions, and also provide a way to measure the quality of these solutions.

Acknowledgements Financial support provided by EPSRC, Leverhulme Trust and ERC grants ERC- 2012-AdG 321162-HELIOS and HELIOS-DFR00200. We thank Christoph Lampert, and Dinesh Jayaraman for kindly providing the real datasets used here.

References

1. Akata, Z., Perronnin, F., Harchaoui, Z., Schmid, C.: Label-embedding for attribute-based classification. In: Conference on Computer Vision and Pattern Recognition (CVPR) (2013)
2. Argyriou, A., Evgeniou, T., Pontil, M.: Convex multi-task feature learning. Mach. Learn. (ML) **73**(3), 243–272 (2008)
3. Argyriou, A., Micchelli, C.A., Pontil, M.: When is there a representer theorem? vector versus matrix regularizers. J. Mach. Learn. Res. (JMLR) **10**, 2507–2529 (2009)
4. Ben-David, S., Blitzer, J., Crammer, K., Kulesza, A., Pereira, F., Vaughan, J.W.: A theory of learning from different domains. Mach. Learn. (ML) **79**(1–2), 151–175 (2010)
5. Ben-david, S., Blitzer, J., Crammer, K., Sokolova, P.M.: Analysis of representations for domain adaptation. In: Conference on Neural Information Processing Systems (NIPS) (2006)
6. Bosch, A., Zisserman, A., Munoz, X.: Representing shape with a spatial pyramid kernel. In: International conference on Image and video retrieval (CIVR) (2007)
7. Croonenborghs, T., Driessens, K., Bruynooghe, M.: Learning relational options for inductive transfer in relational reinforcement learning. In: International conference on Inductive logic programming (ILP) (2008)
8. Daumé III, H.: Frustratingly easy domain adaptation. In: Annual Meeting of the Association of Computational Linguistics (ACL) (2007)
9. Dietterich, T.G., Bakiri, G.: Solving multiclass learning problems via error-correcting output codes. J. Artif. Intell. Res. **2**(1), 263–286 (1994)
10. Farhadi, A., Endres, I., Hoiem, D., Forsyth, D.: Describing objects by their attributes. In: Conference on Computer Vision and Pattern Recognition (CVPR) (2009)
11. Ferrari, V., Zisserman, A.: Learning visual attributes. In: Conference on Neural Information Processing Systems (NIPS) (2007)
12. Frome, A., Corrado, G., Shlens, J., Bengio, S., Dean, J., Ranzato, M., Mikolov, T.: Devise: a deep visual-semantic embedding model. In: Conference on Neural Information Processing Systems (NIPS) (2013)
13. Fu, Y., Hospedales, T.M., Xiang, T., Gong, S.: Learning multimodal latent attributes. IEEE Trans. Pattern Anal. Mach. Intell. (PAMI) **36**(2), 303–316 (2014)
14. Hariharan, B., Vishwanathan, S., Varma, M.: Efficient max-margin multi-label classification with applications to zero-shot learning. Mach. Learn. (ML) **88**(1), 127–155 (2011)
15. Hwang, S.J., Sha, F., Grauman, K.: Sharing features between objects and their attributes. In: Conference on Computer Vision and Pattern Recognition (CVPR) (2011)
16. Jayaraman, D., Grauman, K.: Zero-shot recognition with unreliable attributes. In: Conference on Neural Information Processing Systems (NIPS) (2014)
17. Jayaraman, D., Sha, F., Grauman, K.: Decorrelating semantic visual attributes by resisting the urge to share. In: Conference on Computer Vision and Pattern Recognition (CVPR) (2014)
18. Jetley, S., Romera-Paredes, B., Jayasumana, S., Torr, P.H.: Prototypical priors: from improving classification to zero-shot learning. In: British Machine Vision Conference (BMVC) (2015)

19. Jiang, J., Zhai, C.: Instance weighting for domain adaptation in nlp. In: Annual Meeting of the Association of Computational Linguistics (ACL) (2007)
20. Kifer, D., Ben-David, S., Gehrke, J.: Detecting change in data streams. In: International Conference on Very Large Data Bases (VLDB) (2004)
21. Lampert, C.H., Nickisch, H., Harmeling, S.: Learning to detect unseen object classes by between-class attribute transfer. In: Conference on Computer Vision and Pattern Recognition (CVPR) (2009)
22. Lampert, C.H., Nickisch, H., Harmeling, S.: Attribute-based classification for zero-shot visual object categorization. IEEE Trans. Pattern Anal. Mach. Intell. (PAMI) **36**(3), 453–465 (2014)
23. Lawrence, N.D., Platt, J.C.: Learning to learn with the informative vector machine. In: International Conference on Machine Learning (ICML) (2004)
24. Liu, J., Kuipers, B., Savarese, S.: Recognizing human actions by attributes. In: Conference on Computer Vision and Pattern Recognition (CVPR) (2011)
25. Lowe, D.G.: Distinctive image features from scale-invariant keypoints. Int. J. Comput. Vis. (IJCV) **60**(2), 91–110 (2004)
26. Mahajan, D., Sellamanickam, S., Nair, V.: A joint learning framework for attribute models and object descriptions. In: International Conference on Computer Vision (ICCV) (2011)
27. Murphy, G.: The Big Book of Concepts. The MIT Press (2004)
28. Palatucci, M., Hinton, G., Pomerleau, D., Mitchell, T.M.: Zero-shot learning with semantic output codes. In: Conference on Neural Information Processing Systems (NIPS) (2009)
29. Pan, S.J., Yang, Q.: A survey on transfer learning. IEEE Trans. Knowl. Data Eng. **22**(10), 1345–1359 (2010)
30. Patterson, G., Hays, J.: Sun attribute database: Discovering, annotating, and recognizing scene attributes. In: Conference on Computer Vision and Pattern Recognition (CVPR) (2012)
31. Raykar, V.C., Krishnapuram, B., Bi, J., Dundar, M., Rao, R.B.: Bayesian multiple instance learning: automatic feature selection and inductive transfer. In: International Conference on Machine Learning (ICML) (2008)
32. Romera-Paredes, B., Aung, H., Bianchi-Berthouze, N., Pontil, M.: Multilinear multitask learning. In: International Conference on Machine Learning (ICML) (2013)
33. Rückert, U., Kramer, S.: Kernel-based inductive transfer. In: European Conference on Machine Learning and Principles and Practice of Knowledge Discovery (ECML–PKDD) (2008)
34. Simonyan, K., Zisserman, A.: Very deep convolutional networks for large-scale image recognition. In: International Conference on Learning Representations (ICLR) (2015)
35. Suzuki, M., Sato, H., Oyama, S., Kurihara, M.: Transfer learning based on the observation probability of each attribute. In: International Conference on Systems, Man and Cybernetics (2014)
36. Wang, Y., Mori, G.: A discriminative latent model of object classes and attributes. In: European Conference on Computer Vision (ECCV) (2010)
37. Yang, Y., Hospedales, T.M.: A unified perspective on multi-domain and multi-task learning. In: International Conference on Learning Representations (ICLR) (2015)

Chapter 3
In the Era of Deep Convolutional Features: Are Attributes Still Useful Privileged Data?

Viktoriia Sharmanska and Novi Quadrianto

Abstract Our answer is, if used for challenging computer vision tasks, attributes are useful privileged data. We introduce a learning framework called *learning using privileged information (LUPI)* to the computer vision field to solve the object recognition task in images. We want computers to be able to learn more efficiently at the expense of providing extra information during training time. In this chapter, we focus on semantic attributes as a source of additional information about image data. This information is privileged to image data as it is not available at test time. Recently, image features from deep convolutional neural networks (CNNs) have become primary candidates for many visual recognition tasks. We will therefore analyze the usefulness of attributes as privileged information in the context of deep CNN features as image representation. We explore two maximum-margin LUPI techniques and provide a kernelized version of them to handle nonlinear binary classification problems. We interpret LUPI methods as learning to identify easy and hard objects in the privileged space and transferring this knowledge to train a better classifier in the original data space. We provide a thorough analysis and comparison of information transfer from privileged to the original data spaces for two maximum-margin LUPI methods and a recently proposed probabilistic LUPI method based on Gaussian processes. Our experiments show that in a typical recognition task such as deciding whether an object is "present" or "not present" in an image, attributes do not lead to improvement in the prediction performance when used as privileged information. In an ambiguous vision task such as determining how "easy" or "difficult" it is to spot an object in an image, we show that attribute representation is useful privileged information for deep CNN image features.

V. Sharmanska (✉) · N. Quadrianto
SMiLe CLiNiC, University of Sussex, BN1 9QJ, Brighton, UK
e-mail: sharmanska.v@gmail.com

N. Quadrianto
e-mail: n.quadrianto@sussex.ac.uk

R.S. Feris et al. (eds.), *Visual Attributes*, Advances in Computer Vision and Pattern Recognition, DOI 10.1007/978-3-319-50077-5_3

3.1 Introduction

Image representations in terms of semantic attributes have gained popularity in computer vision, where they were used for a variety of tasks ranging from solving classification problems based on class descriptions instead of training data (zero-shot learning) [1, 26], enabling interactivity in image search [22], automatically creating (textual) descriptions of images [13, 25], to providing additional data representations to computer vision tasks [18, 32, 42, 44, 53]. In this work, we build on the last aspect where the semantic attribute representation is considered as a source of privileged information about image data.

The framework called *learning using privileged information (LUPI)* was formally introduced by Vapnik et al. [48, 49], and it has not been recognized in the computer vision community until very recently. The concept is inspired by human experience of learning with a teacher, when during learning we have access to training examples and to an additional source of explanation from the teacher. For example, learning a new concept in mathematics is faster when the teacher explains it to us rather than if we only get questions and right answers. After the course, the students should be able to solve new tasks themselves and not rely on the teacher's expertise anymore. Training with a teacher can significantly improve the learning process and ability to generalize for humans and machines [48].

As a general framework, LUPI has been successfully applied to a variety of learning scenarios: data clustering [14], facial feature detection [52], facial expression recognition via boosting [7], metric learning [16], learning to rank [42], Gaussian Processes classification with privileged noise [18], structured estimation problems [15], image categorization with privileged Internet data [28, 31], counting with backpropagation [6], and classification with annotation disagreements [43]. There are several theoretical studies about LUPI exploring its relation with weighted SVM [27], distillation [29], and similarity control when learning with a teacher [48].

In the standard learning setting, we are given input–output training pairs about the task we want to learn, for example, images and category labels for object classification. In the LUPI setting, we have the input–output training pairs plus additional information for each training pair that is *only available during training*. There is no direct limitation on the form of privileged information, i.e., it could be yet another feature representation like attributes, or a completely different modality like text in addition to image data, that is specific for each training instance.

Recently, deep learning techniques, particularly convolutional neural networks, which rely on large data with rich annotations, have produced state-of-the-art image feature representations [19, 23]. Earlier work in LUPI for visual data with privileged semantic attributes information [18, 42, 44] do not use these strong features as an image representation. This chapter will put the LUPI framework in the perspective of deep learning features. In a similar vein, [32, 53] use semantic attributes as auxiliary information for learning deep features and show performance gain in object detection and face alignment tasks. Our paper is complementary to these works as we do not learn original or privileged feature representations, but utilize the best available feature representations to learn a better classifier in the original space.

Approach and contribution
In order to do LUPI, we have to understand how to make use of the data modality that is not available at test time. For example, training a classifier on the privileged data is useless, since there is no way to evaluate the resulting classifier on the test data. At the core of our work lies the assumption that *privileged information allows us to distinguish between* easy *and* hard *examples in the training set.* Assuming that examples that are easy or hard with respect to the privileged information will also be easy or hard with respect to the original data, we enable *information transfer* from the privileged to the original data modality. More specifically, we first define and identify which samples are easy and which are hard for the classification task, and then we incorporate the privileged information into the sample weights that encodes its easiness or hardness.

We formalize the above observation in Sect. 3.3, where we study and compare two maximum-margin learning techniques for LUPI. The first, SVM+, was originally described by Vapnik [49], and the second, *Margin Transfer*, is our contribution. We analyze the core difference of the information transfer in the proposed methods, and how this kind of knowledge about the learning problem can guide the training of an image-based predictor to a better solution. In Sect. 3.4, we present our experiments using semantic attributes as privileged information in two scenarios: object classification and easy-hard recognition. We end with the discussion and conclusions in Sect. 3.5.

3.2 Related Work

In computer vision problems, it is common to have access to multiple sources of information. Sometimes all of them are visual, such as when images are represented by color features as well as by texture features. Sometimes, the modalities are mixed, such as for images with text captions. If all modalities are present both at training and at test time, it is rather straight forward to combine them for better prediction performance. This is studied, e.g., in the fields of *multimodal* or *multi-view* learning. Methods suggested here range from *stacking*, where one simply concatenates the feature vectors of all data modalities, to complex adaptive methods for early or late data fusions [45], including *multiple kernel learning* [50] and *LP-β* [17].

Situations with an asymmetric distribution of information have also been explored. In *weakly supervised* learning, the annotation available at training time is less detailed than the output one wants to predict. This situation occurs, e.g., when trying to learn an *image segmentation* system using only per-image or bounding box annotation [24]. In *multiple instance* learning, training labels are given not for individual examples, but collectively for groups of examples [30]. The inverse situation also occurs: for example in the PASCAL object recognition challenge, it has become a standard technique to incorporate strong annotation in the form of bounding boxes or per-pixel segmentations, even when the goal is just per-image object categorization [11, 37]. Similar to strong and weak supervision, situations in which the data representations differ between training and testing phase can be distinguished by whether one has less or more information available at training time than at test time. The first situation occurs, e.g., in tracking, where temporal continuity can be used at test time that might not have been available at training time [20]. Similarly, it has been shown that image metadata (geolocation, capture time) [5] and an auxiliary feature modality [21] can provide additional information at test time compared to only the image information available at training time.

The situation we are interested in occurs when at training time we have an additional data representation compared to test time. Different settings of this kind have appeared in the computer vision literature, but each was studied in a separate way. For example, for clustering with multiple image modalities, it has been proposed to use CCA to learn a shared representation that can be computed from either of the representations [3]. Similarly the shared representation is also used for cross-modal retrieval [35]. Alternatively, one can use the training data to learn a mapping from the image to the privileged modality and use this predictor to fill in the values missing at test time [8]. Feature vectors made out of semantic attributes have been used to improve object categorization when very few or no training examples are available [26, 51]. In [10] it was shown that annotator rationales can act as additional sources of information during training, as long as the rationales can be expressed in the same data representation as the original data (e.g., characteristic regions within the training images). For the special case where multiple datasets are available at training time, it has been shown how to identify and remove their respective bias, thereby improving the classification performance also on the individual tasks [46]. In considering attributes as auxiliary information for learning feature representation, [32] improve object detection accuracy and [53] boost performance of their facial landmark detection with attributes as an additional supervision. Importantly, [32] remark that *attributes help*, but only if they are used in a proper way. Proper in the sense that attribute mixture types instead of attributes are used as the auxiliary information for learning deep representations. The conjecture is that attributes are too complex for the deep model to learn meaningful features and directly using attributes does not consider the correlation between them [32].

Our work follows a different route than the above approaches. We are not looking for task-specific solutions applicable to a specific form of privileged information and we do not pursue learning feature representations (we assume that we have been given state-of-the-art features). Instead, we aim for a generic method of classifier learning that is applicable to any form of privileged information that is given as additional representations of the training data. We show in the following sections that such frameworks do indeed exist, and in Sect. 3.4 we illustrate how learning with attribute representations can naturally be expressed in the LUPI framework.

3.3 Learning Using Privileged Information

In the following we will formalize the LUPI setup for the task of supervised binary classification. Assume that we are given a set of N training examples, represented by feature vectors $X = \{x_1, \ldots, x_N\} \subset \mathcal{X} = \mathbb{R}^d$, their label annotation, $Y = \{y_1, \ldots, y_N\} \in \mathcal{Y} = \{+1, -1\}$, and additional information also in the form of feature vectors, $X^* = \{x_1^*, \ldots, x_N^*\} \subset \mathcal{X}^* = \mathbb{R}^{d^*}$, where x_i^* encodes the additional information we have about sample x_i. Recent progress addresses the setting where there is no one-to-one correspondence between original and privileged data [41]. In this chapter, we focus on the setting of LUPI where privileged information is paired to each data point. In the context of computer vision, we will consider the examples in $\mathcal{X}$ as images and their features being extracted from the image content, for example, in a form of *bag-of-visual-words* histograms [9], or more recently using a deep convolutional neural network (CNN) architecture [23]. We do not make any specific assumption about the *privileged* data space $\mathcal{X}^*$ yet, and keep the general notation for the feature vectors extracted from visual, verbal or semantic form of privileged information. We will refer to $\mathcal{X}$ and $\mathcal{X}^*$ as original and privileged data spaces, accordingly.

The binary classification task is to learn a prediction function $f : \mathcal{X} \to \mathbb{R}$ from a space $\mathcal{F}$ of possible functions, e.g., all linear classifiers. The goal of LUPI is to use the privileged data, X^*, to learn a better classifier in the original data space $f : \mathcal{X} \to \mathbb{R}$, than one would learn without it. Since the privileged data is only available during training time and comes from a different domain, $\mathcal{X}^*$, than the original space $\mathcal{X}$, it is not possible, e.g., to apply functions defined on $\mathcal{X}$ to $\mathcal{X}^*$ or vice versa. In this work, we describe how to use the privileged data to characterize the training samples in the original data space into easy and hard cases. Knowing this will help us to direct the learning procedure toward better generalization and to learn a function of higher prediction quality.

In the following, we explain two maximum-margin methods for learning with privileged information that fit to this interpretation. The first method was proposed by Vapnik et al. [49] in 2009, and the second method is our proposed alternative model for solving LUPI.

3.3.1 Maximum-Margin Model 1: SVM+

The first model for learning with privileged information, SVM+, [33, 49] is based on a direct observation that a nonlinearly separable (soft margin) support vector machine (SVM) can be turned into a linearly separable (hard margin) SVM if one has access to a so-called *slack oracle*. For clarity of presentation, here we include both the soft margin and the hard margin formulations of SVM

Soft margin SVM

$$\underset{\substack{w\in\mathbb{R}^d, b\in\mathbb{R}\\ \xi_1,\dots,\xi_N}}{\text{minimize}} \ \frac{1}{2}\,\|w\|^2 + C\sum_{i=1}^{N}\xi_i \tag{3.1a}$$

subject to, for all $i = 1, \dots, N,$

$$y_i[\langle w, x_i\rangle + b] \geq 1 - \xi_i, \quad \xi_i \geq 0. \tag{3.1b}$$

Hard margin SVM

$$\underset{w\in\mathbb{R}^d, b\in\mathbb{R}}{\text{minimize}} \ \frac{1}{2}\,\|w\|^2 \tag{3.2a}$$

subject to, for all $i = 1, \dots, N,$

$$y_i[\langle w, x_i\rangle + b] \geq 1. \tag{3.2b}$$

The soft margin SVM classifier is fully characterized by its weight vector w and bias parameter b. However, in the training phase, N slack variables ξ_i—one for each training sample—also need to be estimated. When the number of training examples increases, soft margin SVM solutions are known to converge with a rate of $\mathrm{O}\left(\frac{1}{\sqrt{N}}\right)$ to the optimal classifier [47]. This is in sharp contrast to the hard margin solutions that converge with a faster rate of $\mathrm{O}\left(\frac{1}{N}\right)$. Then one could wonder whether it is possible for the soft margin SVM to have a faster convergence rate, ideally at the same rate as the hard margin SVM. If the answer is positive, the improved soft-margin SVM would require fewer training examples to reach a certain prediction accuracy than a standard one. Intuitively, with $\mathrm{O}\left(\frac{1}{N}\right)$ rate, we will only require 100 samples instead of 10,000 to achieve the same level of predictive performance.

It might not come as a surprise that if we knew the optimal slack values ξ_i in the optimization problem (3.1), for example from an *oracle*, then the formulation can be reduced to the Oracle SVM that resembles the hard margin case (3.2) with the convergence rate $\mathrm{O}\left(\frac{1}{N}\right)$:

Oracle SVM

$$\underset{w\in\mathbb{R}^d,\, b\in\mathbb{R}}{\text{minimize}} \ \frac{1}{2}\,\|w\|^2 \tag{3.3a}$$

subject to, for all $i = 1, \dots, N,$

$$y_i[\langle w, x_i\rangle + b] \geq r_i, \quad \text{where } r_i \text{ is known } (r_i = 1 - \xi_i). \tag{3.3b}$$

Instead of $N + d + 1$ unknowns which include slack variables, we are now estimating only $d + 1$ unknowns which are the actual object of interest, our classifying hyperplane. The interpretation of slack variables is to tell us which training examples are *easy* and which are *hard*. In the above Oracle SVM, we do not have to infer those variables from the data as they are given by the oracle.

The idea of the SVM+ classifier is to use the privileged information as a proxy to the oracle. For this we parameterize the slack for i-th sample $\xi_i = \langle w^*, x_i^*\rangle + b^*$ with unknown w^* and b^*, obtaining the SVM+ training problem

$$\underset{\substack{w\in\mathbb{R}^d, b\in\mathbb{R}\\ w^*\in\mathbb{R}^{d^*}, b^*\in\mathbb{R}}}{\text{minimize}} \ \frac{1}{2}\left(\|w\|^2 + \gamma \|w^*\|^2\right) + C\sum_{i=1}^{N}\langle w^*, x_i^*\rangle + b^* \tag{3.4a}$$

subject to, for all $i = 1, \dots, N$,

$$y_i[\langle w, x_i\rangle + b] \geq 1 - [\langle w^*, x_i^*\rangle + b^*] \tag{3.4b}$$

$$\text{and} \quad \langle w^*, x_i^*\rangle + b^* \geq 0. \tag{3.4c}$$

The above SVM+ parameterizes the slack variables with a finite hypothesis space (a scalar and a weight vector with dimension d^*, for example), instead of allowing them to grow linearly with the number of examples N.

Numerical optimization

The SVM+ optimization problem (3.4) is convex, and can be solved in the dual representation using a standard quadratic programming (QP) solver. For a medium size problem (thousands to hundreds of thousands of samples), a general purpose QP solver might not suffice, and special purpose algorithms have to be developed to solve the QP. In [34], suitable sequential minimal optimization (SMO) algorithms were derived to tackle the problem. However, for the problem size that we are experimenting with (hundreds of samples), we find that using a general purpose QP provided in the `CVXOPT`[1] package is faster than the specialized SMO solver. Therefore, we use the `CVXOPT`-based QP solver for our experiments (Sect. 3.4).

Nonlinear SVM+

Kernelizing and dualizing SVM+ are possible using standard techniques [39]. The dual space objective of the kernelized SVM+ has the following form:

$$\underset{\substack{\alpha_i,\beta_i\in\mathbb{R},\\ i=1,\dots,N}}{\text{maximize}} \ \sum_{i=1}^{N}\alpha_i - \frac{1}{2}\sum_{i,j=1}^{N}\alpha_i\alpha_j y_i y_j K(x_i, x_j)$$

$$- \frac{1}{2\gamma}\sum_{i,j=1}^{N}(\alpha_i + \beta_i - C)(\alpha_j + \beta_j - C)K(x_i^*, x_j^*) \tag{3.5a}$$

$$\text{subject to:} \ \sum_{i=1}^{N}\alpha_i y_i = 0 \tag{3.5b}$$

$$\sum_{i=1}^{N}(\alpha_i + \beta_i - C) = 0 \tag{3.5c}$$

$$\alpha_i \geq 0, \ \beta_i \geq 0 \quad \text{for all } i = 1, \dots, N. \tag{3.5d}$$

Here $K(x_i, x_j)$ and $K(x_i^*, x_j^*)$ are kernels in the original and privileged spaces, α_i and β_i are the dual variables. The SVM+ solution in the dual space is defined as follows:

---

[1] http://cvxopt.org.

$$f(x) = \sum_{i=1}^{N} \alpha_i y_i K(x_i, x) + b. \tag{3.6}$$

The bias term can be computed based on equations in Sect. 1.5.1 of Pechyony and Vapnik [34]. The solution of SVM+ is identical to the solution of SVM trained in the original space using (X, Y) if the constraint $\alpha_i + \beta_i - C = 0$ holds for all data points $i = 1, \dots, N$.

3.3.2 *Maximum-Margin Model 2: Margin Transfer*

We propose a second model called *Margin Transfer* that: (1) can be solved by a sequence of standard SVM solvers; and (2) *explicitly* enforces an easy-hard interpretation for transferring information from the privileged to the original space. For each training example we check whether it is easy to classify or hard to classify based on the margin distance to the classifying hyperplane in the privileged space. Subsequently, we transfer this knowledge to the original space. We hypothesize that knowing a priori which examples are easy to classify and which are hard during learning should improve the prediction performance. This consideration leads us to the Margin Transfer method,[2] summarized in Algorithm 1.

First, we train an ordinary SVM on X^*. The resulting prediction function $f^*(x^*)$ is used to compute the margin distance from the training samples to the classifying hyperplane in the privileged space[3] $\rho_i := y_i f^*(x_i^*)$. Examples with a large values of ρ_i are considered easy to classify, whereas small or even negative values of ρ_i indicate hard or even impossible to classify samples. We then train a standard SVM on X, aiming for a *data-dependent margin* ρ_i transferred from the privileged space rather than enforcing a constant margin of 1. The corresponding optimization problem is as follows:

$$\underset{w \in \mathbb{R}^{d+1},\, \xi_i \in \mathbb{R}}{\text{minimize}} \quad \frac{1}{2}\|w\|^2 + C\sum_{i=1}^{N} \xi_i \tag{3.7a}$$

$$\text{subject to, for all } i = 1, \dots, N$$

$$y_i \langle w, x_i \rangle \geq \rho_i - \xi_i \quad \text{and} \quad \xi_i \geq 0. \tag{3.7b}$$

We omit the explicit computation of the bias term b in the algorithm, assuming it is implicitly added to the weight vector w, and all data points are augmented with a unit

[2]Margin Transfer is an adaptation of the Rank Transfer method [42] proposed for the ranking setup, where the information about easy to separate and hard to separate pairs of examples was transferred.

[3]Note that in the standard SVM formulation one would compute the values of slack variables to know how far the sample is from the hyperplane. As slack variables appear only at the training phase, we deliberately evaluate the prediction function on the same data it was trained on to identify easy and hard samples *at train* time.

Algorithm 1 Margin Transfer from $\mathcal{X}^*$ to $\mathcal{X}$

Input original data X, privileged data X^*, labels Y, tolerance $\varepsilon \geq 0$
$f^* \leftarrow$ SVM (Equation 3.1) trained on (X^*, Y)
$\rho_i = \max\{y_i f^*(x_i^*),\ \varepsilon\}$ *(per-sample margin)*
$f \leftarrow$ SVM (Equation 3.7) trained on (X, Y) using ρ_i instead of unit margin.
Return $f : \mathcal{X} \to \mathbb{R}$

element. One can see that examples with small and negative values of ρ_i have limited influence on w comparing to the standard SVM, because their slacks ξ_i can easily compensate for the inequality constraint. We threshold the negative values of margin distance ρ_i at certain tolerance value $\varepsilon \geq 0$, $\rho_i = \max\{y_i f^*(x_i^*),\ \varepsilon\}$. Our interpretation is that if it was not possible to correctly classify a sample in the privileged space, it will also be impossible to do so in the, presumably weaker, original space. Forcing the optimization to solve a hopeless task would only lead to overfitting and reduced prediction accuracy.

Numerical Optimization

Both learning steps in the *Margin Transfer* method are convex optimization problems. Furthermore, in contrast to SVM+, we can use standard SVM packages to solve them, including efficient methods working in primal representation [4], and solvers based on stochastic gradient descent [40].

For the SVM with data-dependent margin (3.7a) and (3.7b), we do the following reparameterization: we divide each constraint (3.7b) by the corresponding ρ_i, which is possible after thresholding at the nonnegative tolerance value. For our experiments, we threshold at $\varepsilon = 0.1$, thereby preventing numeric instabilities and increasing the computational efficiency of the method. Changing variables from x_i to $\hat{x}_i = \frac{x_i}{\rho_i}$ and from ξ_i to $\hat{\xi}_i = \frac{\xi_i}{\rho_i}$ we obtain the equivalent optimization problem

$$\underset{w\in\mathbb{R}^d,\ \hat{\xi}_i\in\mathbb{R}}{\text{minimize}} \quad \frac{1}{2}\|w\|^2 + C\sum_{i=1}^{N}\rho_i\hat{\xi}_i \tag{3.8a}$$

$$\text{subject to, for all } i = 1, \dots, N$$

$$y_i\langle w, \hat{x}_i\rangle \geq 1 - \hat{\xi}_i \quad \text{and} \quad \hat{\xi}_i \geq 0. \tag{3.8b}$$

This corresponds to standard SVM optimization with training examples $\hat{x}_i$, where each slack variable has an individual weight $C\rho_i$ in the objective. Many existing SVM packages support such per-sample weights, for example, LIBLINEAR [12].

Nonlinear Margin Transfer

In the first step, we train a nonlinear SVM classifier f^* using privileged data (X^*, Y). For each data point, the margin distance is computed the same way as before, $\rho_i = \max\{y_i f^*(x_i^*),\ \varepsilon\}$. Kernelizing and dualizing the objective of the second step (3.7a) and (3.7b) is possible using standard techniques [39]. The dual space objective of the kernelized Margin Transfer has the following form:

$$\underset{\substack{\alpha_i \in \mathbb{R},\\ i=1,\dots,N}}{\text{maximize}} \sum_{i=1}^{N} \alpha_i \rho_i - \frac{1}{2} \sum_{i,j=1}^{N} \alpha_i \alpha_j y_i y_j K(x_i, x_j) \tag{3.9a}$$

$$\text{subject to:} \sum_{i=1}^{N} \alpha_i y_i = 0 \tag{3.9b}$$

$$0 \leq \alpha_i \leq C, \quad \text{for all } i = 1, \dots, N. \tag{3.9c}$$

The Margin Transfer solution in the dual space is defined as follows:

$$f(x) = \sum_{i=1}^{N} \alpha_i y_i K(x_i, x) + b, \tag{3.10}$$

where bias term b is computed as an average value of $y_i \rho_i - \sum_{j=1}^{N} \alpha_j y_j K(x_j, x_i)$ for all $0 < \alpha_i < C$. The solution of kernelized Margin Transfer is identical to the solution of nonlinear SVM trained in the original space using (X, Y) if $\rho_i = 1$ for all data points $i = 1, \dots, N$. In our experiments, we implement the kernelized Margin Transfer method using the `CVXOPT`-based QP solver.

3.3.3 *How Is Information Being Transferred?*

We elaborate on how SVM+ and Margin Transfer instantiate the easy-hard interpretation and how they differ from each other.

Observation 1: Both methods, SVM+ and Margin Transfer, concentrate on learning easy samples and deemphasizing the hard ones.

Though SVM+ and Margin Transfer aim at the same goal, the way this is achieved is different in these two methods. Let us illustrate this by using the oracle analogy. In the SVM+, the oracle gives us the value of the slack function $\mathtt{oracle}_{\text{svm+}}(x_i) := \langle w^*, x_i^* \rangle + b^*$ for example x_i, and in the Margin Transfer, the oracle gives us the margin distance to the classifying hyperplane $\mathtt{oracle}_{\text{MT}}(x_i) := y_i f^*(x_i^*)$.

Suppose we only have two training samples, x_1 and x_2, and we ask the oracles what they perceive about the two samples. Say, in case of SVM+, we get back the following answers: $\mathtt{oracle}_{\text{svm+}}(x_1) = 10.0$ and $\mathtt{oracle}_{\text{svm+}}(x_2) = 0.0$. This means that the first sample is hard (its slack variable is high) and the second one is easy (its slack variable is zero). When we encode this into the optimization problem of SVM+, we can see that the constraint (3.4b) becomes $y_1[\langle w, x_1 \rangle + b] \geq -9$, (effort*less* to satisfy comparing to the unit margin in the standard SVM) for the first sample and $y_2[\langle w, x_2 \rangle + b] \geq 1$ (effort*ful* to satisfy comparing to the standard SVM) for the second one. So this means that the optimization task would more or less ignore the constraint of the first sample (that is hard) and concentrate on satisfying the constraint about the second sample (that is easy).

We repeat the questions to the Margin Transfer oracle and say the answers are: $\texttt{oracle}_{\mathrm{MT}}(x_1) = -5$ and $\texttt{oracle}_{\mathrm{MT}}(x_2) = 8$. Interpreting the oracle's answers lead us to conclude that the first sample is hard (its margin distance is zero or negative) and the second one is easy (its margin distance is positive). When we encode this into the optimization problem of Margin Transfer, the constraint (3.7b) becomes $y_1 \langle w, x_1 \rangle \geq \varepsilon - \xi_1$ (effortless to satisfy) for the first sample and $y_2 \langle w, x_2 \rangle \geq 8 - \xi_2$ (effortful to satisfy) for the second one. As before, the optimization task would ignore the constraints of the hard samples and concentrate on learning the easy ones. This is despite the fact that the SVM+ oracle returns high values for hard samples while the Margin Transfer oracle returns low values for hard samples, and vice versa for easy ones.

Observation 2: Classification performance in the privileged space matters for Margin Transfer but not for SVM+.

At the core of SVM+ lies the idea of imitating the oracle by learning the nonnegative linear regression slack function defined in the privileged space. The information about labels does not come into play when modeling the slack function, so in a sense, we never validate the classification performance in the privileged space. In contrast, in the Margin Transfer method, the performance in the privileged space explicitly guides the training of the predictor in the original data space. Samples that are easy and hard to classify in the privileged space directly define the margin for the samples in the original data space.

3.4 Experiments

In our experimental setting we study attribute annotations as a source of privileged information if these are present at training time but not at test time. We consider two scenarios when solving a binary classification task with attributes as privileged information and discuss them in the following subsections.

Methods. We analyze two max-margin methods of learning using privileged information: the proposed Margin Transfer method, and the SVM+ method [34, 49]. We compare the results with a standard nonlinear SVM when learning on the original space $\mathcal{X}$ directly. To put our results into a broader perspective, we also analyze two baselines with a probabilistic approach to binary classification: Gaussian process classification model (GPC) [36] and its adaptation to LUPI scenario, the GPC+ model [18]. In a probabilistic approach to binary classification, the goal is to model probabilities of a data point belonging to one of two class labels. GPC model turns the output of a Gaussian process into a class probability using a nonlinear activation function. GPC+ models the confidence that the Gaussian process has about any training example by adjusting the slope of the sigmoid-shaped likelihood with respect to privileged information. Training examples that are easy to classify by means of their privileged data cause a faster increasing sigmoid, which means the GPC trusts the training example and tries to fit it well. Examples that are hard to classify result in a slowly increase slope, so the GPC considers the training example less reliable and does not put a lot of effort into fitting its label well.

Model selection. In all methods, we use a Gaussian RBF kernel $k(x, x') = exp(-\frac{1}{\lambda}\|x - x'\|^2)$ with the kernel width parameter λ defined using the median trick, that is a median distance of $\|x_i - x_j\|^2$ over all $i, j = 1, \dots, N$. For methods that utilize privileged information, we define two Gaussian RBF kernels in the original space and in the privileged space accordingly. For maximum-margin LUPI models we perform a joint cross-validation model selection approach for choosing the regularization parameters in the original and privileged spaces. In the SVM+ method these are C and γ defined in Eqs. (3.5), and in the Margin Transfer these are C's in the two-stage procedure, defined in Eqs. (3.1), (3.9). The nonlinear SVM baseline has only one regularization parameter C to be cross validated. We select the parameter C and γ over 5 values linearly spanned in the exponential scale of the interval $\{0, \dots, 7\}$ and $\{-3, \dots, 7\}$ accordingly. In our experiments we use $5 \times$ fivefold cross-validation scheme. The best parameter (or pair of parameters) found is used to retrain the complete training set. Based on our experience, LUPI methods require very thorough model selection. To couple the modalities of privileged and original data spaces properly, the grid search over both parameter spaces has to be exploited. For GPC and GPC+, we found the hyperparameters by optimizing type-II maximum likelihood. There are two hyperparameters in GPC, signal amplitude and noise variance, and five in GPC+, signal amplitude and noise variance in original and privileged spaces, and the mean of GP in the privileged space.

Evaluation metric. To evaluate the performance of the methods we use accuracy, and we report mean and standard error across 10 repeats.

3.4.1 *Object Recognition in Images*

In this experiment, we use a subset of the *Animals with Attributes (AwA)* dataset [26] to perform an object recognition task in images. We focus on the default 10 test classes: *chimpanzee, giant panda, leopard, persian cat, pig, hippopotamus, humpback whale, raccoon, rat*, and *seal* that contain 6180 images in total. As privileged information, we use L_2-normalized 85-dimensional predicted attributes that capture 85 properties of the animals, such as color, texture, shape, body parts, behavior among others. The values of the predicted attributes are obtained by training the DAP model [26] and correspond to probability estimates of the binary attributes in the images of 10 animal classes of interest. Previously, it has been shown that attributes are informative privileged information to image features such as bag-of-visual-words representation obtained from SURF descriptors [18, 42, 44]. In this experiment, we investigate whether the same observation holds when deep CNN features are used as original image representation. For this we use L_2-normalized 4096 dimensional deep CNN features extracted from the fc7 activation layer in CaffeNet [19] pretrained on the ImageNet dataset (ILSVRC12) [38]. The deep CNN features are also used for learning the DAP model.

Table 3.1 *CNNs-Attribute Scenario* for object recognition tasks in images. In this scenario, deep CNN features are used as original image representation and attributes are used as privileged information. The numbers are mean and standard error of the accuracy over 10 runs Bold highlighting indicates difference of at least 0.2% between LUPI and non-LUPI methods. For GPC-based methods, both approaches perform comparably

	SVM-based			GPC-based	
	SVM	MT (ours)	SVM+ [49]	GPC	GPC+ [18]
	CNNs	CNNs + attr	CNNs + attr	CNNs	CNNs + attr
Chimpanzee	94.27 ± 0.28	$\mathbf{94.80 \pm 0.30}$	94.49 ± 0.29	94.77 ± 0.28	94.75 ± 0.29
Giant panda	95.66 ± 0.46	95.66 ± 0.40	95.61 ± 0.46	95.98 ± 0.39	95.96 ± 0.38
Leopard	97.35 ± 0.34	$\mathbf{97.78 \pm 0.30}$	97.27 ± 0.31	97.55 ± 0.36	97.55 ± 0.36
Persian cat	94.27 ± 0.54	93.84 ± 0.59	94.17 ± 0.61	94.42 ± 0.56	94.44 ± 0.56
Pig	86.01 ± 0.53	85.81 ± 0.63	$\mathbf{86.21 \pm 0.53}$	86.04 ± 0.51	85.98 ± 0.49
Hippopotamus	91.11 ± 0.56	90.05 ± 1.00	$\mathbf{91.77 \pm 0.42}$	91.57 ± 0.42	91.59 ± 0.42
Humpback whale	98.16 ± 0.13	97.85 ± 0.08	98.01 ± 0.13	97.98 ± 0.12	97.98 ± 0.12
Raccoon	89.60 ± 0.41	89.49 ± 0.56	$\mathbf{89.85 \pm 0.46}$	90.03 ± 0.63	90.03 ± 0.63
Rat	84.17 ± 0.72	84.24 ± 0.87	83.94 ± 0.75	84.32 ± 0.49	84.24 ± 0.47
Seal	85.15 ± 0.78	84.82 ± 0.58	84.97 ± 0.55	84.75 ± 0.65	84.65 ± 0.67

We train 10 binary classifiers, where each task is a binary classification of one class against the remaining nine classes. We use 36 training and 400 test samples, where we balance the amount of positive and negative samples and draw equal amount of negative samples from each of the remaining classes. We report the results of this experiment in Table 3.1.

Results. As we can see from the Table 3.1, using attributes as privileged information has moderate effect when deep CNN features are used as original image representation. This can be explained by the following observations. A positive effect in Margin Transfer is expected when the classifier performance in the privileged space is higher than in the original space, as it is in a majority of previously studied LUPI scenarios [15, 18, 29, 42, 48]. We credit this to the fact that most LUPI methods including Margin Transfer rely on the performance in the privileged space in order to explore easiness and hardness of the samples. In this experiment, SVM trained using deep CNN features has higher accuracy than SVM trained using attribute representation, in most cases. Moreover, even with little training data, the performance using CNNs image representation is significantly higher than using SURF descriptors, indicating that this binary classification problem is relatively easy to solve using state-of-the-art features. In our next experiment, we explore a more challenging vision task of distinguishing easy from hard instances of an object class.

3.4.2 Recognizing Easy from Hard Images

In this experiment, we focus on differentiating between "easy" and "hard" images of eight classes: *chimpanzee, giant panda, leopard, persian cat, hippopotamus, raccoon, rat* and *seal*. This is a subset of the *AwA* dataset for which the annotation of easy-hard scores is publicly available [44]. The easy-hard annotation is collected using Amazon MTurk user study. In this study, a worker is shown a set of images of one animal class and is asked to rank the images from the easiest to the hardest depending on how difficult it is to spot the animal in the image. Finally, each image gets an easy-hard score in the range from 1 (hardest) to 16 (easiest) as the average score over all worker responses across multiple sets of images.

Setup. This task imitates human learning to distinguish between easy and hard examples of a class. For each animal class, we label half of the images as "easy"(class label $+1$) and half of the images as "hard"(class label -1) with respect to the easy-hard scores, and solve a binary classification problem. We use all available data per class, ranging from 300 (class *rat*) to 900 images (class *giant panda*), to form the $80\,\%/20\,\%$ train/test split. As our feature representation, we use deep CNN features in the original space, and predicted attributes in the privileged space, as detailed in the previous experiment. For completeness we also report the performance when using L_2-normalized 2000-dimensional bag-of-visual-words representation with SURF [2] descriptor as original feature space.

Results. As we can see from the Table 3.2, utilizing attributes as privileged information for easy-hard object recognition task is useful. Overall, the methods that utilize privileged information, MT, SVM+ and GPC+, outperform their counterparts, SVM and GPC, in a majority of cases. There is no clear signal to differentiate easy from hard images of the class *seal*, so we exclude this class from our analysis. As expected, the performance gain between LUPI and non-LUPI methods is more apparent when SURF features are used as original feature space (Table 3.3). In

Table 3.2 *CNNs-Attribute Scenario* Distinguishing easy from hard images with attributes as privileged information. The numbers are mean and standard error of the accuracy over 10 runs

	SVM-based			GPC-based	
	SVM CNNs	MT (ours) CNNs + attr	SVM+ [49] CNNs+attr	GPC CNNs	GPC+ [18] CNNs + attr
Chimpanzee	74.57 ± 0.62	74.43 ± 0.81	$\mathbf{75.36 \pm 0.84}$	$\mathbf{75.64 \pm 0.69}$	75.43 ± 0.57
Giant panda	81.44 ± 0.69	81.33 ± 0.73	$\mathbf{82.45 \pm 0.90}$	81.81 ± 0.65	81.70 ± 0.64
Leopard	$\mathbf{82.08 \pm 0.65}$	81.67 ± 0.73	81.00 ± 0.82	82.08 ± 0.83	82.00 ± 0.86
Persian cat	80.35 ± 0.39	79.93 ± 0.89	80.21 ± 0.65	80.49 ± 0.37	80.35 ± 0.48
Hippopotamus	73.33 ± 1.18	73.19 ± 1.29	73.40 ± 1.10	74.10 ± 1.01	$\mathbf{74.44 \pm 0.97}$
Raccoon	76.67 ± 0.92	77.54 ± 0.75	$\mathbf{78.17 \pm 0.68}$	78.33 ± 0.93	$\mathbf{78.65 \pm 0.91}$
Rat	83.33 ± 1.73	83.00 ± 1.45	84.00 ± 1.72	84.50 ± 1.56	$\mathbf{84.83 \pm 1.55}$
Seal	48.30 ± 1.39	48.10 ± 1.19	46.70 ± 1.04	49.80 ± 0.19	50.00 ± 0.28

Table 3.3 *SURF-Attribute Scenario* Distinguishing easy from hard images with attributes as privileged information. The numbers are mean and standard error of the accuracy over 10 runs

	SVM-based			GPC-based	
	SVM SURF	MT (ours) SURF + attr	SVM+ [49] SURF + attr	GPC SURF	GPC+ [18] SURF + attr
Chimpanzee	65.93 ± 1.06	$\mathbf{66.79 \pm 0.99}$	64.93 ± 1.21	65.64 ± 1.43	65.79 ± 1.39
Giant panda	74.26 ± 0.61	$\mathbf{75.90 \pm 0.62}$	74.84 ± 0.53	75.11 ± 0.63	75.05 ± 0.74
Leopard	69.58 ± 0.88	$\mathbf{70.50 \pm 1.06}$	69.83 ± 1.32	69.42 ± 0.92	$\mathbf{70.25 \pm 1.08}$
Persian cat	65.14 ± 1.11	$\mathbf{67.61 \pm 1.09}$	65.99 ± 0.96	67.04 ± 1.25	67.18 ± 1.28
Hippopotamus	66.25 ± 0.98	65.90 ± 0.61	$\mathbf{66.60 \pm 0.95}$	65.21 ± 0.88	$\mathbf{65.56 \pm 0.77}$
Raccoon	65.79 ± 1.03	$\mathbf{67.86 \pm 0.86}$	66.83 ± 1.24	66.90 ± 0.87	$\mathbf{67.62 \pm 0.94}$
Rat	60.33 ± 1.52	60.33 ± 1.97	$\mathbf{60.83 \pm 1.65}$	60.33 ± 1.65	$\mathbf{61.00 \pm 1.86}$
Seal	52.60 ± 1.78	51.80 ± 1.33	51.60 ± 1.79	50.00 ± 0.00	50.00 ± 0.00

Table 3.4 Average training time in minutes of the experiments in Sect. 3.4.1 (object recognition) and Sect. 3.4.2 (easy-hard recognition). For max-margin methods, the reported time includes model selection via cross-validation procedure. SVM has one hyperparameter, whereas SVM+ and MT have two hyperparameters to be selected. For Gaussian process methods, the time includes model selection via the type-II maximum likelihood estimation. GPC has two hyperparameters, while GPC+ has five hyperparameters to be found

	Object recognition	Easy-hard recognition	
	CNNs-Attribute ≈36 tr. samples (m)	CNNs-Attribute ≈510 tr. samples (m)	SURF-Attribute ≈510 tr. samples (m)
SVM	0.1	2.5	2
MT (ours)	0.6	25	24
SVM+ [49]	0.7	30	24
GPC	6.5	122	50
GPC+ [18]	9.2	380	190

this scenario, the Gaussian process-based methods perform better in comparison to max-margin methods at the cost of higher running time (Table 3.4).

3.5 Conclusion

Previously, when image features were unsupervised, semantic attributes have been shown as informative privileged information in the context of object recognition. In this chapter we showed that when deep CNN features are used as original feature space, attributes embedded in the LUPI framework lead to performance improvement in the challenging easy-hard recognition task, but not so in the standard object present–absent recognition task. Deep CNNs are inherently supervised features in a similar spirit to *per-class* attribute features considered in this work; both are discriminatively trained classifier outputs, hence, they are similarly informative about the object recognition task. In the future, we envision several research directions to be addressed: utilizing *per-sample* attribute features in challenging vision tasks, such as easy-hard recognition and object recognition plus localization [32], supplementing *limited* number of attributes with other sources of privileged information in the LUPI framework.

Acknowledgements We would like to thank Christoph Lampert, Kristian Kersting, and Daniel Hernández-Lobato for discussions and collaborative work on the LUPI framework. We also thank Rogerio Feris for his editorial comments on the manuscript.

References

1. Akata, Z., Reed, S., Walter, D., Lee, H., Schiele, B.: Evaluation of output embeddings for fine-grained image classification. In: Computer Vision and Pattern Recognition (CVPR) (2015)
2. Bay, H., Ess, A., Tuytelaars, T., Van Gool, L.: Speeded-up robust features (SURF). Comput. Vision Image Underst. (CVIU) **110**(3), 346–359 (2008)
3. Blaschko, M.B., Lampert, C.H.: Correlational spectral clustering. In: Computer Vision and Pattern Recognition (CVPR) (2008)
4. Chapelle, O.: Training a support vector machine in the primal. Neural Comput. **19**(5), 1155–1178 (2007)
5. Chen, C.Y., Grauman, K.: Clues from the beaten path: location estimation with bursty sequences of tourist photos. In: Computer Vision and Pattern Recognition (CVPR) (2011)
6. Chen, K., Kämäräinen, J.K.: Learning to count with back-propagated information. In: International Conference on Pattern Recognition (ICPR) (2014)
7. Chen, J., Liu, X., Lyu, S.: Boosting with side information. In: Asian Conference on Computer Vision (ACCV) (2013)
8. Christoudias, M., Urtasun, R., Darrell, T.: Multi-view learning in the presence of view disagreement. In: Uncertainty in Artificial Intelligence (UAI) (2008)
9. Dance, C., Willamowski, J., Fan, L., Bray, C., Csurka, G.: Visual categorization with bags of keypoints. In: European Conference on Computer Vision (ECCV) (2004)
10. Donahue, J., Grauman, K.: Annotator rationales for visual recognition. In: International Conference on Computer Vision (ICCV) (2011)
11. Everingham, M., Gool, L.J.V., Williams, C.K.I., Winn, J.M., Zisserman, A.: The Pascal VOC challenge. Int. J. Comput. Vision (IJCV) **88**, 303–338 (2010)
12. Fan, R.E., Chang, K.W., Hsieh, C.J., Wang, X.R., Lin, C.J.: LIBLINEAR: a library for large linear classification. J. Mach. Lear. Res. (JMLR) **9**, 1871–1874 (2008)
13. Farhadi, A., Endres, I., Hoiem, D., Forsyth, D.A.: Describing objects by their attributes. In: Computer Vision and Pattern Recognition (CVPR) (2009)
14. Feyereisl, J., Aickelin, U.: Privileged information for data clustering. Inf. Sci. **194**, 4–23 (2012)
15. Feyereisl, J., Kwak, S., Son, J., Han, B.: Object localization based on structural SVM using privileged information. In: Conference on Neural Information Processing Systems (NIPS) (2014)
16. Fouad, S., Tino, P., Raychaudhury, S., Schneider, P.: Incorporating privileged information through metric learning. IEEE Trans. Neural Netw. Learn. Syst. **24**(7), 1086–1098 (2013)
17. Gehler, P., Nowozin, S.: On feature combination for multiclass object classification. In: International Conference on Computer Vision (ICCV) (2009)

18. Hernández-Lobato, D., Sharmanska, V., Kersting, K., Lampert, C.H., Quadrianto, N.: Mind the nuisance: Gaussian process classification using privileged noise. In: Conference on Neural Information Processing Systems (NIPS) (2014)
19. Jia, Y., Shelhamer, E., Donahue, J., Karayev, S., Long, J., Girshick, R., Guadarrama, S., Darrell, T.: Caffe: convolutional architecture for fast feature embedding. In: ACM Multimedia (ACM MM) (2014)
20. Kalal, Z., Matas, J., Mikolajczyk, K.: Online learning of robust object detectors during unstable tracking. In: ICCV Workshop On-line learning for Computer Vision (2009)
21. Khamis, S., Lampert, C.H.: CoConut: co-classification with output space regularization. In: British Machine Vision Conference (BMVC) (2014)
22. Kovashka, A., Parikh, D., Grauman, K.: Whittlesearch: interactive image search with relative attribute feedback. Int. J. Comput. Vision (IJCV) **115**(2), 185–210 (2015)
23. Krizhevsky, A., Sutskever, I., Hinton, G.E.: Imagenet classification with deep convolutional neural networks. In: Conference on Neural Information Processing Systems (NIPS) (2012)
24. Kuettel, D., Guillaumin, M., Ferrari, V.: Segmentation propagation in ImageNet. In: European Conference on Computer Vision (ECCV) (2012)
25. Kulkarni, G., Premraj, V., Ordonez, V., Dhar, S., Li, S., Choi, Y., Berg, A.C., Berg, T.L.: Babytalk: understanding and generating simple image descriptions. IEEE Trans. Pattern Anal. Mach. Intell. (T-PAMI) **35**(12), 2891–2903 (2013)
26. Lampert, C.H., Nickisch, H., Harmeling, S.: Attribute-based classification for zero-shot visual object categorization. IEEE Trans. Pattern Anal. Mach. Intell. (T-PAMI) **36**(3), 453–465 (2013)
27. Lapin, M., Hein, M., Schiele, B.: Learning using privileged information: SVM+ and weighted SVM. Neural Netw. **53**, 95–108 (2014)
28. Li, W., Niu, L., Xu, D.: Exploiting privileged information from web data for image categorization. In: European Conference on Computer Vision (ECCV) (2014)
29. Lopez-Paz, D., Bottou, L., Schölkopf, B., Vapnik, V.: Unifying distillation and privileged information. In: International Conference on Learning Representations (ICLR) (2016)
30. Maron, O., Ratan, A.L.: Multiple-instance learning for natural scene classification. In: International Conference on Machine Learning (ICML) (1998)
31. Niu, L., Li, W., Xu, D.: Exploiting privileged information from web data for action and event recognition. Int. J. Comput. Vision (IJCV) **118**(2), 130–150 (2016)
32. Ouyang, W., Li, H., Zeng, X., Wang, X.: Learning deep representation with large-scale attributes. In: International Conference on Computer Vision (ICCV) (2015)
33. Pechyony, D., Vapnik, V.: On the theory of learning with privileged information. In: Conference on Neural Information Processing Systems (NIPS) (2010)
34. Pechyony, D., Vapnik, V.: Fast optimization algorithms for solving SVM+. In: Statistical Learning and Data Science (2011)
35. Quadrianto, N., Lampert, C.H.: Learning multi-view neighborhood preserving projections. In: International Conference on Machine Learning (ICML) (2011)
36. Rasmussen, C.E., Williams, C.K.: Gaussian Processes for Machine Learning. The MIT Press (2006)
37. Russakovsky, O., Lin, Y., Yu, K., Fei-Fei, L.: Object-centric spatial pooling for image classification. In: European Conference on Computer Vision (ECCV) (2012)
38. Russakovsky, O., Deng, J., Su, H., Krause, J., Satheesh, S., Ma, S., Huang, Z., Karpathy, A., Khosla, A., Bernstein, M., Berg, A.C., Fei-Fei, L.: ImageNet large scale visual recognition challenge. Int. J. Comput. Vision (IJCV) **115**(3), 211–252 (2015)
39. Schölkopf, B., Smola, A.J.: Learning with Kernels. The MIT Press (2002)
40. Shalev-Shwartz, S., Singer, Y., Srebro, N.: Pegasos: Primal estimated sub-GrAdient solver for SVM. In: International Conference on Machine Learning (ICML) (2007)
41. Sharmanska, V., Quadrianto, N.: Learning from the mistakes of others: matching errors in cross dataset learning. In: Computer Vision and Pattern Recognition (CVPR) (2016)
42. Sharmanska, V., Quadrianto, N., Lampert, C.H.: Learning to rank using privileged information. In: International Conference on Computer Vision (ICCV) (2013)

43. Sharmanska, V., Hernández-Lobato, D., Hernández-Lobato, J.M., Quadrianto, N.: Ambiguity helps: classification with disagreements in crowdsourced annotations. In: Computer Vision and Pattern Recognition (CVPR) (2016)
44. Sharmanska, V., Quadrianto, N., Lampert, C.H.: Learning to transfer privileged information. arXiv:1410.0389 (2014)
45. Snoek, C.G., Worring, M., Smeulders, A.W.: Early versus late fusion in semantic video analysis. In: ACM Multimedia (ACM MM) (2005)
46. Tommasi, T., Quadrianto, N., Caputo, B., Lampert, C.: Beyond dataset bias: multi-task unaligned shared knowledge transfer. In: Asian Conference on Computer Vision (ACCV) (2012)
47. Vapnik, V.: The Nature of Statistical Learning Theory. Springer (1999)
48. Vapnik, V., Izmailov, R.: Learning using privileged information: similarity control and knowledge transfer. J. Mach. Learn. Res. (JMLR) **16**, 2023–2049 (2015)
49. Vapnik, V., Vashist, A.: A new learning paradigm: learning using privileged information. Neural Netw. **22**(5–6), 544–557 (2009)
50. Vedaldi, A., Gulshan, V., Varma, M., Zisserman, A.: Multiple kernels for object detection. In: International Conference on Computer Vision (ICCV) (2009)
51. Wang, Y., Mori, G.: A discriminative latent model of object classes and attributes. In: European Conference on Computer Vision (ECCV) (2010)
52. Yang, H., Patras, I.: Privileged information-based conditional regression forest for facial feature detection. In: International Conference and Workshops on Automatic Face and Gesture Recognition (FG) (2013)
53. Zhang, Z., Luo, P., Loy, C.C., Tang, X.: Learning deep representation for face alignment with auxiliary attributes. IEEE Trans. Pattern Anal. Mach. Intell. (T-PAMI) **38**(5), 918–930 (2015)

Chapter 4
Divide, Share, and Conquer: Multi-task Attribute Learning with Selective Sharing

Chao-Yeh Chen, Dinesh Jayaraman, Fei Sha and Kristen Grauman

Abstract Existing methods to learn visual attributes are plagued by two common issues: (i) they are prone to confusion by properties that are correlated with the attribute of interest among training samples and (ii) they often learn generic, imprecise "lowest common denominator" attribute models in an attempt to generalize across classes where a single attribute may have very different visual manifestations. Yet, many proposed applications of attributes rely on being able to learn the precise and correct semantic concept corresponding to each attribute. We argue that these issues are both largely due to indiscriminate "oversharing" amongst attribute classifiers along two axes—(i) visual features and (ii) classifier parameters. To address both these issues, we introduce the general idea of *selective sharing* during multi-task learning of attributes. First, we show how selective sharing helps learn decorrelated models for each attribute in a vocabulary. Second, we show how selective sharing permits a new form of transfer learning between attributes, yielding a specialized attribute model for each individual object category. We validate both these instantiations of our selective sharing idea through extensive experiments on multiple datasets. We show how they help preserve semantics in learned attribute models, benefitting various downstream applications such as image retrieval or zero-shot learning.

C.-Y. Chen (✉) · D. Jayaraman (✉) · F. Sha · K. Grauman
The University of Texas at Austin, Austin, TX, USA
e-mail: chaoyeh@cs.utexas.edu

D. Jayaraman
e-mail: dineshj@cs.utexas.edu

F. Sha
e-mail: feisha@cs.ucla.edu

K. Grauman
e-mail: grauman@cs.utexas.edu

R.S. Feris et al. (eds.), *Visual Attributes*, Advances in Computer Vision and Pattern Recognition, DOI 10.1007/978-3-319-50077-5_4

4.1 Introduction

Visual attributes are human-nameable mid-level semantic properties. They include both holistic descriptors, such as "furry", "dark", or "metallic", as well as localized parts, such as "has-wheels" or "has-snout". Because attributes describe object and scene categories in natural language terms, they can be used to describe an unfamiliar object class [9], teach a system to recognize new classes by zero-shot learning as in [25, 32, 36] and in Chap. 2, learn mid-level cues from cross-category images [23], or provide a useful bridge between low-level image features and high-level entities like object or scene categories [9, 22, 25].[1]

All these applications stem from one crucial property of attributes—the fact that they are *shared across object categories*. Typically, the idea is that a system can learn about an attribute from image examples drawn from arbitrary objects, e.g., learning "furry" from bunnies, dogs, and bears alike. In fact, attributes are usually shared not only among some limited set of "seen" categories present in the training data, but among other "unseen" categories too. Thus, it is particularly important to be able to correctly recognize each attribute manifested in diverse configurations that may or may not have been previously observed.

The intent to share features and classifiers raises important challenges specific to attribute learning. On the one hand, as we will soon see, spurious correlated factors (including other attributes) in training data may easily be mistaken for the attribute of interest by a learner, which would prevent generalization, especially to instances of the attribute manifested in unseen classes. Further, even among seen classes, attributes may have different visual manifestations in each category, making it difficult for one shared generic attribute classifier to work well on all classes.

Existing methods follow the same standard discriminative learning pipeline that has been successful in other visual recognition problems, particularly object recognition. Using training images labeled by the attributes they exhibit, low-level image descriptors are extracted, and used to *independently* train a discriminative classifier for each attribute in isolation [5, 9, 22, 23, 25, 32, 33, 36, 38]. A single monolithic model is trained per attribute, which is shared across all object categories. For example, classifiers for "furry" and "dark" attributes may be trained independently with color, texture, and shape features. Each of these classifiers is expected now to apply to new instances, agnostic to the category that each instance belongs to, such as "cat", "human", or "tower". In short, the status quo approach thus uniformly shares both the low-level features across all attributes as well as the attribute classifier across all categories.

In this chapter, we explore the following question: when and to what extent is sharing useful for attribute learning? We show that the standard attribute learning approach suffers from a problem of indiscriminate sharing along two axes: (i) it "overshares" features across distinct attribute classifiers and (ii) it overshares classifier parameters for each attribute across distinct categories. See Fig. 4.1 for a visual

[1] Throughout, we use the term "category" to refer to an object or scene class, whereas an "attribute" is a visual property describing some such category.

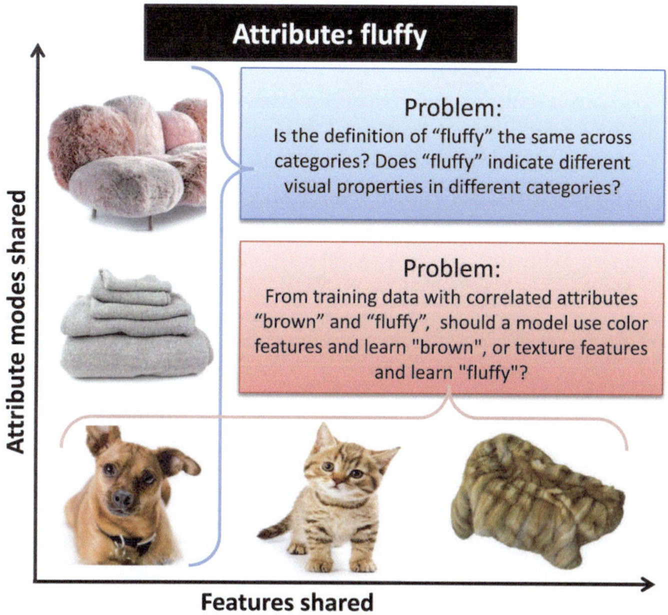

Fig. 4.1 Two problems caused by oversharing the features and attribute modes in attribute learning framework. (i) On the one hand, when attribute models overshare feature supports, it is hard to disambiguate correlated attributes that are semantically very different, such as "brown" and "fluffy" in the example depicted on the horizontal axis. (ii) On the other hand, when attribute classifiers are overshared across object categories, we ignore the fact that the same semantic attribute could have very different visual appearances in different categories

depiction of this problem. We contend that this oversharing approach ignores inter-category and inter-attribute distinctions during attribute learning and thus does not optimally exploit training data.

We propose methods to actively account for the semantic information presented by these distinctions, which allow the learning of better attribute classifiers using the same attribute-labeled training data. Our key idea for improving upon existing attribute learning methods is to make the system "learn the right thing" by avoiding oversharing, using semantic knowledge to decide what to share and what not to share during learning.

We implement this general idea in two separate *multi-task learning* (MTL) schemes to address each of the two problems enumerated above. Multi-task learning methods aim to jointly learn multiple tasks. Whereas typically a multi-task learner strives for greater sharing between tasks, we propose new forms of MTL where the algorithm is intentionally selective about where to share. We show how the concept of selective sharing helps eliminate two major problems that plague the standard attribute recognition approach—namely, (i) disambiguating each attribute from its spurious correlated image properties (Sect. 4.2) and (ii) specializing individual attribute classifiers to fit differences in visual manifestations of the same attribute across different object categories (Sect. 4.3).

Problem #1: Oversharing image features across categories conflates pair(s) of attributes. In the first main contribution of this chapter, we reconsider the standard approach of using the same feature representation for all attributes. Even standard multi-task learning approaches encourage the sharing of features across attributes. This defect makes these approaches especially prone to learning image properties that are *correlated* with the attribute of interest, rather than the attribute itself. In Sect. 4.2, we propose a multi-task learning method informed by attribute semantics to disambiguate correlated attributes while learning attribute vocabularies. It encourages different classifiers to rely on signals from disjoint sets of dimensions in the visual feature space [17].

Problem #2: Oversharing attributes across categories conflates diverse "modes" of same-named attributes. In the second main contribution of this chapter, we reconsider the standard approach of learning one monolithic attribute classifier from training images pooled from all categories. While the notion of a category-independent attribute has certain appeal, are attributes really category-independent? For instance, does fluffiness on a dog look the same as fluffiness on a towel? Are the features that make a high heeled shoe look formal the same as those that make a sandal look formal? In such examples (and many others), while the *linguistic* semantics are preserved across categories, the *visual* appearance of the property is transformed to some degree. That is, some attributes are specialized to the category. This suggests that simply pooling a bunch of training images of any object/scene with the named attribute and learning a discriminative classifier—the status quo approach—will weaken the learned model to account for the "least common denominator" of the attribute's appearance, and, in some cases, completely fail to generalize. In Sect. 4.3, we present a method to learn category-sensitive *analogous attributes*, by exploring the correlations between different attributes and object categories [6].[2]

Thus, both of these approaches implement our key idea of *selective* sharing (of features and models, respectively) when treating attribute learning as a multi-task learning problem. In both approaches, we pursue joint learning of a vocabulary of attributes. Whereas the first approach produces a single attribute model per attribute word, the second approach further formulates the learning of each attribute itself as multiple related tasks corresponding to specialized models of the attribute for each object or scene category. In both cases, easily available semantic information (attribute semantics and category labels, respectively) is exploited to help guide the selective sharing.

Roadmap In the rest of this chapter, we will first zoom in, one by one, to study the two above-listed instantiations of our general idea of selective sharing (as opposed to indiscriminate "oversharing") during attribute learning, delving into their technical approaches and experimental results validating their usefulness. Specifically, in Sect. 4.2, we will focus on our method for learning decorrelated models for a

[2] See Chaps. 12 and 13 for further discussion of the interplay of visual attributes and natural language.

Fig. 4.2 What attribute is present in the first three images, but not the last two? Standard methods attempting to learn "furry" from such images are prone to learn "brown" instead—or some combination of correlated properties. We propose a multi-task attribute learning approach that resists the urge to share features between attributes that are semantically distinct yet often co-occur

vocabulary of visual attributes as described above, and in Sect. 4.3, we will focus on our method for learning category-specific attribute classifiers. In Sect. 4.4, we will zoom back out to look at previous work that is relevant to the ideas discussed in this chapter. Finally, in Sect. 4.5, we will summarize our findings and outline areas for future work that may build on our ideas.

4.2 Learning Decorrelated Attributes

Many applications of visual attributes such as image search and zero-shot learning build on learned models for a *vocabulary* of multiple, diverse attributes, e.g., a detailed textual query in image search might describe various attributes of the desired target image.[3] A key underlying challenge in learning discriminative models of multiple attributes is that the hypothesis space is very large. The standard discriminative model can associate an attribute with any direction in the feature space that happens to separate positive and negative instances in the training dataset, resulting very often in the learning of properties that are spuriously correlated with the attribute of interest. The issue is exacerbated by the fact that many nameable visual properties will occupy the same spatial region in an image. For example, a "brown" object might very well also be "round" and "shiny". In contrast, when learning object categories, each pixel is occupied by just one object of interest, decreasing the possibility of learning incidental classes. Furthermore, even if we attempt stronger training annotations, spatial extent annotation for attributes is harder and more ambiguous than it is for objects. Consider, for example, how one might mark the spatial extent of "pointiness" in the images in Fig. 4.2.

But does it even matter if we inadvertently learn a correlated attribute? After all, weakly supervised object recognition systems have long been known to exploit

[3] Applications of attributes for zero-shot learning and image search are discussed in Chaps. 2 and 5 of this book, respectively.

correlated background features appearing outside the object of interest that serve as "context". For attribute learning, however, it is a problem, on two fronts. First of all, with the large number of possible combinations of attributes (up to 2^k for k binary attributes), we may see only a fraction of plausible ones during training, making it risky to treat correlated cues as a useful signal. In fact, semantic attributes are touted for their extendability to novel object categories, where correlation patterns may easily deviate from those observed in training data. Second, many attribute applications—such as image search [20, 22, 38], zero-shot learning [25], and textual description generation [9]—demand that the named property align meaningfully with the image content. For example, an image search user querying for "pointy-toed" shoes would be frustrated if the system (wrongly) conflates pointiness with blackness due to training data correlations. We contrast this with the object recognition setting, where object categories themselves may be thought of as co-occurring, correlated bundles of attributes. Learning to recognize an object thus implicitly involves learning these correlations.

Given these issues, our goal for the rest of this section is to decorrelate attributes at the time of learning, thus learning attribute classifiers that fire only when the correct semantic property is present. In particular, we want our classifiers to generalize to test images where the attribute co-occurrence patterns may differ from those observed in training. To this end, we propose a multi-task learning framework that encourages each attribute classifier to use a disjoint set of image features to make its predictions. This idea of feature *competition* is central to our approach.

As discussed in Sect. 4.1, whereas conventional models train each attribute classifier independently, and therefore are prone to reusing image features for correlated attributes, our multi-task approach *resists the urge to share*. Instead, it aims to isolate distinct low-level features for distinct attributes in a vocabulary by enforcing a structured sparsity prior over the attributes. We design this prior to leverage side information about the attributes' semantic relatedness, aligning feature *sharing* patterns with semantically close attributes and feature *competition* with semantically distant ones. In the example in Fig. 4.2, the algorithm might discover that dimensions corresponding to color histogram bins should be used to detect "brown", whereas those corresponding to texture in the center of the image might be reserved to detect "furry".

4.2.1 Approach

In the following, we first describe the inputs to our algorithm: the semantic relationships among attributes (Sect. 4.2.1.1) and the low-level image descriptors (Sect. 4.2.1.2). Then we introduce our learning objective and optimization framework (Sect. 4.2.1.3), which outputs a classifier for each attribute in the vocabulary.

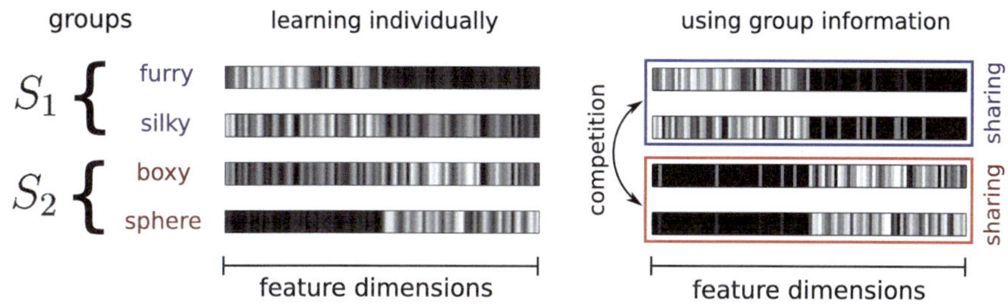

Fig. 4.3 Sketch of our idea. We show weight vectors (absolute value) for attributes learnt by standard (*left*) and proposed (*right*) approaches. The higher the weight (*lighter colors*) assigned to a feature dimension, the more the attribute relies on that feature. In this instance, our approach would help resolve "silky" and "boxy", which are highly correlated in training data and consequently conflated by standard learning approaches

4.2.1.1 Semantic Attribute Groups

Suppose we are learning attribute classifiers[4] for a vocabulary of M nameable attributes, indexed by $\{1, 2, \ldots, M\}$ (see Chaps. 10 and 11 for work investigating ways to develop the attribute vocabulary itself). To represent the attributes' semantic relationships, we use L attribute *groups*, encoded as L sets of indices $S_1, \ldots, S_L$, where each $S_l = \{m_1, m_2, m_3, \ldots\}$ contains the indices of the specific attributes in that group, and $1 \leq m_i \leq M$. While nothing in our approach restricts attribute groups to be disjoint, for simplicity in our experiments each attribute appears in one group only.

If two attributes are in the same group, this reflects that they have some semantic tie. For instance, in Fig. 4.3, S_1 and S_2 correspond to texture and shape attributes, respectively. For attributes describing fine-grained categories, like bird species, a group can focus on domain-specific aspects inherent to the taxonomy—for example, one group for beak shape (hooked, curved, dagger, etc.) and another group for belly color (red belly, yellow belly, etc.). While such groups could conceivably be mined automatically (from text data, WordNet, or other sources), we rely on existing manually defined groups [25, 48] in our experiments (see Fig. 4.6).

As we will see below, group comembership signals to our learning algorithm that the attributes are more likely to share features. For spatially localized attribute groups (e.g., beak shape), this could guide the algorithm to concentrate on descriptors originating from the same-object part; for global attribute groups (e.g., colors), this could guide the algorithm to focus on a subset of relevant feature channels. There might be no such thing as a single "optimal" grouping; rather, we expect such partial side information about semantics to help intelligently decide when to allow sharing.

Our use of attribute label dimension-grouping to exploit relationships among tasks is distinct from and not to be confused with descriptor dimension-grouping to represent *feature* space structure, as in the single-task "group lasso" [55]. While

[4]We use "attribute", "classifier", and "task" interchangeably in this section.

simultaneously exploiting feature space structure could conceivably further improve our method's results, we restrict our focus in this paper to modeling and exploiting *task relationships*.

4.2.1.2 Image Feature Representation

When designating the low-level image feature space where the classifiers will be learned, we are mindful of one main criterion: we want to expose to the learning algorithm *spatially localized* and *channel localized* features. By spatially localized, we mean that the image content within different local regions of the image should appear as different dimensions in an image's feature vector. Similarly, by channel localized, we mean that different types of descriptors (color, texture, etc.) should occupy different dimensions. This way, the learner can pick and choose a sparse set of both spatial regions and descriptor types that best discriminate attributes in one semantic group from another.

To this end, we extract a series of histogram features for multiple feature channels pooled within grid cells at multiple scales. We reduce the dimension of each component histogram (corresponding to a specific window+feature type) using Principal Component Analysis (PCA). This alleviates gains from trivially discarding low-variance dimensions and isolates the effect of attribute-specific feature selection. Since we perform PCA *per channel*, we retain the desired localized modality and location associations in the final representation. More dataset-specific details are in the experiments below in Sect. 4.2.2.

4.2.1.3 Joint Attribute Learning with Feature Sharing and Competition

The input to our learning scheme is (i) the descriptors for N training images, each represented as a D-dimensional vector $\mathbf{x}_n$, (ii) the corresponding (binary) attribute labels for all attributes, which are indexed by $a = 1, \ldots, M$, and (iii) the semantic attribute groups $S_1, \ldots, S_L$. Let $\mathbf{X}_{N\times D}$ be the matrix composed by stacking the training image descriptors. We denote the nth row of $\mathbf{X}$ as the row vector $\mathbf{x}_n$ and the dth column of $\mathbf{X}$ as the column vector $\mathbf{x}^d$. The scalar x_n^d denotes the (n, d)th entry of $\mathbf{X}$. Similarly, the training attribute labels are represented as a matrix $\mathbf{Y}_{N\times M}$ with all entries $\in \{0, 1\}$. The rows and columns of $\mathbf{Y}$ are denoted $\mathbf{y}_n$ and $\mathbf{y}^m$, respectively.

Because we wish to impose constraints on relationships between attribute models, we learn all attributes simultaneously in a multi-task learning setting, where each "task" corresponds to an attribute. The learning method outputs a parameter matrix $\mathbf{W}_{D\times M}$ whose columns encode the classifiers corresponding to the M attributes. We use logistic regression classifiers, with the loss function

$$L(\mathbf{X}, \mathbf{Y}; \mathbf{W}) = \sum_{m,n} \log(1 + \exp((1 - 2y_n^m)\, \mathbf{x}_n^T \mathbf{w}^m)). \tag{4.1}$$

Each classifier has an entry corresponding to the "weight" of each feature dimension for detecting that attribute.

Note that a row $\mathbf{w}_d$ of $\mathbf{W}$ represents the usage of feature dimension d across all attributes; a zero in w_d^m means that feature d is not used for attribute m.

Formulation

Our method operates on the premise that semantically related attributes tend to be determined by (some of) the same image features, and that semantically distant attributes tend to rely on (at least some) distinct features. In this way, the support of an attribute in the feature space—that is, the set of dimensions with nonzero weight—is strongly tied to its semantic associations. Our goal is to effectively exploit the supplied semantic grouping by inducing (i) in-group feature sharing and (ii) between-group competition for features. We encode this as a structured sparsity problem, where structure in the output attribute space is represented by the grouping. Figure 4.3 illustrates the envisioned effect of our approach.

To set the stage for our method, we next discuss two existing sparse feature selection approaches, both of which we will use as baselines in Sect. 4.2.2. The first is a simple adaptation of the single-task lasso method [43]. The original lasso regularizer applied to learning a single attribute m in our setting would be $\|\mathbf{w}^m\|_1$. As is well known, this convex regularizer yields solutions that are a good approximation to sparse solutions that would have been generated by the count of nonzero entries, $\|\mathbf{w}^m\|_0$.

By summing over all tasks, we can extend single-task lasso [43] to the multi-task setting to yield an "all-competing" lasso minimization objective:

$$\mathbf{W}^* = \arg\min_{\mathbf{W}} L(\mathbf{X}, \mathbf{Y}; \mathbf{W}) + \lambda \sum_m \|\mathbf{w}^m\|_1, \tag{4.2}$$

where $\lambda \in \mathbb{R}$ is a scalar regularization parameter balancing sparsity against classification loss. Note that the regularizing second term may be rewritten $\sum_m \|\mathbf{w}^m\|_1 = \sum_d \|\mathbf{w}_d\|_1 = \|\mathbf{W}\|_1$. This highlights how the regularizer is symmetric with respect to the two dimensions of $\mathbf{W}$, and may be thought of, respectively, as (i) encouraging sparsity on each task column $\mathbf{w}^m$ and (ii) imposing sparsity on each feature row $\mathbf{w}_d$. The latter effectively creates competition among all tasks for the feature dimension d.

In contrast, the "all-sharing" ℓ_{21} multi-task lasso approach for joint feature selection [1] promotes sharing among all tasks, by minimizing the following objective function:

$$\mathbf{W}^* = \arg\min_{\mathbf{W}} L(\mathbf{X}, \mathbf{Y}; \mathbf{W}) + \lambda \sum_d \|\mathbf{w}_d\|_2. \tag{4.3}$$

To see that this encourages feature sharing among *all* attributes, note that the regularizer may be written as the ℓ_1 norm $\|\mathbf{V}\|_1 = \sum_d \|\mathbf{w}_d\|_2$, where the single-column matrix $\mathbf{V}$ is formed by collapsing the columns of $\mathbf{W}$ with the ℓ_2 operator, i.e. its dth entry $v_d = \|\mathbf{w}_d\|_2$. The ℓ_1 norm of $\mathbf{V}$ prefers sparse-$\mathbf{V}$ solutions, which in turn means the individual classifiers must only select features that also are helpful to other classifiers. That is, $\mathbf{W}$ should tend to have rows that are either all-zero or all-nonzero.

We now define our objective, which is a semantics-informed intermediate approach that lies between the extremes in Eqs. (4.2) and (4.3) above. Our minimization objective retains the competition-inducing ℓ_1 norm of the conventional lasso across groups, while also applying the ℓ_{21}-type sharing regularizer within every semantic group:

$$\mathbf{W}^* = \arg\min_{\mathbf{W}} L(\mathbf{X}, \mathbf{Y}; \mathbf{W}) + \lambda \sum_{d=1}^{D} \sum_{l=1}^{L} \|\mathbf{w}_d^{S_l}\|_2, \tag{4.4}$$

where $\mathbf{w}_d^{S_l}$ is a row vector containing a subset of the entries in row $\mathbf{w}_d$, namely, those specified by the indices in semantic group S_l. This regularizer restricts the column-collapsing effect of the ℓ_2 norm to within the semantic groups, so that $\mathbf{V}$ is no longer a single-column vector but a matrix with L columns, one corresponding to each group. Figure 4.4 visualizes the idea. Note how sparsity on this $\mathbf{V}$ corresponds to promoting feature competition across unrelated attributes, while allowing sharing among semantically grouped attributes.

Our model unifies the previous formulations and represents an intermediate point between them. With only one group $S_1 = \{1, 2, \ldots, M\}$ containing all attributes, Eq. (4.4) simplifies to Eq. (4.3). Similarly, setting each attribute to belong to its own singleton group $S_m = \{m\}$ produces the lasso formulation of Eq. (4.2). Figure 4.5 illustrates their respective differences in structured sparsity. While standard lasso aims to drop as many features as possible across all tasks, standard "all-sharing" aims to use only features that can be shared by multiple tasks. In contrast, the proposed method seeks features shareable among related attributes, while it resists feature sharing among less related attributes.

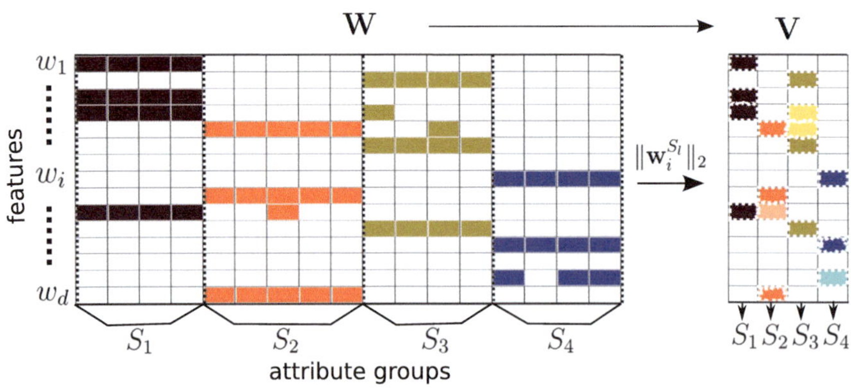

Fig. 4.4 "Collapsing" of grouped columns of the feature selection matrix $\mathbf{W}$ prior to applying the lasso penalty $\sum_l \|\mathbf{v}^l\|_1$. Nonzero entries in $\mathbf{W}$ and $\mathbf{V}$ are *shaded*. *Darkness of shading* in $\mathbf{V}$ represents how many attributes in that group selected that feature

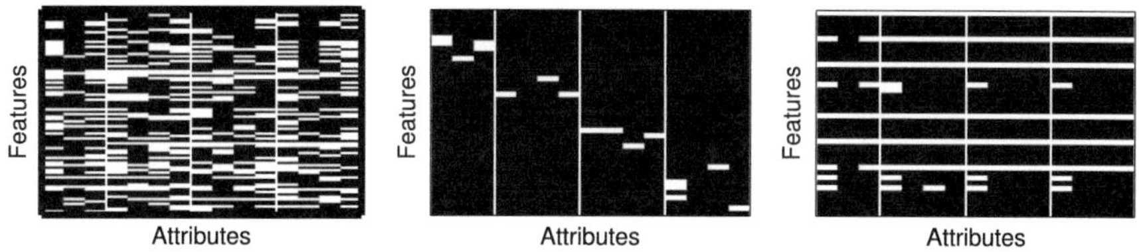

(a) Lasso (Eq. (4.2)) (b) Proposed (Eq. (4.4)) (c) All-sharing (Eq. (4.3))

Fig. 4.5 A part of the **W** matrix (thresholded, absolute value) learned by the different structured sparsity approaches on CUB data. The *thin white vertical lines* separate attribute groups

As we will show in results, this mitigates the impact of incidentally correlated attributes. Pushing attribute group supports away from one another helps decorrelate unrelated attributes *within* the vocabulary. For example, even if "brown" and "furry" always co-occur at training time, there is pressure to select distinct features in their classifiers. Meanwhile, feature sharing within the group essentially pools in-group labels together for feature selection, mitigating the risk of chance correlations—not only within the vocabulary, but also with visual properties (nameable or otherwise) that are not captured in the vocabulary. For example, suppose "hooked beak" and "brown belly" are attributes that often co-occur; if "brown belly" shares a group with the easier to learn "yellow belly", the pressure to latch onto feature dimensions shareable between brown and yellow belly indirectly leads "hooked beak" toward disjoint features.

We stress, however, that the groups are only a prior. While our method prefers sharing for semantically related attributes, it is not a hard constraint, and misclassification loss also plays an important role in deciding which features are relevant.

4.2.1.4 Optimization

Mixed norm regularizations of the form of Eq. (4.4), while convex, are nonsmooth and nontrivial to optimize. Such norms appear frequently in the structured learning literature [1, 3, 19, 55]. As in [19], we reformulate the objective by representing the 2-norm in the regularizer in its dual form, before applying the smoothing proximal gradient descent [7] method to optimize a smooth approximation of the resulting objective. More details are in [17].

4.2.2 *Experiments and Results*

4.2.2.1 Datasets

We use three datasets with 422 total attributes: (i) CUB-200–2011 ("CUB") [48], (ii) Animals with Attributes ("AwA") [25], and (iii) aPascal/aYahoo ("aPY") [9]. Dataset statistics are summarized in Table 4.1. Following common practice, we separate the datasets into "seen" and "unseen" classes. The idea is to learn attributes on one set of seen object classes, and apply them to new unseen objects at test time. This stress tests the generalization power, since correlation patterns will naturally deviate in novel objects. The seen and unseen classes for AwA and aPY come prespecified. For CUB, we randomly select 100 of the 200 classes to be "seen".

4.2.2.2 Features

Section 4.2.1.2 defines the basic feature extraction process. On AwA, we use the features provided with the dataset (global bag-of-words on four channels, 3-level pyramid with $4 \times 4 + 2 \times 2 + 1 = 21$ windows on 2 channels). For CUB and aPY, we compute features with the authors' code [9]. On aPY, we use a one-level pyramid with $3 \times 2 + 1 = 7$ windows on four channels, following [9]. On CUB, we extract features at the provided annotated part locations. To avoid occluded parts, we restrict the dataset to instances that have the most common part visibility configuration (all parts visible except "left leg" and "left eye").

4.2.2.3 Semantic Groups

To define the semantic groups, we rely largely on existing data. CUB specifies 28 attribute groups [48] (head color, back pattern, etc.). For AwA, the authors suggest nine groups in [24] (color, texture, shape, etc.). For aPY, which does not have pre-

Table 4.1 Summary of dataset statistics

	Categories		Attributes		Features	
Datasets	Seen	Unseen	Num (M)	Groups (L)	# Windows	D
CUB-200-2011 (CUB) [48]	100	100	312	28	15	375
Animals with Attributes (AwA) [25]	40	10	85	9	1.21	290
aPascal/aYahoo-restricted (aPY-25) [9]	20	12	25	3	7	105

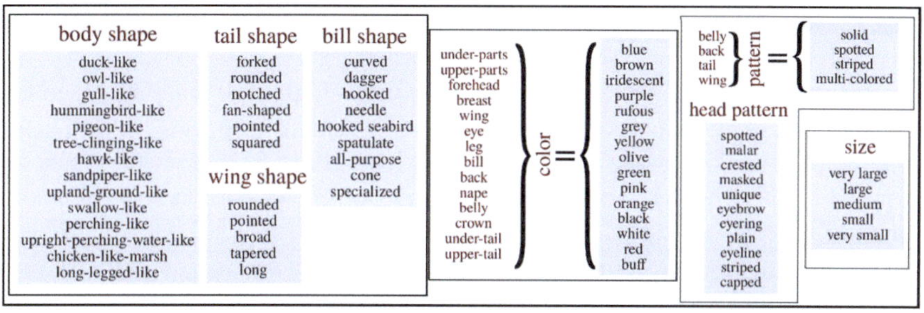

(a) Caltech-UCSD Birds (CUB) groups

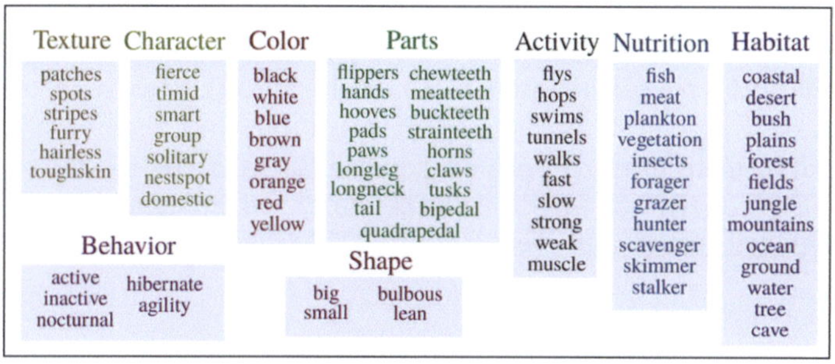

(b) Animals with Attributes (AwA) groups

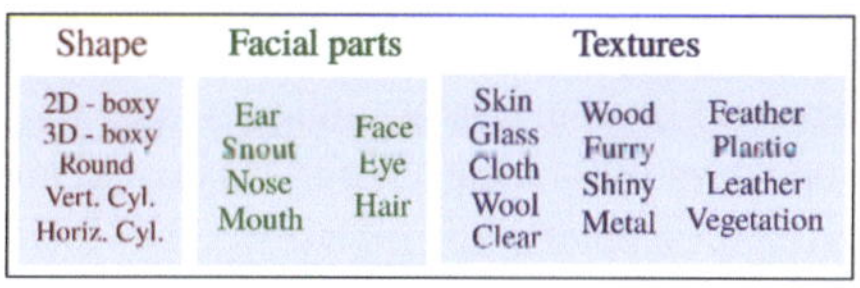

(c) aPascal (aPY-25) groups

Fig. 4.6 Semantic attribute groups on **a** CUB, **b** AwA and **c** aPY-25 datasets, as used in Sect. 4.2.2. Attribute groups are enclosed in *shaded boxes*, and phrases in larger font labeling the *boxes* indicate the rationale for the grouping. Additionally, in **a**, the color and pattern groups, condensed above, are to be interpreted as follows. Each part on the *left*, coupled with the term in the middle (*color/pattern*) represents the title of an attribute group. The predicates on the *right* applied to each part constitute the attributes in the its group, e.g., the "belly-color" attribute group has attributes "belly-color-blue", "belly-color-brown" etc.

specified attribute groups, we group 25 attributes (of the 64 total) into shape, material and facial attribute groups guided by suggestions in [24] ("aPY-25"). The full groups are shown in Fig. 4.6.

As discussed in Sect. 4.2.1.2, our method requires attribute groups and image descriptors to be mutually compatible. For example, grouping attributes based on their locations would not be useful if combined with a bag-of-words description that captures no spatial ordering. However, our results suggest that this compatibility is easy to satisfy. Our approach successfully exploits prespecified attribute groups with independently prespecified feature representations.

4.2.2.4 Baselines

We compare to four methods throughout. Two are single-task learning baselines, in which each attribute is learned separately: (i) "standard": ℓ_2-regularized logistic regression and (ii) "classwise": the object class-label-based feature selection scheme proposed in [9]. The "classwise" method is, to our knowledge, the only previous work that attempts to explicitly decorrelate semantic attributes. For each attribute, the classwise method selects discriminative image features *for each object class*, then pools the selected features to learn the attribute classifier. For example, it first finds features good for distinguishing cars with and without "wheel", then buses with and without "wheel", etc. The idea is that examples from the same class help isolate the attribute of interest. For this baseline, we use logistic regression in the final stage replacing the SVM, for uniformity with the others. The other two baselines are the sparse multi-task methods in Sect. 4.2.1: (iii) "lasso" (Eq. 4.2), and (iv) "all-sharing" (Eq. 4.3). All methods produce logistic regression classifiers and use the same input features. All parameters (λ for all methods, plus a second parameter for [9]) are validated with held out unseen class data.

4.2.2.5 Attribute Detection Accuracy

First, we test basic attribute detection accuracy. For this task, every test image is to be labeled with a binary label for each attribute in the vocabulary. Attribute models are trained on a randomly chosen 60 % of the "seen" class data and tested on three test sets: (i) *unseen*: unseen class instances, (ii) *all-seen*: other instances of seen classes, and (iii) *hard-seen*: a subset of the all-seen set that is designed to consist of outliers within the seen-class distribution. To create the hard-seen set, we first compute a binary class-attribute association matrix as the thresholded mean of attribute labels for instances of each seen class. Then hard sets for each attribute are composed of instances that violate their class-level label for that attribute in the matrix, e.g. albino elephants (gray), cats with occluded ears (ear).

Overall Results: Table 4.2 shows the mean AP scores over all attributes, per dataset.[5] On all three datasets, our method generalizes better than all baselines to unseen classes and hard-seen data.

While the "classwise" technique of [9] helps decorrelate attributes to some extent, improving over "standard" on aPY-25 and CUB, it is substantially weaker than the proposed method. That method assumes that same-object examples help isolate the attribute; yet, if two attributes always co-vary in the same-object examples (e.g., if cars with wheels are always metallic) then the method is still prone to exploit correlated features. Furthermore, the need for sufficient positive and negative attribute examples within each object class can be a practical burden (and makes it inapplicable to AwA). In contrast, our idea to jointly learn attributes and diffuse features between

[5] AwA has only class-level attribute annotations, so (i) the classwise baseline [9] is not applicable and (ii) the "hard-seen" test set is not defined.

Table 4.2 Accuracy scores for attribute detection (AP × 100). Higher is better. U, H, and S refer, respectively, to *unseen*, *hard-seen*, and *all-seen* test sets (Sect. 4.2.2.5). Our approach generally outperforms existing methods, and especially shines when attribute correlations differ between train and test data (i.e., the U and H scenarios)

Datasets	CUB			AwA		aPY-25		
Methods	U	H	S	U	S	U	H	S
Lasso	17.83	25.52	22.19	52.74	61.75	27.13	29.25	31.84
All-sharing [1]	17.78	25.46	22.17	53.78	60.21	26.01	29.34	25.60
Classwise [9]	19.09	27.56	24.06	N/A	N/A	27.29	27.76	35.95
Standard	18.36	27.06	23.69	53.66	**66.87**	27.27	28.45	**37.72**
Proposed	**21.14**	**29.62**	**26.54**	**54.97**	64.80	**29.89**	**33.18**	30.21

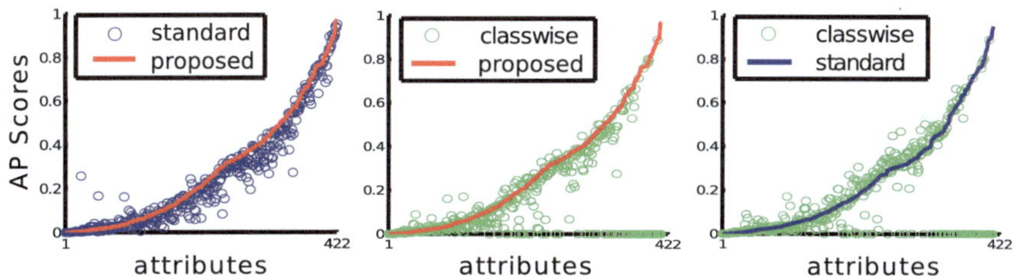

Fig. 4.7 Attribute detection results across all datasets (Sect. 4.2.2.5)

them is less susceptible to same-object correlations and does not make such label requirements. Our method outperforms this state-of-the-art approach on each dataset.

The two multi-task baselines (lasso and all-sharing) are typically weakest of all, verifying that semantics play an important role in deciding when to share. In fact, we found that the all-sharing/all-competing regularization generally hurt the models, leading the validated regularization weights λ to remain quite low.

Figure 4.7 plots the unseen set results for the individual 422 attributes from all datasets. Here we show paired comparisons of the three best performing methods: proposed, classwise [9], and standard. For each plot, attributes are arranged in order of increasing detectability for one method.[6] For nearly all of the 422 attributes, our method outperforms both the standard learning approach (first plot) and state-of-the-art classwise method (second plot).

Evidence of "Learning the Right Thing": Comparing results between the all-seen and hard-seen cases, we see evidence that our method's gains are due to its ability to preserve attribute semantics. On aPY-25 and AwA, our method *underperforms* the standard baseline on the all-seen set, whereas it *improves* performance on the unseen and hard-seen sets. This matches the behavior we would expect from a method that successfully resolves correlations in the training data: it generalizes better on novel

[6]Since "classwise" is inapplicable to AwA, its scores are set to 0 for that dataset (hence the circles along the x-axis in plots 2 and 3).

Fig. 4.8 **a** *Success cases* Annotations shown are our method's attribute predictions, which match ground truth. The logistic regression baseline ("standard") fails on all these cases. **b** *Failure cases* Cases where our predictions (shown) are incorrect and the "standard" baseline succeeds

test sets, sometimes at the cost of mild performance losses on test sets that have similar correlations (where a learner would benefit by learning the correlations).

In Fig. 4.8a, we present qualitative evidence in the form of cases that were mislabeled by the standard baseline but correctly labeled by our approach, e.g., the wedge-shaped "Flatiron" building (row 2, fourth from left) is correctly marked not "3D boxy" and the bird in the muck (row 2, end) is correctly marked as not having "brown underparts" because of the black grime sticking to it. In contrast, the baseline predicts the attribute based on correlated cues (e.g., city scenes are usually boxy, not wedge-shaped) and fails on these images.

Figure 4.8b shows some failure cases. Common failure cases for our method are when the image is blurred, the object is very small or information is otherwise deficient—cases where learning context from co-occurring aspects helps. In the low-resolution "feather" case, for instance, recognizing bird parts might have helped to correctly identify "feather".

Still more qualitative evidence that we preserve semantics comes from studying the features that influence the decisions of different methods. The part-based representation for CUB allows us to visualize the contributions of different bird parts to determine any given attribute. To find locations on instance number n that contribute to positive detection of attribute m, we take the absolute value of the elementwise

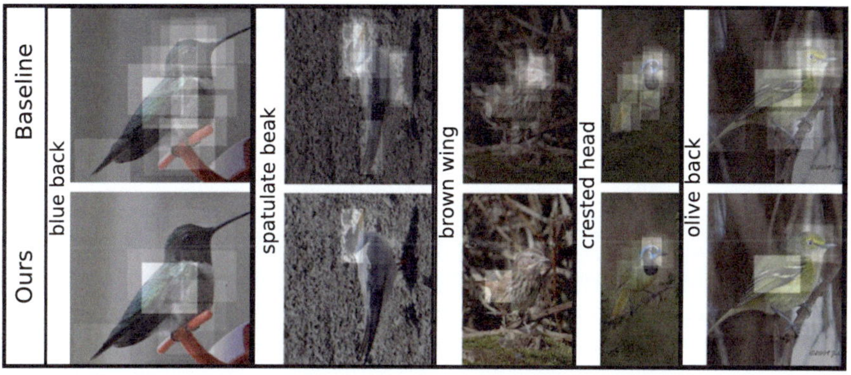

Fig. 4.9 Contributions of bird parts (shown as *highlights*) to the correct detection of specific attributes. Our method looks in the right places more often than the standard single-task baseline

product of descriptor $\mathbf{x}_n$ with the attribute weight vector $\mathbf{w}^m$—denote this $\mathbf{h}$. Each feature dimension is mapped onto the bird part it was computed from, in a mapping f. For each part p, we then compute its weight as $l_p = \sum_{f(i)=p} |h_i|$. These part weights are visualized as highlights in Fig. 4.9.

Our method focuses on the proper spatial regions associated with the bird parts, whereas the baseline picks up on correlated features. For example, on the "brown wing" image, while the baseline focuses on the head, our approach almost exclusively highlights the wing.

4.2.2.6 Zero-Shot Object Recognition

Next we show the impact of retaining attribute semantics for zero-shot object recognition. Closely following the setting in [25], the goal is to learn object categories from textual descriptions (e.g., "zebras are striped and four-legged"), but no training images, making attribute correctness crucial. We input attribute probabilities from each method's models to the Direct Attribute Prediction (DAP) framework for zero-shot learning [25].

Table 4.3 shows the results. Our method yields substantial gains in multiclass accuracy on the two large datasets (CUB and AwA). It is marginally worse than "standard" and "classwise" on the aPY-25 dataset, despite our significantly better attribute detection (Sect. 4.2.2.5). We believe that this may be due to recognition with DAP being less reliable when working with fewer attributes, as in aPY-25 (25 attributes).

4.2.2.7 Category Discovery with Semantic Attributes

Finally, we demonstrate the impact on category discovery. Cognitive scientists propose that natural categories are convex regions in *conceptual spaces* whose axes correspond to "psychological quality dimensions" [12]. This motivates us to perform category discovery with attributes. Treating semantic visual attributes as a conceptual space for visual categorization, we cluster each method's attribute presence probabilities (on unseen class instances) using k-means to discover the convex clusters. We set k to the true number of classes. We compare each method's clusters with the true unseen classes on all three datasets. For CUB, we test against both the 100 species (CUB-s) as well as the taxonomic families (CUB-f). Performance is measured using the normalized mutual information (NMI) score which measures the information shared between a given clustering and the true classes without requiring hard assignments of clusters to classes.

Table 4.4 shows the results. Our method performs significantly better than the baselines on all tasks. If we were to instead cluster the ground truth attribute signatures, we get a sense of the upper bound (last row). This shows that (i) visual attributes indeed constitute a plausible "conceptual space" for discovery and (ii) improved attribute learning models could yield large gains for high-level visual tasks.

Before moving on to the second instantiation of our general idea for multi-task learning of attributes without oversharing, here is a summary of what we have learned so far. We have shown how to use semantics to guide attribute learning without oversharing across attributes. Through extensive experiments across multiple datasets,

Table 4.3 Scores on zero-shot object recognition (accuracy). Higher is better

Datasets	CUB	AwA	aPY-25
Methods	[100 cl]	[10 cl]	[12 cl]
Lasso	7.35	25.32	9.88
All-sharing [1]	7.34	19.40	6.95
Classwise [9]	9.15	N/A	20.00
Standard	9.67	26.29	**20.09**
Proposed	**10.70**	**30.64**	19.43

Table 4.4 NMI scores for discovery of unseen categories (Sect. 4.2.2.7). Higher is better (0–100)

Methods / Datasets	CUB-s	AwA	aPY-25	CUB-f
Lasso	54.85	18.91	19.15	35.03
All-sharing [1]	54.82	18.81	17.17	35.08
Classwise [9]	57.46	N/A	19.73	38.62
Standard	56.97	22.39	17.61	37.19
Proposed	**59.44**	**24.11**	**24.76**	**42.81**
GT annotations	64.89	100.00	64.29	49.37

we have verified that: (i) our approach overcomes misleading training data correlations to successfully learn semantic visual attributes and (ii) preserving semantics in learned attributes is beneficial as an intermediate step in high-level tasks.

4.3 Learning Analogous Category-Sensitive Attributes

In the previous section, we showed how to avoid oversharing features across different attributes by our proposed multi-task learning approach. In this section, we will move to a different instantiation of our idea for multi-task learning with selective sharing. Specifically, we will show how to learn *analogous category sensitive attributes*. These analogous attributes aim to prevent another aspect of oversharing: using a single universal attribute model across all object categories.

Intuitively, the conventional approach of universal attribute learning is an oversimplification. For example, as shown in Fig. 4.10, fluffiness on a dog does not look the same as fluffiness on a towel. In this case, the attribute "fluffy" refers to different visual properties in different categories. Whereas above we encourage some features to be shared within certain attributes and keep some features disjoint between certain attributes, here we want to build a category-sensitive attribute for each category. Instead of sharing the attribute across categories, we utilize the correlation between attributes and categories during training.

What would it mean to have category-sensitive attribute predictions? At a glance it sounds like the other extreme from the current norm: rather than a single attribute model for all categories, one would train a single attribute model for each and every category. Furthermore, to learn accurate category-sensitive attributes, it seems to require category-sensitive training. For example, we could gather positive exemplar images for each category+attribute combination (e.g., separate sets of fluffy dog images, fluffy towel images). If so, this is a disappointment. Not only would learning attributes in this manner be quite costly in terms of annotations, but it would also fail to leverage the common semantics of the attributes that remain in spite of their visual distinctions.

To resolve this problem, we introduce a novel form of transfer learning to infer category-sensitive attribute models. Intuitively, even though an attribute's appearance

Fig. 4.10 Is fluffiness on a dog the same as fluffiness on a towel? Existing approaches assume an attribute such as "fluffy" can be used across different categories. However, as seen in here, in reality the same attribute name may refer to different visual properties for different categories

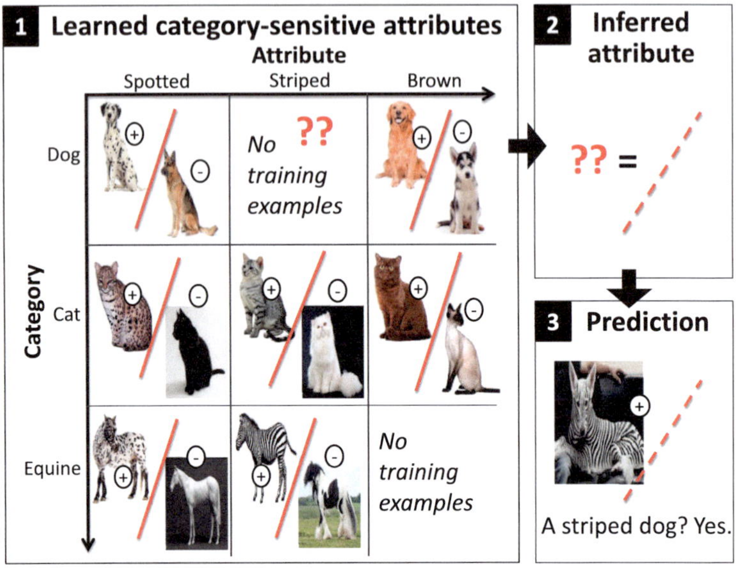

Fig. 4.11 Having learned a sparse set of object-specific attribute classifiers, our approach infers *analogous attribute classifiers*. The inferred models are object-sensitive, despite having no object-specific labeled images of that attribute during training

may be specialized for a particular object, there likely are latent variables connecting it to other objects' manifestations of the property. Plus, some attributes *are* quite similar across some class boundaries (e.g., spots look similar on Dalmatian dogs and Pinto horses). Having learned some category-sensitive attributes, then, we ought to be able to predict how the attribute might look on a new object, *even without labeled examples depicting that object with the attribute*. For example, in Fig. 4.11, suppose we want to recognize striped dogs, but we have no separate curated set of striped-dog exemplars. Having learned "spotted", "brown", etc., classifiers for dogs, cats, and equines, the system should leverage those models to infer what "striped" looks like on a dog. For example, it might infer that stripes on a dog look somewhat like stripes on a zebra but with shading influenced by the shape dogs share with cats.

Based on this intuition, we show how to infer an *analogous attribute*—an attribute classifier that is tailored to a category, even though we lack annotated examples of that category exhibiting that attribute. Given a sparse set of category-sensitive attribute classifiers, our approach first discovers the latent structure that connects them, by factorizing a tensor indexed by categories, attributes, and classifier dimensions. Then, we use the resulting latent factors to complete the tensor, inferring the "missing" classifier parameters for any object+attribute pairings unobserved during training. As a result, we can create category-sensitive attributes with only partial category-sensitive labeled data. Our solution offers a middle ground between completely category-independent training (the norm today [9, 23, 25, 32, 33, 36]) and completely category-sensitive training. We do not need to observe all attributes isolated on each category, and we capitalize on the fact that some categories and some of their attributes share common parameters.

Analogous attributes can be seen as a form of transfer learning. Existing transfer learning approaches for object recognition [2, 4, 10, 27, 30, 34, 44, 50, 53] aim to learn a new object category with few labeled instances by exploiting its similarity to previously learned class(es). While often the source and target classes must be manually specified [2, 4, 50], some techniques automatically determine which classes will benefit from transfer [16, 27, 44], or use class co-occurrence statistics to infer classifier weights to apply to related visual concepts [30]. Different from them, our goal is to reduce labeled data requirements. More importantly, our idea for transfer learning jointly in two label spaces is new, and, unlike the prior work, we can infer new classifiers without training examples. See Sect. 4.4 for further discussion of related work.

4.3.1 Approach

Given training images labeled by their category and one or more attributes, our method produces a series of category-sensitive attribute classifiers. Some of those classifiers are explicitly trained with the labeled data, while the rest are inferred by our method. We show how to create these analogous attribute classifiers via tensor completion.

4.3.1.1 Learning Category-Sensitive Attributes

In existing systems, attributes are trained in a category-independent manner [5, 9, 22, 23, 25, 32, 33, 36, 38]. Positive exemplars consist of images from various object categories, and they are used to train a discriminative model to detect the attribute in novel images. We will refer to such attributes as *universal*.

Here we challenge the convention of learning attributes in a completely category-independent manner. As discussed above, while attributes' visual cues are often shared among *some* objects, the sharing is not universal. It can dilute the learning process to pool cross-category exemplars indiscriminately.

The naive solution to instead train *category-sensitive* attributes would be to partition training exemplars by their category labels, and train one attribute per category. Were labeled examples of all possible attribute+object combinations abundantly available, such a strategy might be sufficient. However, in initial experiments with large-scale datasets, we found that this approach is actually inferior to training a single universal attribute. We attribute this to two things: (i) even in large-scale collections, the long-tailed distribution of object/scene/attribute occurrences in the real world means that some label pairs will be undersampled, leaving inadequate exemplars to build a statistically sound model and (ii) this naive approach completely ignores attributes' interclass semantic ties.

To overcome these shortcomings, we instead use an importance-weighted support vector machine (SVM) to train each category-sensitive attribute. Let each training example $(\mathbf{x}_i, y_i)$ consist of an image descriptor $\mathbf{x}_i \in \Re^D$ and its binary attribute label $y_i \in \{-1, 1\}$. Suppose we are learning "furriness" for dogs. We use examples from all categories (dogs, cats, etc.), but place a higher penalty on violating attribute label constraints for the same category (the dog instances). This amounts to an SVM objective for the hyperplane $\mathbf{w}$:

$$\begin{aligned} \text{minimize} \quad & \left(\frac{1}{2}||\mathbf{w}||^2 + C_s \sum_i \xi_i + C_o \sum_j \gamma_j \right) \\ s.t. \quad & y_i \mathbf{w}^T \mathbf{x}_i \geq 1 - \xi_i; \quad \forall i \in \mathcal{S} \\ & y_j \mathbf{w}^T \mathbf{x}_j \geq 1 - \gamma_j; \quad \forall j \in \mathcal{O} \\ & \xi_i \geq 0; \quad \gamma_j \geq 0, \end{aligned} \tag{4.5}$$

where the sets $\mathcal{S}$ and $\mathcal{O}$ denote those training instances in the same class (dog) and other classes (non-dogs), respectively, and C_s and C_o are slack penalty constants. Note, $\mathcal{S}$ and $\mathcal{O}$ contain both positive and negative examples for the attribute in consideration.

Instance reweighting is commonly used, e.g., to account for label imbalance between positives and negatives. Here, by setting $C_o < C_s$, the out-of-class examples of the attribute serve as a simple prior for which features are relevant. This way we benefit from more training examples when there are few category-specific examples of the attribute, but we are inclined to ignore those that deviate too far from the category-sensitive definition of the property.

4.3.1.2 Object-Attribute Classifier Tensor

Next we define a tensor to capture the structure underlying many such category-sensitive models. Let $m = 1, \ldots, M$ index the M possible attributes in the vocabulary, and let $t = 1, \ldots, T$ index the T possible object/scene categories. Let $\mathbf{w}(t, m)$ denote a category-sensitive SVM weight vector trained for the t-th object and m-th attribute using Eq. (4.5).

We construct a 3D tensor $\mathsf{W} \in \Re^{T \times M \times D}$ using all available category-sensitive models. Each entry w_d^{tm} contains the value of the d-th dimension of the classifier $\mathbf{w}(t, m)$. For a linear SVM, this value reflects the impact of the d-th dimension of the feature descriptor $\mathbf{x}$ for determining the presence/absence of attribute m for the object class t.

The resulting tensor is quite sparse. We can only fill entries for which we have class-specific positive and negative training examples for the attribute of interest. In today's most comprehensive attribute datasets [33, 36], including the SUN dataset discussed in Chap. 11, this means only approximately 25 % of the possible object-attribute combinations can be trained in a category-sensitive manner. Rather than resort to universal models for those "missing" combinations, we propose to use the latent factors for the observed classifiers to synthesize analogous models for the unobserved classifiers, as we explain next.

4.3.1.3 Inferring Analogous Attributes

Having learned how certain attributes look for certain object categories, our goal is to transfer that knowledge to hypothesize how the same attributes will look for other object categories. In this way, we aim to infer analogous attributes: category-sensitive attribute classifiers for objects that lack attribute-labeled data. We pose the "missing classifier" problem as a tensor completion problem.

Matrix (tensor) completion techniques have been used in vision, from bilinear models for separating style and content [11], to multilinear models separating the modes of face image formation (e.g., identity vs. expression vs. pose) [46, 47]. While often applied for visualization, the discovered factors can also be used to impute missing data—for example, to generate images of novel fonts [11] or infer missing pixels for in-painting tasks [28].

Different from the existing work, we want to use tensor factorization to infer *classifiers*, not data instances or labels. This enables a new "zero-shot" transfer protocol: we leverage the latent factors underlying previously trained models to create new analogous ones without any labeled instances. Our goal is to recover the latent factors for the 3D object-attribute tensor W, and use them to impute the unobserved classifier parameters.

Let $\mathbf{O} \in \Re^{K\times T}$, $\mathbf{A} \in \Re^{K\times M}$, and $\mathbf{C} \in \Re^{K\times D}$ denote matrices whose columns are the K-dimensional latent feature vectors for each object, attribute, and classifier dimension, respectively. We assume that w_d^{tm} can be expressed as an inner product of latent factors,

$$w_d^{tm} \approx \langle O_t, A_m, C_d \rangle, \tag{4.6}$$

where a subscript denotes a column of the matrix. In matrix form, we have $\mathsf{W} \approx \sum_{k=1}^{K} O^k \circ A^k \circ C^k$, where a superscript denotes the row in the matrix, and $\circ$ denotes the vector outer product.

The latent factors of the tensor W are what affect how the various attributes, objects, and image descriptors co-vary. What might they correspond to? We expect some will capture mixtures of two or more attributes, e.g., factors distinguishing how "spots" appear on something "flat" versus how they appear on something "bumpy". The latent factors can also capture useful clusters of objects, or supercategories, that exhibit attributes in common ways. Some might capture other attributes beyond the M portrayed in the training images—namely, those that help explain structure in the objects and other attributes we have observed.

We use Bayesian probabilistic tensor factorization [52] to recover the latent factors. Using this model, the likelihood for the explicitly trained classifiers (Sect. 4.3.1.1) is

$$p(\mathsf{W}|\mathbf{O}, \mathbf{A}, \mathbf{C}, \alpha) = \Pi_{t=1}^{T} \Pi_{m=1}^{M} \Pi_{d=1}^{D} \left[\mathcal{N}(w_d^{tm} | \langle O_t, A_m, C_d \rangle, \alpha^{-1}) \right]^{I_{tm}},$$

where $\mathcal{N}(w|\mu, \alpha)$ denotes a Gaussian with mean μ and precision α, and $I_{tm} = 1$ if object t has an explicit category-sensitive model for attribute m, and $I_{tm} = 0$ otherwise. For each of the latent factors O_t, A_m, and C_d, we use Gaussian priors. Let Θ represent all their means and covariances. Following [52], we compute a distribution for each missing tensor value by integrating out all model parameters and hyperparameters, given all the observed attribute classifiers:

$$p(\hat{w}_d^{tm} | \mathsf{W}) = \int p(\hat{w}_d^{tm} | O_t, A_m, C_d, \alpha) p(\mathbf{O}, \mathbf{A}, \mathbf{C}, \alpha, \Theta | \mathsf{W}) \; d\{\mathbf{O}, \mathbf{A}, \mathbf{C}, \alpha, \Theta\}.$$

After initializing with the MAP estimates of the three factor matrices, this distribution is approximated using Markov chain Monte Carlo (MCMC) sampling:

$$p(\hat{w}_d^{tm} | \mathsf{W}) \approx \sum_{l=1}^{L} p(\hat{w}_d^{tm} | O_n^{(l)}, A_m^{(l)}, C_d^{(l)}, \alpha^{(l)}). \tag{4.7}$$

Each of the L samples $\{O_t^{(l)}, A_m^{(l)}, C_d^{(l)}, \alpha^{(l)}\}$ is generated with Gibbs sampling on a Markov chain whose stationary distribution is the posterior over the model parameters and hyperparameters. We use conjugate distributions as priors for all the Gaussian hyperparameters to facilitate sampling. See [52] for details.

We use these factors to generate analogous attributes. Suppose we have no labeled examples showing an object of category t with attribute m (or, as is often the case, we have so few that training a category-sensitive model is problematic). Despite having no training examples, we can use the tensor to directly infer the classifier parameters

$$\hat{\mathbf{w}}(t, m) = [\hat{w}_1^{tm}, \ldots, \hat{w}_D^{tm}], \tag{4.8}$$

where each $\hat{w}_d^{tm}$ is the mean of the distribution in Eq. (4.7).

4.3.1.4 Discussion

In this approach, we use factorization to infer *classifiers* within a tensor representing two interrelated label spaces. Our idea has two key useful implications. First, it leverages the interplay of both label spaces to generate new classifiers without seeing any labeled instances. This is a novel form of transfer learning. Second, by working directly in the classifier space, we have the advantage of first isolating the low-level image features that are informative for the observed attributes. This means the input training images can contain realistic (unannotated) variations. In comparison, existing data tensor approaches often assume a strict level of alignment; e.g., for faces, examples are curated under t specific lighting conditions, m specific expressions, etc. [46, 47].

Our design also means that the analogous attributes can transfer information from multiple objects and/or attributes simultaneously. That means, for example, our model is not restricted to transferring the fluffiness of a dog from the fluffiness of a cat; rather, its analogous model for dog fluffiness might just as well result from transferring a mixture of cues from carpet fluffiness, dog spottedness, and cat shape.

In general, transfer learning can only succeed if the source and target classes are related. Similarly, we will only find an accurate low-dimensional set of factors if some common structure exists among the explicitly trained category-sensitive models. Nonetheless, a nice property of our formulation is that even if the tensor is populated with a variety of classes—some with no ties—analogous attribute inference can still succeed. Distinct latent factors can cover the different clusters in the observed classifiers. For similar reasons, our approach naturally handles the question of "where to transfer": sources and targets are never manually specified. Below, we consider the impact of building the tensor with a large number of semantically diverse categories versus a smaller number of closely related categories.

4.3.2 *Experiments and Results*

We evaluate our approach on two datasets: the attribute-labeled portion of ImageNet [36] and SUN Attributes [33]. The latter is presented in detail in Chap. 11. See Fig. 4.12, for example, images of these two datasets. The datasets do not contain data for all possible category-attribute pairings. Figure 4.13 shows which are available: there are 1,498 and 6,118 pairs in ImageNet and SUN, respectively. The sparsity of these matrices actually underscores the need for our approach, if one wants to learn category-sensitive attributes.

4.3.2.1 Category-Sensitive Versus Universal Attributes

First we test whether category-sensitive attributes are even beneficial. We explicitly train category-sensitive attribute classifiers using importance-weighted SVMs, as described in Sect. 4.3.1.1. This yields 1,498 and 6,118 classifiers for ImageNet and SUN, respectively. We compare their predictions to those of universal attributes, where we train one model for each attribute. When learning an attribute, both models have access to the exact same images; the universal method ignores the category labels, while the category-sensitive method puts more emphasis on the in-category examples.

Table 4.5 ("Category-sens." and "Universal" columns) shows the results, in terms of mean average precision across all 84 attributes and 664 categories. Among those, our category-sensitive models meet or exceed the universal approach 76 % of the

Fig. 4.12 Example images of ImageNet [36] and SUN attributes [33] dataset

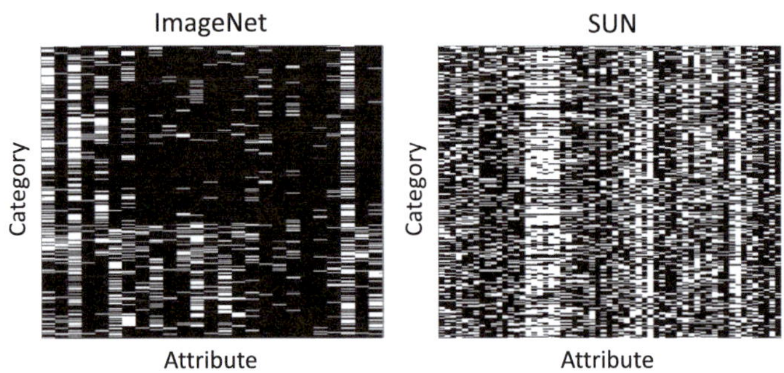

Fig. 4.13 Data availability: *white entries* denote category-attribute pairs that have positive and negative image exemplars. In ImageNet, most *vertical stripes* are color attributes, and most *horizontal stripes* are man-made objects. In SUN, most *vertical stripes* are attributes that appear across different scenes, such as vacationing or playing, while *horizontal stripes* come from scenes with varied properties, such as airport and park

time. This indicates that the status quo [9, 23, 25, 32, 33, 36] pooling of training images across categories is indeed detrimental.

4.3.2.2 Inferring Analogous Attributes

The results so far establish that category-sensitive attributes are desirable. However, the explicit models above are *impossible to train for 18,000 of the ~26,000 pos-*

Table 4.5 Accuracy (mAP) of attribute prediction. Category-sensitive models improve over standard universal models, and our inferred classifiers nearly match their accuracy with no training image examples. Traditional forms of transfer ("Adopt similar" and "One-shot" columns) fall short, showing the advantage of exploiting the 2D label space for transfer, as we propose

	Datasets		Trained explicitly		Trained via transfer			
	# Categ (N)	# Attr (M)	Category-sens.	Universal	Inferred (Ours)	Adopt similar	One-shot	Chance
ImageNet	384	25	**0.7304**	0.7143	**0.7259**	0.6194	0.6309	0.5183
SUN	280	59	**0.6505**	0.6343	**0.6429**	N/A	N/A	0.5408

sible attributes in these datasets. This is where our method comes in. It can infer all remaining 18,000 attribute models even without class-specific labeled training examples.

We perform leave-one-out testing: in each round, we remove one observed classifier (a white entry in Fig. 4.13), and infer it with our tensor factorization approach. Note that even though we are removing one at a time, the full tensor is always quite sparse due to the available data. Namely, only 16 % (in ImageNet) and 37 % (in SUN) of all possible category-sensitive classifiers can be explicitly trained.

Table 4.5 ("Category-sens.", "Universal", and "Inferred (Ours)" columns) shows this key result. In this experiment, the explicitly trained category-sensitive result is the "upper bound"; it shows how well the model trained with real category-specific images can do. We see that our inferred analogous attributes ("Inferred (Ours)" column) are nearly as accurate, yet use zero category-specific labeled images. They approximate the explicitly trained models well. Most importantly, our inferred models remain more accurate than the universal approach. Our inferred attributes again meet or exceed the universal model's accuracy 79 % of the time.

We stress that our method infers models for *all* missing attributes. That is, using the explicitly trained attributes, it infers another 8, 064 and 10, 407 classifiers on ImageNet and SUN, respectively. While the category-sensitive method would require approximately 160, 000 and 200, 000 labeled examples (20 labeled examples per classifier) to train those models, our method uses zero.

Table 4.5 also compares our approach to conventional transfer learning. The first transfer baseline infers the missing classifier simply by adopting the category-sensitive attribute of the category that is semantically closest to it, where semantic distance is measured via WordNet using [8] (not available for SUN). For example, if there are no furry-dog exemplars, we adopt the wolf's "furriness" classifier. The second transfer baseline additionally uses one category-specific image example to perform "one-shot" transfer (e.g., it trains with both the furry-wolf images plus a furry-dog example). Unlike the transfer baselines, our method uses neither prior knowledge about semantic distances nor labeled class-specific examples. We see that our approach is substantially more accurate than both transfer methods. This result highlights the benefit of our novel approach to transfer, which leverages both label spaces (categories and their attributes) simultaneously.

Which attributes does our method transfer? That is, which objects does it find to be analogous for an attribute? To examine this, we first take a category j and identify its neighboring categories in the latent feature space, i.e., in terms of Euclidean distance among the columns of $\mathbf{O} \in \Re^{K \times T}$. Then, for each neighbor i, we sort its attribute classifiers ($\mathbf{w}(i, :)$, real or inferred) by their maximal cosine similarity to any of category j's attributes $\mathbf{w}(j, :)$. The resulting shortlist helps illustrate which attribute+category pairs our method expects to transfer to category j.

Figure 4.14 shows four such examples, with one representative image for each category. We see neighboring categories in the latent space are often semantically related (e.g., syrup/bottle) or visually similar (e.g., airplane cabin/conference center); although our method receives no explicit side information on semantic distances, it discovers these ties through the observed attribute classifiers. Some semantically more distant neighbors (e.g., platypus/rorqual, courtroom/cardroom) are also discovered to be amenable to transfer. The words in Fig. 4.14 are the neighboring categories' top three analogous attributes for the numbered category to their left (*not* attribute predictions for those images). It seems quite intuitive that these would be suited for transfer.

Next we look more closely at where our method succeeds and fails. Figure 4.15 shows the top (bottom) five category+attribute combinations for which our inferred classifiers most increase (decrease) the AP, per dataset. As expected, we see our method most helps when the visual appearance of the attribute on an object is quite

Fig. 4.14 Analogous attribute examples for ImageNet (*top*) and SUN (*bottom*). Words above each neighbor indicate the three most similar attributes (learned or inferred) between leftmost query category and its neighboring categories in latent space. For these four examples, [Query category]:[Neighbor categories] = (*1*) [Bottle]:[filter, syrup, bullshot, gerenuk] (*2*) [Platypus]:[giraffe, ungulate, rorqual, patas] (*3*) [Airplane cabin]:[aquarium, boat deck, conference center, art studio] (*4*) [Courtroom]: [cardroom, florist shop, performance arena, beach house]

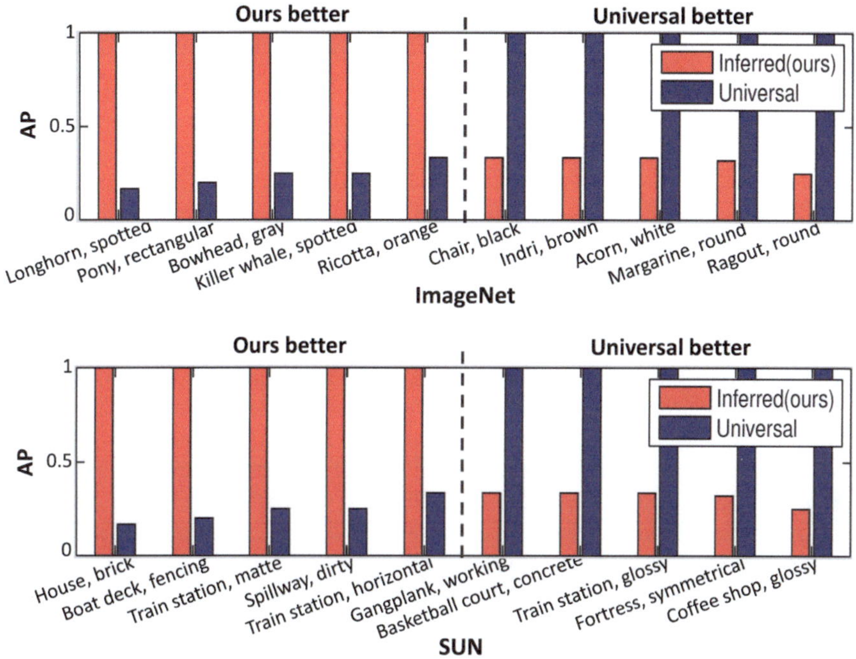

Fig. 4.15 *(Category, attribute)* pairs for which our inferred models most improve (*left*) or hurt (*right*) the universal baseline

Fig. 4.16 Test images that our method (*top row*) and the universal method (*bottom row*) predicted most confidently as having the named attribute (✓ = positive for the attribute, X = negative, according to ground truth.)

different from the common case, such as "spots" on the killer whale. On the other hand, it can detract from the universal model when an attribute is more consistent in appearance, such as "black", or where more varied examples help capture a generic concept, such as "symmetrical".

Figure 4.16 shows qualitative examples that support these findings. We show the image for each method that was predicted to most confidently exhibit the named attribute. By inferring analogous attributes, we better capture object-specific properties. For example, while our method correctly fires on a "smooth wheel", the universal model mistakes a Ferris Wheel as "smooth", likely due to the smoothness of the background, which might look like other classes' instantiations of smoothness.

4.3.2.3 Focusing on Semantically Close Data

In all results so far, we make no attempt to restrict the tensor to ensure semantic relatedness. The fact our method succeeds in this case indicates that it is capable of discovering clusters of classifiers for which transfer is possible, and is fairly resistant to negative transfer.

Still, we are curious whether restricting the tensor to classes that have tight semantic ties could enhance performance. We therefore test two variants: one where we restrict the tensor to closely related objects (i.e., downsampling the rows), and one where we restrict it to closely related attributes (i.e., downsampling the columns). To select a set of closely related objects, we use WordNet to extract sibling synsets for different types of dogs in ImageNet. This yields 42 categories, such as *puppy, courser, coonhound, corgi*. To select a set of closely related attributes, we extract only the color attributes.

Table 4.6 shows the results. We use the same leave-one-out protocol of Sect. 4.3.2.2, but during inference we only consider category-sensitive classifiers among the selected categories/attributes. We see that the inferred attributes are stronger with the category-focused tensor, raising accuracy from 0.7173 to 0.7358, closer to the upper bound. This suggests that among the entire dataset, attributes for which categories differ can introduce some noise into the latent factors. On the other hand, when we ignore attributes unrelated to color, the mAP of the inferred classifiers remains similar. This may be because color attributes use such a distinct set of image features compared to others (like stripes, round) that the latent factors accounting for them are coherent with or without the other classifiers in the mix. From this preliminary test, we can conclude that when semantic side information is available, it could boost accuracy, yet our method achieves its main purpose even when it is not.

Table 4.6 Attribute label prediction mAP when restricting the tensor to semantically close classes. The explicitly trained category-sensitive classifiers serve as an upper bound

Subset	Category-sensitive	Inferred (subset)	Inferred (all)
Categories (dogs)	0.7478	0.7358	0.7173
Attributes (colors)	0.7665	0.7631	0.7628

4.4 Related Work

In this section we describe related work in more detail and highlight contrasts and connections with the two main contributions described above.

4.4.1 Attributes as Semantic Features

A visual attribute is a binary predicate for an image that indicates whether or not a property is present. The standard approach to learn an attribute is to pool images regardless of their object category and train a discriminative classifier [5, 9, 22, 23, 25, 26, 32, 33, 36, 38].

While this design is well motivated by the goal of having attributes that transcend category boundaries, it sacrifices accuracy in practice. We are not aware of any prior work that learns category-sensitive attributes, though class-specific attribute training is used as an intermediate feature generation procedure in [9, 51], prior to training class-independent models.

Recent research focuses on attributes as vehicles of semantics in human–machine communication. For example, using attributes for image search lets a user specify precise semantic queries ("find smiling Asian men" [20, 22, 38] or "find shoes more formal and less shiny than this pair" (Chaps. 5 and 6)); using them to augment standard training labels offers new ways to teach vision systems about objects ("zebras are striped", "this bird has a yellow belly", etc.) [5, 25, 26, 40]; deviations from an expected configuration of attributes may be used to generate textual descriptions of what humans would find remarkable [9, 37]. In all such applications, learning attributes incorrectly (such as by inadvertently learning correlated visual properties) or imprecisely (such as by learning a "lowest common denominator" model shared across all categories) is a real problem; the system and user's interpretations must align for their communication to be meaningful. However, despite all the attention to attribute applications, there is very little work on *how to learn attributes accurately*, preserving their semantics. The approaches presented in Sects. 4.2 and 4.3 show promise for such applications that require "learning the right thing" when learning semantic attributes.

4.4.2 Attribute Correlations

While most methods learn attributes independently, some initial steps have been taken toward modeling their relationships. Modeling co occurrence between attributes helps ensure predictions follow usual correlations, even if image evidence for a certain attribute is lacking (e.g., "has-ear" usually implies "has-eye") [25, 41, 42, 51]. Our goal in decorrelating attributes (Sect. 4.2) is essentially the opposite of these approaches. Rather than equate co-occurrences with true semantic ties, we argue that it is often crucial that the learning algorithm avoid conflating pairs of attributes. This will prevent excessive biasing of the likelihood function toward the training data and thus deal better with unfamiliar configurations of attributes in novel settings.

While attribute learning is typically considered separately from object category learning, some recent work explores how to jointly learn attributes and objects, either to exploit attribute correlations [51], to promote feature sharing [15, 49], or to discover separable features [39, 54]. Our framework in Sect. 4.3 can be seen as a new way to jointly learn multiple attributes, leveraging structure in object-attribute relationships. Unlike any prior work, we use these ties to directly infer category-sensitive attribute models without labeled exemplars.

In [14], analogies between object categories are used to regularize a semantic label embedding. Our method also captures beyond-pairwise relationships, but the similarities end there. In [14], explicit analogies are given as input, and the goal is to enrich the features used for nearest neighbor object recognition. In contrast, our approach in Sect. 4.3 implicitly *discovers* analogical relationships among *object-sensitive attribute classifiers*, and our goal is to generate novel category-sensitive attribute classifiers.

4.4.3 Differentiating Attributes

As discussed above, to our knowledge, the only previous work that attempts to explicitly decorrelate semantic attributes like we attempt in Sect. 4.2 is the classwise method of [9]. For each attribute, it selects discriminative image features *for each object class*, then pools the selected features to learn the attribute classifier. While the idea is that examples from the same class help isolate the attribute of interest, as seen above, this method is susceptible to learning chance correlations among the reduced number of samples of individual classes. Moreover, it requires expensive instancewise attribute annotations. Our decorrelating attributes approach (Sect. 4.2) overcomes these issues, as we demonstrate with experimental comparisons to [9] in Sect. 4.2.2.

While this is the only prior work on decorrelating *semantic* attributes, some unsupervised approaches attempt to diversify discovered (unnamed/non-semantic) "attributes" [9, 29, 54]—for example, by designing object class splits that yield uncorrelated features [54] or converting redundant semantic attributes into discriminative ones [29]. In contrast, our focus in Sect. 4.2 is on jointly learning a specified vocabulary of *semantic* attributes.

4.4.4 Multi-task Learning (MTL)

Multi-task learning jointly trains predictive functions for multiple tasks, often by selecting the feature dimensions ("supports") each function should use to meet some criterion. Most methods emphasize feature *sharing* among all classes [1, 19, 31]; e.g., feature sharing between objects can yield faster detectors [45], and sharing between objects and their attributes can isolate features suitable for both tasks [15, 49]. A few works have begun to explore the value of modeling *negative* correlations [13, 35, 56, 57]. For example, in a hierarchical classifier, feature competition is encouraged via disjoint sparsity or "orthogonal transfer", in order to remove redundancies between child and parent node classifiers [13, 56]. These methods exploit the inherent mutual exclusivity among object labels, which does not hold in our attributes setting. Unlike any of these approaches, in our decorrelating attributes method (Sect. 4.2), we model semantic structure in the target space using multiple task groups.

While most MTL methods enforce joint learning on all tasks, a few explore ways to discover groups of tasks that can share features [16, 18, 21]. Our method for decorrelating attributes (Sect. 4.2) involves grouped tasks, but with two crucial differences: (i) we explicitly model between-group *competition* along with in-group sharing to achieve intergroup decorrelation and (ii) we treat external knowledge about semantic groups as supervision to be exploited during learning. In contrast, the prior methods [16, 18, 21] discover task groups from data, which is prone to suffer from correlations in the same way as a single-task learner.

In Sect. 4.3, we argue for modeling even single attributes through multiple category-specific models, all learned in a multi-task learning framework. While the idea of inferring classifiers for one task from those learned for other tasks is relatively unexplored, [30] recently estimates a classifier for a new class from weighted linear combinations of heuristically selected related class classifiers with the knowledge of co-occurrence statistics in images. Our approach can be seen as a new form transfer learning that leverages the interplay of both the category and attribute label spaces, automatically selecting among and combining previously learned classifiers to generate new classifiers without seeing any labeled instances.

4.5 Conclusion

In this chapter, we have proposed and discussed two new methods to avoid the problem of "oversharing" in attribute learning.

First, we showed a method that exploits semantic relationships among attributes to guide attribute vocabulary learning by selectively sharing features among related attributes and encouraging disjoint supports for unrelated attributes. Our extensive experiments across three datasets validate two major claims for this method: (i) it overcomes misleading training data correlations to successfully learn semantic visual attributes and (ii) preserving semantics in learned attributes is beneficial as an intermediate step in high-level tasks.

Next, we proposed a method to learn category-sensitive attributes rather than the standard monolithic attribute classifier over all categories. To do this, we developed a new form of transfer learning, in which analogous attributes are inferred using observed attributes organized according to two interrelated label spaces. Our tensor factorization approach solves the transfer problem, even when no training examples are available for the decision task of interest. Once again, our results confirm that our approach successfully addresses the category-dependence of attributes and improves attribute recognition accuracy.

The work we have presented suggests a number of possible extensions. The decorrelating attributes approach of Sect. 4.2 may be extended to automatically mine attribute groups from web sources, or using distributed word representations, possibly incorporating ideas like those in Chap. 12. It may also be interesting to generalize the approach to settings where tasks cannot easily be clustered into discrete groups, but, say, pairwise semantic relationships among tasks are known. The analogous attributes approach would be interesting to consider in a one-shot or few-shot setting as well. While thus far we have tested it only in the case where no category-specific labeled examples are available for an attribute we wish to learn, it would be interesting to generalize the model to cases where some image instances are available. For example, such prior observations could be used to regularize the missing classifier parameter imputation step. In addition, we are interested in analyzing the impact of analogous attributes for learning relative properties, such as the fine-grained comparison models explored in Chap. 6.

Finally, a natural question is how the two "selective sharing" ideas presented in this chapter might be brought together. For instance, one might jointly train category-sensitive attribute classifiers with semantics-informed feature sharing between attributes, and then use the factorization method to infer classifiers for the category-attribute pairs for which we lack training examples. Our general idea of controlled sharing among tasks may also be applicable to many general multi-task learning problems that have additional sources of information on task relationships.

Acknowledgements We would like to thank Sung Ju Hwang and Hsiang-Fu Yu for helpful discussions. This research was supported in part by NSF IIS-1065390 and ONR YIP N00014-12-1-0754.

References

1. Argyriou, A., Evgeniou, T., Pontil, M.: Multi-task feature learning. In: Conference on Neural Information Processing Systems (NIPS) (2007)
2. Aytar, Y., Zisserman, A.: Tabula rasa: model transfer for object category detection. In: International Conference on Computer Vision (ICCV) (2011)
3. Bach, F.: Consistency of the group lasso and multiple kernel learning. J. Mach. Learn. Res. (JMLR) **9**, 1179–1225 (2008)

4. Bart, E., Ullman, S.: Cross-Generalization: learning novel classes from a single example by feature replacement. In: Conference on Computer Vision and Pattern Recognition (CVPR) (2005)
5. Branson, S., Wah, C., Schroff, F., Babenko, B., Welinder, P., Perona, P., Belongie, S.: Visual recognition with humans in the loop. In: European Conference on Computer Vision (ECCV) (2010)
6. Chen, C.Y., Grauman, K.: Inferring analogous attributes. In: Conference on Computer Vision and Pattern Recognition (CVPR) (2014)
7. Chen, X., Lin, Q., Kim, S., Carbonell, J.G., Xing, E.P.: Smoothing proximal gradient method for general structured sparse regression. Ann. Appl. Stat. (AAS) (2012)
8. Deng, J., Dong, W., Socher, R., Li, L.J., Li, K., Fei-Fei, L.: ImageNet: a large-scale hierarchical image database. In: Conference on Computer Vision and Pattern Recognition (CVPR) (2009)
9. Farhadi, A., Endres, I., Hoiem, D., Forsyth, D.: Describing objects by their attributes. In: Conference on Computer Vision and Pattern Recognition (CVPR) (2009)
10. Fei-Fei, L., Fergus, R., Perona, P.: A Bayesian approach to unsupervised one-shot learning of object categories. In: International Conference on Computer Vision (ICCV) (2003)
11. Freeman, W.T., Tenenbaum, J.B.: Learning bilinear models for two-factor problems in vision. In: Conference on Computer Vision and Pattern Recognition (CVPR) (1997)
12. Gardenfors, P.: Conceptual spaces as a framework for knowledge representation. In: Mind and Matter. The MIT Press (2004)
13. Hwang, S.J., Grauman, K., Sha, F.: Learning a tree of metrics with disjoint visual features. In: Conference on Neural Information Processing Systems (NIPS) (2011)
14. Hwang, S.J., Grauman, K., Sha, F.: Analogy-preserving semantic embedding for visual object categorization. In: International Conference on Machine Learning (ICML) (2013)
15. Hwang, S.J., Sha, F., Grauman, K.: Sharing features between objects and their attributes. In: Conference on Computer Vision and Pattern Recognition (CVPR) (2011)
16. Jacob, L., Bach, F., Vert, J.: Clustered multi-task learning: a convex formulation. In: Conference on Neural Information Processing Systems (NIPS) (2008)
17. Jayaraman, D., Sha, F., Grauman, K.: Decorrelating Semantic visual attributes by resisting the urge to share. In: Conference on Computer Vision and Pattern Recognition (CVPR) (2014)
18. Kang, Z., Grauman, K., Sha, F.: Learning with whom to share in multi-task feature learning. In: International Conference on Machine Learning (ICML) (2011)
19. Kim, S., Xing, E.: Tree-guided group lasso for multi-response regression with structured sparsity, with an application to eQTL mapping. Ann. Appl. Stat. (AAS) (2012)
20. Kovashka, A., Parikh, D., Grauman, K.: WhittleSearch: Image search with relative attribute feedback. In: Conference on Computer Vision and Pattern Recognition (CVPR) (2012)
21. Kumar, A., III, H.D.: Learning task grouping and overlap in multi-task learning. In: International Conference on Machine Learning (ICML) (2012)
22. Kumar, N., Belhumeur, P., Nayar, S.: Facetracer: A search engine for large collections of images with faces. In: European Conference on Computer Vision (ECCV) (2008)
23. Kumar, N., Berg, A., Belhumeur, P., Nayar, S.: Attribute and simile classifiers for face verification. In: International Conference on Computer Vision (ICCV) (2009)
24. Lampert, C.: Semantic Attributes for Object Categorization (slides). http://ist.ac.at/~chl/talks/lampertvrml2011b.pdf (2011)
25. Lampert, C., Nickisch, H., Harmeling, S.: Learning to detect unseen object classes by between-class attribute transfer. In: Conference on Computer Vision and Pattern Recognition (CVPR) (2009)
26. Lampert, C., Nickisch, H., Harmeling, S.: Attribute-based classification for zero-shot visual object categorization. IEEE Trans. Pattern Anal. Mach. Intell. (PAMI) **36**(3), 453–465 (2014)
27. Lim, J., Salakhutdinov, R., Torralba, A.: Transfer learning by borrowing examples for multiclass object detection. In: Conference on Neural Information Processing Systems (NIPS) (2002)
28. Liu, J., Musialski, P., Wonka, P., Ye, J.: Tensor completion for estimating missing values in visual data. In: International Conference on Computer Vision (ICCV) (2009)

29. Mahajan, D., Sellamanickam, S., Nair, V.: A joint learning framework for attribute models and object descriptions. In: International Conference on Computer Vision (ICCV) (2011)
30. Mensink, T.E.J., Gavves, E., Snoek, C.G.M.: Costa: Co-occurrence statistics for zero-shot classification. In: Conference on Computer Vision and Pattern Recognition (CVPR) (2014)
31. Parameswaran, S., Weinberger, K.: Large margin multi-task metric learning. In: Conference on Neural Information Processing Systems (NIPS) (2010)
32. Parikh, D., Grauman, K.: Relative attributes. In: International Conference on Computer Vision (ICCV) (2011)
33. Patterson, G., Hays, J.: Sun attribute database: discovering, annotating, and recognizing scene attributes. In: Conference on Computer Vision and Pattern Recognition (CVPR) (2012)
34. Quattoni, A., Collins, M., Darrell, T.: Transfer learning for image classification with sparse prototype representations. In: Conference on Computer Vision and Pattern Recognition (CVPR) (2008)
35. Romera-Paredes, B., Argyriou, A., Bianchi-Berthouze, N., Pontil, M.: Exploiting unrelated tasks in multi-task learning. In: International Conference on Artificial Intelligence and Statistics (AISTATS) (2012)
36. Russakovsky, O., Fei-Fei, L.: Attribute learning in large-scale datasets. In: ECCV Workshop on Parts and Attributes (2010)
37. Saleh, B., Farhadi, A., Elgammal, A.: Object-centric anomaly detection by attribute-based reasoning. In: Conference on Computer Vision and Pattern Recognition (CVPR) (2013)
38. Scheirer, W., Kumar, N., Belhumeur, P., Boult, T.: Multi-attribute spaces: calibration for attribute fusion and similarity search. In: Conference on Computer Vision and Pattern Recognition (CVPR) (2012)
39. Sharmanska, V., Quadrianto, N., Lampert, C.: Augmented attributes representations. In: European Conference on Computer Vision (ECCV) (2012)
40. Shrivastava, A., Singh, S., Gupta, A.: Constrained semi-supervised learning using attributes and comparative attributes. In: European Conference on Computer Vision (ECCV) (2012)
41. Siddiquie, B., Feris, R., Davis, L.: Image ranking and retrieval based on multi-attribute queries. In: Conference on Computer Vision and Pattern Recognition (CVPR) (2011)
42. Song, F., Tan, X., Chen, S.: Exploiting relationship between attributes for improved face verification. In: British Machine Vision Conference (BMVC) (2011)
43. Tibshirani, R.: Regression shrinkage and selection via the lasso. In: RSS Series B (1996)
44. Tommasi, T., Orabona, F., Caputo, B.: Safety in numbers: learning categories from few examples with multi model knowledge transfer. In: Conference on Computer Vision and Pattern Recognition (CVPR) (2010)
45. Torralba, A., Murphy, K., Freeman, W.: Sharing visual features for multiclass and multiview object detection. IEEE Trans. Pattern Anal. Mach. Intell. (PAMI) **29**(5), 854–869 (2007)
46. Vasilescu, M.A.O., Terzopoulos, D.: Multilinear analysis of image ensembles: tensorfaces. In: European Conference on Computer Vision (ECCV) (2002)
47. Vlasic, D., Brand, M., Pfister, H., Popović, J.: Face transfer with multilinear models. ACM Trans. Graphics **24**(3), 426–433 (2005)
48. Wah, C., Branson, S., Welinder, P., Perona, P., Belongie, S.: The Caltech-UCSD Birds-200-2011 Dataset. Tech. Rep, California Institute of Technology (2011)
49. Wang, G., Forsyth, D.: Joint learning of visual attributes, object classes and visual saliency. In: Conference on Computer Vision and Pattern Recognition (CVPR) (2009)
50. Wang, G., Forsyth, D., Hoiem, D.: Comparative object similarity for improved recognition with few or no examples. In: Conference on Computer Vision and Pattern Recognition (CVPR) (2010)
51. Wang, Y., Mori, G.: A discriminative latent model of object classes and attributes. In: European Conference on Computer Vision (ECCV) (2010)
52. Xiong, L., Chen, X., Huang, T., Schneider, J., Carbonell, J.: Temporal collaborative filtering with Bayesian probabilistic tensor factorization. In: International Conference on Data Mining (SDM) (2010)

53. Yang, J., Yan, R., Hauptmann, A.: Cross-domain video concept detection using adaptive svms. In: ACM Multimedia (ACM MM) (2007)
54. Yu, F., Cao, L., Feris, R., Smith, J., Chang, S.F.: Designing category-level attributes for discriminative visual recognition. In: Conference on Computer Vision and Pattern Recognition (CVPR) (2013)
55. Yuan, M., Lin, Y.: Model selection and estimation in regression with grouped variables. In: RSS Series B (2006)
56. Zhou, D., Xiao, L., Wu, M.: Hierarchical classification via orthogonal transfer. In: International Conference on Machine Learning (ICML) (2011)
57. Zhou, Y., Jin, R., Hoi, S.: Exclusive lasso for multi-task feature selection. In: International Conference on Artificial Intelligence and Statistics (AISTATS) (2010)

Part II
Relative Attributes and Their Application to Image Search

Chapter 5
Attributes for Image Retrieval

Adriana Kovashka and Kristen Grauman

Abstract Image retrieval is a computer vision application that people encounter in their everyday lives. To enable accurate retrieval results, a human user needs to be able to communicate in a rich and noiseless way with the retrieval system. We propose semantic visual attributes as a communication channel for search because they are commonly used by humans to describe the world around them. We first propose a new feedback interaction where users can directly comment on how individual properties of retrieved content should be adjusted to more closely match the desired visual content. We then show how to ensure this interaction is as informative as possible, by having the vision system ask those questions that will most increase its certainty over what content is relevant. To ensure that attribute-based statements from the user are not misinterpreted by the system, we model the unique ways in which users employ attribute terms, and develop personalized attribute models. We discover clusters among users in terms of how they use a given attribute term, and consequently discover the distinct "shades of meaning" of these attributes. Our work is a significant step in the direction of bridging the semantic gap between high-level user intent and low-level visual features. We discuss extensions to further increase the utility of attributes for practical search applications.

5.1 Introduction

Semantic visual attributes are properties of the world akin to adjectives (e.g. "furry," "metallic," "smiling," "natural," etc.) Humans naturally explain the world to each other with attribute-driven descriptions. For example, a person might say "Give me the *red* cup" or "I wanted shoes that were *more formal*" or "The actor I am thinking

A. Kovashka (✉)
University of Pittsburgh, Pittsburgh, USA
e-mail: kovashka@cs.pitt.edu

K. Grauman
The University of Texas at Austin, Austin, USA
e-mail: grauman@cs.utexas.edu

R.S. Feris et al. (eds.), *Visual Attributes*, Advances in Computer Vision and Pattern Recognition, DOI 10.1007/978-3-319-50077-5_5

of is *older*." Thus, attributes are meaningful to humans. Importantly, they can also be captured with computational models. As such, they are an excellent channel for communication between the user and the system. This property is exploited by a number of works that apply attributes for semantic image retrieval [7, 26, 30, 45, 50, 55, 60].

Image retrieval is a task in which a human user poses a query using either text or an image to a search engine, and the engine returns image results. Search is necessary because there is simply too much visual data on the web today, and browsing it to find relevant content is infeasible. When people perform a search, they usually have a very specific idea of what they want to retrieve, and this idea cannot be captured by simple tags or keywords, which are usually category labels. The traditional categories we use in computer vision are insufficiently descriptive of the user's information need because they are too coarse-grained. For example, a user might want to buy shoes that satisfy certain properties like color, heel height, texture, etc., and these properties cannot be captured by even the most fine-grained categories that might reasonably exist in the world. Similarly, the user might search for stock photography to include in a presentation, and she likely has a very detailed idea of what the photograph she wants to include should look like. Alternatives to keyword search include asking the user to point to examples, which is infeasible because when the user's target is specific or complex, examples may not be available. Another alternative is to trust users to draw readily so they can illustrate what they want to find, but unfortunately this is an unrealistic expectation. Thus, search via some form of language-based interaction remains a very appealing option.

It is infeasible to pre-assign tags to images that are sufficient to satisfy any future query. Further, due to the "semantic gap" between the system's low-level image representation and the user's high-level concept, one-shot retrieval performed by matching images to keywords is unlikely to get the right results. Typically retrieval systems allow the user to iteratively provide feedback on the results retrieved in each round. In this interactive form of search, users mark some images as "relevant" and others as "irrelevant", and the system adapts its relevance ranking function accordingly [5, 14, 31, 33, 52, 63, 70]. Instead of requesting feedback on some user-chosen subset of the current results, some methods perform active selection of the images to display for feedback, by exploiting the uncertainty in the system's current model of relevance to find useful exemplars [5, 14, 33, 63, 70].

However, this form of feedback is limited as it forces the retrieval system to guess *what about* the images was relevant or irrelevant. For example, when a user searches for "black shoes", retrieves a pair of pointy high-heeled black shoes, and marks them as irrelevant, this might be because she did not want these shoes to be "pointy", or because she wanted them to be "flat". However, the system does not know which, and this uncertainty will negatively impact the next set of image results. Furthermore, existing methods which *actively select* the images for feedback use an *approximation* for finding the optimal uncertainty reduction, whether in the form of uncertainty sampling [63] or by employing sampling or clustering heuristics [5, 14]. Finally, such methods only consider binary feedback ("this is relevant"/"this is irrelevant"), which is imprecise.

Below, we introduce a method for refining image search results via attributes. A user initiates the search, for instance by providing a set of keywords involving objects or attributes, and the system retrieves images that satisfy those keywords. After the initialization, the user performs relevance feedback; the form of this feedback is where our method's novelty lies. We propose a new approach which allows the user to give rich feedback based on relative attributes. For example, she can say "Show me images like this, but *brighter in color*." This descriptive statement allows the system to adjust the properties of the search results in exactly the way which the user envisions. Notice this new form of feedback is much more informative than the "relevant/irrelevant" binary relevance feedback that previous methods allowed.

Attribute-based search has been explored in [30, 50, 55, 60], but while one-shot attribute-based queries allow a user to more precisely state their goal compared to category-based queries, the full descriptive power of attributes cannot be utilized without a way to quantify to what extent they are present and to *refine* a search after the query is issued. Furthermore, existing work in attribute-based search [28, 50, 55, 60] assumes one classifier is sufficient to capture all the variability within a given attribute term, but researchers find there is substantial disagreement between users regarding attribute labels [6, 13, 23, 46]. We show how to prevent this disagreement from introducing noise on the user-system communication channel.

Towards the broad goal of interactive search with attributes, we address a number of technical challenges. First, we use attributes to provide a channel on which the user can communicate her information need precisely and with as little effort as possible. We find that, compared to traditional binary relevance feedback, attributes enable more powerful relevance feedback for image search (Sect. 5.2), and show how to further select this feedback so it is as informative as possible (Sect. 5.3). Unlike existing relevance feedback for image retrieval [5, 14, 16, 31, 52, 62, 70], the attribute-based feedback we propose allows the user to communicate with the retrieval system precisely *how* a set of results lack what the user is looking for. We also investigate how users use the attribute vocabulary during search, and ensure that the models learned for each attribute align with how a user employs the attribute name, which is determined by the user's individual perception of this attribute (Sect. 5.4). We automatically discover and exploit the commonalities that exist in user perceptions of the same attribute, to reveal the "shades of meaning" of an attribute and learn more robust models (Sect. 5.5). Due to their computational efficiency, the methods we develop are highly relevant to practical applications.

5.2 Comparative Relevance Feedback Using Attributes

In [26], we propose a novel mode of feedback where a user directly describes how high-level properties of image results should be adjusted in order to more closely match her envisioned target images. Using the relevance feedback paradigm, the user first initializes the search with some keywords: either the name of the general class of interest ("shoes") or some multi-attribute query ("black high-heeled shoes").

Alternatively, the user can provide an image or a sketch [9], and we can use existing query-by-example approaches [37, 48] to retrieve an initial set of results. The system ranks the database images with respect to how well they match the text-based or image-based query. Our system's job is to refine this initial set of results, through user-given feedback. If no text-based or image-based initialization is possible, the search simply begins with a random set of images for feedback.

The top-ranked images are then displayed to the user, and the feedback-refinement loop begins. For example, when conducting a query on a shopping website, the user might state: "I want shoes like these, but *more formal*." When browsing images of potential dates on a dating website, she can say: "I am interested in someone who looks like this, but with *longer hair* and *more smiling*." When searching for stock photos to fit an ad, she might say: "I need a scene *similarly bright* as this one and *more urban* than that one." See Fig. 5.1. Using the resulting constraints in the multi-dimensional attribute space, the system updates its relevance function, re-ranks the pool of images, and displays to the user the images which are most relevant. In this way, rather than simply state which images are (ir)relevant, the user employs semantic terms to say *how* they are so. We call the approach *WhittleSearch*, since it allows users to "whittle away" irrelevant portions of the visual feature space via precise, intuitive statements of their attribute preferences.

Throughout, let $\mathcal{D} = \{I_1, \dots, I_N\}$ refer to the pool of N database images that are ranked by the system using its current scoring function $S_t : I_i \rightarrow \mathbb{R}$, where t denotes the iteration of refinement. $S_t(I_i)$ captures the likelihood that image I_i is relevant to the user's information need, given all accumulated feedback received in iterations $1, \dots, t-1$. Note that S_t supplies a (possibly partial) ordering on the images in $\mathcal{D}$.

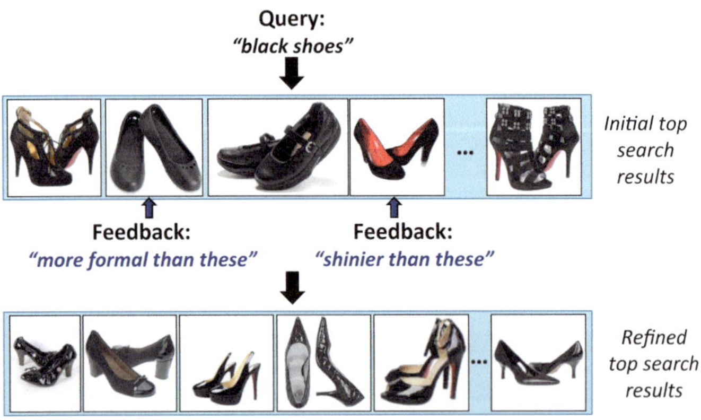

Fig. 5.1 WhittleSearch allows users to refine image search using relative attribute feedback. In this example, the user initiated the search with the query "*black shoes*," retrieved some results, and then asked the system to show images that are "more formal" than the second result and "shinier" than the fourth result. The system then refined the set of search results in accordance with the user's descriptive feedback. Image reprinted with permission

At each iteration t, the top $L < N$ ranked images $\mathcal{T}_t = \{I_{t1}, \ldots, I_{tL}\} \subseteq \mathcal{D}$ are displayed to the user for further feedback, where $S_t(I_{t1}) \geq S_t(I_{t2}) \geq \cdots \geq S_t(I_{tL})$. A user then gives feedback of her choosing on any or all of the L results in $\mathcal{T}_t$. We refer to $\mathcal{T}_t$ interchangeably as the *reference set* or *top-ranked set*.

Offline, our system learns a set of ranking functions, each of which predicts the relative strength of a nameable attribute in an image (e.g. the degree of "shininess," "furriness," etc.). First, we describe how relative attribute models are learned, and then how we use these models to enable a new mode of relevance feedback.

5.2.1 *Learning to Predict Relative Attributes*

We assume we are given a vocabulary of M attributes $A_1, \ldots, A_M$, which may be generic or domain-specific for the image search problem of interest.[1] For example, a domain-specific vocabulary for shoe shopping could contain attributes such as "shininess," "heel height," "colorfulness," etc., whereas for scene descriptions it could contain attributes like "openness," "naturalness," and "depth". It would be too expensive to manually annotate all images with their attribute strength, so we learn to extrapolate from a small set of annotations to a prediction function over all database images as follows.

For each attribute A_m, we obtain supervision on a set of image pairs (i, j) in the training set $\mathcal{I}$. We ask human annotators to judge whether that attribute has a stronger presence in image i or j, or if it is equally strong in both.[2] On each pair we collect five redundant responses from multiple annotators on Amazon Mechanical Turk (MTurk), in order to elicit the most common perception of the attribute and reduce the impact of noisy responses; we use only those responses for which most labelers agree. This yields a set of ordered image pairs $O_m = \{(i, j)\}$ such that $(i, j) \in O_m \implies i \succ j$, i.e. image i has stronger presence of attribute A_m than j. Note that making *comparative* judgments is often more natural for annotators than assigning *absolute* scores reflecting how much the attribute A_m is present [44]. Our approach extends the learning process proposed in [44] to incorporate *image-level* (rather than category-level) relative comparisons, which we show in [27] to more reliably capture those attributes that do not closely follow category boundaries.

Next, we employ the large-margin formulation of [20] to learn a ranking function for each attribute that orders images in increasing order of attribute strength. The function is of the form $a_m(\boldsymbol{x}_i) = \boldsymbol{w}_m^T \boldsymbol{x}_i$, where each image I_i is represented in $\mathbb{R}^d$ by a feature vector $\boldsymbol{x}_i$. We seek a vector $\boldsymbol{w}_m$ for each $m = 1, \ldots, M$ that enforces a large margin between images at nearby ranks, while also allowing the maximum number of

[1] To derive an attribute vocabulary, one could use [43] which automatically generates splits in visual space and learns from human annotations whether these splits can be described with an attribute; [46] which shows pairs of images to users on Amazon's Mechanical Turk platform and aggregates terms which describe what one image has and the other does not have; or [1, 41] which mine text to discover attributes for which reliable computer models can be learned.

[2] The annotations are available at http://vision.cs.utexas.edu/whittlesearch/.

the following constraints to be satisfied: $\forall (i, j) \in O_m : \mathbf{w}_m^T \boldsymbol{x}_i > \mathbf{w}_m^T \boldsymbol{x}_j$. The ranking objective in [20] is reminiscent of standard SVM training and is solved with similar methods; see [20, 27] for details. We apply the learned functions $a_1, \ldots, a_M$ to an image's feature descriptor $\boldsymbol{x}$, in order to predict the extent to which each attribute is present in any novel image. Note that this training is a one-time offline process.

The predicted attribute values $a_m(\boldsymbol{x}_i)$ are what we can observe for image I_i. They are a function of (but distinct from) the "true" latent attribute strengths $A_m(I_i)$. Using standard features and kernels, we find that 75 % of held-out ground truth comparisons are preserved by attribute predictors trained with ~200 pairs.

More sophisticated techniques for learning attribute models can be applied. For example, multiple attributes can be modeled jointly [3, 66]. Chapter 4 describes an approach for decorrelating attribute models, Chap. 6 proposes a method to learn fine-grained attribute differences, and [34] proposes to use random forests to improve relative attributes. In [30], the authors describe how to discover localized attributes using a pre-defined set of candidate face regions (e.g. mouth, eyes), and the authors of [54] mine for discriminative object parts. One can also develop a method to directly learn the spatial support of attributes by capturing human intuition about this support, or by discovering what image features change smoothly to make an attribute "appear" in images [67]. Recent work uses deep networks to predict attributes [11, 42, 57, 58], and to adapt attributes across domains [4, 35].

5.2.2 Relative Attribute Feedback

With the ranking functions learned above, we can now map any image from $\mathcal{D}$ into an M-dimensional space, where each dimension corresponds to the relative rank prediction for one attribute. It is in this feature space we propose to handle query refinement from a user's feedback.

To refine the current search results, the user surveys the L top-ranked images in the displayed set $\mathcal{T}_t$, and uses some of them as reference images to express her desired visual result. The feedback is of the form "What I want is more/less m than image I_{t_f}", where m is an attribute name, and I_{t_f} is an image in $\mathcal{T}_t$ (the subscript t_f denotes it is a reference image at iteration t). Let $\mathcal{F} = \{(I_{t_f}, m, r)\}_1^K$ denote the set of all accumulated comparative constraints at each iteration, where r is the user response $r \in$ {"more", "less"}.[3] The conjunction of all such user feedback statements is used to update the relevance scoring function.

Let $G_{k,i} \in \{0, 1\}$ be a binary random variable representing whether image I_i satisfies the k-th feedback constraint. For example, if the user's k-th comparison on attribute m yields response r = "more", then $G_{k,i} = 1$ if the database image I_i has attribute m more than the corresponding reference image I_{t_f}. The estimate of relevance is thus proportional to the probability that any of the $|\mathcal{F}|$ feedback comparisons are satisfied:

[3] In Sect. 5.3, we extend this approach to also allow "equally" responses.

$$S_T(I_i) = \sum_{k=1}^{|\mathcal{F}|} P(G_{k,i} = 1 | I_i, \mathcal{F}_k). \tag{5.1}$$

Using Iverson bracket notation, we compute the probability that an individual constraint is satisfied as:

$$P(G_{k,i} = 1 | I_i, \mathcal{F}_k) = \begin{cases} [a_m(I_i) > a_m(I_{t_f})] & \text{if } r = \text{"more"} \\ [a_m(I_i) < a_m(I_{t_f})] & \text{if } r = \text{"less"}. \end{cases} \tag{5.2}$$

This simply reflects that images having the appropriate amount of property m are more relevant than those that do not. In the next iteration, we show at the top of the results page those images that satisfy all constraints, followed by images satisfying all but one constraint, etc. The feedback loop is repeated, accepting any additional feedback on the newly top-ranked images, until the user's target image is found or the budget of interaction effort is expended. The final output is a sorting of the database images in $\mathcal{D}$ according to their likelihood of being relevant.

Note that these similarity constraints differ from traditional binary relevance feedback, in that they single out an individual attribute. Each attribute feedback statement carves out a relevant region of the M-dimensional attribute feature space, *whittling away* images not meeting the user's requirements. Further, the proposed form of relative attribute feedback refines the search in ways that a straightforward multi-attribute [30, 55, 60] query cannot. If a user simply stated the attribute labels of interest ("show me black shoes that are shiny and high-heeled"), one can retrieve the images whose attribute predictions meet those criteria, but since the user's description is in absolute terms, it cannot be refined based on the retrieved images. In contrast, with access to relative attributes as a mode of communication, for every new set of reference images returned by the system, the user can further refine his description. Similarly to multi-attribute queries, faceted browsing—where the retrieval system organizes documents or products according to several properties (facets) and allows the user to query with different combinations of the facets [64]—is also a form of keyword search with fixed values for the attribute properties. However, this form of search does not suffice when a user's preferences are very specific and possibly subjective, i.e. it may be difficult to quantize attributes as multiple-valued facets and determine what lies within a range of 0.2–0.4 of "pointiness."

5.2.3 Experimental Validation

We analyze how the proposed relative attribute feedback can enhance image search compared to classic binary feedback. We use three datasets: the Shoes dataset from the Attribute Discovery Dataset [1], the Public Figures dataset of human faces [29] (PubFig), and the Outdoor Scene Recognition dataset of natural scenes [40] (OSR). The Shoes data contains 14,658 shoe images from like.com, and we use Amazon's

Mechanical Turk to annotate the data with ten relative attributes ("pointy at the front," "open," "bright in color," "ornamented," "shiny," "high at the heel," "long on the leg," "formal," "sporty," "feminine"). For PubFig we use the subset from [44], which contains 772 images from 8 people and 11 attributes ("masculine-looking," "young," "smiling," "chubby," "pointy nose," etc.). OSR consists of 2,688 images from 8 categories and 6 attributes ("natural," "open," "close-depth," etc.); these attributes are used in [44]. For the image features $\boldsymbol{x}$, we use GIST [40] and LAB color histograms for Shoes and PubFig, and GIST alone for OSR, since the scenes do not seem well characterized by color.

For each query we select a random *target image* and score how well the search results match that target after feedback. This target stands in for a user's mental model; it allows us to prompt multiple subjects for feedback on a well-defined visual concept, and to precisely judge how accurate results are. We measure the NDCG@K [21] correlation between the full ranking computed by S_t and a ground truth ranking that reflects the perceived relevance of all images in $\mathcal{D}$.

As a baseline, we use a "binary relevance feedback" approach that is intended to represent traditional approaches such as [5, 14, 52, 62, 63]. In a binary relevance feedback model, the user identifies a set of relevant images $\mathcal{R}$ and a set of irrelevant images $\bar{\mathcal{R}}$ among the current reference set $\mathcal{T}_t$. In this case, the scoring function S_t^b is a classifier (or some other statistical model), and the binary feedback supplies positive (the images in $\mathcal{R}$) and negative (the images in $\bar{\mathcal{R}}$) training examples for that classifier. We employ a support vector machine (SVM) classifier for the binary feedback model due to its strong performance in practice.

We use two methods to generate feedback statements in order to evaluate our method and the baseline. First, we gather attribute comparisons from users on MTurk. Second, to allow testing on a larger scale without incurring a large monetary cost, we also generate feedback automatically, by simulating user responses. For relative constraints, we randomly sample constraints based on the predicted relative attribute values, checking how the target image relates to the reference images. For binary feedback, we analogously sample positive/negative reference examples based on their image feature distance to the true target. When scoring rank, we add Gaussian noise to the predicted attributes (for our method) and the SVM outputs (for the baseline), to coarsely mimic people's uncertainty in constraint generation.

In Fig. 5.2, we show the rank correlation for our method and the baseline as a function of the number of feedback statements, using 100 queries and automatically generated feedback. A round of feedback consists of a relative attribute constraint (for our method) or a binary relevance label on one image (for the baseline). For all datasets, both methods clearly improve with more feedback, but the precision enabled by attribute feedback yields larger gains in accuracy. The result is intuitive, since with our method users can better express *what about* the reference image is (ir)relevant to them, whereas with binary feedback they cannot.[4]

[4]As another point of comparison against existing methods, a multi-attribute query baseline that ranks images by how many binary attributes they share with the target image achieves NDCG scores that are 40 % weaker on average than our method when using 40 feedback constraints.

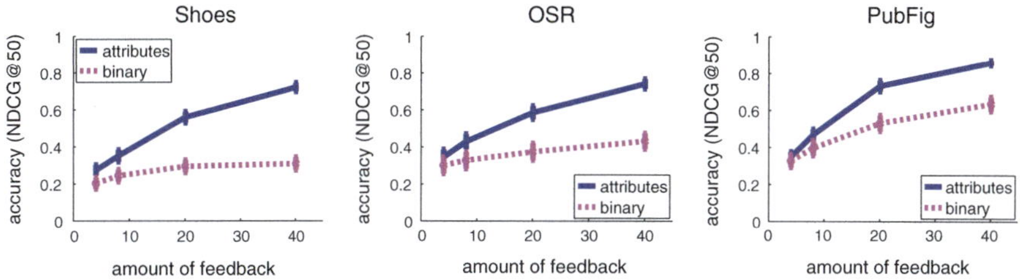

Fig. 5.2 Impact of the amount of feedback: while more feedback enhances both methods, the proposed attribute feedback yields faster gains per unit of feedback. Image reprinted with permission

We see similar results when using the feedback generated by real users on MTurk. Attribute feedback largely outperforms binary feedback, and does similarly well on OSR. One possible reason is that people seem to have more confusion interpreting the attribute meanings (e.g. "amount of perspective" on a scene is less intuitive than "shininess" on shoes). In Sects. 5.4 and 5.5, we propose methods that help account for these ambiguities and differences in user perception.

In [27], we analyze the performance of our system when rather than a batch of feedback statements in a single iteration, one statement is given at a time, and the system iterates. Our method outperforms the binary feedback baseline for all datasets, but on PubFig our advantage is slight, likely due to the strong category-based nature of the PubFig data, which makes it more amenable to binary feedback, i.e. adding positive labels on exemplars of the same person as the target image is quite effective.

Note that while feedback using language (in the form of relative attributes) is clearly richer and more informative than binary relevance feedback, some aspects of desired visual content may be hard to capture in words. In such cases, binary feedback, while imprecise, might offer a more natural alternative. In [26], we propose a hybrid feedback approach that combines relative attribute and binary feedback. Further, one could utilize work in modeling perceptual similarity [18, 61] to more accurately estimate the user's visual need based on examples that the user identifies.

5.3 Actively Guiding the User's Relevance Feedback

Having presented the basic system using relative attribute feedback for image search, we now consider the question of *which images* ought to receive the user's feedback. Notably, the images believed to be most *relevant* need not be most *informative* for reducing the system's uncertainty. As a result, it might be more beneficial to leave the choice of reference images on which to seek feedback to the system. Thus, we next explore how the system can best select the feedback it requests. The method and results in this section first appeared in [23].

The goal of *actively* selecting images for feedback is to solicit feedback on those exemplars that would most improve the system's notion of relevance. Many existing methods exploit classifier uncertainty to find useful exemplars (e.g. [33, 63, 70]), but they have two limitations. First, they elicit traditional binary feedback which is imprecise, as discussed above. This makes it ambiguous how to extrapolate relevance predictions to other images, which in turn clouds the active selection criterion. Second, since ideally they must scan all database images to find the most informative exemplars, they are computationally expensive and often resort to sampling or clustering heuristics [5, 14, 51] or to the over-simplified uncertainty sampling [63] which does not guarantee global uncertainty reduction over the full dataset.

Building on the WhittleSearch concept we introduced above, we next introduce a novel approach that addresses these shortcomings. As before, we assume the user initiates a search and the goal of our method is to then refine the results. We propose to actively guide the user through a coarse-to-fine search using a relative attribute image representation. At each iteration of feedback, the user provides a *visual comparison* between the attribute in her envisioned target and a "pivot" exemplar, where a pivot separates all database images into two balanced sets. Instead of asking the user to choose both the image and attribute for feedback, in this approach we ask the system to make this choice, so the user is presented with a single image and a single attribute and simply has to provide the value of the comparison ("more", "less", or "equally"). In other words, the system interacts with the user through multiple-choice questions of the form: "Is the image you are looking for *more*, *less*, (or *equally*) A than image I?", where A is a semantic attribute and I is an exemplar from the database being searched. The system actively determines along which of multiple attributes the user's comparison should next be requested, based on the expected information gain that would result. We show how to limit the scan for candidate questions to just one image (the *pivot*) per attribute. Thus, the active selection method is efficient both for the system (which analyzes a small number of candidates per iteration) and the user (who locates his content via a small number of well-chosen interactions). See Fig. 5.3.

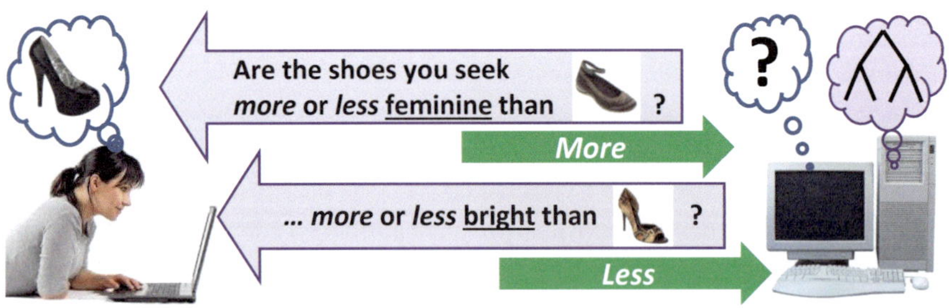

Fig. 5.3 The active version of WhittleSearch requests feedback in the form of visual attribute comparisons between the user's target and images selected by the system. To formulate the optimal questions, it unifies an entropy reduction criterion with binary search trees in attribute space. Image reprinted with permission

5.3.1 Attribute Binary Search Trees

We use the same notation as in Sect. 5.2. $A_m(I_i)$ denotes the true strength and $a_m(I_i)$ the predicted strength of an attribute m in image I_i. We construct one binary search tree for each attribute $m = 1, \ldots, M$. The tree recursively partitions all database images into two balanced sets, where the key at a given node is the median relative attribute value within the set of images passed to that node. To build the m-th attribute tree, we start at the root with all database images, sort them by their attribute values $a_m(I_1), \ldots, a_m(I_N)$, and identify the median value. Let I_p denote the "pivot" image (the one that has the median attribute strength). The images I_i for which $a_m(I_i) \leq a_m(I_p)$ are passed to the left child, and those for which $a_m(I_i) > a_m(I_p)$ are passed to the right child. The splitting repeats recursively, each time storing the next pivot image and its relative attribute value at the appropriate node. Note that the relative attribute ranker training and search tree construction are offline procedures.

One could devise a search procedure that requests a comparison to the pivot at each level of a single attribute tree and eliminates the appropriate portion of the database depending on the user's response. However, such pruning is error-prone because (1) the attribute predictions may not be identical to the attribute strengths a user will perceive, and (2) such pruning ignores the information gain that could result by intelligently choosing the attribute along which a comparison is requested. Instead, we will show how to use comparisons to the pivots in our binary search trees, in order to probabilistically refine the system's prediction of the relevance/irrelevance of database images to the user's goal.

5.3.2 Predicting the Relevance of an Image

The output of our search system will be a sorting of the database images $I_i \in \mathcal{D}$ according to their probability of relevance, given the image content and all user feedback. As before, $\mathcal{F} = \{(I_{p_m}, r)\}_{k=1}^{T}$ denotes the set of comparative constraints accumulated in the T rounds of feedback so far. The k-th item in $\mathcal{F}$ consists of a pivot image I_{p_m} for attribute m, and a user response $r \in \{$"more", "less", "equally"$\}$. $G_{k,i} \in \{0, 1\}$ is a binary random variable representing whether image I_i satisfies the k-th feedback constraint. Let $y_i \in \{1, 0\}$ denote the binary label for image I_i, which reflects whether it is relevant to the user (matches her target), or not. The probability of relevance is the probability that all T feedback comparisons in $\mathcal{F}$ are satisfied, and for numerical stability, we use a sum of log probabilities: $\log P(y_i = 1|I_i, \mathcal{F}) = \sum_{k=1}^{T} \log P(G_{k,i} = 1|I_i, \mathcal{F}_k)$. This equation is similar to the definition of $S_T(I_i)$ in Sect. 5.2, but we now use a soft score denoting whether an image satisfies a constraint, in order to account for the fact that predicted attributes can deviate from true perceived attribute strengths. The probability that the k-th individual constraint is satisfied given that the user's response was r for pivot I_{p_m} is:

$$P(G_{k,i} = 1 | I_i, \mathcal{F}_k) = \begin{cases} P(A_m(I_i) > A_m(I_p)) & \text{if } r = \text{“more”} \\ P(A_m(I_i) < A_m(I_p)) & \text{if } r = \text{“less”} \\ P(A_m(I_i) = A_m(I_p)) & \text{if } r = \text{“equally”}. \end{cases} \tag{5.3}$$

To estimate these probabilities, we map the differences of attribute predictions, i.e. $a_m(I_i) - a_m(I_p)$ (or $|a_m(I_i) - a_m(I_p)|$ for “equally”) to probabilistic outputs, using Platt’s method [47].

5.3.3 Actively Selecting an Informative Comparison

Our system maintains a set of M current pivot images (one per attribute tree) at each iteration, denoted $\mathcal{P} = \{I_{p_1}, \ldots, I_{p_M}\}$. Given the feedback history $\mathcal{F}$, we want to predict the information gain across all N database images that would result from asking the user how her target image compares to each of the current pivots in $\mathcal{P}$. We will request a comparison for the pivot that minimizes the expected entropy when used to augment the current set of feedback constraints. Note that selecting a pivot corresponds to selecting both an image as well as an attribute along which we want it to be compared; I_{p_m} refers to the pivot for attribute m.

The entropy given feedback $\mathcal{F}$ is:

$$H(\mathcal{F}) = -\sum_{i=1}^{N} \sum_{\ell} P(y_i = \ell | I_i, \mathcal{F}) \log P(y_i = \ell | I_i, \mathcal{F}), \tag{5.4}$$

where $\ell \in \{0, 1\}$. Let R be a random variable denoting the user’s response, $R \in$ {“more”, “less”, “equally”}. We select the next pivot for comparison as:

$$I_p^* = \arg\min_{I_{p_m} \in \mathcal{P}} \sum_{r} P(R = r | I_{p_m}, \mathcal{F}) \;\; H(\mathcal{F} \cup (I_{p_m}, r)). \tag{5.5}$$

Optimizing Eq. 5.5 requires estimating the likelihood of each of the three possible user responses to a question we have not issued yet. In [23], we describe and evaluate three strategies to estimate it; here we describe one. We use cues from the available feedback history to form a “proxy” for the user, essentially borrowing the probability that a new constraint is satisfied from previously seen feedback. Let I_b be the database image which the system currently ranks highest, i.e. the image that maximizes $P(y_i = 1 | I_i, \mathcal{F})$. We can use this image as a proxy for the target, and compute:

$$P(R = r | I_{p_m}, \mathcal{F}) = P(G_{c,b} = 1 | I_b, \mathcal{F}_c), \tag{5.6}$$

where c indexes the candidate new feedback for a (yet unknown) user response R.

At each iteration, we present the user with the pivot selected with Eq. 5.5 and request the specified attribute comparison. Using the resulting feedback, we first update $\mathcal{F}$ with the user's new image-attribute-response constraint. Then we either replace the pivot in $\mathcal{P}$ for that attribute with its appropriate child pivot (i.e. the left or right child in the binary search tree if the response is "less" or "more", respectively) or terminate the exploration of this tree (if the response is "equally"). The approach iterates until the user is satisfied with the top-ranked results, or until all of the attribute trees have bottomed out to an "equally" response from the user.

The cost of our selection method per round of feedback is $O(MN)$, where M is the size of the attribute vocabulary, N is the database size, and $M \ll N$. For each of $O(M)$ pivots which can be used to complement the feedback set, we need to evaluate expected entropy for all N images. In contrast, a traditional information gain approach would scan all database items paired with all attributes, requiring $O(MN^2)$ time. In comparison to other error reduction methods [2, 5, 14, 25, 39, 51], our method can exploit the structure of rankable visual properties for substantial computational savings.

5.3.4 Experimental Validation

We use the same data and experimental setup as in Sect. 5.2, but now we measure the *percentile rank* each method assigns to the target at each iteration. We compare our method ACTIVE ATTRIBUTE PIVOTS against:

- ATTRIBUTE PIVOTS, a version of our method that cycles through pivots in a round-robin fashion;
- ACTIVE ATTRIBUTE EXHAUSTIVE, which uses entropy to select questions like our method, but evaluates all possible MxN candidate questions;
- TOP, which selects the image that has the current highest probability of relevance and pairs it with a random attribute;
- PASSIVE, which selects a random (image, attribute) pair;
- ACTIVE BINARY FEEDBACK, which asks the user whether the exemplar is similar to the target, and chooses the image with decision value closest to 0, as in [63]; and
- PASSIVE BINARY FEEDBACK, which works as above, but randomly selects the images for feedback.

To thoroughly test the methods, we conduct experiments where we simulate the user's responses, similar to Sect. 5.2. Figure 5.4 shows that our method finds the target image more efficiently than any of the baselines. Consistent with results in the previous section, our method significantly outperforms binary relevance feedback. Interestingly, we find that PASSIVE BINARY FEEDBACK is stronger than its active counterpart, likely because images near the decision boundary were often negative, whereas the passive approach samples more diverse instances. Our method substantially improves over the TOP approach, which shows that relative attribute feedback alone does not offer the most efficient search if uninformative feedback is given; and

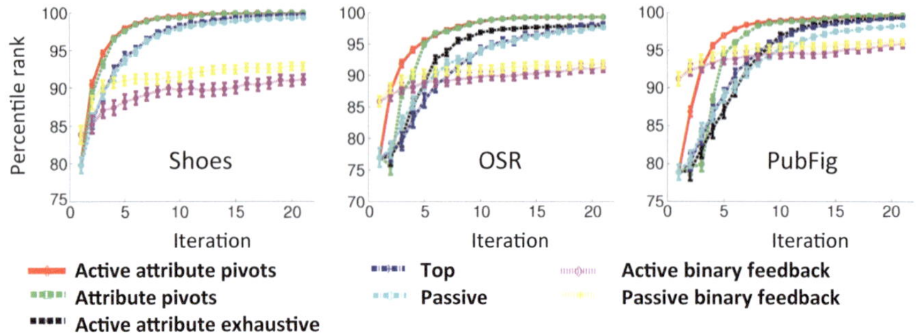

Fig. 5.4 Comparison to existing interactive search methods (higher and steeper curves early on are better). Image reprinted with permission

over ATTRIBUTE PIVOTS, which indicates that actively interleaving the trees allows us to focus on attributes that better distinguish the relevant images. It also outperforms ACTIVE ATTRIBUTE EXHAUSTIVE[5] likely because the attribute trees serve as a form of regularization, helping our method focus on those comparisons that *a priori* may be most informative. The active exhaustive approach considers entropy reduction resulting from feedback on each possible database image in turn, and can be misled by outliers that seem to have high expected information gain. Furthermore, our method is orders of magnitude faster. On the Shoes, OSR and PubFig datasets, our method only requires 0.05, 0.01 and 0.01 s respectively to make its choice in a single iteration. In contrast, the exhaustive methods requires 656.27, 28.20 and 3.42 s.

We present live experiments with real MTurk users in [23]. In those experiments, we achieve a 100–200 raw rank improvement on two datasets, and a negligible 0–10 raw rank loss on PubFig, compared to the strongest baseline, TOP. This is very encouraging given the noise in MTurk responses and the difficulty of predicting all attributes reliably. Our information gain predictions on PubFig are imprecise since the facial attributes are difficult for both the system and people to compare reliably (e.g. it is hard to say who among two white people is whiter).

In [27], we show a comparison of the active pivots method presented in this section, and the passive WhittleSearch method presented in the previous section. Overall we find that the pivots method saves users more time, but also asks harder questions, which results in less confident responses from users, and in turn this could lead to erroneous search results. However, our pivots approach reduces the entropy of the system over the relevance of database images faster than the passive method from Sect. 5.2. The choice of which method to use for a given application can be made depending on how long it takes to browse a page of image results, as shown in [27].

[5]The exhaustive baseline was too expensive to run on all 14K Shoes. On a 1000-image subset, it does similarly as on the other datasets.

Our system actively guides the search based on visual comparisons, helping a user navigate the image database via relative semantic properties. We experimentally demonstrate the utility of this approach. However, there are several possible improvements that can further increase utility as well as the search experience of a user. First, two measures of confidence can be incorporated into the active selection formulation: the confidence of attribute models, and the confidence of user responses. The first would ensure that our selection is not mislead by noisy attribute predictions, while the second would allow the down-weighing of user responses which may be erroneous. Further, we could allow the user to give different weight to responses about different attributes, if these attributes are more important to the search task than others. In this way, information gain would be higher for attributes that have accurate models and are key to the user's search goal.

Further, we could define a mixed-initiative framework for search where we are not forced to choose between the user having control over the feedback (as in Sect. 5.2) or the system having this control (as in this section), but can rather alternate between these two options, depending on whether the user or system can provide a more meaningful next feedback statement. For example, if the system's estimate of what the user's response should be is incorrect for three consecutive iterations, or if the best potential information gain is lower than some threshold, perhaps the system should relinquish control. On the other hand, if the user does not see any reference images that seem particularly useful for feedback, she should give up control.

5.4 Accounting for Differing User Perceptions of Attributes

In the previous sections, we described the power of relative attribute statements as a form of relevance feedback for search. However, no matter what potential power of feedback we offer a user, search efficiency will suffer if there is noise on the communication channel between the user and the system, i.e. if the user says "A" and the system understands "B".

Researchers collecting attribute-labeled datasets report significant disagreement among human annotators over the "true" attribute labels [10, 13, 46]. The differences may stem from several factors: the words for attributes are imprecise (when is the cat "overweight" vs. "chubby"?), and their meanings often depend on context (the shoe appears "comfortable" for a wedding, but not for running) and even cultures (languages have differing numbers of color words, ranging from two to eleven). Further, they often stretch to refer to quite distinct object categories (e.g. "pointy" pencil vs. "pointy" shoes). For all such reasons, people inevitably craft their own definitions for visual attributes. Failing to account for user-specific notions of attributes will lead to discrepancies between the user's precise intent and the message received by the system.

Existing methods learn only a single "mainstream" view of each attribute, forcing a consensus through majority voting. This is the case whether using binary [13, 15, 32] or relative [44] attributes. For binary properties, one takes the majority vote on the attribute present/absent label. For relative properties, one takes a majority vote on the attribute more/less label. Note that using relative attributes does not resolve the ambiguity problem. The point in relative attributes is that people may agree best on comparisons or strengths, not binary labels, but relative attributes too assume that there is some single, common interpretation of the property and hence a single ordering of images from least to most [attribute] is possible.

In this section, we propose to model attributes in a user-specific way, in order to capture the inherent differences in perception. The most straightforward approach for doing so is to learn one function per attribute and per user, from scratch, but this is not scalable. Instead, we pose user-specific attribute learning as an *adaptation* problem. We leverage any commonalities in perception to learn a *generic* prediction function, then use a small number of user-labeled examples to adapt that model into a *user-specific* prediction function. In technical terms, this amounts to imposing regularizers on the learning objective favoring user-specific model parameters that are similar to the generic ones, while still satisfying the user-specific label constraints. In this fashion, the system can learn the user's perception with fewer labels than if it used a given user's data alone.

Adaptation [17, 68] requires that the source and target tasks be related, such that it is meaningful to constrain the target parameters to be close to the source's. In our setting the assumption naturally holds: an attribute is semantically meaningful to all annotators, just with (usually slight) perceptual variations among them.

5.4.1 Adapting Attributes

As before, we learn each attribute of interest separately (i.e. one classifier for "white", another for "pointy"). An adapted function is user-specific, with one distinct function for each user. Let D' denote the set of images labeled by majority vote that are used to learn the generic model. We assume the labeled examples originate from a pool of many annotators who collectively represent the "common denominator" in attribute perception. We train a generic attribute model $f'(\boldsymbol{x}_i)$ from D'. Let D denote the set of user-labeled images, which is typically disjoint from D'. Our adaptive learning objective will take a D and f' as input, and produce an adapted attribute f as output. In this section, we describe how to adapt binary attributes; see [22] for an analogous formulation for adapting relative attributes.

The generic data $D' = \{\boldsymbol{x}'_i, y'_i\}_{i=1}^{N'}$ consists of N' labeled images, with $y'_i \in \{-1, +1\}$. Let f' denote the generic binary attribute classifier trained with D'. For a linear support vector machine (SVM), we have $f'(\boldsymbol{x}) = \boldsymbol{x}^T \boldsymbol{w}'$. To adapt the parameters $\boldsymbol{w}'$ to account for user-specific data $D = \{\boldsymbol{x}_i, y_i\}_{i=1}^{N}$, we use the Adaptive SVM [68] objective function:

$$\min_{w} \frac{1}{2}\|w - w'\|^2 + C\sum_{i=1}^{N} \xi_i, \tag{5.7}$$
$$\text{subject to} \quad y_i x_i^T w \geq 1 - \xi_i, \forall i, \xi_i \geq 0,$$

where w denotes the desired user-specific hyperplane, and C is a constant controlling the tradeoff between misclassification on the user-specific training examples and the regularizer. Note that the objective expands the usual large-margin regularizer $\|w\|^2$ to additionally prefer that w be similar to w'. In this way, the generic attribute serves as a prior for the user-specific attribute, such that even with small amounts of user-labeled data we can learn an accurate predictor.

The optimal w is found by solving a quadratic program to maximize the Lagrange dual objective function. This yields the Adaptive SVM decision function: $f(x) = f'(x) + \sum_{i=1}^{N} \alpha_i y_i x^T x_i$, where α denotes the Lagrange multipliers that define w. Hence, the adapted attribute prediction is a combination of the generic model's prediction and similarities between the novel input x and (selected) user-specific instances x_i. Intuitively, a larger weight on a user-specific support vector x_i is more likely when the generic model f' mispredicts x_i. Thus, user-specific instances that deviate from the generic model will have more impact on f. For example, suppose a user mostly agrees with the generic notion of "formal" shoes, but, unlike the average annotator, is also inclined to call loafers "formal". Then the adapted classifier will likely exploit some user-labeled loafer image(s) with nonzero α_i when predicting whether a shoe would be perceived as formal by that user.

The adaptation strategy promotes efficiency in two ways. First, the human labeling cost is low, since the effort of the extensive label collection required to train the generic models is distributed among many users. Meanwhile, each user only needs to provide a small amount of labeled data. In experiments, we see substantial gains with as few as 12 user-labeled examples. Second, training time is substantially lower than training each user model from scratch by pooling the generic and user-specific data. The cost of training the "big" generic SVM is amortized across all user-specific functions. The efficiency is especially valuable for personalized search.

We obtain the user-specific labeled data D in two ways: by explicitly asking annotators to label informative images (either an uncertain or diverse pool), and by implicitly mining for such data in a user's history. See [22] for details.

We use the adapted attributes to personalize image search results. Compared to using generic attributes, the personalized results should more closely align with the user's perception, leading to more precise retrieval of relevant images. For binary attributes, we use the user-specific classifiers to retrieve images that match a multi-attribute query, e.g. "I want images with attributes X, Y, and not Z". For relative attributes, we use the adapted rankers to retrieve images that agree with comparative relevance feedback, similar to Sects. 5.2 and 5.3. In both cases, the system sorts the database images according to how confidently the adapted attribute predictions agree with the attribute constraints mentioned in the query or feedback. Note that one can directly incorporate our adapted attributes into any existing attribute-search method [26, 30, 55, 60].

5.4.2 Experimental Validation

We conduct experiments with 75 unique users on two large datasets: the Shoes dataset and 12 attributes from the SUN Attributes dataset [46], which contains 14,340 scenes. To form descriptors $\boldsymbol{x}$ for Shoes, we use the GIST and color histograms as before. For SUN, we concatenate features provided by [46]: GIST, color, and base HOG and self-similarity. We cross-validate C for all models, per attribute and user. We compare our USER- ADAPTIVE approach to three methods:

- GENERIC, which learns a model from the generic majority vote data D' only;
- GENERIC+, which adds more generic data to D' (one generic label for each user-specific label our method uses); and
- USER- EXCLUSIVE, which uses the same user-specific data as our method, but learns a user-specific model from scratch, without the generic model.

We evaluate generalization accuracy: will adapted attributes better agree with a user's perception in novel images? To form a generic model for each dataset, we use 100–200 images (or pairs, in the case of relative Shoes attributes) labeled by majority vote. We collect user-specific labels on 60 images/pairs, from each of 10 (Shoes) or 5 (SUN) workers on MTurk. We reserve 10 random user-labeled images per user as a test set in each run. We measure accuracy across 300 random splits.

In Fig. 5.5, we show representative results for individual attributes and individual users. We plot test accuracy as a function of the amount of additional training data beyond the generic pool D'. GENERIC remains flat, as it gets no additional data. For binary attributes, chance is 50 %; for relative it is 33 %, since there are three possible responses ("more", "less", "equally"). Overall, our method more accurately predicts the labels on the held-out user-specific images than any of the baselines. The

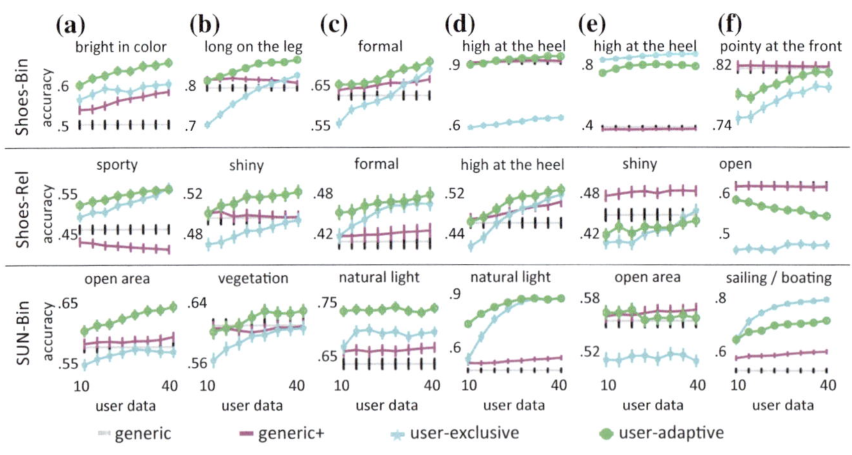

Fig. 5.5 Attribute prediction accuracy per attribute and per user, as more training data is added. Image reprinted with permission

advantage of adapted attributes over the generic model supports our main claim: we need to account for users' individual perception when learning attributes. Further, the advantage over the user-exclusive model shows that our approach successfully leverages "universal" perception as a prior; learning from scratch is inferior, particularly if very few user-specific labels are available (see the leftmost point of all plots). With more user-specific labels, the non-adaptive approach can sometimes catch up (see "sporty" in column (a)), but at the expense of a much higher burden on each user. Finally, the GENERIC+ baseline confirms that our method's advantage is not simply a matter of having more data available. GENERIC+ usually gives GENERIC a bump, but much less than USER- ADAPTIVE. For example, on "bright in color", our method improves accuracy by up to 26 %, whereas GENERIC+ only gains 14 %.

We do see some failure cases though, as shown in columns (e) and (f). The failures are by definition rather hard to analyze. That's because by focusing on user-specific perception, we lose any ability to filter noisy label responses (e.g. with voting). So, when a user-adapted model misclassifies, we cannot rule out the possibility that the worker herself was *inconsistent with her personal perception* of the attribute in that test case. Nonetheless, we do see a trend in the failure cases—weaker USER-EXCLUSIVE classifiers. As a result, our model can start to underperform GENERIC, pulled down by (what are possibly inconsistent) user responses, as seen by a number of cases where USER- EXCLUSIVE remains close to chance. Another reason for failure (with respect to the user-exclusive model) are user responses which were the opposite of generic responses, where the generic prior can cause negative transfer for our method (see "high at the heel" in column (e)). Note that the success of adaptation depends not just on the attribute being learned, but also on individual users, e.g. "high at the heel" in columns (d, e) and "open area" in columns (a, e). One could devise a method that automatically determines when the generic model should be used as a prior.

We find that user-adapted attributes are often strongest when test cases are hardest. See [22] for details. We also show that correctly capturing attribute perception is important for accurate search. Search is a key application where adapted attributes can alleviate inconsistencies between what the user says, and what the (traditionally majority-vote-trained) machine understands. The generalization power of the adapted attributes translates into the search setting: our method is substantially better at finding the images relevant to the user. This result demonstrates how our idea can benefit a number of prior binary attribute search systems [30, 55, 60] and our relative attribute relevance feedback search.

5.5 Discovering Attribute Shades of Meaning

So far, we have discussed generic attribute models, which assume that all users perceive the attribute in the same way; and user-specific models, which assume that each user's perception is unique. However, while users differ in how they perceive and

Fig. 5.6 Our attribute shade discovery method uses the crowd to discover factors responsible for an attribute's presence, then learns predictive models based on these visual cues. For example, for the attribute *open*, the method will discover shades of *meaning*, e.g. peep-toed (*open* at toe) versus slip-on (*open* at heel) versus sandal-like (*open* at toe *and* heel), which are three visual definitions of openness. Since these shades are not coherent in terms of their global descriptors, they would be difficult to discover using traditional image clustering

use attributes, it is likely that there are some commonalities or groupings between them in terms of how they interpret and utilize the attribute vocabulary. We find evidence for this in work on linguistic relativity [12], which examines how culture influences how we describe objects, shape properties of animals, colors, etc. For example, Russian has two words for what would be shades of "blue" in English, while other languages do not strongly distinguish "blue" and "green". In other words, if asked whether an object in some image is "blue" or not, people of different countries might be grouped around different answers. We refer to such groupings of users as "schools of thought".

We can use the groupings of users to discover the "shades of meaning" of an attribute, since users in the same "school" likely subscribe to the same interpretation of the attribute.[6] An attribute "shade" is a visual interpretation of an attribute name that one or more people apply when judging whether that attribute is present in an image. For example, for the attribute "open" in Fig. 5.6, we might discover that some users have peep-toed shoes in mind when they say "open", while others have flip-flops in mind when they use the same word. Note that for many attributes, such ambiguities in language use cannot be resolved by adjusting the attribute definitions, since people *use the same definition differently*.

In order to discover schools, we first collect a set of sparse annotations from a large pool of users. We then perform matrix factorization over these labels, and obtain a description of each user that captures the underlying latent factors contributing to the user's annotations. We cluster users in this latent factor space, and each cluster becomes a "school."

After we discover the schools of users, we personalize each attribute model towards these schools, rather than towards individual users. Focusing on the commonalities between users allows the system to learn the *important* biases that users have in interpreting the attribute, as opposed to minor differences in labeling which may stem from factors other than a truly different interpretation.

[6]Below we use the terms "school" and "shade" interchangeably.

5.5.1 Collecting Personal Labels and Label Explanations

We build a Mechanical Turk interface to gather the labels. We use 12 attributes from the Shoes and SUN Attributes datasets that can be defined concisely in language, yet may vary in their visual instantiations. We sample 250–1000 images per attribute. Workers are shown definitions of the attributes from a web dictionary, but no example images. Then, given an image, the worker must provide a binary label, i.e. she must state whether the image does or does not possess a specified attribute. Additionally, for a random set of 5 images, the worker must explain her label in free-form text, and state which image most has the attribute and why. These questions both slow the worker down, helping quality control, and also provide valuable ground truth data for evaluation. To help ensure self-consistency in the labels, we exclude workers who fail to consistently answer 3 repeated questions sprinkled among the 50. This yields annotations from 195 workers per attribute on average.

5.5.2 Discovering Schools and Training Per-School Adapted Models

We use the label data to discover latent factors, which are needed to recover the shades of meaning, separately for each attribute. We retain each worker's ID, the indices of images she labeled, and how she labeled them. Let M denote the number of unique annotators and N the number of images seen by at least one annotator. Let $\mathbf{L}$ be the $M \times N$ label matrix, where $L_{ij} \in \{0, 1, ?\}$ is a binary attribute label for image j by annotator i. A ? denotes an unlabeled example (on average only 20 % of the possible image-worker pairs are labeled).

We suppose there is a small number D of unobserved factors that influence the annotators' labels. This reflects that their decisions are driven by some mid-level visual cues. For example, when deciding whether a shoe looks "ornate", the latent factors might include presence of buckles, amount of patterned textures, material type, color, and heel height. Assuming a linear factor model, the label matrix $\mathbf{L}$ can be factored as the product of an $M \times D$ annotator latent factor matrix $\mathbf{A}^T$ and a $D \times N$ image latent factor matrix $\mathbf{I}$: $\mathbf{L} = \mathbf{A}^T\mathbf{I}$. We use the probabilistic matrix factorization algorithm (PMF) [53] to factor this partially observed matrix, by finding the best rank-D approximation. We fix $D = 50$, then use the default parameter settings.

We represent each annotator i in terms of her association with each discovered factor, i.e. the "latent feature vector" for annotator i is $A_i \in \Re^D$, the i-th column of $\mathbf{A}$. It represents how much each of the D factors influences that annotator when she decides if the named attribute is present. We pose shade discovery as a grouping problem in the space of these latent features. We apply K-means to the columns of $\mathbf{A}$ to obtain clusters $\{\mathcal{S}_1, \ldots, \mathcal{S}_K\}$. We set K automatically per attribute based on the optimal silhouette coefficient within $K = \{2, \ldots, 15\}$. By clustering in the low-dimensional latent space, the method identifies the "schools of thought" underlying the discrete set of labels the annotators provided.

Finally, we use the positive exemplars in each school to train a predictive model, which can then detect when the particular attribute shade is present in novel images. We train school-specific classifiers that adapt the consensus model. Each school $\mathcal{S}_k$ is represented by the total pool of images that its annotators labeled as positive. Several annotators in the cluster may have labeled the same image, and their labels need not agree. Thus, we perform majority vote (over just the annotators in $\mathcal{S}_k$) to decide whether an image is positive or negative for the shade. We use the images to train a discriminative classifier, using the adaptive SVM objective of Yang et al. [68] to regularize its parameters to be similar to those of the consensus model, as in Sect. 5.4. In other words, we are now personalizing to schools of users, as opposed to individual users. When we need to predict how a user will judge the presence/absence of an attribute, e.g. during image search, we apply the adapted shade model *for the school to which the user belongs*. Compared to user-adaptive models, each shade model typically leverages more training data than a single user provides. This lets us effectively "borrow" labeled instances from the user's neighbors in the crowd. Further, the within-school majority vote can be seen as a form of quality control, where we assume consistency within the group. This helps reduce noise in an individual user's labeling.

The images within a shade can be visually diverse from the point of view of typical global image descriptors, since annotators attuned to that shade's latent factors could have focused on arbitrarily small parts of the images, or arbitrary subsets of feature modalities (e.g. color, shape, texture). For example, one shade for "open" might focus on shoe toes, while another focuses on shoe heels. Similarly, one shade for "formal" capturing the notion that dark-colored shoes are formal would rely on color alone, while another capturing the notion that shoes with excessively high heels are not formal would rely on shape alone. An approach that attempts to discover shades based on image clustering, as well as non-semantic attribute discovery approaches [8, 38, 43, 49, 59, 69], would be susceptible to the more obvious splits in the feature space which need not directly support the semantic attribute of interest, and would not be able to group images according to these perceived, possibly subtle, cues. Furthermore, discovery methods would be biased by the choice of features, e.g. the set of salient splits in color histogram space would be quite different than those discovered in a dense SIFT feature space. In contrast, our method partitions the images *semantically*, so even though the training images may be visually diverse, standard discriminative learning methods let us isolate the informative features.

Note that it would be challenging to manually enumerate the attribute shades with words. For example, when asked to explain why an image is "ornamented", an annotator might comment on the "buckle" or "bow"; yet the latent shade of "ornamented" underlying many users' labels is more abstract and encompasses combinations of such concrete mid-level cues. Our method uses the structure in the labels to automatically discover these shades.

5.5.3 *Experimental Validation*

We demonstrate shades' utility for improving attribute prediction. We compare to the methods from Sect. 5.4, as well as two alternative shade formation baselines—ATTRIBUTE DISCOVERY, where we cluster images in the attribute space discovered by a state-of-the-art non-semantic attribute discovery method [49], and IMAGE CLUSTERS, an image clustering approach inspired by [36]. We run 30 trials, sampling 20 % of the available labels to obtain on average 10 labels per user.

Table 5.1 shows the results. Our shade discovery is more reliable than GENERIC, which is the status quo attribute learning approach. For "open", we achieve an 8-point gain over GENERIC and USER- EXCLUSIVE, which indicates both how different user perceptions of this attribute are, as well as how useful it is to rely on schools rather than individual users. SHADES also outperform our USER- ADAPTIVE approach. While that method learns personalized models, shades leverage *common perceptions* and thereby avoid overfitting to a user's few labeled instances. Finally, neither alternative shade formation method is competitive with our approach. These results demonstrate that for all attributes evaluated, mapping a person's use of an attribute to a shade allows us to *predict attribute presence more accurately*. This is achieved at no additional expense for the user.

Figure 5.7 visualizes two shades each, for four of the attributes (see [24] for more). The images are those most frequently labeled as positive by annotators in a shade $\mathcal{S}_k$. The (stemmed) words are those that appear most frequently in the annotator explanations for that shade, after we remove words that overlap between the two shades. We see the shades capture nuanced visual sub-definitions of the attribute words. For example, for the attribute "ornate," one shade focuses on straps/buckles (top shade), while another focuses on texture/print/patterns (bottom shade). For "open," one shade includes open-heeled shoes, while another includes sandals which are open at the

Table 5.1 Accuracy of predicting perceived attributes, with standard error in parentheses

Attribute	SHADES	GENERIC	USER- EXC	USER- ADP	ATTR DISC	IMG CLUST
Pointy	**76.3** (0.3)	74.0 (0.4)	67.8 (0.2)	74.8 (0.3)	74.5 (0.4)	74.3 (0.4)
Open	**74.6** (0.4)	66.5 (0.5)	65.8 (0.2)	71.6 (0.3)	68.5 (0.4)	68.3 (0.4)
Ornate	**62.8** (0.7)	56.4 (1.1)	59.6 (0.5)	61.1 (0.6)	58.3 (0.8)	58.6 (0.7)
Comfortable	**77.3** (0.6)	75.0 (0.7)	68.7 (0.5)	75.5 (0.6)	76.0 (0.7)	75.4 (0.6)
Formal	**78.8** (0.5)	76.2 (0.7)	69.6 (0.4)	77.1 (0.4)	77.4 (0.6)	77.0 (0.6)
Brown	**70.9** (1.0)	69.5 (1.2)	61.9 (0.5)	68.5 (0.9)	69.3 (1.2)	69.8 (1.2)
Fashionable	**62.2** (0.9)	58.5 (1.4)	60.5 (1.3)	62.0 (1.4)	61.2 (1.4)	61.5 (1.1)
Cluttered	**64.5** (0.3)	60.5 (0.5)	58.8 (0.2)	63.1 (0.4)	60.4 (0.7)	60.8 (0.7)
Soothing	**62.5** (0.4)	61.0 (0.5)	55.2 (0.2)	61.5 (0.4)	61.1 (0.4)	61.0 (0.5)
Open area	**64.6** (0.6)	62.9 (1.0)	57.9 (0.4)	63.5 (0.5)	63.5 (0.8)	62.8 (0.9)
Modern	**57.3** (0.8)	51.2 (0.9)	56.2 (0.7)	56.2 (1.1)	52.5 (0.9)	52.0 (1.1)
Rustic	**67.4** (0.6)	66.7 (0.5)	63.4 (0.5)	67.0 (0.5)	67.2 (0.5)	67.2 (0.5)

Fig. 5.7 Top words and images for two shades per attribute (*top* and *bottom* for each attribute)

front *and* back. In SUN, the "open area" attribute can be either outside (top) or inside (bottom). For "soothing," one shade emphasizes scenes conducive to relaxing activities, while another focuses on the aesthetics of the scene.

See [24] for results that demonstrate the advantage of using shades for attribute-based search and for an analysis of the purity of the discovered shades. These results show the importance of our shade discovery approach for interactive search: for a user to reliably find "formal" shoes, the system must correctly estimate "formal" in the database images. If the wrong attribute shade is predicted, the wrong image is retrieved. In general, detecting shades is key whenever linguistic attributes are required, which includes applications beyond image search as well (e.g. zero-shot recognition).

In our experiments, we assume that the pool of annotators is fixed, so we can map annotators to schools or shades during the matrix factorization procedure. However, new users could join after that procedure has taken place, so how can we map such new users to a shade? Of course, a user must provide at least some attribute labels to benefit from the shade models, since we need to know which shade to apply. One approach is to add the user to the user-image label matrix $\mathbf{L}$ and re-factor. Alternatively, we can use the more efficient folding-in heuristic [19]. We can appropriately copy the user's image labels into a $1 \times N$ vector $\mathbf{u}$, where we fill in missing label values by the most common response (0 or 1) for that image from already known users, similarly to an idea used by [44]. We can then compute the product of $\mathbf{u}$ and the image latent factor matrix $\mathbf{I}$, resulting in a representation of this new user in the latent factor space. After finding this representation, we use the existing set of cluster centers, and find the closest cluster center for the new user. We can then perform the personalization approach for this user as before, and thus any new user can also receive the benefit from our school discovery. We leave as future work the task of testing our system with late-comer new users.

5.6 Discussion and Conclusion

In this chapter, we proposed an effective new form of feedback for image search using relative attributes. In contrast to traditional binary relevance feedback which restricts the user's input to labeling images as "relevant" or "not relevant", our approach allows the user to precisely indicate how the results compare with her mental model. Next, we studied how to select the reference images used for feedback so the provided feedback is as informative to the retrieval system as possible. Today's visual search systems place the burden on the user to initiate useful feedback by labeling images as relevant, and often prioritize showing the user pleasing results over striving to obtain useful feedback. In contrast, we guide the user through a coarse-to-fine search via visual comparisons, and demonstrate this enables accurate results to be retrieved faster. Further, we showed how to bridge the human and machine perception of attributes by accounting for the variability in user attribute perceptions. While existing work assumes that users agree on the attribute values of images and thus build a single monolithic model per attribute, we develop personalized attribute models. Our results on two compelling datasets indicate that (1) people do indeed have varying shades of attribute meaning, (2) transferring generic models makes learning those shades more cost-effective than learning from scratch, and (3) accounting for the differences in user perception is essential in image search applications. Finally, we show how to discover people's shared biases in perception, then exploit them with visual classifiers that can generalize to new images. The discovered shades of attribute meaning allow us to tailor attribute predictions to the user's "school of thought," boosting the accuracy of detecting attributes.

While attributes are an excellent channel for interactive image retrieval, several issues remain to be solved in order to unleash attributes' full power for practical applications. First, the accuracy of attribute-based search is still far from satisfactory, and it is not acceptable for real users. For example, in [23], after 5 iterations of feedback, the viewer still has to browse between 9 and 14 % of the full dataset in order to find the exact image she is looking for. (In contrast, in our simulated experiment using perfect attribute models with added noise, only between 2 and 5 % of the dataset needs to be browsed.) To address this problem, we need to develop more accurate attribute models. Deep learning methods might enable us to make better use of existing annotations, but an orthogonal solution is to learn *richer annotations*, by involving humans more directly in training models that truly understand what these attributes mean.[7] We also need ways to visualize attributes, similar to visualizing object detection models [65], to ensure that the model aligns with the meaning that a human ascribes to the attribute, rather than a property *correlated* with the attribute.

A second problem with existing attribute-based work is that users are confined to using a small vocabulary of attributes to describe the world. We need to enable users to define new attributes on the fly during search, and propose techniques for

[7]Note that non-semantic attributes [49, 56, 69] are not readily applicable for applications that require human-machine communication as they do not have human-interpretable names.

efficiently learning models for these newly defined attributes. One approach for the latter is to utilize existing models for *related* attributes as a prior for learning new attribute models.

Acknowledgements This research was supported by ONR YIP grant N00014-12-1-0754 and ONR ATL grant N00014-11-1-0105. We would like to thank Devi Parikh for her collaboration on WhittleSearch and feedback on our other work, as well as Ray Mooney for his suggestions for future work.

References

1. Berg, T.L., Berg, A.C., Shih, J.: Automatic attribute discovery and characterization from noisy web data. In: European Conference on Computer Vision (ECCV) (2010)
2. Branson, S., Wah, C., Schroff, F., Babenko, B., Welinder, P., Perona, P., Belongie, S.: Visual recognition with humans in the loop. In: European Conference on Computer Vision (ECCV) (2010)
3. Chen, L., Zhang, Q., Li, B.: Predicting multiple attributes via relative multi-task learning. In: Conference on Computer Vision and Pattern Recognition (CVPR) (2014)
4. Chen, Q., Huang, J., Feris, R., Brown, L.M., Dong, J., Yan, S.: Deep domain adaptation for describing people based on fine-grained clothing attributes. In: Conference on Computer Vision and Pattern Recognition (CVPR) (2015)
5. Cox, I., Miller, M., Minka, T., Papathomas, T., Yianilos, P.: The bayesian image retrieval system, PicHunter: theory, implementation, and psychophysical experiments. IEEE Trans. Image Process. **9**(1), 20–37 (2000)
6. Curran, W., Moore, T., Kulesza, T., Wong, W.K., Todorovic, S., Stumpf, S., White, R., Burnett, M.: Towards recognizing "cool": can end users help computer vision recognize subjective attributes or objects in images? In: Intelligent User Interfaces (IUI) (2012)
7. Douze, M., Ramisa, A., Schmid, C.: Combining attributes and fisher vectors for efficient image retrieval. In: Conference on Computer Vision and Pattern Recognition (CVPR) (2011)
8. Duan, K., Parikh, D., Crandall, D., Grauman, K.: Discovering localized attributes for fine-grained recognition. In: Conference on Computer Vision and Pattern Recognition (CVPR) (2012)
9. Eitz, M., Hildebrand, K., Boubekeur, T., Alexa, M.: Sketch-based image retrieval: benchmark and bag-of-features descriptors. IEEE Trans. Vis. Comput. Graph. **17**(11), 1624–1636 (2011)
10. Endres, I., Farhadi, A., Hoiem, D., Forsyth, D.A.: The benefits and challenges of collecting richer object annotations. In: Conference on Computer Vision and Pattern Recognition (CVPR) Workshops (2010)
11. Escorcia, V., Niebles, J.C., Ghanem, B.: On the relationship between visual attributes and convolutional networks. In: Conference on Computer Vision and Pattern Recognition (CVPR) (2015)
12. Everett, C.: Linguistic relativity: evidence across languages and cognitive domains. In: Mouton De Gruyter (2013)
13. Farhadi, A., Endres, I., Hoiem, D., Forsyth, D.A.: Describing objects by their attributes. In: Conference on Computer Vision and Pattern Recognition (CVPR) (2009)
14. Ferecatu, M., Geman, D.: Interactive search for image categories by mental matching. In: International Conference on Computer Vision (ICCV) (2007)
15. Ferrari, V., Zisserman, A.: Learning visual attributes. In: Conference on Neural Information Processing Systems (NIPS) (2007)

16. Fogarty, J., Tan, D.S., Kapoor, A., Winder, S.: Cueflik: interactive concept learning in image search. In: Conference on Human Factors in Computing Systems (CHI) (2008)
17. Geng, B., Yang, L., Xu, C., Hua, X.S.: Ranking model adaptation for domain-specific search. IEEE Trans. Knowle. Data Eng. **24**(4), 745–758 (2012)
18. Heim, E., Berger, M., Seversky, L., Hauskrecht, M.: Active perceptual similarity modeling with auxiliary information. In: arXiv preprint arXiv:1511.02254 (2015)
19. Hofmann, T.: Probabilistic latent semantic analysis. In: Uncertainty in Artificial Intelligence (UAI) (1999)
20. Joachims, T.: Optimizing search engines using click through data. In: International Conference on Knowledge Discovery and Data Mining (KDD) (2002)
21. Kekalainen, J., Jarvelin, K.: Cumulated gain-based evaluation of IR techniques. ACM Trans. Inf. Syst. **20**(4), 422–446 (2002)
22. Kovashka, A., Grauman, K.: Attribute adaptation for personalized image search. In: International Conference on Computer Vision (ICCV) (2013)
23. Kovashka, A., Grauman, K.: Attribute pivots for guiding relevance feedback in image search. In: International Conference on Computer Vision (ICCV) (2013)
24. Kovashka, A., Grauman, K.: Discovering attribute shades of meaning with the crowd. Int. J. Comput. Vis. **114**, 56–73 (2015)
25. Kovashka, A., Vijayanarasimhan, S., Grauman, K.: Actively selecting annotations among objects and attributes. In: International Conference on Computer Vision (ICCV) (2011)
26. Kovashka, A., Parikh, D., Grauman, K.: WhittleSearch: image search with relative attribute feedback. In: Conference on Computer Vision and Pattern Recognition (CVPR) (2012)
27. Kovashka, A., Parikh, D., Grauman, K.: WhittleSearch: interactive image search with relative attribute feedback. Int. J. Comput. Vis. **115**, 185–210 (2015)
28. Kumar, N., Belhumeur, P.N., Nayar, S.K.: FaceTracer: a search engine for large collections of images with faces. In: European Conference on Computer Vision (ECCV) (2008)
29. Kumar, N., Berg, A.C., Belhumeur, P.N., Nayar, S.K.: Attribute and simile classifiers for face verification. In: International Conference on Computer Vision (ICCV) (2009)
30. Kumar, N., Berg, A.C., Belhumeur, P.N., Nayar, S.K.: Describable visual attributes for face verification and image search. IEEE Trans. Pattern Anal. Mach. Intell. **33**(10), 1962–1977 (2011)
31. Kurita, T., Kato, T.: Learning of personal visual impression for image database systems. In: International Conference on Document Analysis and Recognition (ICDAR) (1993)
32. Lampert, C., Nickisch, H., Harmeling, S.: Learning to detect unseen object classes by between-class attribute transfer. In: Conference on Computer Vision and Pattern Recognition (CVPR) (2009)
33. Li, B., Chang, E., Li, C.S.: Learning image query concepts via intelligent sampling. In: International Conference on Multimedia and Expo (ICME) (2001)
34. Li, S., Shan, S., Chen, X.: Relative forest for attribute prediction. In: Asian Conference on Computer Vision (ACCV) (2013)
35. Liu, S., Kovashka, A.: Adapting attributes using features similar across domains. In: Winter Conference on Applications of Computer Vision (WACV) (2016)
36. Loeff, N., Alm, C.O., Forsyth, D.A.: Discriminating image senses by clustering with multimodal features. In: Association for Computational Linguistics (ACL) (2006)
37. Ma, W.Y., Manjunath, B.S.: Netra: a toolbox for navigating large image databases. Multimedia Syst. **7**(3), 184–198 (1999)
38. Mahajan, D., Sellamanickam, S., Nair, V.: A joint learning framework for attribute models and object descriptions. In: International Conference on Computer Vision (ICCV) (2011)
39. Mensink, T., Verbeek, J., Csurka, G.: Learning structured prediction models for interactive image labeling. In: Conference on Computer Vision and Pattern Recognition (CVPR) (2011)
40. Oliva, A., Torralba, A.: Modeling the shape of the scene: a holistic representation of the spatial envelope. Int. J. Comput. Vis. **42**, 145–175 (2001)
41. Ordonez, V., Jagadeesh, V., Di, W., Bhardwaj, A., Piramuthu, R.: Furniture-geek: understanding fine-grained furniture attributes from freely associated text and tags. In: Winter Conference on Applications of Computer Vision (WACV) (2014)

42. Ozeki, M., Okatani, T.: Understanding convolutional neural networks in terms of category-level attributes. In: Asian Conference on Computer Vision (ACCV) (2014)
43. Parikh, D., Grauman, K.: Interactively building a discriminative vocabulary of nameable attributes. In: Conference on Computer Vision and Pattern Recognition (CVPR) (2011)
44. Parikh, D., Grauman, K.: Relative attributes. In: International Conference on Computer Vision (ICCV) (2011)
45. Parikh, D., Grauman, K.: Implied feedback: learning nuances of user behavior in image search. In: International Conference on Computer Vision (ICCV) (2013)
46. Patterson, G., Hays, J.: Sun attribute database: discovering, annotating, and recognizing scene attributes. In: Conference on Computer Vision and Pattern Recognition (CVPR) (2012)
47. Platt, J.C.: Probabilistic output for support vector machines and comparisons to regularized likelihood methods. In: Advances in Large Margin Classifiers (1999)
48. Rasiwasia, N., Moreno, P.J., Vasconcelos, N.: Bridging the gap: query by semantic example. IEEE Trans. Multimedia **9**(5), 923–938 (2007)
49. Rastegari, M., Farhadi, A., Forsyth, D.A.: Attribute discovery via predictable discriminative binary codes. In: European Conference on Computer Vision (ECCV) (2012)
50. Rastegari, M., Parikh, D., Diba, A., Farhadi, A.: Multi-attribute queries: to merge or not to merge? In: Conference on Computer Vision and Pattern Recognition (CVPR) (2013)
51. Roy, N., McCallum, A.: Toward optimal active learning through sampling estimation of error reduction. In: International Conference on Machine Learning (ICML) (2011)
52. Rui, Y., Huang, T.S., Ortega, M., Mehrotra, S.: Relevance feedback: a power tool for interactive content-based image retrieval. IEEE Trans. Circ. Syst. Video Technol. (1998)
53. Salakhutdinov, R., Mnih, A.: Bayesian probabilistic matrix factorization using Markov chain Monte Carlo. In: International Conference on Machine Learning (ICML) (2008)
54. Sandeep, R.N., Verma, Y., Jawahar, C.: Relative parts: distinctive parts for learning relative attributes. In: Conference on Computer Vision and Pattern Recognition (CVPR) (2014)
55. Scheirer, W., Kumar, N., Belhumeur, P.N., Boult, T.E.: Multi-attribute spaces: calibration for attribute fusion and similarity search. In: Conference on Computer Vision and Pattern Recognition (CVPR) (2012)
56. Schwartz, G., Nishino, K.: Automatically discovering local visual material attributes. In: Conference on Computer Vision and Pattern Recognition (CVPR) (2015)
57. Shankar, S., Garg, V.K., Cipolla, R.: Deep-carving: discovering visual attributes by carving deep neural nets. In: Conference on Computer Vision and Pattern Recognition (CVPR) (2015)
58. Shao, J., Kang, K., Loy, C.C., Wang, X.: Deeply learned attributes for crowded scene understanding. In: Conference on Computer Vision and Pattern Recognition (CVPR) (2015)
59. Sharmanska, V., Quadrianto, N., Lampert, C.: Augmented attribute representations. In: European Conference on Computer Vision (ECCV) (2012)
60. Siddiquie, B., Feris, R., Davis, L.: Image ranking and retrieval based on multi-attribute queries. In: Conference on Computer Vision and Pattern Recognition (CVPR) (2011)
61. Tamuz, O., Liu, C., Belongie, S., Shamir, O., Kalai, A.T.: Adaptively learning the crowd kernel. In: International Conference on Machine Learning (ICML) (2011)
62. Tieu, K., Viola, P.: Boosting image retrieval. In: Conference on Computer Vision and Pattern Recognition (CVPR) (2000)
63. Tong, S., Chang, E.: Support vector machine active learning for image retrieval. In: ACM Multimedia (2001)
64. Tunkelang, D.: Faceted search. In: Synthesis Lectures on Information Concepts, Retrieval, and Services (2009)
65. Vondrick, C., Khosla, A., Malisiewicz, T., Torralba, A.: Hoggles: visualizing object detection features. In: International Conference on Computer Vision (ICCV) (2013)
66. Wang, X., Ji, Q.: A unified probabilistic approach modeling relationships between attributes and objects. In: International Conference on Computer Vision (ICCV) (2013)
67. Xiao, F., Lee, Y.J.: Discovering the spatial extent of relative attributes. In: International Conference on Computer Vision (ICCV) (2015)

68. Yang, J., Yan, R., Hauptmann, A.G.: Adapting SVM classifiers to data with shifted distributions. In: IEEE International Conference on Data Mining (ICDM) Workshops (2007)
69. Yu, F., Cao, L., Feris, R., Smith, J., Chang, S.F.: Designing category-level attributes for discriminative visual recognition. In: Conference on Computer Vision and Pattern Recognition (CVPR) (2013)
70. Zhou, X.S., Huang, T.S.: Relevance feedback in image retrieval: a comprehensive review. In: Multimedia Systems (2003)

Chapter 6
Fine-Grained Comparisons with Attributes

Aron Yu and Kristen Grauman

Abstract Given two images, we want to predict which exhibits a particular visual attribute more than the other—even when the two images are quite similar. For example, given two beach scenes, which looks *more calm*? Given two high-heeled shoes, which is *more ornate*? Existing relative attribute methods rely on global ranking functions. However, rarely will the visual cues relevant to a comparison be constant for all data, nor will humans' perception of the attribute necessarily permit a global ordering. At the same time, not every image pair is even orderable for a given attribute. Attempting to map relative attribute ranks to "equality" predictions is non-trivial, particularly since the span of indistinguishable pairs in attribute space may vary in different parts of the feature space. To address these issues, we introduce *local learning* approaches for fine-grained visual comparisons, where a predictive model is trained on the fly using only the data most relevant to the novel input. In particular, given a novel pair of images, we develop local learning methods to (1) infer their relative attribute ordering with a ranking function trained using only analogous labeled image pairs, (2) infer the optimal "neighborhood," i.e., the subset of the training instances most relevant for training a given local model, and (3) infer whether the pair is even distinguishable, based on a local model for *just noticeable differences* in attributes. Our methods outperform state-of-the-art methods for relative attribute prediction on challenging datasets, including a large newly curated shoe dataset for fine-grained comparisons. We find that for fine-grained comparisons, *more* labeled data is not necessarily preferable to isolating the *right* data.

A. Yu (✉) · K. Grauman
University of Texas at Austin, Austin, USA
e-mail: aron.yu@utexas.edu

K. Grauman
e-mail: grauman@cs.utexas.edu

R.S. Feris et al. (eds.), *Visual Attributes*, Advances in Computer Vision and Pattern Recognition, DOI 10.1007/978-3-319-50077-5_6

6.1 Introduction

Attributes are visual properties describable in words, capturing anything from material properties (*metallic*, *furry*), shapes (*flat*, *boxy*), expressions (*smiling*, *surprised*), to functions (*sittable*, *drinkable*). Since their introduction to the recognition community [19, 35, 37], attributes have inspired a number of useful applications in image search [32, 34, 35, 50], biometrics [11, 45], and language-based supervision for recognition [6, 37, 43, 49].

Existing attribute models come in one of two forms: categorical or relative. Whereas categorical attributes are suited only for clear-cut predicates, such as *male* or *wooden*, relative attributes can represent "real-valued" properties that inherently exhibit a spectrum of strengths, such as *serious* or *sporty*. These spectra allow a computer vision system to go beyond recognition into comparison. For example, with a model for the relative attribute *brightness*, a system could judge which of two images is *brighter* than the other, as opposed to simply labeling them as bright/not bright.

Attribute comparisons open up a number of interesting possibilities. In biometrics, the system could interpret descriptions like, "the suspect is *taller* than him" [45]. In image search, the user could supply semantic feedback to pinpoint his desired content: "the shoes I want to buy are like these but *more masculine*" [34], as discussed in Chap. 5 of this book. For object recognition, human supervisors could teach the system by relating new objects to previously learned ones, e.g., "a mule has a tail *longer than* a donkey's" [6, 43, 49]. For subjective visual tasks, users could teach the system their personal perception, e.g., about which human faces are *more attractive* than others [1].

One typically learns a relative attribute in a learning-to-rank setting; training data is ordered (e.g., we are told image A has it more than B), and a ranking function is optimized to preserve those orderings. Given a new image, the function returns a score conveying how strongly the attribute is present [1, 10, 14, 18, 34, 38, 41, 43, 46, 47]. While a promising direction, the standard ranking approach tends to fail when faced with *fine-grained visual comparisons*. In particular, the standard approach falls short on two fronts: (1) it cannot reliably predict comparisons when the novel pair of images exhibits subtle visual differences, and (2) it does not permit equality predictions, meaning it is unable to detect when a novel pair of images are so similar that their difference is indistinguishable. The former scenario includes both the case where the images are globally similar, making all distinctions fine-grained, as well as the case where the images are very similar only in terms of the attribute of interest.

Why do existing global ranking functions experience difficulties making fine-grained attribute comparisons? The problem is that while a single learned function tends to accommodate the gross visual differences that govern the attribute's spectrum, it cannot simultaneously account for the many fine-grained differences among closely related examples, each of which may be due to a distinct set of visual cues. For example, what makes a slipper appear *more comfortable* than a high heel is

Fig. 6.1 A global ranking function may be suitable for *coarse* ranking tasks, but *fine-grained* ranking tasks require attention to subtle details—and which details are important may vary in different parts of the feature space. We propose a local learning approach to train comparative attributes based on fine-grained analogous pairs

different than what makes one high heel appear more comfortable than another; what makes a mountain scene appear *more natural* than a highway is different than what makes a suburb more natural than a downtown skyscraper (Fig. 6.1).

Furthermore, at some point, fine-grained differences become so subtle that they become indistinguishable. However, existing attribute models assume that all images are orderable. In particular, they assume that *at test time*, the system can and should always distinguish which image in a pair exhibits the attribute more. Imagine you are given a pile of images of Barack Obama, and you must sort them according to where he looks most to least *serious*. Can you do it? Surely there will be some obvious ones where he is more serious or less serious. There will even be image pairs where the distinction is quite subtle, yet still perceptible, thus fine-grained. However, you are likely to conclude that forcing a *total* order is meaningless: while the images exhibit different degrees of the attribute seriousness, at some point the differences become indistinguishable. It is not that the pixel patterns in indistinguishable image pairs are literally the same—they just cannot be characterized consistently as anything other than "equally serious" (Fig. 6.2). As we discuss in detail in Sect. 6.5, computational models for indistinguishability of attributes present substantial challenges.

We contend that such fine-grained comparisons are critical to get right, since this is where modeling relative attributes ought to have great power. Otherwise, we could just learn coarse categories of appearance ("bright scenes," "dark scenes") and manually define their ordering. In particular, fine-grained visual comparisons are valuable for sophisticated image search and browsing applications, such as distinguishing subtle properties between products in an online catalog, as well as analysis tasks involving nuanced perception, such as detecting slight shades of human facial expressions or distinguishing the identifying traits between otherwise similar-looking people.

In light of these challenges, we introduce *local learning* algorithms for fine-grained visual comparisons. Local learning is an instance of "lazy learning," where

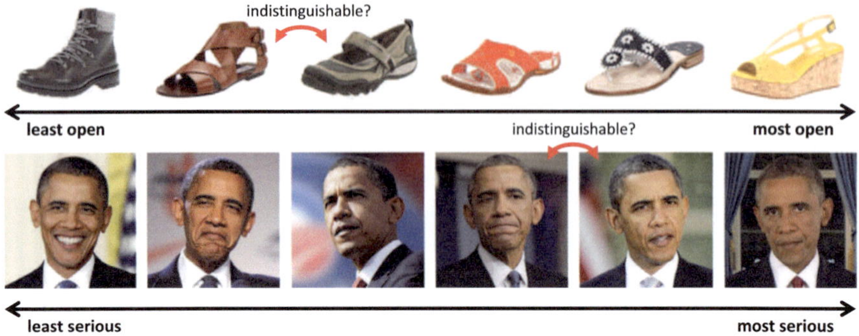

Fig. 6.2 At what point is the strength of an attribute indistinguishable between two images? While existing relative attribute methods are restricted to inferring a total order, in reality there are images that look different but where the attribute is nonetheless perceived as "equally strong." For example, in the fourth and fifth images of Obama, is the difference in *seriousness* noticeable enough to warrant a relative comparison?

one defers processing of the training data until test time. Rather than estimate a single global model from all training data, local learning methods instead focus on a subset of the data most relevant to the particular test instance. This helps learn fine-grained models tailored to the new input, and makes it possible to adjust the capacity of the learning algorithm to the local properties of the data [7]. Local methods include classic nearest neighbor classification as well as various novel formulations that use only nearby points to either train a model [2, 3, 7, 24, 57] or learn a feature transformation [16, 17, 25, 51] that caters to the novel input.

The local learning methods we develop in this chapter address the questions of (1) how to compare an attribute in highly similar images as well as (2) how to determine when such a comparison is not possible. To learn fine-grained ranking functions for attributes, given a novel test pair of images, we first identify *analogous* training pairs using a learned attribute-specific metric. Then we train a ranking function on the fly using only those pairs [54]. Building on this framework, we further explore how to predict the local *neighborhood* itself—essentially answering the "how local" question. Whereas existing local learning work assumes a fixed number of proximal training instances are most relevant, our approach infers the relevant set as a whole, both in terms of its size and composition [55]. Finally, to decide when a novel pair is indistinguishable in terms of a given attribute, we develop a Bayesian approach that relies on local statistics of orderability to learn a model of *just noticeable difference* (JND) [56].

Roadmap The rest of the chapter proceeds as follows. In Sect. 6.2, we discuss related work in the areas of relative attributes, local learning, and fine-grained visual learning. In Sect. 6.3, we provide a brief overview of the relative attributes ranking framework. In Sects. 6.4 and 6.5, we discuss in detail our proposed approaches for fine-grained visual comparisons and equality prediction using JND. Finally, we conclude in Sects. 6.6 and 6.7 with further discussion and future work. The work described in this chapter originally was presented in our previous conference papers [54–56].

6.2 Related Work

Attribute Comparison Attribute comparison has gained attention in the last several years. The original "relative attributes" approach learns a global linear ranking function for each attribute [43]. Pairwise supervision is used for training: a set of pairs ordered according to their perceived attribute strength is obtained from human annotators, and a ranking function that preserves those orderings is learned. Given a novel pair of images, the ranker indicates which image has the attribute more. It is extended to nonlinear ranking functions in [38] by training a hierarchy of rankers with different subsets of data, then normalizing predictions at the leaf nodes. In [14], rankers trained for each feature descriptor (color, shape, texture) are combined to produce a single global ranking function. In [47], part-based representations weighted specifically for each attribute are used instead of global features.

Aside from learning to rank formulations, researchers have applied the Elo rating system for biometrics [45], and regression over "cumulative attributes" for age and crowd density estimation [11].

All the prior methods produce a single global function for each attribute, whereas we propose to learn local functions tailored to the comparison at hand. While some implementations (including [43]) augment the training pool with "equal" pairs to facilitate learning, notably no existing work attempts to discern distinguishable from indistinguishable pairs at test time. As we will see below, doing so is nontrivial.

Fine-Grained Visual Tasks Work on fine-grained visual *categorization* aims to recognize objects in a single domain, e.g., bird species [9, 20]. While such problems also require making distinctions among visually close instances, our goal is to compare attributes, not categorize objects.

In the facial attractiveness ranking method of [10], the authors train a hierarchy of SVM classifiers to recursively push a image into buckets of more/less attractive faces. The leaf nodes contain images "unrankable" by the human subject, which can be seen as indistinguishability for the specific attribute of human attractiveness. Nonetheless, the proposed method is not applicable to our problem. It learns a ranking model specific to a single human subject, whereas we learn a subject-independent model. Furthermore, the training procedure [10] has limited scalability, since the subject must rank *all* training images into a partial order; the results focus on training sets of 24 images for this reason. In our domains of interest, where thousands or more training instances are standard, getting a reliable global partial order on all images remains an open challenge.

Variability in Visual Perception The fact that humans exhibit inconsistencies in their comparisons is well known in social choice theory and preference learning [8]. In existing global models [1, 10, 14, 18, 34, 38, 41, 43, 47], intransitive constraints would be unaccounted for and treated as noise. While the HodgeRank algorithm [28] also takes a global ranking approach, it estimates how much it suffers from cyclic inconsistencies, which is valuable to know how much to trust the final ranking function. However, that approach does not address the fact that the features relevant to a comparison are not uniform across a dataset, which we find is critical for fine-grained comparisons.

We are interested in modeling attributes where there *is* consensus about comparisons, only they are subtle. Rather than personalize a model toward an observer [1, 10, 31], we want to discover the (implicit) map of where the consensus for JND boundaries in attributes exists. The attribute calibration method of [48] post-processes attribute classifier outputs so they can be fused for multi-attribute search. Our method is also conscious that differences in attribute outputs taken at "face value" can be misleading, but our goal and approach are entirely different.

Local Learning In terms of learning algorithms, lazy local learning methods are relevant to our work. Existing methods primarily vary in how they exploit the labeled instances nearest to a test point. One strategy is to identify a fixed number of neighbors most similar to the test point, then train a model with only those examples (e.g., a neural network [7], SVM [57], ranking function [3, 24], or linear regression [2]). Alternatively, the nearest training points can be used to learn a transformation of the feature space (e.g., Linear Discriminant Analysis); after projecting the data into the new space, the model is better tailored to the query's neighborhood properties [16, 17, 25, 51]. In *local selection* methods, strictly the subset of nearby data is used, whereas in *locally weighted* methods, all training points are used but weighted according to their distance [2]. For all these prior methods, a test case is a new data point, and its neighboring examples are identified by nearest neighbor search (e.g., with Euclidean distance). In contrast, we propose to learn local ranking functions for comparisons, which requires identifying analogous neighbor *pairs* in the training data. Furthermore, we also explore how to *predict* the variable-size set of training instances that will produce an effective discriminative model for a given test instance.

In information retrieval, local learning methods have been developed to sort documents by their relevance to query keywords [3, 17, 24, 39]. They take strategies quite similar to the above, e.g., building a local model for each cluster in the training data [39], projecting training data onto a subspace determined by the test data distribution [17], or building a model with only the query's neighbors [3, 24]. Though a form of ranking, the problem setting in all these methods is quite different from ours. There, the training examples consist of queries and their respective sets of ground truth "relevant" and "irrelevant" documents, and the goal is to learn a function to rank a keyword query's relevant documents higher than its irrelevant ones. In contrast, we have training data comprised of paired comparisons, and the goal is to learn a function to compare a novel query pair.

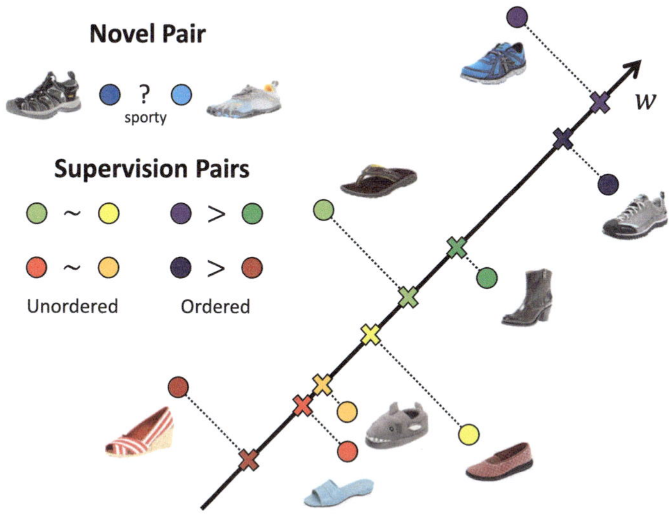

Fig. 6.3 Illustration of a learned linear ranking function trained from ordered pairs. The goal is to learn a ranking function $R_{\mathcal{A}}(x)$ that satisfies both the ordered and unordered pairwise constraints. Given a novel test pair, the real-valued ranking scores of the images are compared to determine their relative ordering

Metric Learning The question "what is relevant to a test point?" also brings to mind the metric learning problem. Metric learning methods optimize the parameters of a distance function so as to best satisfy known (dis)similarity constraints between training data [4]. Most relevant to our work are those that learn *local* metrics; rather than learn a single global parameterization, the metric varies in different regions of the feature space. For example, to improve nearest neighbor classification, in [22] a set of feature weights is learned for each individual training example, while in [52, 53] separate metrics are trained for clusters discovered in the training data. Such methods are valuable when the data is multimodal and thus ill-suited by a single global metric. In contrast to our approach, however, they learn local models offline on the basis of the fixed training set, whereas our approaches dynamically train new models as a function of the novel queries (Fig. 6.3).

6.3 Ranking Functions for Relative Attributes

First we describe how attribute comparisons can be addressed with a learning to rank approach, as originally proposed by Parikh and Grauman [43]. Ranking functions will also play a role in our solution, and the specific model we introduce next will further serve as the representative traditional "global" approach in our experiments.

Our approach addresses the relative comparison problem on a per attribute basis.[1] As training data for the attribute of interest $\mathcal{A}$ (e.g., *comfortable*), we are given a pool of ground truth comparisons on pairs of images. Then, given a novel pair of images, our method predicts which exhibits the attribute more, that is, which of the two images appears *more comfortable*, or if the images are equal, or in other words, *totally indistinguishable*. We first present a brief overview of Relative Attributes [43] as it sets the foundation as a baseline global ranking approach.

The Relative Attributes approach treats the attribute comparison task as a learning to rank problem. The idea is to use ordered pairs (and optionally "equal" pairs) of training images to train a ranking function that will generalize to new images. Compared to learning a regression function, the ranking framework has the advantage that training instances are themselves expressed comparatively, as opposed to requiring a rating of the absolute strength of the attribute per training image.

For each attribute $\mathcal{A}$ to be learned, we take as input two sets of annotated training image pairs. The first set consists of ordered pairs, $\mathcal{P}_o = \{(i, j)\}$, for which humans perceive image i to have the attribute more than image j. That is, each pair in $\mathcal{P}_o$ has a "noticeable difference". The second set consists of unordered, or "equal" pairs, $\mathcal{P}_e = \{(m, n)\}$, for which humans cannot perceive a difference in attribute strength. See Sect. 6.4.3 for discussion on how such human-annotated data can be reliably collected.

Let $x_i \in \mathbb{R}^d$ denote the d-dimensional image descriptor for image i, such as a GIST descriptor or a color histogram, and let $R_{\mathcal{A}}$ be a linear ranking function:

$$R_{\mathcal{A}}(x) = w_{\mathcal{A}}^T x. \tag{6.1}$$

Using a large-margin approach based on the SVM-Rank framework [29], the goal for a global relative attribute is to learn the parameters $w_{\mathcal{A}} \in \mathbb{R}^d$ that optimize the rank function parameters to preserve the orderings in $\mathcal{P}_o$, maintaining a margin between them in the 1D output space, while also minimizing the separation between the unordered pairs in $\mathcal{P}_e$. By itself, the problem is NP-hard, but [29] introduces slack variables and a large-margin regularizer to approximately solve it. The learning objective is:

$$\begin{aligned} \text{minimize} \quad & \left(\tfrac{1}{2}\|w_{\mathcal{A}}\|_2^2 + C\left(\sum \xi_{ij}^2 + \sum \gamma_{m,n}^2\right)\right) \\ s.t. \quad & w_{\mathcal{A}}^T(x_i - x_j) \geq 1 - \xi_{ij}; \quad \forall (i, j) \in \mathcal{P}_o \\ & |w_{\mathcal{A}}^T(x_m - x_n)| \leq \gamma_{pq}; \quad \forall (m, n) \in \mathcal{P}_e \\ & \xi_{ij} \geq 0; \quad \gamma_{mn} \geq 0, \end{aligned} \tag{6.2}$$

where the constant C balances the regularizer and ordering constraints, and γ_{pq} and ξ_{ij} denote slack variables. By projecting images onto the resulting hyperplane $w_{\mathcal{A}}$, we obtain a 1D global ranking for that attribute, e.g., from least to most *comfortable*.

[1] See Chap. 4 for discussion on methods for jointly training multiple attributes.

Given a test pair (x_r, x_s), if $R_{\mathcal{A}}(x_r) > R_{\mathcal{A}}(x_s)$, then image r exhibits the attribute more than image s, and vice versa. While [43] uses this linear formulation, it is also kernelizable and so can produce nonlinear ranking functions.

Our local approach defined next draws on this particular ranking formulation, which is also used in both [43] and in the hierarchy of [38] to produce state-of-the-art results. Note however that our local learning idea would apply similarly to alternative ranking methods.

6.4 Fine-Grained Visual Comparisons

Existing methods train a global ranking function using all available constraints $\mathcal{P}_o$ (and sometimes $\mathcal{P}_e$), with the implicit assumption that more training data should only help better learn the target concept. While such an approach tends to capture the coarse visual comparisons, it can be difficult to derive a single set of model parameters that adequately represents both these big-picture contrasts *and* more subtle fine-grained comparisons (recall Fig. 6.1). For example, for a dataset of shoes, it will map all the sneakers on one end of the *formal* spectrum, and all the high heels on the other, but the ordering among closely related high heels will not show a clear pattern. This suggests there is an interplay between the model capacity and the density of available training examples, prompting us to explore local learning solutions.

In the following, we next introduce our local ranking approach (Sect. 6.4.1) and the mechanism to selecting fine-grained neighboring pairs with attribute-specific metric learning (Sect. 6.4.2). On three challenging datasets from distinct domains, including a newly curated large dataset of 50,000 Zappos shoe images that focuses on fine-grained attribute comparisons (Sect. 6.4.3), we show our approach improves the state-of-the-art in relative attribute predictions (Sect. 6.4.4). After the results, we briefly overview an extension of the local attribute learning idea that learns the *neighborhood* of relevant training data that ought to be used to train a model on the fly (Sect. 6.4.5).

6.4.1 Local Learning for Visual Comparisons

The solution to overcoming the shortcomings of existing methods discussed above is not simply a matter of using a higher capacity learning algorithm. While a low capacity model can perform poorly in well-sampled areas, unable to sufficiently exploit the dense training data, a high capacity model can produce unreliable (yet highly confident) decisions in poorly sampled areas of the feature space [7]. Different properties are required in different areas of the feature space. Furthermore, in our visual ranking domain, we can expect that as the amount of available training data increases, more human subjectiveness and ordering inconsistencies will emerge, further straining the validity of a single global function.

Our idea is to explore a local learning approach for attribute ranking. The idea is to train a ranking function tailored to each novel pair of images $X_q = (x_r, x_s)$ that we wish to compare. We train the custom function using only a subset of all labeled training pairs, exploiting the data statistics in the neighborhood of the test pair. In particular, we sort all training pairs $\mathcal{P}_\mathcal{A}$ by their similarity to (x_r, x_s), then compose a local training set $\mathcal{P}'_\mathcal{A}$ consisting of the top K neighboring pairs, $\mathcal{P}'_\mathcal{A} = \{(x_{k1}, x_{k2})\}_{k=1}^{K}$. We explain in the next section how we define similarity between pairs. Then, we train a ranking function using Eq. 6.2 on the fly, and apply it to compare the test images. Thus, while the capacity of the trained models will be fixed throughout the feature space, crucially, the composition of their training sets and the resulting models will vary.

While simple, our framework directly addresses the flaws that hinder existing methods. By restricting training pairs to those visually similar to the test pair, the learner can zero in on features most important for that kind of comparison. Such a fine-grained approach helps to eliminate ordering constraints that are irrelevant to the test pair. For instance, when evaluating whether a high-topped athletic shoe is more or less *sporty* than a similar-looking low-topped one, our method will exploit pairs with similar visual differences, as opposed to trying to accommodate in a single global function the contrasting sportiness of sneakers, high heels, and sandals (Fig. 6.4).

6.4.2 Selecting Fine-Grained Neighboring Pairs

A key factor to the success of the local rank learning approach is how we judge similarity between pairs. Intuitively, we would like to gather training pairs that are somehow *analogous* to the test pair, so that the ranker focuses on the fine-grained visual differences that dictate their comparison. This means that not only should individual members of the pairs have visual similarity, but also the visual contrasts between the two test pair images should mimic the visual contrasts between the two training pair images. In addition, we must account for the fact that we seek comparisons along a particular attribute, which means only certain aspects of the image appearance are relevant; in other words, Euclidean distance between their global image descriptors is likely inadequate.

To fulfill these desiderata, we define a paired distance function that incorporates attribute-specific metric learning. Let $X_q = (x_r, x_s)$ be the test pair, and let $X_t = (x_u, x_v)$ be a labeled training pair for which $(u, v) \in \mathcal{P}_\mathcal{A}$. We define their distance as:

$$D_\mathcal{A}\left(X_q, X_t\right) = \min\left(D'_\mathcal{A}\left((x_r, x_s), (x_u, x_v)\right), D'_\mathcal{A}\left((x_r, x_s), (x_v, x_u)\right)\right), \quad (6.3)$$

where $D'_\mathcal{A}$ is the product of the two items' distances:

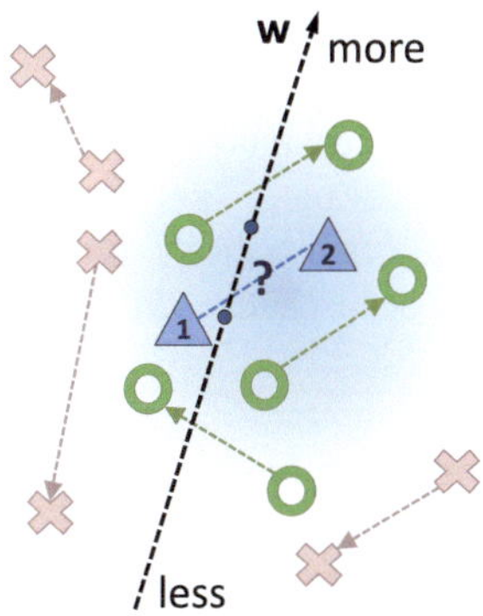

(a) Local Approach

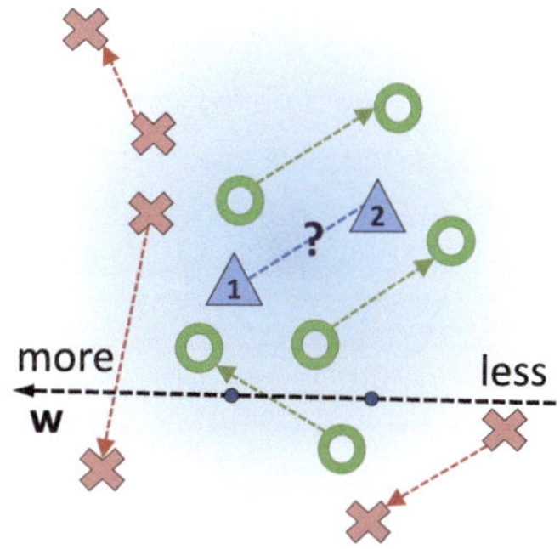

(b) Global Approach

Fig. 6.4 Given a novel test pair (*blue* △) in a learned metric space, our local approach **a** selects only the most relevant neighbors (*green* ○) for training, which leads to ranking test image 2 over 1 in terms of *sporty*. In contrast, the standard global approach defined in Sect. 6.3 **b** uses all training data (*green* ○ and *red* ×) for training; the unrelated training pairs dilute the training data. As a result, the global model accounts largely for the coarse-grained differences, and incorrectly ranks test image 1 over 2. The end of each arrow points to the image with *more* of the attribute (sporty). Note that the rank of each point is determined by its *projection* onto w

$$D'_{\mathcal{A}}\left((x_r, x_s), (x_u, x_v)\right) = d_{\mathcal{A}}(x_r, x_u) \times d_{\mathcal{A}}(x_s, x_v). \tag{6.4}$$

The product reflects that we are looking for pairs where each image is visually similar to one of those in the novel pair. It also ensures that the constraint pairs are evaluated for distance as a pair instead of as individual images.[2] If both query training couplings are similar, the distance is low. If some image coupling is highly dissimilar, the distance is greatly increased. The minimum in Eq. 6.3 and the swapping of $(x_u, x_v) \rightarrow (x_v, x_u)$ in the second term ensure that we account for the unknown ordering of the test pair; while all training pairs are ordered with $R_{\mathcal{A}}(x_u) > R_{\mathcal{A}}(x_v)$, the first or second argument of X_q may exhibit the attribute more. When learning

[2]A more strict definition of "analogous pair" would further constrain that there be low distortion between the vectors connecting the query pair and training pair, respectively, i.e., forming a parallelogram in the metric space. This is similarly efficient to implement. However, in practice, we found the stricter definition is slightly less effective than the product distance. This indicates that some variation in the intra-pair visual differences are useful to the learner.

a local ranking function for attribute $\mathcal{A}$, we sort neighbor pairs for X_q according to $D_{\mathcal{A}}$, then take the top K to form $\mathcal{P}'_{\mathcal{A}}$.

When identifying neighbor pairs, rather than judge image distance $d_{\mathcal{A}}$ by the usual Euclidean distance on global descriptors, we want to specialize the function to the particular attribute at hand. That's because often a visual attribute does not rely equally on each dimension of the feature space, whether due to the features' locations or modality. For example, if judging image distance for the attribute *smiling*, the localized region by the mouth is likely most important; if judging distance for *comfort* the features describing color may be irrelevant. In short, it is not enough to find images that are globally visually similar. For fine-grained comparisons we need to focus on those that are similar in terms of the property of interest.

To this end, we learn a Mahalanobis metric:

$$d_{\mathcal{A}}(x_i, x_j) = (x_i - x_j)^T \mathbf{M}_{\mathcal{A}} (x_i - x_j), \tag{6.5}$$

parameterized by the $d \times d$ positive definite matrix $\mathbf{M}_{\mathcal{A}}$. We employ the information-theoretic metric learning (ITML) algorithm [15], due to its efficiency and kernelizability. Given an initial $d \times d$ matrix $\mathbf{M}_{\mathcal{A}_0}$ specifying any prior knowledge about how the data should be compared, ITML produces the $\mathbf{M}_{\mathcal{A}}$ that minimizes the LogDet divergence $D_{\ell\mathrm{d}}$ from that initial matrix, subject to constraints that similar data points be close and dissimilar points be far:

$$\begin{aligned} \min_{M_{\mathcal{A}} \succeq 0} \quad & D_{\ell\mathrm{d}}(\mathbf{M}_{\mathcal{A}}, \mathbf{M}_{\mathcal{A}_0}) \\ s.t. \quad & d_{\mathcal{A}}(x_i, x_j) \leq c \quad (i, j) \in \mathcal{S}_{\mathcal{A}} \\ & d_{\mathcal{A}}(x_i, x_j) \geq \ell \quad (i, j) \in \mathcal{D}_{\mathcal{A}}. \end{aligned} \tag{6.6}$$

The sets $\mathcal{S}_{\mathcal{A}}$ and $\mathcal{D}_{\mathcal{A}}$ consist of pairs of points constrained to be similar and dissimilar, and ℓ and c are large and small values, respectively, determined by the distribution of original distances. We set $\mathbf{M}_{\mathcal{A}_0} = \Sigma^{-1}$, the inverse covariance matrix for the training images. To compose $\mathcal{S}_{\mathcal{A}}$ and $\mathcal{D}_{\mathcal{A}}$, we use image pairs for which human annotators found the images similar (or dissimilar) *according to the attribute* $\mathcal{A}$. While metric learning is usually used to enhance nearest neighbor classification (e.g., [23, 27]), we employ it to gauge perceived similarity along an attribute.

Figure 6.6 shows example neighbor pairs. They illustrate how our method finds training pairs analogous to the test pair, so the local learner can isolate the informative visual features for that comparison. Note how holistically, the neighbors found with metric learning (FG-LocalPair) may actually look less similar than those found without (LocalPair). However, in terms of the specific attribute, they better isolate the features that are relevant. For example, images of the same exact person need not be most useful to predict the degree of *smiling*, if others better matched to the test pair's expressions are available (last example). In practice, the local rankers trained with learned neighbors are substantially more accurate.

Fig. 6.5 Sample images from each of the high-level shoe categories of UT-Zap50K

6.4.3 Fine-Grained Attribute Zappos Dataset

Having explained the basic approach, we now describe a new dataset amenable to fine-grained attributes. We collected a new UT Zappos50K dataset (**UT-Zap50K**[3]) specifically targeting the fine-grained attribute comparison task. The dataset is fine-grained due to two factors: (1) it focuses on a narrow domain of content, and (2) we develop a two-stage annotation procedure to isolate those comparisons that humans find perceptually very close.

The image collection is created in the context of an online shopping task, with 50,000 catalog shoe images from Zappos.com. For online shopping, users care about precise visual differences between items. For instance, it is more likely that a shopper is deciding between two pairs of similar men's running shoes instead of between a woman's high heel and a man's slipper. The images are roughly 150×100 pixels and shoes are pictured in the same orientation for convenient analysis. For each image, we also collect its meta-data (shoe type, materials, manufacturer, gender, etc.) that are used to filter the shoes on Zappos.com.

Using Mechanical Turk (mTurk), we collect ground truth comparisons for 4 relative attributes: *open*, *pointy at the toe*, *sporty*, and *comfortable*. The attributes are selected for their potential to exhibit fine-grained differences. A worker is shown two images and an attribute name, and must make a relative decision (more, less, equal) and report the confidence of his decision (high, mid, low). We repeat the same comparison for 5 workers in order to vote on the final ground truth. We collect 12,000 total pairs, 3,000 per attribute. After removing the low confidence or agreement pairs, and "equal" pairs, each attribute has between 1,500 to 1,800 total ordered pairs (Fig. 6.5).

Of all the possible $50{,}000^2$ pairs we could get annotated, we want to prioritize the fine-grained pairs. To this end, first, we sampled pairs with a strong bias (80 %) toward intra-category and -gender images (based on the meta-data). We call this collection **UT-Zap50K-1**. We found ~40 % of the pairs came back labeled as "equal" for each attribute. While the "equal" label can indicate that there's no perceivable difference in the attribute, we also suspected that it was an easy fallback response for cases that required a little more thought—that is, those showing fine-grained differences. Thus, we next posted the pairs rated as "equal" (4,612 of them) back onto mTurk as new tasks, but *without* the "equal" option. We asked the workers to look closely, pick one

[3]UT-Zap50K dataset and all related data are publicly available for download at `vision.cs.utexas.edu/projects/finegrained`.

image over the other, and give a one sentence rationale for their decisions. We call this set **UT-Zap50K-2**.

Interestingly, the workers are quite consistent on these pairs, despite their difficulty. Out of all 4,612 pairs, only 278 pairs had low confidence or agreement (and so were pruned). Overall, 63 % of the fine-grained pairs (and 66 % of the coarser pairs) had at least 4 out of 5 workers agree on the same answer with above average confidence. This consistency ensures we have a dataset that is both fine-grained as well as reliably ground truthed.

Compared to an existing Shoes attribute dataset [5] with relative attributes [34], UT-Zap50K is about 3.5× larger, offers meta-data and 10× more comparative labels, and most importantly, specifically targets fine-grained tasks. Compared to existing popular relative attribute datasets like PubFig [36] and Outdoor Scenes [42], which contain only category-level comparisons (e.g., "Viggo *smiles* less than Miley") that are propagated down uniformly to all image instances, UT-Zap50K is distinct in that annotators have made *image-level* comparisons (e.g., "this particular shoe image is *more pointy* than that particular shoe"). The latter is more costly to obtain but essential for testing fine-grained attributes thoroughly.

In the next section we use UT-Zap50K as well as other existing datasets to test our approach. Later in Sect. 6.5 we will discuss extensions to the annotations that make it suitable for the just noticeable difference task as well (Fig. 6.6).

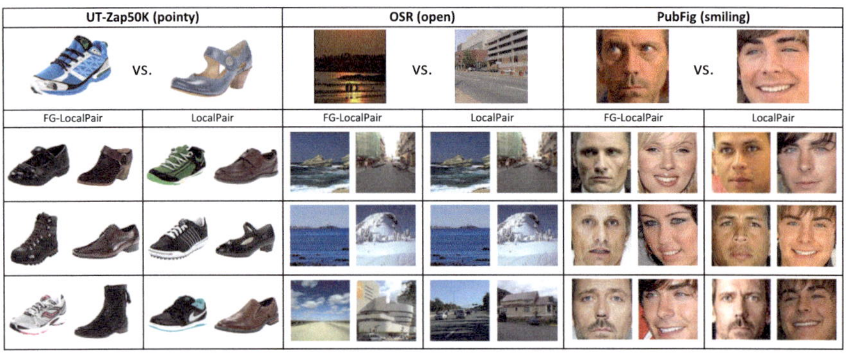

Fig. 6.6 Example fine-grained neighbor pairs for three test pairs (*top row*) from the datasets tested in this chapter. We display the top 3 pairs per query. FG-LocalPair and LocalPair denote results with and without metric learning (ML), respectively. **UT-Zap50K pointy**: ML puts the comparison focus on the tip of the shoe, caring less about the look of the shoe as a whole. **OSR open**: ML has less impact, as openness in these scenes relates to their whole texture. **PubFig smiling**: ML learns to focus on the mouth/lip region instead of the entire face. For example, while the LocalPair (non-learned) metric retrieves face pairs that more often contain the same people as the top pair, those instances are nonetheless less relevant for the fine-grained smiling distinction it requires. In contrast, our FG-LocalPair learned metric retrieves nearby pairs that may contain different people, yet are instances where the degree of smiling is most useful as a basis for predicting the relative smiling level in the novel query pair

6.4.4 *Experiments and Results*

To validate our method, we compare it to two state-of-the-art methods as well as informative baselines.

6.4.4.1 Experimental Setup

Datasets We evaluate on three datasets: **UT-Zap50K**, as defined above, with concatenated GIST and color histogram features; the Outdoor Scene Recognition dataset [42] (**OSR**); and a subset of the Public Figures faces dataset [36] (**PubFig**). OSR contains 2,688 images (GIST features) with 6 attributes, while PubFig contains 772 images (GIST + Color features) with 11 attributes. We use the exact same attributes, features, and train/test splits as [38, 43]. Our choice of features is based on the intent to capture spatially localized textures (GIST) as well as global color distributions, though of course alternative feature types could easily be employed in our framework.

Setup We run for 10 random train/test splits, setting aside 300 ground truth pairs for testing and the rest for training. We cross-validate C for all experiments, and adopt the same C selected by the global baseline for our approach. We use no "equal" pairs for training or testing rankers. We report accuracy in terms of the percentage of correctly ordered pairs, following [38]. We present results using the same labeled data for all methods.

For learning to rank, our *total* training pairs $\mathcal{P}_{\mathcal{A}}$ consist of only ordered pairs $\mathcal{P}_o$. For ITML, we use the ordered pairs $\mathcal{P}_{\mathcal{A}}$ for rank training to compose the set of dissimilar pairs $\mathcal{D}_{\mathcal{A}}$, and the set of "equal" pairs to compose the similar pairs $\mathcal{S}_{\mathcal{A}}$. We use the default settings for c and ℓ in the authors' code [15]. The setting of K determines "how local" the learner is; its optimal setting depends on the training data and query. As in prior work [7, 57], we simply fix it for all queries at $K = 100$ (though see Sect. 6.4.5 for a proposed generalization that learns the neighborhood size as well). Values of $K = 50$–200 give similar results.

Baselines We compare the following methods:

- **FG-LocalPair**: the proposed fine-grained approach.
- **LocalPair**: our approach without the learned metric (i.e., $\mathbf{M}_{\mathcal{A}} = \mathbb{I}$). This baseline isolates the impact of tailoring the search for neighboring pairs to the attribute.
- **RandPair**: a local approach that selects its neighbors randomly. This baseline demonstrates the importance of selecting relevant neighbors.
- **Global**: a global ranker trained with all available labeled pairs, using Eq. 6.2. This is the Relative Attributes method [43]. We use the authors' public code.
- **RelTree**: the nonlinear relative attributes approach of [38], which learns a hierarchy of functions, each trained with successively smaller subsets of the data. Code is not available, so we rely on the authors' reported numbers (available for OSR and PubFig).

Table 6.1 Results for the UT-Zap50K dataset

	Open	Pointy	Sporty	Comfort
(a) UT-Zap50K-1 with ***coarser*** pairs				
Global [43]	87.77	89.37	91.20	89.93
RandPair	82.53	83.70	86.30	84.77
LocalPair	88.53	88.87	92.20	90.90
FG-LocalPair	**90.67**	**90.83**	**92.67**	**92.37**
(b) UT-Zap50K-2 with ***fine-grained*** pairs				
Global [43]	60.18	59.56	62.70	**64.04**
RandPair	61.00	53.41	58.26	59.24
LocalPair	71.64	59.56	61.22	59.75
FG-LocalPair	**74.91**	**63.74**	**64.54**	62.51

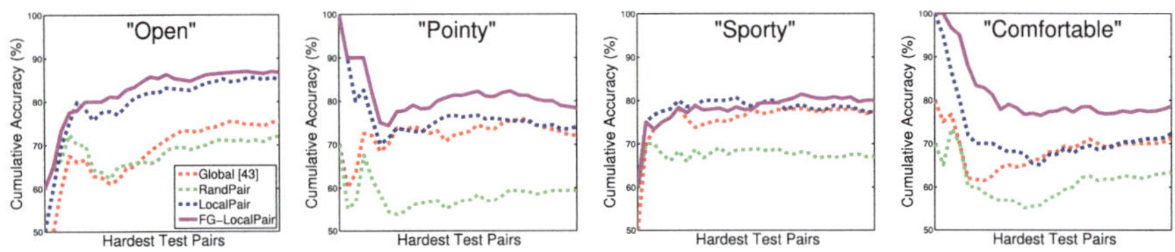

Fig. 6.7 Accuracy for the 30 hardest test pairs on UT-Zap50K-1

6.4.4.2 Zappos Results

Table 6.1a shows the accuracy on UT-Zap50K-1. Our method outperforms all baselines for all attributes. To isolate the more difficult pairs in UT-Zap50K-1, we sort the test pairs by their intra-pair distance using the learned metric; those that are close will be visually similar for the attribute, and hence more challenging. Figure 6.7 shows the results, plotting cumulative accuracy for the 30 hardest test pairs per split. We see that our method has substantial gains over the baselines (about 20 %), demonstrating its strong advantage for detecting subtle differences. Figure 6.8 shows some qualitative results.

We proceed to test on even more difficult pairs. Whereas Fig. 6.7 focuses on pairs difficult according to the learned metric, next we focus on pairs difficult according to our human annotators. Table 6.1b shows the results for UT-Zap50K-2. We use the original ordered pairs for training and all 4,612 fine-grained pairs for testing (Sect. 6.4.3). We outperform all methods for 3 of the 4 attributes. For the two more objective attributes, *open* and *pointy*, our gains are sizeable—14 % over Global for *open*. We attribute this to their localized nature, which is accurately captured by our learned metrics. No matter how fine-grained the difference is, it usually comes down to the top of the shoe (*open*) or the tip of the shoe (*pointy*). On the other hand, the subjective attributes are much less localized. The most challenging one is *comfort*, where our method performs slightly worse than Global, in spite of being better on

Fig. 6.8 Example pairs contrasting our predictions to the Global baseline's. In each pair, the top item is *more sporty* than the bottom item according to ground truth from human annotators. (*1*) We predict correctly, Global is wrong. We detect subtle changes, while Global relies only on overall shape and color. (*2*) We predict incorrectly, Global is right. These coarser differences are sufficiently captured by a global model. (*3*) Both methods predict incorrectly. Such pairs are so fine-grained, they are difficult even for humans to make a firm decision

the coarser pairs (Table 6.1a). We think this is because the locations of the subtleties vary greatly per pair.

6.4.4.3 Scenes and PubFig Results

We now shift our attention to OSR and PubFig, two commonly used datasets for relative attributes [34, 38, 43]. The paired supervision for these datasets originates from categorywise comparisons [43], and as such there are many more training pairs—on average over 20,000 per attribute.

Tables 6.2 and 6.3 show the accuracy for PubFig and OSR, respectively. See [54] for attribute-specific precision recall curves. On both datasets, our method outperforms all the baselines. Most notably, it outperforms RelTree [38], which to our knowledge is the very best accuracy reported to date on these datasets. This particular result is compelling not only because we improve the state-of-the-art, but also

Table 6.2 Accuracy comparison for the OSR dataset. FG-LocalPair denotes the proposed approach

	Natural	Open	Perspective	LgSize	Diagonal	ClsDepth
RelTree [38]	95.24	92.39	87.58	88.34	89.34	89.54
Global [43]	95.03	90.77	86.73	86.23	86.50	87.53
RandPair	92.97	89.40	84.80	84.67	84.27	85.47
LocalPair	94.63	93.27	88.33	89.40	90.70	89.53
FG-LocalPair	**95.70**	**94.10**	**90.43**	**91.10**	**92.43**	**90.47**

Table 6.3 Accuracy comparison for the PubFig dataset

	Male	White	Young	Smiling	Chubby	F.Head
RelTree [38]	85.33	82.59	84.41	83.36	78.97	88.83
Global [43]	81.80	76.97	83.20	79.90	76.27	87.60
RandPair	74.43	65.17	74.93	73.57	69.00	84.00
LocalPair	81.53	77.13	83.53	82.60	78.70	89.40
FG-LocalPair	**91.77**	**87.43**	**91.87**	**87.00**	**87.37**	**94.00**

	Brow	Eye	Nose	Lip	Face	
RelTree [38]	81.84	83.15	80.43	81.87	86.31	
Global [43]	79.87	81.67	77.40	79.17	82.33	
RandPair	70.90	73.70	66.13	71.77	73.50	
LocalPair	80.63	82.40	78.17	79.77	82.13	
FG-LocalPair	**89.83**	**91.40**	**89.07**	**90.43**	**86.70**	

because RelTree is a nonlinear ranking function. Hence, we see that local learning with linear models is performing better than global learning with a nonlinear model. With a lower capacity model, but the "right" training examples, the comparison is better learned. Our advantage over the global Relative Attributes linear model [43] is even greater.

On OSR, RandPair comes close to Global. One possible cause is the weak supervision from the categorywise constraints. While there are 20,000 pairs, they are less diverse. Therefore, a random sampling of 100 neighbors seems to reasonably mimic the performance when using all pairs. In contrast, our method is consistently stronger, showing the value of our learned neighborhood pairs.

While metric learning (ML) is valuable across the board (FG-LocalPair > LocalPair), it has more impact on PubFig than OSR. We attribute this to PubFig's more localized attributes. Subtle differences are what makes fine-grained comparison tasks hard. ML discovers the features behind those subtleties *with respect to each attribute*. Those features could be spatially localized regions or particular image cues (GIST vs. color). Indeed, our biggest gains compared to LocalPair (9 % or more) are on *white*, where we learn to emphasize color bins, or *eye*/*nose*, where we learn to emphasize the GIST cells for the part regions. In contrast, the LocalPair method compares the face images as a whole, and is liable to find images of the same person as more relevant, regardless of their properties in that image (Fig. 6.6).

6.4.4.4 Runtime Evaluation

Learning local models on the fly, though more accurate for fine-grained attributes, does come at a computational cost. The main online costs are finding the nearest neighbor pairs and training the local ranking function. For our datasets, with $K = 100$ and 20,000 total labeled pairs, this amounts to about 3 s. There are straightforward ways to improve the runtime. The neighbor finding can be done rapidly using well known hashing techniques, which are applicable to learned metrics [27]. Furthermore, we could precompute a set of representative local models. For example, we could cluster the training pairs, build a local model for each cluster, and invoke the suitable model based on a test pair's similarity to the cluster representatives. We leave such implementation extensions as future work.

6.4.5 *Predicting Useful Neighborhoods*

This section expands on the neighbor selection approach described in Sect. 6.4.2, briefly summarizing our NIPS 2014 paper [55]. Please see that paper for more details and results.

As we have seen above, the goal of local learning is to tailor the model to the properties of the data surrounding the test instance. However, so far, like other prior work in local learning we have made an important core assumption: that the instances most *useful* for building a local model are those that are *nearest* to the test example. This assumption is well-motivated by the factors discussed above, in terms of data density and intra-class variation. Furthermore, as we saw above, identifying training examples solely based on proximity has the appeal of permitting specialized similarity functions (whether learned or engineered for the problem domain), which can be valuable for good results, especially in structured input spaces.

On the other hand, there is a problem with this core assumption. By treating the individual nearness of training points as a metric of their utility for local training, existing methods fail to model how those training points will actually be employed. Namely, the relative success of a locally trained model is a function of the entire *set* or *distribution* of the selected data points—not simply the individual pointwise nearness of each one against the query. In other words, the ideal target subset consists of a set of instances that together yield a good predictive model for the test instance. Thus, local neighborhood selection ought to be considered jointly among training points.

Based on this observation, we have explored ways to *learn* the properties of a "good neighborhood". We cast the problem in terms of large-scale multi-label classification, where we learn a mapping from an individual instance to an indicator vector over the entire training set that specifies which instances are jointly useful to the query. The approach maintains an inherent bias toward neighborhoods that are local, yet makes it possible to discover subsets that (i) deviate from a strict nearest neighbor ranking and (ii) vary in size. We stress that learning what a good *neighbor* looks like (metric learning's goal) is distinct from learning what a good *neighborhood* looks like (our goal). Whereas a metric can be trained with pairwise constraints indicating what should be near or far, jointly predicting the instances that ought to compose a neighborhood requires a distinct form of learning.

The overall pipeline includes three main phases, shown in Fig. 6.9. (1) First, we devise an empirical approach to generate ground truth training neighborhoods (x_n, y_n) that consist of an individual instance x_n paired with a set of training

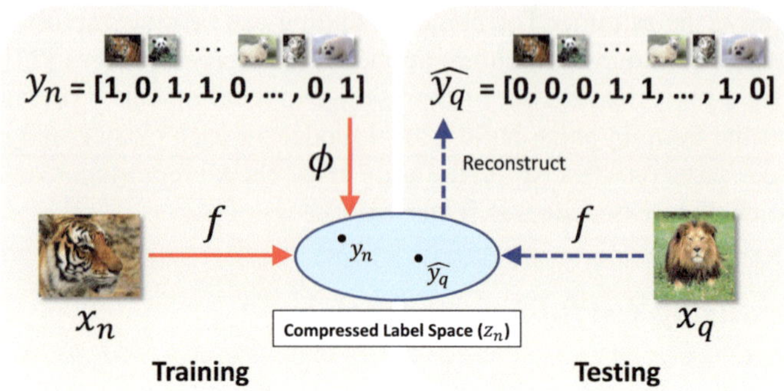

Fig. 6.9 Overview of our compressed sensing based approach. y_n and $\hat{y_q}$ represent the M-dimensional neighborhood indicator vectors for a training and testing instance, respectively. ϕ is a $D \times M$ random matrix where D denotes the compressed indicators' dimensionality. f is the learned regression function used to map the original image feature space to the compressed label space. By reconstructing back to the full label space, we get an estimate of $\hat{y_q}$ indicating which labeled training instances together will form a good neighborhood for the test instance x_q

instance indices capturing its target "neighbors", the latter being represented as a M-dimensional indicator vector y_n, where M is the number of labeled training instances. (2) Next, using the Bayesian compressed sensing approach of [30], we project y_n to a lower dimensional compressed label space z_n using a random matrix ϕ. Then, we learn regression functions $f_1(x_n)$, ..., $f_D(x_n)$ to map the original features x_n to the compressed label space. (3) Finally, given a test instance x_q, we predicts its neighborhood indicator vector $\hat{y_q}$ using ϕ and the learned regression functions f. We use this neighborhood of points to train a classifier on the fly, which in turn is used to categorize x_q.[4]

In [55] we show substantial advantages over existing local learning strategies, particularly when attributes are multimodal and/or its similar instances are difficult to match based on global feature distances alone. Our results illustrate the value in estimating the size and composition of discriminative neighborhoods, rather than relying on proximity alone. See our paper for the full details [55].

6.5 Just Noticeable Differences

Having established the strength of local learning for fine-grained attribute comparisons, we now turn to task of predicting when a comparison is even possible. In other words, given a pair of images, the output may be one of "more," "less," or "equal."

While some pairs of images have a clear ordering for an attribute (recall Fig. 6.2), for others the difference may be indistinguishable to human observers. Attempting

[4]Note that the neighborhood learning idea has been tested thus far only for classification tasks, though in principle applies similarly to ranking tasks.

to map relative attribute ranks to equality predictions is nontrivial, particularly since the span of indistinguishable pairs in an attribute space may vary in different parts of the feature space. In fact, as discussed above, despite the occasional use of unordered pairs for training,[5] it is assumed in prior work that all test images will be orderable. However, the real-valued output of a ranking function as trained in Sect. 6.3 will virtually never be equal for two distinct inputs. Therefore, even though existing methods may learn to produce similar rank scores for equal pairs, it is unclear how to determine when a novel pair is "close enough" to be considered unorderable.

We argue that this situation calls for a model of *just noticeable difference* among attributes. Just noticeable difference (JND) is a concept from psychophysics. It refers to the amount a stimulus has to be changed in order for it to be detectable by human observers at least half the time. For example, JND is of interest in color perception (which light sources are perceived as the same color?) and image quality assessment (up to what level of compression do the images look ok?). JNDs are determined empirically through tests of human perception. For example, JND in color can be determined by gradually altering the light source just until the human subject detects that the color has changed [21].

Why is it challenging to develop a computational model of JND for relative attributes? At a glance, one might think it amounts to learning an optimal threshold on the difference of predicted attribute strengths. However, this begs the question of how one might properly and densely sample real images of a complex attribute (like *seriousness*) to gradually walk along the spectrum, so as to discover the right threshold with human input. More importantly, an attribute space need not be *uniform*. That is, depending on where we look in the feature space, the magnitude of attribute difference required to register a perceptible change may vary. Therefore, the simplistic "global threshold" idea falls short. Analogous issues also arise in color spaces, e.g., the famous MacAdam ellipses spanning indistinguishable colors in the CIE x, y color space vary markedly in their size and orientation depending on where in the feature space one looks (leading to the crafting of color spaces like CIE Lab that are more uniform). See Fig. 6.10.

We next introduce a solution to infer when two images are indistinguishable for a given attribute. Continuing with the theme of local learning, we develop a Bayesian approach that relies on *local* statistics of orderability. Our approach leverages both a low-level visual descriptor space, within which image pair proximity is learned, as well as a mid-level visual attribute space, within which attribute distinguishability is represented (Fig. 6.11). Whereas past ranking models have attempted to integrate equality into *training*, none attempt to distinguish between orderable and unorderable pairs at test time.

Our method works as follows. First, we construct a predicted attribute space using the standard relative attribute framework (Sect. 6.3). Then, on top of that model, we combine a likelihood computed in the predicted attribute space (Sect. 6.5.1.1) with a

[5]Empirically, we found the inclusion of unordered pairs during training in [43] to have negligible impact at test time.

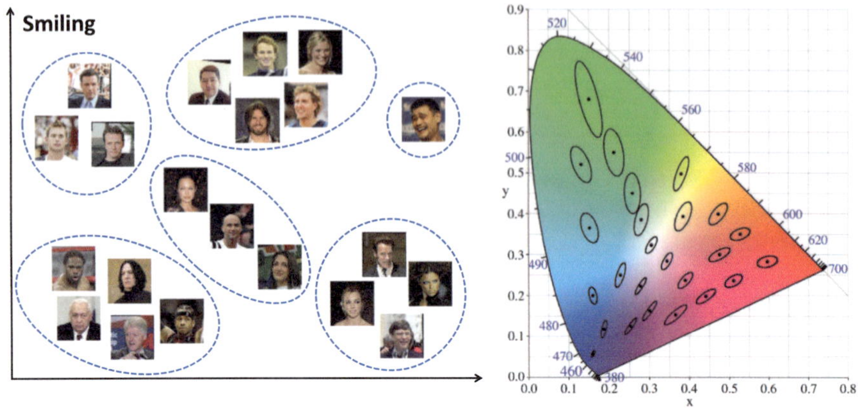

Fig. 6.10 Analogous to the MacAdam ellipses in the CIE x, y color space (*right*) [21], relative attribute space is likely not uniform (*left*). That is, the regions within which attribute differences are indistinguishable may vary in size and orientation across the high-dimensional visual feature space. Here we see the faces within each "equally *smiling*" cluster exhibit varying qualities for differentiating smiles—such as age, gender, and visibility of the teeth—but are still difficult or impossible to order in terms of *smilingness*. As a result, simple metrics and thresholds on attribute differences are insufficient to detect just noticeable differences, as we will see in Sect. 6.5.2.2

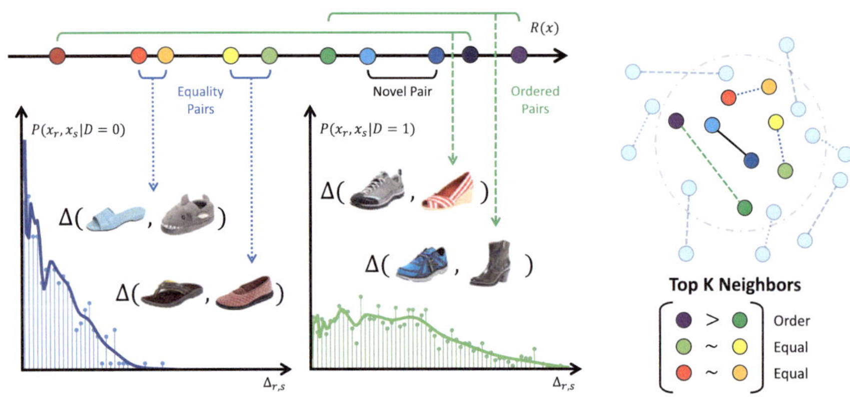

(a) Likelihood Term (b) Prior Term

Fig. 6.11 Overview of our Bayesian approach. (1) Learn a ranking function $R_{\mathcal{A}}$ using all annotated training pairs (Sect. 6.3), as depicted in Fig. 6.3. (2) Estimate the likelihood densities of the equal and ordered pairs, respectively, using the pairwise distances in relative attribute space. (3) Determine the local prior by counting the labels of the analogous pairs in the image descriptor space. (4) Combine the results to predict whether the novel pair is distinguishable (not depicted). Best viewed in color

local prior computed in the original image feature space (Sect. 6.5.1.2). We show our approach's superior performance compared to various baselines for detecting noticeable differences, as well as demonstrate how attribute JND has potential benefits for an image search application (Sect. 6.5.2).

6.5.1 *Local Bayesian Model of Distinguishability*

The most straightforward approach to infer whether a novel image pair is distinguishable would be to impose a threshold on their rank differences, i.e., to predict "indistinguishable" if $|R_{\mathcal{A}}(x_r) - R_{\mathcal{A}}(x_s)| \leq \varepsilon$. The problem is that unless the rank space is uniform, a global threshold ε is inadequate. In other words, the rank margin for indistinguishable pairs need not be constant across the entire feature space. By testing multiple variants of this basic idea, our empirical results confirm this is indeed an issue, as we will see in Sect. 6.5.2.

Our key insight is to formulate distinguishability prediction in a probabilistic, local learning manner. Mindful of the nonuniformity of relative attribute space, our approach uses distributions tailored to the data in the proximity of a novel test pair. Furthermore, we treat the relative attribute ranks as an imperfect mid-level representation on top of which we can learn to target the actual (sparse) human judgments about distinguishability.

Let $D \in \{0, 1\}$ be a binary random variable representing the distinguishability of an image pair. For a distinguishable pair, $D = 1$. Given a novel test pair (x_r, x_s), we are interested in the posterior:

$$P(D|x_r, x_s) \propto P(x_r, x_s|D)P(D), \tag{6.7}$$

to estimate how likely two images are distinguishable. To make a hard decision we take the maximum a posteriori estimate over the two classes:

$$d^* = \arg\max_d P(D = d|x_r, x_s). \tag{6.8}$$

At test time, our method performs a two-stage cascade. If the test pair appears distinguishable, we return the response "more" or "less" according to whether $R_{\mathcal{A}}(x_r) < R_{\mathcal{A}}(x_s)$ (where R is trained in either a global or local manner). Otherwise, we say the test pair is indistinguishable. In this way we unify relative attributes with JND, generating partially ordered predictions in spite of the ranker's inherent totally ordered outputs.

Next, we derive models for the likelihood and prior in Eq. 6.7, accounting for the challenges described above.

6.5.1.1 Likelihood Model

We use a kernel density estimator (KDE) to represent the distinguishability likelihood over image pairs. The likelihood captures the link between the observed rank differences and the human-judged just noticeable differences.

Let $\Delta_{r,s}$ denote the difference in attribute ranks for images r and s:

$$\Delta_{r,s} = |R_{\mathcal{A}}(x_r) - R_{\mathcal{A}}(x_s)|. \tag{6.9}$$

Recall that $\mathcal{P}_o$ and $\mathcal{P}_e$ refer to the sets of ordered and equal training image pairs, respectively. We compute the rank differences for all training pairs in $\mathcal{P}_o$ and $\mathcal{P}_e$, and fit a nonparametric Parzen density:

$$P(x_r, x_s|D) = \frac{1}{|\mathcal{P}|} \sum_{i,j \in \mathcal{P}} K_h \left(\Delta_{i,j} - \Delta_{r,s} \right), \tag{6.10}$$

for each set in turn. Here $\mathcal{P}$ refers to the ordered pairs $\mathcal{P}_o$ when representing distinguishability ($D = 1$), and the equal pairs $\mathcal{P}_e$ when representing indistinguishability ($D = 0$). The Parzen density estimator [44] superimposes a kernel function K_h at each data pair. In our implementation, we use Gaussian kernels. It integrates local estimates of the distribution and resists overfitting. The KDE has a smoothing parameter h that controls the model complexity. To ensure that all density is contained within the positive absolute margins, we apply a positive support to the estimator. Namely, we transform $\Delta_{i,j}$ using a log function, estimate the density of the transformed values, and then transform back to the original scale. See (a) in Fig. 6.11.

The likelihood reflects how well the equal and ordered pairs are separated in the attribute space. However, critically, $P(x_r, x_s|D = 1)$ need not decrease monotonically as a function of rank differences. In other words, the model permits returning a higher likelihood for certain pairs separated by smaller margins. This is a direct consequence of our choice of the nonparametric KDE, which preserves local models of the original training data. This is valuable for our problem setting because in principle it means our method can correct imperfections in the original learned ranks and account for the nonuniformity of the space.

6.5.1.2 Prior Model

Finally, we need to represent the prior over distinguishability. The prior could simply count the training pairs, i.e., let $P(D = 1)$ be the fraction of all training pairs that were distinguishable. However, we again aim to account for the nonuniformity of the visual feature space. Thus, we estimate the prior based only on a subset of data near the input images. Intuitively, this achieves a simple prior for the label distribution in multiple pockets of the feature space:

$$P(D = 1) = \frac{1}{K} |\mathcal{P}'_o|, \tag{6.11}$$

where $\mathcal{P}'_o \subset \mathcal{P}_o$ denotes the set of K neighboring ordered training pairs. $P(D = 0)$ is defined similarly for the indistinguishable pairs $\mathcal{P}_e$. Note that while the likelihood is computed over the pair's rank difference, the locality of the prior is with respect to the image descriptor space. See (b) in Fig. 6.11.

To localize the relevant pocket of the image space, we adopt the metric learning strategy detailed in Sect. 6.4.2. Using the learned metric, pairs analogous to the novel input (x_r, x_s) are retrieved based on a product of their individual Mahalanobis distances, so as to find pairs whose members both align.

6.5.2 Experiments and Results

We present results on the core JND detection task (Sect. 6.5.2.2) on two challenging datasets and demonstrate its impact for an image search application (Sect. 6.5.2.3).

6.5.2.1 Experimental Setup

Datasets and Ground Truth Our task requires attribute datasets that (1) have instance-level relative supervision, meaning annotators were asked to judge attribute comparisons on individual pairs of images, not object categories as a whole and (2) have pairs labeled as "equal" and "more/less." To our knowledge, our UT-Zap50K and LFW-10 [47] are the only existing datasets satisfying those conditions.

To train and evaluate just noticeable differences, we must have annotations of utmost precision. Therefore, we take extra care in establishing the (in)distinguishable ground truth for both datasets. We perform preprocessing steps to discard unreliable pairs, as we explain next. This decreases the total volume of available data, but it is essential to have trustworthy results.

The **UT-Zap50K** dataset is detailed in Sect. 6.4.3. As ordered pairs $\mathcal{P}_o$, we use all coarse and fine-grained pairs for which all 5 workers agreed and had high confidence. Even though the fine-grained pairs might be visually similar, if all 5 workers could come to agreement with high confidence, then the images are most likely distinguishable. As equal pairs $\mathcal{P}_e$, we use all fine-grained pairs with 3 or 4 workers in agreement and only medium confidence. Since the fine-grained pairs have already been presented to the workers twice, if the workers are still unable to come to an consensus with high confidence, then the images are most likely indistinguishable. The resulting dataset has 4,778 total annotated pairs, consisting of on average 800 ordered and 350 indistinguishable (equal) pairs per attribute.

The **LFW-10** dataset [47] consists of 2,000 face images, taken from the Labeled Faces in the Wild [26] dataset.[6] It contains 10 relative attributes, like *smiling*, *big eyes*, etc., with 1,000 labeled pairs each. Each pair was labeled by 5 people. As ordered pairs $\mathcal{P}_o$, we use all pairs labeled "more" or "less" by at least 4 workers. As equal pairs $\mathcal{P}_e$, we use pairs where at least 4 workers said "equal", as well as pairs with the same number of "more" and "less" votes. The latter reflects that a split in decision signals indistinguishability. Due to the smaller scale of LFW-10, we could not perform as strict of a preprocessing step as in UT-Zap50K; requiring full agreement on ordered pairs would eliminate most of the labeled data. The resulting dataset has 5,543 total annotated pairs, on average 230 ordered and 320 indistinguishable pairs per attribute.

Baselines We are the first to address the attribute JND task. No prior methods infer indistinguishability at test time [32, 38, 43, 46, 47]. Therefore, we develop multiple baselines to compare to our approach:

---

[6] `cvit.iiit.ac.in/projects/relativeParts.`

- **Rank Margin**: Use the magnitude of $\Delta_{r,s}$ as a confidence measure that the pair r, s is distinguishable. This baseline assumes the learned rank function produces a uniform feature space, such that a *global threshold* on rank margins would be sufficient to identify indistinguishable pairs. To compute a hard decision for this method (for F1-scores), we threshold the Parzen window likelihood estimated from the training pairs by ε, the midpoint of the likelihood means.
- **Logistic Classifier** [32]: Train a logistic regression classifier to distinguish training pairs in $\mathcal{P}_o$ from those in $\mathcal{P}_e$, where the pairs are represented by their rank differences $\Delta_{i,j}$. To compute a hard decision, we threshold the posterior at 0.5. This is the method used in [32] to obtain a probabilistic measure of attribute equality. It is the closest attempt we can find in the literature to represent equality predictions, though the authors do not evaluate its accuracy. This baseline also maintains a global view of attribute space.
- **SVM Classifier**: Train a nonlinear SVM classifier with a RBF kernel to distinguish ordered and equal pairs. We encode pairs of images as single points by concatenating their image descriptors. To ensure symmetry, we include training instances with the two images in either order.[7]
- **Mean Shift**: Perform mean shift clustering on the predicted attribute scores $R_{\mathcal{A}}(x_i)$ for all training images. Images falling in the same cluster are deemed indistinguishable. Since mean shift clusters can vary in size, this baseline does *not* assume a uniform space. Though unlike our method, it fails to leverage distinguishability supervision as it processes the ranker outputs.

Implementation Details For UT-Zap50K, we use 960-dim GIST and 30-bin Lab color histograms as image descriptors. For LFW-10, they are 8,300-dim part-based features learned on top of dense SIFT bag of words features (provided by the authors). We reduce their dimensionality to 100 with PCA to prevent overfitting. The part-based features [47] isolate localized regions of the face (e.g., exposing cues specific to the eyes vs. hair). We experimented with both linear and RBF kernels for $R_{\mathcal{A}}$. Since initial results were similar, we use linear kernels for efficiency. We use Gaussian kernels for the Parzen windows. We set all hyperparameters (h for the KDE, bandwidth for Mean Shift, K for the prior) on held-out validation data. To maximize the use of training data, in all results below, we use leave-one-out evaluation and report results over 4 folds of random training–validation splits.

6.5.2.2 Just Noticeable Difference Detection

We evaluate just noticeable difference detection accuracy for all methods on both datasets. Figure 6.12 shows the precision–recall curves and ROC curves, where we pool the results from all 4 and 10 attributes in UT-Zap50K and LFW-10, respectively. Tables 6.4 and 6.5 report the summary F1-scores and standard deviations for each individual attribute. The F1-score is a useful summary statistic for our data due to

[7] We also implemented other encoding variants, such as taking the difference of the image descriptors or using the predicted attribute scores $R_{\mathcal{A}}(x_i)$ as features, and they performed similarly or worse.

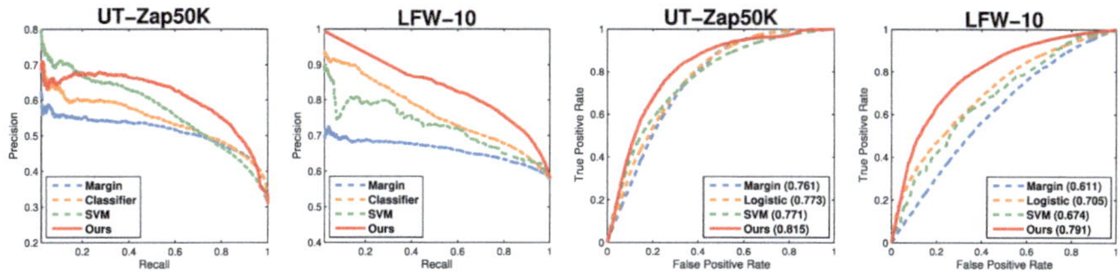

Fig. 6.12 Just noticeable difference detection accuracy for all attributes. We show the precision–recall (*top row*) and ROC curves (*bottom row*) for the shoes (*left*) and faces (*right*) datasets. Legends show AUC values for ROC curves. Note that the Mean Shift baseline does not appear here, since it does not produce confidence values

Table 6.4 JND detection on UT-Zap50K (F1 scores)

	Open	Pointy	Sporty	Comfort	All attributes
Margin	48.95	67.48	66.93	57.09	60.11 ± 1.89
Logistic	10.49	62.95	63.04	45.76	45.56 ± 4.13
SVM	48.82	50.97	47.60	40.12	46.88 ± 5.73
M. Shift	54.14	58.23	60.76	**61.60**	58.68 ± 8.01
Ours	**62.02**	**69.45**	**68.89**	54.63	$\mathbf{63.75 \pm 3.02}$

Table 6.5 JND detection on LFW-10 (F1 scores). NaN occurs when recall = 0 and precision = inf

	Bald	D.Hair	Eyes	GdLook	Masc.	Mouth
Margin	71.10	55.81	74.16	61.36	82.38	62.89
Logistic	75.77	53.26	86.71	64.27	87.29	63.41
SVM	79.06	32.43	89.70	70.98	87.35	70.27
M. Shift	66.37	56.69	54.50	51.29	69.73	68.38
Ours	**81.75**	**69.03**	**89.59**	**75.79**	**89.86**	**72.69**

	Smile	Teeth	F.Head	Young	All attributes	
Margin	60.56	65.26	67.49	**34.20**	63.52 ± 2.67	
Logistic	59.66	64.83	75.00	NaN	63.02 ± 1.84	
SVM	55.01	39.09	79.74	NaN	60.36 ± 9.81	
M. Shift	61.34	65.73	73.99	23.19	59.12 ± 10.51	
Ours	**73.30**	**74.80**	**80.49**	32.89	$\mathbf{74.02 \pm 1.66}$	

the unbalanced nature of the test set: 25 % of the shoe pairs and 80 % of the face pairs are indistinguishable for some attribute.

Overall, our method outperforms all baselines. We obtain sizeable gains—roughly 4–18 % on UT-Zap50K and 10–15 % on LFW-10. This clearly demonstrates the advantages of our local learning approach, which accounts for the nonuniformity of attribute space. The "global approaches," Rank Margin and Logistic Classifier, reveal that a uniform mapping of the relative attribute predictions is insufficient. In spite of the fact that they include equal pairs during training, simply assigning similar scores to indistinguishable pairs is inadequate. Their weakness is likely due both to noise in those mid-level predictions as well as the existence of JND regions that vary in scale. Furthermore, the results show that even for challenging, realistic image data, we can identify just noticeable differences at a high precision and recall, up to nearly 90 % in some cases.

The SVM baseline is much weaker than our approach, indicating that discriminatively learning what indistinguishable image pairs look like is insufficient. This result underscores the difficulty of learning subtle differences in a high-dimensional image descriptor space, and supports our use of the compact rank space for our likelihood model.

Looking at the per attribute results (Tables 6.4 and 6.5), we see that our method also outperforms the Mean Shift baseline. While Mean Shift captures dominant clusters in the spectrum of predicted attribute ranks for certain attributes, for others (like *pointy* or *masculine*) we find that the distribution of output predictions are more evenly spread. Despite the fact that the rankers are optimized to minimize margins for equal pairs, simple post-processing of their outputs is inadequate.

We also see that that our method is nearly always best, except for two attributes: *comfort* in UT-Zap50K and *young* in LFW-10. Of the shoe attributes, *comfort* is perhaps the most subjective; we suspect that all methods may have suffered due to label noise for that attribute. While *young* would not appear to be subjective, it is clearly a more difficult attribute to learn. This makes sense, as youth would be a function of multiple subtle visual cues like face shape, skin texture, hair color, etc., whereas something like *baldness* or *smiling* has a better visual focus captured well by the part features of [47]. Indeed, upon inspection we find that the likelihoods insufficiently separate the equal and distinguishable pairs. For similar reasons, the Logistic Classifier baseline [32] fails dramatically on both *open* and *young*.

Figure 6.13 shows qualitative prediction examples. Here we see the subtleties of JND. Whereas past methods would be artificially forced to make a comparison for the left panel of image pairs, our method declares them indistinguishable. Pairs may look very different overall (e.g., different hair, race, headgear) yet still be indistinguishable *in the context of a specific attribute*. Meanwhile, those that are distinguishable (right panel) may have only subtle differences.

Figure 6.14 illustrates examples of just noticeable difference "trajectories" computed by our method. We see how our method can correctly predict that various instances are indistinguishable, even though the raw images can be quite diverse (e.g., a strappy sandal and a flat dress shoe are equally *sporty*). Similarly, it can detect a difference even when the image pair is fairly similar (e.g., a lace-up sneaker and smooth-front sneaker are distinguishable for *openness* even though the shapes are close) (Fig. 6.15).

Figure 6.16 displays 2D t-SNE [40] embeddings for a subset of 5,000 shoe images based on the original image feature space and our learned attribute space for the attribute *pointy*. To compute the embeddings for our method, we represent each image x_i by its posterior probabilities of being indistinguishable to every other image. i.e., $v(x_i) = [P(D = 0|x_i, x_1), P(D = 0|x_i, x_2), ..., P(D = 0|x_i, x_N)]$ where N is

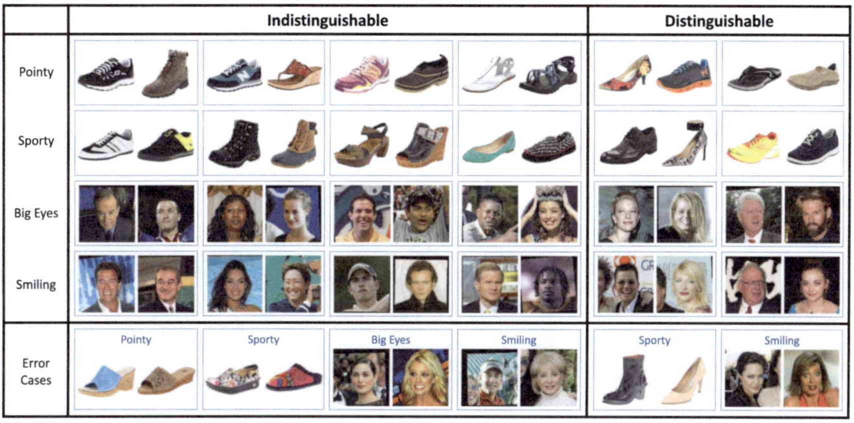

Fig. 6.13 Example predictions. The *top four rows* are pairs our method correctly classifies as indistinguishable (*left panel*) and distinguishable (*right panel*), whereas the Rank Margin baseline fails. Each row shows pairs for a particular attribute. The *bottom row* shows failure cases by our method; i.e., the *bottom left pair* is indistinguishable for pointiness, but we predict distinguishable

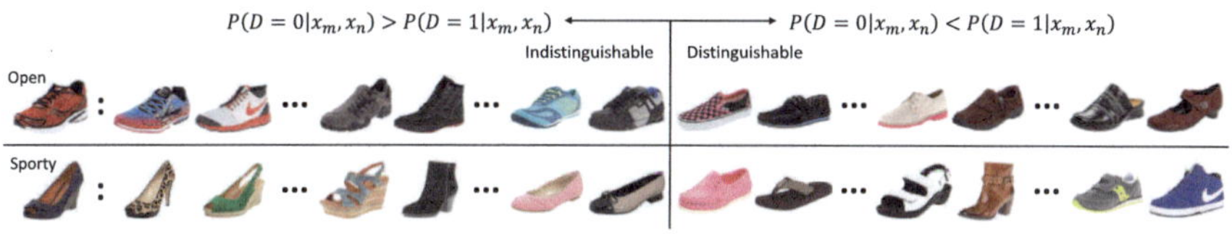

Fig. 6.14 Example just noticeable differences. In each row, we take *leftmost* image as a starting point, then walk through nearest neighbors in relative attribute space until we hit an image that is distinguishable, as predicted by our method. For example, in row 2, our method finds the *left block* of images to be indistinguishable for *sportiness*; it flags the transition from the flat dress shoe to the *pink* "loafer-like sneaker" as being a noticeable difference

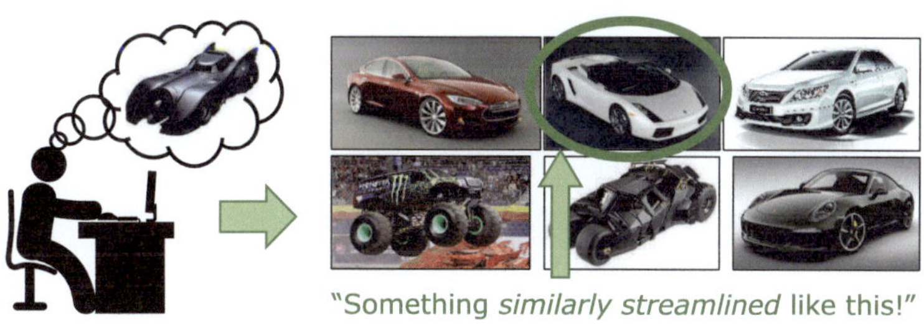

Fig. 6.15 The modified WhittleSearch framework. The user can now express an "equality" feedback, speeding up the process of finding his envisioned target

the total number of images in the embedding. We see that while the former produces a rather evenly distributed mapping without distinct structures, the latter produces a mapping containing unique structures along with "pockets" of indistinguishable images. Such structures precisely reflect the nonuniformity we pointed out in Fig. 6.10.

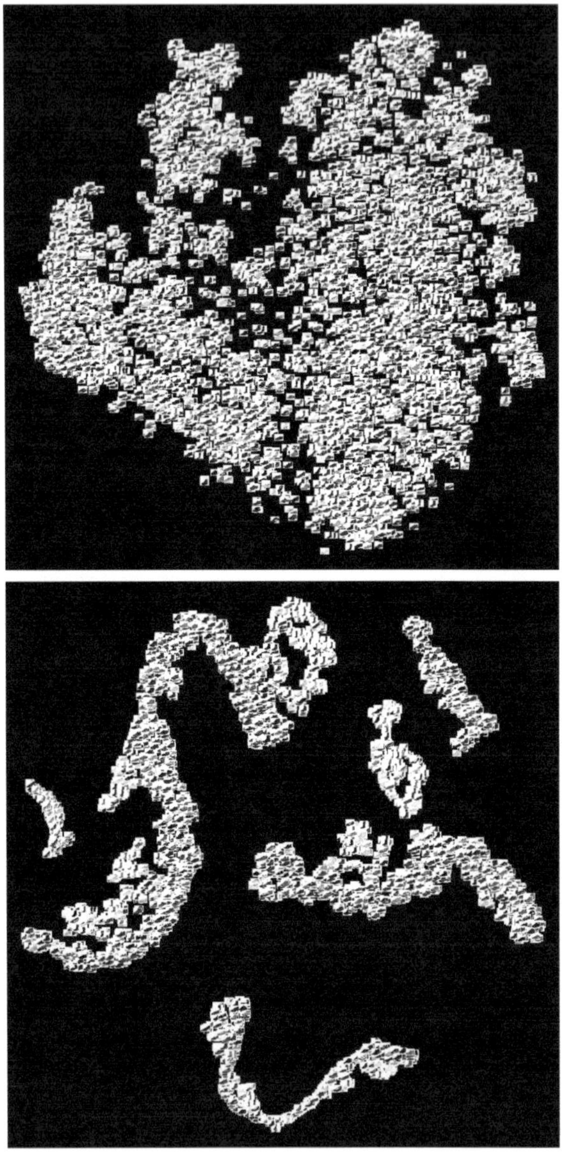

Fig. 6.16 t-SNE visualization of the original feature space (*top*) and our learned attribute space (*bottom*) for the attribute *pointy*. Shoes with similar level of *pointiness* are placed closer together in our learned space, forming loose "pockets" of indistinguishability. Best viewed on PDF

6.5.2.3 Image Search Application

Finally, we demonstrate how JND detection can enhance an image search application. Specifically, we incorporate our model into the WhittleSearch framework of Kovashka et al. [34], overviewed in Chap. 5 of this book. WhittleSearch is an interactive method that allows a user to provide relative attribute feedback, e.g., by telling the system that he wants images "more *sporty*" than some reference image.

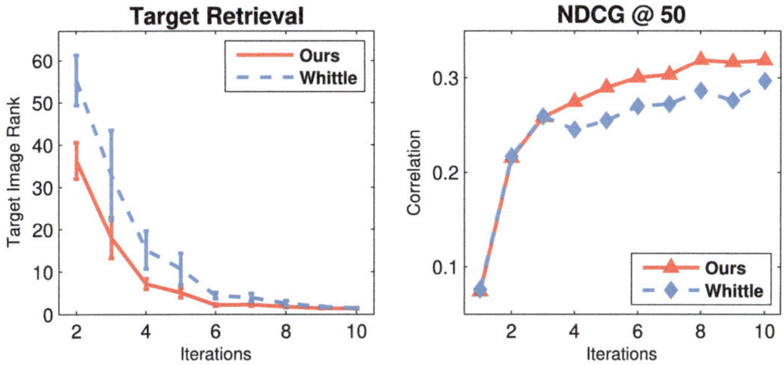

Fig. 6.17 Image search results. We enhance an existing relative attribute search technique called WhittleSearch [34] with our JND detection model. The resulting system finds target images more quickly (*left*) and produces a better overall ranking of the database images (*right*)

The method works by intersecting the relative attribute constraints, scoring database images by how many constraints they satisfy, then displaying the top scoring images for the user to review. See [34] for details.

We augment that pipeline such that the user can express not only "more/less" preferences, but also "equal" preferences (Fig. 6.15). For example, the user can now say, "I want images that are equally *sporty* as image x." Intuitively, enriching the feedback in this manner should help the user more quickly zero in on relevant images that match his envisioned target. To test this idea, we mimic the method and experimental setup of [34] as closely as possible, including their feedback generation simulator.

We evaluate a proof-of-concept experiment on UT-Zap50K, which is large enough to allow us to sequester disjoint data splits for training our method and performing the searches (LFW-10 is too small). We select 200 images at random to serve as the mental targets a user wants to find in the database, and reserve 5,000 images for the database. The user is shown 16 reference images and expresses 8 feedback constraints per iteration.

Figure 6.17 shows the results. Following [34], we measure the relevance rank of the target as a function of feedback iterations (left, lower is better), as well as the similarity of all top-ranked results compared to the target (right, higher is better). We see that JNDs substantially bolster the search task. In short, the user gets to the target in fewer iterations because he has a more complete way to express his preferences—*and* the system understands what "equally" means in terms of attribute perception.

6.6 Discussion

Our results show the promise of local models for addressing fine-grained visual comparisons. We saw how concentrating on the most closely related training instances is valuable for isolating the precise visual features responsible for the subtle distinctions. Our methods expand the viability of local learning beyond traditional classification tasks to include ranking. Furthermore, in an initial step toward eliminating the assumption of locality as the only relevant factor in local learning, we introduced a novel approach to learn the composition and size of the most effective neighborhood conditioned on the novel test input. Finally, we explored how local statistical models can address the "just noticeable difference" problem in attributes, successfully accounting for the nonuniformity of indistinguishable pairs in the feature space.

There are several interesting considerations worthy of further discussion and new research.

While global rankers produce comparable values for all test pairs, our local ranking method's predictions (Sect. 6.4) are test pair specific. This is exactly what helps accuracy for subtle, fine-grained comparisons, and, to some extent, mitigates the impact of inconsistent training comparisons. However, in some applications, it may be necessary to produce a full ordering of many images. In that case, one could try feeding our method's predictions to a rank aggregation technique [12], or apply a second layer of learning to normalize them, as in [11, 14, 38].

One might wonder if we could do as well by training one global ranking function per category within a domain—i.e., one for high heels, one for sneakers, etc. This would be another local learning strategy, but it appears much too restrictive. First of all, it would require category-labeled examples (in addition to the orderings $\mathcal{P}_{\mathcal{A}}$), which may be expensive to obtain or simply not apropos for data lacking clear-cut category boundaries (e.g., is the storefront image an "inside city scene" or a "street scene"?). Furthermore, it would not permit cross-category comparison predictions; we want to be able to predict how images from different categories compare in their attributes, too.

As discussed in Sect. 6.4.4.4, straightforward implementations of lazy local learning come with noticeable runtime costs. In our approach, the main online costs are nearest neighbor search and rank function training. While still only seconds per test case, as larger labeled datasets become available these costs would need to be countered with more sophisticated (and possibly approximate) nearest neighbor search data structures, such as hashing or kd-trees. Another idea is to cache a set of representative models, precomputing offline a model for each prototypical type of new input pair. Such an implementation could also be done in a hierarchical way, letting the system discover a fine-grained model in a coarse to fine manner.

An alternative approach to represent partial orders (and thus accommodate indistinguishable pairs) would be ordinal regression, where training data would consist of ordered equivalence classes of data. However, ordinal regression has severe shortcomings for our problem setting. First, it requires a consistent ordering of all training data (via the equivalence classes). This is less convenient for human annotators and more challenging to scale than the distributed approach offered by learning to rank, which pools any available paired comparisons. For similar reasons, learning to rank is much better suited to crowdsourcing annotations and learning universal (as opposed to person-specific [1, 10], see Chap. 5) predictors. Finally, ordinal regression requires committing to a fixed number of buckets. This makes incremental supervision updates problematic. Furthermore, to represent very subtle differences, the number of buckets would need to be quite large.

Our work offers a way to learn a computational model for just noticeable differences. While we borrow the term JND from psychophysics to motivate our task, of course the analogy is not 100 % faithful. In particular, psychophysical experiments to elicit JND often permit systematically varying a perceptual signal until a human detects a change, e.g., a color light source, a sound wave amplitude, or a compression factor. In contrast, the space of all visual attribute instantiations does not permit such a simple generative sampling. Instead, our method extrapolates from relatively few human-provided comparisons (fewer than 1,000 per attribute in our experiments) to obtain a statistical model for distinguishability, which generalizes to novel pairs based on their visual properties. It remains interesting future work to explore the possibility of generative models for comparative attribute relationships.

Just noticeable difference models—and fine-grained attributes in general—appear most relevant for *domain-specific* attributes. Within a domain (e.g., faces, cars, handbags, etc.), attributes describe fine-grained properties, and it is valuable to represent any perceptible differences (or realize there are none). In contrast, comparative questions about very unrelated things or extra-domain attributes can be nonsensical. For example, do we need to model whether the shoes and the table are *equally ornate*? or whether the dog or the towel is *more fluffy*? Accordingly, we focused our experiments on domains with rich vocabularies of fine-grained attributes, faces and shoes.

Finally, we note that fine-grained differences, as addressed in this chapter, are a separate problem from *subjective* attributes. That is, our methods address the problem where there may be a subtle distinction, yet the distinction is noncontroversial. Other work considers ways in which to personalize attribute models [31, 33] or discover which are subjective properties [13] see Chap. 5). It would be interesting to investigate problems where both subjectivity and fine-grained distinctions interact.

6.7 Conclusion

Fine-grained visual comparisons have many compelling applications, yet traditional global learning methods can fail to capture their subtleties. We proposed several local learning to rank approaches based on analogous training comparisons, and we introduced a new dataset specialized to the problem. On multiple attribute datasets, we find our ideas improve the state of the art.

Acknowledgements We thank Mark Stephenson for his help creating the UT-Zap50K dataset, Naga Sandeep for providing the part-based features for LFW-10, and Ashish Kapoor for helpful discussions. This research is supported in part by NSF IIS-1065390 and ONR YIP Award N00014-12-1-0754.

References

1. Altwaijry, H., Belongie, S.: Relative ranking of facial attractiveness. In: Winter Conference on Applications of Computer Vision (WACV) (2012)
2. Atkeson, C., Moore, A., Schaal, S.: Locally weighted learning. AI Rev. **11**(1), 11–73 (1997)
3. Banerjee, S., Dubey, A., Machchhar, J., Chakrabarti, S.: Efficient and accurate local learning for ranking. In: ACM SIGIR Workshop on Learning to Rank for Information Retrieval (2009)
4. Bellet, A., Habrard, A., Sebban, M.: A survey on metric learning for feature vectors and structured data. Technical report, University of Southern California (2013)
5. Berg, T.L., Berg, A.C., Shih, J.: Automatic attribute discovery and characterization from noisy web data. In: European Conference on Computer Vision (ECCV) (2010)
6. Biswas, A., Parikh, D.: Simultaneous active learning of classifiers and attributes via relative feedback. In: Conference on Computer Vision and Pattern Recognition (CVPR) (2013)
7. Bottou, L., Vapnik, V.: Local learning algorithms. Neural Comput. **4**(6), 888–900 (1992)
8. Boutilier, C.: Preference elicitation and preference learning in social choice. In: Integration of AI and OR Techniques in Constraint Programming for Combinatorial Optimization Problems. Springer (2011)
9. Branson, S., Wah, C., Schroff, F., Babenko, B., Welinder, P., Perona, P., Belongie, S.: Visual recognition with humans in the loop. In: European Conference on Computer Vision (ECCV) (2010)
10. Cao, C., Kwak, I., Belongie, S., Kriegman, D., Ai, H.: Adaptive ranking of facial attractiveness. In: International Conference on Multimedia and Expo (ICME) (2014)
11. Chen, K., Gong, S., Xiang, T., Loy, C.: Cumulative attribute space for age and crowd density estimation. In: Conference on Computer Vision and Pattern Recognition (CVPR) (2013)
12. Conitzer, V., Davenport, A., Kalagnanam, J.: Improved bounds for computing Kemeny rankings. In: Conference on Artificial Intelligence (AAAI) (2006)
13. Curran, W., Moore, T., Kulesza, T., Wong, W., Todorovic, S., Stumpf, S., White, R., Burnett, M.: Towards recognizing "cool": can end users help computer vision recognize subjective attributes or objects in images? In: ACM Conference on Intelligent User Interfaces (2012)
14. Datta, A., Feris, R., Vaquero, D.: Hierarchical ranking of facial attributes. In: International Conference on Automatic Face and Gesture Recognition (FG) (2011)
15. Davis, J.V., Kulis, B., Jain, P., Sra, S., Dhillon, I.: Information-theoretic metric learning. In: International Conference on Machine Learning (ICML) (2007)
16. Domeniconi, C., Gunopulos, D.: Adaptive nearest neighbor classification using support vector machines. In: Conference on Neural Information Processing Systems (NIPS) (2001)
17. Duh, K., Kirchhoff, K.: Learning to rank with partially-labeled data. In: ACM SIGIR Conference on Research and Development in Information Retrieval (2008)
18. Fan, Q., Gabbur, P., Pankanti, S.: Relative attributes for large-scale abandoned object detection. In: International Conference on Computer Vision (ICCV) (2013)
19. Farhadi, A., Endres, I., Hoiem, D., Forsyth, D.: Describing objects by their attributes. In: Conference on Computer Vision and Pattern Recognition (CVPR) (2009)
20. Farrell, R., Oza, O., Zhang, N., Morariu, V., Darrell, T., Davis, L.: Birdlets: Subordinate categorization using volumetric primitives and pose-normalized appearance. In: International Conference on Computer Vision (ICCV) (2011)
21. Forsyth, D., Ponce, J.: Computer Vision: A Modern Approach. Prentice Hall (2002)
22. Frome, A., Singer, Y., Malik, J.: Image retrieval and classification using local distance functions. In: Conference on Neural Information Processing Systems (NIPS) (2006)
23. Frome, A., Singer, Y., Sha, F., Malik, J.: Learning globally-consistent local distance functions for shape-based image retrieval and classification. In: International Conference on Computer Vision (ICCV) (2007)
24. Geng, X., Liu, T., Qin, T., Arnold, A., Li, H., Shum, H.: Query dependent ranking using K-nearest neighbor. In: ACM SIGIR Conference on Research and Development in Information Retrieval (2008)

25. Hastie, T., Tibshirani, R.: Discriminant adaptive nearest neighbor classification. IEEE Trans. Pattern Anal. Mach. Intell. (PAMI) **18**(6), 607–616 (1996)
26. Huang, G.B., Ramesh, M., Berg, T., Learned-Miller, E.: Labeled faces in the wild: a database for studying face recognition in unconstrained environments. Technical report, University of Massachusetts, Amherst (2007)
27. Jain, P., Kulis, B., Grauman, K.: Fast image search for learned metrics. In: Conference on Computer Vision and Pattern Recognition (CVPR) (2008)
28. Jiang, X., Lim, L., Yao, Y., Ye, Y.: Statistical ranking and combinatorial hodge theory. Math. Program. **127**(1), 203–244 (2011)
29. Joachims, T.: Optimizing search engines using clickthrough data. In: Knowledge Discovery in Databases (PKDD) (2002)
30. Kapoor, A., Jain, P., Viswanathan, R.: Multilabel classification using Bayesian compressed sensing. In: Conference on Neural Information Processing Systems (NIPS) (2012)
31. Kovashka, A., Grauman, K.: Attribute adaptation for personalized image search. In: International Conference on Computer Vision (ICCV) (2013)
32. Kovashka, A., Grauman, K.: Attribute pivots for guiding relevance feedback in image search. In: International Conference on Computer Vision (ICCV) (2013)
33. Kovashka, A., Grauman, K.: Discovering attribute shades of meaning with the crowd. Int. J. Comput. Vis. (IJCV) **114**(1), 56–73 (2015)
34. Kovashka, A., Parikh, D., Grauman, K.: WhittleSearch: Image search with relative attribute feedback. In: Conference on Computer Vision and Pattern Recognition (CVPR) (2012)
35. Kumar, N., Belhumeur, P., Nayar, S.: FaceTracer: A search engine for large collections of images with faces. In: European Conference on Computer Vision (ECCV) (2008)
36. Kumar, N., Berg, A., Belhumeur, P., Nayar, S.K.: Attribute and simile classifiers for face verification. In: International Conference on Computer Vision (ICCV) (2009)
37. Lampert, C., Nickisch, H., Harmeling, S.: Learning to detect unseen object classes by between-class attribute transfer. In: Conference on Computer Vision and Pattern Recognition (CVPR) (2009)
38. Li, S., Shan, S., Chen, X.: Relative forest for attribute prediction. In: Asian Conference on Computer Vision (ACCV) (2012)
39. Lin, H., Yu, C., Chen, H.: Query-dependent rank aggregation with local models. In: Asia Information Retrieval Societies Conference (AIRS) (2011)
40. Maaten, L., Hinton, G.: Visualizing high-dimensional data using t-SNE. J. Mach. Learn. Res. (JMLR) **9**, 2579–2605 (2008)
41. Matthews, T., Nixon, M., Niranjan, M.: Enriching texture analysis with semantic data. In: Conference on Computer Vision and Pattern Recognition (CVPR) (2013)
42. Oliva, A., Torralba, A.: Modeling the shape of the scene: a holistic representation of the spatial envelope. Int. J. Comput. Vis. (IJCV) **42**(3), 145–175 (2001)
43. Parikh, D., Grauman, K.: Relative attributes. In: International Conference on Computer Vision (ICCV) (2011)
44. Parzen, E.: On estimation of a probability density function and mode. Annu. Math. Stat. **33**(3), 1065–1076 (1962)
45. Reid, D., Nixon, M.: Soft biometrics; human identification using comparative descriptions. IEEE Trans. Pattern Anal. Mach. Intell. (PAMI) **36**(6), 1216–1228 (2014)
46. Sadovnik, A., Gallagher, A., Parikh, D., Chen, T.: Spoken attributes: mixing binary and relative attributes to say the right thing. In: International Conference on Computer Vision (ICCV) (2013)
47. Sandeep, R., Verma, Y., Jawahar, C.: Relative parts: distinctive parts for learning relative attributes. In: Conference on Computer Vision and Pattern Recognition (CVPR) (2014)
48. Scheirer, W., Kumar, N., Belhumeur, P., Boult, T.: Multi-attribute spaces: calibration for attribute fusion and similarity search. In: Conference on Computer Vision and Pattern Recognition (CVPR) (2012)
49. Shrivastava, A., Singh, S., Gupta, A.: Constrained semi-supervised learning using attributes and comparative attributes. In: European Conference on Computer Vision (ECCV) (2012)

50. Siddiquie, B., Feris, R., Davis, L.: Image ranking and retrieval based on multi-attribute queries. In: Conference on Computer Vision and Pattern Recognition (CVPR) (2011)
51. Vincent, P., Bengio, Y.: K-Local hyperplane and convex distance nearest neighbor algorithms. In: Conference on Neural Information Processing Systems (NIPS) (2001)
52. Weinberger, K., Saul, L.: Distance metric learning for large margin nearest neighbor classification. J. Mach. Learn. Res. (JMLR) **10**, 207–244 (2009)
53. Yang, L., Jin, R., Sukthankar, R., Liu, Y.: An efficent algorithm for local distance metric learning. In: Conference on Artificial Intelligence (AAAI) (2006)
54. Yu, A., Grauman, K.: Fine-grained visual comparisons with local learning. In: Conference on Computer Vision and Pattern Recognition (CVPR) (2014)
55. Yu, A., Grauman, K.: Predicting useful neighborhoods for lazy local learning. In: Conference on Neural Information Processing Systems (NIPS) (2014)
56. Yu, A., Grauman, K.: Just noticeable differences in visual attributes. In: International Conference on Computer Vision (ICCV) (2015)
57. Zhang, H., Berg, A., Maire, M., Malik, J.: SVM-KNN: Discriminative nearest neighbor classification for visual category recognition. In: Conference on Computer Vision and Pattern Recognition (CVPR) (2006)

Chapter 7
Localizing and Visualizing Relative Attributes

Fanyi Xiao and Yong Jae Lee

Abstract In this chapter, we present a weakly supervised approach that discovers the spatial extent of relative attributes, given only pairs of ordered images. In contrast to traditional approaches that use global appearance features or rely on keypoint detectors, our goal is to automatically discover the image regions that are relevant to the attribute, even when the attribute's appearance changes drastically across its attribute spectrum. To accomplish this, we first develop a novel formulation that combines a detector with local smoothness to discover a set of coherent *visual chains* across the image collection. We then introduce an efficient way to generate additional chains anchored on the initial discovered ones. Finally, we automatically identify the visual chains that are most relevant to the attribute (those whose appearance has high correlation with attribute strength), and create an ensemble image representation to model the attribute. Through extensive experiments, we demonstrate our method's promise relative to several baselines in modeling relative attributes.

7.1 Introduction

Visual attributes are human-nameable object properties that serve as an intermediate representation between low-level image features and high-level objects or scenes [9, 10, 17, 21, 24, 31, 33, 34]. They yield various useful applications including describing an unfamiliar object, retrieving images based on mid-level properties, "zero-shot" learning [24, 30, 31], and human–computer interaction [4, 5]. Researchers have developed systems that model binary attributes [10, 21, 24]—a property's presence/absence (e.g., "is furry/not furry")—and relative attributes [31, 35, 36]—a property's relative strength (e.g., "furrier than").

While most existing computer vision algorithms use global image representations to model attributes (e.g., [24, 31]), we humans, arguably, exploit the benefits

F. Xiao (✉) · Y.J. Lee
University of California Davis, Davis, USA
e-mail: fanyix@cs.ucdavis.edu

Y.J. Lee
e-mail: yjlee@cs.ucdavis.edu

R.S. Feris et al. (eds.), *Visual Attributes*, Advances in Computer Vision and Pattern Recognition, DOI 10.1007/978-3-319-50077-5_7

Fig. 7.1 The *spatial extent* of an attribute consists of the image regions that are most relevant to the existence/strength of the attribute. Thus, an algorithm that can automatically identify the spatial extent of an attribute will be able to more accurately model it

of localizing the relevant image regions pertaining to each attribute (see Fig. 7.1). Indeed, recent work demonstrates the effectiveness of using localized part-based representations [3, 35, 45]. They show that attributes—be it global ("is male") or local ("smiling")—can be more accurately learned by first bringing the underlying object-parts into correspondence, and then modeling the attributes conditioned on those object-parts. For example, the attribute "wears glasses" can be more easily learned when people's faces are in correspondence. To compute such correspondences, pre-trained part detectors are used (e.g., faces [35] and people [3, 45]). However, because the part detectors are trained independently of the attribute, the learned parts may not necessarily be useful for modeling the desired attribute. Furthermore, some objects do not naturally have well-defined parts, which means modeling the part-based detector itself becomes a challenge.

The method in [7] addresses these issues by *discovering* useful, localized attributes. A drawback is that the system requires a human-in-the-loop to verify whether each discovered attribute is meaningful, limiting its scalability. More importantly, the system is restricted to modeling binary attributes; however, relative attributes often describe object properties better than binary ones [31], especially if the property exhibits large appearance variations (see Fig. 7.2).

So, how can we develop robust visual representations for *relative attributes*, without expensive and potentially uninformative pretrained part detectors or humans-in-the-loop? To do so, we will need to automatically identify the visual patterns in each image whose appearance correlates with (i.e., changes as a function of) attribute strength. This is a challenging problem: as the strength of an attribute changes, the object's appearance can change drastically. For example, if the attribute describes

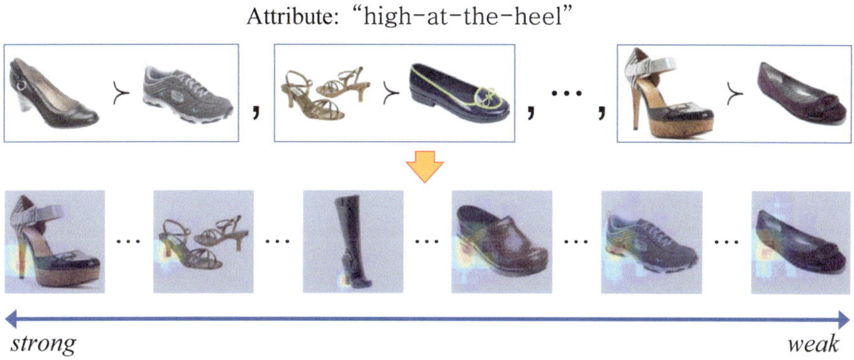

Fig. 7.2 (*top*) Given pairs of images, each ordered according to relative attribute strength (e.g., "higher/lower-at-the-heel"), (*bottom*) our approach automatically discovers the attribute's spatial extent in each image, and learns a ranking function that orders the image collection according to predicted attribute strength

how "high-heeled" a shoe is, then pumps and flats would be on opposite ends of the spectrum, and their heels would look completely different (see Fig. 7.2). Thus, identifying the visual patterns that characterize the attribute is very difficult without a priori knowledge of what a heel is. Moreover, it is even more difficult to do so given only samples of pairwise relative comparisons, which is the typical mode of relative attribute annotation.

In this chapter, we describe a method that automatically discovers the spatial extent of relative attributes in images across varying attribute strengths. The main idea is to leverage the fact that the visual concept underlying the attribute undergoes a *gradual change* in appearance across the attribute spectrum. In this way, we propose to discover a set of local, transitive connections ("visual chains") that establish correspondences between the same object-part, even when its appearance changes drastically over long ranges. Given the candidate set of visual chains, we then automatically select those that together best model the changing appearance of the attribute across the attribute spectrum. Importantly, by combining a subset of the most-informative discovered visual chains, our approach aims to discover the full spatial extent of the attribute, whether it be concentrated on a particular object-part or spread across a larger spatial area.

To our knowledge, no prior work discovers the spatial extent of attributes, given weakly supervised pairwise relative attribute annotations. Toward this goal, important novel components include: (1) a new formulation for discovery that uses both a detector term and a smoothness term to discover a set of coherent visual chains, (2) a simple but effective way of quickly generating new visual chains anchored on the existing discovered ones, and (3) a method to rank and combine a subset of the visual chains that together best capture the attribute. We apply our approach to three datasets of faces and shoes, and outperform state-of-the-art methods that use global image features or require stronger supervision. Furthermore, we demonstrate an application of our approach, in which we can edit an object's appearance conditioned on the discovered spatial extent of the attribute. This chapter expands upon our previous conference paper [43].

7.2 Related Work

In this section, we review related work in visual attributes and visual discovery.

7.2.1 Visual Attributes

Most existing work use global image representations to model attributes (e.g., [24, 31]). Others have demonstrated the effectiveness of *localized* representations. For example, the attribute "mouth open" can be more easily learned when people's mouths are localized. Early work showed how to localize simple color and shape attributes like "red" and "round" [12]. Recent approaches rely on pretrained face/body landmark or "poselet" detectors [3, 16, 20, 21, 45], crowd-sourcing [7], or assume that the images are well-aligned and object/scene-centric [2, 42], which either restricts their usage to specific domains or limits their scalability. Unlike these methods that try to localize *binary* attributes, we instead aim to discover the spatial extent of *relative* attributes, while forgoing any pretrained detector, crowd-sourcing, or object-centric assumptions.

While the "relative parts" approach of [35] shares our goal of localizing relative attributes, it uses strongly supervised pretrained facial landmark detectors, and is thus limited to modeling only facial attributes. Importantly, because the detectors are trained independently of the attribute, the detected landmarks may not necessarily be optimal for modeling the desired attribute. In contrast, our approach aims to directly localize the attribute without relying on pretrained detectors, and thus can be used to model attributes for any object.

7.2.2 Visual Discovery

Existing approaches discover object categories [8, 13, 29, 32, 38], low-level foreground features [27], or mid-level visual elements [6, 37]. Recent work shows how to discover visual elements whose appearance is correlated with time or space, given images that are time-/geo-stamped [26]. Algorithmically, this is the closest work to ours. However, our work is different in three important ways. First, the goal is different: we aim to discover visual chains whose appearance is correlated with *attribute strength*. Second, the form of supervision is different: we are given pairs of images that are ordered according to their relative attribute strength, so unlike [26], we must infer a global ordering of the images. Finally, we introduce a novel formulation and efficient inference procedure that exploits the local smoothness of the varying appearance of the attribute, which we show in Sect. 7.4.4 leads to more coherent discoveries.

7.3 Approach

Given an image collection $S=\{I_1, \ldots, I_N\}$ with pairwise ordered and unordered image-level relative comparisons of an attribute (i.e., in the form of $\Omega(I_i)>\Omega(I_j)$ and $\Omega(I_i)\approx\Omega(I_j)$, where $i, j\in\{1, \ldots, N\}$ and $\Omega(I_i)$ is I_i's attribute strength), our goal is to discover the spatial extent of the attribute in each image and learn a ranking function that predicts the attribute strength for any new image.

This is a challenging problem for two main reasons: (1) we are not provided with any localized examples of the attribute so we must automatically *discover* the relevant regions in each image that correspond to it and (2) the appearance of the attribute can change drastically over the attribute spectrum. To address these challenges, we exploit the fact that for many attributes, the appearance will change gradually across the attribute spectrum. To this end, we first discover a diverse set of candidate *visual chains*, each linking the patches (one from each image) whose appearance changes smoothly across the attribute spectrum. We then select among them the most relevant ones that agree with the provided relative attribute annotations.

There are three main steps to our approach: (1) initializing a candidate set of visual chains, (2) iteratively growing each visual chain along the attribute spectrum, and (3) ranking the chains according to their relevance to the target attribute to create an ensemble image representation. In the following, we describe each of these steps in turn.

7.3.1 *Initializing Candidate Visual Chains*

A visual attribute can potentially exhibit large appearance variations across the attribute spectrum. Take the *high-at-the-heel* attribute as an example: high-heeled shoes have strong vertical gradients while flat-heeled shoes have strong horizontal gradients. However, the attribute's appearance will be quite similar in any local region of the attribute spectrum. Therefore, to capture the attribute across its entire spectrum, we sort the image collection based on predicted attribute strength (we elaborate below), and generate candidate *visual chains* via iterative refinement; i.e., we start with short but visually homogeneous chains of image regions in a local region of the attribute spectrum, and smoothly grow them out to cover the entire spectrum. We generate multiple chains because (1) appearance similarity does not guarantee relevance to the attribute (e.g., a chain of blank white patches satisfies this property perfectly but provides no information about the attribute) and (2) some attributes are better described with multiple image regions (e.g., the attribute "eyes open" may better be described with two patches, one on each eye). We will describe how to select the relevant ones among the multiple candidate chains in Sect. 7.3.3.

We start by first sorting the images in S in descending order of predicted attribute strength—with $\tilde{I}_1$ as the strongest image and $\tilde{I}_N$ as the weakest—using a linear SVM-ranker [15] trained with global image features, as in [31]. To initialize a single chain, we take the top N_{init} images and select a set of patches (one from each image) whose appearance varies smoothly with its neighbors in the chain, by minimizing the following objective function:

$$\min_P C(P) = \sum_{i=2}^{N_{init}} ||\phi(P_i) - \phi(P_{i-1})||_2, \tag{7.1}$$

where $\phi(P_i)$ is the appearance feature of patch P_i in $\tilde{I}_i$, and $P = \{P_1, \ldots, P_{N_{init}}\}$ is the set of patches in a chain. Candidate patches for each image are densely sampled at multiple scales. This objective enforces *local smoothness*: the appearances of the patches in the images with neighboring indices should vary smoothly within a chain. Given the objective's chain structure, we can efficiently find its global optimum using Dynamic Programming (DP).

In the backtracking stage of DP, we obtain a large number of K-best solutions. We then perform a chain-level non-maximum-suppression (NMS) to remove redundant chains to retain a set of K_{init} diverse candidate chains. For NMS, we measure the distance between two chains as the sum of intersection-over-union scores for every pair of patches from the same image. This ensures that different initial chains not only contain different patches from any particular image, but also together spatially cover as much of each image as possible (see Fig. 7.3).

Note that our initialization procedure does not assume any global alignment across the images. Instead the chain alignment is achieved through appearance matching by solving Eq. 7.1.

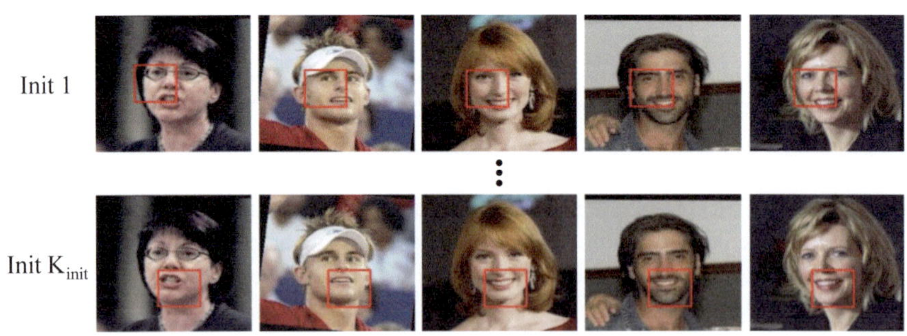

Fig. 7.3 Our initialization consists of a set of diverse visual chains, each varying smoothly in appearance

7.3.2 Iteratively Growing Each Visual Chain

The initial set of K_{init} chains are visually homogeneous but cover only a tiny fraction of the attribute spectrum. We next iteratively grow each chain to cover the entire attribute spectrum by training a model that adapts to the attribute's smoothly changing appearance. This idea is related to *self-paced learning* in the machine learning literature [1, 22], which has been applied to various computer vision tasks such as object discovery and tracking [26, 28, 39].

Specifically, for each chain, we iteratively train a detector and in each iteration use it to grow the chain while simultaneously refining it. To grow the chain, we again minimize Eq. 7.1 but now with an additional term:

$$\min_P C(P) = \sum_{i=2}^{t*N_{iter}} ||\phi(P_i) - \phi(P_{i-1})||_2 - \lambda \sum_{i=1}^{t*N_{iter}} \mathbf{w}_t^T \phi(P_i), \qquad (7.2)$$

where $\mathbf{w}_t$ is a linear SVM detector learned from the patches in the chain from the $(t-1)$-th iteration (for $t = 1$, we use the initial patches found in Sect. 7.3.1), $P = \{P_1, \ldots, P_{t*N_{iter}}\}$ is the set of patches in a chain, and N_{iter} is the number of images considered in each iteration (explained in detail below). As before, the first term enforces local smoothness. The second term is the *detection* term: since the ordering of the images in the chain is only a rough estimate and thus possibly noisy (recall we computed the ordering using an SVM-ranker trained with global image features), $\mathbf{w}_t$ prevents the inference from drifting in the cases where local smoothness does not strictly hold. λ is a constant that trades-off the two terms. We use the same DP inference procedure used to optimize Eq. 7.1.

Once P is found, we train a new detector with all of its patches as positive instances. The negative instances consist of randomly sampled patches whose intersection-over-union scores are lower than 0.3 with any of the patches in P. We use this new detector $\mathbf{w}_t$ in the next growing iteration. We repeat the above procedure T times to cover the entire attribute spectrum. Figure 7.4a illustrates the process of iterative chain growing for the "high-at-the-heel" and "smile" attributes. By iteratively growing the chain, we are able to coherently connect the attribute despite large appearance variations across its spectrum. However, there are two important considerations to make when growing the chain: (1) multimodality of the image dataset and (2) overfitting of the detector.

7.3.2.1 Multimodality of the Image Dataset

Not all images will exhibit the attribute due to pose/viewpoint changes or occlusion. We therefore need a mechanism to rule out such irrelevant images. For this, we use the detector $\mathbf{w}_t$. Specifically, we divide the image set S—now ordered in decreasing attribute strength as $\{\tilde{I}_1, \ldots, \tilde{I}_N\}$—into T *process sets*, each with size N/T. In the t-th iteration, we fire the detector $\mathbf{w}_t$ trained from the $(t-1)$-th iteration across each

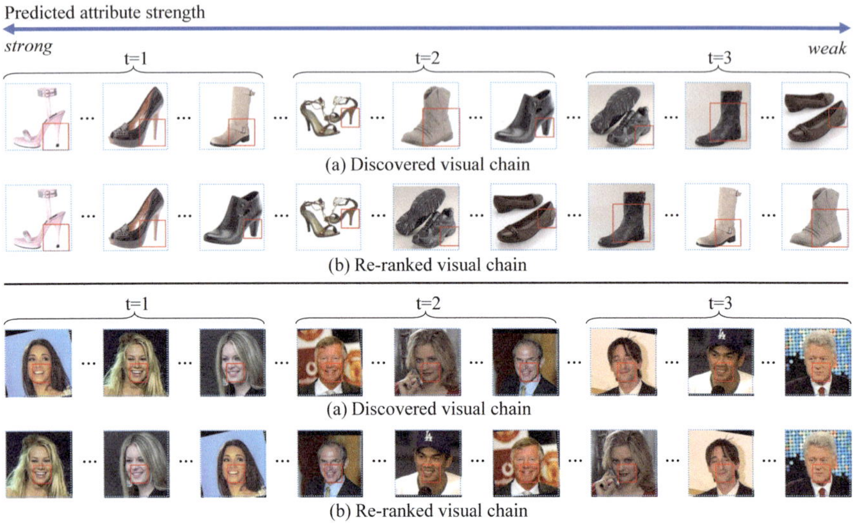

Fig. 7.4 *Top* "high-at-the-heel;" bottom: "smile." **a** We iteratively grow candidate visual chains along the direction of decreasing attribute strength, as predicted by the ranker trained with global image features [31]. **b** Once we obtain an accurate alignment of the attribute across the images, we can train a new ranker conditioned on the discovered patches to obtain a more accurate image ordering

image in the t-th process set in a sliding window fashion. We then add the N_{iter} images with the highest maximum patch detection scores for chain growing in the next iteration.

7.3.2.2 Overfitting of the Detector

The detector can overfit to the existing chain during iterative growing, which means that mistakes in the chain may not be fixed. To combat this, we adopt the *cross-validation* scheme introduced in [37]. Specifically, we split our image collection S into S_1 and S_2, and in each iteration, we run the above procedure first on S_1, and then take the resulting detector and use it to mine the chain in S_2. This produces more coherent chains, and also cleans up any errors introduced in either previous iterations or during chain initialization.

7.3.3 Ranking and Creating a Chain Ensemble

We now have a set of K_{init} chains, each pertaining to a unique visual concept and each covering the entire range of the attribute spectrum. However, some image regions that capture the attribute could have still been missed because they are not easily detectable on their own (e.g., forehead region for "visible forehead"). Thus, we next describe a simple and efficient way to further diversify the pool of chains to increase the chance that such regions are selected. We then describe how to select the most relevant chains to create an ensemble that together best models the attribute.

7.3.3.1 Generating New Chains Anchored on Existing Ones

Since the patches in a chain capture the same visual concept across the attribute spectrum, we can use them as *anchors* to generate new chains by perturbing the patches *locally* in each image with the same perturbation parameters $(\Delta_x, \Delta_y, \Delta_s)$. More specifically, perturbing a patch centered at (x, y) with size (w, h) using parameter $(\Delta_x, \Delta_y, \Delta_s)$ leads to a new patch at location $(x + \Delta_x w, y + \Delta_y h)$, with size $(w \times \Delta_s, h \times \Delta_s)$ (see Fig. 7.5). Note that we get the alignment for the patches in the newly generated chains for free, as they are *anchored* on an existing chain (given that the object is not too deformable). We generate K_{pert} chains for each of the K_{init} chains with Δ_x and Δ_y each sampled from $[-\delta_{xy}, \delta_{xy}]$ and Δ_s sampled from a discrete set χ, which results in $K_{pert} \times K_{init}$ chains in total. To detect the visual concept corresponding to a perturbed chain on any new unseen image, we take the detector of the anchoring chain and perturb its detection using the corresponding perturbation parameters.

7.3.3.2 Creating a Chain Ensemble

Different chains characterize different visual concepts. Not all of them are relevant to the attribute of interest and some are noisy. To select the relevant chains, we rank all the chains according to their relatedness to the target attribute using the image-level relative attribute annotations. For this, we split the original training data into two

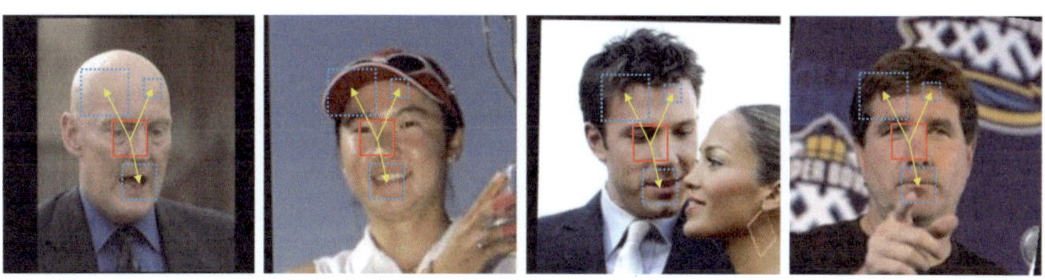

Fig. 7.5 We generate new chains (*blue dashed patches*) anchored on existing ones (*red solid patches*). Each new chain is sampled at some location and scale relative to the chain anchoring it. This not only allows us to efficiently generate more chains, but also allows us to capture visual concepts that are hard to detect in isolation yet still important to model the attribute (e.g., 1st image: the patch at the top of the head is barely detectable due to its low gradient energy, even though it is very informative for "Bald head")

subsets: one for training and the other for validation. For each of the $K_{pert} \times K_{init}$ candidate chains, we train a linear SVM detector and linear SVM-ranker [15, 31]. We then fire the detector on each validation image in a sliding window fashion and apply the ranker on the patch with the maximum detection score to get an estimated attribute strength $\hat{\Omega}(I_i)$ for each image I_i. Finally, we count how many of the pairwise ground-truth attribute orderings agree with our predicted attribute orderings:

$$acc(R, \hat{\Omega}) = \frac{1}{|R|} \sum_{(i,j)\in R} \mathbb{1}[\hat{\Omega}(I_i) - \hat{\Omega}(I_j) \geq 0], \tag{7.3}$$

where $|R|$ is the cardinality of the relative attribute annotation set on the validation data, and $\mathbb{1}[\cdot]$ is the indicator function. We rank each chain according to this validation set accuracy, and select the top K_{ens} chains. To form the final image-level representation for an image, we simply concatenate the feature vectors extracted from the detected patches, each weighted by its chain's validation accuracy. We then train a final linear SVM-ranker using this ensemble image-level representation to model the attribute.

7.4 Results

In this section, we analyze our method's discovered spatial extent of relative attributes, pairwise ranking accuracy, and contribution of local smoothness and perturbed visual chains.

Implementation details.

The feature ϕ we use for detection and local smoothness is HOG [11], with size 8×8 and 4 scales (patches ranging from 40×40 to 100×100 of the original image). For ranker learning, we use both the LLC encoding of dense-SIFT [41] stacked with a two-layer spatial pyramid (SP) grid [25], and *pool-5* activation features from the ImageNet pretrained CNN (Alexnet architecture) implemented using Caffe [14, 19]. (We find the *pool-5* activations, which preserve more spatial information, to be more useful in our tasks than the fully connected layers.) We set $\lambda = 0.05$, $N_{init} = 5$, $N_{iter} = 80$, $K_{init} = 20$, $K_{pert} = 20$, $K_{ens} = 60$, $\delta_{xy} = 0.6$, and $\chi = \{1/4, 1\}$. We find $T = 3$ iterations to be a good balance between chain quality and computation.

Baselines.

Our main baseline is the method of [31] (Global), which learns a relative attribute ranker using global features computed over the whole image. We also compare to the approach of [35] (Keypoints), which learns a ranker with dense-SIFT features computed on facial keypoints detected using the supervised detector of [46], and to the local learning method of [44], which learns a ranker using only the training samples that are close to a given testing sample. For Global [31], we use the authors' code with the same features as our approach (dense-SIFT+LLC+SP and *pool-5* CNN features).

For Keypoints [35] and [44], we compare to their reported numbers computed using dense-SIFT and GIST+color-histogram features, respectively.

Datasets.

LFW-10 [35] is a subset of the *Labeled faces in the wild* (LFW) dataset. It consists of 2000 images: 1000 for training and 1000 for testing. Annotations are available for 10 attributes, with 500 training and testing pairs per attribute. The attributes are listed in Table 7.1.

UT-Zap50K [44] is a large collection of 50,025 shoe images. We use the UT-Zap50K-1 annotation set, which provides on average 1388 training and 300 testing pairs of relative attribute annotations for each of 4 attributes: "Open," "Sporty," "Pointy," and "Comfort."

Shoes-with-Attributes [18] contains 14,658 shoe images from *like.com* and 10 attributes, of which 3 are overlapping with UT-Zap50K: "Open," "Sporty," and "Pointy." Because each attribute has only about 140 pairs of relative attribute annotations, we use this dataset only to evaluate cross-dataset generalization performance in Sect. 7.4.3.

7.4.1 Visualization of Discovered Visual Chains

We first visualize our discovered visual chains for each attribute in LFW-10 and UT-Zap50k. In Fig. 7.6, we show the single top-ranked visual chain, as measured by ranking accuracy on the validation set (see Eq. 7.3), for each attribute. We uniformly sample and order nine images according to their predicted attribute strength using the ranker trained on the discovered image patches in the chain. Our chains are visually coherent, even when the appearance of the underlying visual concept changes drastically over the attribute spectrum. For example, for the attribute "Open" in UT-Zap50k, the top-ranked visual chain consistently captures the opening of the shoe, even though the appearance of that shoe part changes significantly across the attribute spectrum. Due to our precise localization of the attribute, we are able to learn an accurate ordering of the images. While here we only display the top-ranked visual chain for each attribute, our final ensemble image representation combines the localizations of the top 60-ranked chains to discover the full spatial extent of the attribute, as we show in the next section.

7.4.2 Visualization of Discovered Spatial Extent

We next show qualitative results of our approach's discovered spatial extent for each attribute in LFW-10 and UT-Zap50K. For each image, we use a heatmap to display the final discovered spatial extent, where red/blue indicates strong/weak attribute relevance. To create the heatmap, the spatial region for each visual chain is overlaid

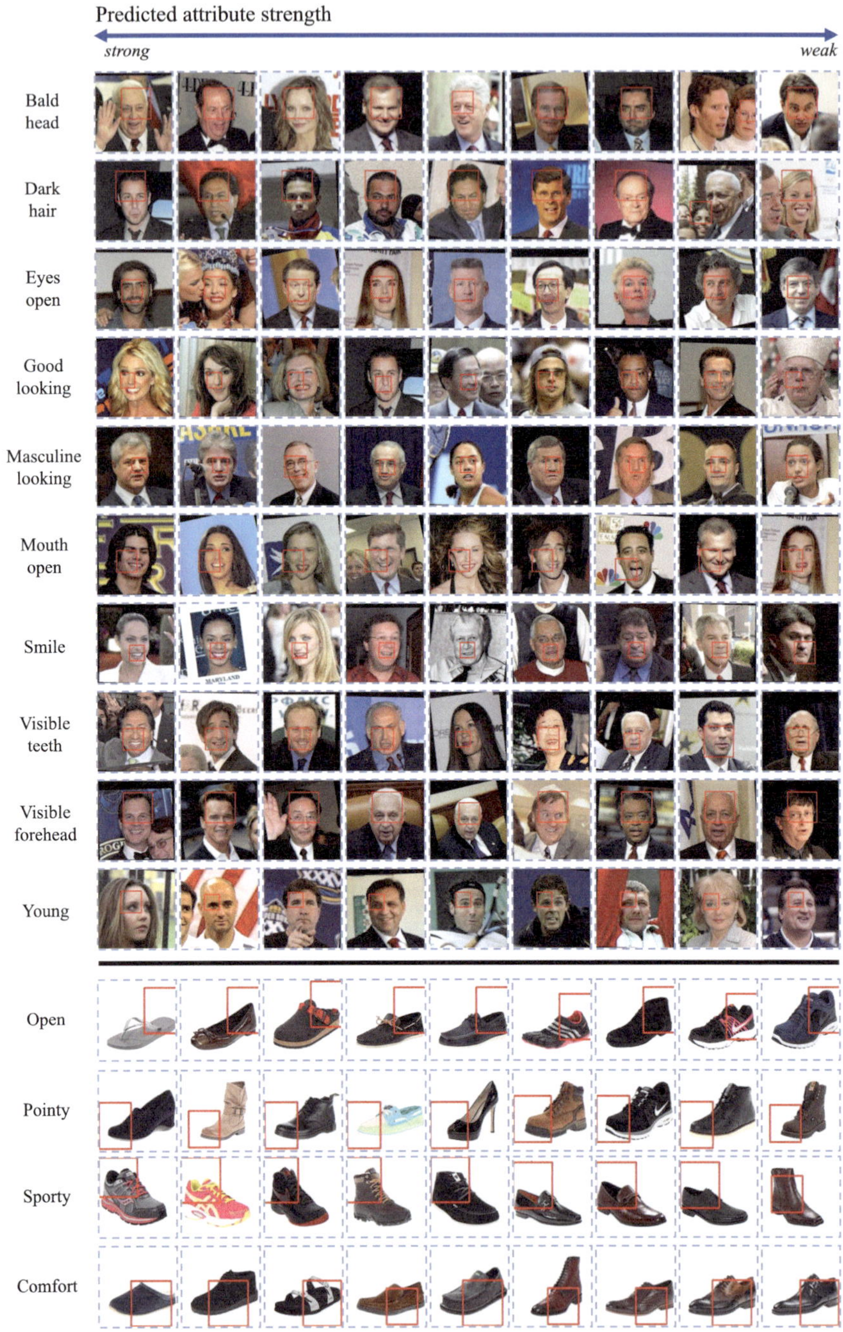

Fig. 7.6 Top-ranked visual chain for each attribute in LFW-10 (*top*) and UT-Zap50K (*bottom*). All images are ordered according to the predicted attribute strength using the ranker trained on the discovered image patches in the chain

Fig. 7.7 (*left*) Detection boxes of the top 60-ranked visual chains for "Smile," using each of their associated detectors. (*right*) The validation score (see Eq. 7.3) of each visual chain is overlaid onto the detected box in the image and summed to create the visualization of the discovered spatial extent of the attribute

by its predicted attribute relevance (as described in Sect. 7.3.3), and then summed up (see Fig. 7.7). Figure 7.8 shows the resulting heatmaps on a uniformly sampled set of unseen test images per attribute, sorted according to predicted attribute strength using our final ensemble representation model.

Clearly, our approach has understood where in the image to look to find the attribute. For almost all attributes, our approach correctly discovers the relevant spatial extent (e.g., for localizable attributes like "Mouth open", "Eyes open", "Dark hair", and "Open", it discovers the corresponding object-part). Since our approach is data-driven, it can sometimes go beyond common human perception to discover non-trivial relationships: for "Pointy", it discovers not only the toe of the shoe, but also the heel, because pointy shoes are often high-heeled (i.e., the signals are highly correlated). For "Comfort", it has discovered that the lack or presence of heels can be an indication of how comfortable a shoe is. Each attribute's precisely discovered spatial extent also leads to an accurate image ordering by our ensemble representation ranker (Fig. 7.8 rows are sorted by predicted attribute strength). There are limitations as well, especially for atypical images: e.g., "Smile" (6th image) and "Visible forehead" (8th image) are incorrect due to mis-detections resulting from extreme pose/clutter. Finally, while the qualitative results are harder to interpret for the more global attributes like "Good looking" and "Masculine looking", we demonstrate through quantitative analyses in Sect. 7.4.4.3 that they occupy a larger spatial extent than the more localizable attributes like "Mouth open" and "Smile". Since the spatial extent of the global attributes is more spread out, the highest-ranked visual chains tend to overlap most at the image centers as reflected by the heatmaps.

In Fig. 7.9, we compare against the Global baseline. We purposely use a higher spatial resolution (20×20) grid for the baseline to make the visualization comparison fair. Since the baseline uses a fixed spatial pyramid rigid grid, it cannot deal with changes in translation or scale of the attribute across different images; it discovers the background clutter to be relevant to "Dark hair" (1st row, 3rd column) and the

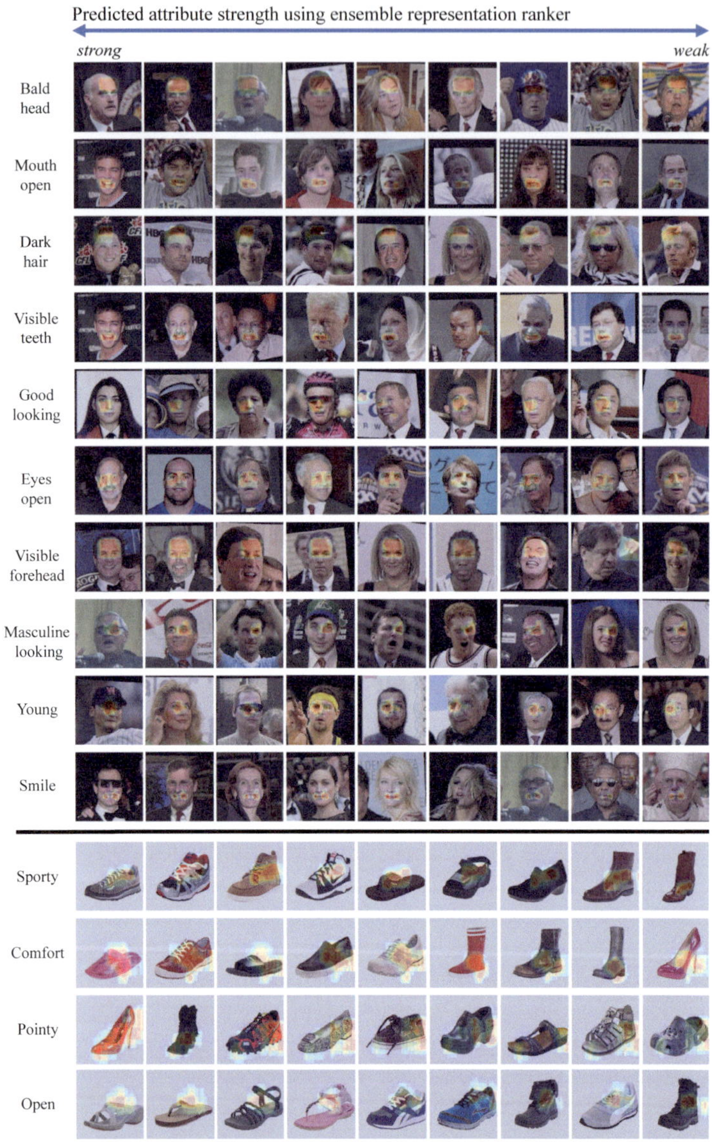

Fig. 7.8 Qualitative results showing our discovered spatial extent and ranking of relative attributes on LFW-10 (*top*) and UT-Zap50K (*bottom*). We visualize our discoveries as heatmaps, where *red/blue* indicates strong/weak predicted attribute relevance. For most attributes, our method correctly discovers the relevant spatial extent (e.g., for "Mouth open," "Dark hair," and "Eyes open," it discovers the corresponding object-part), which leads to accurate attribute orderings. Our approach is sometimes able to discover what may not be immediately obvious to humans: for "Pointy," it discovers not only the toe of the shoe, but also the heel, because pointy shoes are often high-heeled (i.e., the signals are highly correlated). There are limitations as well, especially for atypical images: e.g., "Smile" (6th image) and "Visible forehead" (8th image) are incorrect due to mis-detections resulting from extreme pose or clutter. **Best viewed on pdf**

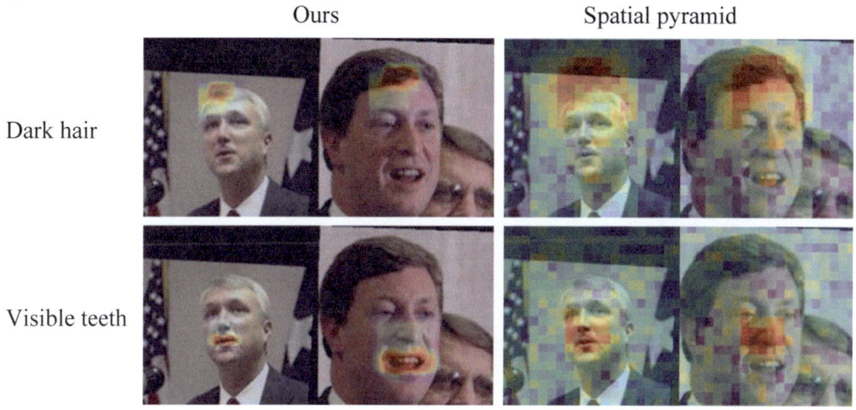

Fig. 7.9 Spatial extent of attributes discovered by our approach versus a spatial pyramid baseline. *Red/blue* indicates strong/weak attribute relevance. Spatial pyramid uses a fixed rigid grid (here 20 × 20), and so cannot deal with translation and scale changes of the attribute across images. Our approach is translation and scale invariant, and so its discoveries are much more precise

nose region to be relevant to "Visible teeth" (2nd row, 4th column). Our approach is translation and scale invariant, and hence its discoveries are much more precise.

7.4.3 Relative Attribute Ranking Accuracy

We next evaluate relative attribute ranking accuracy, as measured by the percentage of test image pairs whose pairwise orderings are correctly predicted (see Eq. 7.3).

We first report results on LFW-10 (Table 7.1). We use the same train/test split as in [35], and compare to the Global [31] and Keypoints [35] baselines. Our approach consistently outperforms the baselines for both feature types. Notably, even with the weaker dense-SIFT features, our method outperforms Global [31] that uses the more powerful CNN features for all attributes except "Masculine looking", which may be better described with a global feature.[1] This result demonstrates the importance of accurately discovering the spatial extent for relative attribute modeling. Compared to Keypoints [35], which also argues for the value of localization, our approach performs better but with less supervision; we do not use any facial landmark annotations during training. This is likely due to our approach being able to discover regions beyond pre-defined facial landmarks, which may not be sufficient in modeling the attributes.

We also report ranking accuracy on UT-Zap50K (Table 7.2). We use the same train/test splits as in [44], and compare again to Global [31], as well as to the local learning method of [44]. Note that Keypoints [35] cannot be easily applied to this

[1]Technically our approach is able to discover relevant regions with arbitrary sizes. However, in practice we are limited by a fixed set of box sizes that we use for chain discovery.

Table 7.1 Attribute ranking accuracy (%) on LFW-10. Our approach outperforms the baselines for both dense-SIFT (*first 3 rows*) and CNN (*last 2 rows*) features. In particular, the largest performance gap between our approach and the Global [31] baseline occurs for attributes with localizable nature, e.g., "Mouth open". Using the same dense-SIFT features, our approach outperforms the Keypoints [35] baseline on 7 of 10 attributes but with less supervision; we do not use any facial landmark annotations for training. *BH—Bald head; DH—Dark hair; EO—Eyes open; GL—Good looking; ML—Masculine looking; MO—Mouth open; S—Smile; VT—Visible teeth; VF—Visible forehead; Y—Young*

	BH	DH	EO	GL	ML	MO	S	VT	VF	Y	Mean
Keypoints [35]+DSIFT	**82.04**	80.56	83.52	68.98	**90.94**	82.04	**85.01**	82.63	83.52	71.36	81.06
Global [31]+DSIFT	68.98	73.89	59.40	62.23	87.93	57.05	65.82	58.77	71.48	66.74	67.23
Ours+DSIFT	78.47	**84.57**	**84.21**	**71.21**	90.80	**86.24**	83.90	**87.38**	**83.98**	**75.48**	**82.62**
Global [31]+CNN	78.10	83.09	71.43	68.73	**95.40**	65.77	63.84	66.46	81.25	72.07	74.61
Ours+CNN	**83.21**	**88.13**	**82.71**	**72.76**	93.68	**88.26**	**86.16**	**86.46**	**90.23**	**75.05**	**84.66**

Table 7.2 Attribute ranking accuracy (%) on UT-Zap50K. Even though our approach outperforms the baselines, the performance gap is not as large as on the LFW-10 dataset, mainly because the images in this dataset are much more spatially aligned. Thus, Global [31] is sufficient to do well on this dataset. We perform another cross-dataset experiment to address this dataset bias, the results of which can be found in Table 7.3

	Open	Pointy	Sporty	Comfort	Mean
Yu and Grauman [44]	90.67	90.83	92.67	92.37	91.64
Global [31]+DSIFT	93.07	92.37	94.50	94.53	93.62
Ours+DSIFT	92.53	**93.97**	95.17	94.23	93.97
Ours+Global+DSIFT	**93.57**	93.83	**95.53**	**94.87**	**94.45**
Global [31]+CNN	94.37	93.97	95.40	95.03	94.69
Ours+CNN	93.80	94.00	96.37	95.17	94.83
Ours+Global+CNN	**95.03**	**94.80**	**96.47**	**95.60**	**95.47**

dataset since it makes use of pretrained landmark detectors, which are not available (and much more difficult to define) for shoes. While our approach produces the highest mean accuracy, the performance gain over the baselines is not as significant compared to LFW-10. This is mainly because all of the shoe images in this dataset have similar scale, are centered on a clear white background, and face the same direction. Since the objects are so well-aligned, a spatial pyramid is enough to capture detailed spatial alignment. Indeed, concatenating the global spatial pyramid feature with our discovered features produces even better results (Ours+Global+DSIFT/CNN).[2]

Finally, we conduct a cross-dataset generalization experiment to demonstrate that our method is more robust to dataset bias [40] compared to Global [31]. We take the detectors and rankers trained on UT-Zap50K, and use them to make predictions on Shoes-with-Attributes. Table 7.3 shows the results. The performance for both methods is much lower because this dataset exhibits shoes with very different styles and much wider variation in scale and orientation. Still, our method generalizes much better than Global [31] due to its translation and scale invariance.

7.4.4 Ablation Studies

In this section, we perform ablation studies to analyze the different components of our approach, and perform additional experiments to further analyze the quality of our method's discoveries and how they relate to human annotations.

[2]Doing the same on LFW-10 produces worse results since the images are not as well-aligned.

Table 7.3 Cross-dataset ranking accuracy (%), training on UT-Zap50K and testing on Shoes-with-Attributes. Our approach outperforms Global [31] with a large margin in this setting (∼10 % points), since our approach is both translation and scale invariant

	Open	Pointy	Sporty	Mean
Global [31]+DSIFT	55.73	50.00	47.71	51.15
Ours+DSIFT	**63.36**	**62.50**	**55.96**	**60.61**
Global [31]+CNN	77.10	72.50	71.56	73.72
Ours+CNN	**80.15**	**82.50**	**88.07**	**83.58**

7.4.4.1 Contribution of each term in Eq. 7.2

We conduct an ablation study comparing our chains with those mined by two baselines that use either only the detection term or only the local smoothness term in Eq. 7.2. For each attribute in LFW-10 and UT-Zap50K, we select the single top-ranked visual chain. We then take the same N_{init} initial patches for each chain, and re-do the iterative chain growing, but *without* the detection or smoothness term. Algorithmically, the detection-only baseline is similar to the style-aware mid-level visual element mining approach of [26].

We then ask a human annotator to mark the outlier detections that do not visually agree with the majority detections, for both our chains and the baselines'. On a total of 14 visual chains across the two datasets, on average, our approach produces 3.64 outliers per chain while the detection-only and smoothness-only baselines produce 5 and 76.3 outliers, respectively. The smoothness-only baseline often drifts during chain growing to develop multiple modes. Figure 7.10 contrasts the detection-only baseline with ours.

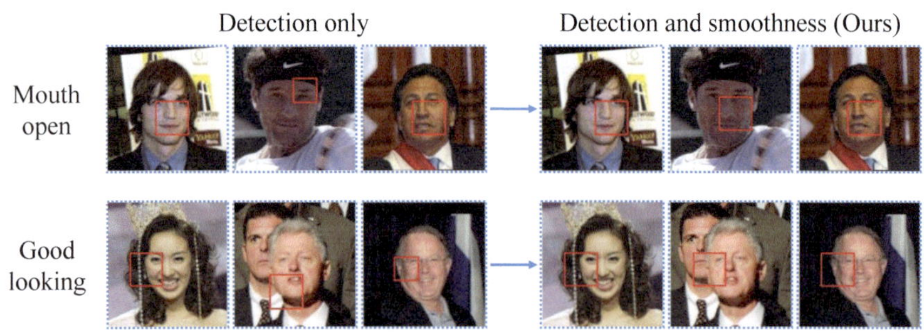

Fig. 7.10 Three consecutive patches in two different visual chains, for "Mouth open" and "Good looking". (*left*) The middle patches are mis-localized due to the confusing patterns at the incorrect locations. (*right*) These errors are corrected by propagating information from neighbors when local smoothness is considered

7.4.4.2 Visual Chain Perturbations

As argued in Sect. 7.3.3, generating additional chains by perturbing the originally mined visual chains is not only an efficient way of increasing the size of the candidate chain pool, but also allows the discovery of non-distinctive regions that are hard to localize but potentially informative to the attribute. Indeed, we find that for each attribute, on average only 4.25 and 2.3 selected in the final 60-chain ensemble are the original mined chains, for UT-Zap50K and LFW-10, respectively. For example, in Fig. 7.8 "Open", the high response on the shoe opening is due to the perturbed chains being anchored on more consistent shoe parts such as the tongue and heel.

7.4.4.3 Spreadness of Subjective Attributes

Since the qualitative results (Fig. 7.8) of the more global attributes are harder to interpret, we next conduct a quantitative analysis to measure the spreadness of our discovered chains. Specifically, for each image, we compute a spreadness score: (# of unique pixels covered by all chains)/(# of pixels in image), and then average this score over all images for each attribute. We find that the global attributes like good_looking, young and masculine_looking have higher spreadness than local ones like mouth_open, eyes_open and smile.

7.4.4.4 Where in the Image Do Humans Look to Find the Attribute?

This experiment tries to answer the above question by analyzing the human annotator rationales provided with the UT-Zap50k dataset. We take "comfort" as our test attribute since its qualitative results in Fig. 7.8 are not as interpretable at first glance. Specifically, we count all noun and adjective word occurrences for the 4970 annotator rationales provided for "comfort", using the Python Natural Language Toolkit (NLTK) part-of-speech tagger. The following are the resulting top-10 word counts: shoe-595, comfortable-587, sole-208, material-205, b-195 heel-184, support-176, foot-154, flexible-140, soft-92. Words like sole, heel and support are all related to heels, which supports the discoveries of our method.

7.4.5 Limitations

While the algorithm described in this chapter is quite robust as we have shown in the above experiments, it is not without limitations. Since our approach makes the assumption that the visual properties of an attribute change gradually with respect to attribute strength, it also implicitly assumes the existence of the same *visual concept* across the attribute spectrum. For example, for the attributes that we study in this chapter, our approach assumes that all images contain either faces or shoes regardless of the strength of the attribute. However, it would be difficult to apply our approach to datasets that do not hold this property, like natural scene images. This is because for an attribute like "natural", there are various visual properties (like forests and mountains, etc.) that are relevant to the attribute but are not consistently present across different images. Therefore, it would be much more challenging to discover visual chains that have the same visual concept whose appearance changes gradually according to attribute strength to link the images together.

Another limitation comes from our approach's dependency on the initial ranking. A rough initial ranking is required for the local smoothness property to hold in the first place. This may not always be the case if the task is too difficult for a global ranker to learn in the beginning (e.g., a dataset that contain highly cluttered images). One potential solution in that case would be to first group the training images into visually similar clusters and then train global rankers within each cluster to reduce the difficulty of ranker learning. The images in each cluster would be ordered according to the corresponding global ranker for initialization, and the rest of our algorithm would remain the same.

7.4.6 Application: Attribute Editor

Finally, we introduce an interesting application of our approach called the *Attribute Editor*, which could potentially be used by designers. The idea is to synthesize a new image, say of a shoe, by editing an attribute to have stronger/weaker strength. This allows the user to visualize the same shoe but e.g., with a pointier toe or sportier look. Figure 7.11 shows examples, for each of 4 attributes in UT-Zap50k, in which a user has edited the query image (shown in the middle column) to synthesize new images that have varying attribute strengths. To do this, we take the highest-ranked visual chain for the attribute, and replace the corresponding patch in the query image with a patch from a different image that has a stronger/weaker predicted attribute strength. For color compatibility, we retrieve only those patches that have similar color along its boundary as that of the query patch. We then blend in the retrieved patch using Poisson blending. The editing results for the "smile" attribute are shown in Fig. 7.12.

Our application is similar to the 3D model editor of [5], which changes only the object-parts that are related to the attribute and keeps the remaining parts fixed. However, the relevant parts in [5] are determined manually, whereas our algorithm discovers them automatically. Our application is also related to the *Transient Attributes* work of [23], which changes the appearance of an image globally (without localization like ours) according to attribute strength.

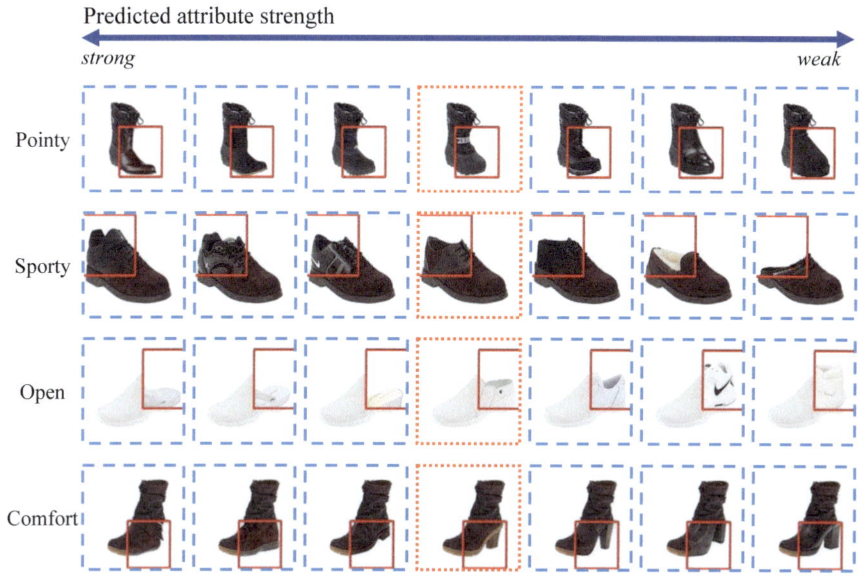

Fig. 7.11 The *middle column* shows the query image whose attribute (automatically localized in *red box*) we want to edit. We synthesize new shoes of varying predicted attribute strengths by replacing the *red box*, which is predicted to be highly relevant to the attribute, while keeping the rest of the query image fixed

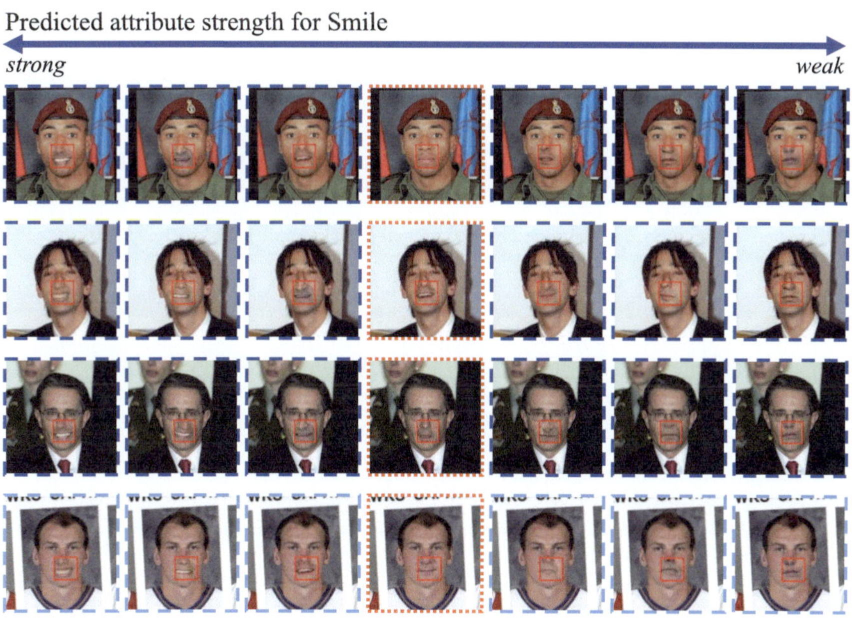

Fig. 7.12 Our attribute editor for "Smile". For the same person, the images from *left* to *right* become less and less smiling

7.5 Conclusion

We presented an approach that discovers the spatial extent of relative attributes. It uses a novel formulation that combines a detector with local smoothness to discover chains of visually coherent patches, efficiently generates additional candidate chains, and ranks each chain according to its relevance to the attribute. We demonstrated our method's effectiveness on several datasets, and showed that it better models relative attributes than baselines that either use global appearance features or stronger supervision.

Acknowledgements The work presented in this chapter was supported in part by an Amazon Web Services Education Research Grant and GPUs donated by NVIDIA.

References

1. Bengio, Y., Louradour, J., Collobert, R., Weston, J.: Curriculum learning. In: International Conference on Machine Learning (ICML) (2009)
2. Berg, T.L., Berg, A.C., Shih, J.: Automatic attribute discovery and characterization from noisy web data. In: European Conference on Computer Vision (ECCV) (2010)
3. Bourdev, L., Maji, S., Malik, J.: Describing people: poselet-based approach to attribute classification. In: International Conference on Computer Vision (ICCV) (2011)
4. Branson, S., Wah, C., Schroff, F., Babenko, B., Welinder, P., Perona, P., Belongie, S.: Visual recognition with humans in the loop. In: European Conference on Computer Vision (ECCV) (2010)
5. Chaudhuri, S., Kalogerakis, E., Giguere, S., Funkhouser, T.: Attribit: content creation with semantic attributes. In: ACM User Interface Software and Technology Symposium (UIST) (2013)
6. Doersch, C., Singh, S., Gupta, A., Sivic, J., Efros, A.A.: What makes Paris look like Paris? ACM Trans. Graph. (SIGGRAPH) **31**(4), 101:1–101:9 (2012)
7. Duan, K., Parikh, D., Crandall, D., Grauman, K.: Discovering localized attributes for fine-grained recognition. In: Conference on Computer Vision and Pattern Recognition (CVPR) (2012)
8. Faktor, A., Irani, M.: "Clustering by composition"—unsupervised discovery of image categories. In: European Conference on Computer Vision (ECCV) (2012)
9. Farhadi, A., Endres, I., Hoiem, D.: Attribute-centric recognition for cross-category generalization. In: Conference on Computer Vision and Pattern Recognition (CVPR) (2010)
10. Farhadi, A., Endres, I., Hoiem, D., Forsyth, D.: Describing objects by their attributes. In: Conference on Computer Vision and Pattern Recognition (CVPR) (2009)
11. Felzenszwalb, P.F., Girshick, R.B., McAllester, D., Ramanan, D.: Object detection with discriminatively trained part based models. IEEE Trans. Pattern Anal. Mach. Intell. (PAMI) **32**(9), 1627–1645 (2010)
12. Ferrari, V., Zisserman, A.: Learning visual attributes. In: Conference on Neural Information Processing Systems (NIPS) (2008)
13. Grauman, K., Darrell, T.: Unsupervised learning of categories from sets of partially matching image features. In: Conference on Computer Vision and Pattern Recognition (CVPR) (2006)
14. Jia, Y., Shelhamer, E., Donahue, J., Karayev, S., Long, J., Girshick, R.B., Guadarrama, S., Darrell, T.: Caffe: Convolutional architecture for fast feature embedding. arXiv preprint arXiv:1408.5093 (2014)

15. Joachims, T.: Optimizing search engines using clickthrough data. In: Knowledge Discovery in Databases (PKDD) (2002)
16. Kiapour, M., Yamaguchi, K., Berg, A.C., Berg, T.L.: Hipster wars: discovering elements of fashion styles. In: European Conference on Computer Vision (ECCV) (2014)
17. Kovashka, A., Grauman, K.: Attribute adaptation for personalized image search. In: International Conference on Computer Vision (ICCV) (2013)
18. Kovashka, A., Parikh, D., Grauman, K.: Whittlesearch: Image search with relative attribute feedback. In: Conference on Computer Vision and Pattern Recognition (CVPR) (2012)
19. Krizhevsky, A., Sutskever, I., Hinton, G.E.: Imagenet classification with deep convolutional neural networks. In: Conference on Neural Information Processing Systems (NIPS) (2012)
20. Kumar, N., Belhumeur, P., Nayar, S.: FaceTracer: A search engine for large collections of images with faces. In: European Conference on Computer Vision (ECCV) (2008)
21. Kumar, N., Berg, A., P.Belhumeur, S.Nayar: Attribute and simile classifiers for face verification. In: International Conference on Computer Vision (ICCV) (2009)
22. Kumar, P., Packer, B., Koller, D.: Self-paced learning for latent variable models. In: Conference on Neural Information Processing Systems (NIPS) (2010)
23. Laffont, P.Y., Ren, Z., Tao, X., Qian, C., Hays, J.: Transient attributes for high-level understanding and editing of outdoor scenes. ACM Trans. Graph. (TOG) **33**(4), 149 (2014)
24. Lampert, C.H., Nickisch, H., Harmeling, S.: Learning to detect unseen object classes by between-class attribute transfer. In: Conference on Computer Vision and Pattern Recognition (CVPR) (2009)
25. Lazebnik, S., Schmid, C., Ponce, J.: Beyond bags of features: spatial pyramid matching for recognizing natural scene categories. In: Conference on Computer Vision and Pattern Recognition (CVPR) (2006)
26. Lee, Y.J., Efros, A.A., Hebert, M.: Style-aware mid-level representation for discovering visual connections in space and time. In: International Conference on Computer Vision (ICCV) (2013)
27. Lee, Y.J., Grauman, K.: Foreground focus: Unsupervised learning from partially matching images. Int. J. Comput. Vis. (IJCV) **85**(2), 143–166 (2009)
28. Lee, Y.J., Grauman, K.: Learning the easy things first: self-paced visual category discovery. In: Conference on Computer Vision and Pattern Recognition (CVPR) (2011)
29. Li, Q., Wu, J., Tu, Z.: Harvesting mid-level visual concepts from large-scale internet images. In: Conference on Computer Vision and Pattern Recognition (CVPR) (2013)
30. Palatucci, M., Pomerleau, D., Hinton, G., Mitchell, T.: Zero-shot learning with semantic output codes. In: Conference on Neural Information Processing Systems (NIPS) (2009)
31. Parikh, D., Grauman, K.: Relative attributes. In: International Conference on Computer Vision (ICCV) (2011)
32. Payet, N., Todorovic, S.: From a set of shapes to object discovery. In: European Conference on Computer Vision (ECCV) (2010)
33. Rastegari, M., Farhadi, A., Forsyth, D.: Attribute discovery via predictable discriminative binary codes. In: European Conference on Computer Vision (ECCV) (2012)
34. Saleh, B., Farhadi, A., Elgammal, A.: Object-centric anomaly detection by attribute-based reasoning. In: Conference on Computer Vision and Pattern Recognition (CVPR) (2013)
35. Sandeep, R.N., Verma, Y., Jawahar, C.V.: Relative parts: distinctive parts for learning relative attributes. In: Conference on Computer Vision and Pattern Recognition (CVPR) (2014)
36. Shrivastava, A., Singh, S., Gupta, A.: Constrained semi-supervised learning using attributes and comparative attributes. In: European Conference on Computer Vision (ECCV) (2012)
37. Singh, S., Gupta, A., Efros, A.A.: Unsupervised discovery of mid-level discriminative patches. In: European Conference on Computer Vision (ECCV) (2012)
38. Sivic, J., Russell, B.C., Efros, A.A., Zisserman, A., Freeman, W.T.: Discovering object categories in image collections. In: Conference on Computer Vision and Pattern Recognition (CVPR) (2005)
39. Supancic, J., Ramanan, D.: Self-paced learning for long-term tracking. In: Conference on Computer Vision and Pattern Recognition (CVPR) (2013)

40. Torralba, A., Efros, A.A.: Unbiased look at dataset bias. In: Conference on Computer Vision and Pattern Recognition (CVPR) (2011)
41. Wang, J., Yang, J., Yu, K., Lv, F., Huang, T., Gong, Y.: Locality-constrained linear coding for image classification. In: Conference on Computer Vision and Pattern Recognition (CVPR) (2010)
42. Wang, S., Joo, J., Wang, Y., Zhu, S.C.: Weakly supervised learning for attribute localization in outdoor scenes. In: Conference on Computer Vision and Pattern Recognition (CVPR) (2013)
43. Xiao, F., Lee, Y.J.: Discovering the spatial extent of relative attributes. In: International Conference on Computer Vision (ICCV) (2015)
44. Yu, A., Grauman, K.: Fine-grained visual comparisons with local learning. In: Conference on Computer Vision and Pattern Recognition (CVPR) (2014)
45. Zhang, N., Paluri, M., Ranzato, M., Darrell, T., Bourdev, L.: PANDA: pose aligned networks for deep attribute modeling. In: Conference on Computer Vision and Pattern Recognition (CVPR) (2014)
46. Zhu, X., Ramanan, D.: Face detection, pose estimation, and landmark localization in the wild. In: Conference on Computer Vision and Pattern Recognition (CVPR) (2012)

Part III
Describing People Based on Attributes

Chapter 8
Deep Learning Face Attributes for Detection and Alignment

Chen Change Loy, Ping Luo and Chen Huang

Abstract Describable face attributes are labels that can be given to a face image to describe its characteristics. Examples of face attributes include gender, age, ethnicity, face shape, and nose size. Predicting face attributes in the wild is challenging due to complex face variations. This chapter aims to provide an in-depth presentation of recent progress and the current state-of-the-art approaches to solving some of the fundamental challenges in face attribute recognition, particularly from the angle of deep learning. We highlight effective techniques for training deep convolutional networks for predicting face attributes in the wild, and addressing the problem of imbalanced distribution of attributes. In addition, we discuss the use of face attributes as rich contexts to facilitate accurate face detection and face alignment in return. The chapter ends by posing an open question for the face attribute recognition challenge arising from emerging and future applications.

8.1 Introduction

Face attribute recognition aims at recognizing describable facial characteristics of a person, including physical appearance, expression, gender, ethnicity, and age range. Solving the face attribute recognition problem has gained a rapid increase of attention in both the academic research communities and the industrial laboratories in recent years.

The problem has many manifestations from different application domains depending on the kind of attributes one is recognizing. For instance, the capability of recog-

C.C. Loy (✉) · P. Luo
Department of Information Engineering, The Chinese University of Hong Kong, Shatin, NT, Hong Kong
e-mail: ccloy@ie.cuhk.edu.hk

P. Luo
e-mail: pluo@ie.cuhk.edu.hk

C. Huang
Robotics Institute, Carnegie Mellon University, Pittsburgh, United States
e-mail: chenh2@andrew.cmu.edu

R.S. Feris et al. (eds.), *Visual Attributes*, Advances in Computer Vision and Pattern Recognition, DOI 10.1007/978-3-319-50077-5_8

nizing describable facial characteristics such as nose size and mouth shape helps to compose descriptions at various levels of specificity for face verification, identification, and retrieval. On the other hand, the problem is related to 'age estimation' when the aim is to estimating the age range (e.g., young, old, mid-twenties) of a target person. Solving the 'expression recognition' problem can be considered as a face attribute recognition problem too. In this specific task, the target attributes are prototypical expressions such as angry, happy, disgust, sad, surprise, fear, and neutral. Recognizing such attributes facilitate the estimation of a person's internal emotional states and intentions. In the context of social signal processing, face attribute recognition can be extended beyond single person's attributes. For instance, recognizing inter-person attributes such as friendly, warm, and dominant, reveals intrinsic relations between two or more persons [84].

Conventional face attribute recognition methods typically begin with the extraction of hand-crafted features at pre-detected facial landmarks. An independently trained classifier such as support vector machine (SVM) is then applied for recognition. For instance, Kumar et al. [38] extracted HOG-like features on various face regions to tackle attribute classification and face verification. To improve the discriminativeness of hand-crafted features, Bourdev et al. [5] built a three-level SVM system to extract high-level information. Existing age estimation methods [11, 27] extracted active appearance model features and formulated a cumulative attribute-aware ridge regression function [11] or discriminative sparse neighbor approximation [27] for estimating age. These approaches generally require careful detection and alignment of face images, and most of them apply to frontal faces only. Solving the face attribute recognition in the wild requires more sophisticated methods since faces can be observed under substantial variations of poses, lightings, and occlusions.

Deep convolutional networks (DCN), or often known as deep convolutional neural networks (CNN), have achieved remarkable performance in many computer vision tasks, such as object detection [23, 53], image classification [25, 57, 61], segmentation [44, 46], and face recognition [59, 60], due to their exceptional capability of capturing abstract concepts invariant to various phenomenon in visual world, e.g., viewpoint, illumination, and clutter. Face attribute recognition, similarly, can enjoy a considerable performance boost by adopting a deep learning framework [45, 48].

In this chapter, we describe the use of DCN for solving some of the fundamental challenges in face attribute recognition. In particular, we present a novel DCN framework for mitigating the class imbalance problem in face attribute recognition in Sect. 8.2. Subsequently, we show that attributes can be exploited as an informative and rich source of context for learning robust deep representations. We show specifically how attributes can benefit face detection (Sect. 8.3) and face alignment (Sect. 8.4). Finally, in Sect. 8.5, we discuss an open question to be solved in order to meet requirements in emerging and future real-world applications.

8.2 Learning to Recognize Face Attributes

Data in vision domain often exhibit highly skewed class distribution, i.e., most data belong to a few majority classes, while the minority classes only contain a scarce amount of instances. Face attribute recognition faces the same problem too—it is comparatively easier to find persons with 'normal-sized nose' attribute on web images than that of 'big-nose.' Without handling the imbalance issue conventional methods tend to be biased toward the majority class with poor accuracy for the minority class.

To counter the negative effects, one often chooses from a few available options. The first option is re-sampling, which aims to balance the class priors by under-sampling the majority class or over-sampling the minority class (or both). The second option is cost-sensitive learning, which assigns higher misclassification costs to the minority class than to the majority. Such schemes are well-known for some inherent limitations. For instance, over-sampling can easily introduce undesirable noise with over-fitting risks, and under-sampling is often preferred but may remove valuable information. Such nuisance factors can be equally applicable to deep representation learning in the face attribute recognition task.

In this section, we present an approach called Large Margin Local Embedding (LMLE) for learning a deep representation given class-imbalanced face attribute data [28].[1] The LMLE method is motivated by the observation that the minority class often contains very few instances with high degree of visual variability. The scarcity and high variability make the genuine neighborhood of these instances easy to be invaded by other imposter nearest neighbors.[2] Specifically, we propose to learn an embedding $f(x) \in \mathbb{R}^d$ with a CNN to ameliorate such invasion. The CNN is trained with instances selected through a quintuplet sampling scheme and the associated triple-header hinge loss. The learned embedding can produce features that preserve not only locality across the same-class clusters but also discrimination between negative and positive attribute classes. We will demonstrate that such 'quintuplet loss' introduces a tighter constraint for reducing imbalance in the local data neighborhood when compared to existing triplet loss. We also study the effectiveness of classic schemes of class re-sampling and cost-sensitive learning in the face attribute recognition context.

8.2.1 A Large Margin Local Embedding Approach

Given a face attribute dataset with an imbalanced class distribution, our goal is to learn an Euclidean embedding $f(x)$ from an image x into a feature space $\mathbb{R}^d$, such that the embedded features preserve locality across the same-class clusters as well

[1]The method is also applicable to other visual recognition problems that encounter imbalanced class distributions.

[2]An imposter of a data point x_i is another data point x_j with a different class label, $y_i \neq y_j$.

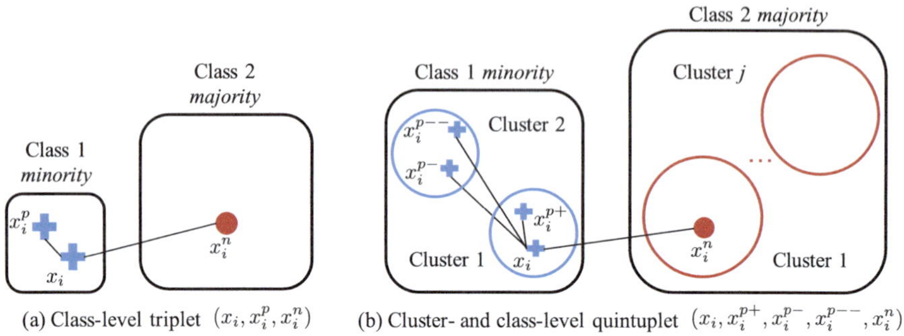

Fig. 8.1 **a** Class-level embedding by triplet versus. **b** cluster- and class-level embedding by quintuplet. We take two different sized classes as example to illustrate the class imbalance. The quintuplet associated with a triple-header hinge loss is found favorable for imbalanced classification

as discrimination between classes to prevent any possible local class imbalance. We constrain this embedding to live on a d-dimensional hypersphere, i.e., $||f(x)||^2 = 1$.

Quintuplet Sampling. To achieve the aforementioned goal, we select quintuplets from the imbalanced data as illustrated in Fig. 8.1b. Each quintuplet is defined as

- x_i : an anchor,
- x_i^{p+} : the anchor's most distant within-cluster neighbor,
- x_i^{p-} : the nearest within-class neighbor of the anchor, but from a different cluster,
- x_i^{p--}: the most distant within-class neighbor of the anchor,
- x_i^n : the nearest between-class neighbor of the anchor.

We wish to ensure that the following relationship holds in the embedding space:

$$D(f(x_i), f(x_i^{p+})) < D(f(x_i), f(x_i^{p-})) < D(f(x_i), f(x_i^{p--})) < D(f(x_i), f(x_i^n)), \tag{8.1}$$

where $D(f(x_i), f(x_j)) = \|f(x_i) - f(x_j)\|_2^2$ is the Euclidean distance.

Such a fine-grained similarity defined by the quintuplet has two merits: (1) The ordering in Eq. (8.1) provides richer information and a stronger constraint than the conventional class-level image similarity. In the latter, two images are considered similar as long as they belong to the same category. In contrast, we require two instances to be close in both class- and cluster-levels to be considered similar. This actually helps build a local classification boundary with the most discriminative local samples. Other irrelevant samples in a class are effectively 'held out' for class separation, making the local boundary robust and insensitive to imbalanced class sizes. (2) The quintuplet sampling is repeated during the CNN training, thus avoiding unnecessary information loss as in traditional random under-sampling. When compared with over-sampling strategies, it introduces no artificial noise. In practice, to ensure adequate learning for all classes, we collect quintuplets for equal numbers of minority- and majority-class samples x_i in one mini-batch.

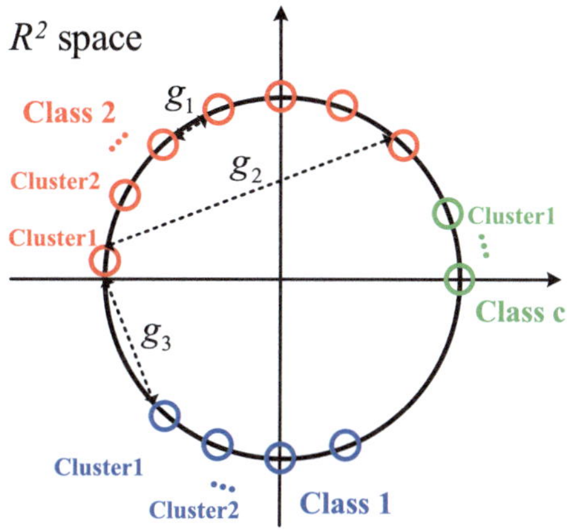

Fig. 8.2 The geometry intuition of margins. Ideally, in the hypersphere embedding space, clusters should collapse into small neighborhoods with safe margin g_1 between one another, and g_2 being the largest within a class, and their containing class is also well separated by a large margin g_3 from other classes

Note in the above, we implicitly assume the imbalanced data are already clustered so that quintuplets can be sampled. In practice, one could obtain the initial clusters for each class by applying k-means on some prior features extracted from e.g., the DeepID2 face recognition model [59]. To make the clustering more robust, an iterative scheme is formulated to refine the clusters using features extracted from the proposed model itself every 5000 iterations. The overall pipeline will be summarized next.

Triple-Header Hinge Loss. To enforce the relationship in Eq. 8.1 during feature learning, we apply the large margin idea using the sampled quintuplets. A *triple-header hinge loss* is formulated to constrain three margins between the four distances, and we solve the following objective function with slack allowed:

$$
\begin{aligned}
&\min \sum_i (\epsilon_i + \tau_i + \sigma_i) + \lambda \|\boldsymbol{W}\|_2^2, \\
&s.t.: \\
&\max\left(0, g_1 + D(f(x_i), f(x_i^{p+})) - D(f(x_i), f(x_i^{p-}))\right) \leq \epsilon_i, \\
&\max\left(0, g_2 + D(f(x_i), f(x_i^{p-})) - D(f(x_i), f(x_i^{p--}))\right) \leq \tau_i, \\
&\max\left(0, g_3 + D(f(x_i), f(x_i^{p--})) - D(f(x_i), f(x_i^{n}))\right) \leq \sigma_i, \\
&\forall i,\ \epsilon_i \geq 0,\ \tau_i \geq 0,\ \sigma_i \geq 0
\end{aligned} \tag{8.2}
$$

where ϵ_i, τ_i, σ_i are the slack variables, g_1, g_2, g_3 are the margins, $\boldsymbol{W}$ is the parameters of the CNN embedding function $f(\cdot)$, and λ is a regularization parameter.

This formulation can effectively regularize the deep representation learning based on the ordering specified in quintuplets, imposing a tighter constraint than triplets [9, 55, 66]. Ideally, in the hypersphere embedding space, clusters should collapse into small neighborhoods with safe margin g_1 between one another, and g_2 being the largest within a class, and their containing class is also well separated by a large margin g_3 from other classes (see Fig. 8.2). An appealing feature of the proposed learning

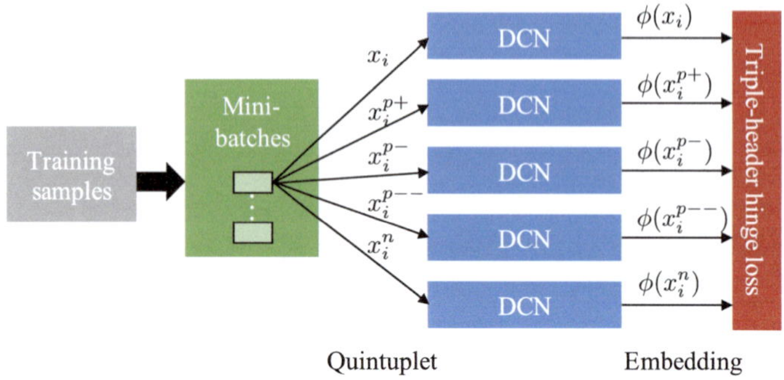

Fig. 8.3 The learning network

algorithm is that the margins can be explicitly determined by a geometric intuition. Suppose there are L training samples in total, class c is of size $L_c, c = 1, \ldots, C$. Let all the classes spread $s \in [0, 1]$ of the entire hypersphere, and we generate clusters of equal-size l for each class. Obviously, the margins' lower bounds are zero. For their upper bounds, g_1^{max} is obtained when all $\lfloor L/l \rfloor$ clusters are squeezed into single points on a proportion s of the sphere. Hence $g_1^{max} = 2\sin(\pi * sl/L)$, and g_2^{max} can be approximated as $2\sin(\pi * s(L_c - l)/L)$ using the triangle inequality. $g_3^{max} = 2\sin(\pi/C)$ when all classes collapse into single points. In practice, we try several decreasing margin combinations before actual training.

The learning network architecture is shown in Fig. 8.3. Given a re-sampled mini-batch, we retrieve for each x_i in it a quintuplet by using a lookup table computed offline. To generate a table of meaningful and discriminative quintuplets, instead of selecting the 'hardest' ones from the entire training set, we select 'semi-hard' ones by computing distances on a random subset (50 %) of training data to avoid those mislabeled or poor quality data. Then each quintuplet member is fed independently into five identical CNNs with shared parameters. Finally, the output feature embeddings are L_2 normalized and used to compute a triple-header hinge loss by Eq. 8.2. Backpropagation is used to update the CNN parameters.

To further ensure equal learning for the imbalanced classes, we assign each sample and its quintuplet in mini-batches a cost such that the *class* weights therein are identical. Below we summarize the learning steps of the LMLE approach. Note that the learning is iterative.

1. Cluster for each class by k-means using the learned features from previous iteration. For the first iteration, we use pre-trained features obtained from a face verification task [59].
2. Generate a quintuplet table using the cluster and class labels from a subset of training data.
3. For CNN training, repeatedly sample mini-batches equally from each class and retrieve the corresponding quintuplets from the offline table.
4. Feed all quintuplets into five identical CNNs to compute loss in Eq. 8.2 with cost-sensitivities.

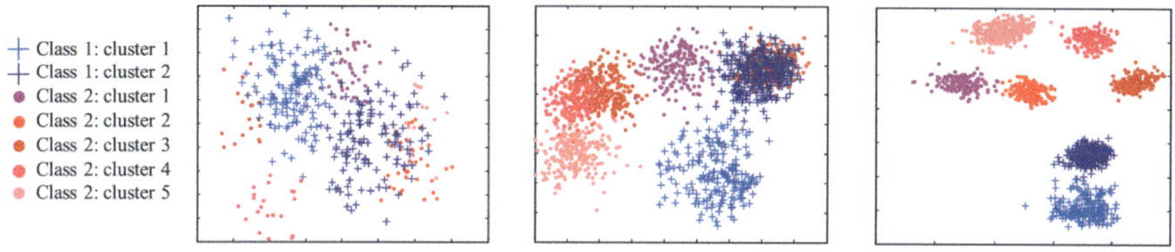

Fig. 8.4 From *left* to *right*: 2D feature embedding of one imbalanced binary face attribute using features obtained from DeepID2 network [59], triplet-based embedding, quintuplet-based LMLE. We only show 2 Positive Clusters (PC) and 5 Negative Clusters (NC) out of a total of 499 clusters to represent the imbalance

5. Backpropagate the gradients to update the CNN parameters and feature embeddings.
6. Alternate between steps 1–2 and steps 3–5 every 5000 iterations until convergence.

Differences between Quintuplet Loss and Triplet Loss. The triplet loss is inspired by Dimensionality Reduction by Learning an Invariant Mapping (DrLIM) [24] and Large Margin Nearest Neighbor (LMNN) [68]. It is widely used in many recent vision studies [9, 55, 66], aiming to bring data of the same class closer, while data of different classes further away (see Fig. 8.1). To enforce such a relationship, one needs to generate mini-batches of triplets, i.e., an anchor x_i, a positive instance x_i^p of the same class, and a negative instance x_i^n of different class, for deep feature learning. We argue that they are rather limited in capturing the embedding structure of imbalanced data, such as that observed in face attribute data. Specifically, the similarity information is only extracted at the *class-level*, which would homogeneously collapse each class irrespective of their different degrees of variations. As a result, the class structures are lost. Moreover, when a class's semantic scope is large but only consists of a few instances with high variability, it is hard to maintain the class-wise margin, leading to potential invasion of imposter neighbors or even domination of the majority class in local neighborhood. By contrast, LMLE generates diverse quintuplets that differ in the membership of clusters as well as classes, operating at both cluster- and class-levels. It is thus capable of better capturing the considerable data variability within each class and reducing any local class imbalance. Figure 8.4 illustrates the advantage of LMLE.

Nearest Neighbor Imbalanced Classification. The above LMLE approach offers crucial feature representations for the following classification to perform well on the imbalanced face attribute data. We choose the simple k-nearest neighbor (kNN) classifier to show the efficacy of the learned features. Better performance is expected with the use of more elaborated classifiers.

A traditional kNN classifier predicts the class label of a query q as the majority label among its kNN in the training set $\mathcal{P} = \{(x_i, y_i)\}_{i=1}^{L}$, where $y_i = 1, \ldots, C$ is the (binary or multi-way) class label of sample x_i. Such kNN rule is appealing due to its non-parametric nature, and it is easy to extend to new classes without retraining. However, the underlying equal-class-density assumption may not be satisfied and will greatly degrade its performance in the imbalanced case. Specifically, the formed decision boundary will be severely biased to majority classes.

To this end, we modify the kNN classifier in two ways: (1) In the well-clustered embedding space LMLE, we treat each cluster as a class-specific exemplar,[3] and perform a fast *cluster-wise* kNN search. (2) Let $\phi(q)$ be query q's local neighborhood defined by its kNN cluster centroids $\{m_i\}_{i=1}^k$. We seek a large margin local boundary among $\phi(q)$, labeling q as the class to which the maximum cluster distance is smaller than the minimum cluster distance to any other class by the largest margin:

$$y_q = -\arg\max_{c=1,\dots,C} \left(\max_{\substack{m_i \in \phi(q) \\ y_i = c}} D(f(q), f(m_i)) - \min_{\substack{m_j \in \phi(q) \\ y_j \neq c}} D(f(q), f(m_j)) \right). \quad (8.3)$$

This large margin local decision offers us two advantages:

(i) *Higher resistance to data imbalance*: Recall that we fix the cluster size l (200 in this study) rather than the number of clusters for each class (to avoid large quantization errors for the minority classes). Thus the $\lfloor L_c/l \rfloor$ clusters generated from different classes $c = 1, \dots, C$ still exhibit class imbalance. The class imbalance issue is partially mitigated here since a classification based on the large margin rule is independent of the class size. It is also very suited to the LMLE representation which is learned under the same rule.

(ii) *Fast speed*: Decision by cluster-wise kNN search is much faster than by sample-wise search.

We summarize the steps for the kNN-based imbalanced classification. For a query q,

1. Find its kNN cluster centroids $\{m_i\}_{i=1}^k$ from all classes.
2. If all the k cluster neighbors belong to the same class, q is labeled by that class and exit.
3. Otherwise, label q as y_q using Eq. 8.3.

Evaluation. We evaluate the effectiveness of the proposed method on a large-scale face attribute dataset. Each face attribute is binary, with severely imbalanced positive and negative samples (e.g., "Bald" attribute: 2 vs. 98 %). We simultaneously predict 40 attributes in a multi-task framework.

For evaluation we collected a large-scale face attribute dataset known as CelebA dataset [45]. It contains 10,000 identities, each with about 20 images. Every face image is annotated with 40 attributes and 5 key points. More information on the dataset can be found in [45].[4] We use the annotated key points to align each image to 55 × 47 pixels. We partition the dataset following [45]: the first 160 thousand

[3] Employing clustering to aid classification is common in the literature [6, 65].

[4] http://mmlab.ie.cuhk.edu.hk/projects/CelebA.html.

images (i.e., 8000 identities) for training, the following 20 thousand for training SVM classifiers for the PANDA [81] and ANet [45], and remaining 20 thousand for testing. We will introduce ANet in Sect. 8.3.1. To account for the imbalanced positive and negative attribute samples, a balanced accuracy is adopted, that is $accuracy = 0.5(t_p/N_p + t_n/N_n)$, where N_p and N_n are the numbers of positive and negative samples, while t_p and t_n are the numbers of true positive and true negative. Note that this evaluation metric differs from that employed in [45], where $accuracy = ((t_p + t_n)/(N_p + N_n))$, which can be biased to the majority class.

We use an CNN architecture identical to that presented in [59], and employ DeepID2 features [59] as prior features for the clustering. Note the prior features for initial clustering are not critical to the final results because we will gradually learn deep features in alternation with their clustering every 5000 iterations. Different prior features generally converge to similar results, but at different speeds. The proposed CNN is trained using batch size 40, momentum 0.9, and $\lambda = 0.0005$ in Eq. 8.2. Class-specific cost is defined as the inverse to class size in a batch. We search $k = 20$ nearest clusters (i.e., $|\phi(q)| = 20$ in Eq. 8.3) for querying.

Table 8.1 Mean per-class accuracy (%) and class imbalance level (=|positive class rate-50|%) of the 40 face attributes on CelebA dataset [45]. Attributes are sorted ascending by the imbalance level. To account for the imbalanced positive and negative attribute samples, a balanced accuracy is adopted, unlike [45]. The results of ANet are therefore different from that reported in [45] (see text for details)

	Attractive	Mouth Open	Smiling	Wear Lipstick	High Cheekbones	Male	Heavy Makeup	Wavy Hair	Oval Face	Pointy Nose	Arched Eyebrows	Black Hair	Big Lips	Big Nose	Young	Straight Hair	Brown Hair	Bags Under Eyes	Wear Earrings	No Beard	Bangs
Imbalance level	1	2	2	3	5	8	11	18	22	22	23	26	26	27	28	29	30	30	31	33	35
Triplet-kNN [55]	83	92	92	91	86	91	88	77	61	61	73	82	55	68	75	63	76	63	69	82	81
PANDA [81]	85	93	98	97	89	99	95	78	66	67	77	84	56	72	78	66	85	67	77	87	92
ANet [45]	87	96	97	95	89	99	96	81	67	69	76	90	57	78	84	69	83	70	83	93	90
LMLE-kNN	88	96	99	99	92	99	98	83	68	72	79	92	60	80	87	73	87	73	83	96	98

	Blond Hair	Bushy Eyebrows	Wear Necklace	Narrow Eyes	5 o'clock Shadow	Receding Hairline	Wear Necktie	Eyeglasses	Rosy Cheeks	Goatee	Chubby	Sideburns	Blurry	Wear Hat	Double Chin	Pale Skin	Gray Hair	Mustache	Bald		**Average**
Imbalance level	35	36	38	38	39	42	43	44	44	44	44	44	45	45	45	46	46	46	48		
Triplet-kNN [55]	81	68	50	47	66	60	73	82	64	73	64	71	43	84	60	63	72	57	75		**72**
PANDA [81]	91	74	51	51	76	67	85	88	68	84	65	81	50	90	64	69	79	63	74		**77**
ANet [45]	90	82	59	57	81	70	79	95	76	86	70	79	56	90	68	77	85	61	73		**80**
LMLE-kNN	99	82	59	59	82	76	90	98	78	95	79	88	59	99	74	80	91	73	90		**84**

Table 8.1 compares the proposed LMLE-kNN method for multi-attribute classification with state-of-the-art methods, namely Triplet-kNN [55], PANDA [81] and the ANet [45], which are trained using the same images and tuned to their best performance. The attributes and their mean per-class accuracy results are given in the order of ascending class imbalance level (=|positive class rate-50|%) to better reflect its effect on performance. It is shown that LMLE-kNN consistently outperforms others across all face attributes, with an average gap of 4 % over the runner-up ANet. Considering most face attributes exhibit high class imbalance with an average positive class rate of 23 %, such improvements are nontrivial and prove the representation power of the LMLE-based deep features on imbalanced data. Although PANDA and ANet are capable of learning a robust representation by model ensembling and multi-task learning respectively, these methods ignore the imbalance issue and thus struggle for highly imbalanced attributes, e.g., 'Bald.' Compared with the closely related triplet sampling method [55], quintuplet sampling better preserves the embedding locality and discrimination on imbalanced data. The advantage is more evident when observing the relative accuracy gains over other methods in Fig. 8.5. The gains tend to increase with higher class imbalance level.

We further conduct an ablation test to demonstrate the benefits of quintuplet loss and the applied re-sampling and cost-sensitive schemes. As can be observed in Table 8.2, while favorable performance is obtained using the classic schemes, we find that the proposed quintuplet loss leads to much larger performance gains than the popular triplet loss does over standard softmax. This strongly supports the necessity of imposing additional cluster-wise relationships as in quintuplets. Such constraints can better preserve local data neighborhood than triplets, which is critical

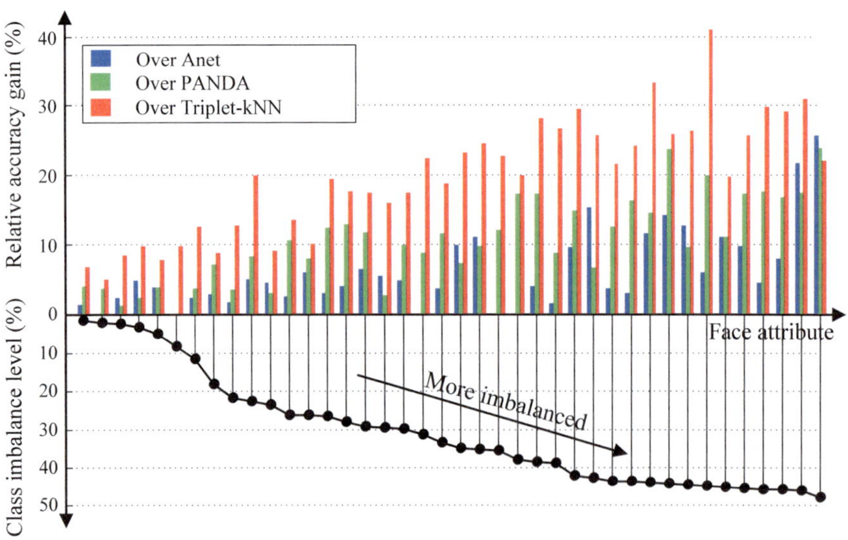

Fig. 8.5 Relative accuracy gains over competitors on the sorted 40 face attributes in Table 8.1

Table 8.2 Ablation tests on attribute classification (average accuracy—%)

Methods	Loss only	Loss + resample	Loss + resample + cost
Softmax	68.07	69.43	70.16
Triplet	71.29	71.75	72.43
Quintuplet	81.31	83.39	**84.26**

for ameliorating the invasion of imposter neighbors in the face attribute recognition problem. It is worth noting that for the cost-sensitive scheme, when applied to strictly balanced data from a re-sampled mini-batch, it would have no effects since the class weights are already equal. However, in the case of predicting multiple face attributes, class-balanced data for one attribute will be almost certainly imbalanced for the other attributes, whose costs can then help.

Summary. In this section, we have discussed the importance of handling the class imbalance issue inherent in the attribute recognition problem. Contemporary deep representation learning methods typically resort to class re-sampling or cost-sensitive learning. Through extensive experiments, we have validated their effectiveness and further demonstrated that the proposed triple-header loss with quintuple sampling works remarkably well in comparison to existing approaches for learning a deep representation from imbalanced attribute data. In the same context, the proposed method has also been shown superior to the triplet loss, which is commonly adopted for large margin learning. We attribute the effectiveness to the unique capability of the loss in preserving locality across clusters and discrimination between classes. Next, we show that attributes can be exploited as an informative and rich source of context for learning robust deep representations. We show specifically how attributes can benefit face detection (Sect. 8.3) and face alignment (Sect. 8.4).

8.3 Face Attributes for Face Localization and Detection

In Sect. 8.2, we assume face detection is performed (using an off-the-shelf face detector [41]) prior to the attribute recognition step. In essence, face localization or detection is a crucial step for face attribute recognition. These two problems are typically treated as isolated problems in existing literature [4, 5, 13, 37, 48, 81]. Current methods first detect face parts and extract features from each part and then the extracted local features are concatenated to train classifiers. For example, Kumar et al. [37] predicted face attributes by extracting hand-crafted features from ten face parts. Zhang et al. [81] recognized human attributes by employing hundreds of poselets [5] to align human body parts. In this section, we demonstrate that face detection and face attribute recognition are highly correlated tasks in two aspects. First, cascading face localization and attribute recognition improves each other. Second, attributes facilitate the detection of facial parts, making face detection robust to large pose variations and occlusions.

8.3.1 A Cascaded Approach for Face Localization and Attribute Recognition

To understand why rich attribute information enables accurate face localization, one could consider the examples in Fig. 8.6. If only a single detector [41, 49] is used to classify all the positive and negative samples in Fig. 8.6a, it is difficult to handle complex face variations. Therefore, multi-view face detectors [73] were developed in Fig. 8.6b, i.e., face images in different views are handled by different detectors. View labels were used in training detectors and the whole training set was divided into subsets according to views. If views are treated as one type of face attributes, learning a face representation by predicting attributes with deep models actually extends this idea to an extreme. As shown in Fig. 8.6c, a neuron (or a group of neurons)[5] in a CNN functions as a detector of an attribute. When a subset of neurons are activated, they indicate the existence of a particular attribute configuration. For instance, Fig. 8.7 visualizes the neurons in the fully-connected layer of a CNN trained for attribute prediction. The neurons are ranked by their responses in descending order with respect to test images. It is observed that these neurons collectively express diverse high-level meanings to explain the test images. The neurons at different layers can form many activation patterns, implying that the whole set of face images can be divided into many subsets based on attribute configurations, and each activation pattern corresponds to one subset (e.g., 'pointy nose,' 'rosy cheek,' and 'smiling'). Therefore, it is not surprising that neurons learned by attributes lead to effective representations for face localization.

We introduce a deep learning framework for joint face localization and attribute prediction in the wild [45]. It cascades two CNNs, LNet and ANet, which are fine-tuned jointly with attribute tags, but pre-trained differently. LNet is pre-trained by massive general object categories for face localization, while ANet is pre-trained by massive face identities for attribute prediction. This framework reveals valuable facts on learning a face representation. First, it shows how the performances of face localization (LNet) and attribute prediction (ANet) can be improved by different pre-training strategies. Second, it reveals that although the filters of LNet are fine-tuned only with image-level attribute tags, their response maps over the entire images have strong indication of face locations. This fact enables training LNet for face localization with only image-level annotations, but without face bounding boxes or landmarks, which are required by existing attribute recognition methods. Third, it also demonstrates that the high-level hidden neurons of ANet automatically discover semantic concepts after pre-training with massive face identities, and such concepts

[5]The layers of a CNN have neurons arranged in 3 dimensions: width, height, and the third dimension of an activation volume.

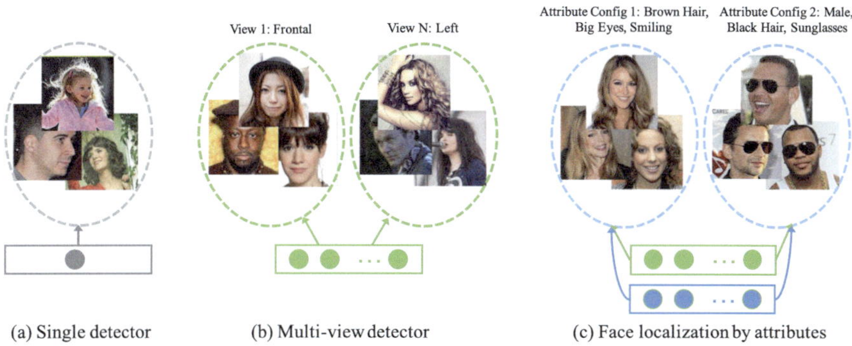

Fig. 8.6 Rich attribute information enables accurate face localization through capturing and dividing the face space into finer subsets of different attribute configurations

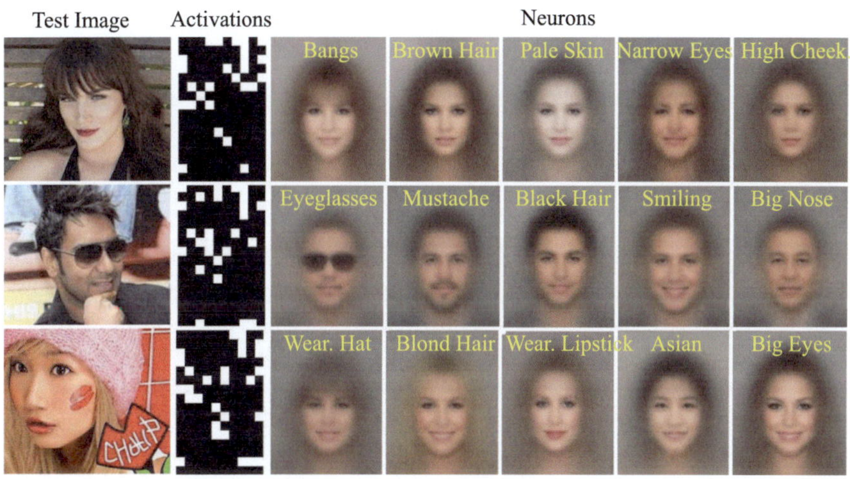

Fig. 8.7 The activations of neurons in CNN capture attribute configurations of different faces. In particular, attributes presented in each test image are explained by a sparse linear combination of these concepts. For instance, the first image is described as 'a lady with bangs, brown hair, pale skin, narrow eyes and high cheekbones'

are significantly enriched after fine-tuning with attribute tags. Each attribute can be well explained with a sparse linear combination of these concepts.

Network Structure Overview. Figure 8.8 illustrates our pipeline where LNet locates the entire face region in a coarse-to-fine manner as shown in (a) and (b), while ANet extracts features for attribute recognition as shown in (c). Different from existing works that rely on accurate face and landmark annotations, LNet is trained in a weakly supervised manner with only image-level annotations. Specifically, it is pre-trained with one thousand object categories of ImageNet [16] and fine-tuned by image-level attribute tags. The former step accounts for background clutter, while

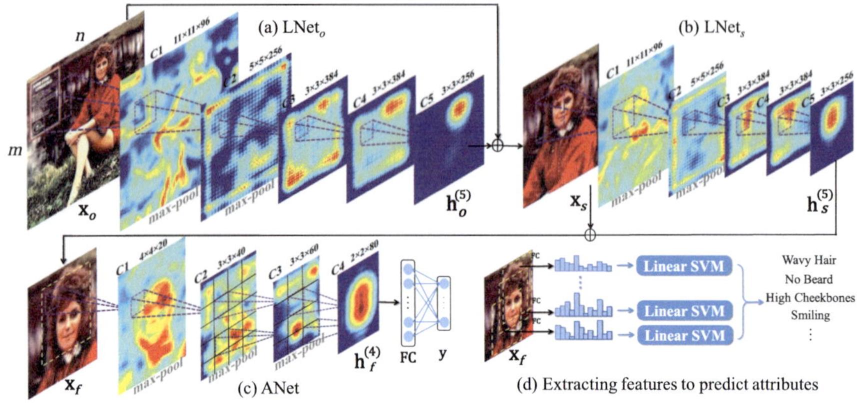

Fig. 8.8 The pipeline of joint learning face localization and attribute prediction

the latter step learns features robust to complex face variations. Learning LNet in this way not only significantly reduces data labeling, but also improves the accuracy of face localization. Both LNet$_o$ and LNet$_s$ have network structures similar to AlexNet [36], whose hyper-parameters are specified in Fig. 8.8a, b respectively. The high activations in the averaged response maps of the fifth convolutional layer (C5) of LNet$_o$ indicate the head-and-shoulders region, while the activations of C5 of LNet$_s$ indicate faces. Moreover, the input $\mathbf{x}_o$ of LNet$_o$ is a $m \times n$ image, while the input $\mathbf{x}_s$ of LNet$_s$ is the head-shoulder region, which is localized by LNet$_o$ and resized to 227×227. The localization is obtained through searching a threshold, such that a window with a response larger than this threshold corresponds to the region of interest.

As illustrated in Fig. 8.8c, ANet is learned to predict attributes $\mathbf{y}$ by providing the input face region $\mathbf{x}_f$, which is detected by LNet$_s$ and properly resized. Specifically, multi-view versions (the four corner patches, the center patch, and their horizontal flips) [36] of $\mathbf{x}_f$ are utilized to train ANet. Furthermore, ANet contains four convolutional layers, where the filters of C1 and C2 are globally shared and the filters of C3 and C4 are locally shared. The effectiveness of local filters have been demonstrated in many face- related tasks [58, 62]. To handle complex face variations, ANet is pre-trained by distinguishing massive face identities, which facilitates the learning of discriminative features.

Figure 8.8d outlines the procedure of attribute recognition. ANet extracts a set of feature vectors (FCs) by cropping overlapping patches on $\mathbf{x}_f$. Support Vector Machines (SVMs) [21] are trained to predict attribute values given each FC. The final prediction is obtained by averaging all these values, to cope with small misalignment of face localization.

Pre-training LNet. Both LNet$_o$ and LNet$_s$ are pre-trained with 1,000 general object categories from the ImageNet Large Scale Visual Recognition Challenge (ILSVRC) 2012 [16], containing 1.2 million training images and 50 thousands validation images. All the data is employed for pre-training except one-third of the validation data for choosing hyper-parameters [36]. We augment data by cropping ten patches from each image, including one patch at the center and four at the corners, and their horizontal flips. We adopt softmax for object classification, which is optimized by stochastic gradient descent (SGD) with backpropagation (BP) [40]. As shown in Fig. 8.9a.2, the averaged response map in C5 of LNet_o already indicates locations of objects including human faces after pre-training.

Fine-tuning LNet. Both LNet_o and LNet_s are fine-tuned with attribute tags. Additional output layers are added to the LNets individually for fine-tuning and then removed for evaluation. LNet_o adopts the full image $\mathbf{x}_o$ as input while LNet_s uses the region with high responses (determined by thresholding) $\mathbf{x}_s$ in the averaged response map in C5 of LNet_o as input, which roughly correspond to head-shoulders. The cross-entropy loss is used for attribute classification, i.e. $L = \sum_{i=1} \mathbf{y}_i \log p(\mathbf{y}_i|\mathbf{x}) + (1-\mathbf{y}_i) \log \left(1 - p(\mathbf{y}_i|\mathbf{x})\right)$, where $p(\mathbf{y}_i = 1|\mathbf{x}) = \frac{1}{1+\exp(-f(\mathbf{x}))}$ is the probability of the i-th attribute given image $\mathbf{x}$. As shown in Fig. 8.9a.3, the response maps after attribute fine-tuning become cleaner and smoother, suggesting that the filters learned by attribute tags can detect face patterns with complex variations. To appreciate the effectiveness of pre-training, we also include the averaged response map in C5 when trained from scratch with attribute tags but without pre-training in Fig. 8.9a.4. It cannot separate face regions from background and other body parts well.

Thresholding and Proposing Windows. We show that the responses of C5 in LNet are discriminative enough to separate faces and background by simply searching a threshold, such that a window with a response larger than this threshold corresponds to a face and otherwise is background. To determine the threshold, we select 2000 images, each of which contains a single face, and 2000 background images from the SUN dataset [69]. For each image, EdgeBox [88] is adopted to propose 500 candidate windows, each of which is measured by a score that sums over its response values normalized by its window size. A larger score indicates the localized pattern is more likely to be a face. Each image is then represented by the maximum score over all its windows. In Fig. 8.9b, the histogram of the maximum scores shows that these scores

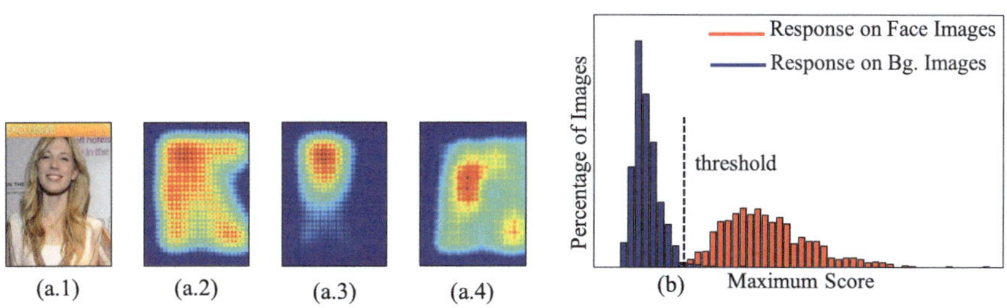

Fig. 8.9 **a.1** Original image, **a.2–a.4** are averaged response maps in C5 of LNet_o after pre-training (**a.2**), fine-tuning (**a.3**) and directly training from scratch with attribute tags but without pre-training (**a.4**). **b** Threshold used to separate faces from non-faces

clearly separate face images from background images. The threshold is chosen as the decision boundary as shown in Fig. 8.9b.

Evaluation. We evaluate the effectiveness of using attributes to facilitate face localization. We employ the CelebA dataset [45], which contains ten thousand identities, each of which has 20 images. There are two hundred thousand images in total. A subset of images from CelebA (twenty thousand images from one thousand randomly chosen identities) are employed to compare the face localization performance of LNet with three widely adopted face detectors, including DPM [49], ACF Multiview [73], SURF Cascade [41], and a commercial product (Face++) [20]. We evaluate them by using Receiver Operating Characteristic (ROC) curves when $IoU^6 \geq 0.5$. As plotted in Fig. 8.10a, when *False Positives Per Image*, $FPPI = 0.01$, the true positive rates of Face++ and LNet are 85 and 93 %; when $FPPI = 0.1$, our method outperforms the other three methods by 11, 9 and 22 % respectively. We also investigate how these methods perform with respect to the overlap ratio (IoU), following [49, 88]. Figure 8.10c shows that LNet generally provides more accurate face localization, leading to good performance in the subsequent attribute prediction. LNet significantly outperforms LNet (without pre-training) by 74 % when the overlap ratio equals to 0.5, which validates the effectiveness of pre-training. We then explore the influence of the number of attributes on localization. Figure 8.10d illustrates that rich attribute information facilitates face localization.

To examine the generalization ability of LNet, we collect another 3,876 face images for testing, namely MobileFaces, where the images are captured by the cameras of mobile phones. These images are collected from an image domain different to the CelebA dataset. Several examples of MobileFaces are shown in Fig. 8.11b and the corresponding ROC curves are plotted in Fig. 8.10b. We observe that LNet consistently performs better and still gains 7 % improvement ($FPPI = 0.1$) compared with other face detectors. As demonstrated in Fig. 8.11, LNet accurately localize faces in the wild except some failure cases due to extreme poses and large occlusions.

8.3.2 *From Facial Parts Responses to Face Detection*

In Sect. 8.3.1, we demonstrated that face attribute recognition benefits face localization. In this section, we introduce a deep learning approach, *Faceness* [77, 78], to further show that face attributes help in localizing distinct facial parts. The localized facial parts are robust to large pose variations and occlusions. The combination of local parts' responses improve face detection. An example is given in Fig. 8.12.

The Faceness's pipeline consists of three stages, i.e. generating partness maps, ranking candidate windows by faceness scores, and refining face proposals for face detection. In the first stage as shown in Fig. 8.13, a full image $\mathbf{x}$ is used as input to five CNNs. Note that all the five CNNs can share deep layers to save computational

[6] IoU indicates Intersection over Union.

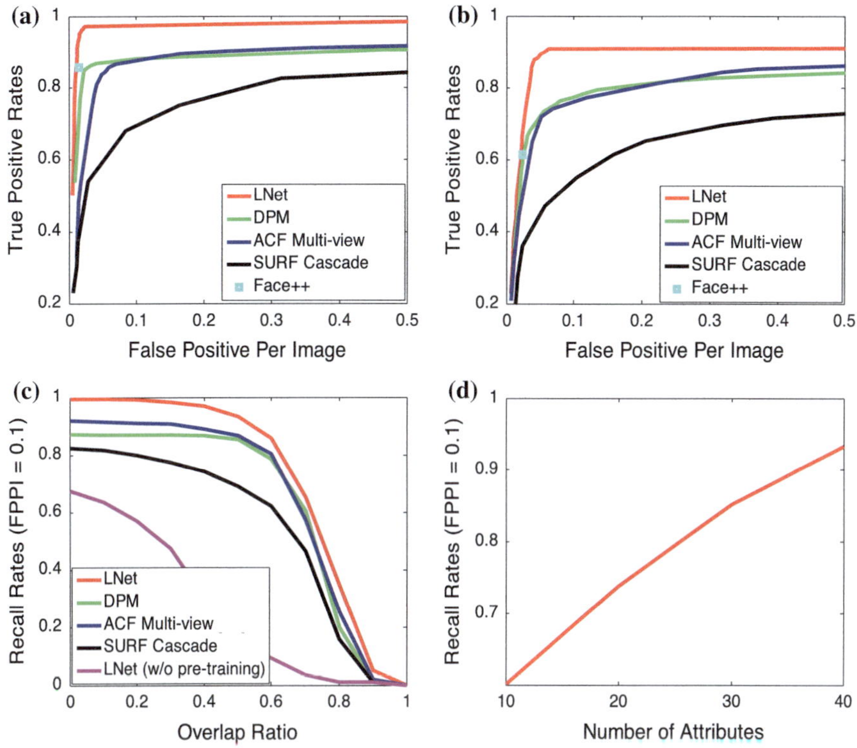

Fig. 8.10 Receiver operating characteristic curves on **a** CelebA and **b** MobileFaces datasets. **c** Recall rates with respect to overlap ratio ($FPPI = 0.1$). **d** Recall rates with respect to the number of attributes ($FPPI = 0.1$)

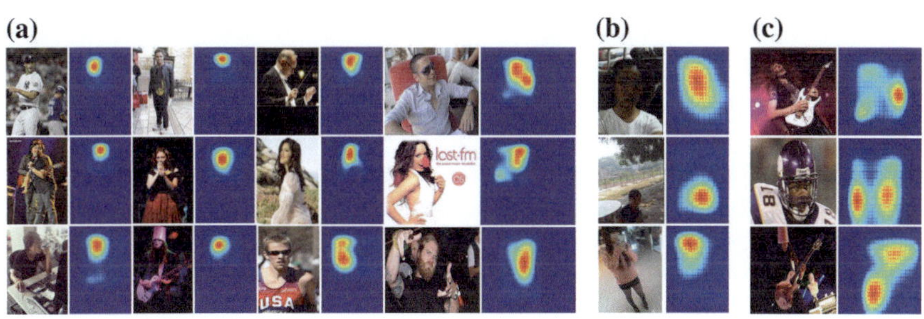

Fig. 8.11 Examples of face localization of LNet, including **a** CelebA, **b** MobileFaces, and **c** some failure cases

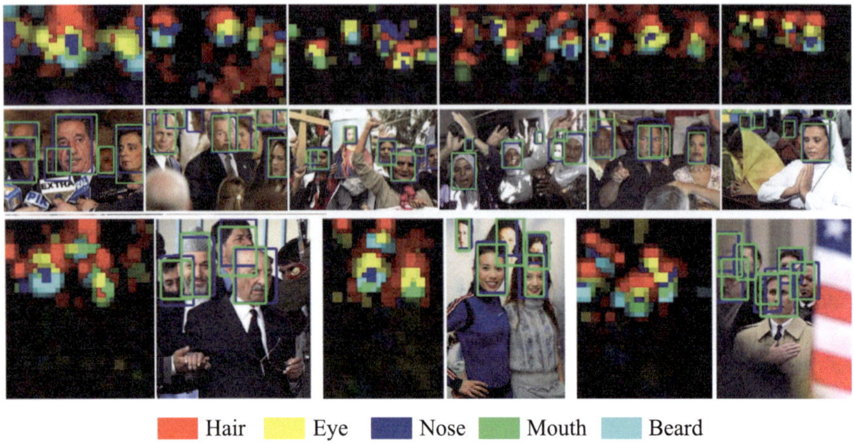

Fig. 8.12 We introduce a deep convolutional network for face detection, which achieves high recall of faces even under severe occlusions and head pose variations. The key to the success of our approach is the new mechanism for scoring face likeliness based on deep network responses on local facial parts. The part-level response maps (we call it 'partness' map) are generated by our deep network given a full image without prior face detection. All these occluded faces are difficult to handle by conventional approaches

time. Each CNN outputs a partness map, which is obtained by weighted averaging over all the label maps at its top convolutional layer. Each of these partness maps indicates the location of a specific facial component presented in the image, e.g., hair, eyes, nose, mouth, and facial hair, denoted by $\mathbf{h}^a$, $\mathbf{h}^e$, $\mathbf{h}^n$, $\mathbf{h}^m$, and $\mathbf{h}^b$, respectively. We combine all these partness maps through max pooling into a face label map $\mathbf{h}^f$, which clearly designates faces' locations.

In the second stage, given a set of candidate windows that are generated by existing object proposal methods such as [1, 64, 88], we rank these windows according to their faceness scores, which are extracted from the partness maps with respect to different facial parts configurations, as illustrated in Fig. 8.14. For example, as visualized in Fig. 8.14, a candidate window 'A' covers a local region of $\mathbf{h}^a$ (i.e., hair) and its faceness score (this is for a part, not the holistic face) is calculated by dividing the values at its upper part with respect to the values at its lower part, because hair is more likely to present at the top of a face region. Note that the spatial configuration of faces, e.g., lower and upper parts as illustrated in Fig. 8.14 can be learned from data. More details are provided in [77]. A final faceness score of 'A' is obtained by averaging over the scores of these parts. In this case, a large number of false positive windows can be pruned. In the last stage, the proposed candidate windows are refined by training a multi-task CNN, where face classification and bounding box regression are jointly optimized.

Learning Partness Maps. The partness maps can be learned in multiple ways. The most straightforward manner is to use the image and its pixelwise segmentation

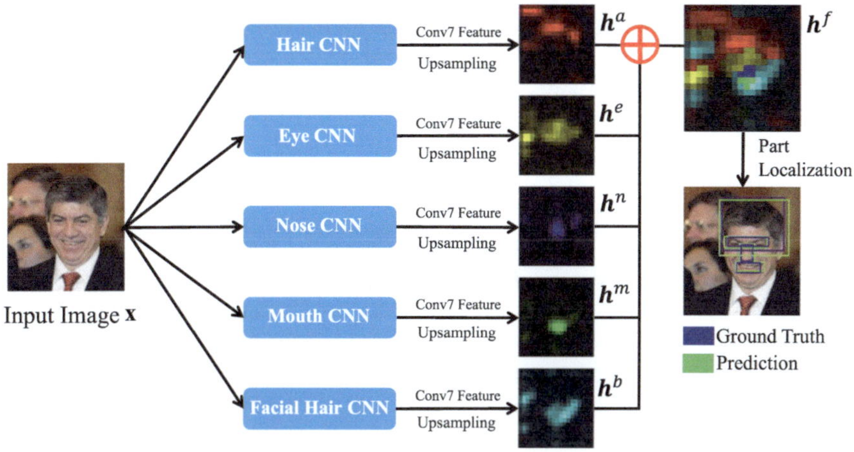

Fig. 8.13 The pipeline of generating part response maps and part localization. Different CNNs are trained to handle different facial parts, but they can share deep layers for computational efficiency

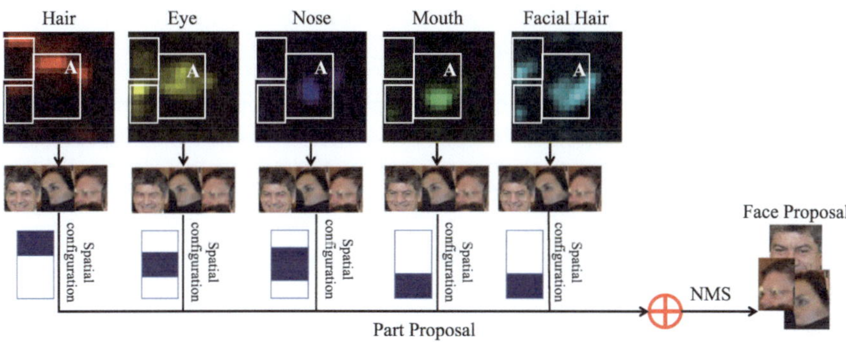

Fig. 8.14 The pipeline for generating face proposals

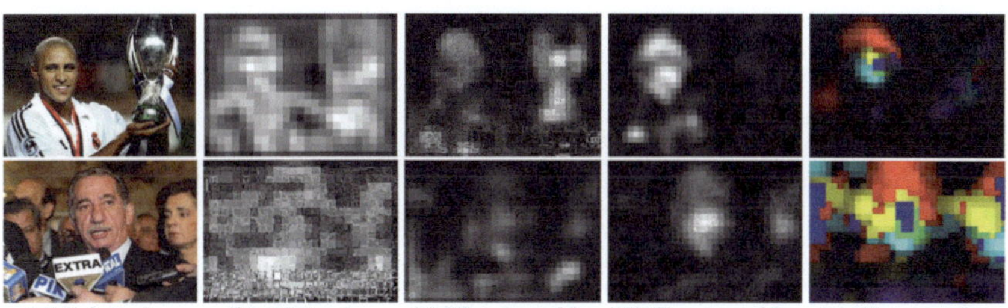

(a) Original image (b) Without pre-trained model (c) Fine-tuned by classifying face vs. non-face images (d) Fine-tuned by classifying 25 face attributes (e) Fine-tuned by classifying grouped face attributes w.r.t facial parts

Fig. 8.15 The responses or partness maps obtained by using different types of supervisions label map as input and target, respectively. This setting is widely employed in image labeling [22, 51]. However, it requires label maps with pixelwise annotations, which are expensive to collect. Another setting is image-level classification (i.e. faces and non-faces), as shown in Fig. 8.15c. It works well when the training images are well-aligned [59]. Nevertheless, it suffers from complex background clutter because the supervisory information is not sufficient to account for complex face variations. Its learned feature maps contain too much noise, which overwhelms the actual faces' locations. Attribute learning in Fig. 8.15d extends the binary classification in (c) to the extreme by using a combination of attributes to capture face variations. For instance, an 'Asian' face can be distinguished from a 'Caucasian' face. However, our experiments demonstrate that this setting is not robust to occlusion. Hence, as shown in Fig. 8.15e, Faceness extends (d) by partitioning attributes into groups based on facial components. For instance, 'black hair,' 'blond hair,' 'bald,' and 'bangs' are grouped together, as all of them are related to hair. The grouped attributes are summarized in Table 8.3. In this case, different face parts can be modeled by different CNNs (with option to share some deep layers). If one part is occluded, the face region can still be localized by CNNs of other parts. Note that although we have multiple attributes in each attribute group, a part CNN in Fig. 8.13 only produces a single output to indicate the presence of a part.

Face Detection. The proposed windows achieved by faceness measure have high recall rate. To improve it further, we refine these windows by joint training face classification and bounding box regression using a CNN similar to the AlexNet [36]. In particular, we fine-tune AlexNet using face images from AFLW [35] and person-free images from PASCAL VOC 2007 [19]. For face classification, a proposed window is assigned with a positive label if the IoU between it and the ground truth bounding box is larger than 0.5; otherwise it is negative. For bounding box regression, each proposal is trained to predict the positions of its nearest ground truth bounding box. If the proposed window is a false positive, the CNN outputs a vector of $[-1, -1, -1, -1]$. We adopt the Euclidean loss and cross-entropy loss for bounding box regression and face classification, respectively.

Table 8.3 Facial attributes grouping

Facial part	Facial attributes
Hair	Black hair, Blond hair, Brown hair, Gray hair, Bald, Wavy hair, Straight hair, Receding hairline, Bangs
Eye	Bushy eyebrows, Arched eyebrows, Narrow eyes, Bags under eyes, Eyeglasses
Nose	Big nose, Pointy nose
Mouth	Big lips, Mouth slightly open, Smiling, Wearing lipstick
Facial hair	No beard, Goatee, 5 o'clock shadow, Mustache, Sideburns

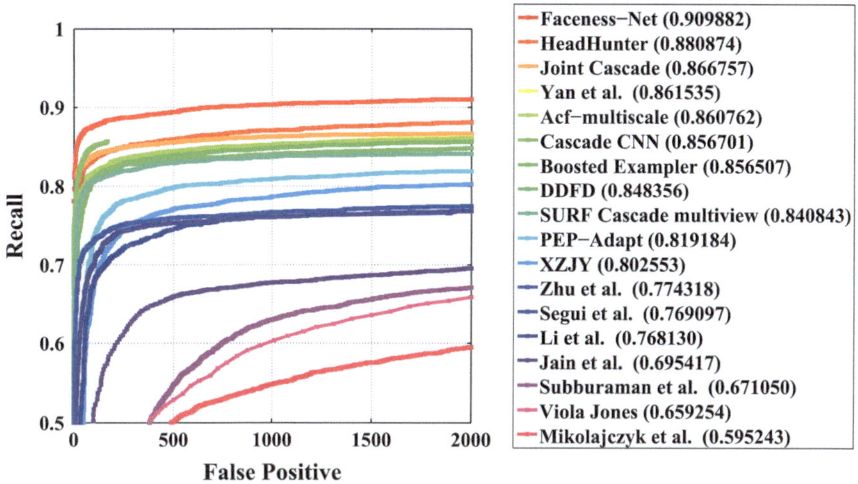

(a) FDDB

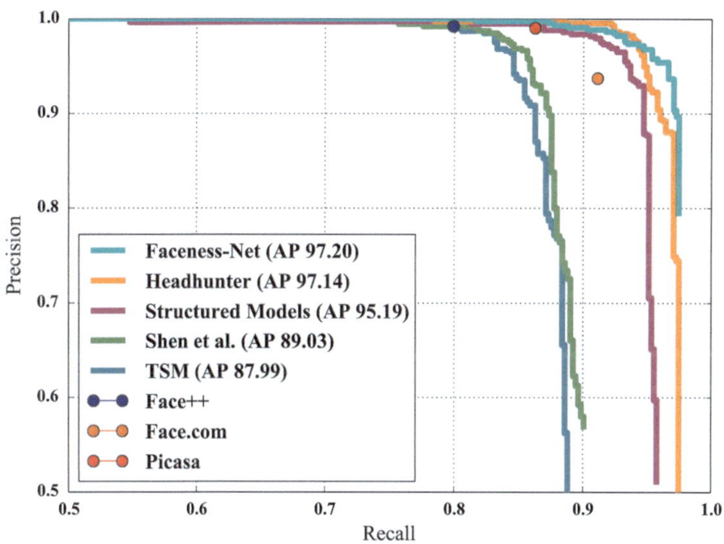

(b) AFW

Fig. 8.16 **a** Comparisons on FDDB dataset. **b** Comparisons on AFW dataset

Evaluation. We conduct face detection experiments on two datasets: FDDB [31] and AFW [87]. We adopt the PASCAL VOC precision–recall protocol for evaluation. We compare Faceness-Net against all published methods [10, 32, 41–43, 49, 56, 71, 73, 87] in the FDDB. For the AFW we compare with (1) deformable part based methods, e.g., structure model [72] and Tree Parts Model (TSM) [87]; (2) cascade-based methods, e.g., Headhunter [49]. Figure 8.16a, b show that Faceness-Net outperforms all previous approaches by a considerable margin, especially on the FDDB dataset.

Summary. In this section, we discussed two attribute-aware deep networks, which are pre-trained with generic objects or identities and then fine-tuned with global or specific part-level binary attributes. It is interesting to observe that these networks could generate response maps in deep layers that strongly indicate the locations of the face or its parts, without any explicit face/part supervisions. Thanks to this unique capability, we are able to train face detector that is robust to severe occlusion and face variations in unconstrained environment. Next we will discuss how face alignment can benefit from attribute learning.

8.4 Face Attributes for Face Alignment

Face alignment, or detecting semantic facial landmarks (e.g., eyes, nose, mouth corners) is a fundamental component in many face analysis tasks, such as face verification [47] and face recognition [30]. Though great strides have been made in this field, robust facial landmark detection remains a formidable challenge in the presence of partial occlusion and large head pose variations [12, 76] (Fig. 8.17a). Landmark detection is traditionally approached as a single and independent problem. Popular approaches include template fitting approaches [14, 63, 79, 87] and regression-based methods [7, 8, 15, 75, 80, 85, 86]. Deep models have been applied as well. For example, Sun et al. [58] propose to detect facial landmarks by coarse-to-fine regression using a cascade of CNNs. This method shows superior accuracy compared to previous methods [3, 8] and existing commercial systems. Nevertheless, the method requires a complex and unwieldy cascade architecture of deep models.

Facial landmark detection can be influenced by a number of heterogeneous and subtly correlated factors. Changes on a face are often governed by the same rules determined by the intrinsic facial structure. For instance, when a kid is smiling, his mouth is widely opened (the second image in Fig. 8.17a). Effectively discovering and exploiting such an intrinsically correlated facial attribute would help in detecting the mouth corners more accurately. Indeed, the input and solution spaces of face alignment can be effectively divided given auxiliary face attributes. In a small experiment, we average a set of face images according to different attributes, as shown in Fig. 8.17b. The frontal and smiling faces show the mouth corners, while there are no specific details for the image averaged over the whole dataset. Given the rich auxiliary attributes, treating facial landmark detection in isolation is counterproductive.

To this end, we consider optimizing facial landmark detection (the main task) by leveraging auxiliary information from attribute inference tasks. Potential auxiliary tasks include head pose estimation, gender classification, age estimation, facial expression recognition, or in general, the prediction of facial attributes. Given the multiple tasks, we employ DCN given its natural capability in handling joint features learning and multi-objective inference. We can formulate a cost function that encom-

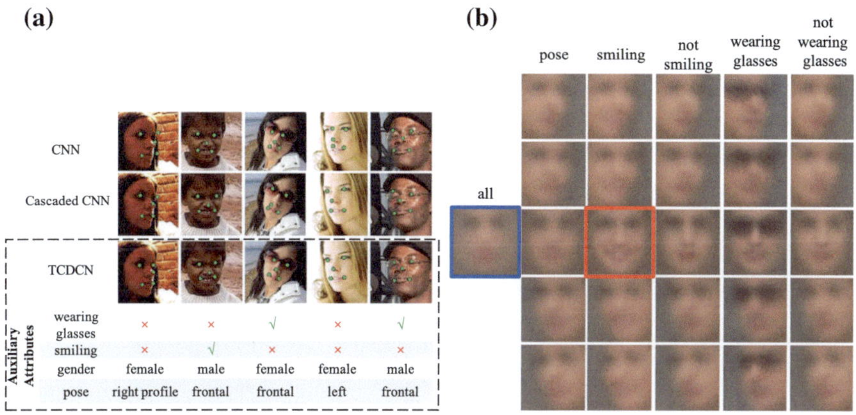

Fig. 8.17 **a** Examples of facial landmark detection by a single conventional CNN, the cascaded CNN [58], and the proposed Tasks-Constrained Deep Convolutional Network (TCDCN). More accurate detection can be achieved by optimizing the detection task jointly with related/auxiliary tasks. **b** Average face images with different attributes. The image in *blue rectangle* is averaged among the whole training faces, while the one in *red* is from the smiling faces with frontal pose. It indicates that the input and solution space can be effectively divided into subsets, which are in different distributions. This lowers the learning difficulty

passes all the tasks and use the cost function in the network backpropagation learning. Designing the network requires some special care. First, the different tasks of face alignment and attribute inference are inherently different in learning difficulties. For instance, learning to identify 'wearing glasses' attribute is easier than determining if one is smiling. Second, as highlighted in Sect. 8.2, we rarely have attributes with similar number of positive/negative cases. For instance, male/female classification enjoys more balanced samples than facial expression recognition. Consequently, different tasks have different convergence rates. In many cases we observe that the joint learning with a specific auxiliary task improves the convergence of landmark detection at the beginning of the training procedure, but become ineffective when the auxiliary task training encounters local minima or over-fitting. Continuing the training with all tasks jeopardizes the network convergence, leading to poor landmark detection performance.

8.4.1 *Attribute Tasks-Constrained Deep Convolutional Network*

To exploit the rich attributes for constraining face alignment, we develop a *Tasks-Constrained Deep Convolutional Network* (TCDCN) [82, 83].

Network Structure Overview. Formally, we cast facial landmark detection as a nonlinear transformation problem, which transforms raw pixels of a face image to positions of dense landmarks. The proposed network is illustrated in Fig. 8.18, showing that the highly nonlinear function is modeled as a DCN, which is pre-trained by five landmarks and attributes, and subsequently fine-tuned to predict the dense landmarks. Since dense landmarks are expensive to label, the pre-training step is essential because it prevents DCN from over-fitting to small datasets. In general, the pre-training and fine-tuning procedures are similar, except that the former step initializes filters by a standard normal distribution, while the latter step initializes filters using the pre-trained network. In addition, the pre-training stage employs both sparse landmarks and attributes as targets, while the fine-tuning stage only uses dense landmarks.

We describe the pre-training stage as follows. As shown in Fig. 8.18, DCN extracts a high-level representation $\mathbf{x} \in \mathbb{R}^{D\times 1}$ on a face image I using a set of filters $\mathbf{K} = \{\mathbf{k}_s\}_{s=1}^{S}$, $\mathbf{x} = \phi(I|\mathbf{K})$, where $\phi(\cdot)$ is the nonlinear transformation learned by DCN. With the extracted feature $\mathbf{x}$, we jointly estimate landmarks and attributes, where landmark detection is the main task and attribute prediction is the auxiliary task. Let $\{y^m\}_{m=1}^{M}$ denote a set of real values, representing the x-, y-coordinates of the landmarks, and let $\{l^t\}_{t=1}^{T}$ denote a set of binary labels of the face attributes, $\forall l^t \in \{0, 1\}$. We have a weight matrix $\mathbf{W} = [\mathbf{w}_1^y, \mathbf{w}_2^y, ..., \mathbf{w}_M^y, \mathbf{w}_1^l, \mathbf{w}_2^l, ..., \mathbf{w}_T^l]$, where each column vector corresponds to the parameters for detecting a landmark or pre-

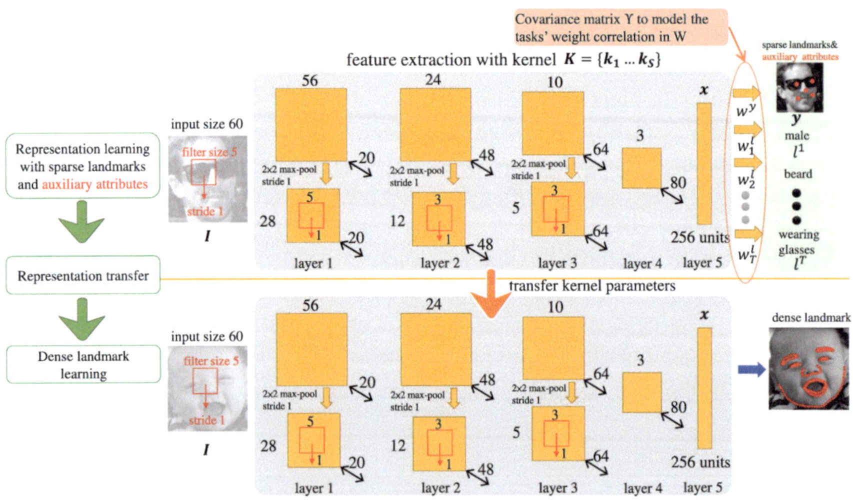

Fig. 8.18 This figure shows the process of transferring representation from a network pre-trained with images annotated with sparse landmarks and attributes (*the top part*), to a new network for dense landmark learning (*the bottom part*). For both networks, a 60×60 image is taken as input. In the first layer, we convolve it with 20 different 5×5 filters, using a stride of 1. The obtained feature map is $56 \times 56 \times 20$, which is subsampled to $28 \times 28 \times 20$ with a 2×2 max-pooling operation. Similar operations are repeated in layer 2, 3, 4, as the parameters shown in the figure. The last layer is fully connected. Then the output is obtained by regression

dicting an attribute based on a generalized linear model [50]. The proposed network considers the following aspects to make the learning effective:

- *Dynamic task coefficient*—Unlike existing multi-task deep models that treat all tasks as equally important, we assign and weight each auxiliary task with a coefficient λ_t, $t = 1...T$, where T is the number of tasks. The coefficient is adaptively and dynamically adjusted based on training and validation errors achieved so far in the learning process. Thus a task that is deemed not beneficial to the main task is prevented from contributing to the network learning. A halted task may be resumed automatically if it is found useful again during the learning process. This approach can be seen as a principled and flexible way of achieving 'early stopping' for a specific task.
- *Inter-task correlation modeling*—We additionally model the relatedness of heterogeneous tasks in a covariance matrix Υ in the objective function. Different from the dynamic task coefficient that is concerned with the learning convergence, inter-task correlation modeling helps better exploiting the relation between tasks to achieve better feature learning.

Objective Function. Given a set of face images and their labels, we jointly estimate the filters **K** in the DCN, the weight matrix **W**, the task covariance matrix Υ, and the dynamic coefficients $\Lambda = \{\lambda_t\}_{t=1}^{T}$. We skip the detailed derivation of the objective function. Interested readers can refer to [83]. The objective function we need to optimize is given as follows:

$$\begin{aligned} \underset{\mathbf{K},\mathbf{W},\Lambda,\Upsilon\succeq\mathbf{0}}{\operatorname{argmin}} & \sum_{i=1}^{N}\sum_{m=1}^{M}(y_i^m - \mathbf{w}_m^{y\,\mathsf{T}}\mathbf{x}_i)^2 \\ & - \sum_{i=1}^{N}\sum_{t=1}^{T}\lambda_t\left\{l_i^t \ln f(\mathbf{w}_t^{l\,\mathsf{T}}\mathbf{x}_i) + (1-l_i^t)\ln\left(1 - f(\mathbf{w}_t^{l\,\mathsf{T}}\mathbf{x}_i)\right)\right\} \\ & + \operatorname{tr}(\mathbf{W}\Upsilon^{-1}\mathbf{W}^{\mathsf{T}}) + D\ln|\Upsilon| + \sum_{s=1}^{S}\mathbf{k}_s^{\mathsf{T}}\mathbf{k}_s + \sum_{t=1}^{T}(\lambda_t - \mu_t)^2. \end{aligned} \tag{8.4}$$

The first and second terms are the least square and cross-entropy loss functions for the main task (landmark regression) and the auxiliary tasks (attribute classification), respectively. Here $f(x) = 1/(1+\exp\{-x\})$. Note that we additionally consider the optimization of task covariance matrix Υ so as to capture the correlations between landmark detection and auxiliary attributes. The dynamic coefficient λ_t of a task is optimized through adjustment based on the mean μ_t, which can be written as

$$\mu_t = \rho \times \frac{E_{val}^t(j-\tau) - E_{val}^t(j)}{E_{val}^t(j-\tau)} \times \frac{E_{tr}^t(j-\tau) - E_{tr}^t(j)}{E_{tr}^t(j-\tau)}, \tag{8.5}$$

Table 8.4 Annotated face attributes in the MAFL dataset

Group	Attributes
Eyes	Bushy eyebrows, arched eyebrows, narrow eyes, bags under eyes, eyeglasses
Nose	Big nose, pointy nose
Mouth	Mouth slightly open, no beard, smiling, big lips, mustache
Global	Gender, oval face, attractive, heavy makeup, chubby
Head pose	Frontal, left, left profile, right, right profile

where $E^t_{val}(j)$, and $E^t_{tr}(j)$ are the values of the loss function of task t on the validation set and training set, respectively, at the j-th learning iteration. The ρ is a constant scale factor, and τ controls a training strip of length τ. The second term in Eq. (8.5) represents the tendency of the validation error. If the validation error drops rapidly within a period of length τ, the value of the first term is large, indicating that training should be emphasized as the task is valuable. Similarly, the third term measures the tendency of the training error. We show the benefits of task covariance matrix and dynamic coefficient in the evaluation section.

Evaluation. To facilitate the training and evaluation of TCDCN, we construct a dataset, Multi-Attribute Facial Landmark (MAFL),[7] by annotating 22 facial attributes on 20,000 faces randomly chosen from the CelebA dataset [45]. The attributes are listed in Table 8.4 and all the attributes are binary, indicating the attribute is presented or not. We divide the attributes into four groups to facilitate the following analysis. The grouping criterion is based on the main face region influenced by the associated attributes. In addition, we divide the face into one of five categories according to the degree of yaw rotation. This results in the fifth group named as 'head pose.' All the faces in the dataset are accompanied with five facial landmarks locations (eyes, nose, and mouth corners), which are used as the target of the face alignment task. We randomly select 1,000 faces for testing and the rest for training. We report our results on two popular metrics [85], i.e. mean error and failure rate. The mean error is measured by the distances between estimated landmarks and the ground truth, and normalized with respect to the inter-ocular distance. Mean error larger than 10 % is reported as a failure.

To examine the influence of auxiliary tasks, we evaluate different variants of the proposed model. In particular, the first variant is trained only on facial landmark detection. We train another five model variants on facial landmark detection along with the auxiliary tasks in the groups 'eyes,' 'nose,' 'mouth,' 'global,' 'head pose,' respectively. In addition, we synthesize a task with random objective and train it along with the facial landmark detection task, which results in the sixth model variant. The full model is trained using all the attributes. For simplicity, we name each variant by facial landmark detection (FLD) and the auxiliary tasks, such as 'FLD only,' 'FLD+eyes,' 'FLD+pose,' 'FLD+all.'

[7]Data and codes of this work are available at http://mmlab.ie.cuhk.edu.hk/projects/TCDCN.html.

It is evident from Fig. 8.19 that optimizing landmark detection with auxiliary tasks is beneficial. In particular, 'FLD+all' outperforms 'FLD' by a large margin, with a reduction of over 7 % in failure rate. When a single auxiliary task group is present, 'FLD+pose' and 'FLD+global' perform better than the others. This is not surprising since the pose variation affects locations of all landmarks directly and the 'global' attribute group influences the whole face region. The other auxiliary tasks such as 'eyes' and 'mouth' are observed to have comparatively smaller influence to the final performance, since they mainly capture local information of the face. As for 'FLD+random' the performance is hardly improved. This result shows that the main task and auxiliary task need to be related for any performance gain in the main task.

In addition, we show the relative improvement caused by different groups of attributes for each landmark in Fig. 8.20. In particular, we define relative improvement $= \frac{\text{reduced error}}{\text{original error}}$, where the original error is produced by the model of 'FLD only.' We can observe a trend that each group facilitates landmark localization in the corresponding face region. For example, for the group 'mouth,' the benefits are mainly observed at the corners of mouth. This observation is intuitive since attributes like smiling drives the lower part of the faces, more than the upper facial region. The learning of these attributes develops a shared representation that describes the lower facial region, which in turn facilitates the localization of corners of mouth. Similarly, the improvement of eye location is much more significant than mouth and nose for the attribute group 'eye.' However, we observe the group 'nose' improves the eye and mouth localization remarkably. This is mainly because the nose is in the center of the

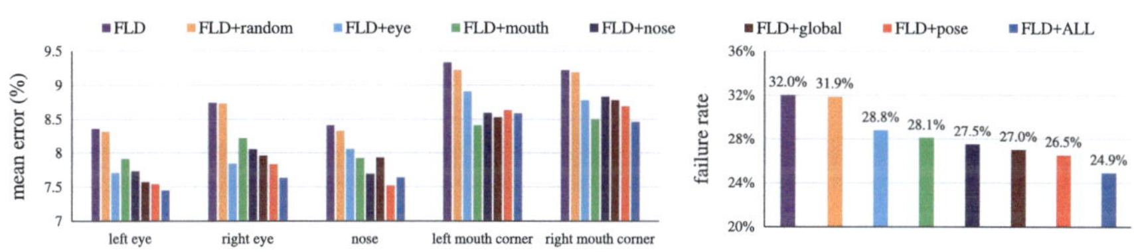

Fig. 8.19 Comparison of different model variants of TCDCN: the mean error over different landmarks (*left*), and the overall failure rate (*right*)

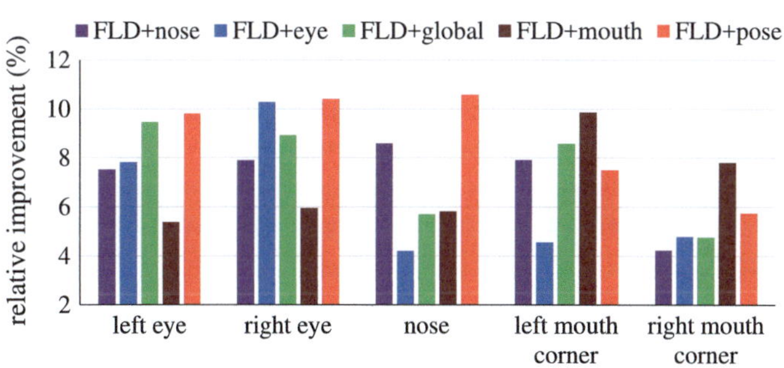

Fig. 8.20 Improvement over different landmarks by different attribute groups

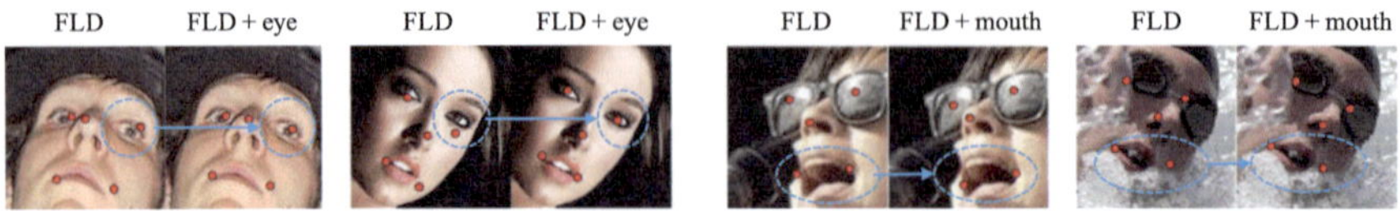

Fig. 8.21 Examples of improvement by attribute groups 'eye' and 'mouth'

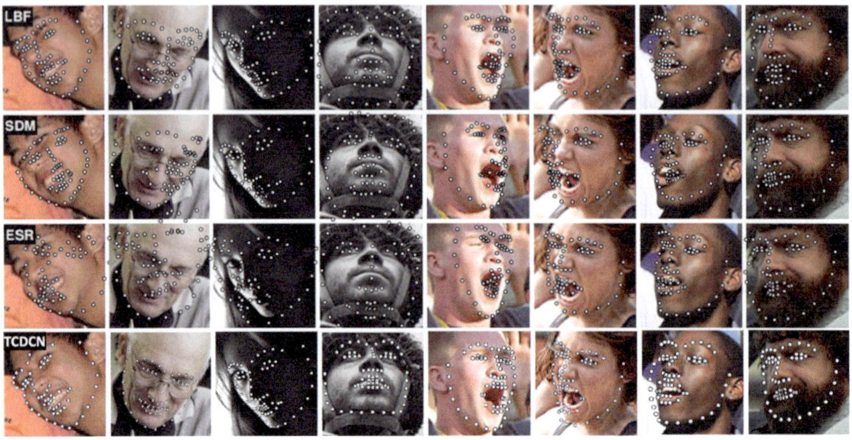

Fig. 8.22 Results of ESR [8], SDM [70], LBF [52] and our method on the IBUG faces [54]

face, and there exists constrains between the nose location and other landmarks. The horizontal coordinate of the nose is likely to be the mean of the eyes in a frontal face. As for the groups of 'pose' and 'global', the improvement is significant in all landmarks. Figure 8.21 depicts improvements led by adding 'eye' and 'mouth' attributes. Figure 8.22 shows more examples, demonstrating the effectiveness of TCDCN under various face variations.

We compare the proposed TCDCN against various state-of-the-art methods on the popular 300-W benchmark [54], following the same protocol in [52]. In particular, the training set of 300-W contains 3,148 faces, including the AFW [87], the training sets of LFPW [3], and the training sets of Helen [39]. The test set contains 689 faces, including IBUG, the testing sets of LFPW, and the testing sets of Helen. The comparisons are summarized in Table 8.5. For the challenging subset (IBUG faces) TCDCN produces a significant error reduction of over 10 % in comparison to the state-of-the-art approach [85]. As can be seen from Fig. 8.22, the proposed method exhibits superior capability of handling difficult cases with large head rotation and exaggerated expressions, thanks to the shared representation learning with auxiliary face attributes.

Benefits of Dynamic Tasks Coefficient and Inter-Task Correlation Learning. We compare the dynamic tasks coefficient with the task-wise early stopping proposed in the earlier version of this work [82]. As shown in Table 8.6, the dynamic task coef-

Table 8.5 Mean errors (%) on 300-W [54] dataset (68 landmarks)

Method	Common subset	Challenging subset	Fullset
CDM [79]	10.10	19.54	11.94
DRMF [2]	6.65	19.79	9.22
RCPR [7]	6.18	17.26	8.35
GN-DPM [63]	5.78	–	–
CFAN [80]	5.50	16.78	7.69
ESR [8]	5.28	17.00	7.58
SDM [70]	5.57	15.40	7.50
ERT [34]	–	–	6.40
LBF [52]	4.95	11.98	6.32
CFSS [85]	**4.73**	9.98	5.76
TCDCN	4.80	**8.60**	**5.54**

Table 8.6 Comparison of mean error ($\times 10^{-2}$) on MAFL dataset under different network configurations

	Without inter-task correlation learning	With inter-task correlation learning
Task-wise early stopping [82]	8.35	8.21
Dynamic task coefficient	8.07	7.95

ficient achieves better performance than the task-wise early stopping scheme. This is because the new method is more dynamic in coordinating the different auxiliary tasks across the whole training process. In addition, we also show the mean errors of facial landmark localization with and without inter-task correlation learning (without correlation learning means that we simply apply multiple tasks as targets and do not use the term of Υ in Eq. (8.4)). It demonstrates the effectiveness of task correlation learning.

Summary. Instead of learning facial landmark detection in isolation, we have shown that more robust landmark detection can be achieved through joint learning with heterogeneous but subtly correlated auxiliary tasks, such as expression, demographic, and head pose. The proposed Tasks-Constrained DCN allows errors of auxiliary tasks to be backpropagated in deep hidden layers for constructing a shared representation to be relevant to the main task. We also show that by learning a dynamic task coefficient, we can utilize the auxiliary tasks in a more efficient way. Thanks to learning with the auxiliary attributes, the proposed model is more robust to faces with severe occlusions and large pose variations compared to existing methods.

8.5 Discussion

This chapter has presented a viable approach for addressing the face attribute recognition problem, together with an extensive discussion of exploiting such attributes to facilitate other face analysis tasks in return. These techniques and approaches by no means have covered exhaustively all the open problems associated with solving face attribute recognition.

A key challenge is to recognize attributes from low-resolution images. Specifically, human experts seek and rely upon matching characteristics, such as discrete hair styles, and facial features for human recognition and identification. In practice, most surveillance cameras are installed to capture far-view field so as to maximize the scene coverage. Consequently, a detectable face of interest may only occupy tiny amount pixels of the whole image (e.g. 20×20 or even smaller), especially for standard definition surveillance videos. Given the low-resolution and potentially blurred images, describing and matching characteristics becomes an exceptionally difficult and challenging task for both human and machine to perform. How to achieve robust attribute recognition even on low-resolution images? While existing face hallucination [26, 29, 33, 67, 74] or image super-resolution methods [17, 18] could be a potential solution, these studies concern about human perceived quality but not machine perception, thus existing methods do not guarantee good attribute recognition performance. In addition, the performance of existing image hallucination remains poor due to the large variations in appearance, illumination and pose, as well as motion and out of focus blurs. Without the guidance of face structures and attributes, the hallucination output would not be realistic and contain clear artifacts. It is thus an interesting direction to explore the joint learning of face hallucination and attribute prediction so that the two tasks could help and regularize each other.

References

1. Arbeláez, P., Pont-Tuset, J., Barron, J.T., Marques, F., Malik, J.: Multiscale combinatorial grouping. In: Conference on Computer Vision and Pattern Recognition (CVPR) (2014)
2. Asthana, A., Zafeiriou, S., Cheng, S., Pantic, M.: Robust discriminative response map fitting with constrained local models. In: Conference on Computer Vision and Pattern Recognition (CVPR) (2013)
3. Belhumeur, P.N., Jacobs, D.W., Kriegman, D.J., Kumar, N.: Localizing parts of faces using a consensus of exemplars. IEEE Trans. Pattern Anal. Mach. Intell. **35**(12), 2930–2940 (2013)
4. Berg, T., Belhumeur, P.N.: Poof: Part-based one-versus-one features for fine-grained categorization, face verification, and attribute estimation. In: Conference on Computer Vision and Pattern Recognition (CVPR) (2013)
5. Bourdev, L., Maji, S., Malik, J.: Describing people: a poselet-based approach to attribute classification. In: International Conference on Computer Vision (ICCV) (2011)
6. Boureau, Y.L., Roux, N.L., Bach, F., Ponce, J., LeCun, Y.: Ask the locals: multi-way local pooling for image recognition. In: International Conference on Computer Vision (ICCV) (2011)
7. Burgos-Artizzu, X., Perona, P., Dollár, P.: Robust face landmark estimation under occlusion. In: International Conference on Computer Vision (ICCV) (2013)

8. Cao, X., Wei, Y., Wen, F., Sun, J.: Face alignment by explicit shape regression. In: Conference on Computer Vision and Pattern Recognition (CVPR) (2012)
9. Chechik, G., Shalit, U., Sharma, V., Bengio, S.: An online algorithm for large scale image similarity learning. In: Conference on Neural Information Processing Systems (NIPS) (2009)
10. Chen, D., Ren, S., Wei, Y., Cao, X., Sun, J.: Joint cascade face detection and alignment. In: European Conference on Computer Vision (ECCV) (2014)
11. Chen, K., Gong, S., Xiang, T., Loy, C.C.: Cumulative attribute space for age and crowd density estimation. In: Conference on Computer Vision and Pattern Recognition (CVPR) (2013)
12. Chrysos, G.G., Antonakos, E., Snape, P., Asthana, A., Zafeiriou, S.: A comprehensive performance evaluation of deformable face tracking "in-the-wild". arXiv preprint arXiv:1603.06015 (2016)
13. Chung, J., Lee, D., Seo, Y., Yoo, C.D.: Deep attribute networks. In: NIPS Workshop on Deep Learning and Unsupervised Feature Learning (2012)
14. Cootes, T.F., Edwards, G.J., Taylor, C.J.: Active appearance models. IEEE Trans. Pattern Anal. Mach. Intell. **23**(6), 681–685 (2001)
15. Cootes, T.F., Ionita, M.C., Lindner, C., Sauer, P.: Robust and accurate shape model fitting using random forest regression voting. In: European Conference on Computer Vision (ECCV) (2012)
16. Deng, J., Dong, W., Socher, R., Li, L.J., Li, K., Fei-Fei, L.: Imagenet: a large-scale hierarchical image database. In: Conference on Computer Vision and Pattern Recognition (CVPR) (2009)
17. Dong, C., Loy, C.C., He, K., Tang, X.: Learning a deep convolutional network for image super-resolution. In: European Conference on Computer Vision (ECCV) (2014)
18. Dong, C., Loy, C.C., He, K., Tang, X.: Image super-resolution using deep convolutional networks. IEEE Trans. Pattern Anal. Mach. Intell. **38**(2), 295–307 (2015)
19. Everingham, M., Van Gool, L., Williams, C.K., Winn, J., Zisserman, A.: The pascal visual object classes (VOC) challenge. Int. J. Comput. Vis. **88**(2), 303–338 (2010)
20. Face++: http://www.faceplusplus.com/
21. Fan, R.E., Chang, K.W., Hsieh, C.J., Wang, X.R., Lin, C.J.: Liblinear: a library for large linear classification. J. Mach. Learn. Res. **9**, 1871–1874 (2008)
22. Farabet, C., Couprie, C., Najman, L., LeCun, Y.: Learning hierarchical features for scene labeling. IEEE Trans. Pattern Anal. Mach. Intell. **35**(8), 915–1929 (2013)
23. Girshick, R.: Fast R-CNN. In: International Conference on Computer Vision (ICCV) (2015)
24. Hadsell, R., Chopra, S., LeCun, Y.: Dimensionality reduction by learning an invariant mapping. In: Conference on Computer Vision and Pattern Recognition (CVPR) (2006)
25. He, K., Zhang, X., Ren, S., Sun, J.: Deep residual learning for image recognition. arXiv preprint arXiv:1512.03385 (2015)
26. Hu, Y., Lam, K.M., Qiu, G., Shen, T.: From local pixel structure to global image super-resolution: a new face hallucination framework. IEEE Trans. Image Process. **20**(2), 433–445 (2011)
27. Huang, C., Loy, C.C., Tang, X.: Discriminative sparse neighbor approximation for imbalanced learning. arXiv preprint arXiv:1602.01197 (2016)
28. Huang, C., Loy, C.C., Tang, X.: Learning deep representation for imbalanced classification. In: Conference on Computer Vision and Pattern Recognition (CVPR) (2016)
29. Huang, H., He, H., Fan, X., Zhang, J.: Super-resolution of human face image using canonical correlation analysis. Pattern Recogn. **43**(7), 2532–2543 (2010)
30. Huang, Z., Zhao, X., Shan, S., Wang, R., Chen, X.: Coupling alignments with recognition for still-to-video face recognition. In: International Conference on Computer Vision (ICCV), pp. 3296–3303 (2013)
31. Jain, V., Learned-Miller, E.: FDDB: a benchmark for face detection in unconstrained settings. university of massachusetts. Technical report, Amherst, Tech. Rep. UM-CS-2010-009 (2010)
32. Jain, V., Learned-Miller, E.: Online domain adaptation of a pre-trained cascade of classifiers. In: Conference on Computer Vision and Pattern Recognition (CVPR) (2011)
33. Jin, Y., Bouganis, C.S.: Robust multi-image based blind face hallucination. In: Conference on Computer Vision and Pattern Recognition (CVPR) (2015)

34. Kazemi, V., Josephine, S.: One millisecond face alignment with an ensemble of regression trees. In: Conference on Computer Vision and Pattern Recognition (CVPR) (2014)
35. Koestinger, M., Wohlhart, P., Roth, P.M., Bischof, H.: Annotated facial landmarks in the wild: a large-scale, real-world database for facial landmark localization. In: First IEEE International Workshop on Benchmarking Facial Image Analysis Technologies (2011)
36. Krizhevsky, A., Sutskever, I., Hinton, G.E.: Imagenet classification with deep convolutional neural networks. In: Conference on Neural Information Processing Systems (NIPS) (2012)
37. Kumar, N., Berg, A.C., Belhumeur, P.N., Nayar, S.K.: Attribute and simile classifiers for face verification. In: International Conference on Computer Vision (ICCV) (2009)
38. Kumar, N., Berg, A.C., Belhumeur, P.N., Nayar, S.K.: Describable visual attributes for face verification and image search. IEEE Trans. Pattern Anal. Mach. Intell. **33**(10), 1962–1977 (2011)
39. Le, V., Brandt, J., Lin, Z., Bourdev, L., Huang, T.S.: Interactive facial feature localization. In: European Conference on Computer Vision (ECCV) (2012)
40. LeCun, Y., Boser, B., Denker, J.S., Henderson, D., Howard, R.E., Hubbard, W., Jackel, L.D.: Handwritten digit recognition with a back-propagation network. In: Conference on Neural Information Processing Systems (NIPS) (1990)
41. Li, J., Zhang, Y.: Learning SURF cascade for fast and accurate object detection. In: Conference on Computer Vision and Pattern Recognition (CVPR) (2013)
42. Li, H., Hua, G., Lin, Z., Brandt, J., Yang, J.: Probabilistic elastic part model for unsupervised face detector adaptation. In: International Conference on Computer Vision (ICCV) (2013)
43. Li, H., Lin, Z., Brandt, J., Shen, X., Hua, G.: Efficient boosted exemplar-based face detection. In: Conference on Computer Vision and Pattern Recognition (CVPR) (2014)
44. Liu, Z., Li, X., Luo, P., Loy, C.C., Tang, X.: Semantic image segmentation via deep parsing network. In: International Conference on Computer Vision (ICCV) (2015)
45. Liu, Z., Luo, P., Wang, X., Tang, X.: Deep learning face attributes in the wild. In: International Conference on Computer Vision (ICCV) (2015)
46. Long, J., Shelhamer, E., Darrell, T.: Fully convolutional networks for semantic segmentation. In: Conference on Computer Vision and Pattern Recognition (CVPR) (2015)
47. Lu, C., Tang, X.: Surpassing human-level face verification performance on LFW with gaussianface. arXiv preprint arXiv:1404.3840 (2014)
48. Luo, P., Wang, X., Tang, X.: A deep sum-product architecture for robust facial attributes analysis. In: International Conference on Computer Vision (ICCV) (2013)
49. Mathias, M., Benenson, R., Pedersoli, M., Van Gool, L.: Face detection without bells and whistles. In: European Conference on Computer Vision (ECCV) (2014)
50. McCullagh, P., Nelder, J.A., McCullagh, P.: Generalized linear models. Chapman and Hall London (1989)
51. Mnih, V., Hinton, G.: Learning to label aerial images from noisy data. In: International Conference on Machine Learning (ICML) (2012)
52. Ren, S., Cao, X., Wei, Y., Sun, J.: Face alignment at 3000 fps via regressing local binary features. In: Conference on Computer Vision and Pattern Recognition (CVPR) (2014)
53. Ren, S., He, K., Girshick, R., Sun, J.: Faster R-CNN: towards real-time object detection with region proposal networks. In: Conference on Neural Information Processing Systems (NIPS) (2015)
54. Sagonas, C., Tzimiropoulos, G., Zafeiriou, S., Pantic, M.: 300 faces in-the-wild challenge: the first facial landmark localization challenge. In: International Conference on Computer Vision Workshop (2013)
55. Schroff, F., Kalenichenko, D., Philbin, J.: FaceNet: a unified embedding for face recognition and clustering. In: Conference on Computer Vision and Pattern Recognition (CVPR) (2015)
56. Shen, X., Lin, Z., Brandt, J., Wu, Y.: Detecting and aligning faces by image retrieval. In: Conference on Computer Vision and Pattern Recognition (CVPR) (2013)
57. Simonyan, K., Zisserman, A.: Very deep convolutional networks for large-scale image recognition. arXiv preprint arXiv:1409.1556 (2014)

58. Sun, Y., Wang, X., Tang, X.: Deep convolutional network cascade for facial point detection. In: Conference on Computer Vision and Pattern Recognition (CVPR) (2013)
59. Sun, Y., Chen, Y., Wang, X., Tang, X.: Deep learning face representation by joint identification-verification. In: Conference on Neural Information Processing Systems (NIPS) (2014)
60. Sun, Y., Wang, X., Tang, X.: Deeply learned face representations are sparse, selective, and robust. In: Conference on Computer Vision and Pattern Recognition (CVPR) (2015)
61. Szegedy, C., Liu, W., Jia, Y., Sermanet, P., Reed, S., Anguelov, D., Erhan, D., Vanhoucke, V., Rabinovich, A.: Going deeper with convolutions. In: Conference on Computer Vision and Pattern Recognition (CVPR) (2015)
62. Taigman, Y., Yang, M., Ranzato, M., Wolf, L.: Deepface: closing the gap to human-level performance in face verification. In: Conference on Computer Vision and Pattern Recognition (CVPR) (2014)
63. Tzimiropoulos, G., Pantic, M.: Gauss-newton deformable part models for face alignment in-the-wild. In: Conference on Computer Vision and Pattern Recognition (CVPR) (2014)
64. Uijlings, J.R., van de Sande, K.E., Gevers, T., Smeulders, A.W.: Selective search for object recognition. Int. J. Comput. Vis. **104**(2), 154–171 (2013)
65. Wang, J., Yang, J., Yu, K., Lv, F., Huang, T., Gong, Y.: Locality-constrained linear coding for image classification. In: Conference on Computer Vision and Pattern Recognition (CVPR) (2010)
66. Wang, J., Song, Y., Leung, T., Rosenberg, C., Wang, J., Philbin, J., Chen, B., Wu, Y.: Learning fine-grained image similarity with deep ranking. In: Conference on Computer Vision and Pattern Recognition (CVPR) (2014)
67. Wang, N., Tao, D., Gao, X., Li, X., Li, J.: A comprehensive survey to face hallucination. Int. J. Comput. Vis. **106**(1), 9–30 (2014)
68. Weinberger, K.Q., Saul, L.K.: Distance metric learning for large margin nearest neighbor classification. J. Mach. Learn. Res. **10**, 207–244 (2009)
69. Xiao, J., Hays, J., Ehinger, K.A., Oliva, A., Torralba, A.: SUN database: large-scale scene recognition from abbey to zoo. In: Conference on Computer Vision and Pattern Recognition (CVPR) (2010)
70. Xiong, X., Torre, F.: Supervised descent method and its applications to face alignment. In: Conference on Computer Vision and Pattern Recognition (CVPR) (2013)
71. Yan, J., Lei, Z., Wen, L., Li, S.: The fastest deformable part model for object detection. In: Conference on Computer Vision and Pattern Recognition (CVPR) (2014)
72. Yan, J., Zhang, X., Lei, Z., Li, S.Z.: Face detection by structural models. Image Vis. Comput. **32**(10), 790–799 (2014)
73. Yang, B., Yan, J., Lei, Z., Li, S.Z.: Aggregate channel features for multi-view face detection. In: International Joint Conference on Biometrics (IJCB) (2014)
74. Yang, C.Y., Liu, S., Yang, M.H.: Structured face hallucination. In: Conference on Computer Vision and Pattern Recognition (CVPR) (2013)
75. Yang, H., Patras, I.: Sieving regression forest votes for facial feature detection in the wild. In: International Conference on Computer Vision (ICCV) (2013)
76. Yang, H., Jia, X., Loy, C.C., Robinson, P.: An empirical study of recent face alignment methods. arXiv preprint arXiv:1511.05049 (2015)
77. Yang, S., Luo, P., Loy, C.C., Tang, X.: From facial parts responses to face detection: a deep learning approach. In: International Conference on Computer Vision (ICCV) (2015)
78. Yang, S., Luo, P., Loy, C.C., Tang, X.: Wider face: a face detection benchmark. In: Conference on Computer Vision and Pattern Recognition (CVPR) (2016)
79. Yu, X., Huang, J., Zhang, S., Yan, W., Metaxas, D.N.: Pose-free facial landmark fitting via optimized part mixtures and cascaded deformable shape model. In: International Conference on Computer Vision (ICCV) (2013)
80. Zhang, J., Shan, S., Kan, M., Chen, X.: Coarse-to-fine auto-encoder networks (CFAN) for real-time face alignment. In: European Conference on Computer Vision (ECCV) (2014)
81. Zhang, N., Paluri, M., Ranzato, M., Darrell, T., Bourdev, L.: PANDA: pose aligned networks for deep attribute modeling. In: Conference on Computer Vision and Pattern Recognition (CVPR) (2014)

82. Zhang, Z., Luo, P., Loy, C.C., Tang, X.: Facial landmark detection by deep multi-task learning. In: European Conference on Computer Vision (ECCV) (2014)
83. Zhang, Z., Luo, P., Loy, C.C., Tang, X.: Learning deep representation for face alignment with auxiliary attributes. IEEE Trans. Pattern Anal. Mach. Intell. **38**(5), 918–930 (2015)
84. Zhang, Z., Luo, P., Loy, C.C., Tang, X.: Learning social relation traits from face images. In: International Conference on Computer Vision (ICCV) (2015)
85. Zhu, S., Li, C., Loy, C.C., Tang, X.: Face alignment by coarse-to-fine shape searching. In: Conference on Computer Vision and Pattern Recognition (CVPR) (2015)
86. Zhu, S., Li, C., Loy, C.C., Tang, X.: Unconstrained face alignment via cascaded compositional learning. In: Conference on Computer Vision and Pattern Recognition (CVPR) (2016)
87. Zhu, X., Ramanan, D.: Face detection, pose estimation, and landmark localization in the wild. In: Conference on Computer Vision and Pattern Recognition (CVPR) (2012)
88. Zitnick, C.L., Dollár, P.: Edge boxes: locating object proposals from edges. In: European Conference on Computer Vision (ECCV) (2014)

Chapter 9
Visual Attributes for Fashion Analytics

Si Liu, Lisa M. Brown, Qiang Chen, Junshi Huang, Luoqi Liu and Shuicheng Yan

Abstract In this chapter, we describe methods that leverage clothing and facial attributes as mid-level features for fashion recommendation and retrieval. We introduce a system called *Magic Closet* for recommending clothing for different occasions, and a system called *Beauty E-Expert* for hairstyle and facial makeup recommendation. For fashion retrieval, we describe a cross-domain clothing retrieval system, which receives as input a user photo of a particular clothing item taken in unconstrained conditions, and retrieves the exact same or similar item from online shopping catalogs. In each of these systems, we show the value of attribute-guided learning and describe approaches to transfer semantic concepts from large-scale uncluttered annotated data to challenging real-world imagery.

S. Liu (✉)
State Key Laboratory of Information Security, Institute of Information Engineering, Chinese Academy of Sciences, Beijing, China
e-mail: liusi@iie.ac.cn

L.M. Brown
IBM T. J. Watson Research Center, New York, England
e-mail: lisabr@us.ibm.com

Q. Chen · J. Huang · L. Liu · S. Yan
Qihoo 360 Artificial Intelligence Institute, Beijing, China
e-mail: chenqiang-iri@360.cn

J. Huang
e-mail: huangjunshi@360.cn

L. Liu
e-mail: llq667@gmail.com

S. Yan
e-mail: yanshuicheng@360.cn

R.S. Feris et al. (eds.), *Visual Attributes*, Advances in Computer Vision and Pattern Recognition, DOI 10.1007/978-3-319-50077-5_9

9.1 Motivation and Related Work

Visual analysis of people, in particular the extraction of facial and clothing attributes [5, 6, 14, 37], is a topic that has received increasing attention in recent years by the computer vision community. The task of predicting fine-grained facial attributes has proven effective in a variety of application domains, such as content-based image retrieval [16], and person search based on textual descriptions [9, 35]. We refer to Chap. 8 for a detailed analysis of methods for processing facial attributes.

Regarding the automated analysis of clothing images, several methods have been proposed for context-aided people identification [10], fashion style recognition [13], occupation recognition [32], and social tribe prediction [17]. Clothing parsing methods, which produce semantic labels for each pixel in the input image, have also received significant attention in the past few years [20, 21, 26, 27, 38]. In the surveillance domain, matching clothing images across cameras is a core subtask for the well-known person reidentification problem [18, 31].

In this chapter, we demonstrate the effectiveness of clothing and facial attributes as mid-level features for fashion analytics and retail applications. This is an important area due to the accelerated growth of e-commerce applications and their enormous financial potential.

Within this application domain, several recent methods have successfully used visual attributes for product retrieval and search. Berg et al. [2] discover attributes of accessories such as shoes and hand bags by mining text and image data from the Internet. Liu et al. [24] describe a system for retrieving clothing items from online shopping catalogs. Kovashka et al. [15] developed a system called "Whittle-Search", which is able to answer queries such as "Show me shoe images like these, but sportier". They used the concept of relative attributes proposed by Parikh and Grauman [29] for relevance feedback. More details about this system is described in Chap. 5. Attributes for clothing have been explored in several recent papers [3–5]. They allow users to search visual content based on fine-grained descriptions, such as a "blue striped polo-style shirt".

Attribute-based representations have also shown compelling results for matching images of people across domains [19, 31]. The work by Donahue and Grauman [7] demonstrates that richer supervision conveying annotator rationales based on visual attributes improves recognition performance. Sharmanska et al. [30] explored attributes and rationales as a form of privileged information [34], considering a learning to rank framework. Along this direction, in one of the applications considered in this chapter, we show that cross-domain image retrieval can benefit from feature learning that simultaneously optimizes a loss function that takes into account visual similarity and attribute classification.

Next, we will describe how visual attributes can serve as a powerful image representation for fashion recommendation and retrieval. We start by describing two systems for clothing and makeup recommendation, respectively, and then show an attribute-guided learning method for cross-domain clothing retrieval.

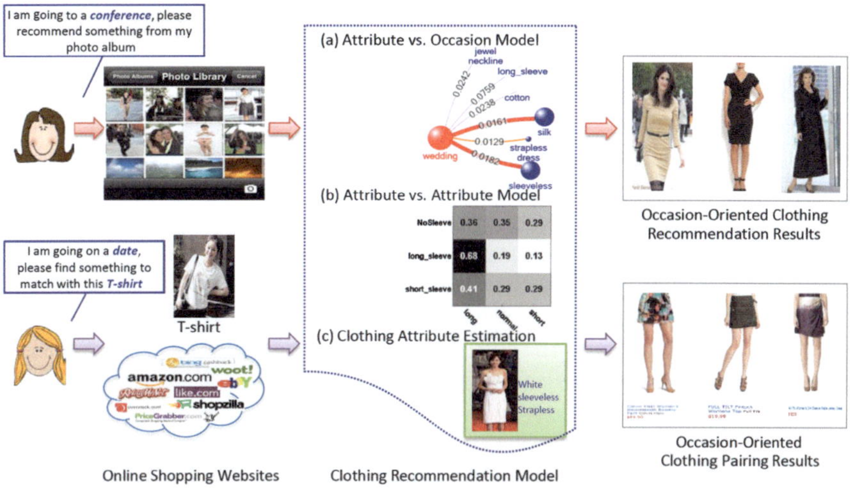

Fig. 9.1 Two typical clothing recommendation scenarios for Magic Closet. (*Top panel*) Clothing suggestion: given an occasion, the most suitable clothing combinations from the user's photo album are suggested. (*Bottom panel*) Clothing pairing: given an occasion and a reference clothing item, the clothing most suitable for the occasion and most matched with the reference clothing is recommended from online shopping websites

9.2 Recommendation Systems

In this section, we describe two recommendation systems based on attribute prediction. In both cases, we use attributes as an intermediate representation to leverage semantic knowledge from a large expert database. In the first case, we detail a system to recommend clothing from a user's collection for a given special occasion such as a wedding, funeral or conference. We construct a latent SVM model where each potential function in the latent SVM is defined specifically for the clothing recommendation task. We use low-level visual features to predict intermediate clothing attributes such as color, pattern, material, or collar type, which in turn are used to predict the best choice of outfit for the given occasion from the user's closet or from online shopping stores.

In the second case, we develop a system to recommend hairstyle and makeup selections for a user's image without makeup and with either short or bound hair. Again, we use visual features to predict intermediate attribute features for this task. In this scenario, we use a multiple tree-structured super-graphs model to estimate facial/clothing attributes such as a high forehead, flat nose bridge, or collar shape, which in turn are used to predict the most suitable high-level beauty attributes such as hair length or color, lip gloss color or the eye shadow template class.

9.2.1 "Hi, magic closet, tell me what to wear!"

Problem: Only a few existing works target the clothing recommendation task. Some online websites[1] can support the service of recommending the most suitable clothing for an occasion. However, their recommendation tools are mainly based on dress codes and common sense. Magic Closet is the first system to automatically investigate the task of occasion-oriented clothing recommendation and clothing pairing by mining the matching rules among semantic attributes from real images.

Magic Closet mainly addresses two clothing recommendation scenarios. The first scenario is *clothing suggestion*. As shown in the top panel of Fig. 9.1, a user specifies an occasion and the system will suggest the most suitable outfits from the user's own photo album. The second scenario is *clothing pairing*. As shown in the bottom panel of Fig. 9.1, a user inputs an occasion and one reference clothing item (such as a T-shirt the user wants to pair), and then the most matched clothing from the online shopping website is returned (such as a skirt). The returned clothing should aesthetically pair with the reference clothing well and also be suitable for the specified occasion. As a result, the Magic Closet system can serve as a plug-in application in any online shopping website for shopping recommendation.

Two key principles are considered when designing Magic Closet. One is *wearing properly*. Wearing properly means putting on some suitable clothing, which conforms to normative *dress codes*[2] and common sense. The other is *wearing aesthetically*. There are some aesthetic rules which need to be followed when one pairs the upper body clothing and lower body clothing. For example, it looks weird to wear a red coat and a green pants together.

Recommendation Model: In the model learning process, to narrow the semantic gap between the low-level visual features of clothing and the high-level occasion categories, we propose to utilize mid-level clothing attributes. Here 7 multivalue clothing attributes are defined, including the category attribute (e.g., "jeans", "skirts") and detail attributes, describing certain properties of clothing (e.g., color, pattern).

We propose to learn the clothing recommendation model through a unified latent Support Vector Machine (SVM) framework [23]. The model integrates four potentials: (1) visual features versus attribute, (2) visual features versus occasion, (3) attributes versus occasion, and (4) attribute versus attribute. Here the first three potentials relate to clothing-occasion matching and the last one describes the clothing-clothing matching. Embedding these matching rules into the latent SVM model explicitly ensures that the recommended clothing satisfies the requirement of *wearing properly* and *wearing aesthetically* simultaneously.

A training clothing image is denoted as a tuple $(\mathbf{x}, \mathbf{a}_u, \mathbf{a}_l, \mathbf{o})$. Here $\mathbf{x}$ corresponds to the visual features from the whole body clothing, which is formed by directly concatenating the upper body clothing feature $\mathbf{x}_u$ and lower body clothing feature $\mathbf{x}_l$, namely $\mathbf{x} = [\mathbf{x}_u; \mathbf{x}_l]$. We extract 5 types of features from 20 upper body parts and 10 lower body parts detected using the methodology in [39]. The features include

[1]http://www.dresscodeguide.com/.

[2]Dress codes are written and unwritten rules with regards to clothing.

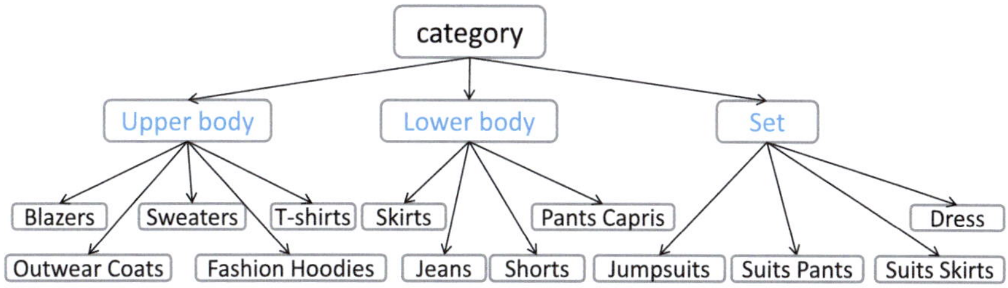

Fig. 9.2 Clothing category attributes. All the attributes are organized in a tree structure and only the leaf nodes are considered in this work

	Attribute Name	Attribute Values			Attribute Name	Attribute Values	
GLOBAL	**Color**	Red	Orange		**Material**		
		Black	White	Yellow		Cotton	Chiffon
		Green	Brown	Gray		Silk	Woolen
		Blue	Purple	Multi-color		Denim	Leather
	Pattern	Vertical	Plaid	Horizontal			
		Drawing	Plain	Floral print			
UPPER	**Collar**	Strapless	V-shape	One-shoulder	**Sleeve**	Long	Short
		Jewel	Round	Shirt collar		Sleeveless	
LOWER	**Length**	Long	Median	Short			

Fig. 9.3 Detail attributes considered in this work

Histograms of Oriented Gradient (HOG), Local Binary Pattern (LBP), color moment, color histogram, and skin descriptor. More specifically, each human part is first partitioned into several smaller, spatially evenly distributed regular blocks. Features extracted from all the blocks are finally concatenated into a 28,770 dimensional feature vector to represent a human part. The block-based features can roughly preserve relative position information inside each human part.

The occasion categories of the clothing are represented by $\mathbf{o} \subset \mathcal{O}$, where $\mathcal{O}$ denotes the finite occasion category set. Note that each clothing may have multiple occasion category labels. The attributes of the upper body clothing are denoted by a vector $\mathbf{a}_u = [a_1^u, \ldots, a_{K_u}^u]^T$, where K_u is the number of attributes considered for the upper body clothing. Each attribute describes certain characteristic of the upper body clothing, e.g., color, collar. Similarly, the attributes of the lower body clothing are denoted as a vector $\mathbf{a}_l = [a_1^l, \ldots, a_{K_l}^l]^T$. All the attributes considered in this work are listed in Figs. 9.2 and 9.3. We denote the attribute set for the upper body and lower body as $\mathcal{A}^u$ and $\mathcal{A}^l$, respectively. Note that each attribute is multivalued and we represent each attribute by a multidimensional binary value vector in the model learning process. For example, the attribute "color" has 11 different values, e.g., red, orange, etc. Then we represent the "color" attribute by an 11-dimensional vector with each element corresponding to one specific type of color.

Given N training examples $\{(\mathbf{x}^{(n)}, \mathbf{a}_u^{(n)}, \mathbf{a}_l^{(n)}, \mathbf{o}^{(n)})\}_{n=1}^N$, our goal is to learn a model that can be used to recommend the most suitable clothing for a given occasion label $o \in \mathcal{O}$, which considers clothing-occasion and clothing–clothing matching simultaneously. Formally speaking, we are interested in learning a scoring function $f_{\mathbf{w}} : \mathcal{X} \times \mathcal{O} \rightarrow \mathbb{R}$, over an image $\mathbf{x}$ and a user specified occasion label o, where $\mathbf{w}$ are the parameters of $f_{\mathbf{w}}$. Here $\mathcal{X}$ denotes the clothing image space. During testing, $f_{\mathbf{w}}$ can be used to suggest the most suitable clothing $\mathbf{x}^*$ from $\mathcal{X}^t$ (candidate clothing repository) for the given occasion o as $\mathbf{x}^* = \text{argmax}_{\mathbf{x} \in \mathcal{X}^t} f_{\mathbf{w}}(\mathbf{x}, o)$. While for the clothing pairing recommendation, given specified lower body clothing $\mathbf{x}_l$, $f_{\mathbf{w}}$ can select the most suitable upper body clothing $\mathbf{x}_u^*$ as $\mathbf{x}_u^* = \text{argmax}_{\mathbf{x}_u \in \mathcal{X}_u^t} f_{\mathbf{w}}([\mathbf{x}_u; \mathbf{x}_l], o)$, where $\mathcal{X}_u^t$ denotes the candidate upper body clothing repository. For the lower body clothing pairing, it works similarly.

The recommendation function is defined as follows:

$$\mathbf{w}^T \Phi(\mathbf{x}, \mathbf{a}_u, \mathbf{a}_l, o) = \mathbf{w}_o^T \phi(\mathbf{x}, o) + \sum_{j \in \mathcal{A}^u \cup \mathcal{A}^l} \mathbf{w}_{a_j}^T \varphi(\mathbf{x}, a_j) + \sum_{j \in \mathcal{A}^u \cup \mathcal{A}^l} \mathbf{w}_{o,a_j}^T \omega(a_j, o) + \sum_{(j,k) \in \mathcal{E}} \mathbf{w}_{j,k}^T \psi(a_j^u, a_k^l). \quad (9.1)$$

In this model, the parameter vector $\mathbf{w}$ is the concatenation of the parameters in all the factors. $\Phi(\mathbf{x}, \mathbf{a}_u, \mathbf{a}_l, o)$ is the concatenation of $\phi(\mathbf{x}, o)$, $\varphi(\mathbf{x}, a_j)$, $\omega(a_j, o)$ and $\psi(a_j^u, a_k^l)$. It is a feature vector depending on the images $\mathbf{x}$, the attributes $\mathbf{a}_u$, $\mathbf{a}_l$ and occasion label o. The model presented in Eq. (9.1) simultaneously considers the dependencies among visual features, attributes, and occasions. In particular, its first term predicts occasion from visual features; the second term describes the relationship between visual features and attributes; the third term captures the relationship between attributes and occasion. The last term expresses the dependencies between the attributes of upper and lower body clothing. Instead of predicting the occasion from visual features or attributes directly, we mine much richer matching rules among them explicitly. The impacts of different relationships on the matching score in Eq. (9.1) are automatically determined in the learning process, therefore, the four relationships are not treated equally.

Model Learning and Inference: In this work, we adopt the latent SVM formulation to learn the model as in [8]:

$$\begin{aligned} &\min_{\mathbf{w},\xi} \beta \|\mathbf{w}\|^2 + \sum_{n=1}^{N} \xi^{(n)} \\ &\text{s.t.} \;\; \max_{\mathbf{a}_u,\mathbf{a}_l} \mathbf{w}^T \Phi(\mathbf{x}^{(n)}, \mathbf{a}_u, \mathbf{a}_l, \mathbf{o}^{(n)}) - \max_{\mathbf{a}_u,\mathbf{a}_l} \mathbf{w}^T \Phi(\mathbf{x}^{(n)}, \mathbf{a}_u, \mathbf{a}_l, o) \\ &\geq \Delta(o, \mathbf{o}^{(n)}) - \xi^{(n)}, \quad \forall n, \forall o \in \mathcal{O}, \end{aligned} \quad (9.2)$$

where β is the tradeoff parameter controlling the amount of regularization, and $\xi^{(n)}$ is the slack variable for the n-th training sample to handle the soft margin. Such an objective function requires that the score of clothing for a suitable occasion should be much higher than for a non-suitable occasion. $\Delta(o, \mathbf{o}^{(n)})$ is a loss function defined as

$$\Delta_{0/1}(\mathbf{o}^{(n)}, o) = \begin{cases} 1 & \text{if } o \notin \mathbf{o}^{(n)} \\ 0 & \text{otherwise} \end{cases}$$

In Eq. 9.2, we aim to learn a discriminative occasion-wise scoring function on each pair of clothing (more specifically, on their features and inferred attributes) such that the scoring function can rank clothing correctly by maximizing the score difference between suitable ones and unsuitable ones for the interest occasion.

After learning the model, we can use it to score any image-occasion pair $(\mathbf{x}, o)$. The score is inferred as $f_{\mathbf{w}}(\mathbf{x}, o) = \max_{\mathbf{a}_u, \mathbf{a}_l} \mathbf{w}^T \Phi(\mathbf{x}, \mathbf{a}_u, \mathbf{a}_l, o)$. Thus after specifying the occasion o, we can obtain a rank of the clothing from the user's clothing photo album. In particular, given the parameter model $\mathbf{w}$, we need to solve the following inference problem during recommendation:

$$\{\mathbf{a}_u^*, \mathbf{a}_l^*\} = \operatorname*{argmax}_{\mathbf{a}_u, \mathbf{a}_l} \mathbf{w}^T \Phi(\mathbf{x}, \mathbf{a}_u, \mathbf{a}_l, o),$$

which can be solved by linear programming since the attributes form a tree structure [36]. And then the clothing obtaining the highest score will be suggested, namely

$$\mathbf{x}^* = \operatorname*{argmax}_{\mathbf{x}} \left\{ \max_{\mathbf{a}_u, \mathbf{a}_l} \mathbf{w}^T \Phi(\mathbf{x}, \mathbf{a}_u, \mathbf{a}_l, o) \right\}. \tag{9.3}$$

Similarly, for the clothing pairing recommendation, given a specified upper body clothing $\mathbf{x}_u$ and the occasion o, the most suitable lower body clothing $\mathbf{x}_l^*$ is paired as:

$$\mathbf{x}_l^* = \operatorname*{argmax}_{\mathbf{x}_l} \left\{ \max_{\mathbf{a}_u, \mathbf{a}_l} \mathbf{w}^T \Phi\left([\mathbf{x}_u; \mathbf{x}_l], \mathbf{a}_u, \mathbf{a}_l, o\right) \right\}. \tag{9.4}$$

The upper body clothing recommendation for a given lower body clothing is conducted in a similar way.

Evaluation Metric and Baselines: We compare the proposed Magic Closet system with two linear SVM-based models. The first baseline is a feature-occasion multiclass linear SVM which predicts occasion from visual features directly without considering attributes. After training based on $\{\mathbf{x}^{(n)}, \mathbf{o}^{(n)}\}_{n=1}^N$, given an occasion, all the clothing in the repository are ranked according to the output confidence score of the feature-occasion SVM. The second baseline feature-attribute-occasion SVM is composed of a two-layer linear SVM. The first-layer SVM linearly maps visual features to attribute values, which is trained based on $\{\mathbf{x}^{(n)}, \mathbf{a}_u^{(n)}, \mathbf{a}_l^{(n)}\}_{n=1}^N$. Then the visual features are converted into attribute confidence score vectors via such first-layer SVM. The second-layer SVM is trained on these attribute confidence vectors to predict their occasion labels. Similar to feature-occasion SVM, all clothing in the repository are ranked based on the output of the two-layer feature-attribute-occasion SVM. We evaluate their performance via Normalized Discounted Cumulative Gain (NDCG), which is commonly used to evaluate ranking systems.

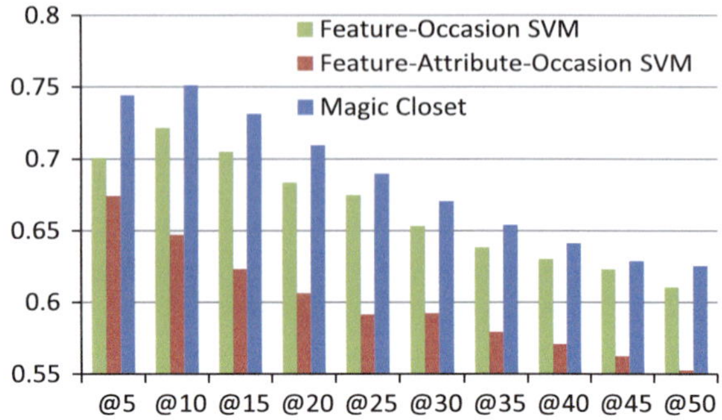

Fig. 9.4 Comparison of Magic Closet with two baselines on the clothing suggestion task (NDCG vs. # returned samples)

Experiment 1: Occasion-Oriented Clothing Suggestion To evaluate the performance of the proposed method, we collect a dataset, which is split into three subsets. The first subset WoW_Full includes 9,469 images containing visible full-body. The second subset, denoted as WoW_Upper, contains 8,421 images with only upper body, such as T-shirts, Fashion hoodies. And the 6,527 images containing lower body clothing, such as Jeans and Skirts, are put into WoW_Lower. According to different sources of data, WoW_Upper is further split into two subsets, one is WoW_Upper_DP where all the images are Daily Photos (DP), which are crawled from popular photo sharing websites, while the other one is WoW_Upper_OS, the photos of which are crawled from Online Shopping (OS) websites. Similarly, both WoW_Lower and WoW_Full subsets are further split into DP and OS subsets in the same way. Though in a practical system all the clothing photos are from the same user, here in order to comprehensively evaluate the Magic Closet system for suggesting clothing with different attributes, we simulate the suggestion scenario on WoW_Full_DP dataset, which contains 6, 661 images from multiple users. We evenly split the WoW_Full_DP subset into two groups. The first half WoW_Full_DP_1 together with WoW_Full_OS (containing 2, 808 images) are used for training the latent SVM-based model embedded in Magic Closet. The second half of WoW_Full_DP_1 is used as testing set. Each set of clothes is annotated with an occasion label, e.g., dating or conference. Given an occasion, the clothing from the set which maximizes the score function in Eq. (9.3) is suggested by Magic Closet.

Quantitative evaluation results of the clothing suggestion are shown in Fig. 9.4. From the results, we can make the following observations. (1) The feature-occasion SVM consistently outperforms the feature-attribute-occasion SVM. This is because the visual features we adopt possess relatively strong discriminative power and their high dimensionality benefits linear classification. We also observe that it is harder to construct a linear relationship between low-dimensional attribute confidence vectors and occasions. (2) The proposed latent SVM model outperforms the two baseline models significantly. This result well demonstrates the effectiveness of the proposed model in mining matching rules among features, attributes, occasions, and utilizing their correlation in occasion-oriented clothing suggestion.

Fig. 9.5 Comparison of Magic Closet with baselines for clothing pairing (NDCG vs. # returned samples)

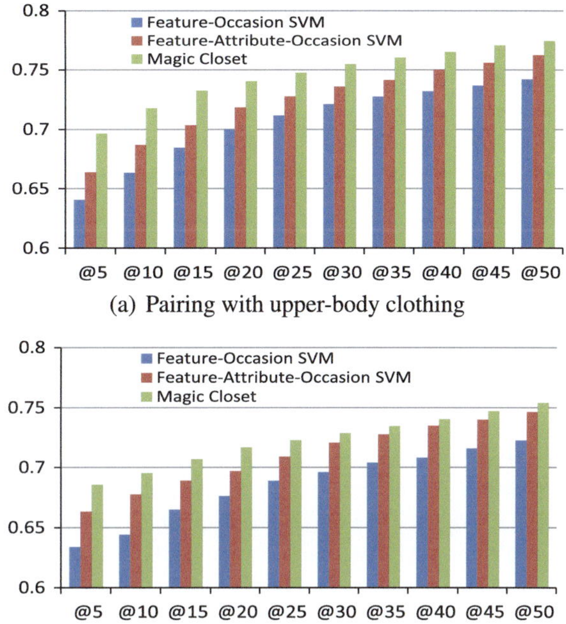

(a) Pairing with upper-body clothing

(b) Pairing with lower-body clothing

Experiment 2: Occasion-Oriented Clothing Pairing To simulate this scenario, we collect 20 images (10 upper body and 10 lower body) as the queries. Summing up across 8 occasions, the total number of queries is 160. The repository consists of clothing from online shopping dataset, including two subsets WoW_Upper_OS (2,500 images) and WoW_Lower_OS (3,791 images). In clothing pairing, for each query of upper/lower body clothing, we provide the rank of the candidate lower/upperbody clothing in the online shop dataset. The rank is calculated based on the pairs aesthetic score and suitableness for the specified occasion, as evaluated in Eq. 9.4. To obtain the ranking ground truth of the returned clothing, we do not require our labelers (40 people aging from 19 to 40) to score each candidate pair. We adopt the group-wise labeling strategy: given an occasion, we randomly show 8 clothing as a group to the labelers. So, labelers only need to rank the clothing within each group and the final rank is obtained. Such strategy can alleviate the burden of labelers significantly. Each pair is labeled at least 10 times and thus the potential inaccurate rank can be eliminated via averaging.

Figure 9.5 shows the NDCG value w.r.t. the increasing number of returned samples of the baseline models and the Magic Closet system. From the figure, we can have the following observations. (1) For the two baseline methods, the feature-attribute-occasion SVM performs significantly better than the feature-occasion SVM. This is because that the feature-occasion SVM is a linear model. The calculated pairing score equals to $\mathbf{w}^T[\mathbf{x}_u; \mathbf{x}_l] = \mathbf{w}_u^T\mathbf{x}_u + \mathbf{w}_l^T\mathbf{x}_l$. The maximization of this score w.r.t. $\mathbf{x}_l$ is independent of $\mathbf{x}_u$. Therefore, for a specified occasion, for different queries, the returned results are identical. However, due to the good performance of feature-occasion SVM in occasion prediction, it can still return suitable clothing for the occasion. Thus its performance is still acceptable. While for the feature-attribute-occasion SVM, since the features are mapped to the attribute space at first, this issue is alleviated. Moreover, the attribute-based features are more robust to cross-domain variation (DP vs. OS). (2) The proposed Magic Closet outperforms the two baseline models. This result is as expected since Magic Closet can better capture matching rules among attributes and thus recommend more aesthetic clothing pairs.

9.2.2 "Wow You Are so Beautiful Today!"

We have built a system called Beauty e-Experts, a fully automatic system for hairstyle and facial makeup recommendation and synthesis [25]. Given a user-provided frontal face image with short/bound hair and no/light makeup, the Beauty e-Experts system can not only recommend the most suitable hairdo and makeup, but also show the synthetic effects. The interface of the Beauty e-Experts system is shown in Fig. 9.6. The main challenge in this problem is how to model the complex relationships among different beauty and facial/clothing attributes for reliable recommendation and natural synthesis.

To obtain enough knowledge for beauty modeling, we build the Beauty e-Experts Database, which contains 1,505 attractive female photos with a variety of beauty attributes and facial/clothing attributes annotated [25]. Based on this Beauty e-Experts Dataset, two problems are considered for the Beauty e-Experts system: what to recommend and how to wear, which describe a similar process of selecting hairstyle and cosmetics in our daily life. For the what-to-recommend problem, we propose a multiple tree-structured super-graphs model to explore the complex relationships among the high-level beauty attributes, mid-level facial/clothing attributes, and low-level image features, and then based on this model, the most compatible beauty attributes for a given facial image can be efficiently inferred. For the how-to-wear problem, an effective and efficient facial image synthesis module is designed to seamlessly synthesize the recommended hairstyle and makeup into the user facial image.

Beauty attributes, facial/clothing attributes, and features: To obtain beauty knowledge from our dataset, we comprehensively explore different beauty attributes on these images, including various kinds of hairstyles and facial makeups. We carefully organize these beauty attributes and set their attribute values based on some basic observations or preprocessing on the whole dataset. Table 9.1 lists the names and values of all the beauty attributes considered in the work. For the first four beauty attributes in Table 9.1, their values are set intuitively, and for the last five ones, their values are obtained by running the k-means clustering algorithm on the training dataset for the corresponding features. We show the visual examples of specific attribute values for some beauty attributes in Fig. 9.7.

Fig. 9.6 Overall illustration of the proposed Beauty e-Experts system. Based on the user's facial and clothing characteristics, the Beauty e-Experts system automatically recommends the suitable hairstyle and makeup products for the user, and then produces the synthesized visual effects

Table 9.1 A list of the high-level beauty attributes

Name	Values
Hair length	Long, medium, short
Hair shape	Straight, curled, wavy
Hair bangs	Full, slanting, center part, side part
Hair volume	Dense, normal
Hair color	20 classes
Foundation	15 classes
Lip gloss	15 classes
Eye shadow color	15 classes
Eye shadow template	20 classes

We further explore a set of mid-level facial/clothing attributes to narrow the gap between the high-level beauty attributes and the low-level image features. Table 9.2 lists all the mid-level facial/clothing attributes annotated for the dataset. These mid-

Table 9.2 A list of mid-level facial/clothing attributes considered in this work

Names	Values
Forehead	High, normal, low
Eyebrow	Thick, thin
Eyebrow length	Long, short
Eye corner	Upcurved, downcurved, normal
Eye shape	Narrow, normal
Ocular distance	Hypertelorism, normal, hypotelorism
Cheek bone	High, normal
Nose bridge	Prominent, flat
Nose tip	Wide, narrow
Mouth opened	Yes, no
Mouth width	Wide, normal
Smiling	Smiling, neutral
Lip thickness	Thick, normal
Fatness	Fat, normal
Jaw shape	Round, flat, pointed
Face shape	Long, oval, round
Collar shape	Strapless, v-shape, one-shoulder, high-necked, round, shirt collar
Clothing pattern	Vertical, plaid, horizontal, drawing, plain, floral print
Clothing material	Cotton, chiffon, silk, woolen, denim, leather, lace
Clothing color	Red, orange, brown, purple, yellow, green, gray, black, blue, white, pink, multicolor
Race	Asian, Western

level attributes mainly focus on the facial shapes and clothing properties, which are kept fixed during the recommendation and the synthesis process.[3]

After the annotation of the high-level beauty attributes and mid-level facial/clothing attributes, we further extract various types of low-level image features on the clothing and facial regions for each image in the Beauty e-Experts Dataset to facilitate further beauty modeling. The clothing region of an image is automatically determined based on its geometrical relationship with the face region. Specifically, the following features are extracted for image representation:

- RGB color histogram and color moments on the clothing region.
- Histograms of oriented gradients (HOG) and local binary patterns (LBP) features on the clothing region.
- Active shape model [28] based-shape parameters.
- Shape context [1] features extracted at facial points.

[3] Although the clothes of a user can be changed to make one look more beautiful, they are kept fixed in our current Beauty e-Experts system.

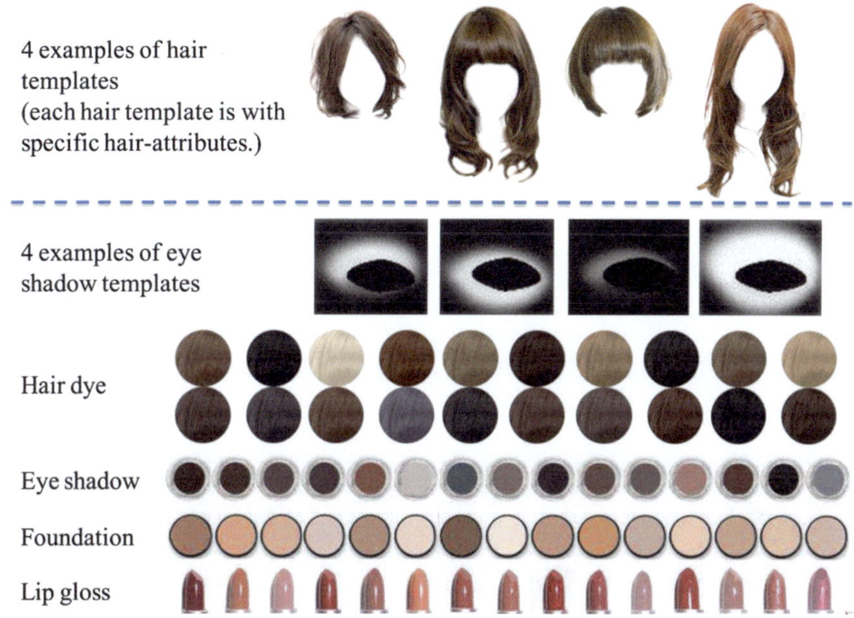

Fig. 9.7 Visual examples of the specific values for some beauty attributes

All the above features are concatenated to form a feature vector of 7,109 dimensions, and then Principal Component Analysis (PCA) is performed for dimensionality reduction. The compressed feature vector with 173 dimensions and the annotated attribute values are then fed into an SVM classifier to train a classifier for each attribute.

The Recommendation Model: Based on the beauty attributes and facial/clothing attributes, we propose to learn a multiple tree-structured super-graphs model to explore the complex relationships among these attributes. Based on the recommended results, an effective and efficient facial image synthesis module is designed to seamlessly synthesize the recommended results into the user facial image and show it back to the user. The whole system processing flowchart is illustrated in Fig. 9.8.

A training beauty image is denoted as a tuple $(\langle \mathbf{x}, \mathbf{a}^r \rangle, \mathbf{a}^b)$. Here $\mathbf{x}$ is the image features extracted from the raw image data; $\mathbf{a}^r$ and $\mathbf{a}^b$ denote the set of the facial/clothing attributes and beauty attributes, respectively. Each attribute may have multiple different values, *i.e.*, $a_i \in \{1, \ldots, n_i\}$, where n_i is the number of attribute values for the i-th attribute. The facial/clothing attributes $\mathbf{a}^r$ act as the mid-level cues to narrow the gap between the low-level image features $\mathbf{x}$ and the high-level beauty attributes $\mathbf{a}^b$. The recommendation model needs to uncover the complex relationships among the low-level image features, mid-level facial/clothing attributes and high-level beauty attributes, and make the final recommendation for a given image.

We model the relationships among the low-level image features, the mid-level facial/clothing attributes, and the high-level beauty attributes from a probabilistic

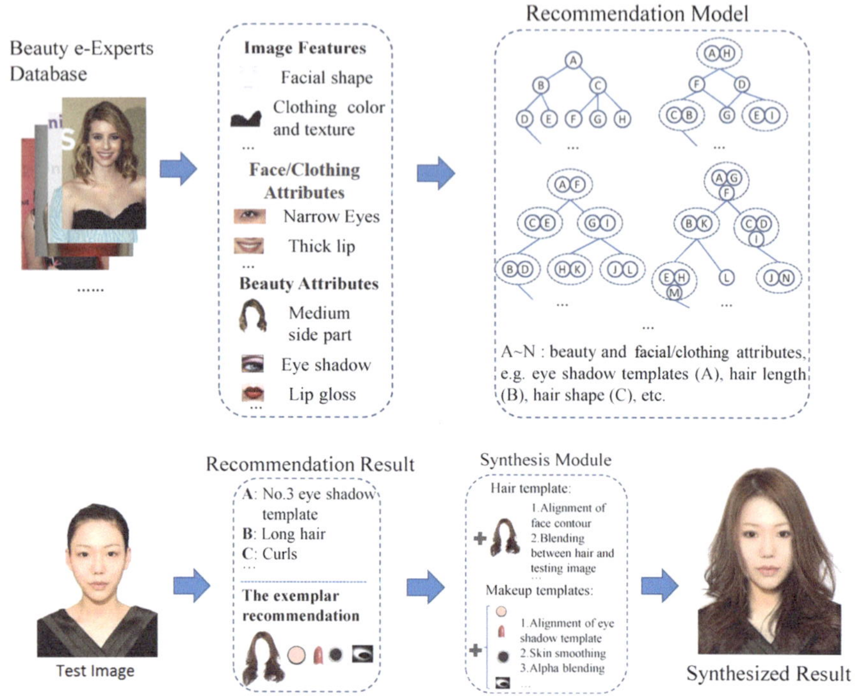

Fig. 9.8 System processing flowchart. We first collect the Beauty e-Experts Database of 1,505 facial images with different hairstyles and makeup effects. With the extracted facial and clothing features, we propose a multiple tree-structured super-graphs model to express the complex relationships among beauty and facial/clothing attributes. The results from multiple individual super-graphs are fused based on a voting strategy. In the testing stage, the recommended hair and makeup templates for the testing face are then applied to synthesize the final visual effects

perspective. The aim of the recommendation system is to estimate the probability of beauty attributes, together with facial/clothing attributes, given the image features, i.e., $p\left(\mathbf{a}^b, \mathbf{a}^r|\mathbf{x}\right)$, which can be modeled using the Gibbs distribution,

$$p\left(\mathbf{a}^b, \mathbf{a}^r|\mathbf{x}\right) = \frac{1}{Z(\mathbf{x})} \exp\left(-E\left(\mathbf{a}^b, \mathbf{a}^r, \mathbf{x}\right)\right), \tag{9.5}$$

where $Z(\mathbf{x}) = \sum_{\mathbf{a}^b, \mathbf{a}^r} \exp\left(-E\left(\mathbf{a}^b, \mathbf{a}^r, \mathbf{x}\right)\right)$, also known as the partition function, is a normalizing term dependent on the image features, and $E(\mathbf{a}^b, \mathbf{a}^r, \mathbf{x})$ is an energy function measuring the compatibility among the beauty attributes, facial/clothing attributes, and image features. The beauty recommendation results can be obtained by finding the most likely joint beauty attribute state $\hat{\mathbf{a}}^b = \arg\max_{\mathbf{a}^b} \max_{\mathbf{a}^r} p\left(\mathbf{a}^b, \mathbf{a}^r|\mathbf{x}\right)$.

The capacity of this probabilistic model fully depends on the structure of the energy function $E(\mathbf{a}^b, \mathbf{a}^r, \mathbf{x})$. Here we propose to learn a general super-graph structure to build the energy function which can theoretically be used to model any relationships among the low-level image features, mid-level facial/clothing attributes, and high-level beauty attributes. To begin with, we give the definition of a super-graph.

Definition 9.1 Super-graph: a super-graph $\mathcal{G}$ is a pair $\mathcal{G} = (\mathcal{V}, \mathcal{E})$ where $\mathcal{V}$ is called super-vertexes, consisting of a set of nonempty subsets of a basic node set, and $\mathcal{E}$ is called super-edges, consisting of a set of two-tuples, each of which contains two different elements in $\mathcal{V}$.

It can be seen that a super-graph is actually a generalization of a graph in which a vertex can have multiple basic nodes and an edge can connect any number of basic nodes. When all the super-vertexes only contain one basic node, and each super-edge is forced to connect to only two basic nodes, the super-graph then becomes a traditional graph. A super-graph can be naturally used to model the complex relationships among multiple factors, where the factors are denoted by the vertexes and the relationships are represented by the super-edges.

Definition 9.2 k-order super-graph: for a super-graph $\mathcal{G} = (\mathcal{V}, \mathcal{E})$, if the maximal number of vertexes involved by one super-edge in $\mathcal{E}$ is k, $\mathcal{G}$ is said to be a k-order super-graph.

Based on the above definitions, we propose to use the super-graph to characterize the complex relationships among the low-level image features, mid-level facial/clothing attributes, and high-level beauty attributes in our problem. For example, pairwise correlations can be sufficiently represented by a 2-order super-graph (traditional graph), while other more complex relationships, such as one-to-two and two-to-two relationships, can be represented by other higher order super-graphs. Denote the basic node set A as the union of the beauty attributes and facial/clothing attributes, i.e., $A = \{a_i | a_i \in \mathbf{a}^r \cup \mathbf{a}^b\}$. Suppose the underlying relationships among all the attributes are represented by a super-graph $\mathcal{G} = (\mathcal{V}, \mathcal{E})$, where $\mathcal{V} = \{\mathbf{a}_i | \mathbf{a}_i \subset A\}$. $\mathbf{a}_i$ is a set of non-empty subsets of A. Note that we use $\mathbf{a}_i$ to denote a non-empty attribute set and a_i to denote a single attribute. $\mathcal{E}$ is the super-edge set that models their relationships, the energy function can then be defined as,

$$E\left(\mathbf{a}^b, \mathbf{a}^r, \mathbf{x}\right) = \sum_{\mathbf{a}_i \in \mathcal{V}} \phi_i\left(\mathbf{a}_i, \mathbf{x}\right) + \sum_{(\mathbf{a}_i, \mathbf{a}_j) \in \mathcal{E}} \phi_{ij}\left(\mathbf{a}_i, \mathbf{a}_j\right). \tag{9.6}$$

The first summation term is called FA (feature to attribute) potential, which is used to model the relationships between the attributes and low-level image features, and the second one is called AA (attribute to attribute) potential and is used to model the complex relationships among different attributes represented by the super-edges. $\phi_i\left(\mathbf{a}_i, \mathbf{x}\right)$ and $\phi_{ij}\left(\mathbf{a}_i, \mathbf{a}_j\right)$ are the potential functions of the corresponding inputs, which can be learned in different ways. Generally, the FA potential $\phi_i\left(\mathbf{a}_i, \mathbf{x}\right)$ is usually modeled as a generalized linear function in the form like

$$\phi_i\left(\mathbf{a}_i = \mathbf{s}_i, \mathbf{x}\right) = \psi_{\mathbf{a}_i}\left(\mathbf{x}\right)^\top \mathbf{w}_i^{\mathbf{s}_i}, \tag{9.7}$$

where $\mathbf{s}_i$ is the values for attribute subset $\mathbf{a}_i$, $\psi_{\mathbf{a}_i}(\mathbf{x})$ is a set of feature mapping functions for the attributes in $\mathbf{a}_i$ using SVM on the extracted features, and $\mathbf{w}_i$ is the FA weight parameters to be learned for the model. And the AA potential function $\phi_i(\mathbf{a}_i, \mathbf{a}_j)$ is defined by a scalar parameter for each joint state of the corresponding super-edge,

$$\phi_{ij}(\mathbf{a}_i = \mathbf{s}_i, \mathbf{a}_j = \mathbf{s}_j) = w_{i,j}^{\mathbf{s}_i \mathbf{s}_j}, \tag{9.8}$$

where $w_{i,j}^{\mathbf{s}_i \mathbf{s}_j}$ is a scalar parameter for the corresponding joint state of $\mathbf{a}_i$ and $\mathbf{a}_j$ with the specific value $\mathbf{s}_i$ and $\mathbf{s}_j$.

The learning of the super-graph-based energy function includes learning the structure and the parameters in the potential functions.

Model Learning: Structure Learning. For a super-graph built on a basic node set $A = \{a_1, \ldots, a_M\}$ with M elements, we find a k-order tree-structured super-graph for these vertexes. We first calculate the mutual information between each pair of vertexes, and denote the results in the adjacency matrix form, i.e., $W = \{w_{ij}\}_{1 \le i,j \le M}$. Then we propose a two-stage algorithm to find the k-order tree-structured super-graph.

In the *first stage*, we aim to find the candidate set of basic node subsets $\mathcal{V} = \{\mathbf{a}_i | \mathbf{a}_i \subset A\}$, which will be used to form the super-edges. The objective here is to find the set of subsets that has the largest amount of total mutual information in the result k-order super-graph. Here we first define a function that calculates the mutual information of a subset set with a specified mutual information matrix,

$$f(\mathcal{V}, W) = \sum_{|\mathbf{a}_i| \ge 2} \sum_{a_j, a_k \in \mathbf{a}_i} w_{jk}. \tag{9.9}$$

Based on this definition, we formulate the candidate set generation problem as the following optimization problem

$$\begin{aligned} &\underset{\mathcal{V}}{\text{argmax}} \quad f(\mathcal{V}, W), \\ &\text{s.t. } |\mathbf{a}_i| \le \lfloor \frac{k+1}{2} \rfloor, \forall i, \\ &|\mathcal{V}| \le m, \end{aligned} \tag{9.10}$$

where the first inequation is from the k-order constraint from the result super-graph, $\lfloor \cdot \rfloor$ is the floor operator, and the parameter m in the second inequation is used to ensure that the generated subsets have a reasonable size to cover all the vertexes and make the inference on the result super-graph more efficient. Specifically, its value can be set as

$$m = \begin{cases} M, & k = 2, \\ 2\lceil M/(k-1) \rceil, & \text{otherwise}, \end{cases} \tag{9.11}$$

where $\lceil \cdot \rceil$ is the ceil operator. To solve this optimization problem, we design a k-means like iterative optimization algorithm to find the solution. The algorithm first initializes some random vertex subsets and then reassigns each vertex to the subsets that result in maximal mutual information increment; if one vertex subset has more than $\lfloor (k+1)/2 \rfloor$ elements, it will be split into two subsets; if the total cardinality of the vertex subset set is larger than $2\lceil M/(k-1) \rceil$, two subsets with the smallest cardinalities will be merged into one subset. This procedure is repeated until convergence.

The *second stage* of the two-stage algorithm first calculates the mutual information between the element pair that satisfies the order restrictions in each vertex subset. The order constraint is that the maximal number of vertexes involved by one super-edge in $\mathcal{E}$ is k. Then it builds a graph by using the calculated mutual information as adjacency matrix, and the maximum spanning tree algorithm is adopted to find its tree-structured approximation.

The above two-stage algorithm is run many times by setting different k values and initializations of subsets, which then generates multiple tree-structured super-graphs with different orders and structures. In order to make the parameter learning tractable, the maximal k-value K is set to be equal to 5.

Model Learning: Parameter Learning. For each particular tree-structured super-graph, its parameter set, including the parameters in the FA potentials and the AA potentials, can be denoted in a whole as $\boldsymbol{\Theta} = \{\mathbf{w}_i^{\mathbf{s}_i}, w_{ij}^{\mathbf{s}_i\mathbf{s}_j}\}$. We adopt the maximal likelihood criterion to learn these parameters. Given N i.i.d. training samples $\mathbf{X} = \{\langle \mathbf{x}_n, \mathbf{a}_n^r \rangle, \mathbf{a}_n^b\}$, we need to minimize the loss function

$$
\begin{aligned}
\mathcal{L} &= \frac{1}{N}\sum_{n=1}^{N} \mathcal{L}_n + \frac{1}{2}\lambda \sum_{i,\mathbf{s}_i} \|\mathbf{w}_i^{\mathbf{s}_i}\|_2^2 \\
&= \frac{1}{N}\sum_{n=1}^{N} \{-\ln p\left(\mathbf{a}_n^b, \mathbf{a}_n^r | \mathbf{x}_n\right)\} + \frac{1}{2}\lambda \sum_{i,\mathbf{s}_i} \|\mathbf{w}_i^{\mathbf{s}_i}\|_2^2,
\end{aligned}
\tag{9.12}
$$

where $\mathcal{L}_n$ is the loss for each sample (expanded in the second line of the equation), λ is the tradeoff parameter between the regularization term and log-likelihood and its value is chosen by k-fold validation on the training set. Since the energy function is linear with respect to the parameters, the log-likelihood function is concave and the parameters can be optimized using gradient-based methods. The gradient of the parameters can be computed by calculating their marginal distributions. Denoting the value of attribute $\mathbf{a}_i$ for training image n as $\hat{\mathbf{a}}_i$, we have

$$
\frac{\partial \mathcal{L}_n}{\partial \mathbf{w}_i^{\mathbf{s}_i}} = \left(\left[\hat{\mathbf{a}}_i = \mathbf{s}_i\right] - p\left(\mathbf{a}_i = \mathbf{s}_i | \mathbf{x}_n\right)\right) \psi_{\mathbf{a}_i}\left(\mathbf{x}_n\right), \tag{9.13}
$$

$$
\frac{\partial \mathcal{L}_n}{\partial w_{ij}^{\mathbf{s}_i\mathbf{s}_j}} = \left[\hat{\mathbf{a}}_i = \mathbf{s}_i, \hat{\mathbf{a}}_j = \mathbf{s}_j\right] - p\left(\mathbf{a}_i = \mathbf{s}_i, \mathbf{a}_j = \mathbf{s}_j | \mathbf{x}_n\right), \tag{9.14}
$$

where $[\cdot]$ is the Iverson bracket notation, i.e., $[\cdot]$ equals 1 if the expression is true, and 0 otherwise.

Based on the calculation of the gradients, the parameters can be learned from different gradient-based optimization algorithms. In the experiments, we use the implementation by Schmidt[4] to learn these parameters. The learned parameters, together with the corresponding super-graph structures, form the final recommendation model.

Inference: Here each learned tree-structured super-graph model can be seen as a beauty expert. Given an input testing image, the system first extracts the feature vector $\mathbf{x}$, and then each beauty expert makes its recommendation by performing inference on the tree structure to find the maximum posteriori probability of $p\left(\mathbf{a}^b, \mathbf{a}^r | \mathbf{x}\right)$. The recommendation results output by all the Beauty e-Experts are then fused by majority voting to make the final recommendation to the user.

The Synthesis Module: With the beauty attributes recommended by the multiple tree-structured super-graphs model, we further synthesize the final visual effect of hairstyle and makeup for the testing image. To this end, each makeup attribute forms a template which can be directly obtained from a dataset. These obtained hair and makeup templates are then fed into the synthesis process, which mainly has two steps: alignment and alpha blending.

In the alignment step, both of the hairstyle and the makeup templates need to be aligned with the testing image. For hair template alignment, a dual linear transformation procedure is proposed to put the hair template on the target face in the testing image. For the makeup templates alignment, only the eye shadow template needs to be aligned to the eye region in the testing image. Other makeup templates can be directly applied to the corresponding regions based on the face keypoint detection results. In the alpha blending step, the final result is synthesized with hair template, makeup, and the testing face.

Experiments and Results: For the recommendation model in the Beauty e-Experts system, we also implement some alternatives using multiclass SVM, neural network, and latent SVM. Figure 9.9 plots the comparison results of our proposed model and other baselines. The performance is measured by NDCG, which is widely used to evaluate ranking systems. From the results, it is observed that our model and latent SVM significantly outperforms multiclass SVM and neural network. From Fig. 9.9 it can be further found that our model has overall better performance than the latent SVM method, especially in the top 15 recommendations. With higher order relationships embedded, our model can express more complex relationship among different attributes. In addition, by employing multiple tree-structured super-graphs, our model obtains more robust recommendation results.

We then compare the hairstyle and makeup synthesis results with a few commercial systems, including Instant Hair Makeover (IHM),[5] Daily Makeover (DM),[6] and the virtual try-on website (TAAZ).[7] As shown in Fig. 9.10, the first column are the test images, and the other four columns are the results generated by DM, IHM, TAAZ,

[4]http://www.di.ens.fr/~mschmidt/Software/UGM.html.

[5]http://www.realbeauty.com/hair/virtual/hairstyles.

[6]http://www.dailymakeover.com/games-apps/games.

[7]http://www.taaz.com.

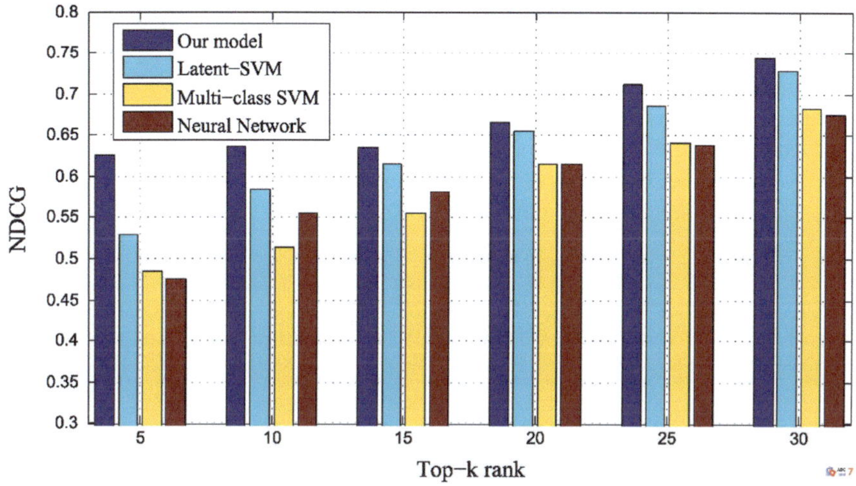

Fig. 9.9 NDCG values of multiple tree-structured super-graphs model and three baselines. The *horizontal axis* is the rank of top-*k* results, while the *vertical axis* is the corresponding NDCG value. Our proposed method achieves better performance than the latent SVM model and other baselines

Fig. 9.10 Contrast results of synthesized effect among commercial systems and our paper

and our system, respectively. The reason why we select these three systems is that only these three can synthesize both the hairstyle and makeup effects. The makeup and hairstyle templates used in the synthesis process are selected with some user interactions to ensure that all the four methods share similar makeups and hairstyles. It can be seen that, even after some extra user interactions, the results generated from these three websites have obvious artifacts. The selected hair templates cannot cover the original hair area. IHM cannot even handle the mouth open cases.

9.3 Fine-Grained Clothing Retrieval System

In this section, we describe a fine-grained clothing retrieval system [12]. In a similar fashion to the recommendation work described in the previous section, we use a large-scale annotated dataset with many attributes to transfer knowledge to a noisy real-world domain. In particular, given an offline clothing image from the "street" domain, the goal is to retrieve the same or similar clothing items from a large-scale gallery of professional online shopping images, as illustrated in Fig. 9.11. We propose a Dual Attribute-aware Ranking Network (DARN) consisting of two subnetworks, one for each domain, whose retrieval feature representations are driven by semantic attribute learning.

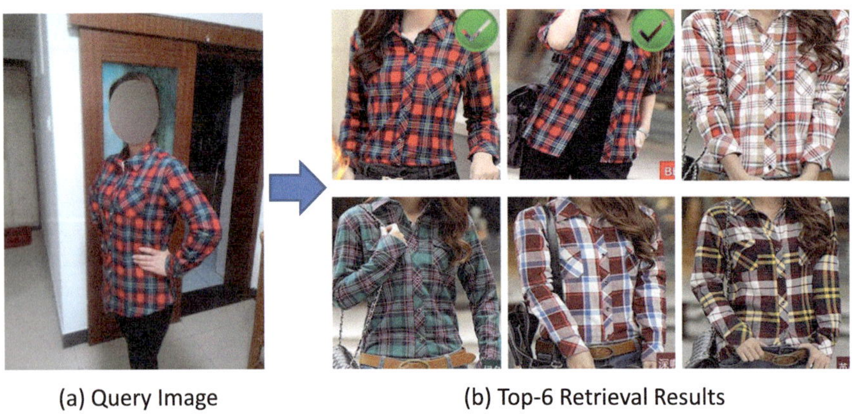

Fig. 9.11 Cross-domain clothing retrieval. **a** Query image from daily photos. **b** Top-6 product retrieval results from the online shopping domain. The proposed system finds the exact same clothing item (first two images) and ranks the ones with similar attributes as top results

9.4 Data Collection

We have collected about 453,983 online upper-clothing images in high-resolution (about 800×500 on average) from several online shopping websites. Generally, each image contains a single frontal-view person. From the text surrounding the images, semantic attributes (e.g., clothing color, collar shape, sleeve shape, clothing style) are extracted and parsed into $\langle key, value \rangle$ pairs, where each *key* corresponds to an attribute category (e.g., color), and the *value* is the attribute label (e.g., red, black, white). Then, we manually pruned the noisy labels, merged similar labels based on human perception, and removed those with a small number of samples. After that, 9 categories of clothing attributes are extracted and the total number of attribute values is 179. As an example, there are 56 values for the color attribute.

The specified attribute categories and example attribute values are presented in Table 9.3. This large-scale dataset annotated with fine-grained clothing attributes is used to learn a powerful semantic representation of clothing, as we will describe in the next section.

Recall that the goal of our retrieval problem is to find the online shopping images that correspond to a given query photo in the "street" domain uploaded by the user. To analyze the discrepancy between the images in the shopping scenario (online images) and street scenario (offline images), we collect a large set of offline images with their online counterparts. The key insight to collect this dataset is that there are many customer review websites where users post photos of the clothing they have purchased. As the link to the corresponding clothing images from the shopping store is available, it is possible to collect a large set of online–offline image pairs.

We initially crawled 381,975 online–offline image pairs of different categories from the customer review pages. Then, after a data curation process, where several annotators helped removing unsuitable images, the data was reduced to 91,390 image pairs. For each of these pairs, fine-grained clothing attributes were extracted from the online image descriptions. As can be seen, each pair of images depict the same

Table 9.3 Clothing attribute categories and example values. The number in brackets is the total number of values for each category

Attribute categories	Examples (total number)
Clothes button	Double Breasted, Pullover, … (12)
Clothes category	T-shirt, Skirt, Leather Coat … (20)
Clothes color	Black, White, Red, Blue … (56)
Clothes length	Regular, Long, Short … (6)
Clothes pattern	Pure, Stripe, Lattice, Dot … (27)
Clothes shape	Slim, Straight, Cloak, Loose … (10)
Collar shape	Round, Lapel, V-Neck … (25)
Sleeve length	Long, Three-quarter, Sleeveless … (7)
Sleeve shape	Puff, Raglan, Petal, Pile … (16)

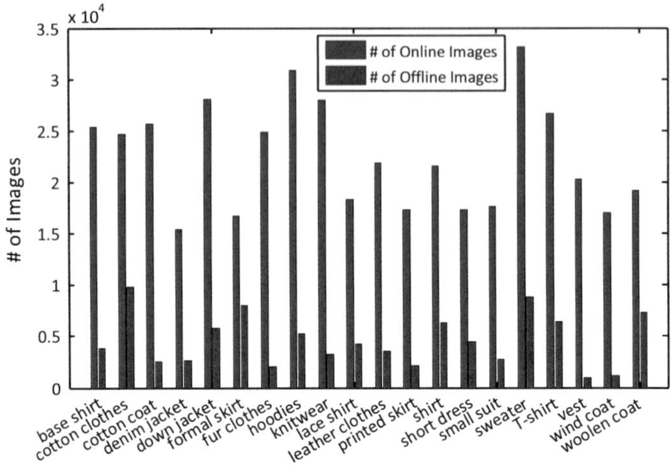

Fig. 9.12 The distribution of online–offline image pairs

clothing, but in different scenarios, exhibiting variations in pose, lighting, and background clutter. The distribution of the collected online–offline images is illustrated in Fig. 9.12. Generally, the number of images of different categories in both scenarios are almost in the same order of magnitude, which is helpful for training the retrieval model.

In summary, our dataset is suitable to the clothing retrieval problem for several reasons. First, the large amount of images enables effective training of retrieval models, especially deep neural network models. Second, the information about fine-grained clothing attributes allows learning of semantic representations of clothing. Last but not least, the online–offline images pairs bridge the gap between the shopping scenario and the street scenario, providing rich information for real-world applications.

9.4.1 Dual Attribute-Aware Ranking Network

In this section, the Dual Attribute-aware Ranking Network (DARN) is introduced for retrieval feature learning. Compared to existing deep features, DARN simultaneously integrates semantic attributes with visual similarity constraints into the feature learning stage, while at the same time modeling the discrepancy between domains.

Network Structure. The structure of DARN is illustrated in Fig. 9.13. Two subnetworks with similar Network-in-Network (NIN) models [22] are constructed as its foundation. During training, the images from the online shopping domain are fed into one subnetwork, and the images from the street domain are fed into the other. Each subnetwork aims to represent the domain-specific information and generate high-level comparable features as output. The NIN model in each subnetwork

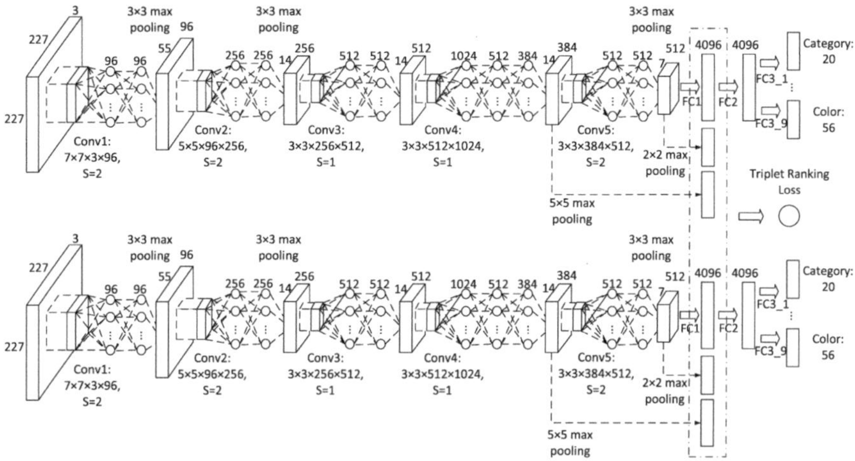

Fig. 9.13 The specific structure of DARN, which consists of two subnetworks for images of the shopping scenario and street scenario, respectively. In each subnetwork, it contains a NIN network, including all the convolutional layers, followed by two fully connected layers. The tree-structure layers are put on top of each network for attribute learning. The output features of each subnetwork, i.e., FC1, Conv4-5, are concatenated and fed into the triplet ranking loss across the two subnetworks

consists of five stacked convolutional layers followed by MLPConv layers as defined in [22], and two fully connected layers (FC1, FC2). To increase the representation capability of the intermediate layer, the fourth layer, named Conv4, is followed by two MLPConv layers.

On top of each subnetwork, we add tree-structured fully connected layers to encode information about semantic attributes. Given the semantic features learned by the two subnetworks, we further impose a triplet-based ranking loss function, which separates the dissimilar images with a fixed margin under the framework of *learning to rank*. The details of semantic information embedding and the ranking loss are introduced next.

Semantic Information Embedding. In the clothing domain, attributes often refer to the specific description of certain parts (e.g., collar shape, sleeve length) or clothing (e.g., clothes color, clothes style). Complementary to the visual appearance, this information can be used to form a powerful semantic representation for the clothing retrieval problem. To represent the clothing in a semantic level, we design tree-structure layers to comprehensively capture the information of attributes and their full relations.

Specifically, we transmit the FC2 response of each subnetwork to several branches, where each branch represents a fully connected network to model each attribute separately. In this tree-structured network, the visual features from the low-level layers are shared among attributes; while the semantic features from the high-level layers are learned separately. The number of neurons in the output-layer of each branch equals the number of corresponding attribute values. Since each attribute has a single value, the cross-entropy loss is used in each branch. Note that the values of some attributes may be missing for some clothing images. In this case, the gradients from the corresponding branches are simply set to zero.

During the training stage, the low-level representation of clothing images is extracted layer by layer. As the activation transfers to the higher layers, the representation becomes more and more abstract. Finally, the distinctive characteristic of each attribute is modeled in each branch. In the back-propagation, the gradient of loss from each attribute w.r.t. the activation of FC2 layer are summed up and transferred back for weight update.

Learning to Rank with Semantic Representation: In addition to encoding the semantic representation, we apply the learning to rank framework on DARN for retrieval feature learning. Specifically, the triplet-based ranking loss is used to constrain the feature similarity of image triplets. Denoting a and b the features of an offline image and its corresponding online image, respectively, the objective function of the triplet ranking loss is:

$$Loss(a, b, c) = max(0, m + dist(a, b) - dist(a, c)), \tag{9.15}$$

where c is the feature of the dissimilar online image, $dist(\cdot, \cdot)$ represents the feature distance, e.g., Euclidean distance, and m is the margin, which is empirically set as 0.3 according to the average feature distance of image pairs. Basically, this loss function imposes that the feature distance between an online–offline clothing pair should be less than that of the offline image and any other dissimilar online image by at least margin m.

In this way, we claim that the triplet ranking loss has two advantages. First and obviously, the desirable ranking ordering can be learned by this loss function. Second, as the features of online and offline images come from two different subnetworks, this loss function can be considered as the constraint to guarantee the comparability of features extracted from those two subnetworks, therefore bridging the gap between the two domains.

We found that the response of FC1 layer, i.e., the first fully connected layer, achieves the best retrieval result. Therefore, the triplet ranking loss is connected to the FC1 layer for feature learning. However, the response from the FC1 layer encodes global features, implying that subtle local information may be lost, which is especially relevant for discriminating clothing images. To handle this problem, we claim that local features captured by convolutions should also be considered. Specifically, the max-pooling layer is used to down-sample the response of the convolutional layers into $3 \times 3 \times f_n$, where f_n is the number of filters in the n-th convolutional layer. Then, the down-sampled response is vectorized and concatenated with the global features. Lastly, the triplet ranking loss is applied on the concatenated features of every triplet. In our implementation, we select the pooled response map of Conv4 and Conv5, i.e., the last two convolutional layers, as local features.

9.4.2 *Clothing Detection*

As a preprocessing step, the clothing detection component aims to eliminate the impact of cluttered backgrounds by cropping the foreground clothing from images, before feeding them into DARN. Our method is an enhanced version of the R-CNN approach [11], which has recently achieved state-of-the-art results in object detection.

Analogous to the R-CNN framework, clothing proposals are generated by selective search [33], with some unsuitable candidates discarded by constraining the range of size and aspect ratio of the bounding boxes. Similar to Chen et al. [5], we process the region proposals by a NIN model. However, our model differs in the sense that we use the attribute-aware network with tree-structured layers as described in the previous section, in order to embed semantic information as extra knowledge.

Based on the attribute-aware deep features, support vector regression (SVR) is used to predict the intersection over union (IoU) of clothing proposals. In addition, strategies such as the discretization of IoU on training patches, data augmentation, and hard example mining, are used in our training process. As post-processing, bounding box regression is employed to refine the selected proposals with the same features used for detection.

9.4.3 *Cross-Domain Clothing Retrieval*

We now describe the implementation details of our complete system for cross-domain clothing retrieval.

Training Stage. The training data is comprised of online–offline clothing image pairs with fine-grained clothing attributes. The clothing area is extracted from all images using our clothing detector, and then the cropped images are arranged into triplets.

In each triplet, the first two images are the online–offline pairs, with the third image randomly sampled from the online training pool. As the same clothing images have an unique ID, we sample the third online image until getting a different ID than the online–offline image pair. Several such triplets construct a training batch, and the images in each batch are sequentially fed into their corresponding subnetwork according to their scenarios. We then calculate the gradients for each loss function (cross-entropy loss and triplet ranking loss) w.r.t. each sample, and empirically set the scale of gradients from those loss functions as 1. Lastly, the gradients are back propagated to each individual subnetwork according to the sample domain.

We pre-trained our network as well as the baseline networks used in the experiments on the ImageNet dataset (ILSVRC-2014), as this yields improved retrieval results when compared to random initialization of parameters.

End-to-end Clothing Retrieval. We have set up an end-to-end real-time clothing retrieval demo on our local server. In our retrieval system, 200,000 online clothing images cropped by the clothing detector are used to construct our retrieval gallery. Given the cropped online images, the concatenated responses from FC1 layer, pooled Conv4 layer, and pooled Conv5 layer of one subnetwork of DARN corresponding to shop scenario are used as the representation features. The same processes are operated on the query image, except that the other subnetwork of DARN is used for retrieval feature extraction. We then l_2 normalize the features from different layers for each image. PCA is used to reduce the dimensionality of the normalized features (17,920-D for DARN with Conv4-5) into 4,096-D, which conducts a fair comparison with other deep features using FC1 layer output only. Based on the preprocessed features, the Euclidean distance between query and gallery images is used to rank the images according to the relevance to the query.

9.4.4 Experiments and Results

For the retrieval experiment, about 230,000 online images and 65,000 offline images are sampled for network training. In the training process, each offline image and its online counterpart are collected, with the dissimilar online image randomly sampled from the 230,000 online pool to construct a triplet. To make the retrieval result convincing, the rest 200,000 online images are used as the retrieval gallery.

For clothing retrieval, the approach using Dense-SIFT (DSIFT) + fisher vector (FV) is selected as traditional baseline. To analyze the retrieval performance of deep features, we compare pretrained networks including AlexNet (*pretrained CNN*) and *pretrained NIN*. We denote the overall solution as Dual Attribute-aware Ranking Network (*DARN*), the solution without dual structure as Attribute-aware Ranking Network (*ARN*), the solution without dual structure and the ranking loss function as Attribute-aware Network (*AN*). We further evaluate the effectiveness of DARN in terms of different configurations w.r.t. the features used, *DARN* using the features obtained from FC1, *DARN with Conv4* using the features from FC1+Conv4, and *DARN with Conv4-5* using the features from FC1+Conv4+Conv5. It is worth noting that the dimension of all features is reduced to 4096 by PCA to have a fair comparison.

Figure 9.14 shows the full detailed top-k retrieval accuracy results for different baselines as well as their proposed methods. We vary k as the tuning parameter as it is an important indicator for a real system.

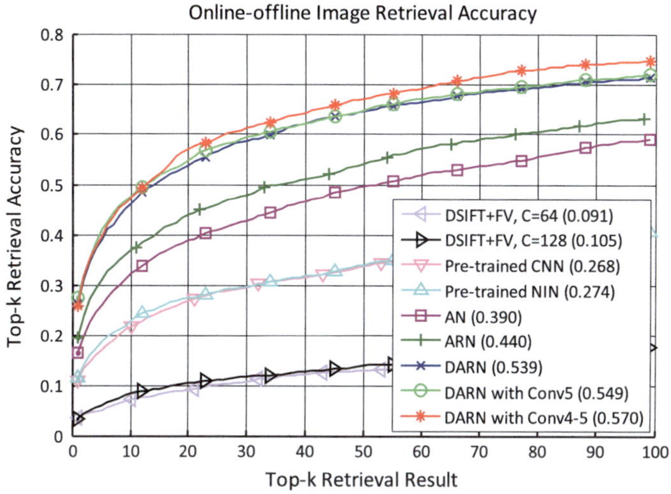

Fig. 9.14 The top-k retrieval accuracy on 200,000 retrieval gallery. The number in the parentheses is the top-20 retrieval accuracy

9.5 Summary

In this chapter, we reviewed fashion attribute prediction and its applications in fashion recommendation and fashion retrieval. We introduced two recommendation systems. The first system is called Beauty E-expert, a fully automatic system for hairstyle and facial makeup recommendation. The second system is called Magic Closet, which is an occasion-oriented clothing recommendation system. For fashion retrieval, a fine-grained clothing retrieval system was developed to retrieve the same or similar clothing items from online shopping stores based on a user clothing photo. In each of these systems, we described an approach to transfer knowledge from a large ground truth dataset to a specific challenging real-world scenario. Visual features were used to learn semantic fashion attributes and their relationships to images from a similar but more challenging user domain. By simultaneously embedding semantic attribute information and visual similarity constraints, we have been able to construct practical real-world systems for fashion analytics.

References

1. Belongie, S., Malik, J., Puzicha, J.: Shape context: a new descriptor for shape matching and object recognition. In: Conference on Neural Information Processing Systems (NIPS) (2000)
2. Berg, T.L., Berg, A.C., Shih, J.: Automatic attribute discovery and characterization from noisy web data. In: European Conference on Computer Vision (ECCV) (2010)
3. Bourdev, L., Maji, S., Malik, J.: Describing people: a poselet-based approach to attribute classification. In: International Conference on Computer Vision (ICCV) (2011)

4. Chen, H., Gallagher, A., Girod, B.: Describing clothing by semantic attributes. In: European Conference on Computer Vision (ECCV) (2012)
5. Chen, Q., Huang, J., Feris, R., Brown, L., Dong, J., Yan, S.: Deep domain adaptation for describing people based on fine-grained clothing attributes. In: Conference on Computer Vision and Pattern Recognition (CVPR) (2015)
6. Datta, A., Feris, R., Vaquero, D.: Hierarchical ranking of facial attributes. In: IEEE International Conference on Automatic Face and Gesture Recognition (FG) (2011)
7. Donahue, J., Grauman, K.: Annotator rationales for visual recognition. In: International Conference on Computer Vision (ICCV) (2011)
8. Felzenszwalb, P., McAllester, D., Ramanan, D.: A discriminatively trained, multiscale, deformable part model. In: Conference on Computer Vision and Pattern Recognition (CVPR) (2008)
9. Feris, R., Bobbitt, R., Brown, L., Pankanti, S.: Attribute-based people search: lessons learnt from a practical surveillance system. In: International Conference on Multimedia Retrieval (ICMR) (2014)
10. Gallagher, A., Chen, T.: Clothing cosegmentation for recognizing people. In: Conference on Computer Vision and Pattern Recognition (CVPR) (2008)
11. Girshick, R., Donahue, J., Darrell, T., Malik, J.: Rich feature hierarchies for accurate object detection and semantic segmentation. In: Conference on Computer Vision and Pattern Recognition (CVPR) (2014)
12. Huang, J., Feris, R.S., Chen, Q., Yan, S.: Cross-domain image retrieval with a dual attribute-aware ranking network. In: International Conference on Computer Vision (ICCV) (2015)
13. Kiapour, M., Yamaguchi, K., Berg, A., Berg, T.: Hipster wars: discovering elements of fashion styles. In: European Conference on Computer Vision (ECCV) (2014)
14. Kiapour, M.H., Han, X., Lazebnik, S., Berg, A.C., Berg, T.L.: Where to buy it: matching street clothing photos in online shops. In: International Conference on Computer Vision (ICCV) (2015)
15. Kovashka, A., Parikh, D., Grauman, K.: Whittlesearch: Image search with relative attribute feedback. In: Conference on Computer Vision and Pattern Recognition (CVPR) (2012)
16. Kumar, N., Berg, A., Belhumeur, P., Nayar, S.: Attribute and simile classifiers for face verification. In: International Conference on Computer Vision (ICCV) (2009)
17. Kwak, I., Murillo, A., Belhumeur, P., Kriegman, D., Belongie, S.: From bikers to surfers: visual recognition of urban tribes. In: British Machine Vision Conference (BMVC) (2013)
18. Layne, R., Hospedales, T., Gong, S.: Person re-identification by attributes. In: British Machine Vision Conference (BMVC) (2012)
19. Li, A., Liu, L., Wang, K., Liu, S., Yan, S.: Clothing attributes assisted person re-identification. IEEE Trans. Circ. Syst. Video Technol. (TCSVT) **25**(5), 869–878 (2014)
20. Liang, X., Liu, S., Shen, X., Yang, J., Liu, L., Lin, L., Yan, S.: Deep human parsing with active template regression. IEEE Trans. Pattern Anal. Mach. Intell. (PAMI) **37**(12), 2402–2414 (2015)
21. Liang, X., Xu, C., Shen, X., Yang, J., Liu, S., Tang, J., Lin, L., Yan, S.: Human parsing with contextualized convolutional neural network. In: International Conference on Computer Vision (ICCV) (2015)
22. Lin, M., Chen, Q., Yan, S.: Network in network. In: International Conference on Learning Representations (ICLR) (2014)
23. Liu, S., Feng, J., Song, Z., Zhang, T., Lu, H., Xu, C., Yan, S.: Hi, magic closet, tell me what to wear! In: ACM Multimedia (ACM MM) (2012)
24. Liu, S., Song, Z., Liu, G., Xu, C., Lu, H., Yan, S.: Street-to-shop: cross-scenario clothing retrieval via parts alignment and auxiliary set. In: Conference on Computer Vision and Pattern Recognition (CVPR) (2012)
25. Liu, L., Xing, J., Liu, S., Xu, H., Zhou, X., Yan, S.: Wow! you are so beautiful today! ACM Trans. Multimedia Comput, Commun. Appl. (TOMM) **11**(1s), 20 (2014)
26. Liu, S., Feng, J., Domokos, C., Xu, H., Huang, J., Hu, Z., Yan, S.: Fashion parsing with weak color-category labels. IEEE Trans. Multimedia (TMM) **16**(1), 253–265 (2014)

27. Liu, S., Liang, X., Liu, L., Shen, X., Yang, J., Xu, C., Lin, L., Cao, X., Yan, S.: Matching-cnn meets knn: Quasi-parametric human parsing. In: Conference on Computer Vision and Pattern Recognition (CVPR) (2015)
28. Milborrow, S., Nicolls, F.: Locating facial features with an extended active shape model. In: European Conference on Computer Vision (ECCV) (2008)
29. Parikh, D., Grauman, K.: Relative attributes. In: International Conference on Computer Vision (ICCV) (2011)
30. Sharmanska, V., Quadrianto, N., Lampert, C.H.: Learning to rank using privileged information. In: International Conference on Computer Vision (ICCV) (2013)
31. Shi, Z., Hospedales, T., Xiang, T.: Transferring a semantic representation for person re-identification and search. In: Conference on Computer Vision and Pattern Recognition (CVPR) (2015)
32. Song, Z., Wang, M., Hua, X., Yan, S.: Predicting occupation via human clothing and contexts. In: International Conference on Computer Vision (ICCV) (2011)
33. Uijlings, J.R., van de Sande, K.E., Gevers, T., Smeulders, A.W.: Selective search for object recognition. Int. J. Comput. Vision (IJCV) **104**(2), 154–171 (2013)
34. Vapnik, V., Vashist, A.: A new learning paradigm: learning using privileged information. Neural Netw. **22**(5), 544–557 (2009)
35. Vaquero, D., Feris, R., Brown, L., Hampapur, A.: Attribute-based people search in surveillance environments. In: Workshop on Applications of Computer Vision (WACV) (2009)
36. Wang, Y., Mori, G.: Max-margin hidden conditional random fields for human action recognition. In: Conference on Computer Vision and Pattern Recognition (CVPR) (2009)
37. Wang, J., Chen, Y., Feris, R.: Walk and learn: facial attribute representation learning from egocentric video and contextual data. In: Conference on Computer Vision and Pattern Recognition (CVPR) (2016)
38. Yamaguchi, K., Kiapour, M.H., Ortiz, L.E., Berg, T.L.: Parsing clothing in fashion photographs. In: Conference on Computer Vision and Pattern Recognition (CVPR) (2012)
39. Yang, Y., Ramanan, D.: Articulated pose estimation with flexible mixtures-of-parts. In: Conference on Computer Vision and Pattern Recognition (CVPR) (2011)

Part IV
Defining a Vocabulary of Attributes

Chapter 10
A Taxonomy of Part and Attribute Discovery Techniques

Subhransu Maji

Abstract This chapter surveys recent techniques for discovering a set of *Parts and Attributes* (PnAs) in order to enable fine-grained visual discrimination between its instances. *Part and Attribute* (PnA)-based representations are popular in computer vision as they allow modeling of appearance in a compositional manner, and provide a basis for communication between a human and a machine for various interactive applications. Based on two main properties of these techniques a unified taxonomy of PnA discovery methods is presented. The first distinction between the techniques is whether the PnAs are semantically aligned, i.e., if they are human interpretable or not. In order to achieve the semantic alignment these techniques rely on additional supervision in the form of annotations. Techniques within this category can be further categorized based on if the annotations are language-based, such as *nameable* labels, or if they are language-free, such as *relative similarity comparisons*. After a brief introduction motivating the need for PnA based representations, the bulk of the chapter will be dedicated to techniques for PnA discovery categorized into *non-semantic*, *semantic language-based*, and *semantic language-free* methods. Throughout the chapter we will illustrate the trade-offs among various approaches though examples from the existing literature.

10.1 Introduction

This chapter surveys a number of part-based and attribute-based models proposed in the last decade in the context of visual recognition, learning, and description for human-computer interaction. Part-based representations have been very successful for various recognition tasks ranging from detecting objects in cluttered scenes [9, 34], segmenting objects [16, 107], recognizing scene categories [45, 72, 77, 92], to recognizing fine-grained attributes of objects [10, 98, 111]. Parts provide robustness to occlusion—the head of a person can be detected even when the legs are occluded. Parts can also be composed in different ways enabling generalization to

---

S. Maji (✉)
University of Massachusetts, Amherst, USA
e-mail: smaji@cs.umass.edu

R.S. Feris et al. (eds.), *Visual Attributes*, Advances in Computer Vision and Pattern Recognition, DOI 10.1007/978-3-319-50077-5_10

novel viewpoints, poses, and articulations of objects. Two popular methods, namely the *Deformable Part-based Model* (DPM) of Felzenszwalb et al. [34] and the *poselets* of Bourdev et al. [9, 11], exploit this property to build robust object detectors.

The compositional nature of part-based models is also the basis for *Convolutional Neural Networks* (CNNs). While traditional part-based models can be seen as shallow networks where the representations are hand-designed, CNNs learn all the model parameters from raw pixels to image labels in an end-to-end manner using a deeper architecture. When trained on large labeled datasets, deep CNNs have led to breakthrough results on a number of recognition tasks [44, 48, 87], and are currently the dominant approach for nearly all visual recognition problems.

Beyond recognition, a set of parts provides a means for a human to indicate the pose and articulation of an object. This is useful for recognition with humans "in the loop" where a person can annotate a part of the object to guide recognition. For instance, Branson et al. [13] interactively categorize birds by asking users to click on discriminative parts leading to significant improvement over the computer vision only baseline. In such cases it is desirable that the parts represent semantically aligned concepts since it involves communication with a human.

Along with parts, *visual attributes* provide a means to model the appearance of objects. The word "attribute" is extremely generic as it can refer to any property that might be associated with an object. Attributes can describe an entire object or a part, e.g., a tall person or a long nose. Attributes can refer to low-level properties such as color and texture, or high-level properties such as age and gender of a person. Attributes can be shared across categories, e.g., both a dog and a cat can be "furry", allowing the description of previously unseen categories. Semantically aligned attributes provide a basis for learning interpretable visual classifiers [33], create classifiers for unseen categories [52], debugging recognition systems through attribute-based explanations [3, 76], and providing human feedback during learning and inference [14, 46, 51, 78].

Thus, PnAs provide a rich compositional way of describing and recognizing categories. Techniques for PnA discovery are necessary as the desired set of parts and attributes often depend on the underlying task. While it may not be necessary to model the gender, hair-style, or the eye color of a person for detecting them, it may be useful for identifying a particular individual. One motivating reason for the unified treatment of PnAs in this chapter is that their roles are interchangeable for recognition and description. For instance, in order to distinguish between a red-beaked and a yellow-beaked bird, one could have two parts, "red beak" and "yellow beak" and no attributes, or a single part "beak" with two attributes, red and yellow. Therefore, from a representation point of view it is more fruitful to think of the joint space induced by various part-attribute interactions instead of each one of them independently. In other words we can think of attributes being localized, i.e. associated with a part, or not.

The next section provides an overview of the rest of the chapter, and describes a unified taxonomy of recent PnA discovery methods.

10.1.1 Overview

Although there are many ways to categorize the vast number of methods for PnA discovery in the literature, the particular one described in this chapter was chosen because it is especially useful for fine-grained domains which are our main focus. Often these domains have a rich structure described through language, visual illustrations, and other modalities, which can be used to guide representation learning. Translating all this information to useful visual properties is one of the main challenges of these methods. The proposed taxonomy categorizes various PnA methods based on

- the degree to which the models explicitly try to achieve *semantic alignment* or *interpretability* of the underlying PnAs,
- the nature of the source of semantics, i.e. if they are language-based or not.

When semantic alignment is not the primary goal, the PnAs can be thought of as a intermediate representation of the appearance of objects. Example methods for part discovery in this setting include DPMs [34], and CNNs [48, 56]. Here the learned parts factorize the appearance variation within the category and are learned without additional supervision apart from the category labels at the object or image level. Hence, semantic alignment is not guaranteed and parts that arise tend to represent visually salient patterns. Similarly non-semantic attributes can be thought of as the coordinates in a transformed space of images optimized for the recognition task. Such methods are described in Sects. 10.2.1 and 10.2.2.

Language is a natural source of semantics. Although the vocabulary of parts and attributes that arise in language are a result of multiple phenomena, they provide a rich source of interpretable visual PnAs. For instance, parts of animals can be based on the names of anatomical parts. Various existing datasets that contain part annotations follow this strategy. This include the *Caltech-UCSD Birds* (CUB) dataset [100], *OID:Airplanes* dataset [98], and part annotations of animals in PASCAL VOC dataset [9, 20]. Similarly, attributes can be based on common color, texture, and shape terms used in language, or can be highly specialized language-based properties of the category. For example, the CUB dataset annotates parts of birds with color attributes, while the Berkeley "attributes of people" dataset [10] contains attributes describing gender, clothing, age, etc. We review techniques for collecting language-based attribute and part annotations in Sects. 10.3.1 and 10.3.4 respectively.

Task-specific language-based PnAs can also be *discovered* by analyzing descriptions of objects (Sect. 10.3.2). For example, Berg et al. [6] analyze captioned images on the web to discover attributes. Nameable attributes may also be discovered *interactively* by asking annotators to *name* the principal directions of variations within the data [79], by selecting a subset of attributes that frequently discriminate instances [80], or by analyzing descriptions of differences between instances [63]. We review such techniques in Sect. 10.3.3.

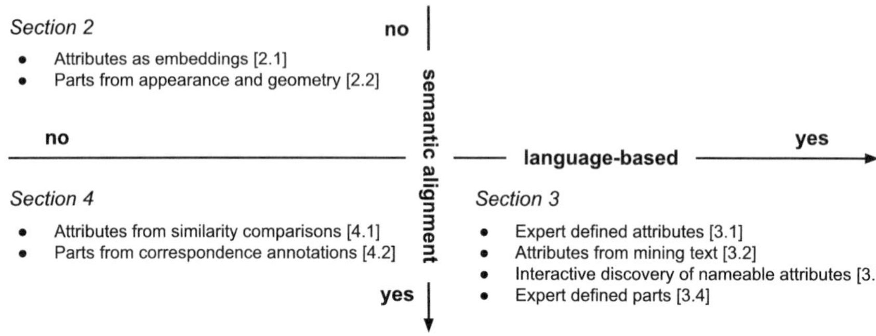

Fig. 10.1 A taxonomy of PnA discovery techniques discussed in this chapter based on the degree of semantic alignment (y-axis) and if they are language-based (x-axis). Various sections and subsections in this chapter are listed within each quadrant

Beyond language, semantic alignment of PnAs may also be achieved by collecting language-free annotations (Sect. 10.4). An example of this is through similarity comparisons of the form *"is A more similar to B than C"*. The coordinates of the embedded space that reflects these similarity comparisons can be viewed as an semantic attribute [101] (Sect. 10.4.1). Another example is when an annotator clicks on landmarks between pairs of instances. Such data can be collected without having to name the parts providing a way to annotate parts for categories that do not have a well defined set of *nameable* parts [65]. The resulting pairwise correspondence data can be used for learning semantic part appearance models (Sect. 10.4.2).

Figure 10.1 shows the taxonomy pictorially. Existing approaches are divided into three main categories: *non-semantic PnAs* (Sect. 10.2), *semantic language-based PnAs* (Sect. 10.3), and *semantic language-free PnAs* (Sect. 10.4). Within each category we further organize approaches into various sections to illustrate the scenarios when they are applicable and the computational *versus* annotation-cost trade-offs they offer. We describe some open questions and conclude in Sect. 10.5.

10.2 Non-semantic PnAs

A common theme underlying techniques for non-semantic PnA discovery is that the parts and attributes arise out of a framework where the goal is a *factorized* representation of the appearance space. Pictorially, one can think of PnAs as an intermediate representation between the images and high-level semantics. The factorization results in better computational efficiency, statistical efficiency, and robustness of the overall model.

10.2.1 Attributes as Embeddings

A typical strategy of learning attributes in this setting is to constrain the intermediate representation to be low-dimensional or sparse. Techniques for dimensionality reduction, such as *k-means* [59], *Principal Component Analysis* (PCA) [42], *Locality Sensitive Hashing* [37], *auto-encoders* [4], and *spectral clustering* [68], can be applied to obtain compact embeddings.

An early application of such approach for recognition is the eigenfaces of Turk and Pentland [97]. PCA is applied to a large number of *aligned* frontal faces to learn a low-dimensional space corresponding to the first few PCA basis. These capture the major axes of variations, some of which are aligned to factors such as lighting, or facial expression. The low-dimensional embedding was used for face recognition in their setting. One can use an image representation such as Fisher Vector [81, 82] instead of pixel values before dimensionality reduction for additional invariance. These techniques have no explicit control over the semantic alignment of the representation, and are not guaranteed to lead to interpretable attributes.

In a *task-specific setting* the intermediate representation can be optimized for the final performance. An example of this is a two-layer neural network for image classification that takes raw pixels as input and produces class probabilities via an intermediate layer which can be seen as attributes.

There are many realizations of this strategy in the literature that vary in the specifics of the architecture and the nature of the task. For example, the "picodes" approach of Bergamo et al. [7] learns a compact binary descriptor (e.g., 16 bytes) that has a good object recognition performance. Attributes are parametrized as $a(\mathbf{x}) = \mathbf{1}[\mathbf{w}^T\mathbf{x} > 0]$, for some weight vector $\mathbf{w}$ for an input representation $\mathbf{x}$. Rastegari et al. [86] use a similar parameterization but use a notion of "predictability" measured as attributes that achieve high separation between classes as the objective. Yu et al. [109] learn attributes by formulating it as a matrix factorization problem.

Experiments reported in the above work show that the task-driven attributes achieve better performance compared to unsupervised methods for attribute discovery on datasets such as Caltech-256 [40] and ImageNet [28]. Moreover, they provide a compact representation of images for efficient retrieval and other applications.

10.2.2 Part Discovery Based on Appearance and Geometry

In addition to appearance, part-based models can take into account the geometric relationships between the parts during learning. In the unsupervised, or task-free setting, parts may be obtained by clustering local patches using any unsupervised method such as k-means, spectral clustering, etc. This is the one of the key steps in the bag-of-visual-words representation of images [24] and their variants such as the Fisher Vector [81, 82] and Vector of Locally Aggregated Descriptors (VLAD) [43], which are some of the early successful image representations.

Geometric information can be added during the clustering process to account for spatial consistency, e.g., by coarsely quantizing the space using a spatial pyramid [55], or by appending the coordinates of the local patches (called "spatial augmentation") to the appearance before clustering [90, 91]. Parts may also be discovered via correspondences between pairs of instances obtained by some low-level matching procedure. For instance, Berg et al. [5] discover important regions in images by considering geometrically consistent feature matches across instances.

Another example of a model that combines appearance and geometry for part learning is the DPM of Felzenszwalb et al. [34]. The model has been widely used for object detection in cluttered scenes. A category is modeled as a mixture of components, each of which is represented as a "root" template and a collection of "parts" that can move independently relative to the root template. The tree-like structure of the model allows efficient inference through distance transforms. The parameters of the model are learned through an iterative procedure where the component membership, part positions, and appearances models are updated in order to obtain good separation between positive examples and the background. Figure 10.2a shows two components learned for person detection on the PASCAL VOC dataset [32]. The compositional architecture of the DPM led to significant improvements over the monolithic template-based detector of Dalal and Triggs [25].

Another example for task-driven part discovery is the "discriminative patches" approach of Singh et al. [92]. Here parts are initialized by clustering appearance, and through a process of positive and hard-negative mining the part appearances

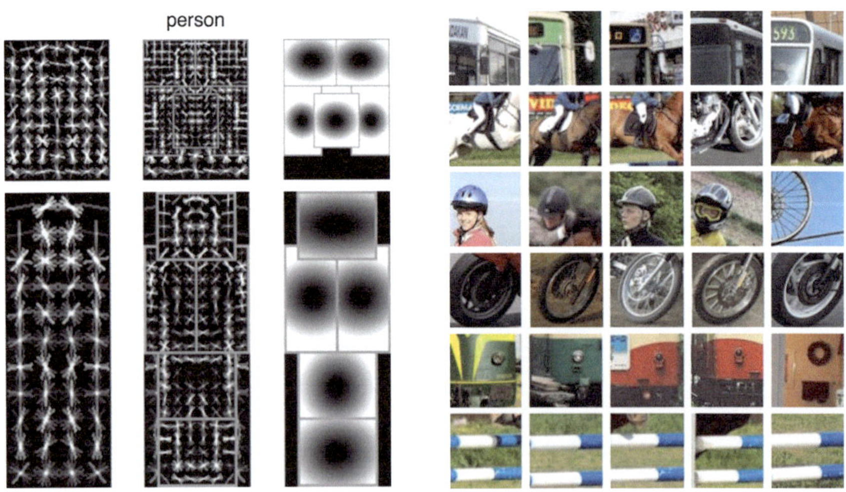

(a) Figure source: Felzenszwalb et al. [34]   (b) Figure source: Gupta et al. [92]

Fig. 10.2 **a** Two components of the deformable part-based model learned for the person category. The "root" and "part" templates are show using the HOG feature visualization (*left* and *middle*) and the spatial model is shown on the *right*. **b** Examples of discriminative patches discovered for various classes in the PASCAL VOC dataset are iteratively refined. Finally parts that are *frequent* and help *discriminate* among classes are selected. Figure 10.2b shows example discriminative patches discovered for the PASCAL VOC dataset. The authors demonstrate good performance on image classification datasets, such as PASCAL VOC, MIT Indoor scenes [83], using a representation that records the activation of discriminative patches at different locations and scales (similar to a bag-of-visual-words model [24]).

Since these methods primarily rely on appearance and geometric consistency, the discovered parts may not be aligned to semantics. For instance, the DPM requires that each object have the same set of parts even if the object is partially occluded. Hence the model uses a part to both recognize a part of the object or its occluder. Similarly, discriminative patches are visually consistent parts according to the underlying *Histograms of Oriented Gradient* (HOG) features [25] and hence two patches that are visually dissimilar but belong to the same semantic category are unlikely to be grouped as the same part. For example, two kinds of car wheels, or two styles of windows, will be represented using two or more parts.

Convolutional Neural Networks (CNNs) can be seen as part-based model trained in an end-to-end manner, i.e. starting from a pixel representation to class labels. The hierarchy of convolution and max-pooling layers resemble the computation of a deformable part-based model. Indeed, the DPM can be seen as a particular instantiation of a CNN since both HOG (see Mahendran and Vedaldi [62]) and the DPM computations (see Girshick et al. [38]) can be written as shallow CNNs. However, after the recent breakthrough result of Krishevsky et al. [48] on the ImageNet classification dataset [28], CNNs have become the architecture of choice for nearly all visual recognition tasks [12, 23, 39, 44, 60, 87, 94, 111, 112].

CNNs trained in a supervised manner can be seen to simultaneously learn parts and attributes. For instance, visualizations of the "AlexNet CNN" [48] by Zeiler and Fergus [110], as seen in Fig. 10.3, reveal units that activate strongly on parts such as human and dog faces, as well as attributes such as "text" and "grid-like". Recent works, such as the *bilinear CNNs* [57] show that discriminative localized attributes emerge when these models are fine-tuned for fine-grained recognition tasks. Figure 10.4 shows example filters learned when these mdoels are trained on birds [100], cars [47], and airplane [64] datasets. The remarkable performance of CNNs shows that considering part and attribute discovery *jointly* can have significant benefits.

10.3 Semantic Language-Based PnAs

Language is the source of categories for virtually all modern datasets in computer vision. The widely used ImageNet dataset reflects the hypernymy-hierarchy ("is a" relationships) of nouns in WordNet—a lexical database of words in English organized in a variety of ways [67]. Naturally, language is also a source of PnAs useful for a high-level description of objects, scenes, materials, and other visual phenomenon. For example, a cat can be described as a four-legged furry animal. This human-

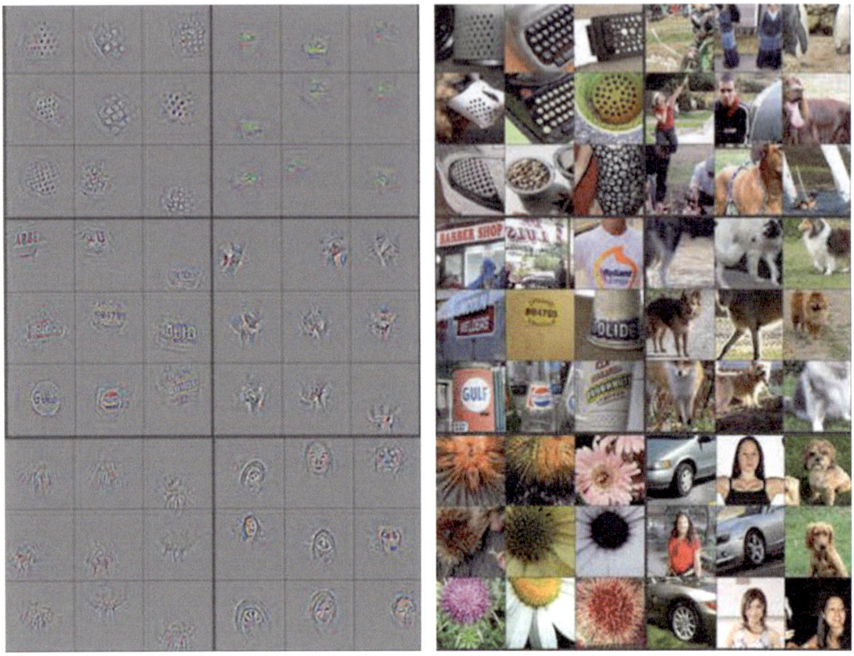

Fig. 10.3 Visualizations of the top activations of six *conv5* units of the AlexNet CNN [48] trained on ImageNet dataset [28]. For each image patch on the *left* the locations of where that are responsible for the activations are also shown on the *left*. The units strongly respond to parts such as dog and human faces, as well as attributes such as "grid-like" and "text". Figure source: Zeiler and Fergus [110]

Fig. 10.4 Visualizions of the top activations of several units of the "bilinear CNN" (B-CNN [D,M] model) [57] fine-tuned on birds [100] (*left*), cars [47] (*middle*), and airplane [64] (*right*) datasets. Each row shows the patches in the training data with the highest activations for a particular unit of the "D network" (See [57] for details). The units correspond to various localized attributes ranging from *yellow-red stripes* (row 4) and particular beak shapes (row 8) for birds, wheel detectors (rows 6, 8, 9) for cars, to propeller (rows 1, 4) and vertical-stabilizer types (row 8) for airplanes

interpretable description of learned models provides a means for communication between a human and machine during learning and inference. Below we overview several applications of language-based PnAs from the literature.

10.3.1 Expert Defined Attributes

An early example of language-based attributes in the computer vision community was for describing texture. Bajscy proposed attributes such as orientation, contrast, size, and spacing of structural elements in periodic textures [2]. Tamura et al. [95] identified six visual attributes of textures namely *coarseness, contrast, directionality, linelikeness, regularity,* and *roughness*. Amadasun and King derived computational models for five properties of texture, namely, *coarseness, contrast, business, complexity,* and *texture strength* [1].

Recently, Cimpoi et al. [22] extended the set of describable attributes to include 47 different words based on the work of Rao and Lohse [85]. Other texture attributes such as material properties have been used to construct datasets such as *CUReT* [26], *UIUC* [54], *UMD* [105], *Outex* [69], *Drexel Texture Database* [71], *KTH-TIPS* [17, 41] and *Flickr Material Dataset* (FMD) [89]. In all the above cases experts identified the set of language terms as attributes based on domain knowledge, or in some cases through human studies [85].

Beyond textures, language-based attributes have since been proposed for a variety of other datasets and applications. Farhadi et al. [33] describe object categories with *shape*, *part-names* and *material attributes*. Lampert et al. [52] proposed the *Animals with Attributes* (AwA) dataset consisting of variety of animals with shared attributes such as color, food habits, size, etc. The *Caltech-UCSD Birds* (CUB) dataset [100] consists of hundreds of species of birds labeled with attributes such as the shape the beak, color of the wings, etc. The *OID:Airplanes* [98] dataset consists of airplanes labeled with attributes such as number of wings, type of wheels, shapes of parts, etc. Attributes such as gender, eye color, hair syle, etc., have been used by Kumar et al. [49] to recognize, describe, and retrieve faces. Other examples include attributes of people [10], human actions [58], clothing style and fashion [19, 106], urban tribes [50], and asthetics [30].

A challenge is using language-based attributes to the degree of specialization to be considered. For instance, while an attribute of airplane such as the *shape of the nose* can be understood by most people, an attribute such as the *type of the aluminum alloy used in manufacturing* can only be understood by a domain expert. Similarly, the scientific names of parts of animals are typically known only to a domain expert. While common attributes have the advantage that they can be annotated by "crowdsourcing", they may lack the precision needed for fine-grained discrimination between closely related categories. Bridging the gap between expert-defined and commonly used attributes remains an open question. In the context of object categories this aspect has been studied by Ordonez et al. [70] where they learn common names

(a) Figure source: Berg et al. [6] (b) Figure source: Divvala et al. [31]

Fig. 10.5 **a** Automatically discovered handbag attributes from [6], sorted by "visualness" measured as the predictability of the attribute based on visual features. **b** Automatically mined visual attributes for various categories from books [31]

("entry-level categories") by analyzing the frequency of usage in text on the Internet, e.g. *grampus griseus* is translated to a *dolphin*.

10.3.2 Attribute Discovery by Automatically Mining Text

Language-based attributes may also be mined from large sets of images with captions. Ferrari and Zisserman [36] mine attributes of texture and color from descriptions on the web. Berg et al. [6] obtain attributes by mining frequently occurring phrases from captioned images and estimating if they are visually salient by training a classifier to predict the attribute from images (Fig. 10.5a). In the process they also characterize if the attributes are localized or not. Text on the Internet from online books, Wikipedia articles, etc., have been mined to discover attributes for objects [31] (Fig. 10.5b), semantic affordances of objects and actions [18], and other common-sense properties of the visual world [21].

10.3.3 Interactive Discovery of Nameable Attributes

While captioned images are a great source of attributes, the vast majority of categories are not well represented in captioned images on the web. In such situations one can aim to discover nameable attributes *interactively*. Parikh and Grauman [73] show annotators images that vary along a projection of the underlying features and ask them to describe it if possible (Fig. 10.6a). To be effective the method requires a feature space whose projections are likely to be semantically correlated.

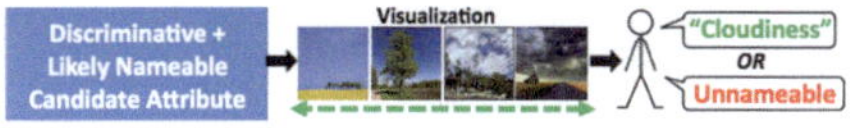

(a) Figure source: Parikh and Grauman [73]

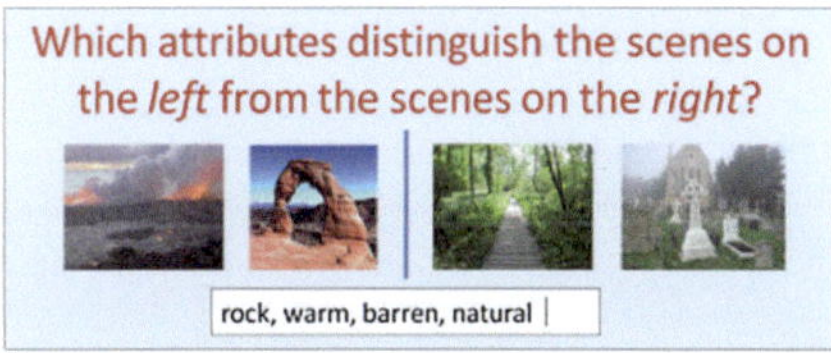

(b) Figure source: Patterson and Hays [80]

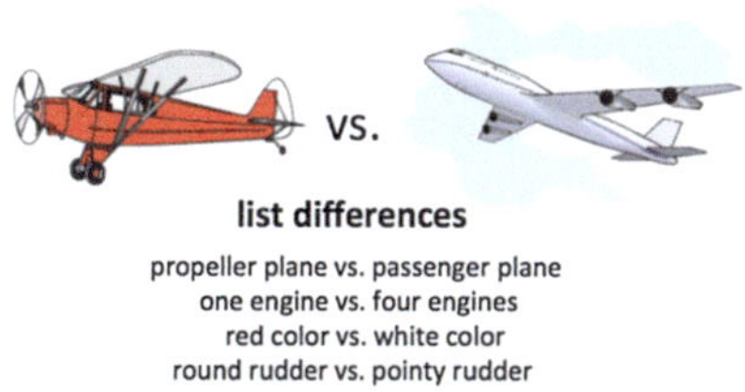

(c) Figure source: Maji [63]

Fig. 10.6 Interactive attribute discovery. Annotators are asked to **a** *name what varies* in the images from *left* to *right* [73], **b** *select attributes* that distinguish images on the *left* from the *right* [80], and **c** *describe the differences* between pairs of instances [63]. The collected data is analyzed to discover a set of *nameable* attributes

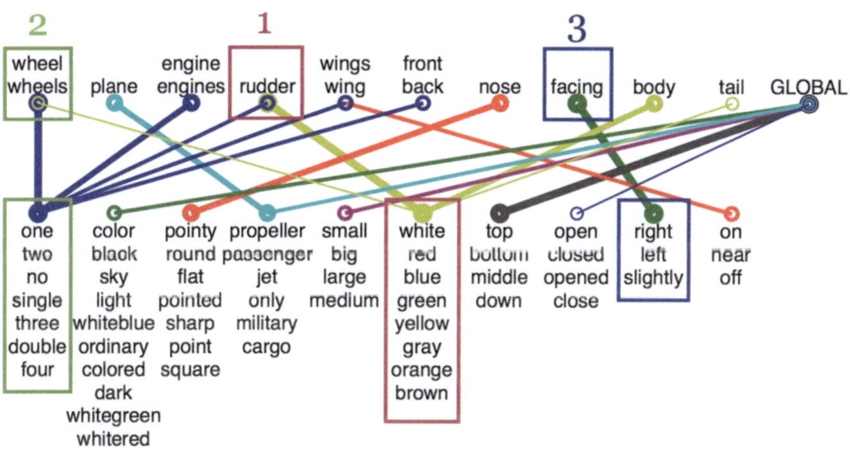

Fig. 10.7 The vocabulary of parts (*top row*) and their attributes (*bottom row*) discovered by from sentence pairs describing the differences between images in *OID:Airplanes* dataset [98]. The three most discriminative attributes are also shown. Figure source: Maji [63]

Patterson and Hays [80] start from a set of attributes mined from natural language descriptions and ask annotators to select five attributes that distinguish images from various scene classes in the SUN database. Thus attributes suited for discrimination within the set of images can be discovered (Fig. 10.6b).

A similar strategy was used in my earlier work [63] where annotators were asked to describe the visual differences between pairs of images (Fig. 10.6c) revealing fine-grained properties useful for discrimination. The collected data was mined to discover a lexicon of parts and attributes by analyzing the *frequency* and *co-occurrence* of words in the descriptions (Fig. 10.7).

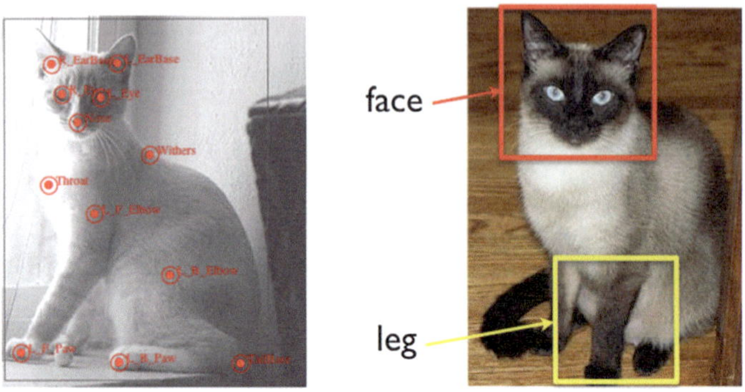

Fig. 10.8 Two methods for collecting part annotations. On the *left*, the positions of set of landmarks are annotated. On the *right*, bounding-boxes for parts are annotated

10.3.4 Expert Defined Parts

Like attributes, language-based parts have been widely used in computer vision for modeling articulated objects. An early example of this is *pictorial structure* model for detecting people in images where parts were based on the human anatomy [35]. A modeling decision that is unique compared to attributes is the choice of the spatial extent, scale, pose, and other visual phenomenon, for a given semantic part.

Broadly, there are commonly used methods for collecting part annotations (Fig. 10.8). The first is *landmark-based* where positions of landmarks, such as joint positions of humans, or fiducial points for faces are annotated. The second is *bounding-box-based* where part bounding-boxes are explicitly labeled to define the extent of each part. The bounding-boxes may be further refined to reflect the pixel-wise support or segmentation of the parts.

When landmarks are provided one could simply assume that parts correspond to these landmarks. This strategy has been applied for modeling faces with fiducial points [113], articulated people with deformable part-based models [35, 108], etc. Another strategy is to discover parts that correspond to frequently occurring configuration of landmarks. The *poselets* approach combines this strategy with a procedure to select a set of *diverse* and *discriminative parts* for the task of person detection [9]. The discovered poselets are different from both landmarks and anatomical parts (Fig. 10.9a). For instance, a part consisting of *half the profile face and the right shoulder* is a valid poselet. These patterns can capture distinctive appearances that arise due to self-occlusion, foreshortening, and other phenomenon which are hard to model in a traditional part-based model.

When bounding-boxes are provided there is relatively little flexibility in part discovery. Much work in this setting has focused on effectively modeling appearance through a mixture of templates. Additional annotations, such as viewpoint, pose, or shape, can be used to guide mixture model learning. For instance, Vedaldi et al. [98] show that using shape and viewpoint annotations to initialize

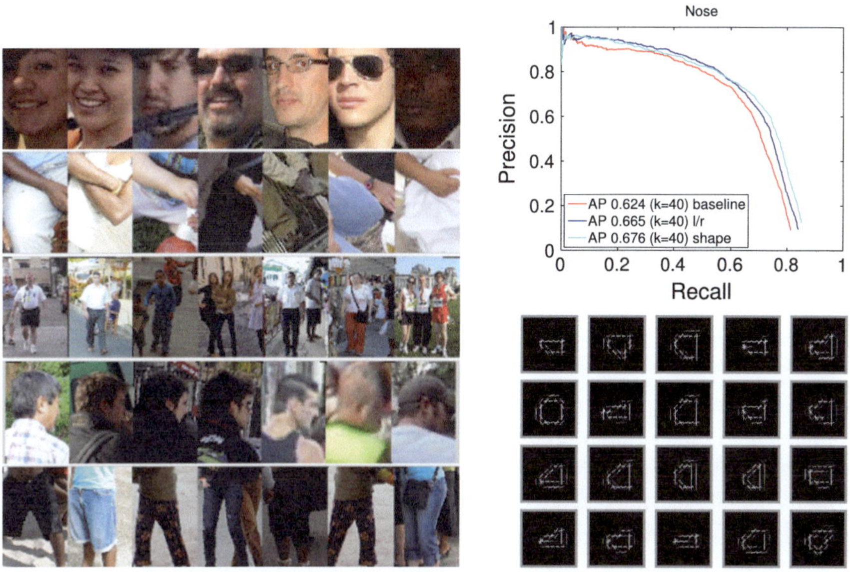

(a) Discovered poselets for person detection (b) Detection using part mixtures

Fig. 10.9 Visual part discovery from annotations. **a** Poselets discovered for detecting people using landmark annotations on the PASCAL VOC dataset. Figure source: Bourdev et al. [9]. **b** Detection AP using $k = 40$ mixture components based on aspect-ratio clustering, *left-right* clustering, and supervised shape clustering. Nose shape clusters learned by EM are shown in the *bottom*. Figure source: Vedaldi et al. [98]

HOG-based parts improves detection accuracy compared to the aspect-ratio based clustering (Fig. 10.9b).

10.4 Semantic Language-Free PnAs

Language-based PnAs, when applicable, provide a rich semantic representation of objects. However language alone may not be sufficient to capture the full range of visual phenomena. Consider the space of colors defined by the [R, G, B] values. Berlin and Kay in their seminal work [8] analyzed the words used to describe color across widely across languages. While languages like English have many words to describe color, there are languages that have very few words, including an extreme case of language with only have two words ("bright" and "dull") to describe color leading to a gross simplification of the color space. Similarly, restricting one to nameable parts poses challenges in annotating categories that are structurally diverse. It would require significant effort to define a set of parts that apply to all chairs, or all buildings, since the resulting set of parts would have to very large to account for the diversity within the category. Moreover, the parts are unlikely to have intuitive names, e.g. "top-right corner of the left handle".

In this section we overview methods to discover semantically aligned PnA without restricting oneself to language-based interfaces. The underlying approach is to collect annotations relative to another. Such annotations provide constraints which can be utilized to guide the alignment of the representation to semantics. We describe several examples of such approaches.

10.4.1 Attribute Discovery from Similarity Comparisons

Similarity comparisons of the form *"A is more similar to B than C"*, can be used to obtain annotations without relying on language. These can be used to transform the data into an Euclidean space that respects the similarity constrains using methods for *distance metric learning* [27, 104], *large-margin nearest neighbor* learning [103], t-STE [61], *Crowd Kernel Learning* [96], etc.

Figure 10.10 shows a visualization of the categories in the CUB dataset using a two-dimensional embedding learned from crowdsourced similarity comparisons between images [101]. Each image-level similarity constraint is converted to a category-level similarity constraint by using the category labels of the images from which an embedding is learned using t-STE. A group of points on the bottom-right corresponds to perching birds, while another group on the bottom-left corresponds to gull-like birds.

Since a representation learned in such manner respects the underlying perceptual similarity, it can be used as a means of interacting with a user for fine-grained recognition. Wah et al. [101] build an interface where users interactively recognize bird species by selecting the most similar image in a display. The underlying perceptual embedding is used to select the images to be displayed in each iteration. The authors show that the method requires fewer questions to get to the right answer than an attribute-based interface of Branson et al. [14].

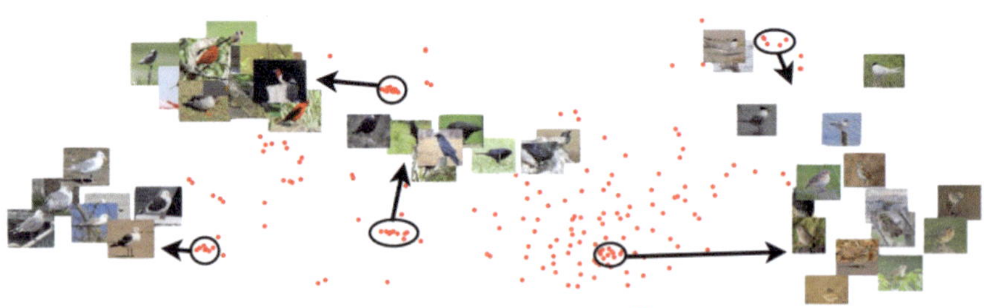

Fig. 10.10 A visualization of the first two dimensions of the 200-node category-level similarity embedding. Visually similar classes tend to belong to coherent clusters (circled and shown with selected representative images). Figure source: Wah et al. [101] (Best viewed digitally with zoom)

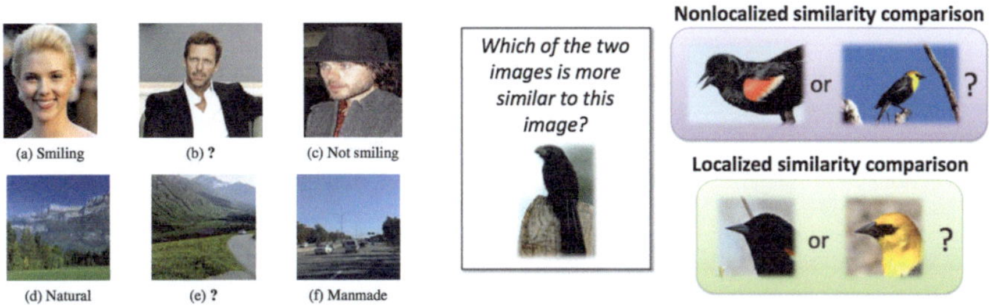

(a) Relative attributes (b) Non-localized and localized similarity

Fig. 10.11 **a** In the *relative attributes* framework an attribute is measured relative to other images, e.g. is the person in the image smiling more, or less, than the other images. Figure source: Parikh and Grauman [74]. **b** *Global* or *localized similarity comparisons* are used to learn a perceptual embedding of the entire object or parts respectively. Figure source: Wah et al. [102]

A drawback of similarity comparisons is that there can be considerable ambiguity in the task since there are many ways to compare images. Most methods for learning embeddings do not take this into account and hence are less robust to annotations collected via "crowdsouring" which can have significant noise. A number of approaches aim to reduce this ambiguity by providing additional instructions to the annotators.

The *relative attributes* approach of Parikh and Grauman [74] guides similarity comparisons by focusing on a particular describable attribute. An example annotation task is: *is A smiling more than B*, as seen in Fig. 10.11a. Such annotations are used to learn a ranking function, or a one dimensional embedding, of images corresponding to the attribute. Relative attributes bridge the gap between categorical attributes and low-dimensional semantic embeddings, and have been used for interactive search and learning of visual attributes [46, 75].

Wah et al. [101] guide similarity comparisons by restricting the image to a *part of the object*, as seen in Fig. 10.11b, to obtain a semantic embedding of parts. The authors use parts discovered using the *discriminative patches* approach [92], but part annotations can be used instead when available. The authors show that localized perceptual similarities provides a richer way of indicating closeness to a test image and leads to better efficiency during interactive recognition tasks.

10.4.2 Part Discovery from Correspondence Annotations

Traditional methods for annotating parts require a set of nameable parts. When such parts are not readily available one can instead label correspondences between pairs of instances. Maji and Shakhanrovich [65, 66] show that when annotators are asked to mark correspondences between image pairs within a category, the result is fairly consistent across annotators, even when the names of parts are not known (Fig. 10.12a).

(a) Pairwise correspondence annotations

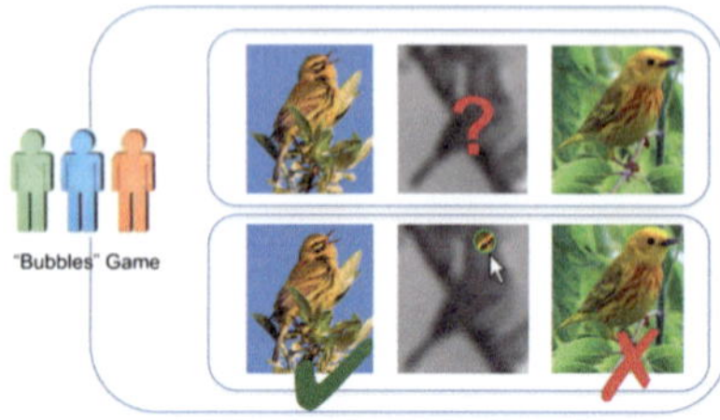

(b) The "Bubbles" game

Fig. 10.12 **a** Annotators click on *corresponding regions* between to indicate parts [65, 66]. **b** The *Bubbles game* shows annotators a blurry image in the middle and asks which one of the two categories, *left* or *right*, does it belong to. The user can click on a region of the blurry image to reveal what is underneath. These clicks reveal the discriminative regions within an image which is used to learn a part-based representation called the *BubblesBank*. Figure source: Deng et al. [29]

Annotators rely on semantics beyond visual similarity to mark correspondences—two windows are matched even though they are visually different.

Methods for part discovery that rely on appearance and geometry can be extended to take into account the pairwise constraints obtained from such correspondence annotations. The authors propose an approach were the patches corresponding to a semantic part are iteratively updated while respecting the underlying matches between image pairs. The resulting discovered patches are both visually and semantically aligned and can be used for rich part-based analysis of objects, including for detection and segmentation [66].

Another method that implicitly obtains correspondences is the *BubbleBank* approach of Deng et al. [29]. Annotators are shown two images A and B, and asked which of the two is the category of the third image (Fig. 10.12b). The caveat is that the third image is blurry, but the user can click on parts of the image to reveal what is underneath. Since, in order to accurately recognize the category corresponding parts have to be compared such annotations reveal the salient regions or parts for a given category. These clicks are used to create the *BubbleBank* representation, a set of parts centered around the frequently clicked locations, and applied for fine-grained recognition.

10.5 Conclusion

The chapter summarizes the current techniques for PnA discovery by categorizing them into three broad categories. The methods described are most relevant for describing and recognizing fine-grained categories, but this is by no means a complete account of existing methods. Unsupervised part-based methods alone have a rich history and even within the DPM family methods vary on how they model part appearance and geometric relationships between parts. See Ramanan [84] for a excellent survey of classical part-based models.

Similarity, a sub-field of Human-Computer Interaction (HCI) designs "games with purpose" to annotate properties of images including attributes and part labels. A well known example is the *ESP game* [99] where a pair of annotators *independently* tag images and get rewarded only if the tags match. This makes it competitive encouraging participation and reduces vandalism. Some frameworks discussed in this chapter such as pairwise correspondence for part annotations, describing the differences for attribute discovery, and the *Bubbles* game, fall into this category. For a good overview of such techniques see the lecture notes by Law and Ahn [53].

We also did not cover methods that discover the structure of objects by analyzing its motion over time. This has been well studied in *robotics* to discover the kinematic structure of articulated objects [15, 93]. Although this works best at the instance-level, the strategy has been used to discover parts within a category [88].

Finally, a number of recent works discover PnAs within the framework of deep CNNs for fine-grained recognition [12, 57, 111, 112]. Although these methods have been very successful, they bring a new set of challenges. One of them is training models for a new domain when limited labeled data is available. Factorization of the appearance using parts and attributes, either using labels provided explicitly through annotations, or implicitly in the model, continues to be the method of choice for such situations.

Acknowledgements Subhransu Maji acknowledges funding from NSF IIS-1617917 and a UMass Amherst startup grant, and thanks Gregory Shakhnarovich, Catherine Wah, Serge Belongie, Erik Learned-Miller, and Tsung-Yu Lin for helpful discussions.

References

1. Amadasun, M., King, R.: Textural features corresponding to textural properties. IEEE Trans. Syst. Man Cybern. **19**(5), 1264–1274 (1989)
2. Bajcsy, R.: Computer description of textured surfaces. Morgan Kaufmann Publishers Inc. (1973)
3. Bansal, A., Farhadi, A., Parikh, D.: Towards transparent systems: semantic characterization of failure modes. In: European Conference on Computer Vision (ECCV) (2014)
4. Bengio, Y.: Learning deep architectures for AI. Found. Trends Mach. Learn. **2**(1), 1–127 (2009)
5. Berg, A.C., Berg, T.L., Malik, J.: Shape matching and object recognition using low distortion correspondences. In: Conference on Computer Vision and Pattern Recognition (CVPR) (2005)
6. Berg, T., Berg, A., Shih, J.: Automatic attribute discovery and characterization from noisy web data. European Conference on Computer Vision (ECCV) (2010)
7. Bergamo, A., Torresani, L., Fitzgibbon, A.W.: Picodes: Learning a compact code for novel-category recognition. In: Conference on Neural Information Processing Systems (NIPS) (2011)
8. Berlin, B., Kay, P.: Basic color terms: their universality and evolution. University of California Press (1991)
9. Bourdev, L., Maji, S., Brox, T., Malik, J.: Detecting people using mutually consistent poselet activations. In: European Conference on Computer Vision (ECCV) (2010)

10. Bourdev, L., Maji, S., Malik, J.: Describing people: a poselet-based approach to attribute classification. In: International Conference on Computer Vision (ICCV) (2011)
11. Bourdev, L., Malik, J.: Poselets: Body part detectors trained using 3d human pose annotations. In: Conference on Computer Vision and Pattern Recognition (CVPR) (2009)
12. Branson, S., Horn, G.V., Belongie, S., Perona, P.: Bird species categorization using pose normalized deep convolutional nets. In: British Machine Vision Conference (BMVC) (2014)
13. Branson, S., Van Horn, G., Wah, C., Perona, P., Belongie, S.: The ignorant led by the blind: a hybrid human-machine vision system for fine-grained categorization. Int. J. Comput. Vis. (IJCV) **108**(1–2), 3–29 (2014)
14. Branson, S., Wah, C., Schroff, F., Babenko, B., Welinder, P., Perona, P., Belongie, S.: Visual recognition with humans in the loop. In: European Conference on Computer Vision (ECCV) (2010)
15. Broida, T., Chellappa, R.: Estimating the kinematics and structure of a rigid object from a sequence of monocular images. IEEE Trans. Pattern Anal. Mach. Intell. (TPAMI) **6**, 497–513 (1991)
16. Brox, T., Bourdev, L., Maji, S., Malik, J.: Object segmentation by alignment of poselet activations to image contours. In: Conference on Computer Vision and Pattern Recognition (CVPR) (2011)
17. Caputo, B., Hayman, E., Mallikarjuna, P.: Class-specific material categorisation. In: International Conference on Computer Vision (ICCV) (2005)
18. Chao, Y.W., Wang, Z., Mihalcea, R., Deng, J.: Mining semantic affordances of visual object categories. In: Conference on Computer Vision and Pattern Recognition (CVPR) (2015)
19. Chen, H., Gallagher, A., Girod, B.: Describing clothing by semantic attributes. In: European Conference on Computer Vision (ECCV) (2012)
20. Chen, X., Mottaghi, R., Liu, X., Fidler, S., Urtasun, R., et al.: Detect what you can: Detecting and representing objects using holistic models and body parts. In: Conference on Computer Vision and Pattern Recognition (CVPR) (2014)
21. Chen, X., Shrivastava, A., Gupta, A.: Neil: Extracting visual knowledge from web data. In: International Conference on Computer Vision (ICCV) (2013)
22. Cimpoi, M., Maji, S., Kokkinos, I., Mohamed, S., Vedaldi, A.: Describing textures in the wild. In: Conference on Computer Vision and Pattern Recognition (CVPR) (2014)
23. Cimpoi, M., Maji, S., Kokkinos, I., Vedaldi, A.: Deep filter banks for texture recognition, description, and segmentation. Int. J. Comput. Vis. **118**(1), 65–94 (2016)
24. Csurka, G., Dance, C.R., Dan, L., Willamowski, J., Bray, C.: Visual categorization with bags of keypoints. In: Proc. ECCV Workshop on Statistical Learning in Computer Vision (2004)
25. Dalal, N., Triggs, B.: Histograms of oriented gradients for human detection. In: Conference on Computer Vision and Pattern Recognition (CVPR) (2005)
26. Dana, K.J., van Ginneken, B., Nayar, S.K., Koenderink, J.J.: Reflectance and texture of real world surfaces. ACM Trans. Graphics **18**(1), 1–34 (1999)
27. Davis, J.V., Kulis, B., Jain, P., Sra, S., Dhillon, I.S.: Information-theoretic metric learning. In: International Conference on Machine Learning (ICML) (2007)
28. Deng, J., Dong, W., Socher, R., Li, L.J., Li, K., Fei-Fei, L.: ImageNet: a large-scale hierarchical image database. In: Conference on Computer Vision and Pattern Recognition (CVPR) (2009)
29. Deng, J., Krause, J., Fei-Fei, L.: Fine-grained crowdsourcing for fine-grained recognition. In: Conference on Computer Vision and Pattern Recognition (CVPR) (2013)
30. Dhar, S., Ordonez, V., Berg, T.L.: High level describable attributes for predicting aesthetics and interestingness. In: Conference on Computer Vision and Pattern Recognition (CVPR) (2011)
31. Divvala, S.K., Farhadi, A., Guestrin, C.: Learning everything about anything: Webly-supervised visual concept learning. In: Conference on Computer Vision and Pattern Recognition (CVPR) (2014)
32. Everingham, M., Eslami, S.M.A., Van Gool, L., Williams, C.K.I., Winn, J., Zisserman, A.: The pascal visual object classes challenge: a retrospective. Int. J. Comput. Vis. (IJCV) **111**(1), 98–136 (2015)

33. Farhadi, A., Endres, I., Hoiem, D., Forsyth, D.: Describing objects by their attributes. In: Conference on Computer Vision and Pattern Recognition (CVPR) (2009)
34. Felzenszwalb, P.F., Grishick, R.B., McAllester, D., Ramanan, D.: Object detection with discriminatively trained part based models. IEEE Trans. Pattern Anal. Mach. Intell. (TPAMI) (2010)
35. Felzenszwalb, P.F., Huttenlocher, D.P.: Pictorial structures for object recognition. Int. J. Comput. Vis. **61**(1), 55–79 (2005)
36. Ferrari, V., Zisserman, A.: Learning visual attributes. In: Conference on Neural Information Processing Systems (NIPS) (2007)
37. Gionis, A., Indyk, P., Motwani, R., et al.: Similarity search in high dimensions via hashing. In: International Conference on Very Large Data Bases (VLDB) (1999)
38. Girshick, R., Iandola, F., Darrell, T., Malik, J.: Deformable part models are convolutional neural networks. In: Conference on Computer Vision and Pattern Recognition (CVPR) (2015)
39. Girshick, R.B., Donahue, J., Darrell, T., Malik, J.: Rich feature hierarchies for accurate object detection and semantic segmentation. In: Conference on Computer Vision and Pattern Recognition (CVPR) (2014)
40. Griffin, G., Holub, A., Perona, P.: Caltech-256 Object Category Dataset (2007)
41. Hayman, E., Caputo, B., Fritz, M., Eklundh, J.O.: On the significance of real-world conditions for material classification. European Conference on Computer Vision (ECCV) (2004)
42. Hotelling, H.: Analysis of a complex of statistical variables into principal components. J. Educ. Psychol. **24**(6), 417 (1933)
43. Jégou, H., Douze, M., Schmid, C., Pérez, P.: Aggregating local descriptors into a compact image representation. In: Conference on Computer Vision and Pattern Recognition (CVPR) (2010)
44. Jia, Y., Shelhamer, E., Donahue, J., Karayev, S., Long, J., Girshick, R., Guadarrama, S., Darrell, T.: Caffe: Convolutional architecture for fast feature embedding. In: Proceedings of the ACM International Conference on Multimedia (2014)
45. Juneja, M., Vedaldi, A., Jawahar, C., Zisserman, A.: Blocks that shout: Distinctive parts for scene classification. In: Conference on Computer Vision and Pattern Recognition (CVPR) (2013)
46. Kovashka, A., Parikh, D., Grauman, K.: WhittleSearch: Image search with relative attribute feedback. In: Conference on Computer Vision and Pattern Recognition (CVPR) (2012)
47. Krause, J., Stark, M., Deng, J., Fei-Fei, L.: 3d object representations for fine-grained categorization. In: International Conference on Computer Vision Workshops (ICCVW) (2013)
48. Krizhevsky, A., Sutskever, I., Hinton, G.E.: Imagenet classification with deep convolutional neural networks. In: Conference on Neural Information Processing Systems (NIPS) (2012)
49. Kumar, N., Berg, A., Belhumeur, P., Nayar, S.: Describable visual attributes for face verification and image search. IEEE Trans. Pattern Anal. Mach. Intell. (TPAMI) **33**(10), 1962–1977 (2011)
50. Kwak, I.S., Murillo, A.C., Belhumeur, P.N., Kriegman, D., Belongie, S.: From bikers to surfers: visual recognition of urban tribes. In: British Machine Vision Conference (BMVC) (2013)
51. Lad, S., Parikh, D.: Interactively guiding semi-supervised clustering via attribute-based explanations. In: European Conference on Computer Vision (ECCV) (2014)
52. Lampert, C.H., Nickisch, H., Harmeling, S.: Learning to detect unseen object classes by between-class attribute transfer. In: Conference on Computer Vision and Pattern Recognition (CVPR) (2009)
53. Law, E., Ahn, L.v.: Human computation. Synth. Lect. Artif. Intell. Mach. Learn. **5**(3), 1–121 (2011)
54. Lazebnik, S., Schmid, C., Ponce, J.: A sparse texture representation using local affine regions. IEEE Trans. Pattern Anal. Mach. Intell. (TPAMI) **28**(8), 2169–2178 (2005)
55. Lazebnik, S., Schmid, C., Ponce, J.: Beyond bags of features: spatial pyramid matching for recognizing natural scene categories. In: Conference on Computer Vision and Pattern Recognition (CVPR) (2006)

56. LeCun, Y., Bottou, L., Bengio, Y., Haffner, P.: Gradient-based learning applied to document recognition. Proc. IEEE **86**(11), 2278–2324 (1998)
57. Lin, T.Y., RoyChowdhury, A., Maji, S.: Bilinear CNN models for fine-grained visual recognition. In: International Conference on Computer Vision (ICCV) (2015)
58. Liu, J., Kuipers, B., Savarese, S.: Recognizing human actions by attributes. In: Conference on Computer Vision and Pattern Recognition (CVPR) (2011)
59. Lloyd, S.P.: Least squares quantization in PCM. IEEE Trans. Inf. Theory **28**(2), 129–137 (1982)
60. Long, J., Shelhamer, E., Darrell, T.: Fully convolutional networks for semantic segmentation. In: Conference on Computer Vision and Pattern Recognition (CVPR) (2015)
61. van der Maaten, L., Weinberger, K.: Stochastic triplet embedding. In: International Workshop on Machine Learning for Signal Processing (MLSP) (2012)
62. Mahendran, A., Vedaldi, A.: Understanding deep image representations by inverting them. In: Conference on Computer Vision and Pattern Recognition (CVPR) (2015)
63. Maji, S.: Discovering a lexicon of parts and attributes. In: Second International Workshop on Parts and Attributes, ECCV 2012 (2012)
64. Maji, S., Rahtu, E., Kannala, J., Blaschko, M., Vedaldi, A.: Fine-grained visual classification of aircraft. arXiv preprint arXiv:1306.5151 (2013)
65. Maji, S., Shakhnarovich, G.: Part annotations via pairwise correspondence. In: 4th Workshop on Human Computation, AAAI (2012)
66. Maji, S., Shakhnarovich, G.: Part discovery from partial correspondence. In: Conference on Computer Vision and Pattern Recognition (CVPR) (2013)
67. Miller, G.A.: Wordnet: a lexical database for english. Commun. ACM **38**(11), 39–41 (1995)
68. Ng, A.Y., Jordan, M.I., Weiss, Y., et al.: On spectral clustering: analysis and an algorithm. In: Conference on Neural Information Processing Systems (NIPS) (2002)
69. Ojala, T., Pietikainen, M., Maenpaa, T.: Multiresolution gray-scale and rotation invariant texture classification with local binary patterns. IEEE Trans. Pattern Anal. Mach. Intell. (TPAMI) **24**(7), 971–987 (2002)
70. Ordonez, V., Liu, W., Deng, J., Choi, Y., Berg, A.C., Berg, T.L.: Predicting entry-level categories. Int. J. Comput. Vis. **115**(1), 29–43 (2015)
71. Oxholm, G., Bariya, P., Nishino, K.: The scale of geometric texture. In: European Conference on Computer Vision (ECCV) (2012)
72. Pandey, M., Lazebnik, S.: Scene recognition and weakly supervised object localization with deformable part-based models. In: International Conference on Computer Vision (ICCV) (2011)
73. Parikh, D., Grauman, K.: Interactively building a discriminative vocabulary of nameable attributes. In: Conference on Computer Vision and Pattern Recognition (CVPR) (2011)
74. Parikh, D., Grauman, K.: Relative attributes. In: International Conference on Computer Vision (ICCV) (2011)
75. Parikh, D., Kovashka, A., Parkash, A., Grauman, K.: Relative attributes for enhanced human-machine communication. In: Conference on Artificial Intelligence (AAAI) (2012)
76. Parikh, D., Zitnick, C.: Human-debugging of machines. In: Second Workshop on Computational Social Science and the Wisdom of Crowds (2011)
77. Parizi, S.N., Oberlin, J.G., Felzenszwalb, P.F.: Reconfigurable models for scene recognition. In: Conference on Computer Vision and Pattern Recognition (CVPR) (2012)
78. Parkash, A., Parikh, D.: Attributes for classifier feedback. In: European Conference on Computer Vision (ECCV) (2012)
79. Parkhi, O.M., Vedaldi, A., Zisserman, A., Jawahar, C.V.: Cats and dogs. In: Conference on Computer Vision and Pattern Recognition (CVPR) (2012)
80. Patterson, G., Hays, J.: SUN attribute database: discovering, annotating, and recognizing scene attributes. In: Conference on Computer Vision and Pattern Recognition (CVPR) (2012)
81. Perronnin, F., Dance, C.R.: Fisher kernels on visual vocabularies for image categorization. In: Conference on Computer Vision and Pattern Recognition (CVPR) (2007)

82. Perronnin, F., Sánchez, J., Mensink, T.: Improving the Fisher kernel for large-scale image classification. In: European Conference on Computer Vision (ECCV) (2010)
83. Quattoni, A., Torralba, A.: Recognizing indoor scenes. In: Conference on Computer Vision and Pattern Recognition (CVPR) (2009)
84. Ramanan, D.: Part-based models for finding people and estimating their pose. In: Visual Analysis of Humans, pp. 199–223. Springer (2011)
85. Rao, A.R., Lohse, G.L.: Towards a texture naming system: identifying relevant dimensions of texture. Vis. Res. **36**(11), 1649–1669 (1996)
86. Rastegari, M., Farhadi, A., Forsyth, D.: Attribute discovery via predictable discriminative binary codes. In: European Conference on Computer Vision (ECCV) (2012)
87. Razavin, A.S., Azizpour, H., Sullivan, J., Carlsson, S.: CNN features off-the-shelf: an astounding baseline for recognition. In: DeepVision Workshop (2014)
88. Ross, D.A., Tarlow, D., Zemel, R.S.: Learning articulated structure and motion. Int. J. Comput. Vis. **88**(2), 214–237 (2010)
89. Sharan, L., Rosenholtz, R., Adelson, E.H.: Material perception: what can you see in a brief glance? J. Vis. **9**:784(8) (2009)
90. Simonyan, K., Parkhi, O.M., Vedaldi, A., Zisserman, A.: Fisher vector faces in the wild. In: British Machine Vision Conference (BMVC) (2013)
91. Simonyan, K., Vedaldi, A., Zisserman, A.: Deep Fisher networks for large-scale image classification. In: Advances in Neural Information Processing Systems (2013)
92. Singh, S., Gupta, A., Efros, A.: Unsupervised discovery of mid-level discriminative patches. In: European Conference on Computer Vision (ECCV) (2012)
93. Sturm, J.: Learning kinematic models of articulated objects. In: Approaches to Probabilistic Model Learning for Mobile Manipulation Robots, pp. 65–111. Springer (2013)
94. Su, H., Maji, S., Kalogerakis, E., Learned-Miller, E.: Multi-view convolutional neural networks for 3d shape recognition. In: International Conference on Computer Vision (ICCV) (2015)
95. Tamura, H., Mori, S., Yamawaki, T.: Textural features corresponding to visual perception. IEEE Trans. Syst. Man Cybern. **8**(6), 460–473 (1978)
96. Tamuz, O., Liu, C., Belongie, S., Shamir, O., Kalai, A.T.: Adaptively learning the crowd kernel. In: International Conference on Machine Learning (ICML) (2011)
97. Turk, M., Pentland, A.: Eigenfaces for recognition. J. Cogn. Neurosci. **3**(1), 71–86 (1991)
98. Vedaldi, A., Mahendran, S., Tsogkas, S., Maji, S., Girshick, R., Kannala, J., Rahtu, E., Kokkinos, I., Blaschko, M.B., Weiss, D., Taskar, B., Simonyan, K., Saphra, N., Mohamed, S.: Understanding objects in detail with fine-grained attributes. In: Conference on Computer Vision and Pattern Recognition (CVPR) (2014)
99. Von Ahn, L.: Games with a purpose. Computer **39**(6), 92–94 (2006)
100. Wah, C., Branson, S., Welinder, P., Perona, P., Belongie, S.: The Caltech-UCSD Birds-200-2011 Dataset. Tech. Rep. CNS-TR-2011-001, California Institute of Technology (2011)
101. Wah, C., Horn, G.V., Branson, S., Maji, S., Perona, P., Belongie, S.: Similarity comparisons for interactive fine-grained categorization. In: Computer Vision and Pattern Recognition (2014)
102. Wah, C., Maji, S., Belongie, S.: Learning localized perceptual similarity metrics for interactive categorization. In: Winter Conference on Applications of Computer Vision (WACV) (2015)
103. Weinberger, K.Q., Blitzer, J., Saul, L.K.: Distance metric learning for large margin nearest neighbor classification. In: Conference on Neural Information Processing Systems (NIPS) (2006)
104. Xing, E.P., Jordan, M.I., Russell, S., Ng, A.Y.: Distance metric learning with application to clustering with side-information. In: Conference on Neural Information Processing Systems (NIPS) (2002)
105. Xu, Y., Ji, H., Fermuller, C.: Viewpoint invariant texture description using fractal analysis. Int. J. Comput. Vis. (IJCV) **83**(1), 85–100 (2009)
106. Yamaguchi, K., Kiapour, M.H., Berg, T.: Paper doll parsing: Retrieving similar styles to parse clothing items. In: International Conference on Computer Vision (ICCV) (2013)

107. Yang, Y., Hallman, S., Ramanan, D., Fowlkes, C.C.: Layered object models for image segmentation. IEEE Trans. Pattern Anal. Mach. Intell. (TPAMI) **34**(9), 1731–1743 (2012)
108. Yang, Y., Ramanan, D.: Articulated human detection with flexible mixtures of parts. IEEE Trans. Pattern Anal. Mach. Intell. (TPAMI) **35**(12), 2878–2890 (2013)
109. Yu, F.X., Cao, L., Feris, R.S., Smith, J.R., Chang, S.F.: Designing category-level attributes for discriminative visual recognition. In: Conference on Computer Vision and Pattern Recognition (CVPR) (2013)
110. Zeiler, M.D., Fergus, R.: Visualizing and understanding convolutional networks. In: European Conference on Computer Vision (ECCV) (2014)
111. Zhang, N., Donahue, J., Girshick, R., Darrell, T.: Part-based R-CNNs for fine-grained category detection. In: European Conference on Computer Vision (ECCV) (2014)
112. Zhang, N., Paluri, M., Rantazo, M., Darrell, T., Bourdev, L.: Panda: Pose aligned networks for deep attribute modeling. In: Conference on Computer Vision and Pattern Recognition (CVPR) (2014)
113. Zhu, X., Ramanan, D.: Face detection, pose estimation, and landmark localization in the wild. In: Conference on Computer Vision and Pattern Recognition (CVPR) (2012)

Chapter 11
The SUN Attribute Database: Organizing Scenes by Affordances, Materials, and Layout

Genevieve Patterson and James Hays

Abstract One of the core challenges of computer vision is understanding the content of a scene. Often, scene understanding is demonstrated in terms of object recognition, 3D layout estimation from multiple views, or scene categorization. In this chapter we instead reason about scene *attributes*—high-level properties of scenes related to affordances ('shopping,' 'studying'), materials ('rock,' 'carpet'), surface properties ('dirty,' 'dry'), spatial layout ('symmetrical,' 'enclosed'), lighting ('direct sun,' 'electric lighting'), and more ('scary,' 'cold'). We describe crowd experiments to first determine a taxonomy of 102 interesting attributes and then to annotate binary attributes for 14,140 scenes. These scenes are sampled from 707 categories of the SUN database and this lets us study the interplay between scene attributes and scene categories. We evaluate attribute recognition with several existing scene descriptors. Our experiments suggest that scene attributes are an efficient feature for capturing high-level semantics in scenes.

11.1 Attribute-Based Representations of Scenes

Scene representations are vital to enabling many data-driven graphics and vision applications. There is important research on *low-level* representations of scenes (i.e., visual features) such as the gist descriptor [18] or spatial pyramids [14]. Typically, low-level features are used to classify scenes into a single-scene category. For example, a scene could be described by the category label 'village' or 'mountain.' Category labels can be a useful way to briefly describe the context of a scene. However, there

G. Patterson (✉)
Brown University, 112 Waterman St., Providence, RI, USA
e-mail: gen@cs.brown.edu

J. Hays
Georgia Institute of Technology, 801 Atlantic Dr NW, Atlanta, GA, USA
e-mail: hays@gatech.edu

R.S. Feris et al. (eds.), *Visual Attributes*, Advances in Computer Vision and Pattern Recognition, DOI 10.1007/978-3-319-50077-5_11

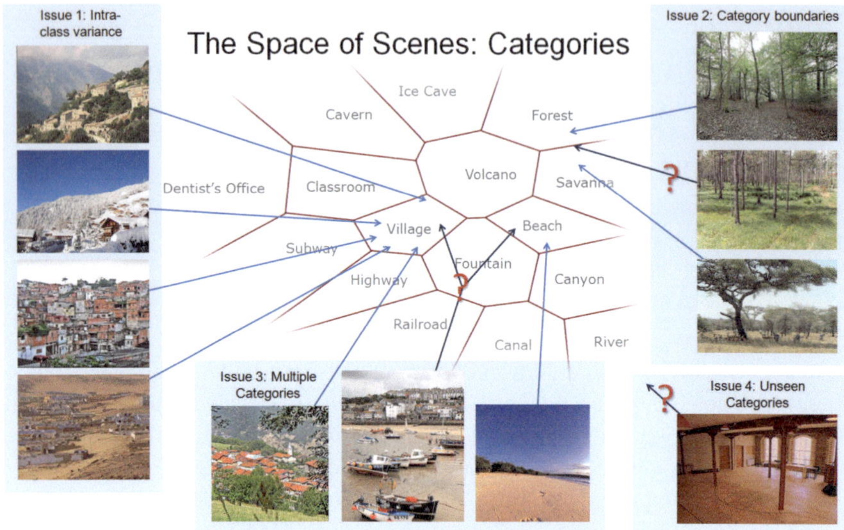

Fig. 11.1 Visualization of a hypothetical space of scenes embedded in 2D and partitioned by categories

are limitations to using a single category label to try to describe everything that is happening in a scene. In this chapter, we explore a different approach, attribute-based representation of scenes.

Scene attributes shake up the standard category-based recognition paradigm. Figure 11.1 illustrates the limitations of a strictly category-based description of scenes. Categorical scene representations have several potential shortcomings: (1) Important intra-class variations such as the dramatic differences between four 'village' scenes cannot be captured, (2) hard partitions break up the continuous transitions between many scene types such as 'forest' and 'savanna,' (3) an image can depict multiple, independent categories such as 'beach' and 'village,' and (4) it is difficult to reason about unseen categories, whereas attribute-based representations lend themselves towards zero-shot learning [11, 12].

An attribute-based representation of scenes addresses these problems by expressing variation within a scene category. Using attributes, we can describe scenes using many attribute labels instead of simple binary category membership. We can also use attributes to describe new scene categories not seen at training time (zero-shot learning), which would be impossible with a category-based representation.

It is worth noting that the presence of a particular attribute can be ambiguous in a scene, just like category membership can be ambiguous. Scenes only have one category label, though, and with hundreds of categories (as with the SUN database) the ground truth category is often unclear. But with a large taxonomy of attributes, most tend to be unambiguous for a particular scene. In this work we largely treat attributes as binary (either present or not), but when annotators disagree (see Fig. 11.7) it tends

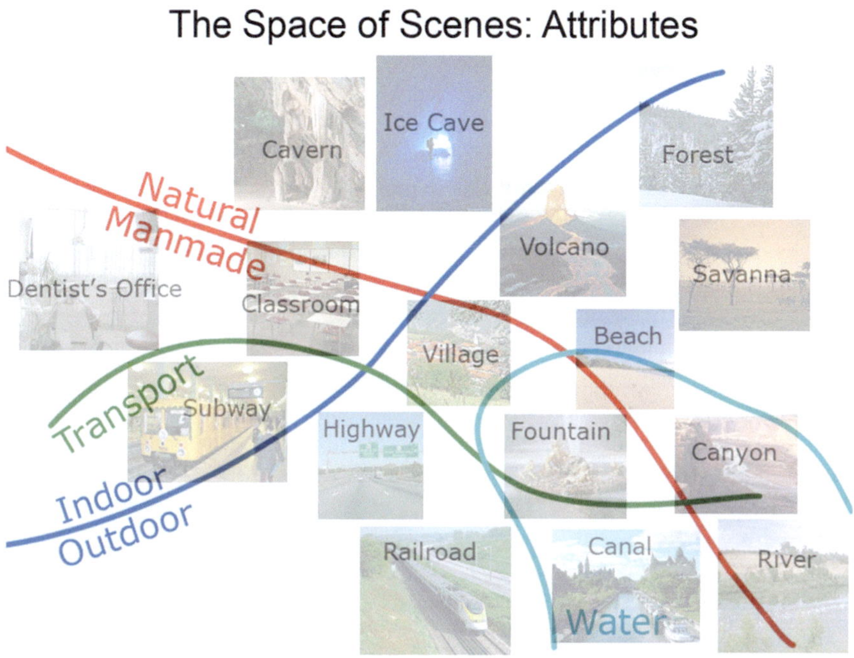

Fig. 11.2 Hypothetical space of scenes partitioned by attributes rather than categories. In reality, this space is much higher dimensional and there are not clean boundaries between attribute presence and absence

to be because the attribute is partially present (e.g., a slightly 'dirty' room or a partly 'indoors' patio). This real-valued notion of attribute presence is natural and in contrast to categorical representations where membership is usually strict.

Our work is inspired by *attribute-based* representations of objects [1, 4–7, 11, 25, 28], faces [10], and actions [15, 32], as an alternative or complement to category-based representations. Attribute-based representations are especially well suited for scenes because *scenes are uniquely poorly served by categorical representations*. For example, an object usually has unambiguous membership in one category. One rarely observes *issue 2* (e.g., this object is on the boundary between sheep and horse) or *issue 3* (e.g., this object is both a potted plant and a television).

In the domain of scenes, an attribute-based representation might describe an image with 'concrete,' 'shopping,' 'natural lighting,' 'glossy,' and 'stressful' in contrast to a categorical label such as 'store.' Figure 11.2 visualizes the space of scenes partitioned by attributes rather than categories. Note, the attributes do not follow category boundaries. Indeed, that is one of the appeals of attributes—they can describe intra-class variation (e.g., a canyon might have water or it might not) and inter-class relationships (e.g., both a canyon and a beach could have water). As stated by Ferrari and Zisserman, "recognition of attributes can complement category-level recognition and therefore improve the degree to which machines perceive visual objects" [7].

In order to explore the use of scene attributes, we build a dataset of scene images labeled with a large vocabulary of scene attributes. Later sections in this chapter describe the creation and verification of the SUN attribute database in the spirit of analogous database creation efforts such as ImageNet [2], LabelMe [26], and Tiny Images [29].

A small set of scene attributes was explored in Oliva and Torralba's seminal 'gist' paper [18] and follow-up work [19]. Eight 'spatial envelope' attributes were found by having participants manually partition a database of eight scene categories. These attributes such as openness, perspective, and depth were predicted using the gist scene representation. Greene and Oliva show that these global scene attributes are predictive of human performance on a rapid basic-level scene categorization task. They argue that global attributes of the type we examine here are important for human perception, saying, "rapid categorization of natural scenes may not be mediated primarily though objects and parts, but also through global properties of structure and affordance," [8]. In this context 'affordance' is used to mean the capacity of a scene to enable an activity. For example, a restaurant affords dining and an empty field affords playing football.

Russakovsky and Fei-Fei identify the need to discover visual attributes that generalize between categories in [25]. Using a subset of the categories from ImageNet, Russakovsky and Fei-Fei show that attributes can both discriminate between unique examples of a category and allow sets of categories to be grouped by common attributes. In [25] attributes were mined from the WordNet definitions of categories. The attribute discovery method described in this chapter instead identifies attributes directly with human experiments. In the end we discover a larger set of attributes, including attributes that would be either too common or too rare to be typically included in the definition of categories.

More recently, Parikh and Grauman [21] argue for 'relative' rather than binary attributes. They demonstrate results on the eight category outdoor scene databases, but their training data is limited—they do not have per-scene attribute labels and instead provide attribute labels at the category level (e.g., highway scenes should be more 'natural' than street scenes). This undermines one of the potential advantages of attribute-based representations—the ability to describe intra-class variation. In this chapter we discover, annotate, and recognize 15 times as many attributes using a database spanning 90 times as many categories where *every scene* has independent attribute labels.

Lampert et al. demonstrate how attributes can be used to classify unseen categories [11]. Lampert et al. show that attribute classifiers can be learned independent of category, and then later test images can be classified as part of an unseen category with the simple knowledge of the expected attributes of the unseen category. This opens the door for classification of new categories without using visual training examples to learn those unseen categories. In Sect. 11.6 we examine the performance of our scene attributes for zero-shot learning by recognizing test images from categories in our dataset without seeing visual examples for those scene categories.

Our scene attribute investigation is organized as follows. First, we derive a taxonomy of 102 scene attributes from crowdsourced experiments (Sect. 11.2). Next, we use crowdsourcing to construct our attribute-labeled dataset on top of a significant subset of the SUN database [31] spanning 707 categories and 14,140 images (Sect. 11.3). We visualize the distribution of scenes in attribute space (Sect. 11.4).

We train and test classifiers for predicting attributes (Sect. 11.5). Furthermore, in Sect. 11.6 we explore the use of scene attributes for scene classification and the zero-shot learning of scene categories. We compare how scene classifiers derived using scene attributes confuse scene categories similar to how human respondents confuse categories. This chapter is based on research originally presented in a CVPR conference publication [22] and a longer, more detailed IJCV journal publication [23].

Since the original release of the SUN attribute database there have been several interesting studies which use it. Zhou et. al demonstrate state-of-the-art performance for scene attribute recognition and scene classification with the Places database [33]. In their paper, Zhou et al. introduce a very large scene dataset containing over 7 million scene images. This dataset enables the authors to train new convolutional neural network (CNN) features that outperform earlier systems on scene-centric recognition tasks including scene attribute recognition.

The SceneAtt dataset expands the SUN attribute dataset by adding more outdoor scene attributes [30]. The scene attributes discovered in later sections of this chapter are also used to support several different kinds of in-the-wild recognition systems. Kovashka et al. use the SUN attributes in their pipeline to improve personalized image search [9]. Zhou et al. use the SUN attributes as features for identifying the city in which an image was taken in [34]. Mason et al. and our own IJCV paper on the SUN attributes use the attributes as input to novel image captioning pipelines [17, 23].

These are some of the largest and most successful projects that build on or take inspiration from the SUN attribute dataset. In the next sections, we will introduce readers to the scene attributes that helped to push forward research in scene and attribute understanding.

11.2 Building a Taxonomy of Scene Attributes from Human Descriptions

Our first task is to establish a taxonomy of scene attributes for further study. The space of attributes is effectively infinite but the majority of possible attributes (e.g., "Was this photo taken on a Tuesday," "Does this scene contain air?") are not interesting. We are interested in finding discriminative attributes which are likely to distinguish scenes from each other (not necessarily along categorical boundaries). We limit ourselves to *global, binary* attributes. This limitation is primarily economic—we collect millions of labels and annotating binary attributes is more efficient than annotating real-valued or relative attributes. None-the-less, by averaging the binary labels from multiple annotators we produce a real-valued confidence for each attribute.

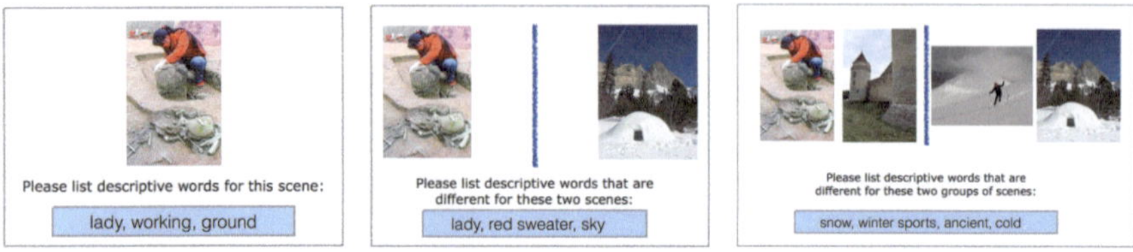

(a) Open-ended description User Interface (b) One vs.One Comparison User Interface (c) Two vs.Two Comparison User Interface

Fig. 11.3 *Attribute Collection UIs.* These are examples of the Mechanical Turk user interfaces used to collect scene attributes

To determine which attributes are most relevant for describing scenes we perform open-ended image description tasks on Amazon Mechanical Turk (AMT). First we establish a set of 'probe' images for which we will collect descriptions. There is one probe image for every category, selected for its canonical appearance. We want a set of images which is maximally diverse and representative of the space of scenes. For this reason the probe images are the images which human participants found to be most typical of 707 SUN dataset categories [3].

We initially ask AMT workers to provide text descriptions of the individual probe images. From thousands of such tasks (hereafter HITs, for human intelligence tasks) it emerges that people tend to describe scenes with five types of attributes: (1) materials (e.g., cement, vegetation), (2) surface properties (e.g., rusty) (3) functions or affordances (e.g., playing, cooking), (4) spatial envelope attributes (e.g., enclosed, symmetric), and (5) object presence (e.g., cars, chairs). An example of the open-ended text description UI is shown in Fig. 11.3a.

Within these broad categories we focus on *discriminative* attributes. To find such attributes we develop a simplified, crowdsourced version of the 'splitting task' used by [18]. The simplest UI for that task is shown in Fig. 11.3b. Unfortunately, asking crowd workers to describe the difference between two images resulted in overly specific descriptions of the contents of a particular image. For example, in Fig. 11.3b the worker correctly stated that there is a red sweater in one image but not in the other, which is not helpful for our task because 'red sweater' does not describe the scene.

To overcome that problem, we show AMT workers two groups of scenes (Fig. 11.3c). We ask workers to list attributes of each type (material, surface property, affordance, spatial envelope, and object) that are present in one group but not the other. The images show typical scenes from distinct, random categories. Such attributes would not be broadly useful for describing other scenes. We found that having two random scene images in each set elicited a diverse, broadly applicable set of attributes.

The attribute gathering task was repeated over 6000 times. From the thousands of raw discriminative attributes reported by participants we manually collapse nearly synonymous responses (e.g., dirt and soil) into single attributes. We omit attributes related to aesthetics rather than scene content. For this study we also omit the object presence attributes from further discussion because prediction of object presence,

Fig. 11.4 *Scene Attributes.* A word cloud of all the scene attributes where the area of the word is proportional to its popularity in the dataset (word cloud made using the software available at www.wordle.net by Jonathan Feinberg)

i.e., object classification, has been thoroughly investigated (Additionally, the SUN database already has dense object labels for most scenes.). Our participants did not report all of the spatial envelope attributes found by [18], so we manually add binary versions of those attributes so that our taxonomy is a superset of prior work. In total, we find 38 materials, 11 surface properties, 36 functions, and 17 spatial layout attributes. Attributes which were reported in less than 1% of trials were discarded (Fig. 11.4).

11.3 Building the SUN Attribute Database

With our taxonomy of attributes finalized we create the first large-scale database of attribute-labeled scenes. We build the SUN attribute database on top of the existing SUN categorical database [31] for two reasons: (1) to study the interplay between attribute-based and category-based representations and (2) to ensure a diversity of scenes. We annotate 20 scenes from each of the 717 SUN categories. Of the full SUN database, which has over 900 categories, only 717 contain at least 20 instances. Our goal is to collect ground truth annotations for all of the 102 attributes for each scene in our dataset. In total we gather more than four million labels. This necessitates a crowdsourced annotation strategy and we once again utilize AMT.

The Attribute annotation task. The primary difficulty of using a large, non-expert workforce is ensuring that the collected labels are accurate while keeping the annotation process fast and economical [27]. From an economic perspective, we want to have as many images labeled as possible for the lowest price. From a quality perspective, we want workers to easily and accurately label images. We find that particular UI design decisions and worker instructions significantly impacted throughput and quality of results. After several iterations, we choose a design where workers are presented with a grid of four dozen images and are asked to consider only a single attribute at a time. Workers are asked to click on images which exhibit the attribute in question. Before working on our HITs, potential annotators are required to pass a quiz covering the fundamentals of attribute identification and image labeling. The quiz asked users to select the correct definition of an attribute after they were shown the definition and example pictures. Users were also graded on how many images they could identify containing a given attribute. The quiz closely resembled the attribute labeling task. An example of our HIT user interface is shown in Fig. 11.5.

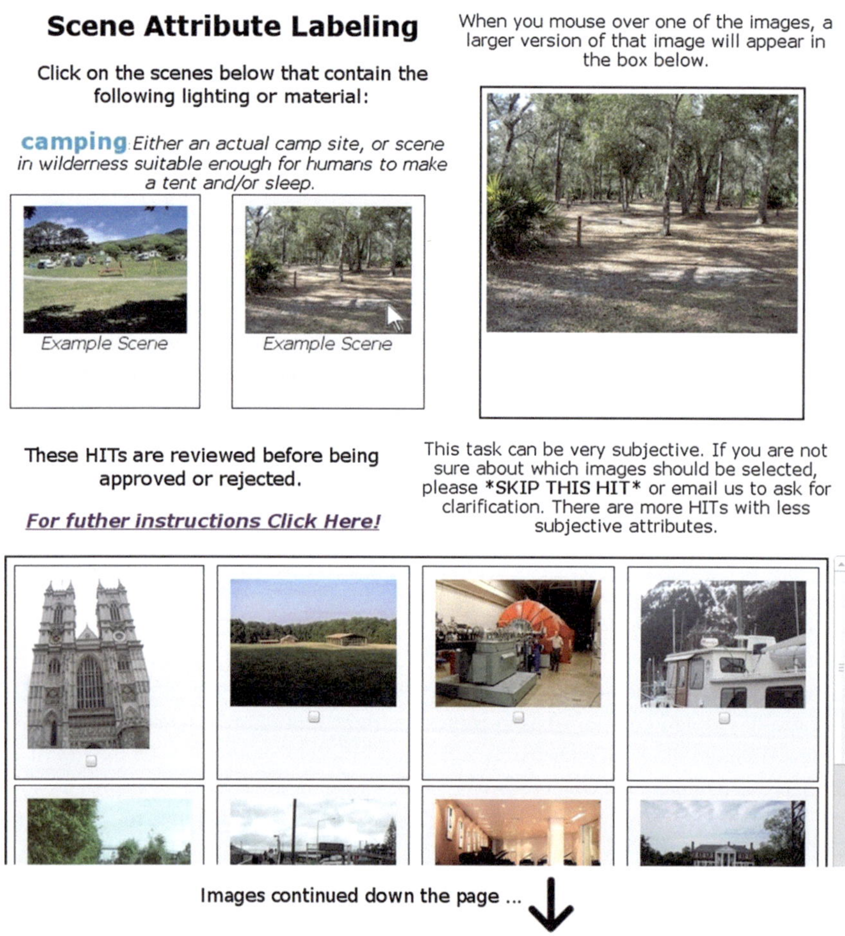

Fig. 11.5 *Annotation interface for AMT workers*. The particular attribute being labeled is prominently shown and defined. Example scenes which contain the attribute are shown. The worker cannot scroll these definitions or instructions off of their screen. When workers mouse over a thumbnail a large version appears in the preview window in the *top right corner*

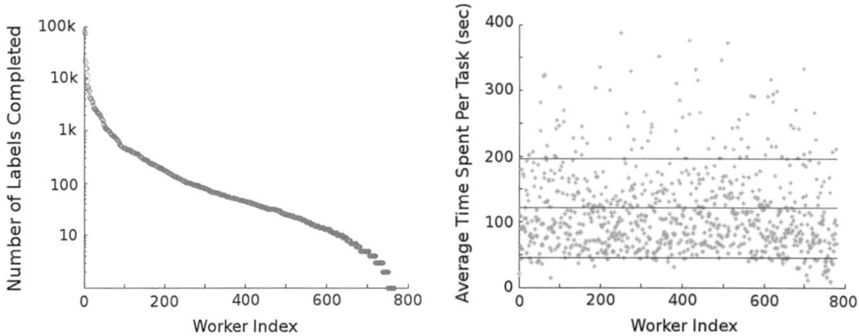

(a) The total number of labels completed by each worker.

(b) The average time (sec) each worker spent on a HIT of image labels.

Fig. 11.6 These plots visualize our criteria for identifying suspicious workers to grade. Figure 11.6a shows the heavy-tailed distribution of worker contributions to the database. The top workers spent hundreds of hours on our HITs. The *red line* in plot 11.6b demarcates the average work time across all workers, and the *blue lines* mark the positive and negative standard deviations from the mean. Work time statistics are particularly useful from identifying scam workers as they typically rush to finish HITs

Even after the careful construction of the annotation interface and initial worker screening, many workers' annotations are unreasonable. We use several techniques to filter out bad workers and then cultivate a pool of *trusted* workers:

Filtering bad workers. Deciding whether or not an attribute is present in a scene image is sometimes an ambiguous task. This ambiguity combined with the financial incentive to work quickly leads to sloppy annotation from some workers. In order to filter out those workers who performed poorly, we flag HITs which are outliers with respect to annotation time or labeling frequency.

Some attributes, such as 'ice' or 'fire,' rarely appear and are visually obvious and thus those HITs can be completed quickly. Other attributes, such as 'man-made' or 'natural light,' occur in more than half of all scenes thus the expected completion time per HIT is higher. We use the behavioral trends shown in Fig. 11.6 to help filter out poorly performing workers. We only use workers who give higher quality labels. This choice is supported by research such as [13] where good workers were shown to be faster *and* more accurate than the average of many workers.

Figure 11.7 qualitatively shows the result of our annotation process. To quantitatively assess accuracy we manually grade ~600 random positive and ~600 random negative AMT annotations in the database. The population of labels in the dataset is not even (8 % positive, 92 % negative). This does not seem to be an artifact of our interface (which defaults to negative), but rather it seems that scene attributes follow a heavy-tailed distribution with a few being very common (e.g., 'natural') and most being rare (e.g., 'wire').

We graded equal numbers of positive and negative labels to understand if there was a disparity in accuracy between them. For both types of annotation, we find

Fig. 11.7 The images in the table above are grouped by the number of positive labels (votes) they received from AMT workers. From *left* to *right* the visual presence of each attribute increases. AMT workers are instructed to positively label an image if the functional attribute is *likely to occur* in that image, not just if it is actually occurring. For material, surface property, or spatial envelope attributes, workers were instructed to positively label images only if the attribute is present

$\sim$93 % of labels to be reasonable, which means that we as experts would agree with the annotation.

In the following sections, our experiments rely on the consensus of multiple annotators rather than individual annotations. This increases the accuracy of our labels. For each of our 102 attributes, we manually grade 5 scenes where the consensus was positive (2 or 3 votes) and likewise for negative (0 votes). In total we grade 1020 images. We find that if 2 out of 3 annotations agree on a positive label, that label is reasonable $\sim$95 % of the time. Many attributes are very rare, and there would be a significant loss in the population of the rare attributes if consensus was defined as 3/3 positive labels. Allowing for 2/3 positive labels to be the consensus standard increases the population of rare attributes without degrading the quality of the labels.

11.4 Exploring Scenes in Attribute Space

Now that we have a database of attribute-labeled scenes we can attempt to visualize that space of attributes. In Fig. 11.9 we show all 14,340 of our scenes projected onto two dimensions by t-distributed stochastic neighbor embedding (t-SNE) [16]. Each subplot in Fig. 11.9 highlights the population of all images with a given attribute (Fig. 11.8).

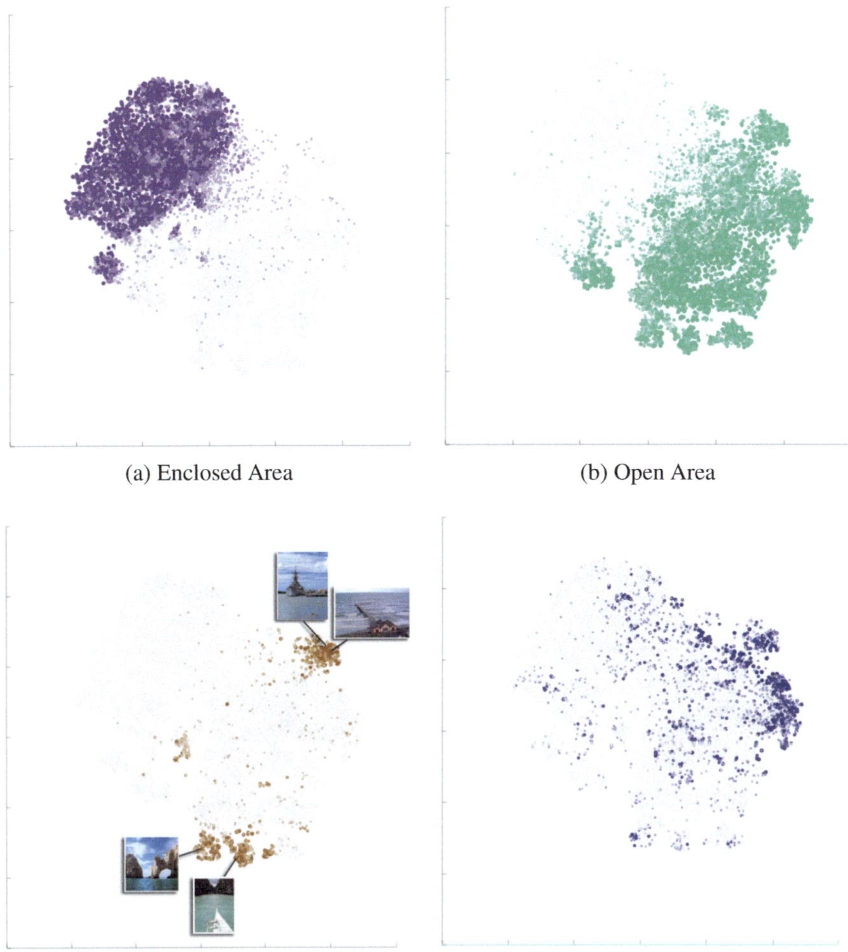

(a) Enclosed Area

(b) Open Area

(c) Sailing/Boating

(d) Transporting Thingsor People

Fig. 11.8 *Distributions of scenes with the given attribute.* This set of plots highlights the populations of images with the listed attributes. Each point is represented by their 102-dimensional attribute vector, reduced to a 2D projection using t-SNE. Grey points are images that do not contain the given attribute. The boldness of the colored points is proportional to the amount of votes given for that attribute in an image, e.g., darkest colored points have three votes. 'Enclosed area' and 'open area' seem to have a strong effect on the layout of scenes in "attribute space." As one might hope, they generally occupy mutual exclusive areas. It is interesting to note that 'sailing/boating' occurs in two distinct regions which correspond to open water scenes and harbor scenes

To better understand where images with different attributes live in attribute space, Fig. 11.8 illustrates where dataset images that contain different attributes live in this 2D version of the attribute feature space.

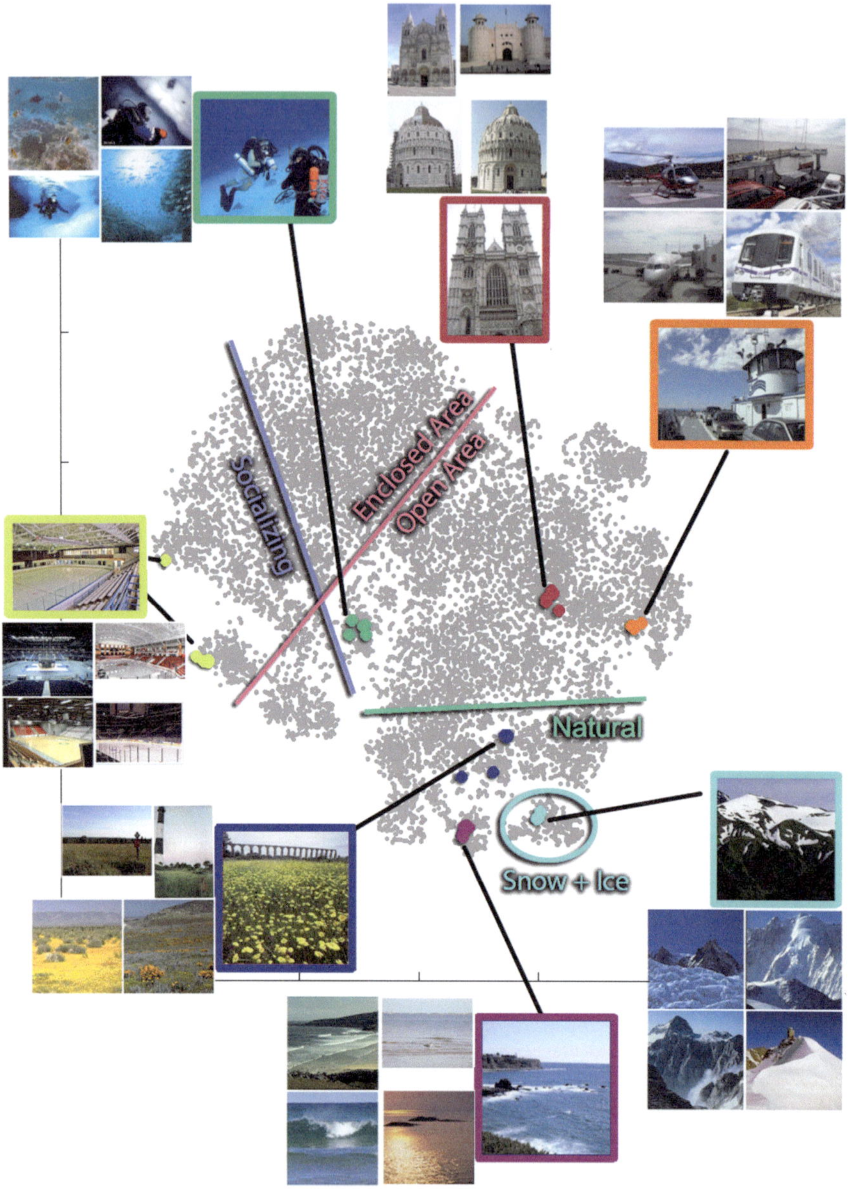

Fig. 11.9 *2D visualization of the SUN attribute dataset*. Each image in the dataset is represented by the projection of its 102-dimensional attribute feature vector onto two dimensions using t-distributed stochastic neighbor embedding [16]. There are groups of nearest neighbors, each designated by a color. Interestingly, while the nearest-neighbor scenes in attribute space are semantically very similar, for most of these examples (underwater_ocean, abbey, coast, ice skating rink, field_wild, bistro, office) *none* of the nearest neighbors actually fall in the same SUN database category. The *colored border lines* delineate the approximate separation of images with and without the attribute associated with the border

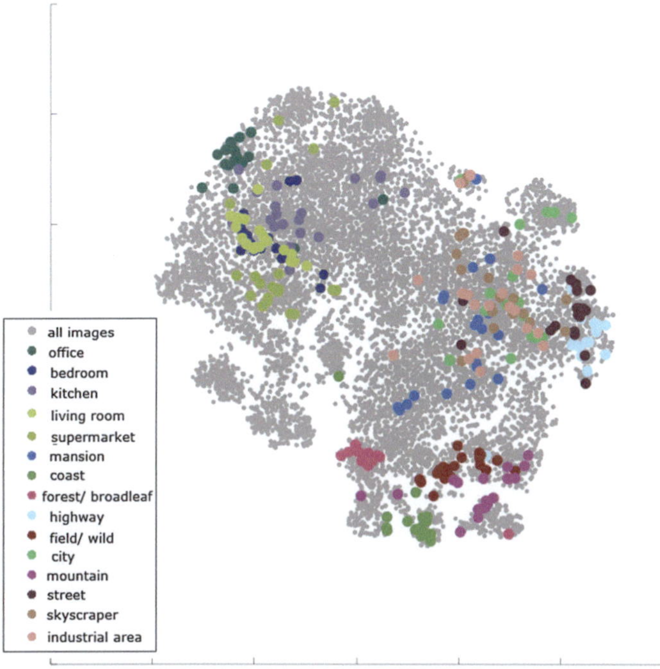

Fig. 11.10 *2D visualization of 15 scene categories.* 20 images from each of the listed scene categories are displayed in a 2D t-SNE visualization of attribute feature space. It is interesting to see how some categories, such as 'office,' 'coast,' and 'forest/broadleaf,' are tightly clustered, while others, such as 'bedroom,' 'living room,' and 'kitchen' have greater overlap when represented by scene attributes

Figure 11.10 shows the distribution of images from 15 scene categories in attribute space. The particular scene categories were chosen to be close to those categories in the 15 scene benchmarks [14]. In this low-dimensional visualization, many of the categories have considerable overlap (e.g., bedroom with living room, street with highway, city with skyscraper). This is reasonable because these overlapping categories share affordances, materials, and layouts. With the full 102-dimensional attribute representation, these scenes could still be differentiated and we examine this task in Sect. 11.6.

11.5 Recognizing Scene Attributes

A motivation for creating the SUN attribute dataset is to enable deeper understanding of scenes. For scene attributes to be useful they need to be machine recognizable. To assess the difficulty of scene attribute recognition we perform experiments using the baseline low-level features used for category recognition in the original paper introducing the SUN database [31]. Our classifiers use a combination of kernels generated from gist, HOG 2×2, self-similarity, and geometric context color histogram features. (See [31] for feature details). These four features were chosen because they are each individually powerful and because they can describe distinct visual phenomena.

How hard is it to recognize Attributes? To recognize attributes in images, we create an individual classifier for each attribute using random splits of the SUN attribute dataset for training and testing data. Note that our training and test splits are scene category agnostic—for the purpose of this section we simply have a pool of 14,340 images with varying attributes. We treat an attribute as present if it receives at least two votes, i.e., consensus is established, and absent if it receives zero votes. As shown in Fig. 11.7, images with a single vote tend to be in a transition state between the attribute being present or absent so they are excluded from these experiments.

We train and evaluate independent classifiers for each attribute. Correlation between attributes could make 'multi-label' classification methods advantageous, but we choose to predict attributes independently for the sake of simplicity.

To train a classifier for a given attribute, we construct a combined kernel from a linear combination of gist, HOG 2×2, self-similarity, and geometric context color histogram feature kernels. Each classifier is trained on 300 images and tested on 50 images and AP is computed over five random splits. Each classifier's train and test sets are half positive and half negative even though most attributes are sparse (i.e., usually absent). We fix the positive to negative ratio so that we can compare the intrinsic difficulty of recognizing each attribute without being influenced by attribute popularity. Figures 11.11 and 11.12 plot the average precision of classifiers for each attribute, given different positive/negative training example ratios. For the balanced 50 % positive/50 % negative training set in Fig. 11.11, the average precision across all attributes is 0.879. The current state-of-the-art method, a CNN trained on the Places database obtains an average precision of 0.915 over all attributes [33].

Some attributes are vastly more popular than others in the real world. To evaluate attribute recognition under more realistic conditions, and to make use of as much training data as the SUN attribute database affords us, we train classifiers on 90 % of the dataset and test on the remaining 10 %. This means that some attributes (e.g., 'natural' will have thousands of positive examples, and others e.g., 'smoke' will have barely 100). Likewise, chance is different for each attribute because the test sets are similarly skewed. The train and test instances for each attribute vary slightly because some images have confident labels for certain attributes and ambiguous labels for others and again we only use scenes with confident ground truth labels for each particular attribute classifier. Figure 11.12 shows the AP scores for these large-scale classifiers. More popular attributes are easier to recognize, as expected. Overall, the average AP scores for different types of attributes are similar—Functions/affordances (AP 0.44), materials (AP 0.51), surface properties (AP 0.50), and spatial envelope (AP 0.62). Average precision is lower than the previous experiment not because the classifiers are worse (in fact, they're better) but because chance is much lower with a test set containing the natural distribution of attributes.

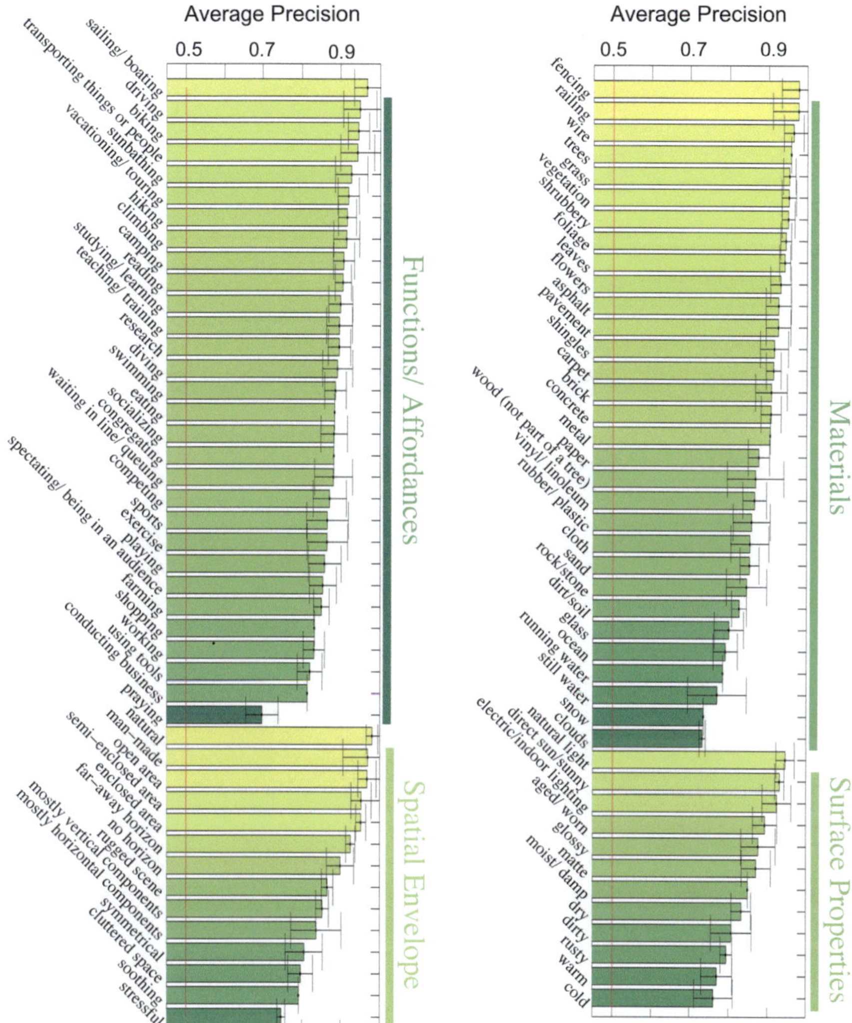

Fig. 11.11 *Average precision for attribute classifiers*. Training and testing sets have a balanced positive to negative example ratio, with 300 training examples and 50 test images per attribute. The AP of chance selection is marked by the *red line*. AP scores are often high even when the visual manifestations of such attributes are subtle. This plot shows that it is possible to recognize global scene attributes. Attributes that occur fewer than 350 times in the dataset were not included in this plot

The classifiers used for Fig. 11.12 and the code used to generate them are publicly available.[1] The attribute classifiers trained on 90 % of the SUN attribute dataset are employed in all further experiments in this chapter.

[1] SUN attribute Classifiers along with the full SUN attribute dataset and associated code are available at www.cs.brown.edu/~gen/sunattributes.html.

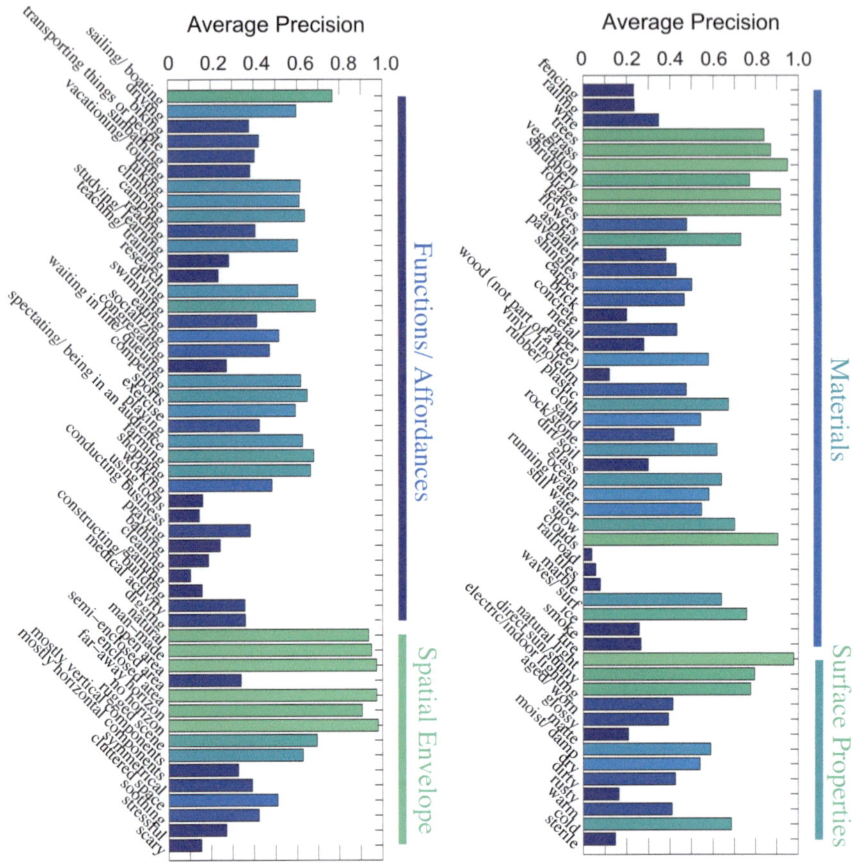

Fig. 11.12 *Average precision for attribute classifiers*. 90 % of the dataset used for training/10 % for test; positive to negative example ratio varies per attribute due to the natural population of each attribute in the dataset. All of the scene attributes are included in this plot. Chance is different for every attribute as they appear with variable frequency in nature. Note that the most difficult to recognize attributes are also the rarest. Many attributes that are not strongly visual such as 'studying,' 'spectating,' or 'farming' are nonetheless relatively easy to recognize

Attribute Classifiers in the Wild. We show qualitative results of our attribute classifiers in Fig. 11.13. Our attribute classifiers perform well at recognizing attributes in a variety of contexts. Most of the attributes with strong confidence are indeed present in the images. Likewise, the lowest confidence attributes are clearly not present. It is particularly interesting that function/affordance attributes and surface property attributes are often recognized with stronger confidence than other types of attributes even though functions and surface properties are complex concepts that may not be easy to define visually. For example, the golf course test image in Fig. 11.13 shows that our classifiers can successfully identify such abstract concepts as 'sports' and 'competing' for a golf course, which is visually quite similar to places

Test Scene Images	Detected Attributes
	*Most Confident Attributes*: vegetation, open area, sunny, sports, natural light, no horizon, foliage, competing, railing, natural *Least Confident Attributes*: studying, gaming, fire, carpet, tiles, smoke, medical, cleaning, sterile, marble
	*Most Confident Attributes*: shrubbery, flowers, camping, rugged scene, hiking, dirt/soil, leaves, natural light, vegetation, rock/stone *Least Confident Attributes*: shingles, ice, railroad, cleaning, marble, sterile, smoke, gaming, tiles, medical
	*Most Confident Attributes*: eating, socializing, waiting in line, cloth, shopping, reading, stressful, congregating, man-made, plastic *Least Confident Attributes*: gaming, running water, tiles, railroad, waves/ surf, building, fire, bathing, ice, smoke
	*Most Confident Attributes*: vertical components, vacationing, natural light, shingles, man-made, praying, symmetrical, semi-enclosed area, aged/ worn, brick *Least Confident Attributes*: railroad, ice, scary, medical, shopping, tiles, cleaning, sterile, digging, gaming
	*Most Confident Attributes*: vertical components, brick, natural light, praying, vacationing, man-made, pavement, sunny, open area, rusty *Least Confident Attributes*: ice, smoke, bathing, marble, vinyl, cleaning, fire, tires, gaming, sterile

Fig. 11.13 *Attribute detection*. For each query, the most confidently recognized attributes (*green*) are indeed present in the test images, and the least confidently recognized attributes (*red*) are either the visual opposite of what is in the image or they are irrelevant to the image

where no sports would occur. Abstract concepts such as 'praying' and 'aged/worn' are also recognized correctly in both the abbey and mosque scenes in Fig. 11.13. Figure 11.14 shows several cases where the most confidently detected attributes are incorrect.

Test Images	Detected Attributes
	*Most Confident Attributes*: swimming, asphalt, open area, sports, sunbathing, natural light, diving, still water, exercise, soothing *Least Confident Attributes*: tiles, smoke, ice, sterile, praying, marble, railroad, cleaning, medical activity, gaming
	*Most Confident Attributes*: cold, concrete, snow, sand, stressful, aged/ worn, dry, climbing, rugged scene, rock/stone *Least Confident Attributes*: medical activity, spectating, marble, cleaning, waves/ surf, railroad, gaming, building, shopping, tiles
	*Most Confident Attributes*: carpet, enclosed area no horizon, electric/indoor lighting, concrete, glossy, cloth, working, dry, rubber/ plastic *Least Confident Attributes*: trees, ocean, digging, open area, scary, smoke, ice, railroad, constructing/ building, waves/ surf

Fig. 11.14 *Failure cases*. In the *top* image, it seems the smooth, *blue regions* of the car appear to have created false positive detections of 'swimming,' 'diving,' and 'still water.' The *bottom* images, unlike all of our training data, is a close-up object view rather than a scene with spatial extent. The attribute classifiers seem to interpret the cat as a mountain landscape and the potato chips bag as several different materials—'carpet,' 'concrete,' 'glossy,' and 'cloth'

In earlier attribute work where the attributes were discovered on smaller datasets, attributes had the problem of being strongly correlated with each other [5]. This is less of an issue with the SUN attribute dataset because the dataset is larger and attributes are observed in many different contexts. For instance, attributes such as "golf" and "grass" are correlated with each other, as they should be. But the correlation is not so high that a "golf" classifier can simply learn the "grass" visual concept, because the dataset contains thousands of training examples where "grass" is present but "golf" is not possible. However, some of our attributes, specifically those related to vegetation, do seem overly correlated with each other because the concepts are not semantically distinct enough.

Figure 11.13 shows many true positive detections. Somewhat surprisingly, many affordance attributes are often estimated correctly and strongly positively for images that contain them. This may be because different activities occur in very distinct looking places. For example, scenes for eating or socializing are distinct from scene for playing sports which are distinct from natural scenes where no human activity is likely to take place. Unsurprisingly, attributes related to vegetation and the shape of the scene are also relatively easy to detect. These attributes are common in the dataset, and their classifiers benefit from the additional training data.

Figure 11.14 shows false positive detections. False negative detections can be inferred from Fig. 11.14. This figure can help us qualitatively understand why attribute recognition may fail. In the first image in Fig. 11.14, there is a broken-down blue car in a field grown wild. This somewhat unusual juxtaposition of a car that looks different from other, working cars in the dataset and a natural-looking scene that wouldn't normally contain cars results in the mis-estimation of the attribute 'swimming.'

The next two images in Fig. 11.14 both fail for reasons of image scale. The images are zoomed in much closer than other images in the SUN dataset which typically try to capture a whole scene. In the case of the cat, it results in the cat being mis-identified as a snowy mountain type landscape and the carpet attribute is not recognized at all.

Figure 11.15 shows the most confident classifications in our test set for various attributes. Many of the false positives, highlighted in red, are reasonable from a visual similarity point of view. 'Cold,' 'moist/damp,' and 'eating' all have false positives that could be reasonably considered to be confusing. 'Stressful' and 'vacationing' have false positives that could be subjectively judged to be correct—a crowded subway car could be stressful, and the New Mexico desert could be a lovely vacation spot.

Correlation of Attributes and Scene Categories. To better understand the relationships between categories and attributes, Table 11.1 lists a number of examples from the SUN 397 categories with the attribute that is most strongly correlated with each category.

The correlation between the scene category and the attribute feature of an input image is calculated using Pearson's correlation. We calculate correlation between the predicted attribute feature vectors for 50 examples from each of the SUN 397 categories and a feature vectors that indicate the category membership of the example images.

Table 11.1 has many interesting examples where an attribute is strongly correlated with visually dissimilar but semantically related categories, such as 'praying' for both the indoor and outdoor church categories. Even attributes that are quite abstract concepts, such as 'socializing' and 'stressful,' are the most strongly correlated attributes for 'pub/indoor' and 'cockpit,' respectively. Scene attributes capture information that is intrinsic to the nature of scenes and how humans interact with them.

11.6 Predicting Scene Categories from Attributes

11.6.1 Predictive Power of Attributes

In this section we measure how well we can predict scene category from *ground truth* scene attributes. While the goal of scene attributes is not necessarily to improve the task of scene categorization, this analysis does give some insight into the interplay

Fig. 11.15 *Top 5 most confident detections in Test Set*. For each attribute, the top five detections from the test set are shown. Images *boxed* in *green* are true positives, and *red* are false positives. Examples of false positives, such as the 'praying' examples, show how attributes are identified in images that arguably contain the attribute, but human annotators disagreed about the attribute's presence; in this case the false positives were a sacristy, which is a room for the storage of religious items, and a cathedral pictured at a distance. The false positive for 'glass' also contain glass, although photographed under glancing illumination, which may have caused the human annotators to mislabel it. For several of the examples, all of the top 5 detections are true positives. The detections for 'brick,' 'metal,' and 'competing' demonstrate the ability of attribute classifiers to recognize the presence of attributes in scenes that are quite visually dissimilar. For 'brick' and 'metal' even the kinds of bricks and metals shown are differ greatly in type, age, and use case. The false positives in the praying example are an art gallery and a monument

between scene categories and scene attributes. In the next experiment, we used the attribute labels made by the crowd workers as the input feature for scene classification. This experiment gives us an upper bound for how useful scene attributes on their own could be for the task of scene classification. In the next subsection, we will *estimate* scene attributes for previously unseen test images and use the *estimated* scene attributes as features for scene classification.

Table 11.1 *Most correlated attributes.* A sampling of scene categories from the SUN 397 dataset listed with their most correlated attribute

Category	Most correlated attributes
Airport terminal	Socializing
Art studio	Cluttered space
Assembly line	Working
Athletic field/outdoor	Playing
Auditorium	Spectating
Ball pit	Rubber/plastic
Baseball field	Sports
Basilica	Praying
Basketball court	Exercise
Bathroom	Cleaning
Bayou	Still water
Bedroom	Carpet
Biology laboratory	Research
Bistro/indoor	Eating
Bookstore	Shopping
Bowling alley	Competing
Boxing ring	Spectating
Campsite	Camping
Canal/natural	Still water
Canal/urban	Sailing/boating
Canyon	Rugged scene
Car interior/backseat	Matte
Car interior/frontseat	Matte
Casino/indoor	Gaming
Catacomb	Digging
Chemistry lab	Research
Chicken coop/indoor	Dirty
Chicken coop/outdoor	Fencing
Cathedral/indoor	Praying
Church/outdoor	Praying
Classroom	Studying/learning
Clothing store	Cloth

(continued)

Table 11.1 (continued)

Category	**Most correlated attributes**
Cockpit	Stressful
Construction site	Constructing/building
Corn field	Farming
Cottage garden	Flowers
Dentists office	Medical activity
Dining room	Eating
Electrical substation	Wire
Factory/indoor	Working
Fastfood restaurant	Waiting in line
Fire escape	Railing
Forest path	Hiking
Forest road	Foliage
Fountain	Running water
Ice skating rink/indoor	Sports
Ice skating rink/outdoor	Cold
Iceberg	Ocean
Lecture room	Studying/learning
Mosque/indoor	Cloth
Mosque/outdoor	Praying
Operating room	Sterile
Palace	Vacationing
Poolroom/establishment	Gaming
Poolroom/home	Gaming
Power plant/outdoor	Smoke
Pub/indoor	Socializing
Restaurant	Eating
Restaurant kitchen	Working
Stadium/football	Spectating
Subway station/platform	Railroad
Underwater/coral reef	Diving
Volcano	Fire
Wheat field	Farming

One hundred binary attributes could potentially distinguish the hundreds SUN dataset scene categories if the attributes were (1) independent and (2) consistent within each category, but neither of these are true. Many of the attributes are correlated (e.g., "farming" and "open area") and there is significant attribute variation within categories. Furthermore, many groups of SUN database scenes would require very specific attributes to distinguish them (e.g., "forest_needleleaf" and

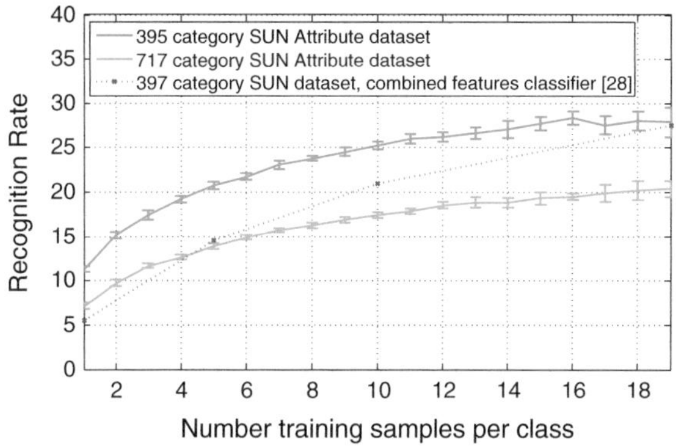

Fig. 11.16 *Category recognition from ground truth attributes using an SVM.* We plot accuracy for the 717 category SUN attribute dataset and for a subset of 395 categories which roughly match the evaluation of the SUN 397 dataset [31] (two categories present in [31] are not part of the SUN attribute dataset). We compare attribute-based recognition to visual recognition by plotting the highest accuracy from [31] (*pink-dotted line*)

"forest_broadleaf"), so it would likely take several hundred attributes to perfectly predict scene categories.

Figure 11.16 shows how well we can predict the category of a scene with *known* attributes as we increase the number of training examples per category. Each image is represented by the ground truth attribute labels collected in Sect. 11.3. We compare this to the classification accuracy using low-level features [31] on the same data set. With one training example per category, attributes are roughly twice as accurate as low-level features. Performance equalizes as the number of training examples approaches 20 per category.

From the results in Fig. 11.16, it is clear that attributes alone are not perfectly suited for scene classification. However, the performance of our attribute-based classifiers hints at the viability of zero-shot learning techniques which have access to attribute distributions for categories but no visual examples. The fact that category prediction accuracy increases significantly with more training examples may be a reflection of intra-class attribute variations.

Attributes allow for the exploration of scenes using information that is complementary to the category labels of those scenes. To the best of our knowledge these experiments are the first to explore the use of attributes as features for scene classification. As with objects [11], attributes also offer the opportunity to learn new scene categories without using any training examples for the new categories. This "zero-shot" learning for scenes will be explored in the next section.

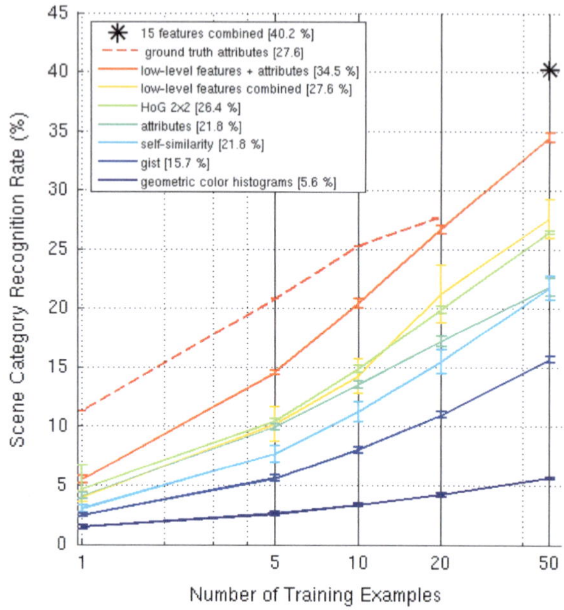

Fig. 11.17 *Scene category recognition rate versus number of training examples.* Classification tested on the SUN 397 dataset [31]. Images that occur in both the SUN 397 and SUN attribute datasets were omitted from the training and test sets of the above classifiers

11.6.2 Scene Classification

Attributes as Features for Scene Classification.
Although our attributes were discovered in order to understand natural scenes more deeply than categorical representations, scene classification remains a challenging and interesting task. As a scene classification baseline, we train one-vs-all non-linear SVMs with the same low-level features used to predict attributes. Figure 11.17 compares this with various classifiers which instead operate on attributes as an intermediate representation.

The simplest way to use scene attributes as an intermediate representation is to run our attribute classifiers on the scene classification training instances and train one-vs-all SVMs in the resulting 102-dimensional space. This "predicted attribute feature" performs better than three of the low-level features, but worse than the HoG 2×2 feature.[2]

In Fig. 11.17 each trend line plots the scene classification accuracy of the associated feature. All predicted features use the same test/train sets, and results averaged over several random test/train splits. When combined with the four low-level features

[2]The images in the SUN attribute dataset were originally taken from the whole SUN dataset, which includes more than 900 scene categories. Thus, some portion of the SUN attribute images also appear in the SUN 397 dataset, which is also a subset of the full SUN dataset. The scene classifiers using low-level and predicted attribute features were trained and tested on the SUN397 dataset minus any overlapping images from the SUN attribute dataset to avoid testing scene classification on the same images used to train attribute classifiers.

originally used in the attribute classifiers, the 'attributes' feature clearly improves performance over a scene classifier that only uses low-level features. This further supports our claim that attributes are encoding important semantic knowledge. Classification accuracy using 15 different low-level features (the same features used in Xiao et al.) plus attribute features at 50 training examples is 40.22 %, slightly beating the 38.0 % accuracy reported in [31].

The current state-of-the-art performance on the SUN 397 benchmark is 56.2 % in the paper introducing the Places dataset [33]. In [33], Zhou et al. use 150 training examples per category. Figure 11.16 shows that perfectly estimated attributes by themselves could achieve nearly 30 % accuracy with only a tenth the number of training examples per category. Scene attributes do a great job of category prediction where there are few training examples available, and CNN-trained features do well with lots of training examples. Scene attributes capture important generalizable visual concepts.

The ground truth feature classifier in Fig. 11.17 deserves slightly more explanation. The ground truth attribute feature in Fig. 11.17 is taken from 10 random splits of the SUN attribute dataset. Thus the number of test examples available for the ground truth feature are $(20 - n_{train})$, where n_{train} is the number of training set images whose attribute labels were averaged to come up with the attribute feature for a given category. As the number of training examples increases, the ground truth feature trend line is less representative of actual performance as the test set is increasingly small. Using ground truth attributes as a feature gives an upper bound on what attribute features could possibly contribute to scene classification.

It is important to note that the low-level features live in spaces that may have thousands of dimensions, while the attribute feature is only 102-dimensional. Partly for this reason, the attribute-based scene classifier seems to benefit less from additional training data than the low-level features. This makes sense, because lower dimensional features have limited expressive capacity and because the attribute distribution for a given category isn't expected to be especially complex (this is, in fact, a motivation for zero-shot learning or easy knowledge transfer between observed and unobserved categories).

Learning to Recognize Scenes without Visual Examples.
In zero-shot learning, a classifier is presented (by some oracle) a ground truth distribution of attributes for a given category rather than any visual examples. Test images are classified as the category whose oracle-annotated feature vector is the nearest neighbor in feature space to the test images' features.

Canonical definitions of zero-shot learning use an intermediate feature space to generalize important concepts shared by categories [11, 20]. Lampert et al. use an attribute representation to enable knowledge transfer between seen and unseen categories, and Palatucci et al. uses phonemes. In these zero-shot learning scenarios, it is prohibitively difficult or expensive to collect low-level feature examples of an exhaustive set of categories. The use of oracle features for those unseen categories is a way to identify them without collecting enough examples to train a classifier.

The goal of zero-shot learning is to learn a classifier $f : \mathcal{X} \rightarrow \mathcal{Z}$ for a label set $\mathcal{Z}$, where some categories in $\mathcal{Z}$ were not seen during training. This is accomplished by learning two transfer functions, $g : \mathcal{X} \rightarrow \mathcal{A}$ and $h : \mathcal{A} \rightarrow \mathcal{Z}$. The set $\mathcal{A}$ is an intermediate feature space like attributes or phonemes. Some oracle provides the labels for the unseen categories in $\mathcal{Z}$ using the feature space of $\mathcal{A}$. In traditional zero-shot learning experiments, instances from the unseen categories in $\mathcal{Z}$ are not used to learn the transfer function $g : \mathcal{X} \rightarrow \mathcal{A}$. This makes sense if obtaining examples of the unseen categories is difficult as in [11, 20].

Because we already had a nearly exhaustive set of scene categories in the SUN attribute dataset, the attribute classifiers were trained using images that belonged to categories that were held out during the "zero-shot" testing of the transfer function $h : \mathcal{A} \rightarrow \mathcal{Z}$. In our "zero-shot" experiment, all of the possible scene category labels in $\mathcal{Z}$ were held out. The experiments conducted using scene attributes as features in this subsection are an expanded version of traditional zero-shot learning, and we have maintained that term to support the demonstration of how a scene category can be identified by it's typical attributes only, without any visual examples of the category. The entire "zero-shot" classification pipeline in this section never involved showing the classifier a visual training example of any scene category. The classifier gets an oracle feature listing the typical attributes of each of the 397 categories.

Our goal is to show that given some reasonable estimate of scene's attributes it is possible to estimate the scene category without using the low-level features to classify the query image. Scene attributes are correlated with scene categories, and query scenes can be successfully classified if only their attributes are known. In this sense our experiment is similar to, but more stringent than canonical knowledge transfer experiments such as in Rohrbach et al. because the scene category labels were not used to help learn the mapping from pixel-features to attributes [24].

Despite the low number of training examples (397, one oracle feature per category, for zero-shot features vs. $n \times 397$ for pixel-level features), the zero-shot classifier shown in Fig. 11.18 performs about as well as the gist descriptor. It does, however,

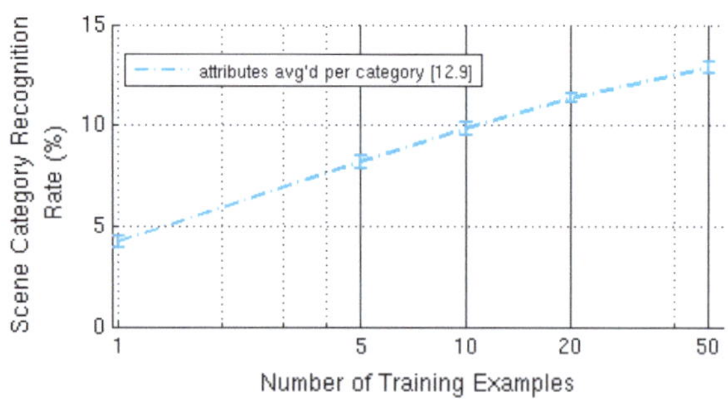

Fig. 11.18 *Scene category recognition without visual examples*. The 'attributes averaged per category' feature is calculated by averaging the predicted attribute features of all of the training instances of a given scene category in the SUN 397 dataset. Test instances are evaluated by selecting the nearest-neighbor scene category feature, and taking that scene category's label

perform significantly worse than the attribute-based classifier trained on n examples of predicted attributes shown in Fig. 11.17. Averaging the attributes into a single "characteristic attribute vector" for each category is quite lossy. In some ways, this supports the argument that there is significant and interesting intra-category variation of scene attributes.

11.7 Discussion

In this chapter, we use crowdsourcing to generate a taxonomy of scene attributes and then annotate more than ten thousand images with individual attribute labels. We explore the space of our discovered scene attributes, revealing the interplay between attributes and scene categories. We measure how well our scene attributes can be recognized and how well predicted attributes work as an intermediate representation for zero-shot learning and image retrieval tasks.

Scene attributes are a fertile, mostly unexplored recognition domain. Many attributes are visually quite subtle, and new innovations in computer vision may be required to automatically recognize them. Even though all of our attribute labels are global, many attributes have clear spatial support (materials) while others may not (functions and affordances). Further experimentation with scene attributes will lead to better ways of describing scenes and the complicated events that take place in them.

Acknowledgements We thank our collaborators Chen Xu and Hang Su for their significant contributions as co-authors on the IJCV submission of our work with Scene Attributes [23]. We also thank Vazheh Moussavi for his insights and contributions in the data annotation process. Genevieve Patterson was supported by the Department of Defense (DoD) through the National Defense Science & Engineering Graduate Fellowship (NDSEG) Program. This work was also funded by NSF CAREER Award 1149853 to James Hays.

References

1. Berg, T., Berg, A., Shih, J.: Automatic attribute discovery and characterization from noisy web data. In: European Conference on Computer Vision (ECCV) (2010)
2. Deng, J., Dong, W., Socher, R., Li, L.J., Li, K., Fei-Fei, L.: ImageNet: a large-scale hierarchical image database. In: Conference on Computer Vision and Pattern Recognition (CVPR) (2009)
3. Ehinger, K.A., Xiao, J., Torralba, A., Oliva, A.: Estimating scene typicality from human ratings and image features. In: 33rd Annual Conference of the Cognitive Science Society (2011)
4. Endres, I., Farhadi, A., Hoiem, D., Forsyth, D.: The benefits and challenges of collecting richer object annotations. In: Advancing Computer Vision with Humans in the Loop (ACVHL) (in conjunction with CVPR) (2010)
5. Farhadi, A., Endres, I., Hoiem, D., Forsyth, D.: Describing objects by their attributes. In: Conference on Computer Vision and Pattern Recognition (CVPR) (2009)
6. Farhadi, A., Endres, I., Hoiem, D.: Attribute-centric recognition for cross-category generalization. In: Conference on Computer Vision and Pattern Recognition (CVPR) (2010)

7. Ferrari, V., Zisserman, A.: Learning visual attributes. In: Conference on Neural Information Processing Systems (NIPS) (2008)
8. Greene, M., Oliva, A.: Recognition of natural scenes from global properties: seeing the forest without representing the trees. Cogn. Psychol. **58**(2), 137–176 (2009)
9. Kovashka, A., Grauman, K.: Attribute adaptation for personalized image search. In: International Conference on Computer Vision (ICCV) (2013)
10. Kumar, N., Berg, A., Belhumeur, P., Nayar, S.: Attribute and simile classifiers for face verification. In: International Conference on Computer Vision (ICCV) (2009)
11. Lampert, C.H., Nickisch, H., Harmeling, S.: Learning to detect unseen object classes by between-class attribute transfer. In: Conference on Computer Vision and Pattern Recognition (CVPR) (2009)
12. Lampert, C.H., Nickisch, H., Harmeling, S.: Attribute-based classification for zero-shot visual object categorization. IEEE Trans. Pattern Anal. Mach. Intell. (TPAMI) **36**(3), 453–465 (2014)
13. Lasecki, W.S., Murray, K.I., White, S., Miller, R.C., Bigham, J.P.: Real-time crowd control of existing interfaces. In: User Interface Software and Technology Symposium (UIST) (2011)
14. Lazebnik, S., Schmid, C., Ponce, J.: Beyond bags of features: spatial pyramid matching for recognizing natural scene categories. In: Conference on Computer Vision and Pattern Recognition (CVPR) (2006)
15. Liu, J., Kuipers, B., Savarese, S.: Recognizing human actions by attributes. In: Conference on Computer Vision and Pattern Recognition (CVPR) (2011)
16. Van der Maaten, L., Hinton, G.: Visualizing data using t-sne. J. Mach. Learn. Res. (JMLR) **9**(2579–2605), 85 (2008)
17. Mason, R., Charniak, E.: Nonparametric method for data-driven image captioning. In: Annual meeting of the Association for Computational Linguistics (ACL) (2014)
18. Oliva, A., Torralba, A.: Modeling the shape of the scene: a holistic representation of the spatial envelope. Int. J. Comput. Vision (IJCV) **42**(3), 145–175 (2001)
19. Oliva, A., Torralba, A.: Scene-centered description from spatial envelope properties. In: 2nd Workshop on Biologically Motivated Computer Vision (BMCV) (2002)
20. Palatucci, M., Pomerleau, D., Hinton, G.E., Mitchell, T.M.: Zero-shot learning with semantic output codes. In: Conference on Neural Information Processing Systems (NIPS) (2009)
21. Parikh, D., Grauman, K.: Interactively building a discriminative vocabulary of nameable attributes. In: Conference on Computer Vision and Pattern Recognition (CVPR) (2011)
22. Patterson, G., Hays, J.: Sun attribute database: discovering, annotating, and recognizing scene attributes. In: Conference on Computer Vision and Pattern Recognition (CVPR) (2012)
23. Patterson, G., Xu, C., Su, H., Hays, J.: The sun attribute database: beyond categories for deeper scene understanding. Int. J. Comput. Vision (IJCV) **108**(1–2), 59–81 (2014)
24. Rohrbach, M., Stark, M., Schiele, B.: Evaluating knowledge transfer and zero-shot learning in a large-scale setting. In: Conference on Computer Vision and Pattern Recognition (CVPR) (2011)
25. Russakovsky, O., Fei-Fei, L.: Attribute learning in largescale datasets. In: ECCV Workshop on Parts and Attributes (2010)
26. Russell, B.C., Torralba, A., Murphy, K.P., Freeman, W.T.: Labelme: a database and web-based tool for image annotation. In: International Conference on Computer Vision (ICCV) (2008)
27. Sorokin, A., Forsyth, D.: Utility data annotation with amazon mechanical turk. In: First IEEE Workshop on Internet Vision at CVPR (2008)
28. Su, Y., Allan, M., Jurie, F.: Improving object classification using semantic attributes. In: British Machine Vision Conference (BMVC) (2010)
29. Torralba, A., Fergus, R., Freeman, W.T.: 80 million tiny images: a large dataset for non-parametric object and scene recognition. IEEE Trans. Pattern Anal. Mach. Intell. (TPAMI) **30**(11), 1958–1970 (2008)
30. Wang, S., Joo, J., Wang, Y., Zhu, S.C.: Weakly supervised learning for attribute localization in outdoor scenes. In: Conference on Computer Vision and Pattern Recognition (CVPR) (2013)
31. Xiao, J., Hays, J., Ehinger, K., Oliva, A., Torralba, A.: SUN database: Large-scale scene recognition from abbey to zoo. In: Conference on Computer Vision and Pattern Recognition (CVPR) (2010)

32. Yao, B., Jiang, X., Khosla, A., Lin, A.L., Guibas, L., Fei-Fei, L.: Human action recognition by learning bases of action attributes and parts. In: International Conference on Computer Vision (ICCV) (2011)
33. Zhou, B., Lapedriza, A., Xiao, J., Torralba, A., Oliva, A.: Learning deep features for scene recognition using places database. In: Conference on Neural Information Processing Systems (NIPS) (2014)
34. Zhou, B., Liu, L., Oliva, A., Torralba, A.: Recognizing city identity via attribute analysis of geo-tagged images. In: European Conference on Computer Vision (ECCV) (2014)

Part V
Attributes and Language

Chapter 12
Attributes as Semantic Units Between Natural Language and Visual Recognition

Marcus Rohrbach

Abstract Impressive progress has been made in the fields of computer vision and natural language processing. However, it remains a challenge to find the best point of interaction for these very different modalities. In this chapter, we discuss how attributes allow us to exchange information between the two modalities and in this way lead to an interaction on a semantic level. Specifically we discuss how attributes allow using knowledge mined from language resources for recognizing novel visual categories, how we can generate sentence description about images and video, how we can ground natural language in visual content, and finally, how we can answer natural language questions about images.

12.1 Introduction

Computer vision has made impressive progress in recognizing large number of objects categories [83], diverse activities [93], and most recently also in describing images and videos with natural language sentences [89, 91] and answering natural language questions about images [48]. Given sufficient training data these approaches can achieve impressive performance, sometimes even on par with humans [28]. However, humans have two key abilities most computer vision system lack. On the one hand humans can easily generalize to novel categories with no or very little training data. On the other hand, humans can rely on other modalities, most notably language, to incorporate knowledge in the recognition process. To do so humans seem to be able to rely on compositionality and transferability, which means they can break up complex problems into components, and use previously learned components in other (recognition) tasks. In this chapter we discuss how attributes can form such components which allow to transfer and share knowledge, incorporate external linguistic knowledge, and decompose the challenging problems of visual description and question answering into smaller semantic units, which are easier to recognize and associate with textual representation.

M. Rohrbach (✉)
UC Berkley EECS and ICSI, Berkeley, USA
e-mail: rohrbach@berkeley.edu

R.S. Feris et al. (eds.), *Visual Attributes*, Advances in Computer Vision and Pattern Recognition, DOI 10.1007/978-3-319-50077-5_12

(a) Semantic attributes allow recognition of novel classes.

(b) Sentence description for an image. Image and caption from MS COCO [8].

Fig. 12.1 Examples for textual descriptions and visual content

Let us first illustrate this with two examples. Attribute descriptions given in the form of hierarchical information (*a mammal*), properties (*striped, black, and white*), and similarities, (*similar to a horse*), allow humans to recognize a visual category, even if they never observed this category before. Given this description in form of attributes most humans would be able to recognize the animal shown in Fig. 12.1a as a *zebra*. Furthermore, once humans know that Fig. 12.1a is a *zebra*, they can describe what it is doing within a natural sentence, even if they never saw example images with captions of zebras before (Fig. 12.1b). A promising way to handle these challenges is to have compositional models which allow interaction between multimodal information at a semantic level.

One prominent way to model such a semantic level are semantic attributes. As the term "*attribute*" has a large variety of definitions in the computer vision literature we define for the course of this chapter as follows.

Definition 12.1 An *attribute* is a semantic unit, which has a visual and a textual representation.

The first part of this definition, the restriction to a semantic unit is important to discriminate attributes from other representations, which do not have human interpretable meaning, such as image gradients, bag of (visual) words, or hidden representations in deep neural networks. We will refer to these as *features*. Of course for a specific feature, one can try to find or associate it with a semantic meaning or unit, but typically it is unknown and once one is able to identify such a association, one has found a representation for this semantic attribute. The restriction to a semantic unit allows to connect to other sources of information on a semantic level, i.e. a level of meaning. In the second part of the definition we restrict it to semantic units which can be both represented textually and visually.[1] This this specific for this chapter as

[1]There are attributes/semantic units, which are not visual but textually, e.g. smells, tastes, tactile sensory inputs, and ones which are visual but not textual, which are naturally difficult to describe

we want to exploit the connection between language and visual recognition. From this definition, it should also be clear that attributes are not distinct from objects, but rather that objects are also attributes, as they obviously are semantic and have a textual and visual representation.

In this chapter, we discuss some of the most prominent directions where language understanding and visual recognition interact. Namely how knowledge mined from language resources can help visual recognition, how we can ground language in visual content, how we can generate language about visual content, and finally how we can answer natural language questions about images, which can be seen as a combination of grounding the question, recognition, and generating an answer. It is clear that these directions cannot cover all potential interactions between visual recognition and language. Other directions include generating visual content from language descriptions (e.g., [45, 102]) or localizing images in text i.e. to find where in a text an image is discussed. In the following we first analyze challenges for combining visual and linguistic modalities; afterward we provide an overview of this chapter which includes a discussion how the different sections relate to each other and to the idea of attributes.

12.1.1 Challenges for Combining Visual and Linguistic Modalities

One of the fundamental differences between the visual and the linguistic modality is the level of abstraction. The basic data unit of the visual modality is a (photographic) image or video which always shows a specific instance of a category, or even more precisely a certain instance for a specific viewpoint, lighting, pose, time, etc. For example, Fig. 12.1a shows one specific instance of the category *zebra* from a side view, eating grass. In contrast to this, the basic semantic unit of the linguistic modality are words (which are strings of characters or phonemes for spoken language, but we will restrict ourselves to written linguistic expressions in this chapter). Although a word might *refer* to a specific instance, the word, i.e. the string, always *represents* a category of objects, activities, or attributes, abstracting from a specific instance. Interestingly this difference, instance versus category level representation, is also what defines one of the core challenges in visual recognition and is also an important topic in computational linguistics. In visual recognition we are interested in defining or learning models which abstract over a specific image or video to understand the visual characteristic of a category. In computational linguistics, when automatically parsing a text, we frequently face the inverse challenge of trying to identify intra

(Footnote 1 continued)
in language, but think of many visual patterns beyond *striped* and *dotted*, for which we do not have name, or the different visual attributes between two people or faces which humans can clearly recognize but which might be difficult to put into words. We also like to note that some datasets such as Animals with Attributes [44] include nonvisual attributes, e.g. *smelly*, which might still improve classification performance as they are correlated to visual features.

and extra linguistic references (co-reference resolution/grounding[2]) of a word or phrase. These problems arise because words typically represent concepts rather than instances and because anaphors, synonyms, hypernyms, or metaphorical expressions are used to refer to the identical object in the real world.

Understanding that the visual and linguistic modalities have different levels of abstraction is important when trying to combine both modalities. In Sect. 12.2 we use linguistic knowledge at category rather than instance level for visual knowledge transfer, i.e. we use linguistic knowledge at the level where it is most expressive that is at level of its basic representation. In Sect. 12.3, when describing visual input with natural language, we put the point of interaction at a semantic attribute level and leave concrete realization of sentences to a language model rather than inferring it from the visual representation, i.e. we recognize the most important components or attributes of a sentence, which are activities, objects, tools, locations, or scenes and then generate a sentence based on these. In Sect. 12.4 we look at a model which grounds phrases which refer to a specific instance by jointly learning visual and textual representations. In Sect. 12.5 we answer questions about images by learning small modules which recognize visual elements which are selected according to the question and linked to the most important components in the questions, e.g. questions words/phrases (*How many*), nouns, (*dog*) and qualifiers (*black*). By this composition in modules or attributes, we create an architecture, which allows learning these attributes, which link visual and textual modality, jointly across all questions and images.

12.1.2 Overview and Outline

In this chapter we explain how linguistic knowledge can help to recognize novel object categories and composite activities (Sect. 12.2), how attributes help to describe videos and images with natural language sentences (Sect. 12.3), how to ground phrases in images (Sect. 12.4), and how compositional computation allows for effective question answering about images (Sect. 12.5). We conclude with directions for future work in Sect. 12.6.

All these directions have in common that attributes form a layer or composition which is beneficial for connecting between textual and visual representations. In Sect. 12.2, for recognizing novel object categories and composite activities, attributes form the layer where the transfer happens. Attributes are shared across known and novel categories, while information mined from different language resources is able to provide the associations between the know categories and attributes at training time to learn attribute classifiers and between the attributes and novel categories at test time to recognize the novel categories.

[2]*Co-reference* is when two or more words refer to the same thing or person within text, while *grounding* looks at how words refer to things outside text, e.g. images.

When describing images and videos (Sect. 12.3), we first learn an intermediate layer of attribute classifiers, which are then used to generate natural language descriptions. This intermediate layer allows us to reason across sentences at a semantic level and in this way to build a model which generates consistent multi-sentence description. Furthermore, we discuss how such an attribute classifier layer allows us to describe novel categories where no paired image-caption data is available.

When grounding sentences in images, we argue that it makes sense to do this on a level of phrases are rather full sentences, as phrases form semantic units, or attributes, which can be well localized in images. Thus, in Sect. 12.4 we discuss how we localize short phrases or referential expressions in images.

In Sect. 12.5 we discuss the task of visual question answering which connects these previous sections, as one has to ground the question in the image and then predict or generate an answer. Here we show how we can decompose the question into attributes which are in this case small neural network components, which are composed in a computation graph to predict the answer. This allows us to share and train the attributes across questions and images, but build a neural network which is specific for a given question.

The order of the following sections weakly follows the historic development, where we start with work which appeared at the time when attributes started to become popular in computer vision [18, 43]. And the last section on visual question answering, a problem which requires more complex interactions between language and visual recognition, has only recently become a topic in the computer vision community [4, 48].

12.2 Linguistic Knowledge for Recognition of Novel Categories

While supervised training is an integral part of building visual, textual, or multimodal category models, more recently, knowledge transfer between categories has been recognized as an important ingredient to scale to a large number of categories as well as to enable fine-grained categorization. This development reflects the psychological point of view that humans are able to generalize to novel[3] categories with only a few training samples [6, 56]. This has recently gained increased interest in the computer vision and machine learning literature, which look at zero-shot recognition (with no training instances for a class) [17, 21, 22, 44, 53, 58, 59], and one- or few-shot recognition [6, 61, 85]. Knowledge transfer is particularly beneficial when scaling to large numbers of classes where training data is limited [21, 53, 66], distinguishing fine-grained categories [13, 19], or analyzing compositional activities in videos [22, 68].

[3] We use "novel" throughout this chapter to denote categories with no or few labeled training instances.

Recognizing categories with no or only few labeled training instances is challenging. In this section we first discuss how we can build attribute classifiers using only category-labeled image data and different language resources which allow recognize novel categories (Sect. 12.2.1). And then, to further improve this transfer learning approach, we discuss how to additionally integrate instance similarity and labeled instances of the novel classes if available (Sect. 12.2.2). Furthermore we discuss what changes have to be made to apply similar ideas to composite activity recognition (Sect. 12.2.3).

12.2.1 Semantic Relatedness Mined from Language Resources for Zero-Shot Recognition

Lampert et al. [43, 44] propose to use attribute-based recognition to allow recognizing unseen categories based on their object-attribute associations. Their Direct Attribute Prediction (DAP) model is visualized in Fig. 12.2. Given images which are labeled with known category labels y and object-attribute associations a_m^y between categories and attributes, we can learn attribute classifier $p(a_m|x_i)$ for an image x_i. This allows to recognize novel categories z if we have associations a_m^z.

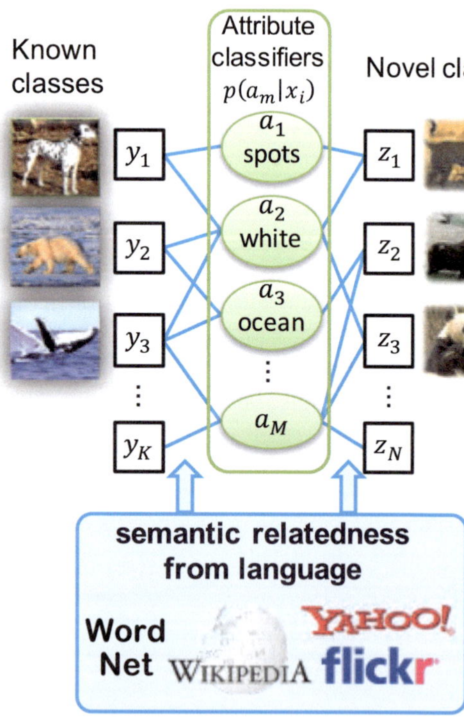

Fig. 12.2 Zero-shot recognition with the Direct Attribute Prediction model [43] allows recognizing unseen classes z using an intermediate layer of attributes a. Instead of manually defined associations between classes and attributes (*cyan lines*), Rohrbach et al. [65] reduce supervision by mining object-attribute association from language resources, such as Wikipedia, WordNet, and image or web search

Table 12.1 Zero-shot recognition on AwA dataset [43]. Results for different language resources to mine association. Trained on 92 images per class, mean area under the ROC curve (AUC) in %

(a) Attribute-based zero-shot recognition

Language resource	Measure	In	AUC
WordNet [20], path	Lin measure [46]	[65]	60.5
Yahoo Web, hit count [54]	Dice coef. [11, 82]	[65]	60.4
Flickr Img, hit count [65]	Dice coef. [11, 82]	[65]	70.1
Yahoo Img, hit count [65]	Dice coef. [11, 82]	[65]	71.0
Wikipedia [65]	ESA [23, 98]	[65]	69.7
Yahoo Snippets [7]	Dice/Snippets [69]	[69]	76.0
Yahoo Img	Expanded attr.	[69]	77.2
Combination	Classifier fusion	[69]	75.9
Combination	Expanded attr.	[69]	79.5
Manual [43]		[69]	79.2

(b) Attributes versus direct similarity, reported in [69]

Images	AUC		
	Test	+ train cls[a]	
Object—attribute associations			
Yahoo Img	71.0	73.2	(+2.2)
Classifier fusion	79.5	78.9	(−0.6)
Manual	79.2	79.4	(+0.2)
Direct similarity			
Yahoo Img	79.9	76.4	(−2.5)
Classifier fusion	75.9	72.3	(−3.6)

[a] Effect of adding images from known classes in the test set as distractors/negatives

To scale the approach to a larger number of classes and attributes, Rohrbach et al. [65, 66, 69] show how these previously manual defined attribute associations a_m^y and a_m^z can be replaced with associations mined automatically from different language resources. Table 12.1a compares several language resources and measures to estimate semantic relatedness to determine if a class should be associated with a specific attribute. Yahoo Snippets [7, 69], which computes co-occurrence statistics on summary snippets returned by search engines, shows the best performance of all single measures. Rohrbach et al. [69] also discuss several fusion strategies to get more robust measures by expanding the attribute inventory with clustering and combining several measures, which can achieve performance on par with manually defined associations (second last versus last line in Table 12.1a).

As an alternative to attributes, Rohrbach et al. [65] also propose to directly transfer information from most similar classes which does not require and intermediate level of attributes. While this achieves higher performance when the test set only contains novel objects, in the more adversarial settings, when the test set also contains images from the known categories, the direct similarity based approach significantly drops in performance as can be seen in Table 12.1b.

Rohrbach et al. [66] extend zero-shot recognition from the 10 unseen categories in the AwA dataset to a setting of 200 unseen ImageNet [9] categories. One of the main challenges in this setting is, that there are no predefined attributes on this dataset available. Rohrbach et al. propose to mine part attributes from WordNet [20] as ImageNet categories correspond to WordNet synsets. Additionally, as the known and unknown classes are leaf nodes of the ImageNet hierarchy, inner nodes can be used to group leaf nodes, similar to attributes. Also, the closest known leaf node categories can transfer to the corresponding unseen leaf category.

An alternative approach is DeViSE [21] which learns an embedding into a semantic skip-gram word-space [55], trained on Wikipedia documents. Classification is achieved by projecting an image in the word-space and taking the closest word as label. Consequently this also allows for zero-shot recognition.

Table 12.2 compares the different approaches. The hierarchical variants [66] performs best, also compared to DeViSE [21] which relies on more powerful CNN [42] features. Further improvements can be achieved by metric learning [53]. As a different application, Mrowca et al. [57] show how such hierarchical semantic knowledge allows to improve large-scale object detection not just classification. While the WordNet hierarchy is very reliable as it was manually created, the attributes are restricted to part attributes and the mining is not as reliably. To improve in this challenging

Table 12.2 Large-scale zero-shot recognition results. Flat error in % and hierarchical error in brackets

Approach/language resource	In	Top-5 error
Hierarchy		
Leaf WordNet nodes	[65]	72.8
Inner WordNet nodes	[65]	66.7
All WordNet nodes	[65]	65.2
+ metric learning	[53]	64.3[a]
Part attributes		
Wikipedia	[65]	80.9
Yahoo Holonyms	[65]	77.3
Yahoo Image	[65]	81.4
Yahoo Snippets	[65]	76.2
All attributes	[65]	70.3
Direct similarity		
Wikipedia	[65]	75.6
Yahoo Web	[65]	69.3
Yahoo Image	[65]	72.0
Yahoo Snippets	[65]	75.5
All measures	[65]	66.6
Label embedding		
DeViSe	[21]	68.2[a]

[a] Note that [21, 53] report on a different set of unseen classes than [65]

setting, we discuss next how one can exploit instance similarity and few labeled examples if available.

Transferring knowledge from known categories to novel classes is challenging as it is difficult to estimate visual properties of the novel classes. Approaches discussed in the previous section cannot exploit instance similarity or few labeled instances, if available. The approach *Propagated Semantic Transfer* (PST) [70] combines four ideas to jointly handle the challenging scenario of recognizing novel categories. First, PST transfers information from known to novel categories by incorporating external knowledge, such as linguistic or expert-specified information, e.g., by a mid-level layer of semantic attributes as discussed in Sect. 12.2.1. Second, PST exploits the manifold structure of novel classes similar to unsupervised learning approaches [80, 94]. More specifically it adapts the graph-based Label Propagation algorithm [99, 101]—previously used only for semi-supervised learning [14]—to zero-shot and few-shot learning. In this transductive setting information is propagated between instances of the novel classes to get more reliable recognition as visualized with the red graph in Fig. 12.3. Third, PST improves the local neighborhood in such graph structures by replacing the raw feature-based representation with a semantic object- or attribute-based representation. And forth, PST generalizes from zero- to few-shot learning by integrating labeled training examples as certain nodes in its graph based propagation. Another positive aspect of PST is that attribute or category models do not have to be retrained if novel classes are added which can be an important aspect e.g. in a robotic scenario.

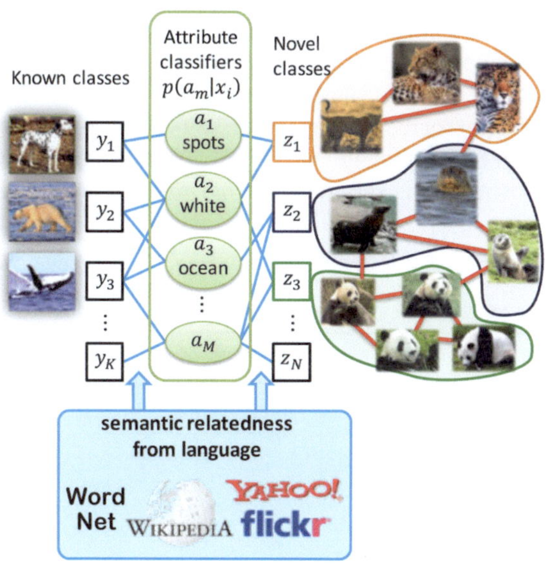

Fig. 12.3 Recognition of novel categories. The approach *Propagated Semantic Transfer* [70] combines knowledge transferred via attributes from known classes (*left*) with few labeled examples in graph (*red lines*) which is build according to instance similarity

12.2.2 Propagated Semantic Transfer

Figure 12.4 shows results on the AwA [43] dataset. We note that in contrast to the previous section the classifiers are trained on all training examples, not only 92 per class. Figure 12.4a shows zero-shot results, where no training examples are available for the novel or in this case unseen classes. The table compares PST with propagating on a graph based on attribute classifier similarity versus image descriptor similarity and shows a clear benefit of the former. This variant also outperform DAP and IAP [44] as well as Zero-Shot Learning [22]. Next we compare PST in the few-shot setting, i.e. we add labeled examples per class. In Fig. 12.4b we compare PST to two label propagation (LP) baselines [14]. We first note that PST (red curves) seamlessly moves from zero-shot to few-shot, while traditional LP (blue and black curves) needs at least one training example. We first examine the three solid lines. The black curve is the best LP variant from Ebert et al. [14] and uses similarity based image features. LP in combination with the similarity metric based on the attribute classifier scores (blue curves) allows to transfer knowledge residing in the classifier trained on the known classes and gives a significant improvement in performance. PST (red curve) additionally transfers labels from the known classes and improves further. The dashed lines in Fig. 12.4b provide results for automatically mined associations between attributes and classes from language resources. It is interesting to note that these automatically mined associations achieve performance very close to the manual defined associations (dashed vs. solid).

Figure 12.5 shows results on the classification task with 200 unseen ImageNet categories. In Fig. 12.5a we compare PST to zero-shot without propagation presented as discussed in Sect. 12.2.1. For zero-shot recognition PST (red bars) improves performance over zero-shot without propagation (black bars) for all language resources and transfer variants. Similar to the AwA dataset, PST also improves over the LP-baseline for few-shot recognition (Fig. 12.5b). The missing LP-baseline on raw features is due to the fact that for the large number of images and high dimensional features the graph construction is very time and memory consuming if not infeasible. In contrast, the attribute representation is very compact and thus computational tractable even with a large number of images.

Approach	Performance AUC	Acc.
DAP [44]	81.4	41.4
IAP [44]	80.0	42.2
Zero-Shot Learning [22]	n/a	41.3
PST [74]		
on image descriptors	81.2	40.5
on attributes	83.7	42.7

(a) Zero-Shot, in %.

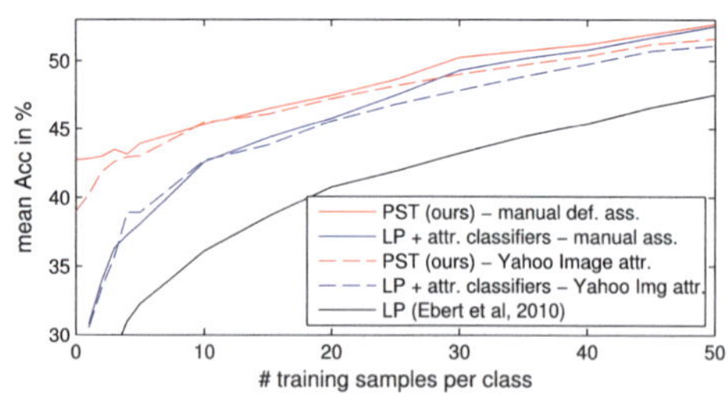

(b) Few-Shot

Fig. 12.4 Zero-shot results on AwA dataset. Predictions with attributes and manual defined associations. Adapted from [70]

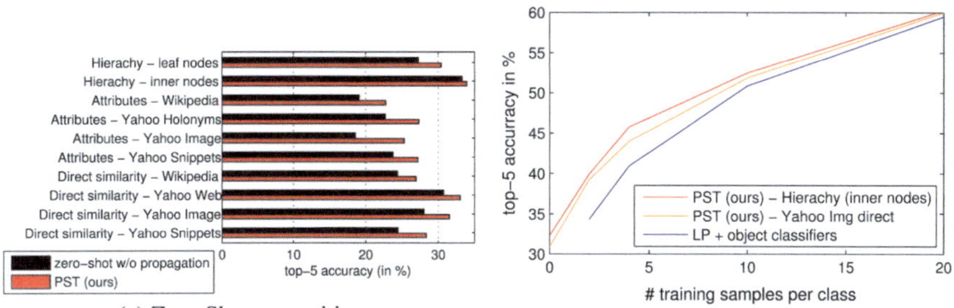

(a) Zero-Shot recognition

(b) Few-Shot recognition

Fig. 12.5 Results on 200 unseen classes of ImageNet. Adapted from [70]

12.2.3 Composite Activity Recognition with Attributes and Script Data

Understanding activities in visual and textual data is generally regarded as more challenging than understanding object categories due to the limited training data, challenges in defining the extend of an activity, and the similarities between activities [62]. However, long-term composite activities can be decomposed in shorter fine-grained activities [68]. Consider, for example, the composite cooking activities *prepare scrambled egg* which can be decomposed in attributes of fine-grained activities (e.g. *open*, *fry*), ingredients (e.g. *egg*), and tools (e.g. *pan*, *spatula*). These attributes can than be shared and transferred across composite activities as visualized in Fig. 12.6 using the same approaches as for objects and attributes discussed in the previous section. However, the representations, both on the visual and on the language side have to change. Fine-grained activities and associated attributes are

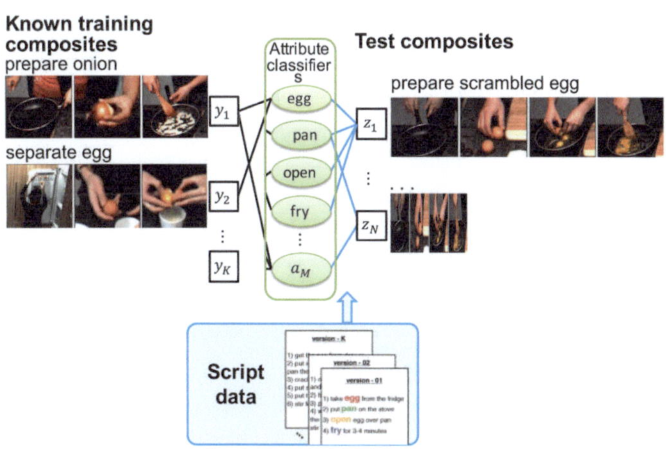

Fig. 12.6 Recognizing composite activities using attributes and script data

Table 12.3 Composite cooking activity classification on MPII Cooking 2 [74], mean AP in %. Top left quarter: fully supervised, right column: reduced attribute training data, bottom section: no composite cooking activity training data, right bottom quarter: true zero shot. Adapted from [74]

Attribute training on	All composites		Disjoint composites	
Activity representation	[93]	[67, 77, 93]	[93]	[67, 77, 93]
With training data for composites				
Without attributes				
(1) SVM	39.8	41.1	–	–
Attributes on gt intervals				
(2) SVM	43.6	52.3	32.3	34.9
Attributes on automatic segmentation				
(3) SVM	49.0	56.9	35.7	34.8
(4) NN	42.1	43.3	24.7	32.7
(5) NN + Script data	35.0	40.4	18.0	21.9
(6) PST + Script data	54.5	57.4	32.2	32.5
No training data for composites				
Attributes on automatic segmentation				
(7) Script data	36.7	29.9	19.6	21.9
(8) PST + Script data	36.6	43.8	21.1	19.3

visually characterized by fine-grained body motions and low interclass variability. In addition to holistic features [93], one consequently should exploit human pose-based [67] and hand-centric [77] features. As the previously discussed language resources do not provide good associations between composite activities and their attributes, Rohrbach et al. [68] collected textual description (*Script data*) of these activities with AMT. From this script, data associations can be computed based on either the frequency statistics or, more discriminate, by term frequency times inverse document frequency (tf∗idf).

Table 12.3 shows results on the MPII Cooking 2 dataset [74]. Comparing the first column (holistic Dense Trajectory features [93]) with the second, shows the benefit of adding the more semantic hand-[77] and pose-[67] features. Comparing line (1) with line (2) or (3) shows the benefit of representing composite activities with attributes as this allows sharing across composite activities. Best performance is achieved with 57.4 % mean AP in line (6) when combining compositional attributes with the Propagated Semantic Transfer (PST) approach (see Sect. 12.2.2) and Script data to determine associations between composites and attributes.

12.3 Image and Video Description Using Compositional Attributes

In this section we discuss how we can generate natural language sentences describing visual content, rather than just giving labels to images and videos as discussed in the previous section. This intriguing task has recently received increased attention in computer vision and computational linguistics communities [89–91] and has a large number of potential applications including human–robot interaction, image and video retrieval, and describing visual content for visually impaired people. In this section we focus on approaches which decouple the visual recognition and the sentence generation and introduce an intermediate semantic layer, which can be seen a layer of attributes (Sect. 12.3.1). Introducing such a semantic layer has several advantages. First, this allows to reason across sentences on a semantic level, which is, as we will see, beneficial for multi-sentence description of videos (Sect. 12.3.2). Second, we can show that when learning reliable attributes, this leads to state-of-the-art sentences generation with high diversity in the challenging scenario of movie description (Sect. 12.3.3). Third, this leads to a compositional structure which allows describing novel concepts in images and videos (Sect. 12.3.4).

12.3.1 Translating Image and Video Content to Natural Language Descriptions

Video Captioning

To address the problem of image and video description, Rohrbach et al. [71] propose a two-step translation approach which first predicts an intermediate semantic attribute layer and then learns how to translate from this semantic representation to natural sentences. Figure 12.7 gives an overview of this two-step approach for videos. First, a rich semantic representation of the visual content including e.g. object and activity attributes is predicted. To predict the semantic representation a CRF models

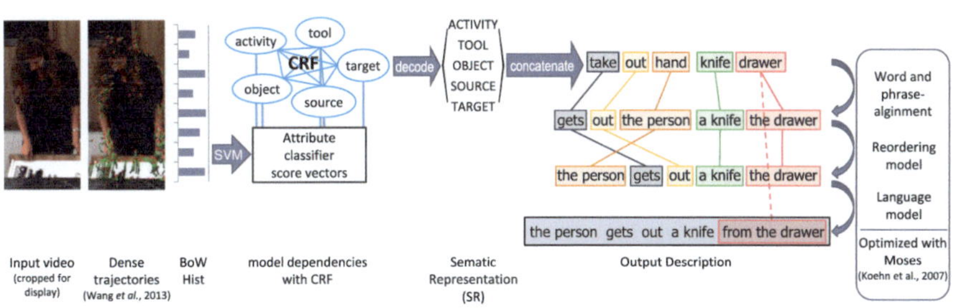

Fig. 12.7 Video description. Overview of the two-step translation approach [71] with an intermediate semantic layer of attributes (SR) for describing videos with natural language. From [64]

the relationships between different attributes of the visual input. And second, the generation of natural language is formulated as a machine translation problem using the semantic representation as source language and the generated sentences as target language. For this a parallel corpus of videos, annotated semantic attributes, and textual descriptions allows to adapt statistical machine translation (SMT) [39] to translate between the two languages. Rohrbach et al. train and evaluate their approach on the videos of the MPII Cooking dataset [67, 68] and the aligned descriptions from the TACoS corpus [62]. According to automatic evaluation and human judgments, the two-step translation approach significantly outperforms retrieval and n-gram-based baseline approaches, motivated by prior work. This similarly can be applied to image description task, however, in both cases it requires an annotated semantic attribute representation. In Sects. 12.3.3 and 12.3.4 we discuss how we can extract such attribute annotations automatically from sentences. An alternative approach is presented by Fang et al. [16] who mine visual concepts for image description by integrating multiple instance learning [52]. Similar to the work presented in the following, Wu et al. [95] learn an intermediate attribute representation from the image descriptions. Captions are then generated solely from the intermediate attribute representation.

12.3.2 Coherent Multi-sentence Video Description with Variable Level of Detail

Most approaches for automatic video description, including the one presented above, focus on generating single sentence descriptions and are not able to vary the descriptions' level of detail. One advantage of the two-step approach with an explicit intermediate layer of semantic attributes is that it allows to reason on this semantic level. To generate coherent multi-sentence descriptions, Rohrbach et al. extend the two-step translation approach to model across-sentence consistency at the semantic level by enforcing a consistent topic, which is the prepared dish in the cooking scenario. To produce shorter or one-sentence summaries, Rohrbach et al. select the most relevant sentences on the semantic level by using tf∗idf (term frequency times inverse document frequency). For an example output on the TACoS Multi-Level corpus [72] see Fig. 12.8. In order to fully automatically do multi-sentence description, Rohrbach et al. propose a simple but effective method based on agglomerative clustering to perform automatic video segmentation. The most important component of good clustering is the similarity measure and it turns out that the semantic attribute classifiers (see Fig. 12.7) are very well suited for that in contrast to Bag-of-Words dense trajectories [92]. This confirm the observation made in Sect. 12.2.2 that attribute classifiers seem to form a good space for distance computations.

To improve performance, Donahue et al. [12] show that the second step, the SMT-based sentence generation, can be replaced with a deep recurrent network to better model visual uncertainty, but still relying on the multi-sentence reasoning on the

Detailed:	A man took a cutting board and knife from the drawer. He took out an orange from the refrigerator. Then, he took a knife from the drawer. He juiced one half of the orange. Next, he opened the refrigerator. He cut the orange with the knife. The man threw away the skin. He got a glass from the cabinet. Then, he poured the juice into the glass. Finally, he placed the orange in the sink.
Short:	A man juiced the orange. Next, he cut the orange in half. Finally, he poured the juice into a glass.
One sentence:	A man juiced the orange.

Fig. 12.8 Coherent multi-sentence descriptions at three levels of detail, using automatic temporal segmentation. See Sect. 12.3.2 for details. From [72].

semantic level. On the TACoS Multi-Level corpus this achieves 28.8 % BLEU@4, compared to 26.9 % [72] with SMT and 24.9 % with SMT without multi-sentence reasoning [71].

12.3.3 Describing Movies with an Intermediate Layer of Attributes

Two challenges arise, when extending the idea presented above to movie description [76], which looks at the problem how to describe movies for blind people. First, and maybe more importantly, there are no semantic attributes annotated as on the kitchen data, and second, the data is more visually diverse and challenging. For the first challenge, Rohrbach et al. [76] propose to extract attribute labels from the description to train visual classifiers to build a semantic intermediate layer by relying on a semantic parsing approach of the description. To additionally accommodate the second challenge of increased visual difficulty, Rohrbach et al. [75] show how to improve the robustness of these attributes or "Visual Labels" by three steps. First, by distinguishing three semantic groups of labels (verbs, objects and scenes) and using corresponding feature representations for each: activity recognition with dense trajectories [93], object detection with LSDA [31], and scene classification with Places-CNN [100]. Second, training each semantic group separately, which removes noisy negatives. And third, selecting only the most reliable classifiers. While Rohrbach et al. use SMT for sentence generation in [76], they rely on a recurrent network (LSTM) in [75].

SMT [67]	Someone is a man, someone is a man.
S2VT [88]	Someone looks at him, someone turns to someone.
Visual labels [66]	Someone is standing in the crowd, a little man with a little smile.
Reference	Someone, back in elf guise, is trying to calm the kids.
SMT [67]	The car is a water of the water.
S2VT [88]	On the door, opens the door opens.
Visual labels [66]	The fellowship are in the courtyard.
Reference	They cross the quadrangle below and run along the cloister.
SMT [67]	Someone is down the door, someone is a back of the door, and someone is a door.
S2VT [88]	Someone shakes his head and looks at someone.
Visual labels [66]	Someone takes a drink and pours it into the water.
Reference	Someone grabs a vodka bottle standing open on the counter and liberally pours some on the hand.

Fig. 12.9 Qualitative results on the MPII Movie Description (MPII-MD) dataset [76]. The "Visual labels" approach [75] which uses an intermediate layer of robust attributes, identifies activities, objects, and places better than related work. From [75]

The Visual Labels approach outperforms prior work [76, 88, 96] on the MPII-MD [76] and M-VAD [86] dataset with respect to automatic and human evaluation. Qualitative results are shown in Fig. 12.9. An interesting characteristic of the compared methods is the size of the output vocabulary, which is *94* for [76], *86* for [88] (which uses an end-to-end LSTM approach without an intermediate semantic representation) and *605* for [75]. Although it is far lower than *6,422* for the human reference sentences, it clearly shows a higher diversity of the output for [75].

12.3.4 Describing Novel Object Categories

In this section we discuss how to describe novel object categories which combines challenges discussed for recognizing novel categories (Sect. 12.2) and generating descriptions (Sect. 12.3.1). State-of-the-art deep image and video captioning approaches (e.g. [12, 16, 50, 89, 91]) are limited to describe objects which appear in caption corpora such as MS COCO [8] which consist of pairs of images and sentences. In contrast, labeled image datasets without sentence descriptions (e.g. ImageNet [10]) or text only corpora (e.g. Wikipedia) cover many more object categories.

Hendricks et al. [30] propose the Deep Compositional Captioner (DCC) to exploit these vision-only and language-only unpaired data sources to describe novel categories as visualized in Fig. 12.10. Similar to the attribute layer discussed in Sect. 12.3.1, Hendricks et al. extract words as labels from the descriptions to learn a "Lexical Layer". The Lexical Layer is expanded by objects from ImageNet [10]. To be able to not only recognize but also generate the description about the novel objects, DCC transfers the word prediction model from semantically closest known word in the Lexical Layer, where similarity is computed with Word2Vec [55]. Interesting to note is, that image captioning approaches such as [12, 91] do use ImageNet data to

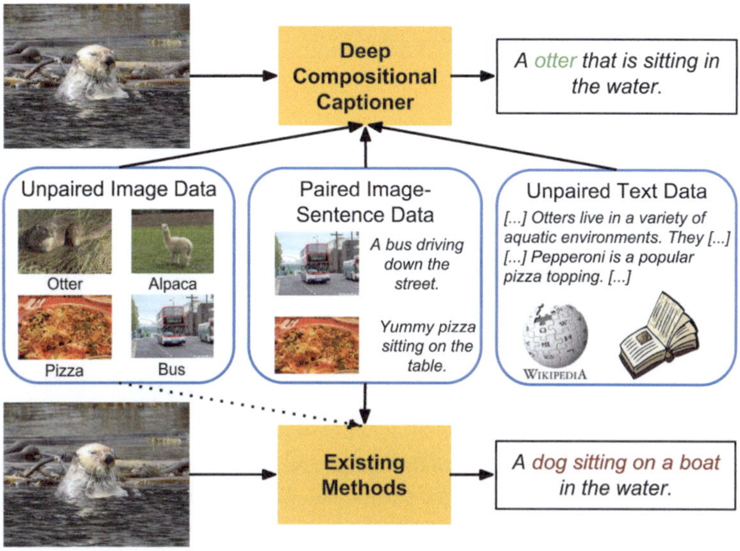

Fig. 12.10 Describing novel object categories which are not contained in caption corpora (like otter). The Deep Compositional Captioner (DCC) [30] uses an intermediate semantic attribute or "lexical" layer to connect classifiers learned on unpaired image datasets (ImageNet) with text corpora (e.g. Wikipedia). This allows it to compose descriptions about novel objects without any paired image-sentences training data. Adapted from [29]

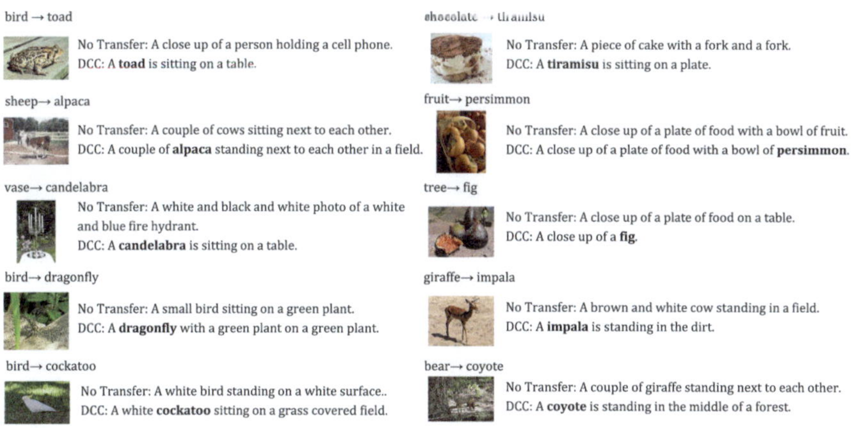

Fig. 12.11 Qualitative results for describing novel ImageNet object categories. DCC [30] compared to an ablation without transfer. X → Y: known word X is transferred to novel word Y. From [29].

(pre-) train the models (indicated with a dashed arrow in Fig. 12.10), but they do not make use of the semantic information but only the learned representation.

Figure 12.11 shows several categories where there exist no captions for training. With respect to quantitative measures, compared to a baseline without transfer, DCC improves METEOR from 18.2 to 19.1 % and F1 score, which measures the appearance of the novel object, from 0 to 34.3 %. Hendricks et al. also show similar results for video description.

12.4 Grounding Text in Images

In this section we discuss the problem of grounding natural language in images. Grounding in this case means that given an image and a natural language sentence or phrase, we aim to localize the subset of the image which corresponds to the input phrase. For example, for the sentence "*A little brown and white dog emerges from a yellow collapsable toy tunnel onto the lawn.*" and the corresponding image in Fig. 12.12a, we want to segment the sentence into phrases and locate the corresponding bounding boxes (or segments) in the image. While grounding has been addressed e.g. in [5, 34, 40, 81], it is restricted to few categories. An exception are Karpathy et al. [36, 37] who aim to discover a latent alignment between phrases in text and bounding box proposals in the image. Karpathy et al. [37] ground dependency-tree relations to image regions using multiple instance learning (MIL) and a ranking objective. Karpathy and Fei-Fei [36] simplify the MIL objective to just the maximal scoring box and replace the dependency tree with a learned recurrent network. These approaches have unfortunately not been evaluated with respect to the grounding performance due to a lack of annotated datasets. Only recently two datasets were released: Flickr30k Entities [60] augments Flickr30k [97] with bounding boxes for

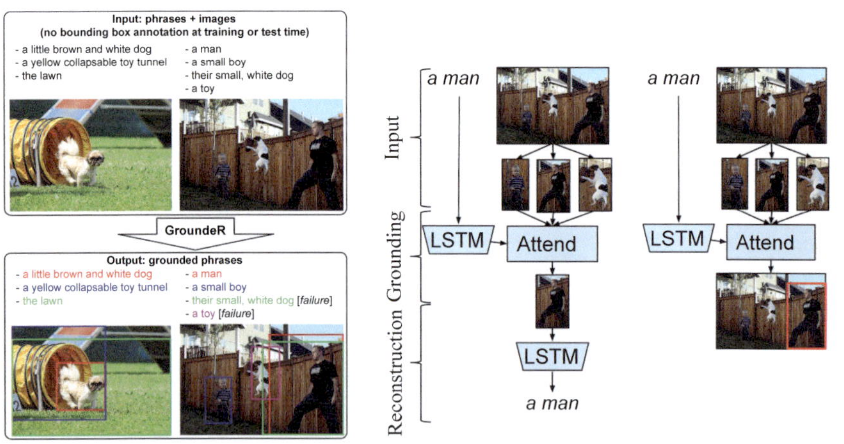

(a) Without bounding box annotations at training or test time GroundeR [65] learns to ground free-form natural language phrases in images.

(b) GroundeR [65] reconstructs phrases by learning to attend to the right box at training time.

(c) GroundeR [65] localizes boxes test time.

Fig. 12.12 Unsupervised grounding by learning to associate visual and textual semantic units. From [73]

Fig. 12.13 Qualitative results for GroundeR unsupervised [73] on Flickr 30k entities [60]. Compact textual semantic units (phrases, e.g. "*a sitting man*") are associated with visual semantic units (bounding boxes). Best viewed in color

all noun phrases present in textual descriptions and ReferItGame [38] has localized referential expressions in images. Even more recent, at the time of writing, efforts are being made to also collect grounded referential expressions for the MS COCO [47] dataset, namely the authors of ReferItGame are in progress of extending their annotations as well as longer referential expressions have been collected by Mao et al. [51]. Similar efforts are also made in the Visual Genome project [41] which provides densely annotated images with phrases.

In the following we focus on how to approach this problem and the first question is, where is the best point of interaction between linguistic elements and visual elements? Following the approaches in [36, 37, 60] a good way to this is to decompose both, sentence and image into concise semantic units or attributes which we can match to each other. For the data as shown in Figs. 12.12a and 12.13, sentences can be split into phrases of typically a few words and images are composed into a larger number of bounding box proposals [87]. An alternative is to integrate phrase grounding in a fully convolutional network, for bounding box prediction [35] or segmentation prediction [33]. In the following, we discuss approaches which focus on how to find the association between visual and linguistic components, rather than the actual segmentation into components. We first look at an unsupervised setting with respect to the grounding task, i.e. we assume that no bounding box annotations are available for training (Sect. 12.4.1), and then we show how to integrate supervision (Sect. 12.4.2). Section 12.4.3 discusses the results.

12.4.1 Unsupervised Grounding

Although many data sources contain images which are described with sentences or phrases, they typically do not provide the spatial localization of the phrases. This is true for both curated datasets such as MSCOCO [47] or large user generated content as e.g. in the YFCC 100M dataset [84]. Consequently, being able to learn from this data without grounding supervision would allow large amount and variety of training data. This setting is visualized in Fig. 12.12a.

For this setting Rohrbach et al. [73] propose the approach GroundeR, which is able to learn the grounding by aiming to reconstruct a given phrase using an attention mechanism as shown in Fig. 12.12b. In more detail, given images paired with natural language phrases (or sentence descriptions), but without any bounding box information, we want to localize these phrases with a bounding box in the image (Fig. 12.12c). To do this, GroundeR learns to attend to a bounding box proposal and, based on the selected bounding box, reconstructs the phrase (Fig. 12.12b). Attention means that the model predicts a weighting over the bounding boxes and then takes the weighted average of the features from all boxes. A softmax over the weights encourages that only one or a few boxes have high weights. As the second part of the model (Fig. 12.12b, bottom) is able to predict the correct phrase only if the first part of the model attended correctly (Fig. 12.12b, top), this can be learned without additional bounding box supervision. At test time we evaluate the grounding performance, i.e. whether the model assigned the highest weight to/attended to the correct bounding box. The model is able to learn these associations as the parameters of the model are learned across all phrases and images. Thus, for a proper reconstruction, the visual semantic units and linguistic phrases have to match, i.e. the models learns what certain visual phrases mean in the image.

12.4.2 Semi-supervised and Fully Supervised Grounding

If grounding supervision (phrase bounding box associations) is available, GroundeR [73] can integrate it by adding a loss over the attention mechanism (Fig. 12.12b, "Attend"). Interestingly, this allows to provide supervision only for a subset of the phrases (semi-supervised) or all phrases (fully supervised).

For supervised grounding, Plummer et al. [60] proposed to learn a CCA embedding [26] between phrases and the visual representation. The Spatial Context Recurrent ConvNet (SCRC) [32] and the approach of Mao et al. [51] use a caption-generation framework to score phrases on a set of bounding box proposals. This allows to rank bounding box proposals for a given phrase or referential expression. Hu et al. [32] show the benefit of transferring models trained on full-image description datasets as well as spatial (bounding box location and size) and full-image context features. Mao et al. [51] show how to discriminatively train the caption-generation framework to better distinguish different referential expression.

12.4.3 Grounding Results

In the following we discuss results on the Flickr 30k Entities dataset [60] and the ReferItGame dataset [38], which both provide ground truth alignment between noun

Table 12.4 Phrase grounding, accuracy in%. VGG-CLS: Pretraining the VGG network [79] for the visual representation on ImageNet classification data only. VGG-DET: VGG further fine-tuned for the object detection task on the PASCAL dataset [15] using Fast R-CNN [25]. VGG + SPAT: VGG-CLS + spatial bounding box features (box location and size)

Approach	Accuracy
(a) Flickr 30k entities dataset [60]	
Unsupervised training	
GroundeR (VGG-CLS) [73]	24.66
GroundeR (VGG-DET) [73]	32.42
Semi-supervised training	
GroundeR (VGG-CLS) [73]	
3.12% annotation	33.02
6.25% annotation	37.10
12.5% annotation	38.67
Supervised training	
CCA embedding [60]	25.30
SCRC (VGG + SPAT) [32]	27.80
GroundeR (VGG-CLS) [73]	41.56
GroundeR (VGG-DET) [73]	47.70
(b) ReferItGame dataset [38]	
Unsupervised training	
LRCN [12] (reported in [32])	8.59
CAFFE-7K [27] (reported in [32])	10.38
GroundeR (VGG + SPAT) [73]	10.44
Semi-supervised training	
GroundeR (VGG + SPAT) [73]	
3.12% annotation	15.03
6.25% annotation	19.53
12.5% annotation	21.65
Supervised training	
SCRC (VGG + SPAT) [32]	17.93
GroundeR (VGG + SPAT) [73]	26.93

phrases (within sentences) and bounding boxes. For the unsupervised models, the grounding annotations are only used at test time for evaluation, not for training. All approaches use the activations of the second last layer of the VGG network [79] to encode the image inside the bounding boxes.

Table 12.4a compares the approaches quantitatively. The unsupervised variant of GroundeR reaches nearly the supervised performance of CCA [60] or SCRC [32] on Flickr 30k Entities, successful examples are shown in Fig. 12.13. For the referential expressions of the ReferItGame dataset the unsupervised variant of GroundeR reaches performance on par with prior work (Table 12.4b) and quickly

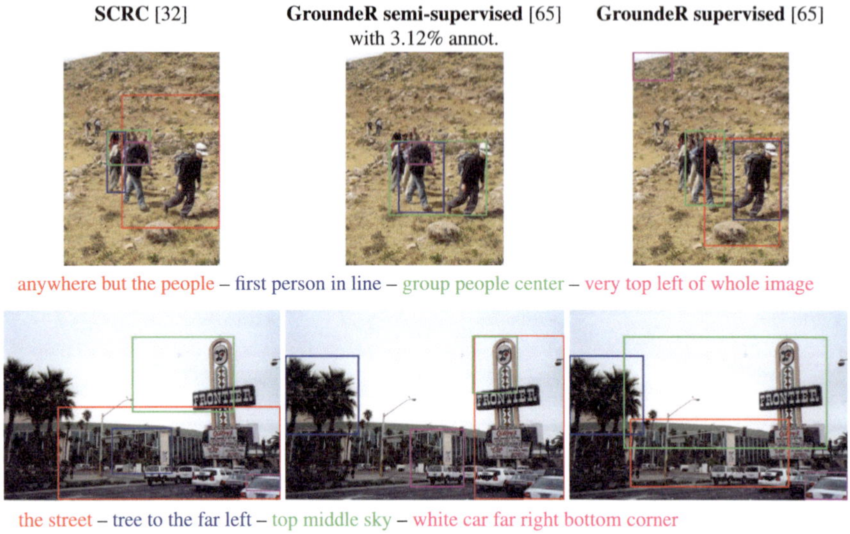

Fig. 12.14 Qualitative grounding results on ReferItGame dataset [38]. Different colors show different referential expressions for the same image. Best viewed in color

gains performance when adding few labeled training annotation (semi-supervised training). In the fully supervised setting GroundeR improves significantly over state of the art on both datasets, which is also reflected in the qualitative results shown in Fig. 12.14.

12.5 Visual Question Answering

Visual question answering is the problem of answering natural language questions about images, e.g. for the question *"Where is the amber cat?"* about the image shown in Fig. 12.15 we want to predict the corresponding answer *on the floor*, or just *floor*. This is a very interesting problem with respect to several aspects. On the one hand it has many applications, such visual search, human–robot interaction, and assisting blind people. On the other hand, it is also an interesting research direction as it requires to relate textual and visual semantics. More specifically it requires to ground the question in the image, e.g. by localizing the relevant part in the image (*amber cat* in Fig. 12.15), and then recognizing and predicting an answer based on the question and the image content. Consequently, this problem requires more complex semantic interaction between language and visual recognition than in previous sections, specifically, the problem requires ideas from grounding (Sect. 12.4) and recognition (Sect. 12.2) or description (Sect. 12.3).

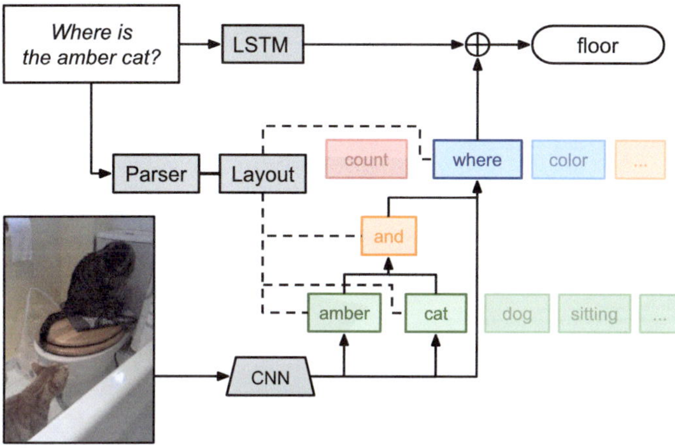

Fig. 12.15 To approach visual question answering, Andreas et al. [3] propose to dynamically create a deep network which is composed of different "modules" (colored boxes). These "modules" represent semantic units, i.e. attributes, which link linguistic units in the question with computational units to do the corresponding visual recognition. Adapted from [1]

Most recent approaches to visual question answering learn a joint hidden embedding of the question and the image to predict the answer [4, 24, 49, 63] where all computation is shared and identical for all questions. An exception to this is proposed by Wu et al. [95], who learn an intermediate attribute representation from the image descriptions, similar to the work discussed in Sects. 12.3.3 and 12.3.4. Interestingly, this intermediate layer of attributes allows to query an external knowledge base to provide additional (textual) information not visible in the image. The embedded textual knowledge base information is combined with the attribute representation and the hidden representation of a caption-generation recurrent network (LSTM) and forms the input to an LSTM-based question–answer encoder–decoder [49].

Andreas et al. [3] go one step further with respect to compositionality and propose to predict a compositional neural network structure from the questions. As visualized in Fig. 12.15 the question "*Where is the amber cat?*" is decomposed into network "modules" `amber`, `cat`, `and`, and `where`. These modules are semantic units, i.e. attributes, which connect most relevant semantic components of the questions (i.e. word or short phrases) with corresponding computation to recognize it in the image. These Neural Module Networks (NMN) have different types of modules for different types of attributes. Different types have different colors in Fig. 12.15. The `find[`*cat*`]` and `find[`*amber*`]` (green) modules take in CNN activations (VGG [79], last convolutional layer) and produce a spatial attention heatmap, while `combine[`*and*`]` (orange) combines two heatmaps to a single one, and `describe[`*where*`]` (blue) takes in a heatmap and CNN features to predict an answer. Note that the distinction between different types, e.g. `find` versus `describe`, which have different kind of computation and different instances, e.g. `find[`*cat*`]` versus `find[`*amber*`]`, which learn different parameters. All parameters are initialized randomly and only trained from question

	test-dev				test
	Y/N	Num	Other	All	All
LSTM	78.7	36.6	28.1	49.8	–
ATT+LSTM	80.6	36.4	42.0	57.2	–
NMN	70.7	36.8	39.2	54.8	–
NMN+LSTM	81.2	35.2	43.3	58.0	–
NMN+LSTM+FT	81.2	38.0	44.0	58.6	**58.7**

LSTM: a question-only baseline
ATT: single `find+describe` for all questions
NMN+LSTM: full model shown in Fig. 12.15
+FT: image features fine-tuned on captions [12]
NMN: ablation w/o LSTM

(a) Results from evaluation server of [4] in %.

how many different lights in various different shapes and sizes?	*what color is the vase?*	*is the bus full of passengers?*
four (four)	green (green)	no (no)

(b) Answers from [1] (ground truth answers in parentheses).

Fig. 12.16 Results on the VQA dataset [4]. Adapted from [1]

answer pairs. Interestingly, in this work attributes are not only distinguished with respect of their type, but also are composed with other attributes in a deep network, whose parameters' are learned end-to-end from examples, here question–answer pairs. In a follow up work, Andreas et al. [2] learn not only the modules, but also what the best network structure is from a set of parser proposals, using reinforcement learning.

In addition to NMN, Andreas et al. [2, 3] also incorporate a recurrent network (LSTM) to model common sense knowledge and dataset bias which has been shown to be important for visual question answering [49]. Quantitative results in Table 12.16(a) indicate that NMNs are indeed a powerful tool to question answering, a few qualitative results can be seen Fig. 12.16b.

12.6 Conclusions

In this chapter we presented several tasks and approaches where attributes enable a connection of visual recognition with natural language on a semantic level. For recognizing novel object categories or activities, attribute can build an intermediate representation which allows incorporating knowledge mined from language resources or script data (Sect. 12.2). For this scenario we saw that semantic attribute classifiers additionally build a good metric distance space useful for constructing instance graphs and learning composite activity recognition models. In Sect. 12.3 we explained how an intermediate level of attributes can be used to describe videos with multiple sentences and at a variable level and allow describing novel object categories. In Sect. 12.4 we presented approaches for unsupervised and supervised grounding of phrases in images. Different phrases are semantically overlapping and the examined approaches try to relate these semantic units by jointly learning representations for the visual and language modalities. Section 12.5 discusses an approach to visual question answering which composes the most important attributes of a question in a compositional computation graph, whose parameters are learned end-to-end only by backpropagating from the answers.

While the discussed approaches take a step toward the challenges discussed in Sect. 12.1.1, there are many future steps ahead. While the approaches in Sect. 12.2 use many advanced semantic relatedness measures minded from diverse language resources they are not jointly trained on textual and visual modalities. Regneri et al. [62] and Silberer et al. [78], as discussed in Chap. 13, take a step in this direction by looking at joint semantic representation from the textual and visual modalities. Section 12.3 presents compositional models for describing videos, but it is only a first step toward automatically describing a movie to a blind person as humans can do it [76], which will require an even higher degree of semantic understanding, and transfer within and between modalities. Section 12.4 describes interesting ideas to grounding in images and it will be interesting to see how this scales to the size of the Internet. Visual question answering (Sect. 12.5) is an interesting emerging direction with many challenges as it requires to solve all of the above, at least to some extend.

Acknowledgements I would like to thank all my coauthors, especially those whose publications are presented in this chapter. Namely, Sikandar Amin, Jacob Andreas, Mykhaylo Andriluka, Trevor Darrell, Sandra Ebert, Jiashi Feng, Annemarie Friedrich, Iryna Gurevych, Lisa Anne Hendricks, Ronghang Hu, Dan Klein, Raymond Mooney, Manfred Pinkal, Wei Qiu, Michaela Regneri, Anna Rohrbach, Kate Saenko, Michael Stark, Bernt Schiele, György Szarvas, Stefan Thater, Ivan Titov, Subhashini Venugopalan, and Huazhe Xu. Marcus Rohrbach was supported by a fellowship within the FITweltweit-Program of the German Academic Exchange Service (DAAD).

References

1. Andreas, J., Rohrbach, M., Darrell, T., Klein, D.: Deep compositional question answering with neural module networks. arXiv:1511.02799 (2015)
2. Andreas, J., Rohrbach, M., Darrell, T., Klein, D.: Learning to compose neural networks for question answering. In: Proceedings of the Conference of the North American Chapter of the Association for Computational Linguistics (NAACL) (2016)
3. Andreas, J., Rohrbach, M., Darrell, T., Klein, D.: Neural module networks. In: Conference on Computer Vision and Pattern Recognition (CVPR) (2016)
4. Antol, S., Agrawal, A., Lu, J., Mitchell, M., Batra, D., Zitnick, C.L., Parikh, D.: Vqa: visual question answering. In: International Conference on Computer Vision (ICCV) (2015)
5. Barnard, K., Duygulu, P., Forsyth, D., De Freitas, N., Blei, D.M., Jordan, M.I.: Matching words and pictures. J. Mach. Learn. Res. (JMLR) **3**, 1107–1135 (2003)
6. Bart, E., Ullman, S.: Single-example learning of novel classes using representation by similarity. In: Proceedings of the British Machine Vision Conference (BMVC) (2005)
7. Chen, H.-H., Lin, M.-S., Wei, Y.-C.: Novel association measures using web search with double checking. In: Proceedings of the Annual Meeting of the Association for Computational Linguistics (ACL) (2006)
8. Chen, X., Fang, H., Lin, T.-Y., Vedantam, R., Gupta, S., Dollar, P., Zitnick, C.L.: Microsoft COCO captions: data collection and evaluation server. arXiv:1504.00325 (2015)
9. Deng, J., Dong, W., Socher, R., Li, L.-J., Li, K., Fei-Fei, L.: Imagenet: a large-scale hierarchical image database. In: Conference on Computer Vision and Pattern Recognition (CVPR) (2009)
10. Deng, J., Berg, A., Li, K., Fei-Fei, L.: What does classifying more than 10,000 image categories tell us? In: European Conference on Computer Vision (ECCV) (2010)

11. Dice, L.R.: Measures of the amount of ecologic association between species. Ecology **26**(3), 297–302 (1945)
12. Donahue, J., Hendricks, L.A., Guadarrama, S., Rohrbach, M., Venugopalan, S., Saenko, K., Darrell, T.: Long-term recurrent convolutional networks for visual recognition and description. In: Conference on Computer Vision and Pattern Recognition (CVPR) (2015)
13. Duan, K., Parikh, D., Crandall, D., Grauman, K.: Discovering localized attributes for fine-grained recognition. In: Conference on Computer Vision and Pattern Recognition (CVPR) (2012)
14. Ebert, S., Larlus, D., Schiele, B.: Extracting structures in image collections for object recognition. In: European Conference on Computer Vision (ECCV) (2010)
15. Everingham, M., Van Gool, L., Williams, C.K., Winn, J., Zisserman, A.: The pascal visual object classes (VOC) challenge. Int. J. Comput. Vis. (IJCV) **88**(2), 303–338 (2010)
16. Fang, H., Gupta, S., Iandola, F.N., Srivastava, R., Deng, L., Dollár, P., Gao, J., He, X., Mitchell, M., Platt, J.C., Zitnick, C.L., Zweig, G.: From captions to visual concepts and back. In: Conference on Computer Vision and Pattern Recognition (CVPR) (2015)
17. Farhadi, A., Endres, I., Hoiem, D., Forsyth, D.: Describing objects by their attributes. In: Conference on Computer Vision and Pattern Recognition (CVPR) (2009)
18. Farhadi, A., Endres, I., Hoiem, D.: Attribute-centric recognition for cross-category generalization. In: Conference on Computer Vision and Pattern Recognition (CVPR) (2010)
19. Farrell, R., Oza, O., Morariu, V., Darrell, T., Davis, L.: Birdlets: subordinate categorization using volumetric primitives and pose-normalized appearance. In: International Conference on Computer Vision (ICCV) (2011)
20. Fellbaum, C.: WordNet: An Electronical Lexical Database. The MIT Press (1998)
21. Frome, A., Corrado, G., Shlens, J., Bengio, S., Dean, J., Ranzato, M., Mikolov, T.: Devise: a deep visual-semantic embedding model. In: Conference on Neural Information Processing Systems (NIPS) (2013)
22. Fu, Y., Hospedales, T.M., Xiang, T., Gong, S.: Learning multimodal latent attributes. IEEE Trans. Pattern Anal. Mach. Intell. (PAMI) **36**(2), 303–316 (2014)
23. Gabrilovich, E., Markovitch, S.: Computing semantic relatedness using wikipedia-based explicit semantic analysis. In: Proceedings of the International Joint Conference on Artificial Intelligence (IJCAI) (2007)
24. Gao, H., Mao, J., Zhou, J., Huang, Z., Wang, L., Xu, W.: Are you talking to a machine? Dataset and methods for multilingual image question answering. In: Conference on Neural Information Processing Systems (NIPS) (2015)
25. Girshick, R.: Fast R-CNN. In: International Conference on Computer Vision (ICCV) (2015)
26. Gong, Y., Wang, L., Hodosh, M., Hockenmaier, J., Lazebnik, S.: Improving image-sentence embeddings using large weakly annotated photo collections. In: European Conference on Computer Vision (ECCV) (2014)
27. Guadarrama, S., Rodner, E., Saenko, K., Zhang, N., Farrell, R., Donahue, J., Darrell, T.: Open-vocabulary object retrieval. In: Robotics: Science and Systems (2014)
28. He, K., Zhang, X., Ren, S., Sun, J.: Delving deep into rectifiers: surpassing human-level performance on imagenet classification. In: International Conference on Computer Vision (ICCV) (2015)
29. Hendricks, L.A., Venugopalan, S., Rohrbach, M., Mooney, R., Saenko, K., Darrell, T.: Deep compositional captioning: describing novel object categories without paired training data. arXiv:1511.05284v1 (2015)
30. Hendricks, L.A., Venugopalan, S., Rohrbach, M., Mooney, R., Saenko, K., Darrell, T.: Deep compositional captioning: describing novel object categories without paired training data. In: Conference on Computer Vision and Pattern Recognition (CVPR) (2016)
31. Hoffman, J., Guadarrama, S., Tzeng, E., Donahue, J., Girshick, R., Darrell, T., Saenko, K.: LSDA: large scale detection through adaptation. In: Conference on Neural Information Processing Systems (NIPS) (2014)
32. Hu, R., Xu, H., Rohrbach, M., Feng, J., Saenko, K., Darrell, T.: Natural language object retrieval. In: Conference on Computer Vision and Pattern Recognition (CVPR) (2015)

33. Hu, R., Rohrbach, M., Darrell, T.: Segmentation from natural language expressions. arXiv:1603.06180 (2016)
34. Johnson, J., Krishna, R., Stark, M., Li, L.-J., Shamma, D., Bernstein, M., Fei-Fei, L.: Image retrieval using scene graphs. In: Conference on Computer Vision and Pattern Recognition (CVPR) (2015)
35. Johnson, J., Karpathy, A., Fei-Fei, L.: Densecap: fully convolutional localization networks for dense captioning. In: Conference on Computer Vision and Pattern Recognition (CVPR) (2016)
36. Karpathy, A., Fei-Fei, L.: Deep visual-semantic alignments for generating image descriptions. In: Conference on Computer Vision and Pattern Recognition (CVPR) (2015)
37. Karpathy, A., Joulin, A., Fei-Fei, L.: Deep fragment embeddings for bidirectional image sentence mapping. In: Conference on Neural Information Processing Systems (NIPS) (2014)
38. Kazemzadeh, S., Ordonez, V., Matten, M., Berg, T.L.: Referitgame: referring to objects in photographs of natural scenes. In: Proceedings of the Conference on Empirical Methods in Natural Language Processing (EMNLP) (2014)
39. Koehn, P.: Statistical Machine Translation. Cambridge University Press (2010)
40. Kong, C., Lin, D., Bansal, M., Urtasun, R., Fidler, S.: What are you talking about? Text-to-image coreference. In: Conference on Computer Vision and Pattern Recognition (CVPR) (2014)
41. Krishna, R., Zhu, Y., Groth, O., Johnson, J., Hata, K., Kravitz, J., Chen, S., Kalanditis, Y., Li, L.-J., Shamma, D.A., Bernstein, M., Fei-Fei, L.: Visual genome: connecting language and vision using crowdsourced dense image annotations. arXiv:1602.07332 (2016)
42. Krizhevsky, A., Sutskever, I., Hinton, G.E.: Imagenet classification with deep convolutional neural networks. In: Conference on Neural Information Processing Systems (NIPS) (2012)
43. Lampert, C., Nickisch, H., Harmeling, S.: Learning to detect unseen object classes by between-class attribute transfer. In: Conference on Computer Vision and Pattern Recognition (CVPR) (2009)
44. Lampert, C.H., Nickisch, H., Harmeling, S.: Attribute-based classification for zero-shot visual object categorization. IEEE Trans. Pattern Anal. Mach. Intell. (PAMI) **36**(3), 453–465 (2014)
45. Liang, C., Xu, C., Cheng, J., Min, W., Lu, H.: Script-to-movie: a computational framework for story movie composition. IEEE Trans. Multimedia **15**(2), 401–414 (2013)
46. Lin, D.: An information-theoretic definition of similarity. In: International Conference on Machine Learning (ICML) (1998)
47. Lin, T.-Y., Maire, M., Belongie, S., Hays, J., Perona, P., Ramanan, D., Dollár, P., Zitnick, C.L.: Microsoft COCO: common objects in context. In: European Conference on Computer Vision (ECCV) (2014)
48. Malinowski, M., Fritz, M.: A multi-world approach to question answering about real-world scenes based on uncertain input. In: Conference on Neural Information Processing Systems (NIPS) (2014)
49. Malinowski, M., Rohrbach, M., Fritz, M.: Ask your neurons: a neural-based approach to answering questions about images. In: International Conference on Computer Vision (ICCV) (2015)
50. Mao, J., Xu, W., Yang, Y., Wang, J., Huang, Z., Yuille, A.: Deep captioning with multimodal recurrent neural networks (m-RNN). In: International Conference on Learning Representations (ICLR) (2015)
51. Mao, J., Huang, J., Toshev, A., Camburu, O., Yuille, A., Murphy, K.: Generation and comprehension of unambiguous object descriptions. In: Conference on Computer Vision and Pattern Recognition (CVPR) (2016)
52. Maron, O., Lozano-Pérez, T.: A framework for multiple-instance learning. In: Conference on Neural Information Processing Systems (NIPS) (1998)
53. Mensink, T., Verbeek, J., Perronnin, F., Csurka, G.: Metric learning for large scale image classification: generalizing to new classes at near-zero cost. In: European Conference on Computer Vision (ECCV) (2012)
54. Mihalcea, R., Moldovan, D.I.: A method for word sense disambiguation of unrestricted text. In: Proceedings of the Annual Meeting of the Association for Computational Linguistics (ACL) (1999)

55. Mikolov, T., Sutskever, I., Chen, K., Corrado, G.S., Dean, J.: Distributed representations of words and phrases and their compositionality. In: Conference on Neural Information Processing Systems (NIPS) (2013)
56. Moses, Y., Ullman, S., Edelman, S.: Generalization to novel images in upright and inverted faces. Perception **25**, 443–461 (1996)
57. Mrowca, D., Rohrbach, M., Hoffman, J., Hu, R., Saenko, K., Darrell, T.: Spatial semantic regularisation for large scale object detection. In: International Conference on Computer Vision (ICCV) (2015)
58. Palatucci, M., Pomerleau, D., Hinton, G., Mitchell, T.: Zero-shot learning with semantic output codes. In: Conference on Neural Information Processing Systems (NIPS) (2009)
59. Parikh, D., Grauman, K.: Relative attributes. In: International Conference on Computer Vision (ICCV) (2011)
60. Plummer, B., Wang, L., Cervantes, C., Caicedo, J., Hockenmaier, J., Lazebnik, S.: Flickr30k entities: collecting region-to-phrase correspondences for richer image-to-sentence models. In: International Conference on Computer Vision (ICCV) (2015)
61. Raina, R., Battle, A., Lee, H., Packer, B., Ng, A.: Self-taught learning: transfer learning from unlabeled data. In: International Conference on Machine Learning (ICML) (2007)
62. Regneri, M., Rohrbach, M., Wetzel, D., Thater, S., Schiele, B., Pinkal, M.: Grounding action descriptions in videos. In: Transactions of the Association for Computational Linguistics (TACL) (2013)
63. Ren, M., Kiros, R., Zemel, R.: Image question answering: a visual semantic embedding model and a new dataset. In: Conference on Neural Information Processing Systems (NIPS) (2015)
64. Rohrbach, M.: Combining visual recognition and computational linguistics: linguistic knowledge for visual recognition and natural language descriptions of visual content. PhD thesis, Saarland University (2014)
65. Rohrbach, M., Stark, M., Szarvas, G., Gurevych, I., Schiele, B.: What helps where—and why? Semantic relatedness for knowledge transfer. In: Conference on Computer Vision and Pattern Recognition (CVPR) (2010)
66. Rohrbach, M., Stark, M., Schiele, B.: Evaluating knowledge transfer and zero-shot learning in a large-scale setting. In: Conference on Computer Vision and Pattern Recognition (CVPR) (2011)
67. Rohrbach, M., Amin, S., Andriluka, M., Schiele, B.: A database for fine grained activity detection of cooking activities. In: Conference on Computer Vision and Pattern Recognition (CVPR) (2012)
68. Rohrbach, M., Regneri, M., Andriluka, M., Amin, S., Pinkal, M., Schiele, B.: Script data for attribute-based recognition of composite activities. In: European Conference on Computer Vision (ECCV) (2012)
69. Rohrbach, M., Stark, M., Szarvas, G., Schiele, B.: Combining language sources and robust semantic relatedness for attribute-based knowledge transfer. In: Proceedings of the European Conference on Computer Vision Workshops (ECCV Workshops), vol. 6553 of LNCS (2012)
70. Rohrbach, M., Ebert, S., Schiele, B.: Transfer learning in a transductive setting. In: Conference on Neural Information Processing Systems (NIPS) (2013)
71. Rohrbach, M., Qiu, W., Titov, I., Thater, S., Pinkal, M., Schiele, B.: Translating video content to natural language descriptions. In: International Conference on Computer Vision (ICCV) (2013)
72. Rohrbach, A., Rohrbach, M., Qiu, W., Friedrich, A., Pinkal, M., Schiele, B.: Coherent multi-sentence video description with variable level of detail. In: Proceedings of the German Confeence on Pattern Recognition (GCPR) (2014)
73. Rohrbach, A., Rohrbach, M., Hu, R., Darrell, T., Schiele, B.: Grounding of textual phrases in images by reconstruction. arXiv:1511.03745 (2015)
74. Rohrbach, M., Rohrbach, A., Regneri, M., Amin, S., Andriluka, M., Pinkal, M., Schiele, B.: Recognizing fine-grained and composite activities using hand-centric features and script data. Int. J. Comput. Vision (IJCV) **119**(3), 346–373 (2015)

75. Rohrbach, A., Rohrbach, M., Schiele, B.: The long-short story of movie description. In: Proceedings of the German Confeence on Pattern Recognition (GCPR) (2015)
76. Rohrbach, A., Rohrbach, M., Tandon, N., Schiele, B.: A dataset for movie description. In: Conference on Computer Vision and Pattern Recognition (CVPR) (2015)
77. Senina, A., Rohrbach, M., Qiu, W., Friedrich, A., Amin, S., Andriluka, M., Pinkal, M., Schiele, B.: Coherent multi-sentence video description with variable level of detail. arXiv:1403.6173 (2014)
78. Silberer, C., Ferrari, V., Lapata, M.: Models of semantic representation with visual attributes. In: Proceedings of the Annual Meeting of the Association for Computational Linguistics (ACL) (2013)
79. Simonyan, K., Zisserman, A.: Very deep convolutional networks for large-scale image recognition. In: International Conference on Learning Representations (ICLR) (2015)
80. Sivic, J., Russell, B.C., Efros, A.A., Zisserman, A., Freeman, W.T.: Discovering object categories in image collections. In: International Conference on Computer Vision (ICCV) (2005)
81. Socher, R., Fei-Fei, L.: Connecting modalities: semi-supervised segmentation and annotation of images using unaligned text corpora. In: Conference on Computer Vision and Pattern Recognition (CVPR) (2010)
82. Sørensen, T.: A method of establishing groups of equal amplitude in plant sociology based on similarity of species and its application to analyses of the vegetation on danish commons. Biol. Skr. **5**, 1–34 (1948)
83. Szegedy, C., Liu, W., Jia, Y., Sermanet, P., Reed, S., Anguelov, D., Erhan, D., Vanhoucke, V., Rabinovich, A.: Going deeper with convolutions. In: Conference on Computer Vision and Pattern Recognition (CVPR) (2015)
84. Thomee, B., Elizalde, B., Shamma, D.A., Ni, K., Friedland, G., Poland, D., Borth, D., Li, L.-J.: Yfcc100m: the new data in multimedia research. Commun. ACM **59**(2), 64–73 (2016)
85. Thrun, S.: Is learning the n-th thing any easier than learning the first. In: Conference on Neural Information Processing Systems (NIPS) (1996)
86. Torabi, A., Pal, C., Larochelle, H., Courville, A.: Using descriptive video services to create a large data source for video annotation research. arXiv:1503.01070v1 (2015)
87. Uijlings, J.R., van de Sande, K.E., Gevers, T., Smeulders, A.W.: Selective search for object recognition. Int. J. Comput. Vision (IJCV) **104**(2), 154–171 (2013)
88. Venugopalan, S., Rohrbach, M., Donahue, J., Mooney, R., Darrell, T., Saenko, K.: Sequence to sequence—video to text. arXiv:1505.00487v2 (2015)
89. Venugopalan, S., Rohrbach, M., Donahue, J., Mooney, R., Darrell, T., Saenko, K.: Sequence to sequence—video to text. In: International Conference on Computer Vision (ICCV) (2015)
90. Venugopalan, S., Xu, H., Donahue, J., Rohrbach, M., Mooney, R., Saenko, K.: Translating videos to natural language using deep recurrent neural networks. In: Proceedings of the Conference of the North American Chapter of the Association for Computational Linguistics (NAACL) (2015)
91. Vinyals, O., Toshev, A., Bengio, S., Erhan, D.: Show and tell: a neural image caption generator. In: Conference on Computer Vision and Pattern Recognition (CVPR) (2015)
92. Wang, H., Kläser, A., Schmid, C., Liu, C.-L.: Action recognition by dense trajectories. In: Conference on Computer Vision and Pattern Recognition (CVPR) (2011)
93. Wang, H., Schmid, C.: Action recognition with improved trajectories. In: International Conference on Computer Vision (ICCV) (2013)
94. Weber, M., Welling, M., Perona, P.: Towards automatic discovery of object categories. In: Conference on Computer Vision and Pattern Recognition (CVPR) (2000)
95. Wu, Q., Shen, C., Hengel, A.V.D., Wang, P., Dick, A.: Image captioning and visual question answering based on attributes and their related external knowledge. arXiv:1603.02814 (2016)
96. Yao, L., Torabi, A., Cho, K., Ballas, N., Pal, C., Larochelle, H., Courville, A.: Describing videos by exploiting temporal structure. arXiv:1502.08029v4 (2015)
97. Young, P., Lai, A., Hodosh, M., Hockenmaier, J.: From image descriptions to visual denotations: New similarity metrics for semantic inference over event descriptions. Trans. Assoc. Comput. Linguist. (TACL) **2**, 67–78 (2014)

98. Zesch, T., Gurevych, I.: Wisdom of crowds versus wisdom of linguists—measuring the semantic relatedness of words. Nat. Lang. Eng. **16**(1), 25–59 (2010)
99. Zhou, D., Bousquet, O., Lal, T.N., Weston, J., Schölkopf, B.: Learning with local and global consistency. In: Conference on Neural Information Processing Systems (NIPS) (2004)
100. Zhou, B., Lapedriza, A., Xiao, J., Torralba, A., Oliva, A.: Learning deep features for scene recognition using places database. In: Conference on Neural Information Processing Systems (NIPS) (2014)
101. Zhu, X., Ghahramani, Z., Lafferty, J.: Semi-supervised learning using Gaussian fields and harmonic functions. In: International Conference on Machine Learning (ICML) (2003)
102. Zitnick, C.L., Parikh, D., Vanderwende, L.: Learning the visual interpretation of sentences. In: International Conference on Computer Vision (ICCV) (2013)

Chapter 13
Grounding the Meaning of Words with Visual Attributes

Carina Silberer

Abstract We address the problem of grounding representations of word meaning. Our approach learns higher level representations in a stacked autoencoder architecture from visual and textual input. The two input modalities are encoded as vectors of attributes and are obtained automatically from images and text. To obtain visual attributes (e.g. has_legs, is_yellow) from images, we train attribute classifiers by using our large-scale taxonomy of 600 visual attributes, representing more than 500 concepts and 700 K images. We extract textual attributes (e.g. *bird, breed*) from text with an existing distributional model. Experimental results on tasks related to word similarity show that the attribute-based vectors can be usefully integrated by our stacked autoencoder model to create bimodal representations which are overall more accurate than representations based on the individual modalities or different integration mechanisms (The work presented in this chapter is based on [89]).

13.1 Introduction

Humans generally possess a rich semantic knowledge of words[1] and concepts[2] which captures the perceivable physical properties (e.g. visual appearance) of their real-world referents and their relations. This knowledge enables us to recognise objects and entities by means of our senses, to interact with them and to verbally convey information about them [65]. An extensive amount of work in cognition research has been devoted to approaches and theories that explain the complex phenomena related to learning, representing and processing aspects of this knowledge,

[1] We use the term *word* to denote any sequence of non-delimiting symbols.
[2] We use the term *concept* to denote the mental representation of objects belonging to basic-level classes (e.g. *dog*), and the term *category* to refer to superordinate-level classes (e.g. ANIMAL).

C. Silberer (✉)
Institute for Language, Cognitition and Computation,
School of Informatics, University of Edinburgh,
Informatics Forum, 10 Crichton Street, Edinburgh EH8 9AB, UK
e-mail: c.silberer@ed.ac.uk

R.S. Feris et al. (eds.), *Visual Attributes*, Advances in Computer Vision
and Pattern Recognition, DOI 10.1007/978-3-319-50077-5_13

and has given rise to different classes of models of meaning representations. Likewise, meaning representations are crucial for many applications of natural language processing, such as information retrieval, document classification, or semantic role labelling [100], which spurred research on models for automatic representation learning.

A major strand of research popular across disciplines focusses on models which induce semantic representations from text corpora. These models are based on the hypothesis that the meaning of words is established by their distributional relation to other words [40]. Despite their widespread use, distributional models of word meaning have been criticised as 'disembodied' in that they are not *grounded* in perception and action [5, 36, 78]. This lack of grounding contrasts with many experimental studies suggesting that meaning is acquired not only from exposure to the linguistic environment but also from our interaction with the physical world [11, 58]. Recent years have seen a surge of interest in models which aim at inducing perceptually grounded semantic representations. Essentially, existing approaches learn meaning representations from multiple views corresponding to different modalities, i.e. linguistic and perceptual input. To approximate the perceptual modality, previous work has relied largely on features automatically extracted from images, or on semantic attributes collected from humans (e.g. is round, is sour). The latter have a long-standing tradition in cognitive science and are thought to represent salient psychological aspects of word meaning including multisensory information. However, their elicitation from human subjects is expensive and limits the scope of computational models to a small number of concepts for which attributes are available.

In this chapter, we present an approach which draws inspiration from the application of natural language attributes in computer vision, and represent images and the concepts depicted by them by automatically predicted attributes.[3] To this end, we created a dataset comprising nearly 700 K images and a taxonomy of 636 visual attributes and use it to train attribute classifiers. In line with the attribute-based approximation of the visual modality, we represent the linguistic modality by textual attributes which we obtain with an off-the-shelf distributional model [4]. We then introduce a neural network-based model, which learns higher level meaning representations by mapping words and images, represented by attributes, into a common embedding space. In contrast to most previous approaches to multimodal learning using different variants of deep networks and data sources, our model is defined at a finer level of granularity—it computes representations for individual words—and is unique in its use of attributes as a means of representing the textual and visual modalities. We demonstrate the effectiveness of the representations learned by our model by evaluating its ability to account for human behaviour on semantic tasks related to word similarity. For this purpose, we created a new evaluation dataset in a large-scale experiment where participants are asked to give two ratings per word pair expressing their semantic and visual similarity, respectively. We hope that this

[3] By the term *attributes* we refer to semantic properties or characteristics of concepts (or categories), expressed by words which people would use to describe their meaning.

dataset and our visual attributes resource will be of use to the computer vision and natural language processing communities.[4]

We first present an overview of related work on models of word meaning. We then describe how we extract visual and textual attributes from images and text data, respectively, and how we use these to represent word meaning. We introduce our model that learns higher level meaning representations using the attribute-based representations as input, and conclude with experimental results and discussion

13.2 Background: Models of Word Meaning

The presented work is related to several classes of models of meaning representations which we review in the following. Common to the first two classes is their induction of word meaning representations on the basis of other natural language words, which occur in text data (Sect. 13.2.1) or are directly produced by humans for individual words (Sect. 13.2.2).

13.2.1 Distributional Models

Distributional models of word meaning specify mechanisms for automatically constructing semantic representations from text corpora. They represent words through vectors which capture their relation to other words, based on the *distributional hypothesis* [40] postulating that words that appear in similar linguistic contexts tend to have related meanings. These vector space models (VSMs) can mathematically compare the meaning of two words by geometrically estimating their similarity, e.g. as the cosine of the angle [21] between their vectors.

A well-known instance of VSMs are constructed by analysing a text corpus and extracting the co-occurrence frequency of each target word with its contextual elements, such as context words or documents (e.g. [63]). Each target word is then represented as a vector whose components correspond to contextual elements and whose entries give their frequency of co-occurrence with the target word, weighted by schemes such as mutual information. The dimensionality of the vector space may further be reduced by means of an appropriate method, such as singular value decomposition (SVD) [21, 59]. VSMs based on co-occurrence counts have been successfully used in many natural language applications (see [100], and the references therein) and in cognitive science on various simulation tasks (see [38]). In our work, we apply a distributional method [4] to extract attribute-centric representations of words from a text corpus.

---

[4]Available at http://homepages.inf.ed.ac.uk/csilbere/resources.html.

In recent years, a variety of models have been proposed that use deep (and shallow) network architectures to learn distributed word representations corresponding to vectors of activation of network units, a.k.a. *word embeddings* [7, 19, 44, 69, 70]. The models embed each word into a continuous space via an embedding matrix to be learned. Typically, the embeddings are initialised randomly and then optimised with respect to predicting the contexts in which the words occur in a text corpus. Mikolov et al.'s [69] skip-gram model has become one of the standard choices for NLP approaches leveraging word representations (see Sect. 13.5.1). These models, however, usually cannot deal with out-of-vocabulary words. Our model learns distributed representations by mapping attribute-based representations into a distributed space and which hence can be applied to encode new words.

13.2.2 Models Based on Human-Produced Attributes

A long-standing tradition in cognitive science is the assumption that meaning representations are based on attributes Mervis and Rosch (e.g. [68]), Sloman et al. (e.g. [91]). These are human-produced natural language properties and typically include visual attributes (e.g. has scales, is yellow, has stripes, made of metal), but also encode knowledge of concepts with respect to other sensory properties (gustatory, acoustic, etc., such as tastes sweet, rattles), and non-perceptual attributes, such as encyclopaedic properties (e.g. is tropical, is poisonous) or taxonomic relations (e.g. a_herbivore). Attribute-based theories of lexical semantic representation[5] [20, 48, 104, inter alia] use such attributes to computationally model phenomena of human cognition, e.g. categorisation and lexical priming. Given the context of this book, it is important to note that these models do not use attributes recognised automatically in, e.g. an image depicting an object to which a word can refer, but rely on the attribute annotations produced by humans for individual words. We will discuss visual attributes from images in Sect. 13.3.

Traditionally, attribute-based representations have been either directly hand-coded by the researchers [18, 92], or induced in shallow neural network models using the attributes as knowledge source to study semantic memory and its impairments (e.g. [82]).

Modern attribute-based models Grondin et al. (e.g. [39]), O'Connor et al. (e.g. [73]), Rogers et al. (e.g. [83]), Taylor et al. (e.g. [99]), Tyler and Moss (e.g. [101]), Voorspoels et al. (e.g. [109]) use data collected in attribute norming studies, in which a large group of humans are presented with a series of words and asked to list relevant attributes of the things to which the words refer [24, 66, 107]. Such *attribute norms*[6] are widely regarded as proxy for sensorimotor experience. They provide a cue to

[5]In the context of semantic representations, attributes are often called features or properties in the literature. For the sake of consistency of the present work, we will adhere to the former term.

[6]They are often termed semantic feature production norms (e.g. [66]) or property norms (e.g. [24]) in the literature.

aspects of human meaning representations which have developed through interaction with the physical environment [66], and are used to verbally convey perceptual and sensorimotor information (e.g. is yellow, smells bad, used by twisting).

Our neural network model induces word representations by augmenting it with attribute-based input vectors. However, to the best of our knowledge, we present the first model to use as input attribute activations automatically extracted from text and image data.

13.2.3 Grounded Semantic Spaces

Grounded semantic spaces are essentially distributional models augmented with perceptual information. Existing models mainly differ with respect to the type of perceptual information used and the way it is integrated with linguistic information.

Some models [2, 41, 90] use attributes norms as an approximation of the perceptual environment. Other models focus on the visual modality and exploit image databases, such as ImageNet [22] or ESP [108]. A few approaches [15, 31] use *visual words* which they derive by clustering SIFT descriptors [62] extracted from images. More recently, models which combine both attribute norms and visual words have also been introduced [84]. In other work [51, 60] representations for the visual modality are obtained directly from image pixels using the feature extraction layers of a deep convolutional neural network (CNN) trained on a labelled object recognition data set. Finally, some models use human generated image tags as a proxy for visual information [13, 41].

As far as the integration mechanism is concerned, the simplest method is to concatenate the vectors corresponding to a word's perceptual and linguistic representation [12, 51]. Other approaches infer bimodal representations over latent variables responsible for the co-occurrence of words over featural dimensions. Bruni et al. [15] concatenate two independently constructed textual and visual spaces and subsequently project them onto a lower dimensional space using SVD. Several models [2, 31, 84] present extensions of Latent Dirichlet Allocation [10], where topic distributions are learned from words *and* other perceptual units treating them both as observed variables. Hill and Korhonen [41] extend the skip-gram network model [69] in an analogous fashion; in Lazaridou et al.'s [60] extension of the skip-gram model the representations are trained to predict linguistic and visual features. In most cases, the visual and textual modalities are decoupled in that they are obtained independently e.g. from text corpora and feature norms or image databases (but see [31], for an exception).

Our model uses stacked autoencoders to learn higher level vector representations from textual and visual input. Rather than simply adding perceptual information to textual data it integrates both modalities *jointly* in a single representation which is desirable, at least from a cognitive perspective. It is unlikely that we have separate representations for different aspects of word meaning [83]. Following earlier work discussed above, we also train our model on independently collated linguistic and visual data. However, in our case, the two modalities are unified in their representation by natural language attributes.

13.3 Representing Word Meaning with Attributes from Images and Text

In our approach to perceptually ground meaning representations of words we focus on the visual modality as a major source of perceptual information, and represent it by visual attributes which we obtain automatically from images, as we describe below. Analogously, we represent the textual modality by means of textual attributes which we automatically extract from text data using an existing distributional method ([4]; Sect. 13.3.2).

Our choice of an attribute-centric approach is motivated by theoretical arguments from cognitive science and computer vision research. From a cognitive perspective, the use of attributes for meaning representations is endorsed by its long-standing tradition in cognitive science, as discussed in Sect. 13.2.2. In brief, attributes are the medium humans naturally use to verbally convey perceptual, taxonomic, sensori-motor, and functional knowledge of concepts. From a computer vision perspective, attributes are advantageous for several reasons. In order to describe visual phenomena (e.g. objects, scenes, faces, actions) in natural language, computer vision algorithms traditionally assign each instance a categorical label (e.g. *apple*, *sunrise*, *Sean Connery*, *drinking*). Attributes, on the other hand, offer a means to obtain semantically more fine-grained descriptions. They can transcend category and task boundaries and thus provide a generic description of visual data and, consequently, their depictions (e.g. both *apples* and *balls* are round, *forks* and *rakes* have a handle and have tines). In addition to facilitating inter-class connections by means of shared attributes, intra-class variations can also be captured, hence offering a means to discriminate between instances of the same category (e.g. *birds* can have long beaks or short beaks). Moreover, attributes allow to generalise to new instances for which there are no training examples available. We can thus say something about depicted entities without knowing their object class. This makes attributes efficient, since they obviate the training of a classifier for each category.

Furthermore, from a modelling perspective, attributes occupy the middle ground between non-linguistic (low- or mid-level) image features and linguistic words. More precisely, attributes constitute a medium that is both, machine detectable and human understandable. They crucially represent image properties, however by being words themselves, they can be easily integrated in any text-based model thus eschewing known difficulties with rendering images into word-like units.

13.3.1 *Visual Attributes from Images*

Initial work on visual attributes for image data [32] focussed on simple colour and texture attributes (e.g. blue, stripes) and showed that these can be learned in a weakly supervised setting from images returned by a search engine when using the attribute as a query. Farhadi et al. [28] were among the first to use visual attributes in an object recognition task. Using an inventory of 64 attribute labels, they developed a dataset of approximately 12,000 instances representing 20 objects from the PASCAL VOC 2008 [26]. Lampert et al. [57] showed that attribute-based representations can be used to classify objects when there are no training examples of the target classes available (*zero-shot learning*; see also Chap. 2 of this book), provided their attributes are known. Their dataset contained over 30,000 animal images and used 85 attributes (e.g. brown, stripes, furry, paws) from the norming study of Osherson et al. [74]. Similar work was done by Parikh and Grauman [75], who use relative attributes indicating their degree of presence in an image compared to other images (e.g. more smiling than; see also Part II of this book). The use of attributes for zero-shot learning was also explored in the context of scene classification ([76], see also Chap. 11) and action recognition [61]. Russakovsky and Fei-Fei [86] learned classifiers for 20 visual attributes on ImageNet [22] with the goal of making visual inter-category connections across a broad range of classes on the basis of shared attributes (e.g. striped animals and striped fabric). The ability of attributes to capture intra-category variations has in turn been leveraged in approaches for face verification [55], domain-specific image retrieval [55, 76, 81], and fine-grained object recognition ([25]; see also Chap. 10). The use of visual attributes extracted from images in models of semantic representations is novel to our knowledge.

13.3.1.1 The Visual Attributes Dataset (VISA)

A key prerequisite for learning attribute classifiers for images is the availability of training data comprising a large number of images along with attribute annotations. Existing image databases of objects and their attributes focus on a small number of categories [28], or on a specific category, such as animals [57], birds [110], faces [54] or clothing items [16]. Some databases provide attribute annotations for scenes ([56, 76], see Chap. 11) or textures [17]. Other, general-purpose image collections cover a broad range of object categories, but provide no [46, 108] or little [22, 86, 87] attribute information.

Since our goal is to develop models that are applicable to many words from different categories, we created a new dataset. It shares many features with previous work [28, 57], but differs in focus and scope, covering a larger number of object classes and attributes. We chose to create the dataset on top of the image ontology ImageNet[7] [22] due to its high coverage of different objects, the high quality of its

[7] Available at http://www.image-net.org.

images (i.e. cleanly labelled and high resolution), and its organisation according to the hierarchical structure of the lexical database WordNet [29].

Concepts and Images We created the dataset for the nominal concepts contained in McRae et al.'s [66] attribute norms (henceforth the McRae norms), as they cover a wide range of concrete concepts including animate and inanimate things (e.g. animals, clothing, vehicles) and are widely established in cognitive science research. Images for the concepts in the McRae norms were harvested from ImageNet [22]. The McRae norms contain 541 concepts out of which 516 appear in ImageNet and are represented by nearly 700 K images overall. The average number of images per concept is 1,310 with the most popular being *closet* (2,149 images) and the least popular *prune* (5 images).

Attribute Annotation Our aim was to develop a set of visual attributes that are both discriminating and cognitively plausible in the sense that humans would generally use them to describe a concrete concept. As a starting point, we thus used the visual attributes from the McRae norms. Attributes capturing non-visual attributes, such as other primary sensory (e.g. sound) or encyclopaedic information, were not taken into account. For example, is_purple is a valid visual attribute for an *eggplant*, whereas a_vegetable is not, since it cannot be visualised. Collating all the visual attributes in the norms resulted in a total of 676. Similar to Lampert et al. [57], we conducted the annotation on a *per-concept* rather than a *per-image* basis (as, e.g. [28]). However, our methodology is slightly different from Lampert et al. [57] in that we did not simply transfer the attributes from the norms to the concepts in question but modified and extended them during the annotation process explained below, using a small fraction of the image data as development set (see Sect. 13.3.1.2 for details on the latter).

For each concept (e.g. *eggplant*), we inspected the images in the development set and chose all visual attributes contained in the McRae norms that applied. If an attribute was generally true for the concept, but the images did not provide enough evidence, the attribute was nevertheless chosen and labelled with <no_evidence>. For example, a *plum* has_a_pit, but most images in ImageNet show plums where only the outer part of the fruit is visible. We added new attributes which were supported by the image data but missing from the initial set as given by the norms. For example, has_lights and has_bumper are attributes of *cars* but are not included in the norms. In general, we were conservative in adding new attributes since our aim was to preserve the cognitive plausibility of the original attribute norms. For this reason, we added entirely new attributes only when we considered them to be on the same level of granularity as the attributes of the McRae norms.

There are several reasons for choosing the described annotation scheme instead of transferring the McRae attributes directly. Firstly, it makes sense to select attributes corroborated by the images. Secondly, by looking at the actual images, we could eliminate errors in the McRae norms. For example, eight study participants erroneously thought that a *catfish* has_scales. Thirdly, during the annotation process, we normalised synonymous attributes (e.g. has_pit and has_stone) and attributes that exhibited negligible variations in meaning (e.g. has_stem and has_stalk). Finally, our aim was to collect an exhaustive list of visual attributes for each concept which is consistent across all members of a category. This is unfortunately not the case in the McRae norms. Participants were asked to list up to 14 different properties that describe a concept. As a result, the attributes of a concept denote the set of properties humans consider most salient. For example, both, *lemons* and *oranges* have_pulp. But the norms provide this attribute only for the second concept.

Annotation proceeded on a category-by-category basis, e.g. first all food-related concepts were annotated, then animals, vehicles, and so on. Two annotators (one of them is the author of this chapter) developed the set of attributes for each category. One annotator first labelled concepts with their attributes as described above, and the other annotator reviewed the annotations, making changes if needed. Finally, annotations were revised and compared per category in order to ensure consistency across all concepts of that category. Attributes were grouped in ten general classes (e.g. anatomy, parts) shown in Fig. 13.1.

Overall, we discarded or modified 262 visual attributes of the McRae norms, and added 294 attributes. On average, each concept was annotated with 15 attributes; approximately 11.5 of these were not part of the set of attributes created by the participants of the McRae norms for that concept even though they figured in the

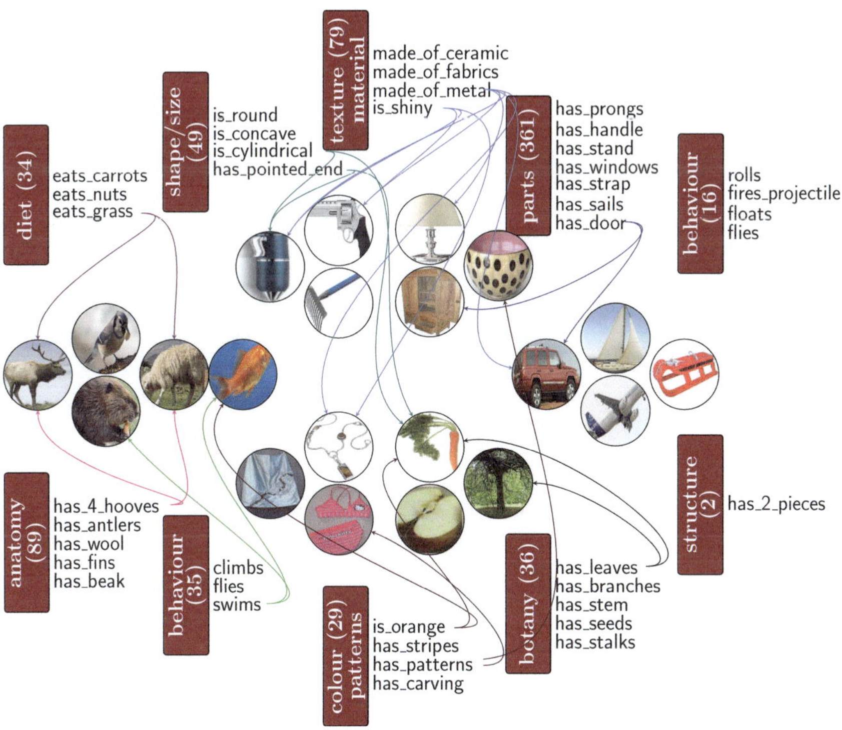

Fig. 13.1 Attribute categories and examples of attribute instances and images. *Parentheses* denote the number of attributes per category

Table 13.1 Human-authored attributes for *bear*, *eggplant*, *car*. <ne> stands for <no_evidence>

	anatomy	has_mouth, has_head, has_nose, has_tail, has_claws has_jaws, has_neck, has_snout, has_feet, has_tongue
	behaviour	eats, walks, climbs, swims, runs
	colour_patterns	is_black, is_brown, is_white
	diet	drinks_water, eats_anything
	shape_size	is_tall, is_large
	botany	has_skin, has_seeds, has_stem, has_leaves, has_pulp
	colour_patterns	purple, white, green, has_green_top
	shape_size	is_oval, is_long
	texture_material	is_shiny
	behaviour	rolls
	colour_patterns	different_colors, is_black, is_red, is_grey, is_blue, is_white
	parts	has_4_wheels, has_steering_wheel, has_seat<ne>, has_windows has_engine<ne>, has_mirror, has_number_plate, has_bonnet has_trunk, has_windshield_wiper, has_roof, has_bumper, has_handle has_belts, has_light, has_windshield, has_door, has_brakes<ne>
	texture_material	made_of_metal

attribute sets of other concepts. Furthermore, on average two McRae attributes per concept were discarded. Examples of concepts and their attributes from our database[8] are shown in Table 13.1.

13.3.1.2 Automatically Extracting Visual Attributes

Data For each concept in the VISA dataset, we partitioned the corresponding images into a training, development, and test set. For most concepts the development set contained a maximum of 100 images and the test set a maximum of 200 images. Concepts with less than 800 images in total were split into $^1/_8$ test and development set each, and $^3/_4$ training set. Image assignments to the splits were done randomly in general. However, we wanted the test set to be composed of as many images with bounding box annotations as possible. We therefore first assigned images for which ImageNet provided bounding boxes to the splits, starting with the test set, before assigning the remaining images. To learn a classifier for a particular attribute, we used all images in the training data, totalling to approximately 550 K images. Images of concepts annotated with the attribute were used as positive examples, and the rest as negative examples.

Training Attribute Classifiers In order to extract visual attributes from images, we followed previous work [28, 57] and learned one classifier for each attribute that had been assigned to at least two concepts in our dataset. We furthermore only considered attribute annotations that were corroborated by the images, that is, we ignored those labelled with <no_evidence>. This amounts to 414 classifiers in total. We used L2-regularised L2-loss linear support vector machines (SVM, [27]) to learn the

[8] Available at http://homepages.inf.ed.ac.uk/s1151656/resources.html.

attribute predictions, and adopted the training procedure of Farhadi et al. [28]. We optimised cost parameter C of each SVM on the training data, randomly partitioning it into a split of 70 % for training, and 30 % for validation. The final SVM for an attribute was trained on the entire training data, i.e. on all positive and negative examples.

Features We used the four different feature types proposed by Farhadi et al. [28],[9] namely colour, texture, visual words, and edges. For each feature type, an image (or an image region) was represented using a histogram based on clustered feature descriptors (bag-of-words approach). Texture descriptors [103] were computed for each pixel and quantised to the nearest 256 k-means centres. Edges were detected using a standard Canny detector and their orientations were quantised into eight bins. Colour descriptors were computed in the LAB colour space. They were sampled for each pixel and quantised to the nearest 128 k-means centres. Visual words were constructed with a HoG spatial pyramid using 2 scales per octave. HoG descriptors were computed using 8×8 blocks and a 4 pixel step size and then quantised into 1000 k-means centres (visual words). Individual histograms were computed for the whole image or a bounding box (if available). With the purpose to represent shapes and locations, six additional histograms were generated for each feature type, by dividing the image (or region) into a grid of three vertical and two horizontal blocks, and computing a histogram for each block in the grid separately. The resulting seven histograms per feature type were finally normalised with the l^2-norm and then stacked together.

Evaluation Figure 13.2 shows classifier predictions for test images from concepts seen by the classifiers during training (top), and from new, i.e. unseen, concepts not part of the VISA dataset (bottom), respectively. We quantitatively evaluated the attribute classifiers by measuring the interpolated average precision (AP, [88]) on the test set. Since the reference annotations contained in VISA are concept-based, we perform the evaluation on the basis of concept-level predictions as the centroid of all attribute predictions for the images belonging to the same concept (see below for details on how we compute the concept-level predictions); specifically, we plot precision against recall based on a threshold.[10] Recall is the proportion of correct attribute predictions whose prediction score exceed the threshold to the true attribute assignments given by VISA. Precision is the fraction of correct attribute predictions to all predictions exceeding the threshold. The AP is the mean of the maximum precision at eleven recall levels [0, 0.1, ..., 1]. The precision/recall curve is shown in Fig. 13.3; the attribute classifiers achieved a mean AP of 0.52.

13.3.1.3 Deriving Visual Representations of Concepts

Note that the classifiers predict attributes on an image-by-image basis; in order to describe a concept w by its visual attributes taking into account multiple images

[9]The code by [28] is available at http://vision.cs.uiuc.edu/attributes/ (last accessed in May 2015).

[10]Threshold values ranged from 0 to 0.9 with 0.1 stepsize.

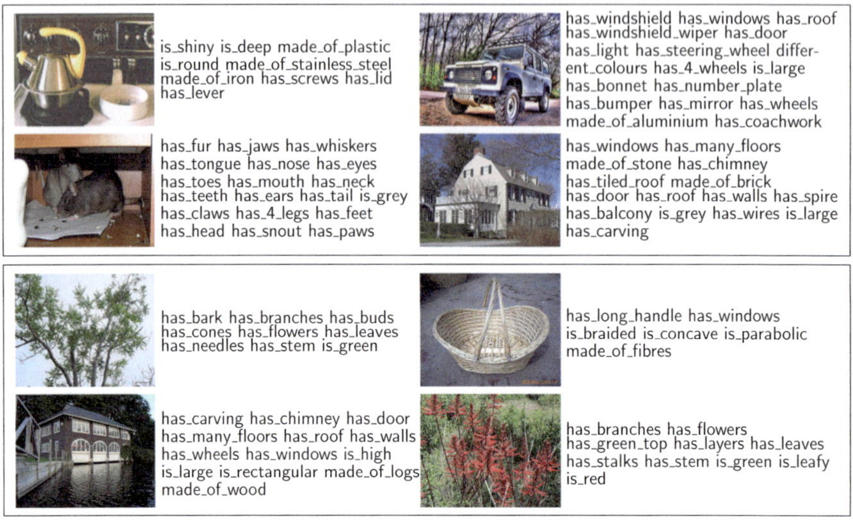

Fig. 13.2 Attribute predictions for concepts seen (from *top left* to *bottom right*: *kettle, rat, jeep, house*), and not seen during training (*ailanthus, boathouse, shopping basket, coraltree)*

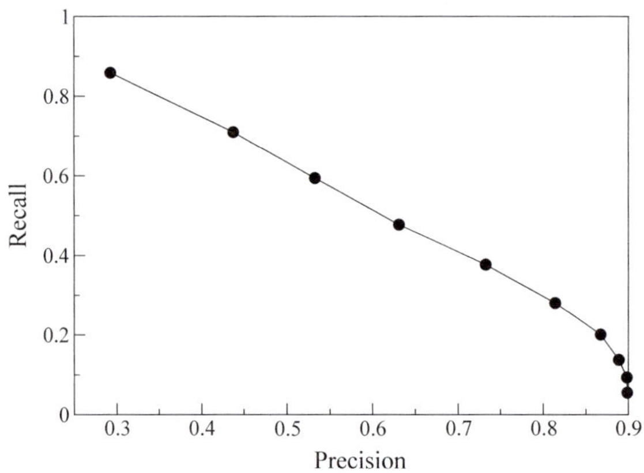

Fig. 13.3 Attribute classifier performance for different thresholds δ (test set)

representing w, we need to aggregate their attributes into a single representation. We use a vector-based representation where each attribute corresponds to a dimension of an underlying semantic space and concepts are represented as points in this attribute space. Just as in text-based semantic spaces, we can thus quantify similarity between two concepts by measuring the geometric distance of their vectors. Since we encode visual attributes, the underlying semantic space is perceptual, and so is the similarity we can measure.

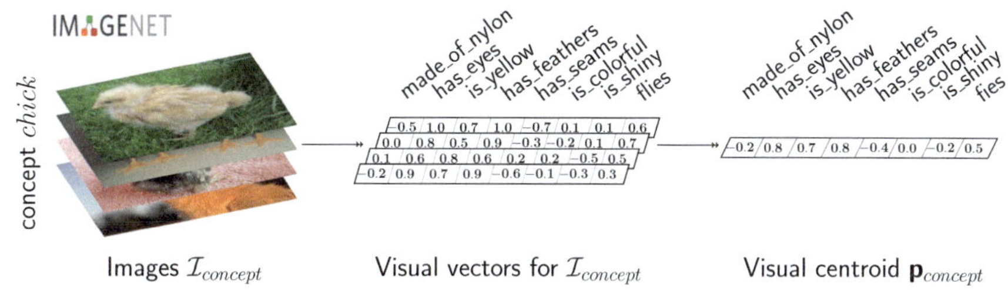

Fig. 13.4 Visual representation for the concept *chick*. Attribute classifiers predict attributes for example images depicting *chicks*. The prediction scores are then converted into vectors (*first arrow*). To compute a single visual attribute vector for a concept, all vectors are aggregated into $\mathbf{p}_{chick}$, respectively, according to Eq. (13.1) (*second arrow*)

We construct visual vector representations as follows. For each image $x_w \in \mathcal{I}_w$ of concept w, we output an A-dimensional vector containing prediction scores $\text{score}_\text{a}(x_w)$ for attributes $a = 1, \ldots, A$.[11] We transform these attribute vectors into a single vector $\mathbf{p}_w \in \mathbb{R}^{1\times A}$ by computing the centroid of all vectors for concept w:

$$\mathbf{p}_w = \Big(\frac{1}{|\mathcal{I}_w|}\sum_{x_w \in \mathcal{I}_w} \text{score}_\text{a}(x_w)\Big)_{a=1,\ldots,A} \tag{13.1}$$

The construction process is illustrated in Fig. 13.4 by the example concept *chick*. In Table 13.2 (second column) we give the six nearest neighbours for six example concepts (first column) from our dataset. Nearest neighbours for a concept were found by measuring the cosine similarity between the visual attribute vectors $\mathbf{p}$ of that concept and all other concepts in our dataset and choosing the six concepts with the highest similarity. For comparison the table also shows the six nearest neighbours when the example concepts are represented by their textual attribute vectors (Table 13.2, third column; see below for their creation) and by their bimodal vector representations as learned with our SAE model (Table 13.2, last column; see Sect. 13.3).

13.3.2 Textual Attributes

Several methods have been developed for automatically extracting norm-like attributes from text using pattern-based approaches and co-occurrence association measures [3], more elaborate natural language processing techniques and Word-

[11]For simplicity, we use the symbol w to denote both, the concept and its index. Analogously, symbol a denotes the attribute and its index.

Table 13.2 Example concepts (column 1) and their six most similar concepts computed on the basis of visual and textual attribute-based representations (columns 2 and 3, respectively) and bimodal representations learned by the SAE model (column 4) in order of decreasing cosine similarity

Concept	Nearest neighbours		
	Visual	Textual	Bimodal (SAE)
ambulance	*van truck taxi bus limousine jeep*	*helicopter trolley van taxi train truck*	*taxi van truck bus train trolley*
bison	*ox bull pony elephant bear cow*	*elk buffalo deer caribou bear otter pig pony*	*buffalo bear elephant caribou deer sheep*
brush	*paintbrush pencil ladle hammer screwdriver pin*	*comb paintbrush vest scissors doll coat*	*comb paintbrush pencil scissors razor pen*
microwave	*oven shelves stove cabinet freezer radio*	*stove oven freezer radio pot colander*	*radio stove oven freezer stereo fridge*
scarf	*gloves shawl socks sweater veil pajamas*	*shawl sweater cloak veil gown robe*	*shawl sweater pajamas skirt socks veil*

Net [23] as well as manual extraction rules [50]. A fully unsupervised template-based approach was proposed by Baroni et al. ([4], *Strudel*) which extracts weighted concept-attribute pairs (e.g. *chick–bird:n*, *chick–brood:v*) from a text corpus. We opted for using Strudel to obtain textual attributes for concepts due to its knowledge-lean approach—it merely expects input texts tagged with parts-of-speech (PoS)—and the fact that it has a bias towards non-perceptual attributes such as actions, functions or situations [4].

Strudel[12] takes as input a set of target concepts and a set of patterns, and extracts a list of attributes for each concept. The attributes are not known a priori, but are directly extracted from the corpus. Unlike many other distributional models, Strudel induces meaning representations that describe a concept via its properties instead of a bag of co-occurring words. Each concept-attribute pair is weighted with a log-likelihood ratio expressing the pair's strength of association.

It is relatively straightforward to obtain a textual semantic space from Strudel's extracted attributes. Specifically, we represent each target word as a vector in a high-dimensional space, where each component corresponds to some textual attribute (entries are set to word-attribute ratio scores). Example representations for the concepts *canary* and *trolley* are shown in Table 13.3. In accordance with the terminology for the visual modality, we will henceforth refer to the Strudel attributes as textual attributes.

[12]The software is available at http://clic.cimec.unitn.it/strudel/.

Table 13.3 Examples of attribute-based representations provided as input to our autoencoders

Visual		eat_seeds	has_beak	has_claws	has_handlebar	has_wheels
	canary	0.05	0.24	0.15	0.00	–0.10
	trolley	0.00	0.00	0.00	0.30	0.32
Textual		bird:n	breed:v	cage:n	chirp:v	fly:v
	canary	0.16	0.19	0.39	0.13	0.13
	trolley	–0.40	0.00	0.00	0.00	0.00
Visual		has_wings	yellow	of_wood		
	canary	0.19	0.34	0.00		
	trolley	0.00	0.00	0.25		
Textual		track:n	ride:v	run:v	rail:n	wheel:n
	canary	0.00	0.00	0.00	0.00	–0.05
	trolley	0.14	0.16	0.33	0.17	0.20

13.4 Visually Grounding Word Meaning with Attributes

In the following, we will present our model for visually grounded meaning representations applies deep learning techniques in a neural network architecture for modality integration, using our attribute-centric representations as input. We introduce the details of our model in Sect. 13.4.3. Our model builds upon autoencoders to learn higher level meaning representations for single words. We first briefly review autoencoders placing emphasis on aspects relevant to our model which we then describe in Sect. 13.4.3.

13.4.1 Multimodal Deep Learning

The use of stacked autoencoders to extract a shared lexical meaning representation is new to our knowledge, although, as we explain below related to a large body of work on multimodal deep learning in network architectures.

Work which focusses on integrating words and images has used a variety of architectures including deep [96, 97] or restricted Boltzmann machines [95], and autoencoders [30]. Similar methods were employed to combine other modalities such as speech and video or images [45, 52, 72, 97].

Although our model is conceptually similar to these studies (especially those applying stacked autoencoders), it differs in at least two aspects. First, many former models learn bimodal representations with the aim to reason about one modality given the respective other modality Huang and Kingsbury (e.g. [45]), Ngiam et al. (e.g. [72]), Sohn et al. (e.g. [95]). In contrast, our goal is to learn bimodal representations in which complimentary and redundant information from different modalities is unified in an optimal way. Second, most approaches deal with a particular end task (e.g. image classification or speech recognition, but see [97] for an exception), and fine-tune the network parameters with an appropriate supervised criterion on top of the joint representations Huang and Kingsbury (e.g. [45]), or use the latter as features for training a conventional classifier Ngiam et al. (e.g. [72]), Sohn et al. (e.g. [95]). In contrast, we fine-tune our autoencoder using a semi-supervised criterion. Specifically, we use a combined objective comprising the reconstruction of the attribute-based input and the classification of the input object. The latter, supervised criterion is used as a means to drive the learning process, as we will explain in more detail later on.

Furthermore, our model is defined at a finer level of granularity than most previous work—it computes representations for *individual* words—and leverages information from decoupled data sources, i.e. image collections and text corpora. Former work on multimodal representation learning builds upon images and their accompanied tags [30, 95, 97], or sentential descriptions of the image content for the purpose of image and description retrieval or description generation [49, 53, 64, 94].

13.4.2 Background

Autoencoders An autoencoder (AE) is an unsupervised feedforward neural network which is trained to reconstruct a given input from its latent distributed representation [6, 85]. It consists of an encoder f_θ which maps an input vector $\mathbf{x}^{(i)}$ to a hidden (*latent*) representation $\mathbf{y}^{(i)} = f_\theta(\mathbf{x}^{(i)}) = s(\mathbf{W}\mathbf{x}^{(i)} + \mathbf{b})$, with s being a nonlinear activation function, such as a sigmoid function, and $\mathbf{W}$ and $\mathbf{b}$ being the weight matrix and an offset vector, respectively. A decoder $g_{\theta'}$ then aims to reconstruct input $\mathbf{x}^{(i)}$ from $\mathbf{y}^{(i)}$, i.e. $\hat{\mathbf{x}}^{(i)} = g_{\theta'}(\mathbf{y}^{(i)}) = s(\mathbf{W}'\mathbf{y}^{(i)} + \mathbf{b}')$. The training objective is the determination of parameters $\hat{\theta} = \{\mathbf{W}, \mathbf{b}\}$ and $\hat{\theta}' = \{\mathbf{W}', \mathbf{b}'\}$ that minimise the average reconstruction error over a set of input vectors $\{\mathbf{x}^{(1)}, ..., \mathbf{x}^{(n)}\}$: $\hat{\theta}, \hat{\theta}' = \arg\min_{\theta,\theta'} \frac{1}{n} \sum_{i=1}^{n} L(\mathbf{x}^{(i)}, g_{\theta'}(f_\theta(\mathbf{x}^{(i)})))$, where L is a loss function, such as cross-entropy. Parameters θ and θ' can be optimised by gradient descent methods.

AEs are a means to learn representations of some input by retaining useful features in the encoding phase which help to reconstruct (an approximation of) the input, whilst discarding useless or noisy ones.

The use of a bottleneck hidden layer to produce under-complete representations of the input is one strategy of guiding parameter learning towards useful representations. The literature describes further strategies, such as constraining the hidden layer to yield sparse representations [80], or *denoising*.

Denoising AEs The training criterion with denoising AEs is the reconstruction of clean input $\mathbf{x}^{(i)}$ given a corrupted version $\tilde{\mathbf{x}}^{(i)}$ [105, 106]. The reconstruction error for an input $\mathbf{x}^{(\mathbf{i})}$ with loss function L then is:

$$err(\mathbf{x}^{(i)}, \tilde{\mathbf{x}}^{(i)}) = L(\mathbf{x}^{(i)}, g_{\theta'}(f_\theta(\tilde{\mathbf{x}}^{(i)}))) \tag{13.2}$$

One possible corruption process is *masking noise*, where the corrupted version $\tilde{\mathbf{x}}^{(i)}$ results from randomly setting a fixed proportion v of units of $\mathbf{x}^{(\mathbf{i})}$ to 0. The underlying idea of denoising AEs is that if a latent representation is capable of reconstructing the actual input from its corruption, it presumably has learned to capture the regularities and interrelations of the structure of the input and can therefore be deemed a good representation.

Stacked AEs Several (denoising) AEs can be used as building blocks to form a deep neural network [8, 106]. For that purpose, the AEs are often pre-trained layer by layer, with the current layer being fed the latent representation yielded by the previous, already pre-trained, AE as input. Using this unsupervised pre-training procedure, initial parameters are found which approximate a good solution. Subsequently, the original input layer and hidden representations of all the AEs are stacked yielding a deep network.

The parameters of this network can be optimised (*fine-tuned*) with respect to the objectives at hand. More precisely, a supervised criterion can be imposed on top of the last hidden layer such as the minimisation of a prediction error on a supervised task [6]. Another approach is to unfold the stacked AEs and fine-tune their parameters with respect to the minimisation of the global reconstruction error [42]. Alternatively, a semi-supervised criterion can be used [79, 93] through combination of the unsupervised training criterion (global reconstruction) with a supervised criterion, that is, the prediction of some target given the latent representation.

13.4.3 Grounded Semantic Representations with Autoencoders

To learn meaning representations of single words from textual and visual input, we employ stacked (denoising) autoencoders. Both input modalities are vector-based representations of the objects the target words refer to (e.g. *canary*). The vector dimensions correspond to textual and visual attributes, as exemplified in Table 13.3.

13.4.3.1 Architecture

We first pre-train a stack of two autoencoders (AEs) for each modality separately. Then, we join the modalities by feeding the latent representations (*encodings*) induced by their respective second AE simultaneously to another AE. Its hidden layer $\check{\mathbf{y}}$ yields word representations that capture the meaning of words across both modalities. In the final training phase, we stack all layers and unfold them in order to fine-tune this SAE. Figure 13.5 illustrates the architecture of the model. As can be seen from the figure, we additionally add a softmax-layer on top of the bimodal encoding layer (shown in the centre of Fig. 13.5, labelled as softmax), which outputs predictions with respect to the object label of an input (e.g. *dog, baseball*). It serves as a supervised training criterion in addition to the unsupervised reconstruction objective during fine-tuning, with the aim of guiding the learning towards descriptive and discriminative (bimodal) representations that capture the structure of the input patterns within and across the two modalities, and discriminate between different objects.

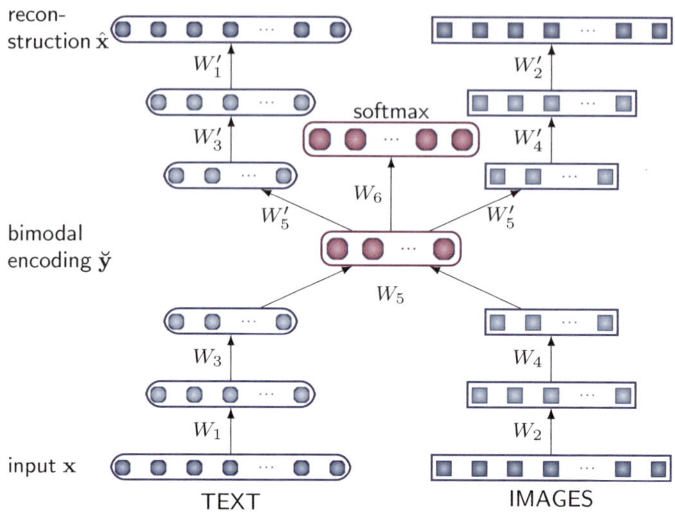

Fig. 13.5 Stacked AE trained with semi-supervised objective. Input to the model are single-word vector representations obtained from text and images. The edges are labelled with the weight matrices to be learned (bias vectors are omitted for the sake of clarity)

After training, a word is represented by its encoding in the bimodal layer, corresponding to a vector $\check{\mathbf{y}}$ of distributed unit activations (shown in the centre of Fig. 13.5). An individual unit of $\check{\mathbf{y}}$ does not represent a nameable attribute, but it is rather part of a pattern formed by the interplay between the visual and linguistic characteristics of the word it represents. Two words can then be compared on the basis of their encodings (e.g. by measuring their cosine similarity), and the more their activation patterns coincide, the more similar the words are assumed to be.

13.4.3.2 Model Details

Unimodal AEs For both modalities, we use the hyperbolic tangent function as activation function for encoder f_θ and decoder $g_{\theta'}$ and an entropic loss function for L. The weights of each autoencoder (AE) are tied, i.e. $\mathbf{W}' = \mathbf{W}^T$. We employ denoising AEs for pre-training the textual modality.

Regarding the visual AE, we derive a new ('denoised') target vector to be reconstructed for each input vector $\mathbf{x}^{(i)}$, and treat $\mathbf{x}^{(i)}$ itself as corrupted input. The target vector is derived as follows: each object o (or concept) in our data is represented by multiple images. Each image in turn is rendered in a visual attribute vector $\mathbf{x}^{(i)}$. The target vector is the weighted aggregation of $\mathbf{x}^{(i)}$ and the centroid $\mathbf{x}^{(o)}$ of all attribute vectors collectively representing object o. This denoising procedure compensates for prediction errors made by the attribute classifiers on individual images. Moreover, not all attributes which are true for a concept are necessarily observable from a relevant image. Attribute predictions for individual images therefore introduce corruption with respect to the overall *concept* they represent.

Bimodal AE The bimodal AE is fed with the concatenated second hidden encodings of the visual and textual modalities as input and maps these to a joint hidden layer $\breve{\mathbf{y}}$ of B units. We normalise both unimodal input encodings to unit length. Again, we use tied weights for the bimodal autoencoder. We also actively encourage the AE to detect dependencies between the two modalities while learning the mapping to the bimodal hidden layer, and therefore apply masking noise to one modality with a masking factor v, so that the corrupted modality optimally has to rely on the other modality in order to reconstruct its missing input features.

Stacked Bimodal AE We finally build a SAE with all pre-trained AEs and fine-tune their parameters with respect to a semi-supervised criterion. That is, we unfold the stacked AE (as shown in Fig. 13.5) and furthermore add a softmax output layer on top of the bimodal layer $\breve{\mathbf{y}}$ that outputs predictions $\hat{\mathbf{t}}$ with respect to the inputs' object labels (e.g. *boat*):

$$\hat{\mathbf{t}}^{(i)} = \frac{\exp(\mathbf{W}^{(6)}\breve{\mathbf{y}}^{(i)} + \mathbf{b}^{(6)})}{\sum_{k=1}^{O} \exp(\mathbf{W}_{k.}^{(6)}\breve{\mathbf{y}}^{(i)} + \mathbf{b}_{k}^{(6)})}, \tag{13.3}$$

with weights $\mathbf{W}^{(6)} \in \mathbb{R}^{O \times B}$, $\mathbf{b}^{(6)} \in \mathbb{R}^{O \times 1}$, where O is the number of unique object labels. The overall objective to be minimised is then the weighted sum of the reconstruction error L_r and the classification error L_c:

$$L = \frac{1}{n}\sum_{i=1}^{n}\left(\delta_r L_r(\mathbf{x}^{(i)}, \hat{\mathbf{x}}^{(i)}) + \delta_c L_c(\mathbf{t}^{(i)}, \hat{\mathbf{t}}^{(i)})\right) + \lambda R \tag{13.4}$$

where δ_r and δ_c are weighting parameters that give different importance to the partial objectives, L_c and L_r are entropic loss functions, and R is a regularisation term with $R = \sum_{j=1}^{5} 2||\mathbf{W}^{(j)}||^2 + ||\mathbf{W}^{(6)}||^2$, i.e. we use an L2 weight decay penalty (penalisation of the sum of squared weights). Finally, $\hat{\mathbf{t}}^{(i)}$ is the object label vector predicted by the softmax function for input vector $\mathbf{x}^{(i)}$, and $\mathbf{t}^{(i)}$ is the correct object label, represented as an O-dimensional *one-hot vector*.[13]

13.4.3.3 Model Properties

Our model benefits from its deep learning architecture, obtaining meaning representations from multiple layers. The first layers operate on individual modalities, whereas the final hidden layer combines them to a bimodal representation. This architecture allows us to test different hypotheses with respect to word meaning. Specifically, we can disentangle the contribution of visual or textual information, for instance by representing words based on their unimodal encoding and contrasting them with their

[13] In a one-hot vector (a.k.a. *1-of-N coding*), exactly one element is one and the others are zero. In our case, the non-zero element corresponds to the object label.

bimodal representation. Related bimodal models have used SVD [15], LDA [84], or kCCA [90] to project the input data into a joint space *directly*. There is no hierarchy of representations with potentially increasing complexity, nor an intermediate unimodal representation naturally connecting the input to the bimodal representation. Similarly to models employing SVD or kCCA, our model can also perform dimensionality-reduction in the course of representation learning by mapping to lower dimensional hidden layers. However, in contrast to SVD, this is performed nonlinearly which we argue allows to model complex relationships between visual and textual data.

Finally, in contrast to other network models which learn word *embeddings* from randomly initialised input, our input vectors are meaningful (they are attribute-based). The model can therefore derive bimodal representations for out-of-vocabulary words, and has furthermore the potential for inductive inference with respect to attributes of new objects Johns and Jones (cf. [47]). For example, the model could be used to infer textual attributes given visual attributes and vice versa. This inference ability follows directly out of the model, without additional assumptions or modifications. Previous models either do not have a simple way of projecting one modality onto a joint space Andrews et al. (e.g. [2]), or altogether lack a mechanism of inferring missing modalities.

13.5 Experiments

Vector-based models aimed at representing the meaning of individual words are commonly evaluated against human judgements on word similarity or linguistic phenomena which are dependent on similarity, such as categorisation [67]. We evaluate our model on a word similarity and a categorisation task.[14]

13.5.1 Experiment 1: Word Similarity

We first give details on the evaluation dataset we used for the similarity task and then explain how our SAE model was trained and describe comparison models.

13.5.1.1 Elicitation of Evaluation Dataset

In this experiment, we collected similarity ratings[15] that capture the concepts contained in the McRae norms. Although several relevant datasets exist, such as the widely used WordSim353 [33] or the more recent Rel-122 norms [98], they contain many abstract words, (e.g. *love–sex* or *arrest–detention*) which are not covered in

[14] See [89] for more experiments.

[15] Available at http://homepages.inf.ed.ac.uk/s1151656/resources.html.

the McRae norms. This is for a good reason, as most abstract words do not have discernible attributes, or at least attributes that participants would agree upon. The new dataset we created consists exclusively of nouns from the McRae norms, and contains similarity ratings for semantic as well as visual similarity.

Materials and Design Initially, we created all possible pairings over the concepts of the McRae norms and computed the semantic relatedness of the corresponding WordNet [29] synsets using Patwardhan and Pedersen's [77] WordNet-based measure. We opted for this specific measure as it achieves high correlation with human ratings and has a high coverage on our nouns. Next, we randomly selected 30 pairs for each concept under the assumption that they are representative of the full variation of semantic similarity. This resulted in 7,576 pairs. We split the pairs into overall 255 tasks; each task consisted of 32 pairs covering examples of weak to very strong semantic relatedness, and furthermore contained at most one instance of each target concept.

Participants and Procedure We used Amazon Mechanical Turk (AMT) to obtain similarity ratings for the word pairs grouped into tasks. Participants were first presented instructions that explained the task and gave examples. They were asked to rate a pair on two dimensions, visual and semantic similarity using a 5-point Likert scale (1 = *highly dissimilar* and 5 = *highly similar*). Note that they were not provided with images depicting the concepts. Each task was completed by five volunteers, all self-reported native English speakers. They were allowed to complete as many tasks as they wanted. A total of 46 subjects (27 women, 18 men, 1 unspecified, mean age: 38.5 years, age range: 18–67) took part in the experiment and completed between one and 147 tasks each. Participants were paid $0.5 per completed task.

Results Examples of the stimuli and elicited mean ratings are shown in Table 13.4. The similarity data was post-processed so as to identify and remove outliers. Similarly to previous work [98], we considered an outlier to be any individual whose mean pairwise correlation coefficient (Spearman's ρ) fell outside two standard deviations from the mean correlation. 11.5 % of the annotations were detected as outliers and removed. After outlier removal, we further examined how well the participants agreed in their similarity judgements. We measured inter-subject agreement as the average pairwise correlation coefficient between the ratings of all annotators for each task. For semantic similarity, the mean correlation was $\rho = 0.76$ (Min = 0.34, Max = 0.97, StD = 0.11) and for visual similarity $\rho = 0.63$ (Min = 0.19, Max = 0.90, StD = 0.14). These results indicate that the participants found the task relatively straightforward and produced similarity ratings with a reasonable level of consistency. For comparison, Patwardhan and Pedersen's [77] measure achieved a coefficient of $\rho = 0.56$ on the dataset for semantic similarity and $\rho = 0.48$ for visual similarity. Finally, the correlation between the mean visual and semantic similarity ratings is $\rho = 0.70$.

13.5.1.2 Comparison Models

We learned meaning representations for the concepts of the McRae norms which are contained in the VISA dataset. As shown in Fig. 13.5, our bimodal stacked

Table 13.4 Mean semantic and visual similarity ratings for the concepts of the McRae norms with varying degrees of similarity. Averaged across experiment participants

Word pairs	Semantic	Visual	Word pairs	Semantic	Visual
pistol–revolver	5.0	5.0	*clarinet–keyboard_(musical)*	4.3	1.3
cup–mug	5.0	4.3	*car–scooter*	4.0	1.7
gloves–mittens	5.0	4.2	*gun–missile*	4.0	1.0
bracelet–chain	2.8	4.0	*screwdriver–wrench*	3.6	1.4
bat_(baseball)–baton	2.8	4.0	*pencil–wand*	1.8	4.0
closet–elevator	1.5	2.8	*bullet–thimble*	1.0	3.0

autoencoder (SAE) model takes as input two (real-valued) vectors representing the visual and textual modalities. Vector dimensions correspond to textual and visual attributes, respectively. We maintained the partition of the VISA image data into training, validation, and test set and acquired visual vectors for each of the sets by means of our attribute classifiers (see Sect. 13.3.1.3). We used the visual vectors of the training and development set for training the AEs, and the vectors for the test set for evaluation. We derived textual attribute vectors by means of Strudel [4] which we ran on a 2009 dump of the English Wikipedia of about 800 M words.[16] We only retained the ten attributes with highest log-likelihood ratio scores for each target word, amounting to a total of 2,362 dimensions for the textual vectors. The textual and visual vectors were scaled to the $[-1, 1]$ range.

Model hyper-parameters[17] were optimised on a subset of the free word association norms collected by [71][18] which covered the McRae norms. These norms were established by presenting participants with a cue word (e.g. *canary*) and asking them to name an associate word in response (e.g. *bird, sing*). For each cue, the norms provide a set of associates and the frequencies with which they were named. During training we used correlation analysis (ρ) to monitor the degree of linear relationship between model cue-associate cosine similarities and human probabilities. The best autoencoder on the word association task obtained a correlation coefficient of $\rho = 0.33$. This model has the following architecture: the textual denoising autoencoder (Fig. 13.5, left-hand side) consists of 700 hidden units which are then mapped to the second hidden layer with 500 units (the corruption parameter was set to $v = 0.1$); the visual autoencoder (see Fig. 13.5, right-hand side) has 170 and 100 hidden units, in the first and second layer, respectively. The 500 textual and 100 visual hidden units feed a bimodal autoencoder containing 500 units, and masking noise was applied to the textual modality with $v = 0.2$. The weighting parameters for the joint training objective of the stacked autoencoder were set to $\delta_r = 0.8$ and $\delta_c = 1$ (see Eq. (13.4)).

[16]The corpus is downloadable from http://wacky.sslmit.unibo.it/doku.php?id=corpora.

[17]We performed random search over combinations of hyper-parameter values.

[18]Available at http://w3.usf.edu/FreeAssociation.

We used the meaning representations obtained from the output of the bimodal layer for the experiment.

We compare our SAE against unimodal autoencoders based solely on textual and visual input (left- and right-hand sides in Fig. 13.5). We also compare our model against a concatenation model as well as two latent inference approaches which differ in their modality integration mechanisms. The first one is based on kCCA with a linear kernel. The second one emulates Bruni et al.'s [15] integration mechanism based on SVD (see below). All these models run on the same data and are given input identical to our model, namely attribute-based textual and visual representations.

We furthermore report results obtained with Bruni et al.'s [15] bimodal distributional model using their publicly available system [14]. Their textual modality is represented by a 30K-dimensional co-occurrence matrix[19] extracted from text corpora, i.e. the ukWaC corpus (2 billion tokens)[20] and WaCkypedia. Note that our attribute-based input relies solely on the latter. The entries of the matrix correspond to the weighted co-occurrence frequency between target and context words. Two words are considered co-occurring if one of them occurs in the window of two content words on each side of the other word. Moreover, they extract visual information, from the ESP game dataset [108] which comprises 100 K images randomly downloaded from the Internet and tagged by humans (the average number of images per tag is 70). The visual modality is represented by bag-of-visual-words histograms built on the basis of clustered SIFT descriptors [62].

Finally, we also compare to Mikolov et al.'s [69] skip-gram model. The model uses a neural network to learn state-of-the-art distributed word embeddings by optimising the training objective of predicting the context words of an input word. It does not integrate any perceptual information, representations are directly inferred from large amounts of text data. In our experiments, we used the 300-dimensional vectors trained on part of the Google News dataset which comprises 100B words.[21] They were trained using negative sampling (the objective is the distinction between the target, i.e. a correct context word, from randomly sampled negative examples), and sub-sampling of frequent words [69].

13.5.1.3 Results

We evaluate the models on the gathered word similarity dataset described in Sect. 13.5.1.1. With each model, we measure the cosine similarity of the given word pairs and correlate these predictions with the mean human similarity ratings using Spearman's rank correlation coefficient (ρ).

Table 13.5 presents our results. As an indicator to how well automatically extracted attributes can approach the effectiveness of clean human generated attributes, we also report results of a model induced from the McRae norms (see the row labelled McRae

---

[19] We thank Elia Bruni for providing us with their data.

[20] From http://wacky.sslmit.unibo.it/doku.php?id=corpora.

[21] The vectors are available at https://code.google.com/p/word2vec/.

Table 13.5 Correlation of model predictions against similarity

Models	Semantic similarity			Visual similarity		
	T	V	T+V	T	V	T+V
McRae	0.71	0.49	0.68	0.58	0.52	0.61
Attributes	0.63	0.62	0.71	0.49	0.57	0.60
SAE	0.67	0.61	0.72	0.55	0.60	0.65
SVD	–	–	0.70	–	–	0.59
kCCA	–	–	0.58	–	–	0.56
Bruni	–	–	0.50	–	–	0.44
Skip-gram	0.73	–	–	0.56	–	–

in the table). Each noun is represented as a vector with dimensions corresponding to attributes elicited by participants of the norming study. Vector components are set to the (normalised) frequency with which participants generated the corresponding attribute. We show results for three models, using all attributes except those classified as visual (columns labelled T), only visual attributes (V), and all available attributes (T + V). The concatenation model (see row Attributes in Table 13.5) is based on the concatenation (T + V) of textual attributes (obtained from Strudel) and visual attributes (obtained from our classifiers; columns T and V, respectively). The automatically obtained textual and visual attribute vectors serve as input to SVD, kCCA and our bimodal stacked autoencoder (SAE). The third row in the table presents three variants of our model trained on textual and visual attributes only (T and V) and on both modalities jointly (T + V) (Table 13.6).

Recall that participants were asked to provide ratings on two dimensions, namely semantic and visual similarity. We would expect the textual modality to be more dominant when modelling semantic similarity and conversely the perceptual modality to be stronger with respect to visual similarity. This is borne out in our unimodal SAEs. The textual SAE correlates better with semantic similarity judgements ($\rho = 0.67$) than its visual equivalent ($\rho = 0.61$). And the visual SAE correlates better with visual similarity judgements ($\rho = 0.60$) compared to the textual SAE ($\rho = 0.55$). Interestingly, the bimodal SAE (T + V) is better than the unimodal variants on both types of similarity judgements, semantic and visual. We hypothesise that both modalities contribute complementary information and that the SAE model is able to extract a shared representation which improves generalisation performance across tasks by learning them jointly. The bimodal autoencoder (SAE, T + V) outperforms all other bimodal models on both similarity tasks. It yields a correlation coefficient of $\rho = 0.72$ on semantic similarity and $\rho = 0.65$ on visual similarity. Human agreement on the former task is 0.76 and 0.63 on the latter. Table 13.7 shows examples of word pairs with highest similarity according to the SAE model.

We also observe that simply concatenating textual and visual attributes (Attributes, T + V) performs competitively with SVD and better than kCCA. This indicates that the attribute-based representation is a powerful predictor on its own. With respect to

Table 13.6 F-score results on ratings for the noun pairs of the McRae norms (Spearman's ρ). Concept categorisation

Models	Categorisation		
	T	V	T+V
McRae	0.52	0.31	0.42
Attributes	0.35	0.37	0.33
SAE	0.36	0.35	0.43
SVD	–	–	0.39
kCCA	–	–	0.37
Bruni	–	–	0.34
Skip-gram	0.37	–	–

Table 13.7 Word pairs with highest semantic and visual similarity according to SAE model. Pairs are ranked from highest to lowest similarity

#	Pair	#	Pair	#	Pair		
1	*pliers–tongs*	5	*chapel–church*	9	*cloak–robe*	13	*horse–pony*
2	*cathedral–church*	6	*airplane–helicopter*	10	*nylons–trousers*	14	*gun–rifle*
3	*cathedral–chapel*	7	*dagger–sword*	11	*cello–violin*	15	*cedar–oak*
4	*pistol–revolver*	8	*pistol–rifle*	12	*cottage–house*	16	*bull–ox*

models that do not make use of attributes, we see that Bruni et al. [15] is out-performed by all other attribute-based systems (columns T+V). Interestingly, skip-gram is the best performing model on the semantic similarity task (column T, first block), but falls short on the visual similarity task.

13.5.2 Experiment 2: Concept Categorisation

Concept learning and categorisation have been subject to many experimental studies and simulation approaches Goldstone et al. (see, e.g. [37], for an overview). Existing models typically focus on a single modality, either perception or language. For example, perceptual information is represented in form of hand-coded (binary) values on a few dimensions Vanpaemel et al. (e.g. [102]), or by images Hsu et al. (e.g. [43]), and linguistic representations are often derived from large text corpora Frermann and Lapata (e.g. [35]). Very few approaches exist that use both, perception and language [15, 111]. In this experiment, we induce semantic categories following a clustering-based approach which uses the bimodal word representations learned by our model.

13.5.2.1 Experimental Setup

To obtain a clustering of nouns into categories, we use Chinese Whispers (CW, [9]), a randomised, agglomerative graph-clustering algorithm. In the categorisation setting, CW produces a hard clustering over a weighted graph whose nodes correspond to words, and edges to cosine similarity scores between vectors representing their meaning. At the beginning, each word forms an own category. All words are then iteratively processed for a few repetitions in which each word is assigned to the category (i.e. cluster) of the most similar neighbour words, as determined by the maximum sum of (edge) weights between the word and the neighbour nodes pertaining to the same category. CW is a non-parametric model, it induces the number of clusters from the data as well as which nouns belong to these clusters. In our experiments, we initialise CW with different graphs resulting from different vector-based representations of the McRae nouns.

We evaluate model output against a gold standard set of categories created by Fountain and Lapata [34]. The dataset contains a classification, (produced by human participants) of the McRae nouns into (possibly multiple) semantic categories (40 in total).[22] We transformed the dataset into hard categorisations by assigning each noun to its most typical category as extrapolated from human typicality ratings Fountain and Lapata [see [34], for details].

We use the SAE model described in Experiment 1. Some performance gains could be expected if (hyper-)parameter optimisation took place separately for each task. However, we wanted to avoid overfitting, and show that our parameters are robust across tasks and datasets. The SAE model is evaluated against the same comparison models described in Experiment 1. We evaluate the clustering solution produced by CW using the F-score measure introduced in the SemEval 2007 task [1]; it is the harmonic mean of precision and recall defined as the number of correct members of a cluster divided by the number of items in the cluster and the number of items in the gold standard class, respectively.

13.5.2.2 Results

Our results on the categorisation task are given in Table 13.6. In this task, simple concatenation of visual and textual attributes does not yield improved performance over the individual modalities (see row Attributes in Table 13.6). In contrast, all bimodal models are better (SVD and SAE) than or equal (kCCA) to their unimodal equivalents and skip-gram. The SAE outperforms both kCCA and SVD by a large margin delivering clustering performance similar to McRae's human produced norms. Table 13.8 shows examples of clusters produced by CW when using vector representations provided by the SAE model. Note that we added the cluster labels manually for illustration purposes.

[22] Available at http://homepages.inf.ed.ac.uk/s0897549/data/.

Table 13.8 Examples of clusters produced by CW using the representations obtained from the SAE model

Category	Words
STICK-LIKE UTENSILS	*baton, ladle, peg, spatula, spoon*
RELIGIOUS BUILDINGS	*cathedral, chapel, church*
WIND INSTRUMENTS	*clarinet, flute, saxophone, trombone, trumpet, tuba*
AXES	*axe, hatchet, machete, tomahawk*
ENTRY POINTS	*door, elevator, gate*
UNGULATES	*bison, buffalo, bull, calf, camel, cow, donkey, elephant, goat, horse, lamb, ox, pig, pony, sheep*

13.6 Conclusions

This chapter presented the use of visual attributes predicted from images as a way of physically grounding word meaning. We described our database (VISA) which comprises visual attribute annotations of concrete nouns and a large set of images depicting objects these nouns refer to. We explained how we obtain visual attribute-based representations of words by means of attribute classifiers which we trained on VISA. Our deep stacked autoencoder architecture then learned visually grounded meaning representations by simultaneously combining these visual attribute representations with attribute vectors derived from text data. To the best of our knowledge, our model is novel in its use of attribute-based input in a deep neural network. Experimental results in two tasks, namely simulation of word similarity and word categorisation, showed that our SAE model yields an overall better fit with behavioural data than unimodal (textual or visual) models, and that it furthermore is more effective than all bimodal comparison models.

Possible future work is to apply our model to image-based applications which could benefit from linguistic information, such as zero-shot learning or basic-level categorisation.

References

1. Agirre, E., Soroa, A.: SemEval-2007 Task 02: Evaluating word sense induction and discrimination systems. In: Proceedings of the Fourth International Workshop on Semantic Evaluations (2007)
2. Andrews, M., Vigliocco, G., Vinson, D.: Integrating experiential and distributional data to learn semantic representations. Psychol. Rev. **116**(3), 463–498 (2009)
3. Barbu, E.: Combining methods to learn feature-norm-like concept descriptions. In: Proceedings of the ESSLLI Workshop on Distributional Lexical Semantics (2008)
4. Baroni, M., Murphy, B., Barbu, E., Poesio, M.: Strudel: a corpus-based semantic model based on properties and types. Cogn. Sci. **34**(2), 222–254 (2010)
5. Barsalou, L.: Perceptual symbol systems. Behav. Brain Sci. **22**, 577–609 (1999)

6. Bengio, Y.: Learning deep architectures for AI. Found. Trends Mach. Learn. **2**(1), 1–127 (2009)
7. Bengio, Y., Ducharme, R., Vincent, P., Janvin, C.: A neural probabilistic language model. J. Mach. Learn. Res. (JMLR) **3**, 1137–1155 (2003)
8. Bengio, Y., Lamblin, P., Popovici, D., Larochelle, H.: Greedy layer-wise training of deep networks. In: Conference on Neural Information Processing Systems (NIPS) (2006)
9. Biemann, C.: Chinese whispers—an efficient graph clustering algorithm and its application to natural language processing problems. In: Proceedings of TextGraphs: The 1st Workshop on Graph Based Methods for Natural Language Processing (2006)
10. Blei, D.M., Ng, A.Y., Jordan, M.I.: Latent Dirichlet allocation. J. Mach. Learn. Res. (JMLR) **3**, 993–1022 (2003)
11. Bornstein, M.H., Cote, L.R., Maital, S., Painter, K., Park, S.-Y., Pascual, L.: Cross-linguistic analysis of vocabulary in young children: Spanish, Dutch, French, Hebrew, Italian, Korean, and American English. Child Dev. **75**(4), 1115–1139 (2004)
12. Bruni, E., Tran, G., Baroni, M.: Distributional semantics from text and images. In: Proceedings of the GEMS 2011 workshop on geometrical models of natural language semantics (2011)
13. Bruni, E., Boleda, G., Baroni, M., Tran, N.: Distributional semantics in technicolor. In: Proceedings of the 50th annual meeting of the association for computational linguistics (2012)
14. Bruni, E., Bordignon, U., Liska, A., Uijlings, J., Sergienya, I.: VSEM: an open library for visual semantics representation. In: Proceedings of the 51st Annual Meeting of the Association for Computational Linguistics: System Demonstrations (2013)
15. Bruni, E., Tran, N., Baroni, M.: Multimodal distributional semantics. J. Artif. Intel. Res. (JAIR) **49**, 1–47 (2014)
16. Chen, H., Gallagher, A., Girod, B.: Describing clothing by semantic attributes. In: European Conference on Computer Vision (ECCV) (2012)
17. Cimpoi, M., Maji, S., Kokkinos, I., Mohamed, S., Vedaldi, A.: Describing textures in the wild. In: Conference on Computer Vision and Pattern Recognition (CVPR) (2014)
18. Collins, A.M., Loftus, E.F.: A spreading-activation theory of semantic processing. Psychol. Rev. **82**(6), 407 (1975)
19. Collobert, R., Weston, J.: A unified architecture for natural language processing: deep neural networks with multitask learning. In: International Conference on Machine Learning (ICML) (2008)
20. Cree, G.S., McRae, K., McNorgan, C.: An attractor model of lexical conceptual processing: simulating semantic priming. Cogn. Sci. **23**(3), 371–414 (1999)
21. Deerwester, S., Dumais, S.T., Furnas, G.W., Landauer, T.K., Harshman, R.: Indexing by latent semantic analysis. J. Am. Soc. Inform. Sci. **41**(6), 391–407 (1990)
22. Deng, J., Dong, W., Socher, R., Li, L., Li, K., Fei-Fei, L.: ImageNet: a large-scale hierarchical image database. In: Conference on Computer Vision and Pattern Recognition (CVPR) (2009)
23. Devereux, B., Pilkington, N., Poibeau, T., Korhonen, A.: Towards unrestricted, large-scale acquisition of feature-based conceptual representations from corpus data. Res. Lang. Comput. **7**(2–4), 137–170 (2009)
24. Devereux, B.J., Tyler, L.K., Geertzen, J., Randall, B.: The centre for speech, language and the brain (CSLB) concept property norms. Behav. Res. Methods (2013)
25. Duan, K., Parikh, D., Crandall, D., Grauman, K.: Discovering localized attributes for fine-grained recognition. In: Conference on Computer Vision and Pattern Recognition (CVPR) (2012)
26. Everingham, M., Van Gool, L., Williams, C.K.I., Winn, J., Zisserman, A.: The PASCAL visual object classes challenge 2008 results (2008)
27. Fan, R., Chang, K., Hsieh, C., Wang, X., Lin, C.: LIBLINEAR: a library for large linear classification. J. Mach. Learn. Res. (JMLR) **9**, 1871–1874 (2008)
28. Farhadi, A., Endres, I., Hoiem, D., Forsyth, D.: Describing objects by their attributes. In: Conference on Computer Vision and Pattern Recognition (CVPR) (2009)
29. Fellbaum, C. (ed.) WordNet: an electronic lexical database. The MIT Press (1998)

30. Feng, F., Li, R., Wang, X.: Constructing hierarchical image-tags bimodal representations for word tags alternative choice. In: Proceedings of the ICML Workshop on Challenges in Representation Learning (2013)
31. Feng, Y., Lapata, M.: Visual information in semantic representation. In: Human Language Technologies: The 2010 Annual Conference of the North American Chapter of the Association for Computational Linguistics (2010)
32. Ferrari, V., Zisserman, A.: Learning visual attributes. In: Conference on Neural Information Processing Systems (NIPS) (2007)
33. Finkelstein, L., Gabrilovich, E., Matias, Y., Rivlin, E., Solan, Z., Wolfman, G., Ruppin, E.: Placing search in context: the concept revisited. ACM Trans. Inform. Syst. **20**(1), 116–131 (2002)
34. Fountain, T., Lapata, M.: Meaning representation in natural language categorization. In: Proceedings of the 31st Annual Conference of the Cognitive Science Society (2010)
35. Frermann, L., Lapata, M.: Incremental Bayesian learning of semantic categories. In: Proceedings of the 14th Conference of the European Chapter of the Association for Computational Linguistics (2014)
36. Glenberg, A.M., Kaschak, M.P.: Grounding language in action. Psychon. Bull. Rev. **9**(3), 558–565 (2002)
37. Goldstone, R.L., Kersten, A., Cavalho, P.F.: Concepts and categorization. In: Healy, A.F., Proctor, R.W. (eds.) Comprehensive Handbook of Psychology, vol. 4: Experimental Psychology, pp. 607–630. Wiley (2012)
38. Griffiths, T.L., Steyvers, M., Tenenbaum, J.B.: Topics in semantic representation. Psychol. Rev. **114**(2), 211–244 (2007)
39. Grondin, R., Lupker, S., Mcrae, K.: Shared features dominate semantic richness effects for concrete concepts. J. Mem. Lang. **60**(1), 1–19 (2009)
40. Harris, Z.S.: Distributional structure. Word **10**(2–3), 146–162 (1954)
41. Hill, F., Korhonen, A.: Learning abstract concept embeddings from multi-modal data: since you probably cant see what I mean. In: Proceedings of the 2014 Conference on Empirical Methods in Natural Language Processing (2014)
42. Hinton, G.E., Salakhutdinov, R.R.: Reducing the dimensionality of data with neural networks. Science **313**(5786), 504–507 (2006)
43. Hsu, A.S., Martin, J.B., Sanborn, A.N., Griffiths, T.L.: Identifying representations of categories of discrete items using Markov Chain Monte Carlo with people. In: Proceedings of the 34th annual conference of the cognitive science society (2012)
44. Huang, E.H., Socher, R., Manning, C.D., Ng, A.Y.: Improving word representations via global context and multiple word prototypes. In: Proceedings of the 50th Annual Meeting of the Association for Computational Linguistics: Long Papers (2012)
45. Huang, J., Kingsbury, B.: Audio-visual deep learning for noise robust speech recognition. In: Proceedings 38th International Conference on Acoustics, Speech, and Signal Processing (2013)
46. Huiskes, M.J., Lew, M.S.: The MIR Flickr retrieval evaluation. In: Proceedings of the 1st ACM International Conference on Multimedia Information Retrieval (2008)
47. Johns, B.T., Jones, M.N.: Perceptual inference through global lexical similarity. Topics Cogn. Sci. **4**(1), 103–120 (2012)
48. Jones, M.N., Willits, J.A., Dennis, S.: Models of semantic memory. In: Busemeyer, J., Townsend, J., Wang, Z., Eidels, A. (eds.) The Oxford Handbook of Computational and Mathematical Psychology, pp. 232–254. Oxford University Press (2015)
49. Karpathy, A., Fei-Fei, L.: Deep visual-semantic alignments for generating image descriptions. In: Conference on Computer Vision and Pattern Recognition (CVPR) (2015)
50. Kelly, C., Devereux, B., Korhonen, A.: Acquiring human-like feature-based conceptual representations from corpora. In: NAACL HLT Workshop on Computational Neurolinguistics (2010)
51. Kiela, D., Bottou, L.: Learning image embeddings using convolutional neural networks for improved multi-modal semantics. In: Proceedings of the 2014 Conference on Empirical Methods in Natural Language Processing (2014)

52. Kim, Y., Lee, H., Provost, E.M.: Deep learning for robust feature generation in audiovisual emotion recognition. In: IEEE International Conference on Acoustics, Speech and Signal Processing (2013)
53. Kiros, R., Salakhutdinov, R., Zemel, R.: Unifying visual-semantic embeddings with multimodal neural language models. NIPS. In: Deep Learning and Representation Learning Workshop (2014)
54. Kumar, N., Belhumeur, P.N., Nayar, S.K.: FaceTracer: a search engine for large collections of images with faces. In: European Conference on Computer Vision (ECCV) (2008)
55. Kumar, N., Berg, A.C., Belhumeur, P.N., Nayar, S.K.: Describable visual attributes for face verification and image search. IEEE Trans. pattern Anal. Mach. Intel. (PAMI) **33**(10), 1962–1977 (2011)
56. Laffont, P.-Y., Ren, Z., Tao, X., Qian, C., Hays, J.: Transient attributes for high-level understanding and editing of outdoor scenes. ACM Trans. Graph. **33**(4), 149:1–149:11 (2014)
57. Lampert, C.H., Nickisch, H., Harmeling, S.: Learning to detect unseen object classes by between-class attribute transfer. In: Conference on Computer Vision and Pattern Recognition (CVPR) (2009)
58. Landau, B., Smith, L., Jones, S.: Object perception and object naming in early development. Trends Cogn. Sci. **2**(1), 19–24 (1998)
59. Landauer, T., Dumais, S.T.: A solution to Plato's problem: the latent semantic analysis theory of acquisition, induction, and representation of knowledge. Psychol. Rev. **104**(2), 211–240 (1997)
60. Lazaridou, A., Pham, N.T., Baroni, M.: Combining language and vision with a multimodal skip-gram model. In: Human Language Technologies: The 2015 Annual Conference of the North American Chapter of the Association for Computational Linguistics (2015)
61. Liu, J., Kuipers, B., Savarese, S.: Recognizing human actions by attributes. In: Conference on Computer Vision and Pattern Recognition (CVPR) (2011)
62. Lowe, D.G.: Distinctive image features from scale-invariant keypoints. Int. J. Comput. Vision (IJCV) **60**(2), 91–110 (2004)
63. Lund, K., Burgess, C.: Producing high-dimensional semantic spaces from lexical co-occurrence. Behav. Res. Methods Instrum. Comput. **28**(2), 203–208 (1996)
64. Mao, J., Xu, W., Yang, Y., Wang, J., Yuille, A.L.: Explain images with multimodal recurrent neural networks. In: Deep Learning and Representation Learning Workshop: NIPS (2014)
65. McRae, K., Jones, M.: Semantic memory. In: Reisberg, D. (ed.) The Oxford Handbook of Cognitive Psychology. Oxford University Press (2013)
66. McRae, K., Cree, G.S., Seidenberg, M.S., McNorgan, C.: Semantic feature production norms for a large set of living and nonliving things. Behav. Res. Methods **37**(4), 547–559 (2005)
67. Medin, D.L., Schaffer, M.M.: Context theory of classification learning. Psychol. Rev. **85**(3), 207–238 (1978)
68. Mervis, C.B., Rosch, E.: Categorization of natural objects. Annu. Rev. Psychol. **32**(1), 89–115 (1981)
69. Mikolov, T., Sutskever, I., Chen, K., Corrado, G.S., Dean, J.: Distributed representations of words and phrases and their compositionality. In: Conference on Neural Information Processing Systems (NIPS) (2013)
70. Mnih, A., Hinton, G.E.: A scalable hierarchical distributed language model. In: Conference on Neural Information Processing Systems (NIPS) (2009)
71. Nelson, D.L., McEvoy, C.L., Schreiber, T.A.: The University of South Florida Word Association, Rhyme, and Word Fragment Norms (1998)
72. Ngiam, J., Khosla, A., Kim, M., Nam, J., Lee, H., Ng, A.: Multimodal deep learning. In: International Conference on Machine Learning (ICML) (2011)
73. O'Connor, C.M., Cree, G.S., McRae, K.: Conceptual hierarchies in a flat attractor network: dynamics of learning and computations. Cogn. Sci. **33**(4), 665–708 (2009)
74. Osherson, D.N., Stern, J., Wilkie, O., Stob, M., Smith, E.E.: Default probability. Cogn. Sci. **2**(15), 251–269 (1991)

75. Parikh, D., Grauman, K.: Relative attributes. In: International Conference on Computer Vision (ICCV) (2011)
76. Patterson, G., Xu, C., Su, H., Hays, J.: The SUN attribute database: beyond categories for deeper scene understanding. Int. J. Comput. Vision (IJCV) **108**(1–2), 59–81 (2014)
77. Patwardhan, S., Pedersen, T.: Using WordNet-based context vectors to estimate the semantic relatedness of concepts. In: Proceedings of the EACL 2006 Workshop on Making Sense of Sense: Bringing Computational Linguistics and Psycholinguistics Together (2006)
78. Perfetti, C.: The limits of co-occurrence: tools and theories in language research. Discourse Processes **25**(2&3), 363–377 (1998)
79. Ranzato, M., Szummer, M.: Semi-supervised learning of compact document representations with deep networks. In: International Conference on Machine Learning (ICML) (2008)
80. Ranzato, M., Poultney, C., Chopra, S., LeCun, Y.: Efficient learning of sparse representations with an energy-based model. In: Conference on Neural Information Processing Systems (NIPS) (2006)
81. Rastegari, M., Diba, A., Parikh, D., Farhadi, A.: Multi-attribute queries: to merge or not to merge? In: Conference on Computer Vision and Pattern Recognition (CVPR) (2013)
82. Rogers, T.T., McClelland, J.L.: Semantic Cognition: A Parallel Distributed Processing Approach. A Parallel Distributed Processing Approach. The MIT Press (2004)
83. Rogers, T.T., Lambon Ralph, M.A., Garrard, P., Bozeat, S., McClelland, J.L., Hodges, J.R., Patterson, K.: Structure and deterioration of semantic memory: a neuropsychological and computational investigation. Psychol. Rev. **111**(1), 205–235 (2004)
84. Roller, S., Schulte im Walde, S.: A Multimodal LDA model integrating textual, cognitive and visual modalities. In: Proceedings of the 2013 Conference on Empirical Methods in Natural Language Processing (2013)
85. Rumelhart, D.E., Hinton, G.E., Williams, R.J.: Learning internal representations by error propagation. In: Rumelhart, D.E., McClelland, J.L. (eds.) Parallel Distributed Processing: Explorations in the Microstructure of Cognition, vol. 1: Foundations, pp. 318–362. The MIT Press (1986)
86. Russakovsky, O., Fei-Fei, L.: Attribute learning in large-scale datasets. In: ECCV International Workshop on Parts and Attributes (2010)
87. Russell, B., Torralba, A., Murphy, K., Freeman, W.: LabelMe: a database and web-based tool for image annotation. Int. J. Comput. Vis. (IJCV) **77**, 157–173 (2008)
88. Salton, G., McGill, M.J.: Introduction to modern information retrieval. McGraw-Hill, Inc. (1986)
89. Silberer, C.: Learning Visually Grounded Meaning Representations. Ph.D. thesis, Institute for Language, Cognition and Computation, School of Informatics, The University of Edinburgh (2015)
90. Silberer, C., Lapata, M.: Grounded models of semantic representation. In: Proceedings of the 2012 Joint Conference on Empirical Methods in Natural Language Processing and Computational Natural Language Learning (2012)
91. Sloman, S.A., Love, B.C., Ahn, W.-K.: Feature centrality and conceptual coherence. Cogn. Sci. **22**(2), 189–228 (1998)
92. Smith, E.E., Shoben, E.J., Rips, L.J.: Structure and process in semantic memory: a featural model for semantic decisions. Psychol. Rev. **81**(3), 214–241 (1974)
93. Socher, R., Pennington, J., Huang, E.H., Ng, A.Y., and Manning, C.D.: Semi-supervised recursive autoencoders for predicting sentiment distributions. In: Proceedings of the Conference on Empirical Methods in Natural Language Processing (2011)
94. Socher, R., Karpathy, A., Le, Q.V., Manning, C., Ng, A.: Grounded compositional semantics for finding and describing images with sentences. Trans. Assoc. Comput. Linguist. **2**, 207–218 (2014)
95. Sohn, K., Shang, W., Lee, H.: Improved multimodal deep learning with variation of information. In: Conference on Neural Information Processing Systems (NIPS) (2014)
96. Srivastava, N., Salakhutdinov, R.: Multimodal learning with deep Boltzmann machines. In: Conference on Neural Information Processing Systems (NIPS) (2012)

97. Srivastava, N., Salakhutdinov, R.: Multimodal learning with deep Boltzmann machines. J. Mach. Learn. Res. (JMLR) **15**, 2949–2980 (2014)
98. Szumlanski, S., Gomez, F., Sims, V.K.: A new set of norms for semantic relatedness measures. In: Proceedings of the 51st Annual Meeting of the Association for Computational Linguistics (2013)
99. Taylor, K.I., Devereux, B.J., Acres, K., Randall, B., Tyler, L.K.: Contrasting effects of feature-based statistics on the categorisation and basic-level identification of visual objects. Cognition **122**(3), 363–374 (2012)
100. Turney, P.D., Pantel, P.: From frequency to meaning: vector space models of semantics. J. Artif. Intell. Res. **37**(1), 141–188 (2010)
101. Tyler, L.K., Moss, H.E.: Towards a distributed account of conceptual knowledge. TRENDS Cogn. Sci. **5**(6), 244–252 (2001)
102. Vanpaemel, W., Storms, G., Ons, B.: A varying abstraction model for categorization. In: Proceedings of the 27th Annual Conference of the Cognitive Science Society (2005)
103. Varma, M., Zisserman, A.: A statistical approach to texture classification from single images. Int. J. Comput. Vis. (IJCV) (Special Issue on Texture Analysis and Synthesis) **62**(1–2), pp. 61–81 (2005)
104. Vigliocco, G., Vinson, D.P., Lewis, W., Garrett, M.F.: Representing the meanings of object and action words: the featural and unitary semantic space hypothesis. Cogn. Psychol. **48**(4), 422–488 (2004)
105. Vincent, P., Larochelle, H., Bengio, Y., Manzagol, P.-A.: Extracting and composing robust features with denoising autoencoders. In: International Conference on Machine Learning (ICML) (2008)
106. Vincent, P., Larochelle, H., Lajoie, I., Bengio, Y., Manzagol, P.: Stacked denoising autoencoders: learning useful representations in a deep network with a local denoising criterion. J. Mach. Learn. Res. (JMLR) **11**, 3371–3408 (2010)
107. Vinson, D.P., Vigliocco, G.: Semantic feature production norms for a large set of objects and events. Behav. Res. Methods **40**(1), 183–190 (2008)
108. von Ahn, L., Dabbish, L.: Labeling images with a computer game. In: Conference on Human Factors in Computing Systems (2004)
109. Voorspoels, W., Vanpaemel, W., Storms, G.: Exemplars and prototypes in natural language concepts: a typicality-based evaluation. Psychon. Bull. Rev. **15**, 630–637 (2008)
110. Wah, C., Branson, S., Welinder, P., Perona, P., Belongie, S.: The Caltech-UCSD Birds-200-2011 Dataset. Technical Report CNS-TR-2011-001, California Institute of Technology (2011)
111. Westermann, G., Mareschal, D.: From perceptual to language-mediated categorization. Philos. Trans. R Soc. B: Biol. Sci. **369**(1634), 20120391 (2014)

Index

R.S. Feris et al. (eds.), *Visual Attributes*, Advances in Computer Vision and Pattern Recognition, DOI 10.1007/978-3-319-50077-5

MIX
Papier aus verantwortungsvollen Quellen
Paper from responsible sources
FSC® C105338

If you have any concerns about our products,
you can contact us on
ProductSafety@springernature.com

In case Publisher is established outside the EU,
the EU authorized representative is:
Springer Nature Customer Service Center GmbH
Europaplatz 3, 69115 Heidelberg, Germany

Printed by Libri Plureos GmbH
in Hamburg, Germany